Also available:

Seventeen Years of Media Consumption (2002–2018): The films

Seventeen Years of Media Consumption (2002–2018): The recordings

First published in 2020
by Scarlatti Tilt
Pulttitie 17, 00820 Helsinki Finland
www.scarlattitilt.com

This is TILT 02.

Thanks to Katarina Meister, Bill Boichel, Daron Gardner, Lewis McGuffie, Brian Miles, Tuukka Asplund, Agnieszka Pokrywka, Patrick McGinley, John and Christine Fail, Michelle and Anthony Failla, John Grzinich, Giles Bailey, Adam Strohm, Doug Mosurak, Andy Beckerman, C. Spencer Yeh, Caleb Waldorf, Jon Wichmann, and everyone else who has been part of this journey.

Seventeen Years of Media Consumption (2002–2018): The books
ISBN: 978-952-69395-1-3

Seventeen Years of Media Consumption (2002-2018):

The books

John W. Fail

"The library will endure; it is the universe. As for us, everything has not been written; we are not turning into phantoms. We walk the corridors, searching the shelves and rearranging them, looking for lines of meaning amid leagues of cacophony and incoherence, reading the history of the past and our future, collecting our thoughts and collecting the thoughts of others, and every so often glimpsing mirrors, in which we may recognize creatures of the information."

— Jorge Luis Borges, *The Library of Babel*

Introduction
to the books

Within this project, this volume is the one I'm most uneasy about putting forth into the world, for the very stupid reason that I hold a postgraduate degree in English literature. And thus, writing about literature is something that I'm supposed to be able to do, properly.

But this isn't always literature, here; this is a collection of books, many that are definitely literature, but with plenty of other entries which are genre fiction, journalism, theory, political tracts, humour writing, comics/graphic novels, or other forms of non-fiction. Some journals and magazines even slipped in here, as my criteria for inclusion are idiosyncratic and hard to define, but can be essentially boiled down to 'has a spine'. Except when it doesn't. For example, I enthusiastically bought every issue of *The Believer* and *The Baffler* for years, and despite the prominent spines, I only listed them a few times. Inconsistencies and exceptions are the nature of this project, as with the films and recordings.

You will notice that I rarely go all-out while commenting on these books. These comments were never meant to be taken as critical essays, though in the films volume I'm clearly willing to espouse lengthy, semi-articulate diatribes about superhero movies and action films. Yet when presented with masterpieces of literature, the art form I bothered to study to advanced degree level, I rarely write more than a paragraph or two, which is usually my immediate reaction upon completion of the tome.

This entire project is called *Seventeen Years of Media Consumption*, and I chose the verb 'consume' as a somewhat ironic, bleak choice to describe the absorption of media objects created by others. In the case of music recordings, it is literally about consumption, since a physical copy of the LP or CD was purchased or given to me. But with the other two categories, I'm using the term slightly metaphorically, and it somehow feels most cynical when applied to books.

Who was it that first referred to books as trophies? Reading is a far more solitary pursuit than the other categories in this project. Films (at least early on) were watched as a social act; recordings are often documents of a life lived through music culture, as much mementos and keepsakes of personal relationships as works of art for me. But apart from that year of studies, reading is something I did alone. I have never even joined a book club.

My relationship to writing goes way, way back. I was a bookworm as a child, reading everything I could get my hands on through libraries (school and public), the Scholastic book service, and whatever else I could find. I devoured great, inspiring children's literature (Ellen Raskin, D. Manus Pinkwater, *The Phantom Tollbooth*) while also loving the endless titles of the various children-who-solve-mysteries series. I wanted to be a writer myself. This has not yet happened. (These books do not count).

Introduction to the books

High school was spent obsessing over Douglas Adams and Kurt Vonnegut, which wasn't the worst way to pass the time. My father introduced me to travel writing, and I loved Bill Bryson in particular. As a University undergraduate, I only managed to take two literature courses — one called 'The Modernist Tradition', which covered Faulkner, Woolf, Henry James, Conrad, and *Dubliners*; the second a special topic on Joyce that included a deep dive into *Ulysses* and a shallow dip into *Finnegans Wake*.

It was during and immediately after this time that I really began to invest my energy into literature. Using the nascent Internet for assistance, I learned everything I could about postmodern fiction, being particularly drawn to 'big' writers such as Gaddis and Pynchon, but also discovering some stranger corners. My life in 2002, when I started logging the material that comprises these books, was a fairly mundane one. I worked a soul-crushing office job, full-time — but one with enough downtime that I could pursue books on the clock, if not actually read them. My friend Andy was really the only person I shared this with; we chatted over AOL Instant Messenger (while at work) about literature that we were reading, and more often about literature that we wanted to read.

A wonderful and now-forgotten time in American Internet commerce was happening around us — the era of half.com. An eBay offshoot, half.com allowed people to list books they wanted to sell in a non-auction format, available to buy anytime, for anyone who wanted them. This, in combination with the US Postal Service's legendary "Media Mail" shipping rates, allowed both Andy and I to order an enormous amount of secondhand books online for 99 cents each + shipping, which was usually less than $2. At one point I was going to my post office box every other day on my lunch break and returning with padded envelopes full of cheap books: Oulipo oddities, Dalkey Archive titles, cult and experimental fiction, and obscure novels purchased because they were recommended by someone online, somewhere, as being similar to Gaddis, or Vollmann, or Harry Mathews.

Neither of us were actually able to read as fast as the books were coming in, but when one can get a paperback for less than $3, why not buy it now and read it later? In addition, my major leisure activity on evenings and weekends was visiting secondhand book and record shops. I was always perusing the new arrivals at Pittsburgh's premier used bookshops, but even better were the weird, cut-out discount houses on the outskirts of town, such as Half-Price Books and Book Country. All sorts of crazy books were purchased at places like this, never for more than a few bucks.

By the time I moved to the UK, I had some pretty impressive trophies on the shelf, though 60% of them I hadn't even opened — yet! I wanted to read everything, eventually, but some titles clearly had to go. I sold off a great deal to one store, receiving over $200 in credit, which stayed on file for me for years (which my father would occasionally cash in, since his name is also John Fail). The remaining books I boxed up and eventually shipped over a few years later, once I ended up in Finland. Some of these are still on the shelf at my studio in Helsinki now. Some were sold in the bookstore I co-operated in Tallinn, Estonia from 2011–2013. Others have ended up at the library of Nida Art Colony in Neringa, Lithuania, to which I began donating books in 2016.

Half.com shut down in 2017, though I stopped using it long before. At some point, big bad Amazon cannibalised the online secondhand book market, and recent increases in shipping rates have made it considerably more difficult to randomly buy a book just because it sounds interesting. My sense of time also changed; I now am more judicious about reading, which I still enjoy more than almost any other activity on earth, but I'm aware that I'm not going to be able to read everything I want to.

I still frequent second-hand bookshops, though. As I don't live in an English speaking country,

I don't have as many opportunities to pass my free time browsing shelves. But whenever I'm in the UK or US I always come back with a pile of books. And I frequent the Helsinki public library, which is pretty good for English books, all things considered.

Perhaps this is a roundabout way to provide some context for what you're holding, the second volume of *Seventeen Years of Media Consumption*. Here, you have listings of 875 books that I read, and what I thought about them at the time. What I wrote then is not necessarily something I'll stand behind today, but there's nothing too controversial here. Unfortunately, there's nothing too insightful either. I don't do any deep readings, nor do I single out beautiful passages; it's rare that I even acknowledge different thought processes within myself.

What I do, as with the other two volumes in this series, is reference other works. Yes, my understanding of art is sadly just a jumble of links to other works of art, a spider-web of connections that contains little actual substance, I fear. The books here are cross-referenced to other titles across the three volumes, with appropriate icons and numbers in the margins as needed. This referencing is somewhat inconsistent — specific titles, if mentioned and existing, will always be referenced, but if it's just a writer or musician namedrop (who may be included here with multiple entries or titles), then there may be a reference, but there may not be. If unsure, trust the indices.

Only books I completed reading are included here, though what 'completed' means may also be a bit blurry (see Appendix B). It's safe to assume I read it cover-to-cover, unless otherwise indicated.

I'm more aware of the omissions here than in the other two volumes. Maybe that's because the time commitment to read a book is greater than with the other categories, so what's not listed is more obvious because of the space it occupies in my memory. Some I only noticed while editing — *Dr. Bloodmoney, The Man in the High Castle,* and *The Penultimate Truth* were all read during my crazed Philip K Dick intake, which happened so rapidly I forgot to list them. I did eventually read (and love) *Catch-22* at some point along the way, but I guess I never wrote it down.

Other omissions are glaring; I don't know how Russell Hoban's *Riddley Walker* slipped through the cracks, as it's referred to numerous times throughout the other entries. I read it some time in spring 2006, during the aforementioned postgraduate course. That was a year where I had nothing to do, officially, except read; the sheer number of books I went through led to some sloppy chronicling. I'm not sure what else isn't here, and I suppose I will never know for sure.

As with the other volumes, there is a narrative to be found here in what I selected for 'consumption' over these years. I never lost my appetite for big, encyclopedic American post-modern novels. But I also started to appreciate more hybrid-style essay writing, as I discovered W.G. Sebald and others like him. Any academic sense of snobbery I may have held has hopefully been washed away (look at the glee that filled me when I dove into the PK Dick period, just after finishing my dissertation); I greatly enjoy 'genre' fiction, and hate even using that term.

Putting this all together has been a joy, though it has been time-consuming, and I'm glad to have it done so I can get back to reading more. As with the other two volumes, I'm grateful to anyone who is interested in this insane, obsessive, and depressingly typical 'male' behaviour. My best hope is that a reader may discover a book here that they wouldn't otherwise have known about, thanks to my own enthusiasm.

Helsinki, September 2019

The books

1. Carpenter's Gothic by William Gaddis
Received: (already owned)
Started: 1 January 2002
Finished: 7 January 2002
It's sad, finishing this book; besides the fact that it was incredibly dark and it made me want to put a gun to my mouth, it's also the last Gaddis novel that I haven't already read, which means I need to re-read them or wait until his posthumous novel is published this fall. That said it was probably the most depressing of his works, not even very funny save for a few extended rants against religion. This shorter work is probably his most conventional book but it also just wasn't that interesting; he was wise to end it after 264 pages because the narrative wouldn't have sustained for very much longer. The story is really about the darkness of man and the modern age, as almost all of the characters are completely unlikeable. It's not one I'll read again any time soon.

2. Marbles in my Underpants by Renee French
Received: 10 January 2002
Started: 10 January 2002
Finished: 10 January 2002
EXTREMELY DISTURBING comics. Some were great, some were just fucking weird.

3. Species of Spaces and Other Pieces by Georges Perec
Received: (already owned)
Started: 13 January 2002
Finished: 15 January 2002
Perec rules! Some of the parts I skipped, like "All the Food I ate in 1974" and the more dull list-type things, but some of the essays were amazing, and the "Winter Journey" thing at the end was killer. I need to read more Perec.

4. The Baron in the Trees by Italo Calvino
Received: (already owned)
Started: 23 January 2002
Finished: 31 January 2002
A nice fairy tale type story, but nothing amazing.

5. Pierrot Mon Ami by Raymond Queneau
Received: (already owned)
Started: 1 February 2002
Finished: 7 February 2002
Great quirky French novel, pretty enjoyable and light but well constructed. Recommended.

6. Free Jazz (The Roots of Jazz) by Ekkehard Jost
Received: 10 February 2002
Started: 10 February 2002
Finished: 16 February 2002
Fantastic analysis of the free jazz masters. Goes more in-depth musically than most people might want but it really gave me a lot of insight.

7. As Serious As Your Life: The Story of the New Jazz by Val Wilmer
Received: 20 February 2002
Started: 21 February 2002
Finished: 25 February 2002
Great study of free jazz musicians; fun and awkward at times but very informative and "real".

8. An Emotional Memoir of Martha Quinn by Alan Licht
Received: 2 March 2002
Started: 2 March 2002
Finished: 2 March 2002
I really liked this! Licht echoes a lot of the thoughts I have had regarding popular culture/music.

9. Dhalgren by Samuel R. Delany
Received: (already owned)
Started: 20 January 2002
Finished: 6 March 2002
I became completely absorbed in Bellona; it really didn't come together until the last 100 pages but it almost knocked me over when it did. So vague, and yet so real.

10. Avant-Garde Jazz Musicians: Performing "Out There" by David G. Such
Received: 20 February 2002
Started: 7 March 2002
Finished: 11 March 2002
Nothing great but had some info on 1980s "out" jazz which was cool. Got into some really stupid discussions of slang, etc.

11. A Smugglers Bible by Joseph McElroy
Received: (already owned)
Started: 6 March 2002
Finished: 14 March 2002
A lot of this was over my head, by stylistically it was incredible. I need to read some more McElroy.

12. Ratner's Star by Don DeLillo
Received: (already owned)
Started: 14 March 2002
Finished: 22 March 2002
The ending lost me. It would have worked better as just a sci-fi novel.

13. Going Native by Stephen Wright
Received: 31 January 2002
Started: 23 March 2002
Finished: 26 March 2002
Some parts I really enjoyed. Fun and quick.

14. The Sinking of Odradek Stadium by Harry Mathews
Received: 27 March 2002
Started: 27 March 2002
Finished: 31 March 2002
I love Harry Mathews. I didn't understand this 100%, so I will have to re-read it.

15. Kangaroo by Yuz Aleshkovsky
Received: 27 March 2002
Started: 1 April 2002
Finished: 5 April 2002
Anarchic, funny Russian novel. Very enjoyable and vulgar.

16. The COINTELPRO Papers: Documents from the FBI's Secret Wars Against Dissent in the United States by Ward Churchill, Jim Vander Wall
Received: 27 February 2002
Started: 5 April 2002
Finished: 9 April 2002
Dry at times but fascinating. I only skimmed the actual letters and I skipped the part about the suppression of the American Indian Movement.

17. This Is Not a Novel by David Markson
Received: 27 March 2002
Started: 8 April 2002
Finished: 9 April 2002
Lots of fun, even though I just view this as a collection of thoughts and facts instead of an "experimental novel".

18. Extended Play: Sounding Off from John Cage to Dr. Funkenstein by John Corbett
Received: 20 February 2002
Started: 21 February 2002
Finished: 11 April 2002
Solid. The interviews are great.

19. Bayamas/Cardinal Polatuo: Two Novels by Stefan Themerson
Received: 10 April 2002
Started: 10 April 2002
Finished: 14 April 2002
Bayamas was great! *CP* was too pedantic and boring.

20. Cigarettes by Harry Mathews
Received: 1 March 2002
Started: 10 April 2002
Finished: 17 April 2002
So very conventional, but still distinctly Harry Mathews. Brilliantly constructed.

21. Harry Potter and the Sorcerer's Stone by J.K. Rowling
Received: 8 May 2002
Started: 8 May 2002
Finished: 12 May 2002

22. Harry Potter and the Chamber of Secrets by J. K. Rowling
Received: 14 May 2002
Started: 14 May 2002
Finished: 15 May 2002

23. Harry Potter and the Prisoner of Azkban by JK Rowling
Received: 16 May 2002
Started: 16 May 2002
Finished: 16 May 2002
Wow! Really great!

24. Harry Potter And The Goblet Of Fire by J. K. Rowling
Received: 17 May 2002
Started: 17 May 2002
Finished: 21 May 2002
Intense. I can't believe how good this was.

25. Understanding Power: The Indispensable Chomsky by Noam Chomsky, Peter Mitchell
Received: 25 May 2002
Started: 26 May 2002
Finished: 30 May 2002
Fantastic. Everyone should read this.

26. The Golden Compass by Philip Pullman
Received: 18 May 2002
Started: 20 May 2002
Finished: 31 May 2002

27. The Subtle Knife by Philip Pullman
Received: 30 May 2002
Started: 31 May 2002
Finished: 1 June 2002
Got really awesome near the end.

28. The Amber Spyglass by Philip Pullman
Received: 30 May 2002
Started: 1 June 2002
Finished: 8 June 2002
A killer trilogy. Maybe I should read more fantasy-type stuff.

29. Lanark: A Life in 4 Books by Alasdair Gray
Received: 13 June 2002
Started: 13 June 2002
Finished: 26 June 2002
I must check out more Gray.

30. Players by Don DeLillo
Received: 4 June 2002
Started: 27 June 2002
Finished: 3 July 2002
A quick DeLillo read.

31. 53 Days by Georges Perec
Received: (already owned)
Started: 11 July 2002
Finished: 13 July 2002
It's so sad that he died.

32. American Elf Volume 1: The Collected Sketchbook Diaries Of James Kochalka by James Kochalka
Received: 7 June 2002
Started: 9 June 2002
Finished: 13 July 2002
This slowly charmed me.

33. Mulligan Stew: A Novel by Gilbert Sorrentino
Received: 4 July 2002
Started: 15 July 2002
Finished: 1 August 2002
A ridiculously self-indulgent rewrite of *At Swim-Two-Birds*. Shades of *Pale Fire*, too. Funny as hell, though.

34. The Stairs: Munich Projection by Peter Greenaway, Elisabeth Schweeger
Received: 1 August 2002
Started: 1 August 2002
Finished: 1 August 2002
I can't really rate it, it's a catalog from an art show.

35. Peter Greenaway: Interviews (Conversations With Filmmakers Series) edited by Vernon Gras, Marguerite Gras
Received: 2 August 2002
Started: 2 August 2002
Finished: 4 August 2002
What a madman.

36. The Winner of the Slow Bicycle Race: The Satirical Writings of Paul Krassner by Paul Krassner
Received: 7 August 2002
Started: 7 August 2002
Finished: 8 August 2002
Amusing at parts but not ground-breaking. I do like this guy a lot, though.

37. Fear Of Drowning By Numbers by Peter Greenaway
Received: 8 August 2002
Started: 9 August 2002
Finished: 9 August 2002
Like a director's commentary track, only a book!

38. Boggs: A Comedy of Values by Lawrence Weschler
Received: 7 August 2002
Started: 10 August 2002
Finished: 10 August 2002
Weschler does it again.

39. Peter Greenaway: Museums and Moving Images by David Pascoe
Received: 8 August 2002
Started: 11 August 2002
Finished: 23 August 2002
Started out weak but got better.

40. Being Naked-Playing Dead: The Art of Peter Greenaway by Alan Woods
Received: 26 August 2002
Started: 26 August 2002
Finished: 28 August 2002
Way better than the other book I read about him.

41. Deterring Democracy by Noam Chomsky
Received: 14 June 2002
Started: 19 August 2002
Finished: 14 September 2002
Solid but somewhat dry. A bit too long and disorganized.

42. Our Beautiful Heroine by Jacques Roubaud
Received: 5 September 2002
Started: 6 September 2002
Finished: 16 September 2002
Sort of dumb, but amusing at parts.

43. The Human Country: New and Collected Stories by Harry Mathews
Received: 11 September 2002
Started: 11 September 2002
Finished: 18 September 2002
Scattered; some amazing stories and some that miss the mark. I'm such a fan at this point...

44. The Lost Scrapbook by Evan Dara
Received: (already owned)
Started: 25 September 2002
Finished: 7 October 2002
Really great, and sort of horrific.

45. The Rush for Second Place: Essays and Occasional Writings by William Gaddis
Received: 7 October 2002
Started: 7 October 2002
Finished: 11 October 2002
Too brief! A lot more political than I expected. Reminded me of Tom Frank at points only more erudite.

46. Strong Motion: A Novel by Jonathan Franzen
Received: 10 October 2002
Started: 10 October 2002
Finished: 17 October 2002
Very good. I wanted to hate Franzen. Dammit.

47. Agape Agape by William Gaddis
Received: 15 October 2002
Started: 17 October 2002
Finished: 18 October 2002
I already need to re-read it. Extremely dense and I didn't really understand it.

48. Gargoyles: A Novel by Thomas Bernhard
Received: 10 October 2002
Started: 18 October 2002
Finished: 27 October 2002
An intense monologue. I should read more Bernhard.

49. 20 Lines a Day by Harry Mathews
Received: 16 November 2002
Started: 16 November 2002
Finished: 21 November 2002
A great insight into a writer and his insecurities, but at this point I think I'm a rabid "fan" so how critical can I be?

50. The Tattooed Potato and Other Clues by Ellen Raskin
Received: 22 November 2002
Started: 22 November 2002
Finished: 23 November 2002
This was one of my favourite books when I was a child; my girlfriend recently got it from the library so I re-read it. It's still wonderful.

51. The Elsewhere Community by Hugh Kenner
Received: 25 November 2002
Started: 1 December 2002
Finished: 2 December 2002
Really nice essays; the ending rants about the internet are sorta "old person".

52. American Music in the Twentieth Century by Kyle Gann
Received: 25 November 2002
Started: 2 December 2002
Finished: 19 December 2002
A good overview; sort of simplistic at times but for learning about more obscure composers it was really interesting.

53. The Complete Lord of the Rings Trilogy : The Fellowship of the Ring — The Two Towers — The Return of the King
by J. R. R. Tolkien
Received: 18 October 2002
Started: 23 November 2002
Finished: 30 December 2002

54. The Corrections: A Novel by Jonathan Franzen
Received: 16 November 2002
Started: 6 January 2003
Finished: 10 January 2003
Stunning, fantastic novel. I loved reading every page.

55. Gold by Peter Greenaway
Received: 21 December 2002
Started: 21 December 2002
Finished: 16 January 2003
Greenaway is a lunatic. Ends on a terrible joke.

56. Omensetter's Luck by William H. Gass
Received: 27 December 2002
Started: 10 January 2003
Finished: 23 January 2003
I think I like Gass more as an essayist. I'm sick of stream-of-consciousness right now.

57. The Baffler Magazine #15: Civilization with a Krag edited by Thomas Frank
Received: 25 January 2003
Started: 27 January 2003
Finished: 28 January 2003
Such a great publication

58. Maldoror by Comte de Lautreamont
Received: 25 December 2002
Started: 24 January 2003
Finished: 10 February 2003
I didn't really like this as much as I thought; maybe I should re-read it someday.

59. Plus by Joseph McElroy
Received: (already owned)
Started: 11 February 2003
Finished: 25 February 2003
Really difficult and strange; I didn't really understand this entirely but the prose was superb.

60. Hopeful Monsters by Nicholas Mosley
Received: 27 December 2002
Started: 25 February 2003
Finished: 2 March 2003
Huge, sprawling, ambitious, and largely successful.

61. Running Dog by Don DeLillo
Received: 2 March 2003
Started: 3 March 2003
Finished: 5 March 2003
A pulpy thriller; good plot idea but bogged down by typical DeLillo bullshit.

62. The Franchiser: A Novel by Stanley Elkin
Received: 2 March 2003
Started: 5 March 2003
Finished: 11 March 2003
I must read more Elkin!

63. Wittgenstein's Mistress by David Markson
Received: 2 March 2003
Started: 11 March 2003
Finished: 16 March 2003

64. Snow White by Donald Barthelme
Received: 28 February 2003
Started: 17 March 2003
Finished: 18 March 2003
Got this for 50 cents!

65. The Hard Life by Flann O'Brien
Received: 2 March 2003
Started: 19 March 2003
Finished: 23 March 2003
Delightful but ultimately forgettable for O'Brien.

66. The Magic Kingdom by Stanley Elkin
Received: 23 March 2003
Started: 23 March 2003
Finished: 27 March 2003
Totally fun, unsentimental satire about dying children. Rather different than *The Franchiser* yet still obviously the same voice.

62, 341

67. Spiels of a/d'un Minuteman by Mike Watt
Received: 4 April 2003
Started: 4 April 2003
Finished: 4 April 2003
A nice, limited edition collection of Watt's lyrics, some writing, and some Pettibon artwork.

68. Stories and Remarks by Raymond Queneau
Received: 2 April 2003
Started: 2 April 2003
Finished: 5 April 2003
Queneau's short stories are wonderful, humorous, absurd; talking dogs, too!

69. The Cyberiad by Stanislaw Lem
Received: 23 March 2003
Started: 29 March 2003
Finished: 14 April 2003
Funny at times, would have loved this more at an earlier age, but some great sci-fi ideas. Reminded me of children's writer D. Manus Pinkwater.

70. The Case of the Persevering Maltese: Collected Essays by Harry Mathews
Received: 9 April 2003
Started: 11 April 2003
Finished: 16 April 2003
Is anything as exciting as a new Harry Mathews book? I read most of this quickly; solid writing of course, some parts amazing. Lots of stuff about Perec and a few pieces on the theory of writing, which were fantastic.

71. The Dick Gibson Show by Stanley Elkin
Received: 13 April 2003
Started: 18 April 2003
Finished: 19 April 2003
A little bit scattered but still so damn enjoyable. A beautiful piece of warped Americana.

72. The Believer, March 2003, Vol. 1, No. 1 edited by Heidi Julavits
Received: 1 May 2003
Started: 1 May 2003
Finished: 2 May 2003
A quite excellent new magazine. I'm anxious to see the next issue!

73. Teitlebaum's Window by Wallace Markfield
Received: 16 March 2003
Started: 21 April 2003
Finished: 6 May 2003
A great coming of age story, very funny and stylistic. I didn't understand all of the Jewish stuff, though.

74. How to Be Alone: Essays by Jonathan Franzen
Received: 13 May 2003
Started: 13 May 2003
Finished: 14 May 2003
A really excellent collection. I have to admit I do like Franzen now and have more in common with him that I'd admit.

75. The Big Book of Losers: Pathetic but True Tales of the World's Most Titanic Failures! by DC Comics
Received: 13 May 2003
Started: 15 May 2003
Finished: 15 May 2003
Another killer collection of historical comics about weird stuff. This whole series is great.

76. The Believer, May 2003, Vol. 1, No. 2 edited by Heidi Julavits
Received: 13 May 2003
Started: 13 May 2003
Finished: 20 May 2003
Not as good as the first issue; only skimmed a few articles (like the Jack White interview).

77. Masters of Atlantis by Charles Portis
Received: 13 May 2003
Started: 16 May 2003
Finished: 21 May 2003
Very funny but not really that substantial. Apparently this is different from the usual Portis. Will read more.

78. Invisible Forms: A Guide to Literary Curiosities by Kevin Jackson
Received: 3 May 2003
Started: 3 May 2003
Finished: 29 May 2003
A clever look at the parts of books you'll never think about. Sort of limited in scope — the author's bias is very apparent — and his humour is both the best and worst thing about the book.

79. State by State With the State: An Uninformed, Poorly Researched Guide to the United States by The State
Received: 25 May 2003
Started: 30 May 2003
Finished: 30 May 2003
A friend gave me this book after we watched *Stella* — it was surprisingly non-sensical, like a Dave Barry book only funnier. Read it in an hour.

80. Poor Things: Episodes from the Early Life of Archibald McCandless M.D. Scottish Public Health Officer by Alasdair Gray
Received: 13 April 2003
Started: 30 May 2003
Finished: 1 June 2003
An amusing novel set as a found document; not nearly as much of a mind-fuck as *Lanark* but still pretty entertaining

81. The Believer June 2003 Vol 1 No 3 edited by Heidi Julavits and Ed Park
Received: 8 June 2003
Started: 8 June 2003
Finished: 9 June 2003
Another solid issue of this publication that I really must appreciate despite the occasional foray into trendy/cute crap. Read almost everything and enjoyed it.

82. The MacGuffin by Stanley Elkin
Received: 1 May 2003
Started: 1 June 2003
Finished: 14 June 2003
Another great Elkin. This time he's really revealing a lot of himself, as the main character's paranoia is incredibly human, fragile, and surprisingly warm. Plus there's a minor mystery in the plot, which is nice but not overdone. And it's funny too, though not as sweeping in its humour as some of the other ones I've read. Another great slice of Americana, this time focusing on city life in a realistic yet "Elkin" way.

83. George Mills by Stanley Elkin
Received: 13 April 2003
Started: 5 May 2003
Finished: 19 June 2003
This was the book that Elkin considered to be his finest; I can certainly see how it's his most accomplished, as the emotional parts really hint at the desperation in his characters. Additionally, the narrative structure is complex without being confusing, a real testament to Elkin's ability to pull the reader through a story. However, I never really identified with George Mills, and the historical glimpses into Mills' ancestry, while sorta the point of the book, weren't really that enjoyable. And overall, it just wasn't FUNNY. I still thought it was great because Elkin is such a talented writer, but I would never recommend this as a starting point.

84. Wigfield: The Can-Do Town That Just May Not by Amy Sedaris, Paul Dinello and Stephen Colbert
Received: 31 May 2003
Started: 13 June 2003
Finished: 19 June 2003
Funny light reading. It's nice to read a total comedy book like this every once in awhile to loosen up, but I hate when they take too long cause I feel like I could/should be reading something "worthwhile".

85. The Believer August 2003 Vol. 1, No. 4 edited by Heidi Julavits
Received: 8 July 2003
Started: 8 July 2003
Finished: 9 July 2003
I should just get a subscription since I buy every issue. I also should stop considering these as books, but since it has a spine... Another solid issue, though I found myself skimming the interviews. A piece on Potocki! (This was worth the cover price.)

86. Lookout Cartridge by Joseph McElroy
Received: (already owned)
Started: 23 June 2003
Finished: 15 July 2003
Finally finished; and I am left pretty much speechless by this amazing masterpiece. McElroy's record of perception is stunning; narrator Cartwright tries to manage all of the interpersonal connections in his head, and likewise you do too; but the constant shifts in time and space make it extremely difficult to follow, and we are left with the feeling that it will all fit together neatly like a detective story if we can only figure it out ourselves. But I couldn't; the last sixty pages were completely overwhelming, dizzying, sinister, yet compelling. This novel succeeds so much because it combines McElroy's stylistic genius with an actual plot, and a damn good one at that. Cartwright is one of the greatest characters of contemporary/pomo literature that I've ever read, and it's a fucking crime that this

book is out of print and hideously obscure.

87. A Box of Matches by Nicholson Baker
Received: 11 July 2003
Started: 16 July 2003
Finished: 16 July 2003
Nicholson Baker truly returns to form. This was a beautiful, contemplative look at the little things in life, and after reading it, I no longer fear middle age, and I really want a fireplace and to live in New England. This was like an American *Mr. Palomar*; I'm glad Baker has returned to his detailed celebration of mundane existence. Highly recommended, and it barely took an hour to read.

88. A Short History of Nearly Everything by Bill Bryson
Received: 15 July 2003
Started: 17 July 2003
Finished: 21 July 2003
It's great to have a new Bill Bryson book to devour, even if it's not as funny as his others. It's a real "popular science" type of book, but his talent at making things interesting is unsurpassed. The writings on natural history, specifically volcanoes, were the best — there's a little bit of humour here and there, but mostly a genuine commitment to explanation. It fascinates me how little we actually know about the world — I guess I had assumed that science was pretty much wrapping things up. It put a lot of things in perspective.

89. Harry Potter and the Order of the Phoenix by J. K. Rowling
Received: 21 July 2003
Started: 21 July 2003
Finished: 22 July 2003
Very fun (and reading 860 pages in 2 days is great work); structurally almost identical to book #4, but much darker. It's interesting to see how she has incorporated basic political ideas into it, as the book touches on not only bureaucracy but also media control and, I guess, terrorism. Maybe I'm crazy to detect a post-9/11 feel to this Harry Potter book but it's definitely not all wine and roses. Also I liked how Harry and Sirius were both becoming self-involved twats, and not just total heroes. Even though Harry makes a mistake in every book, he really makes a mistake in this one. There weren't really any surprises to the story though, and I didn't put the book down thinking "Holy fuck, shit is totally fucked up!" like i did after #4.

90. The Universal Baseball Association, Inc by Robert Coover
Received: 11 July 2003
Started: 22 July 2003
Finished: 29 July 2003
Very fun, light comic novel about a man who is lost in his own world. It says a lot about imagination, faith, and religion as the awesome last chapter takes a diversion. Additionally it was all about baseball, which was fun; it made me really wonder how much worse Waugh was than the rest of us because although he is obsessive about a phony baseball league, we are often obsessive about equally superficial things.

91. The Elementary Particles by Michel Houellebecq
Received: 15 July 2003
Started: 23 July 2003
Finished: 30 July 2003
By the end of this I was sorta like "what the fuck?" I didn't really understand how the narrative was constructed and what he was going for — it had that exaggerated, extremist attitude that French intellectuals often have and while some parts were definitely funny, other parts seemed a bit too dogmatic and they rather pissed me off. The ending was quite stupid, though many may feel it's the strong part of the book, I just saw it as a cop-out and any sort of existential philosophy built up by the other parts seemed irrelevant. I certainly understand why Houellebecq is controversial — because in France, people actually read literature and give a shit about this stuff, which must be nice.

92. Sixty Stories by Donald Barthelme
Received: (already owned)
Started: 19 June 2003
Finished: 31 July 2003
The stories I liked the most were the funniest ones; the ones I liked the second most were just weird; overall I think I liked the earlier, funnier stuff better (just like Woody Allen!) but overall I really enjoyed this — it was great bus reading, as I could just read one or two stories each day. The detached, faux-profound writing just strikes me as hilarious, though he may be trying to actually go for something artistic at time; I really do like Barthelme though and I want to check out the nonfiction stuff my friend

was telling me about.

93. The Dog of the South by Charles Portis
Received: 24 May 2003
Started: 4 August 2003
Finished: 9 August 2003
Hilarious quest novel that mixed the American-style humour of Gaddis with the all-out wackiness of Flann O'Brien. Parts of this reminded me of *The Third Policeman*, specifically the parallel of John Selmer Dix with deSelby. This was way better than *Masters of Atlantis* and more obviously
77 funny — and I would recommend this to anyone. I loved it!

94. Actress in the House by Joseph McElroy
Received: 30 July 2003
Started: 30 July 2003
Finished: 24 August 2003
Writing about this isn't going to be easy; like the other McElroy books I've read it defies explanation, for the plot is relatively irrelevant. This has a phenomenal literary consciousness to it, though at times it because so tough (in the unique difficult way of McElroy) that I wanted to put it down; still, I pushed my way through it and discovered a novel rich with connections, taking a semi-mundane encounter and extrapolating all of the connections between the characters. Daley is such a difficult and obtuse character; even while floating inside his thoughts and memories for 400 pages I didn't really understand him. Still, the connections he makes often take a paranoid tone, reflecting the sinister vision of *Lookout Cartridge* at times. I
86 don't know if I would even recommend this book to someone else. Every word seems so important, and the choppy style really mirrors thoughts well. McElroy is such an incredible literary experience, but you really have to want to read him, and I'm not sure why I pushed myself into his oeuvre so much (but I'm glad I did).

95. Magnetic Field(s) by Ron Loewinsohn
Received: 1 July 2003
Started: 21 August 2003
Finished: 27 August 2003
This book was surreal to read because it felt like a book I have tried to write multiple times; the first section about the thief echoed an aborted short story I started a couple of years ago; the overall flow of the book was exactly like my first novel; and the second part is about an electroacoustic composer, which just seems like something I would write. What I really loved about this book was the way that it was populated with mundane household objects that kept reappearing, suggesting some spooky connections between the characters — a great idea, but I wish the book was 800 pages longer to really develop this and link more characters together. It could be an American *Life: A User's Manual* that way; not that Loewinsohn should strive to emulate other works, but it would really be an accomplishment.

96. Boswell: A Modern Comedy by Stanley Elkin
Received: 13 April 2003
Started: 28 August 2003
Finished: 26 September 2003
Elkin's first novel is more or less a blueprint for what is to follow: hilariously exaggerated protagonists with loud personalities, the tendency to break into monologues, and a sad, fragile side that exposes their weaknesses. This started slow but once it got rolling it had some very funny scenes, and is an interested look at celebrity in the early 1960s. Boswell's feelings about death are the spectre that hangs over the novel, and shades of this are definitely evident in later works like *The Franchiser* and *The
Magic Kingdom*. 62, 341 66

97. The Last Samurai by Helen Dewitt
Received: 9 April 2003
Started: 25 September 2003
Finished: 30 September 2003
This is a fantastic story about a child genius, perhaps caught up a bit in its own erudition but never getting overly ambitious with prose. DeWitt weaves together so many references to science, classics, etc. that it reminds me at times of David Markson's *Wittgenstein's Mistress*, especially in it's 
first person address. The beginning of the 63
book is incredibly delightful and fun; once the son takes over the narrative and begins searching for a father figure it falls into a routine that takes away from the excitement of the book, though it's still quite excellent reading.

98. The Baffler Magazine No. 16 edited by Thomas Frank
Received: 23 September 2003
Started: 23 September 2003
Finished: 2 October 2003
The Baffler seems to be really moving in a business-oriented direction; this probably reflects the interest of Tom Frank. There's some great articles here, especially the one about working for the dot-coms. I tend to think of *The Baffler* as "cultural criticism" first, but i guess business is culture in America.

99. Kalpa Imperial: The Greatest Empire That Never Was by Angelica Gorodischer
Received: 7 October 2003
Started: 7 October 2003
Finished: 2 November 2003
See my pending review in the *Review of Contemporary Fiction* January 2004 issue.

100. Gringos by Charles Portis
Received: 28 July 2003
Started: 2 November 2003
Finished: 10 November 2003
A longer Charles Portis novel, this one followed the adventures of Jimmy Burns, a lackadaisical American who lives in Merida, Mexico. Much like the protagonist of *The

93 *Dog of the South*, Burns lives life his way but doesn't take any shit; however, he's not macho at all. The construction of the characters is really what I like about Portis, and his eccentric characters are the spice that makes the book keep going.

101. Mainlines, Blood Feasts and Bad Taste: A Lester Bangs Reader by Lester Bangs
Received: 8 November 2003
Started: 10 November 2003
Finished: 18 November 2003
Bangs's second collection of writings is every bit as great as the first. He had a remarkable voice, but unlike Meltzer he never became too bogged down by his own negativity. His unpublished essay on the death of Sid Vicious is a very intelligent look at punk that sadly has gone unheard. His writings on music are great, and it's great to see his love for Charlie Haden and

2006 the **Mekons**, but his writings on culture offer a look at someone who lived during a vital time, was in the pulse of things, and never let himself be defined by any stupidity. Of course most of these pieces are about music and culture, and the more wacked out stuff is totally hilarious. The 8 million pieces about the **Rolling Stones** are almost as funny/obsessive as the 8 million pieces about Lou Reed in *Psychotic Reactions*. Of course, there are a few Lou Reed pieces here too.

102. The Believer, Eighth Issue: Neckfire! Vol. 1, No. 8, November 2003 edited by Charles Baxter
Received: 15 November 2003
Started: 18 November 2003
Finished: 19 November 2003
It's good that I'm actually getting around to reading these since I keep buying them. The best piece in here was on the Superman/Jesus myth and *Smallville*; there were some pieces I skipped, as usual. The article about the absence of face in literature was pretty weak and the chart that went with it was also shitty. The David Foster Wallace interview was good, but I can't help thinking how much better it would have been if Dave Eggers didn't conduct it.

103. A Fan's Notes by Frederick Exley
Received: 24 August 2003
Started: 17 November 2003
Finished: 28 November 2003
Frederick Exley managed to summon sympathy from me with this autobiography, thinly disguised as fiction, and that's notable because he's a real asshole. His candid honesty is certainly remarkable; he's in the mold of that sensitive tough guy, like Hemingway, macho as hell but not afraid to lay it out on paper. I mostly felt like I was reading a book that Holden Caufield would have written had he grown up a bit and not changed at all, which was also depressing. Halfway through I thought about how I never read autobiographies by people who have interesting, worthwhile lives, yet I was spending my time reading this. Of course, interesting and worthwhile lives aren't always this entertaining.

104. Three by Perec by Georges Perec
Received: 24 October 2003
Started: 28 November 2003
Finished: 7 December 2003
I was psyched to find this for cheap on half.com. This collects three shorter works into one volume, and I was most excited about *The Exeter Text: Jewels, Secrets, Sex* which is the English translation of *Les Revenentes*, the corollary to *La Disparition*.

Which Moped etc. is an early novella, a very funny rendering of a slightly interesting narrative, though it certainly shows the marks of being "early". *The Exeter Text* is a profound disappointment — while it's still impressive that e is the only vowel, a lot more liberties had to be taken with the English language to make the story work in translation. Of course I accepted these modifications — I was disappointed because it's so damn hard to read that after 30 pages I had to stop. It's certainly a novel idea (or novella idea, ha ha) but pushing through the actual text started to make me dizzy. And reading on, I knew there wasn't going to be any payoff, for the best thing about the text was known before I even read it. The final piece in this book, *A Gallery Portrait,* is the most rewarding. From 1982, it was his last published work, I believe, and continues in the manner that *La Vie mode d'emploi* began. It reminded me of that great Steven Millhauser novella I read a few years ago, only with that Perec wit and a complexity to the artifice. The idea of a huge painting of paintings of paintings (and so on recursively), with slight variations in each iteration, is incredibly Perecian, and I'm glad he got his idea down before his untimely passing.

105. Ancient history: A paraphrase by Joseph McElroy
Received: 1 December 2003
Started: 2 December 2003
Finished: 2 January 2004
I can't believe I found this for only $5 on half.com! McElroy continues to amaze me. Here is another novel that hijacks the concept of narrative, creating a crazy network of mental associations and memories. The "plot" is merely the narrator, Cy, hiding in the apartment of a famous celebrity writer/political figure just moments after his suicide. The book is being written as he hides there, and the "space" of the novel is entirely within Cy's head. His memories are very personal and they occasionally correlate to the celebrity's life, but the genius of this book (like all of McElroy's other novels except for maybe *Lookout*
86 *Cartridge*) is not in the story, but in the style. As disorienting as his other works, I've become somewhat used to his prose after reading a few, so I get a good feel for this "paraphase" (as Cy calls it). There is a rich human side to McElroy's prose that draws largely from his personal experiences — and I'm sure that Cy is David Brooke is Cartwright is Daley is Jospeh McElroy himself. And I didn't have to pay upwards of $50 for this, though it usually fetches that price online. Now if only I can find *Hind's Kidnap*!

106. Bear v. Shark: The Novel by Chris Bachelder
Received: 30 January 2004
Started: 30 January 2004
Finished: 31 January 2004
This book has been on my list for awhile as something that looked like a lot of fun, and it certainly was — a quick read that is over-the-top hilarious and very Barthelme-influenced. Bachelder is a pretty good writer, and he paces it well so it never becomes boring (nor do the relentless metafictional aspects become tiresome). Some parts were just completely hilarious, and this guy could be the next David Foster Wallace (he even makes several references to DFW in the text). Plus, his name sounds like "Box Elder".

1431

107. Searches and Seizures by Stanley Elkin
Received: 24 May 2003
Started: 22 January 2004
Finished: 24 February 2004
Read (slowly) on the bus, which is a pretty good way to take in three novellas. *The Bailbondsman* is not one of Elkin's strongest works, though it is very indicative of his style — a somewhat crazed, overassertive protagonist that captures a weird cross-section of middle America. *The Making of Ashenden* begins as a parody of the rich and turns into a twisted tale of bestiality; I must admit it was pretty entertaining, though again not something I would recommend. It's only *The Condominium* that really stands as one of Elkin's better efforts. And unlike his other protagonists, this one is rather muted, only breaking into soliloquy once I think. While the ending seemed rather sudden, this was definitely the best of the three selections in this volume.

108. The Believer issue 10 edited by Heidi Julavits
Received: 4 January 2004
Started: 3 March 2004
Finished: 3 March 2004
A pretty solid issue; Mishima piece was quite interesting; Xgau's piece on minstrelsy was unsurprisingly shit-boring; other stuff kept my attention, generally. Their cute little one-page "Mammal" and "Child" etc.

pieces are actually really stupid though and I'm pretty tired of them.

109. Infinite Jest by David Foster Wallace
Received: (already owned)
Started: 12 January 2004
Finished: 10 March 2004
Second reading. The first time I read this book, I thought it was hilarious, yet overambitious — nothing I would have considered a masterpiece, but definitely the funniest book I have ever read. And after a second passage through the book's 1100 pages, I find it both a masterpiece and one of the saddest books I have ever read (though still probably the funniest). How the inescapable sorrow of this book escaped my attention the first time I do not know; I guess I was caught up in the novel's quirks. I will go as far as saying that this is the best and most accomplished book that I have ever read from within the past 20 years (not that there is a lot of competition). I certainly love arcane, bizarre encyclopaedic novels, but this is successful on so many levels. DFW is undoubtedly a genius, the prose dazzling in both language and erudition. The imagination that went into this novel is astounding, as is the organization. While it seemed sprawling and inconclusive the first time through, it now reveals itself as a well-crafted book with many deliberate ambiguities. I guess one of the things I liked the most about this book is the sense of mystery; lots is unexplained, and I can accept that there is no definite answer — yet it's still really fun to read, and to look for clues in, and to try to put things together. This sense of the reader as a detective is something that I really enjoy in film and literature, and something that I need to find more of. I wish all of my friends would read this, so I can talk about it with them. The narrative is "anti-confluential" itself, just like the films of James O Incandenza, and the book itself becomes an addiction, as I would crave it's pages when I wasn't reading — making the stories of addiction work. I wish it were twice as long, three times even. I wish there'd be a sequel. 12/12, five stars, amazing, use all the superlatives you like.

110. Mountain R by Jacques Jouet
Received: 13 March 2004
Started: 13 March 2004
Finished: 22 March 2004
What a disappointment! After reading the summary on the Dalkey site I anxiously awaited this book — it sounded like an absurd, hilarious Oulipian novel. Instead I read a tightly focused political satire, which I guess was okay, but nothing remarkable. The book ends on a bit of a non-sequitur, I think, and it certainly wasn't unpleasant reading — but I expected something more zany, given the story. Jouet is an Oulipian but i don't know if this novel was constructed using Oulipo methods — I would guess not.

111. White Teeth: A Novel by Zadie Smith
Received: (already owned)
Started: 25 March 2004
Finished: 4 April 2004
Nice ensemble novel that captures a ethnic cross-section of London in a moving way; humorous, friendly, and clever in it's layout, I really liked this. I think she struggled a little too hard to make the ending into some great coming together of plots, but it was definitely a good novel.

112. Crosscurrents: The Hidden Wiring of Modern Music edited by Rob Young
Received: 4 April 2004
Started: 5 April 2004
Finished: 11 April 2004
The Wire's collected essays are very good indeed; not too academic, giving a rich background into the history of some common threads of current music. I really liked the occult" section with the piece on Harry Smith, but could have done without the last chapter (a bunch of NYC free-jazz worship). I would recommend this to someone interested in experimental music, however.

113. You Shall Know Our Velocity by Dave Eggers
Received: 4 April 2004
Started: 12 April 2004
Finished: 12 April 2004
Read this in 3 hours straight and I loved every page. It's hard to complain about Eggers, cause he is a good writer, and this tale of careless travelling felt especially relevant as I am travelling right now. Hilarious at times, easy to read and wonderfully strange at points.

114. Forty Stories by Donald Barthelme
Received: 21 March 2004
Started: 12 April 2004
Finished: 13 April 2004

While not as consistently great as *60 Stories*, this had some great moments. Barthelme manages to be utterly hilarious for the most part, but a few stories like "Overnight to Distant Cities" really succeed as incredible experimental writing. Of course not every experiment works, but we have to applaud his efforts.

115. The Stones Of Summer by Dow Mossman
Received: 25 March 2004
Started: 13 April 2004
Finished: 16 April 2004
The Stones of Summer truly is a remarkable book, surprisingly powerful in its use of language and meta-textual elements. I was worried that this would be a disappointment, after all of the hype, but I think Moskowitz really did unearth a treasure. While the narrative at times just resembles an Iowan *Portrait of the Artist as a Young Man*, the ending really unravels the story and calls into question all sorts of issues of unreliable narrators, autobiography, etc. But beyond all that, Mossman just uses language in a remarkable way, with some of the most beautiful descriptions of nature and the Midwest that I have ever read.

116. Fathers and Crows. Seven Dreams. A book of North American landscapes by William T. Vollmann
Received: 2 March 2003
Started: 16 April 2004
Finished: 21 April 2004
As much as it's easy to get excited about *Rising Up and Rising Down*, Vollmann's *Seven Dreams* series will probably be even more impressive if it's ever completed. This 800-page novel concerned the Jesuit attempts to convert the Huron in the seventeenth century, and was so incredibly well-researched that it could almost be taught as nonfiction. There were far less fictional flourishes than in *The Rifles*, but it still managed to hold my interest. I was actually pretty amazed at how readable it was, considering how daunting and dry I thought it would be. And it's almost as well documented as his non-fiction, filled with biographical sources, glossaries, and gazetteers. Vollmann's treatment of the Catholic missionaries was interesting — he did not seem to be judgements, actually casting one as a hero through his piousness. But I can't help but think this is Vollmann being a devil's advocate, as the whole book resonated with the atrocities committed by the French and British (though oddly, the Iroquois were really presented as the evil force in the tale).

117. The Public Burning by Robert Coover
Received: (already owned)
Started: 23 April 2004
Finished: 26 April 2004
Wow! This has sat on my shelf for years, and I'm glad I finally attacked it. Coover is totally hilarious, and daring in how he skewers Nixon. Oddly though, Nixon becomes pretty likeable as the protagonist. As far as novels encompassing mid-20th century America, this is tops as far as satire goes. Despite the hilarity within, deep down it felt like a quiet plea against the death penalty, and a strange warning about what America was to become. Highly recommended.

118. Chromos by Felipe Alfau
Received: (already owned)
Started: 30 April 2004
Finished: 3 May 2004
Incredible, a masterpiece. Alfau writes with such erudition, made all the more amazing by the fact that English was his second language. Narratively this novel plays with the idea of fiction, presenting the nested stories that make Potocki so wonderful, and also with a rich feel for European storytelling tradition. But Chromos also succeeds as a story about people between cultures, struggling to find their place in America while retaining their Spanish origins. Highly recommended.

119. Wanderlust: A History of Walking by Rebecca Solnit
Received: 26 November 2003
Started: 3 May 2004
Finished: 4 May 2004
It's nice to read some non-fiction; Solnit takes an interesting idea — the history of walking — and uses this to trace a path throughout art, social action and history. She infuses the writing with a great deal of her own personality, so the book loses some of its academic edge, but she manages to keep the topic coherent because she is such a good writer. Sections on mountain climbing and Las Vegas were especially interesting. A quick read but a

nice break from the heavy fiction.

120. The Letter Left to Me by Joseph McElroy
Received: 12 December 2003
Started: 4 May 2004
Finished: 6 May 2004
A brief, personal McElroy novel about a boy whose father died, and the father wrote him a letter, which is then copied among family and classmates. I guess it's a coming of age novel, for McElroy deals with some adolescent emotions here, although the narrator is still far too McElroyish to be believable as 17 years old. I would recommend this as a starting point for his books because of it's length, though it doesn't have the interconnected mindfuck elements of *Lookout Cartridge*.

121. Take Five by D. Keith Mano
Received: 25 March 2004
Started: 8 April 2004
Finished: 7 May 2004
Absolutely hilarious, and totally offensive. The character of Simon Lynxx manages to break all possible taboos of political correctness; Mano's style is actually somewhat difficult and this took awhile to read, but was constantly funny — like laugh-out-loud funny. Close to Pynchon in it's slapstick moments but even crasser.

122. Dance Dance Dance by Haruki Murakami
Received: 7 May 2004
Started: 7 May 2004
Finished: 7 May 2004
Good; possibly more enjoyable than *Wind-Up Bird*. Murakami's style (or perhaps his translator) is so calm and detached, yet managed to evoke empathy from me for the main character. His surrealist interludes remind me of David Lynch's — the strange stuff feels slightly forced, as opposed to the more natural surrealism of Buñuel for example; yet it was drenched in such clean and readable prose that it wasn't hackneyed.

123. The Age of Wire and String: Stories by Ben Marcus
Received: 5 March 2004
Started: 8 March 2004
Finished: 14 May 2004
I didn't understand this book at all, yet I pored over each page because the writing was so strange that I was motivated to keep reading. Marcus has conjured an eerie world that is calm, dreamy and unique; parts reminded me of early **Peter Greenaway** films in their almost-documentary style, and even though I had no idea what I was reading, I loved it and will read it again, attempting to make some sense.

124. The World According to Garp by John Irving
Received: 7 May 2004
Started: 7 May 2004
Finished: 14 May 2004
I've never read John Irving before and have never had much interest in him. While this was unremarkable stylistically, and had a really cheesy epilogue, the narrative was compelling enough to hold my interest. It's really a book about being a father and being a writer, and was very even-handed in the way it dealt with feminist issues. Good, I guess.

125. The Fortress of Solitude: A Novel by Jonathan Lethem
Received: 17 May 2004
Started: 17 May 2004
Finished: 18 May 2004
My friend was fanatic in her praise of this book — calling it perhaps the best novel she ever read — so I devoured it quickly. And she is right — it is a masterpiece, a real step forward for Lethem, but it doesn't abandon his past quasi-sci-fi elements. It's packed with cultural references and could almost be read as a memoir of the early years of graffiti and hip-hop. The last part is so crowded with music nerd references that it almost loses focus. I spent the entire day reading this and went through almost 600 pages quickly — it was definitely a "can't put it down" type of book.

126. Sabriel by Garth Nix
Received: 24 May 2004
Started: 26 May 2004
Finished: 28 May 2004
Enjoyable teen fantasy that definitely is similar to Phillip Pullmann, though not as well-written and without as much depth to the world. The magic stuff was sort of tossed off and explained too easily, but the "I was a teenage Necromancer" idea works and I will def. read the sequels if I can find them.

127. The Age of Kali by William Dalrymple
Received: 2 June 2004
Started: 2 June 2004
Finished: 3 June 2004
Collection of essays about different distraught parts of India. Dalrymple clearly loves India, but these essays tend to emphasize the negative. Still, it was very readable and his outrage was controlled into a hopeful feeling. Bihar sounds like a really fucked up place.

128. Holy Cow! by Sarah McDonald
Received: 3 June 2004
Started: 3 June 2004
Finished: 5 June 2004
McDonald's Indian travelogue is a hilarious look at India from a very Western perspective; this perspective is really the defining feature of the work, for she goes from completely hating India to loving it for its idiosyncrasies. What I think is most interesting is how she doesn't try to hide behind political correctness or an 'enlightened' viewpoint — she is quite definitely Western and unashamed of it. (I'm more ashamed myself.) Some of the mystical coincidences stretched my ability to believe but her quest for some sort of spirituality was understandable, and her failure to embrace anything was comforting.

129. The Autograph Man by Zadie Smith
Received: 24 May 2004
Started: 6 June 2004
Finished: 9 June 2004
Smith's second novel lacked the sweeping expanse of *White Teeth*, though it tried to
111 be a hell of a lot funnier. The style was a bit quirkier too, though some of the jokes ran thin (such as the 'International Gestures'); the Jewish emphasis was a bit too much for me to follow, and the main plot point with the old 50s actress was really stupid. So overall, I guess I didn't enjoy this book, though it was pleasant enough to read and quite funny at times.

130. Yadav: A Roadside Love Story by Jill Lowe
Received: 3 June 2004
Started: 5 June 2004
Finished: 9 June 2004
I pretty much hated this book. If it was supposed to be a captivating love story, then why did she treat her husband like shit? I mean, it's clear that he is an asshole but why would you actually be that honest about him in print? Clearly the author was terribly conflicted about her decision to marry this drunken hillbilly. She's a terrible writer too, which made it even more painful to get through — and her depictions of rural Haryana farmers was pandering and condescending. Fuck this.

131. The Inscrutable Americans by Anurag Malth
Received: 3 June 2004
Started: 11 June 2004
Finished: 12 June 2004
Hilarious, comic novel that makes fun of America and makes fun of India just as much. The end degenerated into a 1980s sex movie, but it was still pretty funny and I would recommend this to anyone whether they are interested in India or not.

132. The Salmon of Doubt: Hitchhiking the Galaxy One Last Time by Douglas Adams
Received: 7 June 2004
Started: 12 June 2004
Finished: 12 June 2004
I had forgotten how important Douglas Adams was to me when I was 14. I had also forgotten how brilliant he is as a comic writer, and his works hold up well despite my gravitations towards somewhat more "serious" literature as I've grown. I had also forgotten how intelligent he is when writing about science. In 10th grade I decided to re-read *HHGttG* every year forever, but forgot to keep it up as I got older. This really makes me want to dig it out and read it again.

133. Everything Is Illuminated by Jonathan Safran Foer
Received: 3 June 2004
Started: 14 June 2004
Finished: 15 June 2004
I had low expectations, but wow, this was readable. The postmodern structural crap worked really well, and made this great. While mining the emotional territory of the Holocaust is easy material for heavy drama, this novel succeeds still, mostly because of its juxtaposition with very sharp humour. A friend of mine may feel this was irresponsible because of the way it used a nonfictional town but I have no problem with it — this is fiction and if Coover can use
Richard Nixon as a character, Safran Foer is 117

entitled to use a historical village (though it is on his conscience, not mine, heh).

134. No Full Stops in India by Mark Tully
Received: 2 June 2004
Started: 10 June 2004
Finished: 17 June 2004
Tully writes about India from a journalistic perspective, and this is very dull. I get the feeling that he is a stodgy old Brit who loves India, but can never be comfortable enough with his feelings to write in an interesting manner. The first chapter about his servant was fucking dreadful to get through. The other chapters were pretty disorganized, and while I thrashed my way through it, I have no real desire to read any of his other books about India.

135. The Da Vinci code: A novel by Dan Brown
Received: 14 June 2004
Started: 16 June 2004
Finished: 17 June 2004
Terrible! I usually don't read shitty thrillers like this, but I am drawn towards books with a Templar/secret Europe/Illuminati conspiracy side, which this revelled in. The story goes so over the top that it's hard to take it seriously, and I kept comparing it to *Foucault's Pendulum* while I was reading it. And here's an analogy — *The DaVinci Code* is like a shitty American/Hollywood remake of a great European film (being Eco's novel, in this analogy); it removes all ambiguity and makes things simple, so the reader/
86 viewer doesn't have to think. (And *Lookout Cartridge* is like if Alain Resnais made a
232 conspiracy film, and maybe *Illuminatus!* is like an absurdist/experimental version a la Robert Nelson — but my analogy is getting carried away). Conspiracy fiction is my favourite cup of tea, but this was a particularly poor example. Sadly, I found myself continuing to read it, laughing out loud at how cheesy it was but secretly enjoying it.

136. Middle East Illusions: Including Peace in the Middle East? Reflections on Justice and Nationhood by Noam Chomsky
Received: 14 June 2004
Started: 17 June 2004
Finished: 17 June 2004
What has happened to me where I can sit down and knock out an entire Noam Chomsky book in one sitting? Of course this is filled with a thoughtful, logical analysis of the problems in the Middle East, not offering any easy solutions but hoping for a peaceful settlement. I'd like to read some other political writers to see alternate points of view, but few write as well as Chomsky — avoiding dry, academic parts and keeping everything readable and accessible.

137. Platform by Michel Houellebecq
Received: 7 June 2004
Started: 17 June 2004
Finished: 18 June 2004
Oh, Houllebecq. I didn't care for *Atomised* yet I picked this up anyway, and found 91
myself yet again disappointed. Still, it was a quick read and had some incredibly funny comments towards the beginning — humour that is the most misogynistic and misanthropic I have ever read outside of conversations among my friends. The bleak, existential attitude was boring — I read *The Stranger* when I was in high school, thank you. The ending fell apart, though not as badly as his first novel — and the very last pages were so "oh woe is me, life is empty" laughable that I was doing just that — laughing. Still the sex scenes were pretty hot and I suspect this is the major appeal of his work for many people.

138. Something Happened by Joseph Heller
Received: 31 May 2004
Started: 18 June 2004
Finished: 20 June 2004
I've never read Joseph Heller before (somehow I have never gotten around to *Catch-22*) but will have to read more. This was a crushingly honest depiction of the dark side of middle-class affluence. The fears alluded to in this book are shared by all men, yet laid out in such a bare manner it took an incredible amount of guts from Heller. The vulnerability exposed here is shocking, and the neurotic paranoia in here is funny in a very bleak way.

139. The Algebra of Infinite Justice by Arundhati Roy
Received: 14 June 2004
Started: 20 June 2004
Finished: 20 June 2004
Essays about politics and development by a highly acclaimed novelist. I enjoyed this for the India and political content, though Roy has a real flair for drama that charges

all of these essays with an emotional level that is somewhat unprofessional from political writing. The anti-American rants are fairly standard and somewhat unnecessary (I've read a million condemnations of the War on Terror already and don't need anymore, thank you), but her essays exposing the dangers of development projects and dam-building across the Deccan were remarkable, and probably the most important justification for this book to exist.

140. The Star's Tennis Balls by Stephen Fry
Received: 14 June 2004
Started: 21 June 2004
Finished: 22 June 2004
I picked this up cause it was cheap, and because I know Stephen Fry as an actor/comedian; as a novelist he is nothing special, crafting a far-fetched revenge tale with echoes of *The Prisoner*. I wouldn't recommend this or bother with it again, but as light "beach" reading (which is exactly what it was) it was amusing and went down easily.

141. Cobra Road by Trevor Fishlock
Received: 7 June 2004
Started: 22 June 2004
Finished: 23 June 2004
I thought this was going to be a travelogue — and it was, but not a linear one necessarily — rather a series of essays about different places that followed a specific path. The writing was good and insightful — probably a lot less social issue-oriented than other stuff I've read here — and the stuff about Pakistan was really great. Still, the travelling itself is half of the fun here — trains, plains, buses — and I had hoped that Fishlock would focus a bit on this.

142. The Hotel New Hampshire by John Irving
Received: 14 June 2004
Started: 23 June 2004
Finished: 26 June 2004
Wes Anderson must be a huge John Irving fan — this novel is just begging for a film adaptation. It has many of the same themes as Anderson's work, but most closely it shares a similar sense of whimsicality, where seriousness and sentimentality are blended together into a palatable package. Like *Garp* this was fun, dealt with women's issues well, and had an annoying unnecessary epilogue that ties up every possible end of things. Still, a good read though I don't think I will be reading anything else by Irving.

143. Villa Incognito by Tom Robbins
Received: 28 June 2004
Started: 28 June 2004
Finished: 28 June 2004
I read most of this while waiting for my room to be ready. I used to love Tom Robbins in high school, and I think it's with slightly guilty pleasure that I read his new works. This one was pretty insignificant — by this point his themes are tired and he has nothing new to say. The usual quirks and humorous metaphors that make his books so enjoyable were missing; or maybe I am just older? Or I've just graduated to bigger and better stuff now? His last book I remember being a little bit more substantial, but maybe it actually wasn't.

144. Chasing the Monsoon by Alexander Frater
Received: 18 June 2004
Started: 27 June 2004
Finished: 29 June 2004
Frater's travelogue is one of the best I have read about India, probably because it focuses on the monsoon instead of trying to generally capture the entire spirit of India in only 250 pages. His writing is funny, honest, and he comes across as a bit of an asshole at times (but in a good way). Excellent balance of science/meteorology writing and travel narrative, and possibly because his journey partly matched my own I found this really satisfying.

145. Was This Man A Genius? by Julie Hecht
Received: 28 June 2004
Started: 29 June 2004
Finished: 29 June 2004
Basically a long magazine article about Andy Kaufman that was stretched into a book (and double-spaced as well), this is a pretty great insight into Kaufman just before he achieved big success. It's shockingly honest at times (though you can never be sure) and a really interesting relationship developed between the two of them. Kaufman's subversive sense of humour is really inspiring. This only took about 45 minutes to read.

146. Underground: The Tokyo Gas Attack and the Japanese Psyche by Haruki Murakami
Received: 7 June 2004
Started: 30 June 2004
Finished: 30 June 2004
Having now experienced a little of the Japanese mentality I can only emphasize how much better this read for me — but subject matter like this would to be hard to not be compelling. The interviews with survivors were actually a bit tedious, yet upsetting. It's the interviews with Aum members and ex-members that really makes this an incredible read — reading first-hand about what life in a cult is like, and most interestingly learning that many are still believers. In a culture that is so materialistic, it's fascinating to hear about those who are rejecting that, even if it may lead to frightening results.

147. Not-Knowing: The Essays and Interviews by Donald Barthelme
Received: 28 June 2004
Started: 28 June 2004
Finished: 30 June 2004
This book made me excited to apply to grad schools. Barthelme's thoughts on literature are very forward thinking; his general non-fiction writing was pretty funny and not unlike his short stories; the interviews revealed a lot into the creative process. I skimmed some of the film and art reviews for works I wasn't familiar with.

148. Amnesia Moon by Jonathan Lethem
Received: 3 July 2004
Started: 4 July 2004
Finished: 5 July 2004
Lethem's debt to *Dhalgren* is explored here — this is almost a re-write at times, though with an even more emphasized amnesia element. At first I thought it was going to be another generic post-nuclear scenario, but he really wrote a unique world. Not up to his last book's standard of course, but as an early transitional work it's good, and more "literature" than "sci-fi" (though I hate those classifications anyway).

149. The Art of Travel by Alain De Botton
Received: 28 June 2004
Started: 7 July 2004
Finished: 8 July 2004
Very welcome collection of essays about the philosophy of travelling — de Botton is a great writer and he illustrates his concepts with a lot of historical figures. The 18th Century Frenchman who wrote *Journey around my Bedroom* was my favourite part. De Botton highlights some of the darker aspects of travel too, which I have definitely experienced in the past 3 months, and dwells on the nature of observation. Recommended.

150. No Sound Is Innocent by Eddie Prevost
Received: 10 July 2004
Started: 10 July 2004
Finished: 12 July 2004
I guess I am a relativist, but I just don't understand the need to be so dogmatic about music. Prevost's book had some great insights into the creative process of improvised music, but the majority of it was near-impenetrable "meta-musical" narratives. His language is so dense — not even overly academic, just overly wordy — that when you really looked at what he was saying, a lot of the time it wasn't anything ground breaking. And his positions are needlessly absolute at times — especially with his views on the cultural meanings of music, and the integration of traditional folk elements into rock and other genres. While he argues well here, his book seems to deny the most visceral thrills that great music can produce. But someone has to be AMM — someone has to be exploring in this direction, and I am grateful for everything they have given us. The essay about music education was probably the high point of this for me.

151. Party Going by Henry Green
Received: 13 July 2004
Started: 13 July 2004
Finished: 14 July 2004
Very interesting. While reading I found this to be a strange, subtle comedy, mocking the ultra rich in the manner of Wodehouse (I assume; I've never actually read Wodehouse). A lot of the subtext I figured was lost on me. But by the end I realized what a strange, mysterious novel this was. The prose was clean, but disorientating; the narrative dull, yet oddly compelling at the same time. After reading the introduction after finishing it, I was retroactively amazed by this novel (yet another example of literary criticism having too strong of an effect on my own judgement).

152. The Various Lives of Keats and Chapman: Including The Brother by Flann O'Brien
Received: 13 July 2004
Started: 13 July 2004
Finished: 14 July 2004
A collection of excerpts from O'Brien's newspaper columns concerning Keats and Chapman, which are just short farcical stories all set up around some ridiculous pun. I thought about how one friend would love these because he loves when there's a big setup all for one punch line, and some of these puns were brilliant (though some of them I didn't get). *The Brother* is a one-man play adapted from O'Brien's writings, which was okay, but not really written by him so it shouldn't have been presented as such. Quick and fun.

153. The Middle Mind: Why Americans Don't Think for Themselves by Curtis White
Received: 14 July 2004
Started: 14 July 2004
Finished: 18 July 2004
Curtis White doesn't pull any punches in this critique of American middle-class imagination. At times this reads like an extremely spoiled, snobby attack on everything sacred to American liberals (though he is attacking from the left); he delves into political rants often, which are occasionally childish and feel very out of place (I thought academics weren't supposed to do things like this). And I loved it — White articulates many things that seem taboo, and he perfectly expresses my hatred for *American Beauty* and it's mediocre embracing of traditional values masquerading as independent thought (finally, I am not alone!). While I wouldn't recommend this as a solid argument, it's funny and as a case of "preaching to the converted", it's wonderful.

154. Lirael by Garth Nix
Received: 14 July 2004
Started: 18 July 2004
Finished: 20 July 2004
The second volume in this teen fantasy series is a lot more developed than the first, introducing a lot of new characters and storylines. Well-written, though a bit predictable — yet my appetite was whetted for the third book.

155. The Moviegoer by Walker Percy
Received: 14 July 2004
Started: 20 July 2004
Finished: 22 July 2004
This has always been highly acclaimed as a masterpiece of modern fiction, etc. but I never knew much about it until I checked it out on a whim. I loved this novel — I definitely would consider it a masterpiece. Percy's writing is very gentle, and his narrative doesn't do anything tricky yet doesn't have much of a "story" to it anyway; the tiny reflections of the narrator touch on the sense of the "sublime" that Curtis White was raving about in *The Middle Mind* — a contemplation of life's mysteries and celebration of the world. Percy's descriptions of New Orleans are stilted and strange but beautiful, in their own way. Amazing.

153

156. Norwood by Charles Portis
Received: 14 July 2004
Started: 22 July 2004
Finished: 23 July 2004
Reading this book made me actually miss America more than anything else that's happened to me in the past four months. Charles Portis is amazing. He is amazing in a way that it doesn't hit you right away, and only after reading a few of his books did I realize his genius. There is a subtlety to his humour as grand as Wes Anderson's, and a celebration of the maverick American throughout everything. This highbrow treatment of the lowbrow is absolutely wonderful, and I'm sad that I only have one more of his novels left unread.

157. 1982 Janine by Alasdair Gray
Received: 20 July 2004
Started: 23 July 2004
Finished: 26 July 2004
Intense! At first I was like "oh shit, this is basically straight pornography" but as it went on I started to see how, like *Lanark*, it mixes very personal, emotional writing with really insane fantastical meta-fiction. Gray's character, which is clearly not entirely he, is really laid bare and the workings of his mind are presented in a realistic manner. Deep down, this is an extremely sad book and the dirty parts work not as titillation but to strengthen the sorrow. The more meta-fictional/experimental/whatever aspects of Gray's style succeed to convey the disjointedness of the narrator's mind. A fantastic book, on the level of *Lanark* but probably not likely to reach as wide of an audience.

29

158. Abhorsen by Garth Nix
Received: 23 July 2004
Started: 26 July 2004
Finished: 27 July 2004
The third instalment is much grander than the first two, and I have to admit that by the end I was thinking "this is a great fantasy series". Nix shows that his world is very well conceived and he brings personality to his characters without becoming overly sentimental. Will there be a fourth book?

159. Joe Gould's Secret by Joseph Mitchell
Received: 27 July 2004
Started: 27 July 2004
Finished: 28 July 2004
My favourite type of nonfiction writing is like this — showing the most wonderful and ridiculous sides of humanity. This is a treasure — and it reminds me of *Mr. Wilson's Cabinet of Wonders* both stylistically and content-wise. The only bad thing was that it was too short.

160. The Amazing Adventures of Kavalier & Clay by Michael Chabon
Received: 23 July 2004
Started: 28 July 2004
Finished: 31 July 2004
Okay. Why does a book like this win the Pulitzer prize, while a novel like *Hopeful Monsters* is ignored? 60 Chabon's debt to John Irving is apparent, though fortunately he doesn't have to tie up every possible fucking plotline with an annoying epilogue. The story was fine — well planned, with a nice surprising diversion into Antarctica — but his prose was completely unimaginative and bland. I guess I would say that I liked this book in that I found it pleasant, story-wise — but great literature? Come on, this is just like a beach book for the slightly more adventurous. The comic book stuff was well researched, which was nice, and Chabon does well at blending his characters in with history — but the only really interesting idea was of the artist becoming his creation, and it could have been explored a bit more.

161. Cosmic Trigger I: Final Secret of the Illuminati by Robert Anton Wilson
Received: 2 August 2004
Started: 2 August 2004
Finished: 3 August 2004
I don't know why I've waited so long to read these. Wilson is truly a genius; what I found most enlightening about these ideas is that they don't necessarily contradict with my own scepticism. It's easy to misinterpret his writing as a bunch of new age/occult crap, especially since the ideas are so fantastical, but Wilson is adamant that he doesn't actually believe in anything. The idea that the human brain is chemically possible to create realities is certainly a way to look toward the future, and drugs/the occult, if anything, just seem like possible gateways to this. Discordianism also appeals to me even more than before, once realizing that it's not a complicated joke disguised as a new religion, but a new religion disguised as a complicated joke. I will have to re-read this because it's a lot to absorb.

162. Cosmic Trigger II: Down to Earth by Robert Anton Wilson
Received: 2 August 2004
Started: 4 August 2004
Finished: 6 August 2004
Wilson's second book isn't really a continuation of the first one, but merely a collected group of ideas all vaguely related to his usual spiel. There's a far more autobiographical sense to this book, and it took me awhile to get into it; it's really just sort of like a supplemental appendix for the first *Cosmic Trigger* and in no way "essential".

163. Raw Deal: Horrible and Ironic Stories of Forgotten Americans by Ken Smith
Received: 10 August 2004
Started: 11 August 2004
Finished: 12 August 2004
Amusing collection of anecdotes about losers in American history; some were quite interesting, especially the part about how prairie dogs are being systematically exterminated. Sort of reminded me of those *Big Book* comic anthologies, only without the comics. 75

164. Cosmic Trigger III: My Life After Death by Robert Anton Wilson
Received: 2 August 2004
Started: 8 August 2004
Finished: 13 August 2004
The final piece of the *Cosmic Trigger* series explores the UMMO conspiracy while interspersing itself with more essays about reality, illusion, mind expansion and belief. Wilson goes into some rants against political correctness that would make you infer that he has reactionary politics — then

he takes you to task for inferring it, and warns against making jumps in logic. This has a bit less on drugs and the occult than the other two books.

165. Them: Adventures with Extremists by Jon Ronson
Received: 12 August 2004
Started: 12 August 2004
Finished: 14 August 2004
This is the kind of nonfiction work that is so outrageous you doubt it's veracity. Ronson, a Jewish journalist, spends time with neo-Nazis, David Icke, and KKK wizards while slowly getting sucked into the conspiracies about the Bilderburg group. I can't believe he actually infiltrated Bohemian Grove; furthermore that he's published accounts of it. Fantastic!

166. Grand Central Winter: Stories from the Street by Lee Stringer
Received: 12 August 2004
Started: 14 August 2004
Finished: 15 August 2004
Stringer was a homeless crack addict who started writing about his experiences, and they are quite entertaining. He doesn't moralize at all, and he was so intelligent with that he formed a pretty amusing attitude towards his stint on the streets. A good counterpoint to *Travels with Lizbeth* perhaps?

167. Bad Wisdom by Bill Drummond, Mark Manning
Received: 18 August 2004
Started: 19 August 2004
Finished: 24 August 2004
After wanting to read this for years I finally borrowed a copy and got to it. This is much, much crazier than I imagined — full of total sociopathic craziness and more perverse sexual humour than even I can imagine. It's nice seeing Drummond's honesty cut through Mannings's fantasies. And it makes me fascinated by the figure of Bill Drummond even further.

168. The Kinks' The Village Green Preservation Society by Andy Miller
Received: 2 September 2004
Started: 3 September 2004
Finished: 4 September 2004
I guess this is everything you could ask for in a short book written about a single album. Informative and it made me love the record even more.

169. The Believer #12 edited by Heidi Julavits
Received: 7 September 2004
Started: 8 September 2004
Finished: 11 September 2004
Some excellent political content here though I still didn't read it cover-to-cover, especially with the backlog to catch up on.

170. Iceland by Jim Krusoe
Received: 30 September 2004
Started: 30 September 2004
Finished: 10 October 2004
I'm not sure that I loved this book, though it was humorous enough to keep my interest. Krusoe reminds me of Donald Antrim — there's a similar silly but straightforward style, as if it's normal to write like this — where there aren't really jokes in the writing, but just straight descriptions of strange, funny events. There were some interesting things touched on here — memory, for one — but mostly I think it's a book about companionship, and our need for it. Paul is detached enough to move from one close relationship to another, while trying to convince us of his absolutely commitment and devotion.

401, 658

171. Requiem by Curtis White
Received: 30 September 2004
Started: 10 October 2004
Finished: 24 October 2004
White's fiction is funny and features some of the interests I saw in his non-fiction (attacking Terry Gross and the general lack of imagination in the world) but never really comes together. As a postmodern meditation on death and sexuality it's lots of fun, but it's too often derailed by diversions on bestiality and Internet pornography. As an anarchic look at the relationships between classical music composers, modern religion, and fetishes, it's fine. But it's not great as a lasting novel that I would want to read again or recommend.

172. What's the Matter with Kansas?: How Conservatives Won the Heart of America by Thomas Frank
Received: 29 October 2004
Started: 29 October 2004
Finished: 13 November 2004
Fuck. The Democrats need to read this book. Every single one of them. This was

the best look at the contemporary American electorate that I have ever read. Frank's writing style made this very enjoyable — he has a good sense of humour — and it was cool to hear him come out of the closet as a teenage conservative. He may be considered a "rising star" of the Left but I still think he'd be fun to hang out with.

173. Oblivion: Stories by David Foster Wallace
Received: 17 November 2004
Started: 17 November 2004
Finished: 24 November 2004
A new David Foster Wallace collection — a cause for celebration? Some of these stories were great — "The Suffering Channel" and "The Soul Is Not a A Smithy", specifically. Others were almost unreadable. This is the densest book he has ever written — pages and pages go by without any paragraph or line breaks. And some stories achieve what he does best — writing about the inherent sorrow in contemporary America masked through a strange, somewhat irreverent facade. The story "Oblivion" in specific has lots of cute gestures (like putting so many terms in quotes, though that does seem to actually call attention to how we manufacture meaning in so many terms) but ultimately is a moving, human story.

174. Men and Cartoons by Jonathan Lethem
Received: 17 November 2004
Started: 2 December 2004
Finished: 3 December 2004
I'm not sure why I like Jonathan Lethem so much. He's fairly obsessed with superhero comics, which isn't a topic I'm particularly interested in, and he keeps dropping references to "cool" music, which just sort of annoys me. But his writing has the potential to tap into something really 'authentic', even if it's couched in sci-fi genre trappings. This had some really fun stories and it was such a short read there's really nothing to complain about. Of course it's not up to the standard of *The Fortress of Solitude*
125 but it has similar themes and was plenty enjoyable.

175. The Rule of Four by Iain Caldwell, Duncan Thomason
Received: 6 December 2004
Started: 7 December 2004
Finished: 15 December 2004
Why do I continually read books like this when I am always disappointed? Another potentially interesting brainy thriller, a lot more restrained than *DaVinci Code* but
ultimately no more imaginative. The puz- 135
zle at the centre of the story isn't really elaborated on, which is a bit of a copout. Also it's too much of a "college" novel. The *Hypernotomachia Polyphili* content was interesting but so heavily fictionalized, and this proves to be yet another poor substitute for *Foucault's Pendulum*.

176. Mr. Dynamite by Meredith Brosnan
Received: 6 December 2004
Started: 16 December 2004
Finished: 23 December 2004
Very funny character sketch that shows one man's descent into obsession. I don't think we were meant to feel much sympathy for the narrator nor were we supposed to think this was a very well rounded character — the novel is purely a comedy. The writing was very good, in a Meltzer-esque style, with a lot of highbrow references and humour.

177. Hard-Boiled Wonderland and the End of the World: A Novel by Haruki Murakami
Received: 11 May 2002
Started: 1 January 2005
Finished: 9 January 2005
I should read more Murakami since I've liked everything I've read by him, especially this. A very strange narrative, even for Murakami, that was a lot more sci-fi than anything else I've read by him — but it was intercut with an almost Tolkeinesque fantasy half. The parallel narratives were set up well, though I found myself more interested in the *Hardboiled Wonderland* half. It's also interesting how the major action occurs in the middle of the book, and the end is a long, slow decline — sort of like Roeg's *Eureka*. I enjoy the calm detachedness of 
his narrators — it's something that makes 3
more sense after being in Japan for a bit.

178. Vermeer in Bosnia: Selected Writings by Lawrence Weschler
Received: 27 February 2005
Started: 9 January 2005
Finished: 22 January 2005
Lawrence Weschler is such an incredible writer than he can take pretty much any subject and make it interesting. This collection is of more recent material, organized into thematic sections. His writing about

Eastern Europe shows that he understands the complexity of the situations there, and his pieces on Los Angeles actually cast the city in an appealing light. When he writes about an artist, he highlights things I would never have realized about them but in an understated way, not showing them off as much as communicating for them. While this doesn't have the humorous quirks of *Mr Wilson's Cabinet of Wonder*, it's wonderful in an entirely different way.

179. True Grit by Charles Portis
Received: 11 November 2004
Started: 22 January 2005
Finished: 10 February 2005
The saddest thing about Charles Portis is that he only wrote five books. This is his most famous, originally serialized and made into a famous movie with John Wayne, and feels a bit weaker than the rest of them, though different. There's still the same unique sense of humour — the innocent quirks and certain type of character that's in all of his books. It ultimately makes me
93 want to read *The Dog of the South* again.

180. Checkpoint: A Novel by Nicholson Baker
Received: 10 February 2005
Started: 11 February 2005
Finished: 11 February 2005
Nicholson Baker seems to be capable of brilliant novels like *A Box of Matches* and
87 also fun throwaway books like *Vox*. This certainly ranks among the latter. The subject matter made this fun (and angry) and Baker's sense of humour remains (the methods plotted to commit the assassination are completely ludicrous). The controversy wasn't really deserved and it's sad that people overlook his more worthwhile novels because of it.

181. 50 Things You're Not Supposed to Know by Russ Kick
Received: 24 February 2005
Started: 25 February 2005
Finished: 25 February 2005
Another fun Disinformation book, that I stumbled across in the library this morning. I love these cheesy books, especially quick reads like this. I was amazed at how the US dropped two nuclear bombs in North Carolina in the 1960s, and there was some other entertaining facts in there.

182. Kafka on the Shore by Haruki Murakami
Received: 29 March 2005
Started: 24 February 2005
Finished: 6 March 2005
Another vast Haruki Murakami construction that bears a resemblance to *Hard-Boiled*

Wonderland in terms of structure, *Kafka* 177
is perhaps a bit more ambitious. The narrative is sweeping, delving into some of Murakami's familiar territory such as Freudian/sexual complexes, graphic violence, and the cold detached view of the world. Like most of the things I have read, his character progress through the narrative in an unclear, predestined trajectory. There were aspects of this novel that made it feel like one of his best works, such as the *Mulholland Drive*-esque mysteries and

non-resolution, but there were also aspects 126
that I didn't like. The majority of these I will blame on the translation though — Philip Gabriel's prose seems more childlike than Alfred Birnbaum or Jay Rubin's. I also don't understand the need to convert yen to dollars but leave the rest of the context in modern Japan. I don't know if I would recommend this as the first Murakami novel to read but it's certainly enjoyable, and another solid offering by one of the masters of contemporary surrealism.

183. Status Anxiety by Alain De Botton
Received: (already owned)
Started: 7 March 2005
Finished: 19 March 2005
I really like deBotton's approach to writing; he writes about philosophy, but not in a boring way, and illustrates his points with examples from the history of art and philosophy. The central question of this book is "Why are we so concerned with status?", and it points out how with all of the luxuries available in the modern world, we are still unhappy. I think his writing has helped me to frame a lot of my own ideas about my life, and I found it inspirational in that aspect. He mentions several ways to overcome status anxiety — art, politics, religion and bohemia — and it seems like a good way to look at things. I don't think it will ever be possible to completely overcome status anxiety (and maybe not even desirable) but it's good to put things in perspective and think about how the modern Western psyche has developed over the past few centuries.

184. My Life In CIA by Harry Mathews
Received: 9 May 2005
Started: 29 March 2005
Finished: 9 April 2005
A new Harry Mathews book — wow! The only reason it took me so long to read was because Dalkey sent me a Xerox of it and I found the format awkward. I loved the first 50 pages because it was a weird, offbeat memoir about being involved in the French avant-garde in the 1970s. Then I realized that I was reading a novel, not a straight autobiography. Mathews is so amazing when he turns on his weird, contrived humour, and sections of this book were undoubtedly conceived through some sort of Oulipian method. I was totally thrilled by certain passages, and as the novel got more and more ridiculous I kept enjoying it further. As a fan of his other works, I enjoyed it even more so- it felt closer to *Tlooth* than any of his other books, and
240 *Tlooth* is probably my favourite of his. I hope he writes a few more books, soon!

185. Love, Poverty, and War : Journeys and Essays by Christopher Hitchens
Received: 31 May 2005
Started: 30 April 2005
Finished: 3 May 2005
I really enjoy Christopher Hitchens — and I'm glad that I disagree with him on the War on Terror — and this book of essays reaffirmed my faith. He shows his erudition in the literary excerpts, and except for some of the war-themed pieces I found this consistently enjoyable. The essay about testifying against Mother Theresa to the Vatican was hilarious, and the piece on North Korea was absolutely terrifying (yet funny). I really appreciate how dedicated he is to attacking the notion of the hero, and thus his even-handed viewpoint of Winston Churchill was refreshing. There are few writers who despise power and idolatry as much as Hitchens, and every word he writes is like a condemnation. Lefties who have abandoned him because of a policy dispute are really missing out on a great mind.

186. Vanishing Point: A Novel by David Markson
Received: 30 April 2005
Started: 11 May 2005
Finished: 12 May 2005
Every fucking David Markson book is exactly the same. They are great, though. People really seem to consider him to be one of the vanguard experimental novelists, but I don't really see what is so innovative about him. He disposes of plot, character, sure — but to say that his books are much more than collections of observations about the creative process is giving him a bit too much credit. I think *Wittgenstein's Mistress*
was the best one because of the pretext of 63
it, but they're all exactly the same fucking book. He can keep them coming, and I'll keep reading them, but I don't think I'll ever rank him as one of my favourite writers.

187. What the Dormouse Said: How the Sixties Counterculture Shaped the Personal Computer Industry by John Markoff
Received: 5 June 2005
Started: 13 May 2005
Finished: 18 May 2005
The topic of 1960s counterculture and it's influence on the PC industry is very interesting; unfortunately, this book did a poor job of presentation. The biggest flaw is Markoff's writing, which is full of cliches, and felt childish at times. He did a poor job in conveying how these so-called countercultural values actually translated philosophically with these people; it was largely just stories about people inventing new hardware, and then taking acid and having orgies. It also felt like he would occasionally forget what the topic was and then be like "Oh yeah, they hated Vietnam and smoked pot too."

188. Extremely Loud and Incredibly Close: A Novel by Jonathan Safran Foer
Received: 8 June 2005
Started: 18 May 2005
Finished: 22 May 2005
One critic trashed this book so hard that I almost felt bad for Safran Foer, but when reading his overwhelming cleverness here, my sympathy washed away. Of course, I enjoyed reading this — it pushes all of the right buttons like *Amelie* or something, even managing to take 9/11 as a topic and not be completely puerile. There are criticisms galore — many "experimental" techniques that are nothing of the sort, most merely copouts to avoid having to actually write — but the book was so funny, smart and clever that I probably even liked it more than his first one (which I also wanted to hate). Fuck you JSF for writing books like this, because they're too good and bad and inevitable.

189. The Disappointment Artist: Essays by Jonathan Lethem
Received: (already owned)
Started: 1 June 2005
Finished: 3 June 2005
Jonathan Lethem is such a fanboy! This book of essays is mostly about art and culture, including essays about how he saw *Star Wars* 21 times in a summer, and an closing section that explores the relationship we have to media and art. The last essay in particular was so powerful because it's exactly about my life, and the Fortress of Solitude I have built in the Ninth Room, surrounded by the "books and all the records of my lifetime" (to make yet another reference here). His writing is so passionate that it's hard not to love this, and his admissions are so accurate to my own life that it's almost embarrassing at points.

190. Notable American Women: A Novel by Ben Marcus
Received: 8 June 2005
Started: 5 June 2005
Finished: 8 June 2005
I now feel that Ben Marcus is one of the most exciting young experimentalists today; compared to someone like Safran Foer, he's in a different league, and actually creating new meaning as my friend put it. Language hasn't transformed this brilliantly to my eyes in a long time. This still conjured the sense of creation that I enjoy in early Greenaway yet it had a light, almost spiritual touch to the prose (and was funny at times too). Absolutely fucking brilliant, and I can't wait to read what he does next.

191. How We Are Hungry by Dave Eggers
Received: 23 May 2005
Started: 23 May 2005
Finished: 14 June 2005
Eggers' latest collection is unsurprising; I enjoyed a handful of stories and didn't care for the rest. I don't know why this guy thinks he is clever because he "writes" a story of five blank pages. I suppose at this point he is here to stay, so I'd better get used to him. The stories about the one-armed girl in Skye and the mountain climbing expedition were very nice; some of the others amused me, and others still were completely awful.

192. Portnoy's Complaint by Philip Roth
Received: 19 June 2005
Started: 18 July 2005
Finished: 20 July 2005
I had no idea this was so funny — totally over the top, obnoxious politically-incorrect Jewish-orientated humour that had me laughing throughout. At times I'm reminded of Wallace Markfield — and then the novel actually makes a reference to Wallace Markfield! Woody Allen seems second-rate after this. Classic!

193. Harry Potter and the Half-Blood Prince by J.K. Rowling
Received: 18 August 2005
Started: 18 August 2005
Finished: 1 August 2005
The latest Harry Potter book really didn't offer any surprises — I sort of expected the big shocking thing at the end before it even came out. It was still fun, but noticeably more condensed than the last one, and missing a lot of the stuff I really liked about the longer books. There was enough to keep me reading it quickly but I would have to say that this is a step down from the last two.

194. The Mezzanine by Nicholson Baker
Received: (already owned)
Started: 24 August 2005
Finished: 1 September 2005
It's been five years since I read this, and when I was packing up my books to store for the next year it caught my eye and I decided to re-visit it. This is a wonderful book that is both hilariously and mind-expanding, though on a surface level it's a dull, silly exercise in minutiae. Baker's obsession with the mundane reveals a deep philosophy in the way things work, and the simple pleasures in everyday life. This isn't as beautiful of a book as *A Box of Matches* but it's still great and it held up wonderfully on a second read.

195. Murphy by Samuel Beckett
Received: 17 September 2005
Started: 17 September 2005
Finished: 21 September 2005
Quite absurd fun! I had trouble understanding much of this novel, which was very Irish in it's sense of humour, feeling like a good bridge between Joyce and Flann O'Brien. There's a darkly comical feel to the story and the death at the end is strangely

triumphant. I must read more of Beckett's fiction (and I have to, for class).

196. The Good Soldier: A Tale of Passion by Ford Madox Ford
Received: 20 September 2005
Started: 20 September 2005
Finished: 25 September 2005
Quite readable and I guess remarkable because of it's non-linear narrative, which jumps back and forth through flashbacks. The plot is "sad" of course, but not sappy, and the narrator is somewhat unreliable — he comes across as totally daft but I can't help suspect he was dipping his eggs into another basket too.

197. Postwar America: 1945-1971 by Howard Zinn
Received: 27 September 2005
Started: 27 September 2005
Finished: 3 October 2005
This reads like a more in-depth final section of *People's History* and is easy to read and enjoyable. There weren't many things that I didn't already know, though learning about McCarthyism a bit further was interested. Zinn ends the book on a really hopeful note, seeming to believe that the social reforms of the late 60s were the gateway to a better tomorrow. Reading it 30 years later, it's all the more tragic that the country has followed along this path.

198. A History of Bombing by Sven Lindqvist
Received: 11 October 2005
Started: 11 October 2005
Finished: 18 October 2005
We are structuring our Special Topic around this book. It's a brilliant look at the art of aerial bombing throughout history, cut up into chronological chunks and then reassembled through different patterns. The Choose-Your-Own-Adventure format works well because you get a sense of chronology and repetition, but you aren't forced to read the book that way. It benefits the topic, rather than just appearing gimmicky, because of the sense of destruction and displacement cause by bombing. In some ways this is history, in some ways it's also political essay, journalistic, and personal. It succeeds on all levels.

199. Ground Zero by Paul Virilio
Received: 12 October 2005
Started: 19 October 2005
Finished: 20 October 2005
This was easier to read than I thought, and as these things go it was actually pretty enjoyable. However, I still had trouble following it and a lot of things went over my head. I think I really got a few ideas out of it, which oddly enough I was thinking about in relation to the Instal fest, but I don't know how much I missed. It seemed a bit unfocused even within each chapter, as he would proclaim some ideas and then move onto the next, without giving me any way to really tie it together. Perhaps I should try a longer work of his next.

200. Armed with Madness by Mary Butts
Received: 21 October 2005
Started: 22 October 2005
Finished: 23 October 2005
This lost classic of 1920s English modernism is very, very strange — a dark, unresolving story that deals with the modern fascination with the ancient and esoteric in a similar way to Charles Portis, TS Eliot, and Pynchon. The prose was actually quite difficult at time, falling somewhere between Joyce and Gaddis in style, and the ending was very compelling, as the narrative splintered and then re-converged. I would have never heard of this writer if it wasn't for it being assigned, so I am very glad to have had to read this because it definitely is something I will want to read again.

201. Time's Arrow by Martin Amis
Received: 12 October 2005
Started: 23 October 2005
Finished: 24 October 2005
A very entertaining novel that's gimmick is the backwards life of a Nazi War criminal; of course the gimmicky aspects overshadow everything, but are also the most compelling reason to keep reading. The morality of the subject matter is dealt with in a very even manner, without much debate. I would have preferred a little bit more mystery, and a little more of having to figure things out, like that film *Memento*.

202. Darkness Falls from the Air by Nigel Balchin
Received: 24 October 2005
Started: 27 October 2005
Finished: 31 October 2005
Very Hemingway-esque novel of male impotence during the London blitz. While it had a "popular fiction" feel, there were a few tricks involved — I got the sense of an unreliable narrator, mostly. It's an interesting social portrait, and I definitely find the area of sexual freedom during wartime to be interesting.

203. Things Fall Apart by Chinua Achebe
Received: 4 November 2005
Started: 4 November 2005
Finished: 5 November 2005

204. No Longer at Ease by Chinua Achebe
Received: 1 November 2005
Started: 7 November 2005
Finished: 7 November 2005

205. Caught by Henry Green
Received: 11 October 2005
Started: 5 November 2005
Finished: 8 November 2005
My professor's theory is that Green was attempting to write a pastoral novel about the Blitz, but I think he had to radicalize the form by writing about the destruction of nature and the horrors of urbanity instead of the natural world. Incredibly strong use of colour here, and stylistically Green continues to intrigue me because he uses elements present in a lot of writing, but nothing overwhelming, ie: some stream of consciousness, but I wouldn't call him a SofC writer. I really want to read more of his work as soon as this course is over!

206. Slaughterhouse-Five or The Children's Crusade by Kurt Vonnegut Jr.
Received: 9 November 2005
Started: 9 November 2005
Finished: 10 November 2005
First time in maybe eight years that I have read this? Revisiting this in terms of the course I am taking, it's even more fun than I remembered. Perhaps Vonnegut's absurdism comes as a release after the more serious accounts of aerial bombardment I have been reading. The idea of the adynaton is certainly present, as Vonnegut basically says in the introduction that he is writing about Dresden because he feels obligated to, but obviously resorts to a pretty unusual way to talk about it. The horror is glossed over to the point that it becomes more horrifying because it isn't dwelled upon.

207. On the Beach by Nevil Shute
Received: 16 November 2005
Started: 17 November 2005
Finished: 18 November 2005
One of the best dystopian novels I have ever read — I love how the characters cling to the things they hold dear to them in the face of certain doom — objects, bureaucracy, family. A very readable (if uninventive) style makes this a pretty gripping page-turner, despite the fact that nothing really happens in it. And there's not even any chance of a hopeful outcome — from the beginning the cards are stacked against everybody.

208. Welcome to the Desert of the Real: Five Essays on September 11 and Related Dates by Slavoj Zizek
Received: 16 November 2005
Started: 16 November 2005
Finished: 20 November 2005
Very interesting and challenging book, in the same series as the Virilio I read earlier. This attempts to dissect the reaction to 9/11 and argues against both Islamic fundamentalism and Western liberal democracy, showing how the two positions are hopelessly linked. While there were parts of this that were lost on me, and some unclear ideas, I like all of the examples he used and the general style of the writing. I may not have completely grasped his arguments, but I actually really enjoyed reading this.

209. Mao II by Don DeLillo
Received: 11 October 2005
Started: 6 December 2005
Finished: 10 December 2005
Another brilliant and frustrating work by DeLillo. I think my interest in the topic has been enhanced by the course, yet I can't help but wish he avoided his usual stylistic flourishes. This lacks the power of *The Names* or *White Noise* because it seems more confident in that power. There were some very interesting ideas about the commercialisation of terror factions, which I'm sure we'll discuss in seminar, but the more traditional elements of narrative/character felt uncertain, and even a bit unfinished.

219, 482 220

210. Dhalgren by Samuel R. Delany
Received: 9 November 2005
Started: 9 November 2005
Finished: 19 December 2005
On a second read I found this even more of an accomplishment than I previously though. None of the mysteries are any more clear to me, though I suppose that's not the point. The city and the book mirror each other, which will be the gist of the essay I have to write on this. Now, it's time to get started.

211. Crash by J. G. Ballard
Received: 10 January 2006
Started: 10 January 2006
Finished: 15 January 2006
I'm not going to enjoy something just because it's transgressive, but I did enjoy this largely because some of the ideas were so fucked up and complete in Ballard's vision. The irony was not lost on me, and although some parts are slow going I would hardly call it boring. The professor's subsequent seminar on post-modern space was great!

212. Education of a Coach by David Halberstam
Received: 25 December 2005
Started: 15 January 2006
Finished: 18 January 2006
Not particularly well-written, but I suppose it's a book about a football coach written for sports fans. Not that I suggesting football fans aren't intelligent, but they don't need to subscribe to rigorous standards of academic writing. This was enjoyable cause I needed a football fix, but I sort of feel like I could have used my time more wisely.

213. Trout Fishing in America by Richard Brautigan
Received: 7 February 2006
Started: 7 February 2006
Finished: 8 February 2006
My aunt recommended this when I was 15 and I loved it. On a whim I re-read it, wondering "Will it hold up?" and it did — perhaps exceeding my adolescent enjoyment. Perfectly absurd and funny, not too long, and my professor gave me a free copy which totally rules.

214. In Watermelon Sugar by Richard Brautigan
Received: 7 February 2006
Started: 8 February 2006
Finished: 9 February 2006
But *In Watermelon Sugar* is Brautigan's masterpiece, I'd say. The hazy dream world created here is just underwritten enough to let your imagination take hold. The actual plot is fairly minimal — it ends before it really gets going, and the true joy is the world he created. Why can't I live here?

215. The 42nd Parallel: Volume One of the U.S.A. Trilogy by John Dos Passos
Received: 23 January 2006
Started: 30 January 2006
Finished: 14 February 2006

216. The Driver's Seat by Muriel Spark
Received: 16 February 2006
Started: 18 February 2006
Finished: 18 February 2006
Very, very strange! I was fooled by the beginning of the book and its readability, but by the end I was completely absorbed yet no more clear. I feel like I'm often comparing things too much but this struck me as *A Woman Under the Influence* crossed with Buñuel, and also a book. The sense of feminine space is well defined and the disconnection with sexuality and normal human interaction is actually quite convincing. I look forward to discussion on Monday.

416

217. The Passion of New Eve by Angela Carter
Received: 19 February 2006
Started: 19 February 2006
Finished: 20 February 2006

218. More Pricks Than Kicks by Samuel Beckett
Received: 23 February 2006
Started: 23 February 2006
Finished: 27 February 2006
Does Beckett's revelry in intellectual wordplay and artifice mean he is inherently mocking class structure? Both Belacqua and Murphy are heroes who reject any sorts of vocation, and their class backgrounds are irrelevant. Beckett's black humour and callousness towards the plight of the female characters showcases the spectacles of modern society and an unwillingness to commit to a moral judgement. A copout? Brilliant.

219. The Names by Don DeLillo
Received: 17 November 2005
Started: 18 January 2006
Finished: 15 March 2006
My memory of this book was that it was completely amazing and the best DeLillo work by a mile. After re-reading it, I think I experienced the same effect — I wasn't really that into it while I was reading it, but a slow sinking enjoyment came after I finished it. I still think this is his best book (of the ones I've read); it manages to perfectly walk the line between postmodern political relationships and bullshit without crossing over. It's not the warmest of his texts, but that distance is exactly what makes it great. It also touches on systems and numerology without going too deep, again the perfect balance.

220. White Noise by Don DeLillo
Received: 27 April 2006
Started: 5 May 2006
Finished: 9 May 2006
I haven't read this since the pre-listing days so I grabbed it for a weekend read during my Paris trip, figuring it would be a good prequel to beginning a summer working with miserable disaster literature. This novel may actually be the most successful DeLillo novel, but for a good reason — the typical DeLillo pontificating isn't quite as dense here, for the subjects are very human and he's not trying to create an artificial distance between the reader and character as he does in *Players*, *Running Dog*, *The*
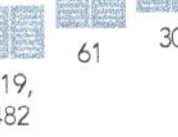
61 30 219, 482
Names, etc. The warmth may be a bit of a false pleasure though, because the novel is completely obsessed with death in every way, a biting way to undercut the family dialogues. This is a new approach to the bleak — instead of opting for black humour, DeLillo confronts the fear, not with acceptance but by trying to study it as much as possible.

221. The Aesthetics of Disappearance by Paul Virilio
Received: 9 April 2006
Started: 10 May 2006
Finished: 10 May 2006
A quick read, though a lot of it went in my brain and out pretty quickly. Virilio attempts to theorize on absence and disappearance, looking through a child's brain and specifically at how cinema measures time. Western society's obsession with speed is addressed as a method, a cause perhaps, of disappearing.

222. Louis Riel: A Comic-Strip Biography by Chester Brown
Received: 17 April 2006
Started: 13 May 2006
Finished: 13 May 2006
Subtitled "A Comic Strip Biography," this examines the life of Louis Riel, who led the Métis independence movement in the late 19th century. Riel was an interesting character — passionately humane, and religious to the point of believing he was a prophet. Brown's style works well to draw the reader into the historic period, and the scenes of battle are mapped out in a way that isn't confusing or overwhelming. This will probably do wonders to promote the idea of comics as literature.

223. The Accident of Art by Sylvère Lotringer, Paul Virilio
Received: 18 May 2006
Started: 19 May 2006
Finished: 19 May 2006
This is great — extremely readable and conversational, which is the best way to read this type of thing. Virilio (who dominates the dialogue) differentiates representation and presentation as two types of iconoclasm in art, and laments the death of a fixed point. It's similar to Jameson's writing on the speed of history, and how nostalgia is permanently in flux.

224. Roadside Picnic by Arkadi Strugatsky, Boris Strugatsky, Arkady Strugatsky
Received: 30 May 2006
Started: 30 May 2006
Finished: 2 June 2006
The novel that *Stalker* is based on is quite a bit different — Tarkovsky certainly tried 165, 486, 505 to find a more allegorical feel in his adaptation. This is a really fascinating, gripping sci-fi novel that is every bit as mysterious and inviting as the film. The language is very straightforward, even a bit coarse, so the more spiritual aspects of the film are filled in by my imagination. The deeper exploration of the characters' backgrounds adds a new dimension, as the Stalker of the novel is a much more warm and empathetic figure.

225. Towards a Philosophy of Photography by Vilem Flusser
Received: 13 May 2006
Started: 27 May 2006
Finished: 4 June 2006
Very clear and straightforward, defining

four major terms: image, apparatus, program and information; looking at chance and how it plays a role in the construction of photographic consciousness and ending with a reflection on freedom and a new methodology for photography in the "post-historical" age.

226. Pure War by Paul Virilio, Sylvère Lotringer
Received: 2 June 2006
Started: 2 June 2006
Finished: 4 June 2006
This didn't have as much to do with my topic but I still enjoyed reading it as "fun" fare; the discussion centred around Virilio's idea of the military class and its dominance in the world. Some interesting points made about the shift from geographic control to temporal, and the contemplation of death.

227. The Falls by Peter Greenaway
Received: 7 June 2006
Started: 8 June 2006
Finished: 21 June 2006
It's definitely easier to take notes on this
88 than the film, but both are great.

228. Solaris by Stanislaw Lem
Received: 22 June 2006
Started: 24 June 2006
Finished: 25 June 2006
My impression is that the film is a radical departure from the novel, but after reading it I don't think that's true. The basic difference is that Tarkovsky emphasized the humanist element, but as far as plot/narrative goes it's pretty spot-on. This wasn't
69 nearly as goofy as *The Cyberiad.*

229. The Thinking Fan's Guide to the World Cup edited by Matt Weiland, Sean Wilsey
Received: 22 June 2006
Started: 22 June 2006
Finished: 7 July 2006
A great collection of essays about all 32 countries in the World Cup, generally structured around the country's relationship with football, though some take different approaches. It had just enough statistics to be useful for reference during the tournament, too. I will buy this in 2010 if they come out with an edition then.

230. The Vision Machine by Paul Virilio
Received: 30 May 2006
Started: 15 July 2006
Finished: 20 July 2006
Short collection of essays about perception and art. The vision machine of the title is the proposed bit of technological equipment that will 'see' for us, and do accurate artificial image recognition. Some very interesting ideas in here about the artificiality of photography, and the power of cinema.

231. Peter Greenaway: Museums and Moving Images by David Pascoe
Received: 1 August 2006
Started: 2 August 2006
Finished: 3 August 2006
Re-reading a book after you get to know the author is weird; I could hear his voice and it felt very natural. It's been a few years but I do think this is one of the best books on Greenaway out there, even though I didn't think much the first time I read it — I could done with more material on *The Falls*, but I suppose that leaves me more 88
opportunity within my dissertation.

232. The Illuminatus! Trilogy: The Eye in the Pyramid, The Golden Apple, Leviathan by Robert Shea, Robert Anton Wilson
Received: 8 July 2006
Started: 8 July 2006
Finished: 26 September 2006
If this isn't my all-time favourite book, it's certainly the most influential on me. I haven't read it in a few years and felt like giving it a go again. Of course, I find new Truths and Lies every time I go through it. Now I'm in the mood to revisit *Cosmic Trigger*
along with the appendices from here! 161, 162, 164, 242, 698

233. Rock and the Pop Narcotic: Testament for the Electric Church by Joe Carducci
Received: 6 October 2006
Started: 7 October 2006
Finished: 22 October 2006
Yeah, I would say this is the best book on rock music I've ever read. I disagree with large portions of it and Carducci's right-wing homophobic vibe clashes with my own politics, but as the best attempt at 'theory' of rock that I've ever seen, this book is unparalleled. His (musical) viewpoint is so unlike my own that it's really opened my eyes to a few things, and I'm

especially impressed at how he tosses off comments without expanding on them that could be entire essays in their own.

234. Ubik by Philip K. Dick
Received: 29 November 2006
Started: 29 November 2006
Finished: 29 November 2006
This is the third and best PK Dick novel I've read; I tore through it in one day, maybe because I was so starved for English-language reading material on this tour. I'm still a bit confused about the narrative but I guess that's what you get from Dick.

235. Vineland by Thomas Pynchon
Received: 31 May 2006
Started: 13 September 2006
Finished: 26 December 2006
A re-read that I took my time with, *Vineland* is almost like a light comic novel at times, uproariously funny and designed around a brilliant parallel reality. The 80s are captured perfectly, even through the fading veneer of 60s counterculture; the television obsessions, the linguistic changes, and the economic attitudes are commented on (unsubtly) by this rambling narrative. Now I'm psyched to tackle the new one, and then *Mason & Dixon* finally!

524 243, 822

236. If on a Winter's Night a Traveler by Italo Calvino
Received: 10 January 2007
Started: 10 January 2007
Finished: 18 January 2007
This is a masterpiece. It manages to be deeply philosophical about the act of reading and the art of fiction, while wrapped up in an Oulipian shell and delivered with a high quotient of the weird style of humour that I love so much. Re-reading this has been a delight and I really should read the rest of Calvino's work.

237. Zazie in the Metro by Raymond Queneau
Received: 1 February 2007
Started: 4 February 2007
Finished: 6 February 2007
French speakers apparently consider this dated because of the slang of its time, but translated, the novelty still resonates in 2007. Queneau's attempt to revolutionize language through the spoken word may not seem that radical today after years of Arno Schmidt and other post-Joycean experimentalists, but the way that he manages to make it all such a fun "romp" justifies it's classic status. Good implications of language as camouflage, with the metro symbolising the subconscious and the hidden, and the child cutting through it like a knife.

238. Cigarettes by Harry Mathews
Received: 7 February 2007
Started: 7 February 2007
Finished: 13 February 2007
I remarked to a classmate that *Cigarettes* was probably my least favourite Mathews work; after reading it again, I think it's now my favourite. The plotted intricacies are actually quite secondary to the actual writing; there are passages here that are so incredibly cruel that they expose the darkest side of humankind. At the same time the sense of play that I love in all of his writing is apparent, though seeping between the incredible power games portrayed.

239. My Life In CIA by Harry Mathews
Received: 7 February 2007
Started: 13 February 2007
Finished: 14 February 2007
A quick re-read was every bit as delightful as the first time. Interesting points raised by my professor – after the great mess of paranoia-themed literature, here is a spy novel entirely devoid of paranoia. So much fun, it should be banned.

240. Tlooth by Harry Mathews
Received: 26 February 2007
Started: 27 February 2007
Finished: 4 March 2007
A revisit to *Tlooth* was about as insane as reading a novel can be. Reading without having to follow the ludicrous plot this time, I was able to let myself be lost in the fucked up, artificial language-world he creates. I can't think of a more absurd reality to live in, and I don't know that I would want to.

241. Micronations by John Ryan, George Dunford, Simon Sellars
Received: 7 March 2007
Started: 8 March 2007
Finished: 11 March 2007
I thought this would be a lot more interesting than it actually is — it's more of a silly look at people who proclaim their own countries, the majority of which are a complete joke. My interest lies more with places

like Sealand and actual countries that are outside of the jurisdiction of recognized nations.

242. Cosmic Trigger I: Final Secret of the Illuminati by Robert Anton Wilson
Received: (already owned)
Started: 19 February 2007
Finished: 12 March 2007
A re-read of this somewhat influential book left me thinking about how any possibilities of higher intelligence I planned to investigate when I first read it in 2004 have been abandoned. The more academic mind I now have sees the sloppy logic of Wilson's writing, but since 'maybe' logic is his philosophy then I can't really complain about it. Still very fun to read, and offering many doorways into occult studies.

243. Against the Day by Thomas Pynchon
Received: 19 December 2006
Started: 27 December 2006
Finished: 17 March 2007
Reading this took two and a half months out of my life, and I loved every minute of it. I think this is probably my favourite Pynchon novel yet (though I still haven't read *M&D*) and I don't know what to even say about it in the space here except that I want to read it again, and this is the first time ever reading where the Internet really enhanced my enjoyment due to the annotations wiki and the read-along blogs.

244. Myths and Memories by Gilbert Adair
Received: 7 March 2007
Started: 18 March 2007
Finished: 21 March 2007
Adair's collection of essays is really fun — the pieces are each 2 or 3 pages, and looking at different "myths" of contemporary British culture. Some were more enjoyable than others and everything was fairly light, yet insightful. The memories section was really good though I didn't understand much of the popular culture referencing; it was nice as a more Anglo-centric *Je me souviens*, though I think both projects are only the start of something and could benefit from more development.

245. Down Under by Bill Bryson
Received: 31 March 2007
Started: 31 March 2007
Finished: 2 April 2007
In preparation for my visit to Australia I re-read this and remembered how much I love Bryson's writing. I was laughing uncontrollably at points, but also amazed at the weird obscure anecdotes and stories that he tells. I suspect that there's a lot even an Australian native would learn from this.

246. A Secret Country: The Hidden Australia by John Pilger
Received: 4 April 2007
Started: 4 April 2007
Finished: 9 April 2007
Pilger is an excellent writer — I expected Chomsky-style politics, but there's a flair for the descriptive that ranks him among the finest observers I've read recently. The reality of Australia is not that surprising to me, as the tendency for men to create evil in this world doesn't shock me — yet I was unaware of the CIA's involvement in the overthrow of the Whitlam government. I look even more forward to arriving.

247. The Fragile Absolute: Or, Why the Christian Legacy is Worth Fighting For by Slavoj Zizek
Received: 7 April 2007
Started: 10 April 2007
Finished: 11 April 2007
Well, I can't say I understood much of this — I read the whole thing on the train, and while large sections of it made sense to me, I wasn't able to piece it together into a coherent argument. I don't know enough about Hegel, Heidegger or any of the other philosophers whose theories provide the underlying structure of this (the same problem I had with *The Parallax View*). Still, it was rewarding in some unexplainable way, and maybe re-reading it will bring some of the ideas more clearly to light.

248. The Call of the Weird: Encounters with Survivalists, Porn Stars, Alien Killers, and Ike Turner by Louis Theroux
Received: 31 March 2007
Started: 14 April 2007
Finished: 14 April 2007
Theroux can actually write, and he does so with a surprising amount of honesty and self-deprecation. A lot of the book reiterated what had happened on the shows, but when he gets around to actually following

up the characters it comes across as humorous and a bit tragic. And remembering the original shows wasn't a bad thing — though he's doing far better work now. I'm curious what he'd be capable of doing in a second book, particularly if he moves away from the subjects of his TV shows and finds some new subjects.

249. Absalom, Absalom! by William Faulkner
Received: (already owned)
Started: 23 March 2007
Finished: 29 April 2007
I finally read this after putting it off for years, and while it was a bit slow-going at times, I got into weird moments where I was practically speed-reading it, just letting the language completely overtake me. The remarkable thing about this novel to me is not so much the language or the narrative themes, but the way in which it questions the veracity of history and language. Perhaps it's a true forbearer to postmodern literature because of that.

250. The Execution Club by Robert Twigger
Received: 14 April 2007
Started: 20 April 2007
Finished: 29 April 2007
I randomly bought this thinking it would be a weird travel book, but it was actually a book about an extinct species of deer. Twigger approached his topic from a Charlie Kaufman *Adaptation*-esque perspective, 116, 1070 which is annoying at times, but occasionally busts on a really brilliant idea. The highlight was the concept of the Extinction Club, a society of people dedicated to extinguishing animal species — it's as fucked up as something out of a Ballard novel, only funnier.

251. Imperial Attitudes by Noam Chomsky
Received: 12 May 2007
Started: 12 May 2007
Finished: 12 May 2007
A quick airport read — but it turned out to be too quick, as I read the entirety of it before my layover ended. It's the typical Chomsky ideas, in thve conversation format which I prefer. He seems to not believe that the neo-cons support free markets, which differs with Adam Curtis' view that they genuinely do believe in the philosophy they espouse. What makes Curtis' documentaries so damning is that they portray the evil of the neocons without even discussing the illegal activities they partake in.

252. RE/Search #11: Pranks! edited by Andrea Juno and V. Vale
Received: 15 May 2007
Started: 16 May 2007
Finished: 27 May 2007
Even though I've already owned this twice, it had been awhile so I bought this and quickly re-read it. This book changed my life — it introduced me to so many countercultural ideas and people that I am still following paths that started with it, 15 years later. And funny enough, the sequel just came out!

253. The Men Who Stare at Goats by Jon Ronson
Received: 16 June 2007
Started: 20 June 2007
Finished: 9 July 2007
Ronson's style gets on my nerves — it's a bit too cute and quirky — and thus the subject matter started to feel almost fictional. It's hard to tell what his embellishments are, and now that I think back, *Them* was written  similarly but the interviews were so fascinat- 165 ing it didn't bug me. This was fun to read however, though I'll be steering far clear of that collection of his Guardian pieces.

254. RE/Search: Pranks 2 edited by V. Vale
Received: 7 July 2007
Started: 7 July 2007
Finished: 14 July 2007
What a disappointment. *Pranks 2* follows up from one of the most influential books  of my entire life, 20 years later, but fails 252 to be focused or entertaining. The lineup isn't nearly as good, and the interviews are more rambling and less philosophical. I still enjoyed reading it, though I would have loved for Boyd Rice to be involved again.

255. Bringing it All Back Home by Ian Clayton
Received: 15 July 2007
Started: 16 July 2007
Finished: 20 July 2007
Ian Clayton's memoir starts off wonderfully, as a stream-of-consciousness collection of early memories mixed in with popular culture references. Later on, it's dragged

into a repetitive list of famous musicians he's met and/or worked with, spoiling the otherwise pleasant contemplations about music and what impact it had on his life. Still, I enjoyed it, as his writing is quick and amusing. I don't really know why his life is supposed to be particularly interesting, and I guess it isn't.

256. A Confederate General from Big Sur by Richard Brautigan
Received: 18 July 2007
Started: 21 July 2007
Finished: 21 July 2007
There is something so incredibly wonderful about Richard Brautigan's classic works, and this first novel of his has it too while also having a bit more narrative than his other works. The dreamy surrealism of *In Watermelon Sugar* is replaced by an ode to Bohemia, practically a proto-Hippie manifesto. The quirky absurdity that I love in his writing is woven into every page.

257. The New Complete Joy of Home Brewing by Charlie Papazian
Received: 24 July 2007
Started: 24 July 2007
Finished: 26 July 2007
Papazian writes with enthusiasm, but he keeps his opinions in check — I expected more of a polemic about the "RIGHT" way to do homebrew, but instead I found a book that was very open and accepting of different methods. This coupled with the "How To Brew" website should give me the theoretical backing I need to get really experimental with my future homebrews.

258. A Walk in the Woods: Rediscovering America on the Appalachian Trail by Bill Bryson
Received: 3 August 2007
Started: 4 August 2007
Finished: 5 August 2007
I read this when it came out and was a bit disappointed by it; going back to it now, I was much more appreciative of Bryson's writing style and his emphasis on the natural world. A pleasure, like all of his work.

259. Harry Potter and the Deathly Hallows by J. K. Rowling
Received: 7 August 2007
Started: 7 August 2007
Finished: 9 August 2007
I really didn't care much for this. I mean, I read it and wanted to keep reading it, but mostly just because I wanted the whole series to be over with. I liked the series overall — I thought it really peaked during the middle few books — but this one wrapped up in a disgustingly saccharine way. I am very happy though that I will never again read another word of JK Rowling.

260. Pyongyang: A Journey in North Korea by Guy Delisle
Received: 24 August 2007
Started: 15 September 1904
Finished: 25 August 2007
Fantastic account of a stay in North Korea that does a lot to whet my appetite for a description of what it must be like to visit Pyongyang. Next I should try to find something about life outside of the city. Delisle's style is great, very much visually reminding me of Kevin Huizenga, and he doesn't get too wrapped up in the format's artifice, letting the experiences carry the narrative.

261. Bill Bryson's African Diary by Bill Bryson
Received: 13 September 2007
Started: 15 September 2007
Finished: 15 September 2007
This quick charity project was pleasant enough, though (as he admits) suffers from a lack of depth. The usual Bryson wit is present, though his focus on the social problems makes it a somewhat more sombre affair. I probably spent more time writing this comment than it actually took to read.

262. Planet of Slums by Mike Davis
Received: 4 September 2007
Started: 4 September 2007
Finished: 17 September 2007
Davis's book is a brilliant study of slum life around the world. It's packed with statistics, almost becoming overwhelming, but then moves on to make an argument against the IMF and the World Bank. The most compelling section for me was on "Slum ecology", detailing the terrible conditions that most people live in. I also liked how he switched from city to city fluidly, without always saying what continent the city is in; I started to get confused, but it actually helped to portray the similarities of slum life all over the world.

263. I Am a Strange Loop by Douglas R. Hofstadter
Received: 17 September 2007
Started: 18 September 2007
Finished: 25 September 2007
Hofstadter ... hmmm, I'm not sure about this guy anymore. This started off really promising, and reminded me a bit of Robert Anton Wilson's arguments in *Cos-*
161, 162, 164, 242, 698 *mic Trigger*. Of course I expected this to deal with extremely scientific terms and conceptual mathematics. There were two math-heavy chapters that I was able to follow, but I started to feel that the book was really speculative, and almost like a pop psychology thing. Also, Hofstadter's writing style began to irritate me, though to his credit he remained clear throughout — but what was with the continual "Dear reader"? I guess I wanted something "harder". I loved *Metamagical Themas* when I was younger, though.

264. The Three Stigmata of Palmer Eldritch by Philip K. Dick
Received: 17 September 2007
Started: 4 October 2007
Finished: 6 October 2007
Each PK Dick book I read feels like an improvement over the last one; am I picking them better, or am I just becoming more familiar with his worldview? The usual concerns are here — paranoia, mind-altering drugs, confusion over what defines human evolution — but the twisted chronology and uncertain reality is perfect here, even more so than *Ubik* I think. I gotta read
234, 653 more Dick.

265. How Mumbo-Jumbo Conquered the World: A Short History of Modern Delusions by Francis Wheen
Received: 6 October 2007
Started: 16 October 2007
Finished: 17 October 2007
Wheen's attack on the disappearance of reason over the past two decades reads like a lengthy article from *The Baffler*. His viewpoint is not so cut-and-dry left, however — he rails against kneejerk left-wing reactions and has some damning criticism of Noam Chomsky. But I loved this book — though it seemed to veer all over the place, there is not a weak chapter, and some sections are incredibly strong (like the attack on academic postmodernism). It begins by talking about the rise of Thatcherism and the Islamic revolution, and I thought the entire book would be about that. But that's material which Adam Curtis has explored well in his television documentaries.

266. Man in the Holocene by Max Frisch
Received: 11 September 2007
Started: 17 October 2007
Finished: 20 October 2007
A beautiful, calm book that contemplates man's relation to the natural world through the metaphor of geology. Memory is a fragile, organic creature here, shown to be constantly shifting; the collection of human knowledge is another big theme that is explored by Geiser, attaching his notes to the wall. Though the prose is very sparse, it's the mark of a great writer when a book can leave a physical effect on a reader. Reading this, I really felt the torrents of rain, sensing the sound and rhythm of a downpour even though I read this at a time when it (strangely) wasn't raining here.

267. The Life and Times of the Thunderbolt Kid: A Memoir by Bill Bryson
Received: 11 August 2007
Started: 23 October 2007
Finished: 24 October 2007
Bryson's autobiography is wonderful reading for a fan like me. The humour is as solid as always, and he dwells on the disappeared America with just the right amount of nostalgia. He never disappoints.

268. Where Dead Voices Gather by Nick Tosches
Received: 5 September 2007
Started: 26 October 2007
Finished: 3 November 2007
Tosches investigates the forgotten lore of Emmett Miller, a minstrel artist who recorded mostly in the late 1920s. Of course, he's much more than a minstrel artist; more like a genre-defying symbol of a lost American heritage, this reads almost like a spooky mystery at times. Tosches's rhetorical, anti-intellectual flourishes are feisty and wonderful at times, but trying and immature at others. Despite his obsession with Miller, by the end I was more focused on the general culture of the minstrel show and what it said about American attitudes towards race and tradition (despite Tosches's best attempts to avoid any sort of politicizing).

269. God Is Not Great: How Religion Poisons Everything by Christopher Hitchens
Received: 2 November 2007
Started: 3 November 2007
Finished: 7 November 2007
I didn't really need to read this but I thought it would be fun, and it was. Hitchens didn't have to preach to this converted (pun intended) but as usual his writing style carries me through. His venom is not held back for anyone, not even Gandhi or the Dalai Lama. And I can't help but agree with him, when he puts it the way he does.

270. Japrocksampler: How the Post-War Japanese Blew Their Minds on Rock 'n' Roll by Julian Cope
Received: 19 September 2007
Started: 9 November 2007
Finished: 17 November 2007
Cope's book was much more enjoyable than I thought; the personal approach never claimed to be anything else, and is writing is far more sharp than his acid-casualty image would suggest. What I liked was how he distinctly avoided any sort of Nipponfile fetishisation, instead concentrating on the music and history. It felt a bit disorganized, slightly repetitive and certainly incomplete, but that's the nature of Julian Cope isn't it? It's made me curious to check out some music like Speed,

1503 Glue and Shinki and made me revisit Les

1588, 1589 Rallizes Denudés, whom I haven't listened to in ages.

271. The Discomfort Zone: A Personal History by Jonathan Franzen
Received: 16 November 2007
Started: 18 November 2007
Finished: 19 November 2007

Reading this after recently reading Bryson's
267 childhood memoir, I can't help but compare the two; while Bryson's is bittersweet and safe, Franzen's feels more honest, more neurotic, and far more philosophical. While I enjoyed the first half of this, the second half hit me like a ton of bricks. Franzen's insights into art, relationships and family are so fucking real, yet delivered with a confidence and honesty rarely found outside of personal storytelling masters like

Spalding Gray or Ross McElwee. I wouldn't
444, 600, 638 have thought this to be such a masterpiece, but it surprised me, and is one of the best books I've read this year.

272. Europe Central by William T. Vollmann
Received: 4 September 2007
Started: 11 September 2007
Finished: 22 November 2007
The epic is over; the dates on this entry are slightly misleading for while it did take me ages to read this, I probably went the whole month of October without touching it. This was actually fairly painful to finish, from the sheer density of it; there were some incredible sections and others that I didn't care for. While Vollmann is no stranger to historical fiction, I don't think he's written so extensively on Europe before, and he unsurprisingly is quite good at it.

273. Falling Man: A Novel by Don DeLillo
Received: 16 November 2007
Started: 23 November 2007
Finished: 26 November 2007
DeLillo probably couldn't wait to tackle 9/11; I thought this would be pathetically desperate, the work of an author taking on a subject that he believed only he was qualified to write about. I read through this novel very quickly, and I can't say that I enjoyed it, but it was significantly better than I thought it would be. It actually felt quite a bit like *Players* or one of his
books from that time, with 9/11 as the cen- 30
trepiece, yet able to touch on more topics than just that. There were some completely cringe-worthy sentences, but even the final section that describes the actual attack was surprisingly tasteful.

274. Martian Time-Slip by Philip K. Dick
Received: 23 November 2007
Started: 26 November 2007
Finished: 27 November 2007
Another great PK Dick novel, this one maybe a little more straightforward than *Palmer Eldritch* or *Ubik*. This one dealt with
themes of race and fidelity more directly 264 234, 653
than anything else I've read by Dick, and I detected a bit of a political leaning. Jack Bohlen is probably the most overall positive character I've yet encountered in Dick; and this has a (more or less) happy ending.

275. Bat Tattoo by Russell Hoban
Received: 6 November 2007
Started: 28 November 2007
Finished: 29 November 2007
I don't know if I cared much for *The Bat Tattoo*. The verbal experimentation of

Riddley Walker was completely absent, and though there were some interesting ideas hinted at (art and creation, objects as symbols, and the relationship between money and art mainly) I don't feel that anything was fully developed. The prose was so straightforward it almost felt like teen fiction, and I couldn't help but feel that this was one of those novels that would get a great review in *The Guardian*. Whenever Hoban dropped something interesting into the narrative, I found that I had lost interest by the time that element was fully realised.

276. Bend Sinister by Vladimir Nabokov
Received: 5 September 2007
Started: 6 September 2007
Finished: 30 November 2007
Nabokov's dystopian nightmare grew on me slowly, as I spent the first half of the book absorbing his beautiful and strange language. The themes have been explored a zillion times, but Nabokov brings his incredible talent for prose and some parts that were strangely absurd and comic (such as Krug's meeting with Paduk). I should read Nabokov more often than once every four years.

277. Under the Volcano: A Novel by Malcolm Lowry
Received: 4 December 2007
Started: 4 December 2007
Finished: 9 December 2007
This is rightly regarded as one of the best novels of the 20th century; it captures a darkness that is absent in many other works in the canon. Lowry's depiction of the Consul pulls no punches, and the dark depiction of Mexico is strangely alluring despite its malevolence. It's not that the prose was particularly special but the overall construction and theme of self-destruction; while staying in a setting removed from the Western first world, there is a powerful relevance.

278. Locos: A Comedy of Gestures by Felipe Alfau
Received: 6 December 2007
Started: 10 December 2007
Finished: 17 December 2007
I make no secret of my love for Alfau's

118

Chromos, an underappreciated masterpiece. This is his other book, which I've been meaning to read for a while. At first I felt that it was going to be quite bad, but by the end the many disparate narrative threads reflected on each other a good bit and I felt a warm appreciation for the collection. Sure, it's nothing on *Chromos*, but it does have some of the magic that I loved about it, specifically his freewheeling depiction of Bohemian eccentricities.

279. Legacy of Ashes: The History of the CIA by Tim Weiner
Received: 6 December 2007
Started: 7 December 2007
Finished: 22 December 2007
Thought the author is a bit annoying, this was an awesome book. It started slow and the writing didn't impress me as the most sophisticated I had ever read, but by the time the Nixon era is described, I was completely drawn in. Told as a narrative, the history of the CIA is actually quite entertaining. The facts are stunning, the ineptitude is unparalleled, and that all of the sources are on the record is even more amazing. This reads as a brief overview of American foreign policy since WWII, which is always a good thing to be acquainted with. The only bit of hope is that the CIA is shown to be much more fragile entity than I always thought.

280. Yellow Back Radio Broke-Down by Ishmael Reed
Received: 19 December 2007
Started: 23 December 2007
Finished: 25 December 2007
My first Ishmael Reed novel was definitely fun — more fun than I expected — yet it didn't completely floor me. I love this type of anarchic, comic novel, but here something was missing. I'm curious to read more by him — and I suspect if I had read this at a different time I might have been more receptive to it. It fits in well thematically (though not stylistically) with other 60s revisionist Westerns, such as Brautigan's work or *McCabe and Mrs. Miller* (close enough to the 60s for me). I think I might try *Mumbo Jumbo*, for it's plot synopsis sounds fascinating in a Pynchon kinda way.

361

281. The Endgame of Globalization by Neil Smith
Received: 19 December 2007
Started: 25 December 2007
Finished: 28 December 2007

282. Valis by Philip K. Dick
Received: 20 December 2007
Started: 2 January 2008
Finished: 5 January 2008
Wow. I expected this — which I put off for awhile until I was 'ready' for it (by reading other Dick novels first) — to be good, but it was completely incredible, and not at all incoherent like I feared. Coming from the tradition of Robert Anton Wilson and *Cosmic Trigger* sorta stuff, *VALIS* gets into 161, 162, 164, 242, 698 some really complex occult ideas, while masquerading as a (somewhat) sci-fi novel. But because it's based on Dick's own experiences, it has such a greater power. Though it's actually fairly optimistic, there's a pain underneath everything — the loneliness of the experience, which is made the more isolated by the creation of characters to share the experiences. There's also some really harrowing descriptions of dislocation from reality, which are old hat after reading a few more Dick novels but more powerful in this one because of his closeness to it. Additionally, he doesn't hide his own involvement with the material.

283. Geometric Regional Novel by Gert Jonke
Received: 17 December 2007
Started: 19 December 2007
Finished: 7 January 2008
I found this slow-going — kinda boring — but by the end I started to really appreciate it. At first I found the bureaucratic parody to be tired and inconsistent, but that's the point. There's some wonderfully Pythonesque humour buried beneath the poetics, and some wonderful poetics buried beneath the bureaucracy. A lot of the 'impact' of this book comes from its subversion of the German 'regional novel' genre, which I know absolutely nothing about. But disregarding that it still held up as a strange synthesis of Butor's *Mobile* and 762 what I've always imagined Austrian postwar fiction to be like (which is based on cultural stereotypes and the one Thomas Bernhard 48 novel that I read).

284. Extreme Brewing: An Enthusiast's Guide to Brewing Craft Beer at Home by Sam Calagione
Received: 10 January 2008
Started: 10 January 2008
Finished: 12 January 2008
I wish I had started with this book when I began homebrewing. The *beginner* beer — the one they walk you through in the first chapter to teach you how to brew — is an intense 9% ale with maple syrup and Belgian candy. There are recipes inside for Midas Touch, India Brown Ale and Raison D'Etre — sadly not the Chicory Stout, but there's a liquorice root stout that I'm sure is pretty similar. The Dogfish Head dude can actually write, and he seems to have a good, open-minded attitude towards brewing (not that I'm surprised by this given his products). I almost feel like I've stumbled across a secret that isn't known on this side of the ocean. I can't wait to brew an extreme beer — I'm thinking of using honey and elderflowers and maybe even some Lyle's Golden Syrup.

285. The Inquisitory by Robert Pinget, Donald Watson
Received: 19 December 2007
Started: 6 January 2008
Finished: 13 January 2008
Supposedly Pinget's greatest work, *The Inquisitory* is a 400 page interrogation that doesn't contain a single full stop (well, I stopped looking after awhile). The device is used in a manner akin to that chapter of *Ulysses*, though without the smirking humour. Pinget uses this interrogation to outline the characters of history of his fictional town, Agapa — his Yoknapatawpha county. Though there's some real moments in here, I found myself bored by the narratives. Hundreds of characters and their histories were described, but nothing was particularly memorable to me. I suspect that it's a fairly realistic portrait of provincial French life, but that's not what I came looking for here.

286. The Age of Wire and String: Stories by Ben Marcus
Received: 20 December 2007
Started: 13 January 2008
Finished: 15 January 2008
Ben Marcus is probably my favourite contemporary writer. This book uses familiar language in one of the most incredible ways I have ever experienced. The end result is a world that is more that surrealist or hypnotic or fantastic — it is almost like pure unaffected creation. *Notable American Women* is even better, but this is also  190, 571 a masterpiece. Though it is a completely singular work, it conjures up similar sensations that I get when watching *The Falls*, or maybe that film *Northfork*. The first time I  88   266, 652 read this I loved it, but reading it a second time allowed me to take it more slowly and

savour the words. Reading this inspires me because it shows the potential of art; I don't care how exaggerated or ridiculous it sounds. I'm gonna re-read *NAW* next and then maybe just read this again — why read anything else?

287. The Moviegoer by Walker Percy
Received: 21 December 2007
Started: 14 January 2008
Finished: 17 January 2008
Re-reading this cemented its place in my pantheon of great books. I picked up on a much darker undercurrent to Bollings this time; the first time through it felt like a southern American version of *L'étranger*, but balanced by a gentle, almost pastoral beauty. I felt the strength of his descriptions of air, light, and smell even stronger this time, which made the dark aspects feel even darker. The detachment extends to an almost predatory treatment of women, yet still strangely celebratory; it's a troubled portrayal, though one that doesn't have to interfere with the connection I made to this text. I've never been interested in any of his other books but maybe I should check one out. I don't usually go for these heavy books about searching for the meaning of life, but that's exactly why I connect with this — because it's not heavy, it's almost ridiculously light-hearted and escapist. By avoiding dealing with anything "real", Percy manages to write about something without actually writing about it.

288. The First Book of Grabinoulor by Pierre Albert-Birot
Received: 20 December 2007
Started: 18 January 2008
Finished: 24 January 2008
Albert-Birot's surrealist classic was fun to read again, with it's nonstop barrage of language and magic. There's some pretty radical positions in here — anarchistic, nihilistic, and extremely sexually liberated — at least for a book from the 1920s. I'd someday like to read the other five books (though I don't think they're translated yet). The poetry in the middle was actually my favourite part.

289. The Shock Doctrine: The Rise of Disaster Capitalism by Naomi Klein
Received: 17 January 2008
Started: 17 January 2008
Finished: 26 January 2008
Klein's look at 'disaster capitalism' is a remarkable effort that excels about the typical political study for several reasons. What I liked most is the way she weaves a narrative throughout, taking the concept of 'shock' beyond a mere metaphor and paralleling economic policies with torture and psychological treatments. Rather than being merely about Iraq and Katrina (as I expected), the first 2/3 of the book consists of case studies in previous nations and their adoption of privatization and corporate rule. I now see Milton Friedman as one of the 20th century's greatest villains (just behind Hitler, Stalin, Kissinger, etc.). The research is impressive and the argument never wavers, though it never feels overly preachy or self-righteous. The studies of Chile and Russia in particular are fascinating and a serious alternative to popular viewpoints. When she does get into Iraq, the outrage is contained enough to be effective; the finger is pointed however, and the accusations are quite damning. Klein doesn't waste space arguing about the morality of the war, instead focusing on the corporate profiteering that resulted from it, which is even more shocking than I had imagined. The final section deals with the recent populist movements in South America and actually leaves me with a great deal of hope for the future (more so than these kinds of books usually do). However, I am left with great doubts that a Democratic administration in America will do anything to alter the course of globalisation. It's rare for me to find a book about politics that is so good I can't put it down, but this is completely excellent and hopefully will be read by a lot of people.

290. Flow My Tears, the Policeman Said by Philip K. Dick
Received: 24 January 2008
Started: 26 January 2008
Finished: 27 January 2008
Another amazing Philip K Dick novel, as confusing as the best of them. Throughout this novel Dick repeatedly addresses issues of amnesia and age; it's clear he had some issues about his own aging at the time of writing. The payoff is a bit underwhelming here — I don't entirely understand the idea behind the drug — but the police state described is among the best I've read yet from Dick.

291. You Don't Love Me Yet: A Novel by Jonathan Lethem
Received: 5 January 2008
Started: 28 January 2008
Finished: 28 January 2008
As a one-day read this was fun enough, but given the high quality of Lethem's other output I felt like this was a real regression. I like Lethem's Philip K Dick obsession, which was absent in this novel (apart from a radio station called KPKD). The first half of the novel felt like it was written by Don DeLillo, with it's extended, 'profound' dialogues and exaggerated social constructs. Then the emphasis on the rock band took over and the entire novel felt very, I dunno, lame. Lethem is certainly older than me, but he seemed to be chronicling a subculture and lifestyle that I myself have already graduated from. I realise that's not a fair criticism and it reeks of arrogance and elitism, but the actions of a rock band in LA feel like the most worn out of ideas. It's awkward too — I've always felt a slight awkwardness in Lethem, as I would feel reading anyone who comes from a similar cultural background as I do, who also directly addresses that background in his/her writing — and it's more pronounced here than in any other book of his. In *The Fortress of Solitude* 125 the comic book and music themes work well, as their fictionalisation feels natural. Maybe it's because I've been so immersed in the world of rock music for so long, but everything felt false and a bit desperate in *You Don't Love Me Yet.*

292. 39 Microlectures: In Proximity of Performance by Matthew Goulish
Received: 19 December 2007
Started: 11 January 2008
Finished: 29 January 2008
Got from library; read half, then it got recalled so I had to borrow it from the friend who recommend it, in order to finish it. Goulash is a member of the Goat Island performance group, and this is a series of vague, short essays about performance and creation. I enjoy reading this type of more theoretical work about art, even if a lot of it feels without substance. There were some good anecdotes and the type of 'oblique strategy'/open style of writing that can be frustrating to read, but actually fairly stimulating when used as part of the creative process. Though I'm coming from a non-performance background myself, there's similar ideas about fluidity and setting that can be applied to any artwork.

293. Our Friends from Frolix 8 by Philip K. Dick
Received: 21 January 2008
Started: 29 January 2008
Finished: 30 January 2008
This is definitely a 'lesser' Dick novel, but still greatly enjoyable. It's made me think about how most of his novels are really about the concept of 'freedom', questioning what it really means in the nature of Buñuel's *The Phantom of Liberty*. In most 25, 352 of his books there is some sort of police state, yet with a twisted catch. Here (as in many of his books), drugs are legal and state-regulated, but alcohol is completely illegal and 'underground'. There wasn't as much of a total reality mindfuck as his best books have, and it felt a bit more Kilgore Trout-like. This is not necessarily bad, but it's not one I think I'll ever re-read.

294. Easy Riders, Raging Bulls by Peter Biskind
Received: 4 January 2008
Started: 31 January 1999
Finished: 4 February 2008
I loved this chronicle of the 70s American film renaissance. There was something just slightly trashy about it, but that was probably unavoidable given the subject matter. The insanity of Coppola, Friedkin, Bogdanovich, Robert Evans, Robert Towne and so many others goes beyond belief. Throughout it all Biskind expresses a real love for the films themselves, and talks a lot about how it all went wrong in the 80s. For someone interested in American film from the 70s this is really indispensible — I wish he had focused more on some of the "lesser" works such as later Altman or Cassavetes films, but I guess it's good he limited the scope to certain titles.

295. The Sweet Forever by George P. Pelecanos
Received: 10 January 2008
Started: 5 February 2008
Finished: 7 February 2008
I wanted to read this because it's by one of *The Wire*'s main writers, who is very highly acclaimed in this genre. Well, this is my first foray into 'crime fiction' and probably my last. This book was abysmal. It wasn't merely bad because of the one-dimensional characters, clichéd stereotypes and appalling dialogue. What really wrecked it for me was the obsession with placing everything into a historical timeframe — in this case, 1986. No more than a few pages

go by before Pelecanos makes a reference to an album, sporting event or TV show. The musical dialogue is particularly bad, such as the punks talking about going to see Black Flag. "Rollins?" one of them says. Just so you know. It reminds me of that Monty Python sketch with the railway time-table-obsessed playwright, whose plays just involve a bunch of characters talking about railway timetables. But really, this was just a really bad book. And given the accolades on the cover, it's probably one of the more renowned of the genre, which doesn't really say a lot about the crime fiction world. I can see how some of the "grit" of this guy's approach might filter into *The Wire*, but thankfully, David Simon is there to induce a good bit of cynicism and deal with the more complex relationships of power, bureaucracy and the self.

296. The Future of the Image by Jacques Ranciere
Received: 8 February 2008
Started: 8 February 2008
Finished: 11 February 2008
Ranciere's treatise on the image was a bit hard for me to follow at first, but once I started taking notes I was able to concentrate on it more and extract some key points. I can't say that I picked up on any overall argument, if there was one, which isn't his fault — he's a clear and lucid writer — but more because I find it difficult to read philosophy/theory when I'm not directly applying it to anything I'm working on. He centred much of the text around the idea of the 'sentence-image', and I'm not certain that I can clearly define it. The chapter on design didn't do anything for me, and his definition of the 'anti-representation' I think I grasp, but more from my own experiences than his writing.

297. The Fowler Family Business by Jonathan Meades
Received: 20 December 2007
Started: 8 February 2008
Finished: 12 February 2008
Jonathan Meades never disappoints me. I preferred this full novel to the collection of stories that I started because I think I generally prefer novels to short stories. But the stories were maybe a bit more adventurous with language; the novel, by having to focus on a narrative for so long maybe sacrificed a bit of experimentation. Still, there were some incredibly Meadesian passages. While I still dream of a book of non-fiction and essays, I'll enjoy reading the rest of his fiction. His imagination is brilliant at creating some of the darkest corners of English life I've ever read, though I probably miss a good bit of it by being American.

298. Noise/Music: A History by Paul Hegarty
Received: 8 February 2008
Started: 13 February 2008
Finished: 14 February 2008
A quick flip to the index reveals the value of this book — what, no Wolf Eyes?!?! Seriously though, Hegarty has set out to write a history of noise in music as he loosely defines noise. And perhaps that is the book's biggest weakness — to him, 'noise' varies between commercial antagonism, harsh social aesthetics, a sense of discomfort — without ever being really pinned down. He most frequently returns to Batallie, describing a sense of negation that has no resolution. Musically, Hegarty sticks strictly to the 20th century though he does step across all genres pretty well. It's really just one man's view, tempered by occasional rants about Adorno's critquie of jazz etc, but it's not a bad viewpoint, and avoids being dismissive. It's the kind of book I imagine we're going to see a lot more of, as this sort of thing is being studied much more these days, but I doubt that most of them will be this readable. His chapter on Merzbow is the highlight of the book, an impassioned, slightly crazed attempt to place Masami Akita in some sort of framework. Also great is his nine-step program to view the Sex Pistols' *The Great Rock and Roll Swindle* as noise, in a way illustrating the absurdity behind the book's entire project. Chapters on Kraturock, jazz and DJ culture, while obviously focused around the writer's biases, weave together a narrative pretty well but without actually teaching me anything new. I wouldn't give this a blazing 5-star review, but it certainly wasn't bad.

299. Design and Crime (and Other Diatribes) by Hal Foster
Received: 13 February 2008
Started: 16 February 2008
Finished: 19 February 2008
Foster's essays run between art meta-criticism to architectural rants, with a bit of cultural studies thrown in. A good bit of this I found hard to focus on; the most interesting essay was the final one about the

perceived 'death' of art. The stuff about art criticism mildly interested me, but I wasn't knowledgeable enough to follow it all. As a history of *Artforum* magazine, I suppose it's a good overview. Foster is a very precise writer and I think I would read this again, maybe after spending some more time with the subjects.

300. The Visual Display of Quantitative Information by Edward R. Tufte
Received: 13 February 2008
Started: 19 February 2008
Finished: 19 February 2008
I checked this out to freshen up on Tufte's ideas, thinking I could apply it to web design (specifically with a project I'm working on with the History of Art department of Glasgow Uni). I can't see a lot of analogies actually, but it was fun to read this again. This is certainly the least colourful of Tufte's books, but it's very much the place to start with his ideas. The other two are checked out of the library but I may brush up on them as well in the next few weeks.

301. The Divine Invasion by Philip K. Dick
Received: 23 February 2008
Started: 23 February 2008
Finished: 23 February 2008
The second book in the *VALIS* trilogy was significantly more fictional than *Valis*, even
282 ridiculously so. Dick's theological concerns become extremely overt here, with the personification of God etc. almost reaching the absurd heights of Pratchett and Gaiman's *Good Omens*. But everytime I thought the story was becoming clichéd or easy, it shifted gears again. The universalization of Dick's internal struggle takes away a bit of its extremism, but I still really enjoyed this. I don't think it has to be read as an acceptance of Christianity; it can be seen as philosophical entertainment using Christian devices.

302. Envisioning Information by Edward R. Tufte
Received: 27 February 2008
Started: 28 February 2008
Finished: 1 March 2008
This is my favourite Tufte book and the only one I own back home. It presents some really fun graphics and charts and states a case not dissimilar to *The Visual Display of Quantitative Information*. I should try
300 to find the third one and complete the trilogy, as the third one is the one I have only read once.

303. Surrealism and Architecture by Thomas Mical
Received: 14 February 2008
Started: 25 February 2008
Finished: 3 March 2008
I pulled this randomly off the shelf because of the title and spent forever paging through it on the bus. It's a pretty hit and miss collection of essays, with most being about architectural motifs in the work of the classic surrealists. Only a few essays hint at the influence of surrealism on architecture, and most of these finish before they get going. The most interesting one to me is about the city of Brasilia; the rest veer between theory-heavy rambling and tenuous connections.

304. The Conspiracy of Art by Jean Baudrillard, Sylvère Lotringer
Received: 28 February 2008
Started: 4 March 2008
Finished: 6 March 2008
This collection of essays was all fixed around one provocative piece Baudrillard wrote, "The Conspiracy of Art," in which he basically declares all art to by null and empty. The reactions are varied but many seem to misunderstand his approach — that he is talking about the anthropological value of art rather than the aesthetic. Like Lotringer's books with Virilio, I found this
most enjoyable when in conversational 223, 226, 390
mode. Baudrillard is anything but obtuse; his viewpoints are clearly stated and not even particularly radical. The stuff at the end about Artaud I didn't get much from, as I'm not very familiar with Artaud. But throughout the rest, I was continually thinking about the trap defined by Baudrillard — the void of contemporary art — and trying to think of ways out of the predicament. Especially after reading the Hal Foster book — I think these two men have pretty different viewpoints, though one is an 'insider' and one is not. I also liked the stuff about Warhol, who I have always taken a bit for granted.

305. Overexposed: Perverting Perversions by Sylvère Lotringer
Received: 4 March 2008
Started: 6 March 2008
Finished: 7 March 2008
Lotringer's book is very curious and quite

entertaining; the strange style in which it's written makes me question it's veracity slightly. Like his interviews with Baudrillard and Virilio, this follows a conversational style which makes it read quickly; it's not always clear who is speaking, especially in one chapter which is an unquoted account of a paedophile (but I thought was Lotringer for the first half of reading it).

306. Ninety-two in the Shade by Thomas Mcguane
Received: 23 February 2008
Started: 10 March 2008
Finished: 12 March 2008
My first proper McGuane novel (my interest was stirred by a *Believer* article awhile back) and I was quite happy with what I found. The humour so often spoken about McGuane's style was distinct and sharp, but not the centrepiece of the book. I would have never thought a story about fishing guides in the Florida Keys would be so entertaining, but it succeeded, reminding me of a lost Coen Brothers script especially in the middle with all the short, episodic scenes. But throughout the narrative lies more than the occasional brilliant turns of phrase — more 'grounded' than the postmodernists of the time and as attenuated as the best words of Kerouac, Walker Percy, or Updike. I'll seek out others, and try to 759 find the film adaptation as well.

307. Radio Free Albemuth by Philip K. Dick
Received: 23 February 2008
Started: 13 March 2008
Finished: 15 March 2008
The last Philip K. Dick novel ends in the most brutal, crushing way possible before offering a glimpse of hope, but I can't overcome my own cynicism to believe in it. Like *Valis* and *The Divine Invasion*, this  301 282 is primarily concerned with direct transmissions from an alien intelligence. If *Valis* was his struggle to come to terms with his own experiences, and *Divine Invasion* was an attempt to place it into a theological context, then *Radio Free Albemuth* takes these experiences back to what he is familiar with — the science-fiction/dystopian context, with a bit of the alternate history thing thrown in. I really enjoyed this novel — it's a fitting swan song to an incredible writing career. I wonder if he had lived for 20 more years, if he would have kept writing and rewriting about Valis; I don't know why this isn't considered part of the trilogy as it seems to fit into place.

308. Norwegian Wood by Haruki Murakami
Received: 24 April 2006
Started: 20 March 2008
Finished: 24 March 2008
This is Murakami's "normal" novel, a coming-of-age story set in 1969-1970 Tokyo and centred around a student's romantic entanglements. It's so conventional compared to what I was expecting that I spent the first half waiting for something 'weird' to happen. Once I realised that this was a different sort of novel, I began to really appreciate it. Without the detached surrealism of his other books, Murakami allows his writerly qualities to really shine. This is the novel that made him hugely successful in Japan, and I can see why — it addresses sex and relationships in a really honest manner. This isn't the type of novel I typically read but it carries a certain magic that I found hard to resist.

309. The Botany of Desire: A Plant's-Eye View of the World by Michael Pollan
Received: 15 March 2008
Started: 25 March 2008
Finished: 2 April 2008
This is my first foray into Michael Pollan, who I became interested in after reading a really good interview in *The Believer*. Here he goes through four plants and talks about how they mirror human desires. There's some pretty interesting history and creative nonfiction writing, including a pot-addled chapter on pot and an exploration of the myth of Johnny Appleseed. It was the final chapter I enjoyed the most, which detailed the emerging debate on genetically modified products via his own planting of the Monsanto NewLeaf potato. I want to read his newer books but the libraries don't carry them here so I may be waiting awhile.

310. Do Androids Dream of Electric Sheep? by Philip K. Dick
Received: 26 March 2008
Started: 2 April 2008
Finished: 4 April 2008
Somehow I've managed to put off Dick's most famous book until now; it is definitely the last of his 'major' works that I haven't read yet, and well-deserving of its accolades. I kept expecting a twist ending that never came, yet I wasn't disappointed in

any way. There are some brilliant ideas in here, like kipple, or useless objects that keep multiplying. I'm gonna watch *Blade Runner* now, which I haven't seen since high school and remember nothing from.

617

311. The Curious Incident of the Dog in the Night-Time by Mark Haddon
Received: 8 July 2006
Started: 4 April 2008
Finished: 4 April 2008
Yes, I quite liked this. At first I was afraid it was going to be too cute, as the child genius/idiot thing seems like quite a trendy subject (cut *The Last Samurai* or Jonathan Safran Foer's 9/11 book) but the bottom line is that I enjoyed it too much to say anything but positive words.

188 97

312. The Shifting Realities of Philip K. Dick: Selected Literary and Philosophical Writings by Philip K. Dick, edited by Lawrence Sutin
Received: 23 February 2008
Started: 5 April 2008
Finished: 11 April 2008
This collection of Dick's nonfiction is really solid. The bits of biographical information are interesting enough that I think I'm going to read some biographies of him; the writings on science fiction are especially rewarding as they attempt to lay out a 'theory' of sci-fi (if such a thing exists). The book gets progressively more difficult to read as it goes on; the meaty essays on reality are the peak, sharing a lot of similar ground to Robert Anton Wilson's writings though with Dick's own interests in Christian theory laid on top. They are fairly disorganised but lay bare Dick's thoughts on his own experiences, making some outrageous claims that I'm sure he truly experienced. The essay on cosmogony was impossible to understand and I skimmed it; I made it through the excerpts from the *Exegesis* but they were dense and difficult as well. (I imagine reading the entire *Exegesis*, were it possible, would be pretty mental) This makes me ready to read more of his fiction.

313. Distant Star by Roberto Bolano
Received: 7 April 2008
Started: 9 April 2008
Finished: 11 April 2008
This is the first Bolaño book I've read; given the hype about him I expected something totally dazzling. This novel was quite enjoyable to read, and raised some interesting questions about the relationship between art and politics. The main character of the novel is ruthlessly avant-garde and ruthlessly bloodthirsty; it's an interesting idea, as avant-garde movements are usually affiliated with the left (well, usually) and Bolaño's character straddled so many movement he became a force of his own. It's interesting how realistic this novel was; I was never sure if the writers and politicians he describes were fictional or not. It's setting in 1970s Chile is of course charged with the blood of Allende and the horrible things that happened there, yet this doesn't become the focal point of the book. I like the contrast between the many poor victims of Pinochet's reign, who unfortunately 'disappeared', with Wieder, who voluntarily disappeared. I can't quite understand how this guy also write an 800 page surrealist masterpiece (or so the hype claims — *2666* doesn't come out in English until this fall) yet this book was strikingly realistic.

397

314. Cantata-140 by Philip K. Dick
Received: 12 April 2008
Started: 12 April 2008
Finished: 12 April 2008
If I can keep reading a Dick novel per day I'll actually get through his entire bibliography well before the end of the year. Though I must admit, at points in *Cantata-140* I was regretting reading it, for it had some of the most dire, turgid, poorly-written parts I've yet encountered in Dick. However, the narrative was brilliant — and quite timely, being that it concerns a black Presidential candidate. This novel is very much about race; as it was written in 1966 it's surely motivated by the civil rights movement (and I suspect the Jim Briskin character is based on MLK). Its clunkyness is probably why it's remembered as one of Dick's minor works, and it certainly doesn't contain any reality-spinning elements like *Palmer Eldritch* or *Ubik*. Originally published as *The Crack in Space*.

264

234, 653

315. I Am Alive and You Are Dead: A Journey into the Mind of Philip K. Dick by Emmanuel Carrere
Received: 12 April 2008
Started: 14 April 2008
Finished: 15 April 2008
This biography doesn't cite any specific sources yet seems to have a complete understanding of Dick's internal thoughts throughout his life, though the author never met Dick. It's also prone to fanciful flights of prose that attempt to capture the distressed mental state of its subject, yet come

off as high school sci-fi poetry. Despite these flaws, this was hard to put down, as Dick's life was completely fascinating. Many of his experiences ended up somewhere in his novels, even with Carrère doesn't specify that. I sorta wish I had read the other Dick biography because it's probably better, yet I doubt I will bother reading a second bio.

316. The Transmigration of Timothy Archer by Philip K. Dick
Received: 15 April 2008
Started: 16 April 2008
Finished: 17 April 2008
This is the proper "final" novel of Philip K Dick and by far the most distinct and singular of his works. For starters, it isn't science fiction at all but rather a meditation on psychology and theology. It's also written from the point of view of a woman. As far as its *writerly* qualities, this is probably the best prose that Dick ever wrote. It rolls with a detached awareness that reminds me a lot of DeLillo's writing, only avoiding some of his excesses. I hesitate to proclaim this to be Dick's best book, but in some ways it's the masterpiece of "serious" literature he wanted to write so badly in the 50s. It's extremely autobiographical and his resemblance to Bishop Pike is only thinly disguised; Dick was obviously working with some residual demons and trying his best to assert a wide spectrum of beliefs in one novel. But is Dick renouncing the fantastic and the supernatural, as his narrator does, or does he present a more ambiguous argument? Furthermore, is this the work of a man who knew his death was imminent? Death pervades every page of this novel — it begins the day after John Lennon was shot and follows the deaths of three major characters, though none of them occur in the novel but are merely talked about. The character of Bill is almost certainly doomed, and Angel's attempts to save him are presented pessimistically, as if we know it will fail. For a novel that deals with death so much, Dick presents the "life after death" idea very cynically, in a way that suggests that it wouldn't even be desirable if at all possible. The Bishop's foundations of faith are shaken, just as the real life Bishop Pike's are, and Dick's faith in fiction falls apart as well. It makes sense that he never wrote again, as there's little left for him to say at this point. Thinking about this as a trilogy with *Valis* and *Divine Invasion* makes it a hell of a weird trilogy — the only concept of Valis here would be the discussions of ancient Christian illumination; what Dick writes is the amnesis, the opposite of his anamnesis. It is a forgetting of his understanding and experiences; it is a return to what is concrete, an attempt to ascertain something grounded. Maybe that makes this the biggest tragedy he ever wrote.

301 282

317. Time Out of Joint by Philip K. Dick
Received: 11 April 2008
Started: 17 April 2008
Finished: 19 April 2008
It's hard not to think about *The Truman Show* when reading this but the same basic concept applies, though with a sci-fi story grafted on. This is apparently a real turning point for Dick, and as it's the earliest of his novels that I've read I can't say for sure. It certainly felt a bit more thorough than his crazed 60s work. It's a nice biting commentary on the placid life of Eisenhower America, and it certainly looks to the future with a strange prescience. The afterword suggests the ending "sci-fi" section was tacked on just so he could get it published, and suggests that it's forced and unnecessary. Maybe this is true; as Dick wrote so many 'serious' novels at this time (all unpublished during his lifetime), it does show in the relative calm of the first 150 pages. As a document of paranoia and conspiracy this also precedes the works of Pynchon and DeLillo; strangely it comes across as a more conventional novel than Pynchon would write despite being about the moon attacking the Earth.

318. A Maze of Death by Philip K. Dick
Received: 17 April 2008
Started: 21 April 2008
Finished: 22 April 2008
What an awesome book! It started slow but then became a very strange murder mystery, with some extreme sci-fi elements that were pretty secondary to the story. This was about human relationships and the religious framework people impose on things; it started to feel ridiculous and gothic as the corpses started piling up. There's some feel to this that makes it 'stand apart' from Dick's other work, maybe the sex or maybe the "thriller" feel to it. The ending isn't a cop out but coulda been handled a bit differently, though I generally hate when people complain about a narrative going a direction they don't like (so I'll shut up).

319. Galactic Pot-Healer by Philip K. Dick
Received: 22 April 2008
Started: 22 April 2008
Finished: 24 April 2008
The saving grace of reading all of these Dick books in succession (and running the risk of actually going insane myself) is that they are so varied. While there are themes that repeat across his fiction, each individual book really stands alone and apart from one or two, they don't feel unnecessary. *Galactic Pot-Healer* is again probably a "minor" work in his canon, yet I felt a special fondness while reading it. The most distinct characteristic of this novel is the humour — it is downright silly, with slapstick humour and weird jokes in the dialogue that made this feel a lot like a Dogulas Adams book. The idea of a deity who kinda fucks up a lot and is extremely fallible is a good one, but it's his personality — he's a *goof* — that made this seem so far removed from the nightmares of *Palmer Eldritch* or *Ubik*. At the beginning it almost felt like a parody of Dick's frequent police states; and I actually thought it was going to have a happy ending for once.

264 234, 653

320. The Spanish Civil War by Frances Lannon
Received: 24 April 2008
Started: 24 April 2008
Finished: 27 April 2008
This "Essential Histories" series covers a war in 99 pages, and while I don't generally care about war, I've wanted to read about the Spanish Civil War for some time. This was (obviously) concise and pretty well written, and it's made me want to learn even more about the conflict. I never realised before how the Spanish Civil War was pretty much the ultimate left-vs-right battle, and how it set the template for the rest of the 20th century. It was *The Hobbit* to World War II's *Lord of the Rings*, to make a crude analogy. I also checked out a book from this series on the Suez Crisis which I might also read — and maybe even start learning about, I dunno, the Thirty Years War.

321. Counter-Clock World by Philip K. Dick
Received: 24 April 2008
Started: 25 April 2008
Finished: 29 April 2008
This was a monster book — it felt epic in scope, and was based around the idea of anti-time. That whole gimmicky aspect, like people undigesting their food, was really inconsistent and didn't really "work", but the novel still played out well as a thriller. Though it dealt with race, religion and marital fidelity head-on, it seemed to take place inside a *koinos kosmos,* which makes this less Dickish than I would have liked. Still I can't say it wasn't great, like all of these novels.

322. The Zap Gun by Philip K. Dick
Received: 24 April 2008
Started: 30 April 2008
Finished: 1 May 2008
It's easy to imagine Dick bashing this book out, his brain riddled with amphetamines and trying to just write as many books as possible. That's not to say I didn't enjoy it — I enjoy them all — but the writing style is very stunted, almost like he meant to go back later and fill things in. There's similar "hoax" material like in *The Penultimate Truth*, though here the weapon industry is presented as linked to toy and commerce (which is pretty realistic) and the society exists in a relatively free (at least for a Dick book) capitalist manner. The most "messed-up" aspect of *The Zap Gun* is that something just isn't right about it — but in this case its' due to sloppy writing rather than a twisted reality-warping vision.

323. The Great Railway Bazaar by Paul Theroux
Received: 29 April 2008
Started: 2 May 2008
Finished: 6 May 2008
This is Paul Theroux's first travel book, where he embarks on a rail journey from London to Vietnam to Japan to Siberia and back to London. This pretty much created the modern travel-writing genre and is surprisingly funny — hilarious actually — even if Theroux's mid-70s attitudes towards other cultures aren't the most politically correct. Unlike a writer such as Bryson, Theroux doesn't have a wide-eyed fascination with his subjects. He is actually somewhat grumpy and cynical, and he writes more about sitting on trains than the actual countries he is visiting. Still, I loved it, and his depictions of India are the most vivid and accurate I've come across.

324. After Dark by Haruki Murakami
Received: 29 April 2008
Started: 8 May 2008
Finished: 12 May 2008
I was really unimpressed by this recent Murakami tome. The childlike narration got on my nerves by the end, and I didn't find the narrative to be engaging. I like other Murakami novels when the calm, detachment of the narrative voice is cut by horror, misery and extreme Freudian psychology. Here it seemed like he was focusing on the adolescents that brought him such success in *Norwegian Wood*, only without the con-
308 text of the historical setting or the depth required to make the characters feel alive. Here, I just didn't care — I wanted to get it over with. His usual mystery and ambiguity just bored me.

325. Eye in the Sky: A Novel by Philip K. Dick
Received: 10 May 2008
Started: 13 May 2008
Finished: 13 May 2008
A friend recommended this specifically (and he's read every single Dick novel) so I was psyched to read it. I see why it stands out — it's definitely on the 'goofy' side of Dick, not as much as *Galactic Pot-Healer*
319 but still strangely fun. At first I thought this was gonna take on some religious themes, but I think Dick was still an atheist when he wrote it, and the deity-led alternate reality in the novel is extreme and ridiculous. This definitely feels like a precursor to *A Maze of Death*; there's the same roundta-
318 ble of psychosis, and the same concept of shared internal worlds. The ending feels a bit rushed and I wasn't completely convinced that I was following it all, but Dick novels aren't really about resolution.

326. Human Smoke: The Beginnings of World War II, the End of Civilization by Nicholson Baker
Received: 13 May 2008
Started: 13 May 2008
Finished: 16 May 2008
I didn't know what to expect from this book, as I guess I never know what to expect from Nicholson Baker. It's quite controversial, probably because it argues that WWII was not a "good" war — if you tend to read it that way. Baker does little writing of his own here, apart from a few sentences between quotes of primary sources (almost all from the *New York Times*). Of course it's his choice of information that makes his argument, painting Churchhill to be a monster of the empire, and the pacifist movement as an oppressed, marginalized voice (which they were).

I found this fascinating — I had trouble tearing myself away from it — in the way that the most gripping thrillers occupy the mind and body. His chronological presentation of information is a simple, yet incredible method for placing the reader in the context of Europe in the 1930s. It's made me rethink the ways in which I learned of World War II — which I guess was the standard public school education. *Human Smoke* is also a great nonfictional complement to Vollmann's *Europe Central*.
I intentionally avoided reading criticism of 272
this before I read it, though I suspect there's a general outrage when anyone questions the unassailable reverence of World War II and "The Greatest Generation," etc. Maybe some feel that Baker — a weirdo novelist with childlike outbursts (*Checkpoint, Vox*)
and whose only previous work of nonfiction 180
is a ridiculous attack on newspaper digitisation — has no place in writing a work of history. But what I think is great about this book is that it illustrates the very instability of history via viewpoints. In a way I think the meta-textual ideas behind this book make it very interesting — perhaps more so than the actual content. It's sourced and noted thoroughly, so what makes this any different than the plethora of pro-WWII texts (at least from an academic point of view)? As always I want to defend Baker; now I am curious to read the criticism.

I'm a pacifist myself, I guess, but his case was a hard one to make without just playing a bunch of historical "What if?" games. Sure, Churchill loved the war and was obsessed with total non-negotiable victory; I also believe that Roosevelt was happy to enter the war and "let' Pearl Harbor happen. And maybe Hitler was prepared to negotiate a peace deal in 1940. But no one can really know what would have happened if the war had ended in 1940 — if Hitler would have stopped after Poland, or if the Holocaust still would have happened (since Britain and US weren't allowing any Jews to resettle there). So it's great that this book debunks a lot of the bullshit myths about it being "the good war", but to condemn it and say that fighting wasn't inevitable is impossible. I don't think the argument is that strong anyway — I think a lot of it feels like Baker trying to understand World War II through his own pacifist eyes — and often presenting both sides of the argument. I think I will probably read this again.

327. Black Mass: Apocalyptic Religion and the Death of Utopia by John Gray
Received: 1 May 2008
Started: 17 May 2008
Finished: 21 May 2008
This book actually was far more about politics than religion, or rather the way that utopian and apocalyptic religious thoughts patterns exist in political ideology. Gray compares the post-Communist view that western liberal democracy is the "only" form of government as being equivalent to saying there is a goal, or a utopia at the end of society. He claims this belief is distinctly Western and then moves through a series of political situations to illustrate his point, from Thatcher's dismantling of the British state to Blair's continuation of her status quo. It all culminates in Bush and Iraq, where rather than simply illustrate how Bush believes America's actions are dictated by God, Gray actually dissects the rhetoric of the war and makes a clear distinction between neo-liberal and neo-conservative. At times it feels a bit jumbled and unfocused, but this was a great book with some really sharp critiques of contemporary political and economic though. At the end it makes a case for a realist approach to civilisation, which I didn't completely understand, and also starts to talk about the need for a post-secular society. I don't think I've ever read an argument against secularism from the left before, and I'd like to see it expanded into it's own book, as Gray tacks it into the frantic concluding chapter.

328. How to Read Lacan by Slavoj Zizek
Received: 30 April 2008
Started: 21 May 2008
Finished: 22 May 2008
Lacan's *Écrits* has been sitting beside my bed for a month but I've found it impenetrable. Luckily, Slavoj Zizek comes to the rescue with this introductory volume that is extremely readable and fantastically entertaining. With his usual references to contemporary politics, film, and low culture, Zizek works through several key concepts of Lacan while peppering it with his brilliant flair and humour. I now feel like Lacan's writing are something that I can comprehend, and actually I feel that they are writings I *should* comprehend. I think I'm going to go on a Zizek kick but try Lacan's seminars first, which are much more approachable than his *écrits*. I actually want to read this "How to Read" again just to make sure it sinks in, and also cause it was so much fun.

329. Philip K. Dick: Exhilaration and Terror of the Postmodern by Christopher Palmer
Received: 12 April 2008
Started: 21 April 2008
Finished: 24 May 2008
This is a proper academic study on Dick — a strange thing to find in the public library — that focuses on postmodern themes in his writing. It looks mostly at *Martian Time-Slip*, with its themes of autism and 274
language, but also at other novels. The writing style is a bit wonky and it's a chore to read, but the writer knows his Dick and really digs into some of the books. The *Valis* trilogy is examined from the point of view of authorship and meta-fiction, rather 282,
than dealing with the religious element, 301, 316
which was a bit disappointing. It took me a month to plough through this because I wasn't really enjoying it, and I ultimately don't know if it really contributed anything to my enjoyment of the Dick oeuvre.

330. Running with Scissors: A Memoir by Augusten Burroughs
Received: 24 May 2008
Started: 25 May 2008
Finished: 26 May 2008
Why autobiography? I've always felt it's a weakness of 'my' generation's approach to art and literature, especially evident in forms such as 'new' journalism and successful memoirs of people who had never done anything interesting before writing them, like Dave Eggers. But this book takes it to a new level by portraying a childhood so warped that it is profoundly disturbing and incredibly funny. Burroughs episodic memoir is very, very dark, and strangely engrossing. It upends my romanticism of Western Massachusetts as an evolved, intellectual haven and shows a dark undercurrent lurking beneath — in this way, it strangely reminds me of *Blue Velvet*. Except 
far more funny — a thirteen-year-old boy 123
getting molested by a 33-year old man has never been this funny before. Burroughs writes with the perfect amount of affect to convey the insanity of his world and the foibles of false maturity. I would gladly read a sequel (or a rebuttal written by one of the other characters).

331. In Defence of Food: The Myth of Nutrition and the Pleasures of Eating by Michael Pollan
Received: 24 May 2008
Started: 27 May 2008
Finished: 27 May 2008
This is completely great. I listened to Pollan's lecture to Google employees online, and this book reiterates a lot of those points, but it's still worth reading because there's a lot more detail, specifically about the lies of 'nutritionism', as he calls it. I've always been extremely sceptical of nutrition claims in food products, but Pollan really backs up his critique with a plethora of sources. His final section, where he outlines his philosophy of eating, is written incredibly well — I think I may be a changed man after reading it. I've always been reluctant to spend more on what I eat, and I'm particularly wary of places that overcharge for some perceived 'natural' approach to food. But there is a hell of a lot of truth to what he writes, and I feel inspired enough to break out my wallet a bit more.

332. The Puppet and the Dwarf: The Perverse Core of Christianity by Slavoj Zizek
Received: 22 May 2008
Started: 22 May 2008
Finished: 28 May 2008
This is part of the 'short circuits' series of books, which encourages unusual readings of texts, or something like that. I feel a bit worn out from this, as I struggled to focus on Zizek's argument but found it constantly evading me. My background in philosophy and psychoanalysis is a layman's, so I was challenged to comprehend all of the twists and turns in this text. And even if I got the gist of what he was saying at one point, I wasn't always to fit it into the larger narrative. I understand the basic core arguments for why he views Christianity as perverse, but I felt that this book was out of my grasp as a whole entity. Still, it was rewarding to read. I jotted down a lot of interesting notes in the first half before giving up and just going along with the ride. I think this was a good follow-up to the *Black Mass*
327 book I just read, because both deal with belief in the way it applies to social order. I will read this again at some point and feel more in control, I guess; in the meantime I'll dance around some other Zizek, for his star shines bright.

333. The Spirit of Terrorism: And Requiem for the Twin Towers by Jean Baudrillard
Received: 22 May 2008
Started: 29 May 2008
Finished: 29 May 2008
This ultra-quick read is from the same Verso series that produced Virilio's *Ground Zero* and Zizek's *Welcome to the Desert of the* 199, 347  *Real*. In two short essays, Baudrillard talks 208 about the symbolic power of terrorism and the aesthetic impact of the World Trade Centre collapse. It's actually fairly lightweight compared to the other two in this series, which I am going to re-read now. If anything I found myself thinking about how "over" 9/11 we are already — much more quickly than I thought — which seems to validate Virilio's views of *dromos*. Baudrillard talks about the then-forthcoming war on terror as the fourth world war, but there aren't many ground-breaking ideas here.

334. The Use and Abuse of History: or How the Past is Taught to Children by Marc Ferro
Received: 29 May 2008
Started: 29 May 2008
Finished: 3 June 2008
Ferro's study looks at how different cultures present their own histories to children, and asks questions about the purpose of such histories. The conclusions are nothing shocking — history is taught to encourage patriotism and smooth over controversy — but the process itself is what makes this so compelling. By selecting quotes from these children's textbooks and then commenting on them, Ferro presents a brief overview of all of these cultures histories and looks at the specific issues of each one, such as the Armenians' sense of identity and the Aborigines own cyclical view. In the process I actually learned a lot of history, though it was so overwhelming I found myself skimming parts and quickly forgetting names and dates. This was written in 1980 and updated slightly to reflect the 1980s and the fall of communism, though I suspect the basic point is still the same.

335. The Cosmic Puppets: A Novel by Philip K. Dick
Received: 12 June 2008
Started: 13 June 2008
Finished: 13 June 2008
Here's one I just TORE through in super quick fashion; it's really quick and kinda lightweight, but a lot more fun than other

317 Dick stuff. Compared to *Time Out of Joint* it's moves way quicker, and instead of wasting any time on character development it just gets into the strangeness. I'll never read this again but it would also make a great movie.

336. Gravity's Rainbow by Thomas Pynchon
Received: (already owned)
Started: 3 June 2008
Finished: 1 July 2008
Obviously there's too much to say here, as reading a novel like this produces a lot of thought. More than usual as it's my third go-around, and even more so because I
337 read it with Weisenburger's annotations. The experience of reading this was incredibly dense as the annotations allowed me to swim in all of the references — though the unreferenced material is no less stunning, containing some incredibly beautiful writing.

337. A Gravity's Rainbow Companion: Sources And Contexts for Pynchon's Novel by Steven C. Weisenburger
Received: 29 May 2008
Started: 3 June 2008
Finished: 1 July 2008
It's not easy to write a 'review' of this book, as it's a list of references/explanations throughout *Gravity's Rainbow*. It
336 enhanced *GR* in the greatest imaginable manner, while still being incomplete (of course). It highlighted themes that I would have never otherwise picked up on, and provided the years worth of scholarship that I would never be able to achieve myself. Weisenburger's own voice is rather muted as he lets Pynchon do the talking, so I can't say I got much of a feel for the 'style' of his annotations. There is apparently an updated version of this that has been expanded, and I may buy it before I give *GR* a fourth 'go'.

338. The Simulacra by Philip K. Dick
Received: 4 May 2008
Started: 2 July 2008
Finished: 3 July 2008
The Simulacra had the potential to be Dick's greatest novel; its construction could have been epic, but it winds up quickly in only 200 pages. If this novel was about twice as long, it would have been amazing. As it is, I liked this a lot and think it's among Dick's better books. Put into 'real' terms (though reading Dick by now has made me sceptical of such terms), you can imagine this as the Hillary Clinton-led future America, with Nazis coming back from the past, representatives from the Ocora label attempting to record a psychokinetic Conlan Nancarrow, and a battle between corporations for the right to build the next George W. Bush. Definitely awesome, and it was nice to see the V-2 rocket make another appearance
in my life so quickly. 336

339. The Game-Players of Titan by Philip K. Dick
Received: 15 April 2008
Started: 5 July 2008
Finished: 5 July 2008
In this thriller, Dick tackles games and chance, but gets into the uncertainty of his best work, with the possibility of alien invaders masquerading as human. It's not that simple, though; there's divisions of trust that extend beyond racial lines, which confuses the protagonist. Like Dick himself, the protagonist is addicted to pills and has extreme, suicidal moods. This planet Earth resembles the empty, dying Earth of *The Penultimate Truth*. I've read three Dick novels in three days and all have been excellent; sadly, I only see two more on my shelf and only a few more after that before I've read them all.

340. Clans of the Alphane Moon by Philip K. Dick
Received: 26 June 2008
Started: 4 July 2008
Finished: 5 July 2008
Another of Dick's better books, I think, *Clans of the Alphane Moon* moved from the story of a crumbling marriage (which passages that surely came from Dick's failed non-fiction books) to a spy thriller. The underlying theme is that of mental illness, as it addresses the settlements on the Alphane Moon as various races, echoing their ailments like a weird caste system. The subplot about writing the TV show is probably a product of Dick's own failure to support himself commercially, and his hero's reluctance is maybe a rationalisation of this failure. The telepathic slime mould reminded me a bit of Glimmung from *Galactic Pot-Healer*, though without
as much silliness to it. Also interesting is 319
that the world in this novel is much less of a totalitarian state than in his other ones, almost as if the mental illness provide enough constraints.

341. The Franchiser: A Novel by Stanley Elkin
Received: 10 June 2008
Started: 22 June 2008
Finished: 7 July 2008
This was the first Elkin novel I ever read, and one that I regard as (probably) his best. I've had an itch to write something about Elkin for a long time now, so I thought I'd revisit this to see if I still felt the magic. I do; very, very much so. I remembered much of this book but I didn't mind reading it again, especially the long monologues. Now I felt I could afford myself the time to savour them, though still moving through them with the propulsion they deserve. The final chapter, attempting to tie up loose ends, is a bit superfluous; the preceding chapter should be the end, as it's one of my favourite parts in any Elkin novel. The long introduction to it, describing the hotel, is like something out of *Life: A User's Manual*; the attention to detail is great and perfect for capturing the vanishing America. This is a novel about the eternal Southland Drive in Lexington; the fading signs of franchises before the corporate sheen took over. It's an America that I am too young for, though I love it and deeply mourn being away from (what is left of) it.

342. In Praise of Shadows by Junichiro Tanizaki
Received: 11 June 2008
Started: 6 July 2008
Finished: 7 July 2008
This short essay looks at aesthetics, specifically the difference between Japanese and American approaches. The part about toilets is great; the stuff about Kabuki interested me less. Its rambling style is nice and I can see how this was really influential; it could be a calming breeze to a lot of Western designers. And this was written in the 30s!

343. Consider the Lobster: And Other Essays by David Foster Wallace
Received: 10 July 2008
Started: 11 July 2008
Finished: 13 July 2008
It's been too long since I've spent some time with David Foster Wallace; this collection of essays makes me want to read 109 *Infinite Jest* AGAIN — I am a glutton for punishment. Opening with the hilarious and disturbing look at the Adult Video industry, the centrepiece of the book is probably his review of an English usage manual, where he gets into the Prescriptivist vs. Descriptivist arguments about correct usage. For once, Wallace's style really benefits the subject, with acronyms, footnotes and Proper Nouns. The essay on the lobster festival turned out to be about animal rights, which must have really pleased *Gourmet* magazine (who commissioned it). The McCain thing is also here, which I saw they're reprinting for the election season; given the current climate it was awesome to read about McCain 8 years ago, and I feared it would be really pro-McCain but it's actually about the cynicism of young voters and the bullshit of the campaign trail. The last essay, about a conservative talk radio host, gets a bit more experimental with the notation style but proves to be a brilliant look at the rise of conservative talk radio while splattered with Wallace's technological interests.

344. America by Jean Baudrillard
Received: 18 June 2008
Started: 18 July 2008
Finished: 23 July 2008
Baudrillard's work on my native country begins as a strange travelogue, with his reflections and contemplations about the Western landscape. I geared myself for something resembling Butor's *Mobile*, but then the tone shifted into a more stan- 762 dard Baudrillard essay style — which is to say it became flowery, dramatic, and provocative yet strangely without a centre. Though he does get into the loneliness of New York City, the recurring image is that of the desert. He compares America to Europe extensively, and sees Reagan as the logical conclusion at the time. The invective is often very anti-American, but there's more balance than seems at first. Though I greatly enjoyed reading this, it does suffer from the usual problems these types of books suffer from — gross generalisations that are actually too vague to even be generalisations, and an extreme, exaggerated lens over culture's impulses (much like Virilio). But I'd read this again and recommend it, for 22 years later it still resonates and there are some passages of pure beauty.

345. The Age of Extremes: A History of the World, 1914-1991 by Eric Hobsbawm
Received: 7 July 2008
Started: 7 July 2008
Finished: 26 July 2008
It was about time I read something by the world's most renowned Marxist historian, and this look at the "Short Twentieth Century" interested me more than his books on previous eras. Covering World War I through the fall of the Soviet Union, Hobsbawm looks at world trends in war, economics, science and the arts. Obviously he can't get into too much detail with such a large scope, but he succeeds in constructing a coherent narrative historical viewpoint. Thought the history is slightly Eurocentric, he shows the effects of change as they ripple through the entire world. For a Marxist, his viewpoint is fairly restrained; in the second half it starts to become more dominant, but he is fiercely critical of the Soviet nightmare and finds some value in capitalism's excesses. Actually, what impressed me the most was his argument that socialist and capitalist systems need each other to challenge and refine themselves; written in the early 90s, this book (wisely) expresses fear at a future with nothing to keep liberal democracy and capitalism in check. First and foremost, Hobsbawm is a social historian, so he manages to convey the effect of actual human lives even when writing about industrialisation or war debts. He doesn't try to build the book around Great personalities (though Hitler, Stalin, and Gorbachev are of course unavoidable); nor does he claim distinct turning points (apart from the three main sections of the book, positioned around the end of World War II and the beginning of the economic decline of the early 1970s). The chapters on science and the arts were good, though they felt like they could have been excised — it was war and money that interested me the most. I don't know if I'll go back and seek out Hobsbawm's older historical works just because this was huge and slow going, but I'm glad I got through this.

346. The Terrible Twos by Ishmael Reed
Received: 3 June 2008
Started: 28 July 2008
Finished: 1 August 2008
This quick read was fun though the language was rather plain; the humour came more from the bizarre scenarios than anything in the language. Written in the early 80s, this is a surreal view of a potential America, taking the promises of 80s consumerism and exaggerating it in a similar manner to *Mr. Freedom*. There's obviously a shock about Reagan's election that is conveyed through the whole novel; the Christmas/Santa Claus theme is a good wrapper for the bitterness.

345, 1082

347. Ground Zero by Paul Virilio
Received: 18 June 2008
Started: 3 August 2008
Finished: 4 August 2008
This was the first work of Virilio's I ever read, back when I started my MLitt programme, and I decided to re-read it just for fun. This is a pretty good introduction to Virilio's ideas and style, as it's very short and accessible. He wrote it a month after 9/11 though you can tell he was already working on it and he rushed it out for the Verso 9/11 series. The stuff about the telecracy and telepresence isn't anything new for Virilio (and it really isn't anything unique to his vision) but it's still interesting, if not fun. I don't know that we'll see all of his visions come to fruition — specifically that artists will become sponsored by corporations and forced to produce new work — but there's always some seeds planted in my mind by even his most idiosyncratic musings.

348. Gilles Deleuze by C. Colebrook
Received: 29 May 2008
Started: 4 June 2008
Finished: 5 August 2008
I've never been able to actually penetrate Deleuze so I figured a book discussing his work might be easier. I think it's important to understand Deleuze to understand the 20th century — his ideas influenced so much though, and his philosophy was pretty ground-breaking. Reading this has still only scratched the surface for me. Colebrook is a clear, lucid writer and at the beginning of each section I am able to follow for a bit before I lose the plot. I read half of this and put it down for a month before finishing it, so I had forgotten a lot too. There are little things I gleamed from it that I will take with me, like the majoritarian vs. minoritarian readings of literature, the univocity of experience (though I'm not sure I completely understand that), etc. I will probably end up reading this again rather than attempt actual Deleuze — in fact, I don't know if I even care to read Deleuze himself. The section at the end with information about post-Deleuzian

writers sounded really interesting, as they are taking his theories and applying them to contemporary film, politics and feminist theory — but I will probably be confusing myself more by jumping straight into that stuff.

349. Freakonomics: A Rogue Economist Explores the Hidden Side of Everything by Steven D. Levitt, Stephen J. Dubner
Received: 4 August 2008
Started: 4 August 2008
Finished: 5 August 2008
This was something I meant to read for ages and finally remembered it and found many copies in the library system. These guys are pretty entertaining writers (I've read their blog sometimes) and the point out some interesting ideas, though there's nothing incredibly amazing besides the abortion as crime deterrent argument in the middle of the book. The survey on children's names was pretty funny too, and the hierarchy of crack dealers is fascinating though really it's the other guy who actually discovered all of that stuff. A quick, light read, and now back to the Bolaño ....

350. Scepticism Inc. by Bo Fowler
Received: 5 July 2008
Started: 10 August 2008
Finished: 11 August 2008
A friend lent me this weird sci-fi/philosophy novel which was a good choice; I enjoyed it in a quick, Douglas Adams-style manner and laughed a bit too. There's nothing particularly literary about it but as a meditation on belief taken to an absurd level, it works well. Now that I think about it, this could pass as a Kurt Vonnegut novel.

351. The Savage Detectives: A Novel by Roberto Bolaño
Started: 30 July 2008
Finished: 12 August 2008
This book came with so much hype that I could not help but approach it sceptically, though I found it's narrative engaging and I had read 300 pages before I even realised it. At times it felt like endless lists of Latin American poets, but for the most part it was a kaleidoscope of voices unified in an incredible portrait of poetry-obsessed people. I can see the similarities to the other one I read by him, though this is obviously on a much wider scope. By the end I was tugging the pages with excitement, though it's the episodic central section that I think was the most mesmerising. I am definitely psyched about *2666* now.

313

397

352. Did Somebody Say Totalitarianism: Five Interventions in the (Mis)Use of a Notion by Slavoj Zizek
Received: 5 August 2008
Started: 13 August 2008
Finished: 18 August 2008
I had to return this to the library before I was able to finish it, so it's not exactly something I can completely review. This was among the more fun Zizek books I've read, even though I didn't understand a lot of it. In general I tend to get into the beginnings of the chapters and slowly lose my way as he gets revved up. The section on discussing the Holocaust was really good though — it related to stuff we talked about in the 'Writing the Disaster' seminar I had in grad school. I'd like to read this again some day when I have the background to fully comprehend it (which is probably what I say about every Zizek book I've read).

353. The End of Mr. Y by Scarlett Thomas
Received: 22 August 2008
Started: 22 August 2008
Finished: 25 August 2008
I meant to start *Atmospheric Disturbances* on the plane but I stupidly left it in my checked luggage, so I bought this after reading a decent review in *The Independent*. This was little more than an airport book dressed up as something better. It discussed Derrida, Heidegger and post-structuralism thoughout but as little more than a stoned grad school discussion around a really cheesy sci-fi narrative. The sexy, deviant, loner PhD student theme, while never exactly anything I read before, came off as a bit of wishful thinking, like it was trying to fulfil some sort of countercultural fantasy. Ultimately I felt this was like Harry Potter for adults, yet I finished reading it till the bitter end. Maybe there was something I secretly enjoyed about it, or maybe I kept hoping for some good writing to finally appear. This reminded me of when I read those shitty Arturo Perez-Reverte novels as a younger man.

356

354. The Art of the Ridiculous Sublime: On David Lynch's Lost Highway by Slavoj Zizek
Received: 2 September 2008
Started: 3 September 2008
Finished: 4 September 2008
This Zizek book repeated a lot of things I've

read in his other works, but it was pretty entertaining anyway. This was probably my single favorite overall Zizek book because it was brief, about a film I liked, and it ended 638 before I started to get confused. I think after bashing my head against all of this stuff I'm starting to see the psychoanalytical approach to film. I don't know if I believe there is much of a purpose to this approach besides fun, but fun is good.

355. Shakey: Neil Young's Biography by Jimmy McDonough
Received: 3 September 2008
Started: 4 September 2008
Finished: 9 September 2008
All this book did to enhance my understanding of Neil Young was to fill in many details, and it did a great job at that. Young didn't seem as insane and monomaniacal as I had thought, and the book was very critical of his behaviours and output. The section about his 80s work was actually really interesting to read; the writer has a similar viewpoint to my own regarding his music so it was nice we clicked.

356. Atmospheric Disturbances: A Novel by Rivka Galchen
Received: 18 August 2008
Started: 27 August 2008
Finished: 10 September 2008
This lived up to the hype — actually it maybe exceeded it — not because of the weird, dreamlike surrealism or the Dick-esque paranoid twists, but because of the way that it addressed marriage and intimacy. This is something that I probably wouldn't have understood if I had read this a few years ago. That Galchen can write a book so fantastically strange and deeply disturbing as a first novel is impressive — that it's a powerful love story disguised as a surreal sci-fi nightmare adds a further level of complexity to it.

357. The Great Derangement: A Terrifying True Story of War, Politics, and Religion at the Twilight of the American Empire by Matt Taibbi
Received: 19 September 2008
Started: 19 September 2008
Finished: 21 September 2008
Taibbi manages to completely nail this particular point in American history, with a cynical-yet-progressive attitude and shitloads of humour. To say I loved this book would be an understatement — Taibbi probably singlehandedly justifies the continued existence of Rolling Stone magazine, and this is something I would recommend to everyone. I think I'm gonna go back and read his earlier book about the Kerry campaign, even if it's a bit dated.

358

358. Spanking the Donkey: Dispatches from the Dumb Season by Matt Taibbi
Received: 24 September 2008
Started: 25 September 2008
Finished: 29 September 2008
Taibbi's earlier book is a mix of his longer campaign-trail pieces from 2004 with some over-the-top satirical columns. His viewpoint is even more pronounced — total disgust with the electoral process and the charade of politics, etc. The end piece is a tournament to crown the shittiest political writer of 2004, which was funny but I skimmed most of it cause it's more for journalism nerds.

359. Lost Cosmonaut: Observations of an Anti-Tourist by Daniel Kalder
Received: 30 September 2008
Started: 4 October 2008
Finished: 4 October 2008
A friend floated me this weird travelogue and I read it on the plane. The author is a caustic Scotsman from Dumferline who has developed a manifesto of "anti-tourism" — a bit overdone really, but the book explores four forgotten republics in the Russian federation — Tatarstan, Mari El, Udmurtia and Kalmyk. Though his style is needless edgy, the material was good enough to carry the book. I can only imagine how good ths would be if it was written by someone who actually cared about the people he was writing about. His intentional omissions on research and his refusal to visit rural areas and actually discover something about the people he was trying to write about definitely hindered the book. Despite this, I wished it were longer (perhaps because I spent 19 hours traveling home).

360. Guided by Voices' Bee Thousand by Marc Woodworth
Received: 30 September 2008
Started: 5 October 2008
Finished: 5 October 2008
This 33 1/3 series is cool, and I was psyched to read an entire book about *Bee Thousand*. However, by the end of 160 pages I felt that it was getting pretty repetitive, despite the author turning over more than

744

half of the book to other voices. Pollard himself weighs in at the beginning, and the other members of GbV are interviewed throughout though they add little to the story. There's a lengthy excerpt from a dead PhD student's work in progress (unless it was fake) and lots of flowery rambling about the majesty of the album. Now, I love this album as much as anyone else listed here — in fact, reading about it at such a level of detail has amplified my own love of it — but 160 pages is just too much. Some of the material in the Pollard section is quoted repeatedly, and yes, I love it, but how much do we need to say about the lyric "And Christ it's a cluttered mess" from "Peep-hole"?

361. Mumbo Jumbo by Ishmael Reed
Received: 3 October 2008
Started: 4 October 2008
Finished: 5 October 2008
Finally, a copy of *Mumbo Jumbo*, which proved surprisingly difficult to come across — nothing in any libraries, and I don't think it's actually in print. A shame too, because this book was completely amazing. The other works I've read by Reed were lighter and a bit zanier — this was still extremely comic, but preoccupied with developing a big historical conspiracy. He researched the hell out of it, as you can see from the copious footnotes/etc. — and the final conspiracy theory detailed at the end is absolutely overwhelming. This reminds me a great deal of the *Illuminatus* trilogy — 232 both on terms of content, and in style. The disjointed, traveling narrative was probably very influential on Shea and Wilson; Reed actually kicks it a gear higher I think by being more focused and pointed. I don't know why Dalkey Archive hasn't reprinted this because it's absolutely essential.

362. Flying to America: 45 More Stories by Donald Barthelme
Received: 29 September 2008
Started: 6 October 2008
Finished: 11 October 2008
This collection brings together all of the stories that aren't in *60* and *40 Stories*. It's 114 92 great that this is finally available, as it eliminates the need to track down out-of-print collections. And while some of the stories in the middle of this book were less than memorable, it's still work reading every word this man ever wrote. A few of these were incredibly brilliant, and resembled the "classics" in the earlier collections — a few of these are classics of their own. This collection definitely tended towards the more humorous side of Barthelme, though there were some non-funny ones that were still great. It's hard to even pick a favourite here, but "To London and Rome" had me doubled over in laughter. I'm looking 194, 467 forward to the non-fiction collection that I bought (though I shipped it here, so it'll be a few weeks before I get to read it).

363. Perfect from Now On: How Indie Rock Saved My Life by John Sellers
Received: 22 October 2008
Started: 22 October 2008
Finished: 24 October 2008
I stumbled across this while browsing Amazon and though it might be fun, maybe the kind of book I would write. But it was terrible. The writer is a smarmy "indie rock" fan who actually knows extremely little about music and wears that fact with pride throughout the book. Everyone feels incredibly special about the experiences that music provided, especially growing up, but he seemed to think that his were somehow special. His anecdotes are dull, and he fills the book with footnotes, supposedly as a tribute to Nicholson Baker's *Mezzanine*, but it's just annoying to read about how he spent a whole day listening to Joy Division to commemorate Ian Curtis' death. I guess it's his close-minded ignorance that annoyed me the most; he talks about how he hates Dylan a ton cause his father liked it, and seems to think that his choice in music is somehow better.

Now, Pavement is probably my favourite band ever for the same sentimental reasons that he writes about, but I could at least convey my special experiences in a much more writerly manner. At least I think so — maybe I too would fall into the trap of thinking anyone else wants to read about this stuff. Really, the only interesting thing that ever happened to him is that he got to hang out with Bob Pollard a bit, and he fills the second half of the book with this. Of course, I kept reading — I can't deny that the part of me that still worships GbV and Pavement enjoyed reading such fanboy drivel. I should get back to Durrell now ....

364. The Omnivore's Dilemma: A Natural History of Four Meals by Michael Pollan
Received: 27 October 2008
Started: 27 October 2008
Finished: 28 October 2008
Michael Pollan rules. This book was like a cross between the other two I've read by him. The opening section about the corn industry was almost upsetting — I knew that the American industrial food system was fucked, but I never knew it was quite so bad. Pollan is very critical, but he writes in an easy, restrained way, letting the facts make the argument. The middle section, on organic food, confirmed my suspicions about the organic hoopla and showed an amazing, but sadly impossible alternative. The section on hunting and foraging was great too — as a vegetarian, reading about Pollan's experience shooting a pig was fairly upsetting, and as passionate as he is about his final meal, I think the description of cleaning the pig is enough to keep me vegetarian forever. I think this was the best of his books and I'm gonna download that documentary about the corn industry.

666

365. At the Same Time: Essays and Speeches by Susan Sontag
Received: 21 October 2008
Started: 21 October 2008
Finished: 2 November 2008
I didn't read this from cover to cover, as a lot of the essays dealt with works of Russian literature I'm not familiar with. I liked the piece about beauty at the beginning, but the section about 9/11 wasn't so impressive. I guess Sontag wrote about 9/11 from the reasonable progressive viewpoint, but it didn't really offer anything new to me.

366. Unknown Quantity by Paul Virilio
Received: 1 September 2008
Started: 31 October 2008
Finished: 2 November 2008
This is the exhibition catalogue from Virilio's disaster museum show, which I read about back when I was writing my dissertation. There's a surprising amount of writing in here amongst the photographs, though it's all typeset in some wacky manner that makes it a bit annoying to read. The Virilio essays here are his definitive writings on accident and art; they're all short and direct, and some of his best ideas in my opinion. The back section is the work of some of the other artists with some writing by a few of them (including Lebbeus Woods). It's a lovely book (though miserable on the inside) and I'm glad to get to check it out finally.

367. Look, Listen, Vibrate, Smile by Domenic Priore
Received: 29 October 2008
Started: 30 October 2008
Finished: 6 November 2008
This is a monster collection of articles, interviews, and other ephemera relating to the period in Beach Boys history where *SMiLE* was developed. I've been really into the Beach Boys lately so I checked this out of the library and I was kind of blown away by how geeky and fanboyish it is. Actually, this is really remarkable even if you're not into the Beach Boys — it's a true labour of love and it predates the Internet so it makes it even more special. There's some great articles in here and insane photos — I don't know how Priore got access to them all. The narrative constructed throughout this — even though it's 99% written by other people besides Priore — is that of the secret history of rock music, and the dream of an alternate reality where the whole world heard *SMiLE* and things evolved differently.

368. The Wrecking Crew: How Conservatives Rule by Thomas Frank
Received: 10 September 2008
Started: 10 September 2008
Finished: 13 November 2008
The great Thomas Frank delivers another excellent attack on the conservative philosophy, this time looking broadly at the rise of the movement and offering a hopeful plan for making America into the liberal state he dreams of. It was weird starting this book in September, in the throws of election fever, then accidentally shipping it to Finland and not actually finishing it until now, when a major nail has been hopefully driven into the conservative movement's coffin. This book sort of followed the story of Jack Abramoff, but not dominantly so. His involvement in defending the regime of South African apartheid is interesting, but even more so was the story of direct mail marketing in the 80s, and the Saipan nightmare. I don't know if I'll read this a second time, so maybe I shouldn't have blown $26 on a hardback — but if there is any political writer who I want to support financially, it would be Tom Frank. I wish there'd be a new issue of *The Baffler* some day ....

369. Poor People by William T. Vollmann
Received: 27 October 2008
Started: 5 November 2008
Finished: 13 November 2008
Vollmann's most recent book of non-fiction resembles *Rising Up, Rising Down* in that it's committed to explaining poverty through some sort of morally defensible framework. This is a lot shorter, however, but every bit as depressing. This is written in Vollmann's usual stilted journalistic style, drawn from his own experiences and punctuated with photographs of his interview subjects. He attempts to discover different types of poverty — systematic, political, spiritual, etc. — and in the book's strongest section, explores an incredibly fucked region of Kazakhstan that has been ravaged by a chemical plant. If I have any criticism, it's that maybe he spends too much time trying to compare the different people he's interviewed — comparing Chinese prostitutes in Tokyo to impoverished Thai families doesn't really make much of a point. At least he only compares them monetarily in the beginning, which is all in a table. Despite his "simple" writing style (as he claims in the final section, where he suggests [correctly, I think] that his readers are all rich), there are still some descriptive passages of stunning complexity, as strange and beautiful as anything in his novels. I continue to hold Vollmann as the most intense, fascinating, "young" living writer (since young means "under 60" in the literary world) and this is just another piece to further this view.

370. Remainder by Tom McCarthy
Received: 16 September 2008
Started: 18 November 2008
Finished: 18 November 2008
This starts off with that kind of calm yet quirky approach that's really prevalent in a lot of contemporary fiction. I used to associate that with the McSweeney's thing but this is British and so was *the Curious Dog in the Night-Time* book, so maybe that's infesting Britain as well. Or maybe I'm trying too hard to look for influence or blame; perhaps these writers just choose to write like this. Anyway, it starts off fairly on-track and slowly becomes more and more obsessive and crazy, and at some point about midway through the book it really starts to click. I think this book works well at creating a fantasy based around process and objects; maybe it's the most ultimately "post-modern" sense in that it removes the centre or the purpose and creates a fiction based around the details and periphery. Not to say the narrator didn't have a purpose or an idea — he very much does and it is the dominating motif of the novel — but it was never completely comprehensible to me, and the ending (not to spoil it for any potential readers) is perfect and appropriate. I could have probably written about this in my Master's dissertation, as there's an unexplained accident and it leads to the themes of transformation and creation (just as seen in *Stalker* and *Dhalgren* etc.).

311

165, 486, 505

9, 210

371. Now Wait for Last Year by Philip K. Dick
Received: 1 April 2008
Started: 26 November 2008
Finished: 26 November 2008
In a way this is one of the 'last' PK Dick novels I'll read — there are a handful of early titles and then his non-fiction and those few hard-to-find works (like the ones he wrote with other people) and his children's book, and then all of the stories — but in the sense of the 'classic' Dick canon, meaning the brilliant run he had beginning with *Time Out of Joint* — this is the last one I haven't read, so I maybe tried to savour it. Actually, I read this in one sitting on a flight to Glasgow and loved every second of it. This is in many ways a 'typical' Dick novel, but it was an excellent example of it. The time-travel content was the best stuff; the novel got a bit twisted and confusing but not too much, as his best books do. The decayed marriage suffered by the main characters was truly painful to read, despite Dick's blunt and awkward prose — I can see that this was a man who had been married 5 times. I guess now it's time to move onto the stories or maybe re-read some of the ones I liked best.

317

372. We Can Build You by Philip K. Dick
Received: 30 June 2008
Started: 21 November 2008
Finished: 26 November 2008
I took a few months off from Dick (ha, ha) and decided to go back and nail these last two just to get them off the shelf. *We Can Build You* is actually one of my least favourite, as it drags on with this strange civil war obsession and it uses the idea of the simulacra in the least developed of any of its other appearances; in *The Simulacra* or *Do Androids Dream*, Dick plays around much more with the question

338 310

of what constitutes humanity. The writing about mental illness (towards the end) is the most interesting aspect, though again he handles the themes better in *Clans of the Alphane Moon* and well, just about every other one of his novels. 340, 784

373. What It Is by Lynda Barry
Received: 30 September 2008
Started: 25 November 2008
Finished: 6 December 2008
Lynda Barry is such a treasure, and this is a masterpiece. It's rare to find a book of comics that transcends the genre so completely — actually there is very little in here that I would even call "comics", as it's really a work of art and philosophy wrapped together in a visually stimulating package. This book takes autobiography and uses it inspirationally; Barry suggests plans for creative work drawing from your own memories and experiences but presents her instructions, or rather her exercises, as a starting point for creating, rather than the end. She collages a lot of sources together but keeps them all from a similar pool, so it feels very thematically cohesive. The troubles of her childhood are addressed but not dwelled on — we're not supposed to feel sorry for her, but rather see how art provided a solution. And the questions that fill this book — questions on every page, some serious and some tossed off — make it a work that engages the reader so they are active and drawn into the book. The exercises in here, designed a bit like a children's activity book, would probably be worth trying — I intend to, actually, as I find writing and drawing difficult and could use the jumpstart. This is the kind of book you can go back to any time and open to a random page and have a million new ideas and directions — almost like an *Oblique Strategies* form of creative stimulus. I'm so glad I have this; it's probably the kind of thing I will go back to until its dog-eared and tattered.

374. Revolutionary Road by Richard Yates
Received: 30 November 2008
Started: 4 December 2008
Finished: 11 December 2008
This book was written in clear, concise language yet described the most brutal of domestic situations — a failing marriage and crushed dreams. It reminded me of Joseph Heller's *Something Happened* of course, yet not entirely focused on the male 138, 855 mind. Maybe it wasn't quite as successful because of its clairvoyance, though it was still a great read. This is one of those 'classics' of the mid-century I've always meant to read — I group it in with *The Moviegoer* in terms of style and theme, though Yates tries to comprehend detachment rather than just describing it. 155, 287, 474 I just saw there's a Hollywood film coming out based on this, which I'm sure will be shit but I may not be able to resist the urge to see it. Or at least download it.

375. Justine by Lawrence Durrell
Received: 9 October 2008
Started: 11 October 2008
Finished: 15 December 2008
The first of these four novels amazed me with it's language — I expected this novel to be cerebral and stylistically experimental, but instead I got succinct yet beautiful descriptive prose. The narrative is a bit less than compelling, but I stayed with it knowing how it would complexify in the subsequent books. I think it reminded me of some of the DH Lawrence stuff I read in grad school, maybe because it's that pre-war British modernist vibe. but while dabbling in topics (infidelity, politics) in a way that wasn't heavy-handed. Curious to see where this goes... [*Balthazar*]: got halfway through this, forgot about it as other things came along. I had to return it to the library as it was overdue. Maybe I'll try these again in the future, as I think you really need to read all 4 to get the full impact.

376. Lint by Steve Aylett
Received: 4 May 2008
Started: 16 December 2008
Finished: 18 December 2008
This book was so good I think I'll be re-reading it for a long time to come. *Lint* is not a parody of a Philip K Dick novel, but more like a parody of a Dick biography. The verbal experimentation is part Wrestling Team, part Marx Brothers, and a large part Samuel Beckett. The absurdity is so extreme it becomes fairly highbrow, but there's a few awful, ridiculous jokes thrown in a well. But it's more than just comedy — there are some amazing ideas and extensions of language present. The narrative was particularly enjoyable to me after reading a Dick biography because there were a lot of elements of Lint's life that are straight from Dick — the *Valis* trilogy appears here as the "Arkwitch" trilogy, and the moment of gnosis Dick experienced happens to Lint 282, 301, 316

too. But there's no real need for knowing that to enjoy this. Right now I want to run out and read every other Steve Aylett book. I had a few some years back when I used to buy shitloads of books but I never read them and unloaded them during one of my moves. I'm kicking myself now. Amazing amazing amazing.

377. MOME Fall 2008 (Vol. 12) edited by Gary Groth, Eric Reynolds
Received: 30 September 2008
Started: 19 December 2008
Finished: 20 December 2008
This issue of *MOME* has some new artists, such as John Vermilyea, who's "Breakfast" story is really funny and done in this action-packed, slightly confusing B&W style. There's a recurring Tom Kazcyniski series about noise (which is okay but could have been better) and a lengthy David B. piece that is beautiful and mysterious. Hornschmeier's story is entertaining in that post-adolescent regret kind of way, but would have probably worked better as a comic than prose with a few illustrations. Another great issue though; from cover to cover, this does not disappoint because if anything is weak then the next piece usually picks up the slack!

378. All About H. Hatterr by G. V. Desani
Received: 20 September 2008
Started: 22 December 2008
Finished: 28 December 2008
This was amazingly rich in the way it destroyed the English language and rebuilt it into something bizarre and, well, Indian. At times the prose was so dizzying it became hard to read; the narrative was comic as well, and it conveyed a real zaniness that only India can offer. In some way it reminded me of Firbank, maybe through the weird linguistic constructions. It wasn't a total deconstruction of English though — it was actually quite readable, and it's a shame this languishes in obscurity.

379. Exit Wounds by Rutu Modan
Received: 28 December 2008
Started: 28 December 2008
Finished: 28 December 2008
This graphic novel is tightly plotted and perfectly paced, but I'm not sure how it sits with me. The ending is abrupt and I was actually shocked that there was nothing more to it, but after thinking about it for a few minutes I don't think it was necessarily a bad thing. This was done entirely on a Wacom tablet, so it's kind of interesting to read a graphic novel that was created without paper, which I tend to think of as the most elemental ingredient of comics. Because of this digital origin, everything feels incredibly clean, though there are a few awkward moments where Modan has to include arrows or some extracurricular indicator of motion. Narratively, it's interesting to read something about contemporary Israeli life, specifically the way that people live with everyday violence and just adapt to it. The constant underbelly of terrorism and conflict is felt, at least by me as a reader, and the religious aspect of Israeli life plays a role that is subdued (due to the nature of the main characters) but inescapable. I'm curious what else Modan will produce; this has definitely interested me in seeing more of her work.

380. Winner of the National Book Award: A Novel of Fame, Honor, and Really Bad Weather by Jincy Willett
Received: 23 June 2007
Started: 28 December 2008
Finished: 29 December 2008
A friend gave this to us as a wedding gift last year, and I just got around to starting it. I'm not sure why he gave us this — maybe he thought she would like it in some sort of warped way, I dunno. This is actually a fairly interesting premise for a novel — a woman is reading a biography of her sister while commenting on it throughout. This is another entry in the canon of twin literature; here though, there's an unreliability aspect with the narrator, and some incredibly dark sexual and psychological territory described. I liked the parts that delved into the psychosis of eating disorders and sexual malevolence more than the quaint stories about New England life.

381. Atom by Steve Aylett
Received: 31 December 2008
Started: 4 January 2009
Finished: 6 January 2009
Maybe this is more 'typical' Aylett — a fucked up, absurd detective story set in a sci-fi world where everything is impossible. I enjoyed this because it was quick; I preferred *Lint* which is just non-stop entertainment, while this attempted to send-up the hardboiled gumshoe genre and actually bored me a little bit with the stereotypes (even though Aylett relentlessly

fucks things up). I enjoyed the narrative enough, especially Atom's multiple stories about his father, but I'm definitely glad it ended when it did. There were a few runs of language that were as fantastic as any part of *Lint*; I love how Aylett employs non-sequiturs carefully. The time loop was also ace.

382. The Rough Guide to the Velvet Underground by Rough Guides
Received: 31 December 2008
Started: 6 January 2009
Finished: 7 January 2009
Rough Guides always put together nice books and this one is no exception. The first half tells the story of the Velvet Underground, pulling no punches in describing about how insanely fucked up Cale and Reed were. Nico, too, comes off as a fucking mess and it all serves to make Moe Tucker look like the most stable, awesome person ever (which I'm sure she is). The second half goes through the discography in detail, including bootlegs, side projects and solo albums. It's pretty funny to read about all the awful Reed/Cale solo albums all at once, though it's made me want to pull out some of my faves (like Cale's *Fear*).
581 It is completely dismissive of Cale's avant/minimalist work with Conrad and Young, but to each his own, I guess.

383. Invisible Republic: Bob Dylan's Basement Tapes by Greil Marcus
Received: 7 January 2009
Started: 8 January 2009
Finished: 11 January 2009
I always kinda thought that this book, and Greil Marcus-like people in general (such as the whole annoying school of "Dylanologists" [which to me sounds like Dylanite + apologist]) are responsible for inflating the basement tapes into something more than just an album — into the enduring myth and symbol that they've become. But then I started listening to the tapes themselves, first the weird falsely-authentic official double album (with Band overdubs and stuff recorded later without Dylan) and then the various messy bootlegs (finally settling on *A Tree With Roots* as the best collection), and I too found myself drawn into an amazing world. I'm not sure if I've fallen victim to the myth or if all of Marcus's inflated language actually illustrates something very real and remarkable that affects me. This book *is* ridiculous, though maybe not as
585 ridiculous as *Lipstick Traces*; once you get past all of his invented fictional scenarios to describe a song, there is some compelling writing about the music itself. I don't really know if it was necessary to compare "Tears of Rage" to a 1630 Puritan sermon by John Winthrop, but who knows, maybe that's exactly what Dylan was inspired by. The middle section of the book isn't about the basement tapes at all, but about the *Anthology of American Folk Music*, specifically Clarence Tom Ashley and Dock Boggs. No amount of rock-writer hyperbole can obfuscate how fascinating that music is, and I found this much more interesting than the stuff about Dylan. It reminded me of my favourite parts of *Where Dead Voices Gather* by Nick Tosches — the sense of 268
mystery that these forgotten, marginalised records carry. For the first half of *Invisible Republic* I felt like Marcus was building up some huge concept of Americana, some ultimately false belief in some sort of mentality or truth that runs as an undercurrent to all of this music and was somehow 'perfected' in the basement tapes. But by the end, I think he treats this pretty sensibly — he is aware of the contradictions and dangers of this way of thinking, and how it's ultimately just identity politics in the disguise of folk music. Despite its flaws, I would probably consider this 'essential' reading of rock literature.

384. Get in the Van: On the Road With Black Flag by Henry Rollins
Received: 30 January 2009
Started: 31 January 2009
Finished: 2 February 2009
I had never read this before and thought it might be a good time; I had no idea what a dark, intense journal this book is. The beginning is great because Rollins is this wide-eyed kid, living the dream of getting asked to sing for his favourite band. After a few tours where they are met with non-stop violence and aggression from both the police and the audiences, he turns into the Henry Rollins we all know — the intense modern primitive who obsesses on rage, strength, and other 'heavy' topics. His writing throughout the book is turgid, but at least the early stuff is forgivable because he has not yet become the *artiste* that he later becomes. And I admit that I found myself skimming some of the later journal entries, especially the surrealistic fantasies at the ends of some. I've never actually been the world's biggest Black Flag fan but after reading this (and the Carducci book) I feel like I really 233, 445

understand where they were coming from. Black Flag were not a punk band, and though they forever changed punk rock, punk rock also forever changed them. Black Flag were too radical to be part of any mere subculture, but the structure of the system they were entrenched them made it impossible for them to ignore it. Thus, show after show of audience members spitting and throwing cups of piss at them, while they struggled through poverty and interpersonal problems because they were trying to express themselves musically. There's an incredible contempt for the audience described in this book, which of course only focuses on the shitheads at these shows; still, it's hard to see Rollins and company as being too whiny when they were faced with such utter depravity every single night.

A friend once said to me that he thought Wolf Eyes were the new Black Flag, in the way that they toured constantly, playing about 100 shows per year and inspiring kids to start similar style bands in every city. That's a good analogy, but Wolf Eyes never had to hide cheese sandwiches from each other, and they aren't faced with hostile audiences. The cultural landscape of America has changed so much since the early 1980s that there can never be a situation like this again; it's not just that multiculturalism and permissiveness have taken over, but rather the speed at which culture accelerates today creates a distance that, while not necessarily always irony, has a similar effect.

385. The Universal Exception by Slavoj Zizek
Received: 20 January 2009
Started: 21 January 2009
Finished: 6 February 2009
I tried to buy this book last year but I accidentally ordered volume 1, *Interrogating the Real*, which is all high level Lacan talk and far beyond my comprehension. This book collects Zizek's political writing, and while challenging, there are some absolutely brilliant insights here. A few of the essays were pretty difficult for me to follow, such as 'The Fetish of the Party' (which breaks down Stalinism through a series of equations). But others were fun and extremely stimulating, though occasionally repetitive. Because he comes from an academic Marxist background, there are some essays about the intellectual legacy of Marxist thought (such as the George Lukacs essay) which aren't particularly relevant to my daily life. There's a couple of interesting but obscure topics — a theory of Stalinism based upon a few musical films produced during the 1940s, and a defense of Laibach. The essays I found most intriguing were the ones that I could relate my own experiences to: 'Attempts to Escape the Logic of Capitalism', 'Multiculturalism', 'A Leftist Plea for Eurocentrism' and 'The Three Faces of Bill Gates'. Bill Gates represents 'frictionless capitalism' (where great amounts of money are made while playing racquetball and sitting in comfy offices, etc.) — and this has replaced actual capitalism as the perceived situation, which is actually worse because the truly violent, exploitative elements of capitalism are no longer felt. If there is a predominant theme through most of these, it's that the dialogue of left vs. right has shifted to eliminate true socialism as an option. The "third way" is referred to mockingly as the "post-socialist" global capitalism of Bill Clinton, the Labour party, and Francis Fukuyama; it feels like the 'second way' has never really been attempted though, as Sovietism/"really existing socialism" is a corruption. Now, with this worldwide economic 'crisis' in effect, I'm curious what Zizek has to say. His viewpoints are progressive but very rooted in ethics/morals; the essay on the current Iraq war rejects the idea that opposition to Saddam Hussein and opposition to the US invasion have to be mutually exclusive; he actually defends Christopher Hitchens' viewpoint, which is weirdly refreshing. I do wish I knew more about philosophy; I fear that he may be misrepresenting Peter Singer in 'The Prospects of Radical Politics Today', so maybe I should read some Singer. This book also reprints an earlier version of 'Welcome to the Desert of the Real' (which was the first thing I ever read by Zizek and got me really interested in his ideas and style) — this version seems even more rambling than the book-length one, but is still great to read 7.5 years after 9/11. As with everything else I've read by Zizek, I can't say I have an overall grasp on his theoretical system (although there is a helpful glossary at the end of this book) but I intend to re-read this, of course.

386. Lost Dimension by Paul Virilio
Received: 17 February 2009
Started: 17 February 2009
Finished: 22 February 2009
A thin and very early Virilio book that lays down many of the ideas that follow in his later books. I took halfassed notes

on this but here I'll try to summarise my thoughts. Being written in the early 80s and largely about technology and speed, there is a certain amount of this book that is 'dated' because he's describing advances in video screen technology, etc., which are all quite common now. However, the usual Virilio prescience is extremely evident, perhaps because this was written so long ago and so much of what he has predicted has come true. There's little ideas in here that are applicable to many of today's Internet based trends (such as the emergence of micronarratives — Virilio predicted blogging and Twitter in 1984!). In the last chapter, 'Critical Space' (which seemed like a weird ending, as it goes off in entirely different directions from the first four chapters), Virilio talks about the decentralisation of the city — something that has certainly come to fruition since the early 80s — and how this will encourage economic deregulation and the disenfranchisement of entire populations. Again, it comes true with startling relevance both in his France and in my America. But the majority of the book deals with what he calls 'architectonic and morphological irruptions'. He expands on the time-lapse/ picnoleptic moment more in *Aesthetics of*
221 *Disappearance* but here he's laying down the fundamental ideas about measurement, distance and perspective — how surfaces and interfaces have changed due to speed, and how tele-presence emerges as a new portal that displaces architectural windows and door. There are some ideas about the accident, something else he develops more. I'm really glad I read this, because I've studied a lot of Virilio but starting back with the early work gives me a better understanding of his ideas. I think I'm going to read a lot of his other works that I never read (or never finished reading, such as *Open Sky*) next.

387. The Teachings of Don B.: Satires, Parodies, Fables, Illustrated Stories, and Plays of Donald Barthelme by Donald Barthelme

Received: 29 September 2008
Started: 24 February 2009
Finished: 6 March 2009

This is the final chapter in the Donald Barthelme story, for me — everything left over that isn't previously collected in *60 Stories,*
362 114 92 *40 Stories, Flying to America, Not-Knowing* or the novels. But that's not to marginalise
147 this material, which is some of the finest that DB ever penned. These pieces are very short, and many are really just short stories that are labelled here as 'satires' (even though a great majority of his short stories could be classified as such). There's some amazingly hilarious pieces, such as his recipes using canned goods, and his deconstructions of psychology, technology and modern life are unparalleled. The plays, in the back, I enjoyed less, but this other version of 'Snow White' was pretty enjoyable and made me want to re-read the novel. I have only a few slim novels left before I will have read everything by Barthelme, but I look forward to reading everything a second or third time.

388. Camp Concentration: A Novel by Thomas M. Disch

Received: 15 September 2008
Started: 15 September 2008
Finished: 11 March 2009

I recently saw a list on io9.com of science-fiction writers that non-SF people/ fans of "serious literature" love. The list was a bit condescending, implying that people who like these writers but don't read any other genre sci-fi are snobby in some way. I'm happy to be considered as such — if "common" genre sci-fi reached the literary heights of Delany, Disch, or DeLillo's sci-fi, then I'd read more of it. Disch was of course on the list because of how "literary" he is, which I believe means he makes frequent allusions to other classic and modernist works while constructing something that is marketed towards sci-fi readers. This novel was pretty incredible, and I don't really know what's "sci-fi" about it except for maybe the fact that it contains a weird intelligence-increasing drug. It is soaked in the protest movement of the 60s and I originally took the protagonist's protestations as against Vietnam, though a later reference suggests a future heating of the Cold War against the Soviets. Regardless of the setting, Disch brilliantly comments on freedom and captivity through the artistic intellect. The ending of the book suddenly jumps into an accelerated voice and really surprised me, as I was setting myself up (from page 1) for a novel of unbelievable bleakness and despair. The dates here suggest that it took me six months to read this, but actually I started it, accidentally packed it in the overseas shipment, and then didn't go back to it until March. Thanks to one friend for lending this to me and to another for urging me to read Disch for the past year and a half — I completely understand why he recommended it to me as a fan of

Dick, as Disch is really similar to Dick from a conceptual point of view but with the added bonus of being a talented stylist and the "literary" aspect io9 somewhat mockingly mentioned.

389. Eunoia by Christian Bök
Received: 13 March 2009
Started: 16 March 2009
Finished: 20 March 2009
Thought not a member of the Oulipo, Bök demonstrates his talents in this slender volume, which is pretty much the most purely Oulipian book I've ever read. Each chapter uses only one vowel, but is also laden with additional constraints (described in the afterword) such as having to use at least 98% of the available words and contain certain themes. Like Perec's *Les Revenen-*
104 *tes*, the prose becomes maddening after just a few pages, but if I can fight the urge to consume quickly and really take in the language, it's actually quite enjoyable. The book is ridiculously brief — 77 pages, and each one only has about a third of it with text, and even that is double-spaced — but it felt substantive enough, being that it would be fairly insane to read anything properly novel-length written like this. The back section of the book has some bonus material — other Oulipian experiments, like using all words in English that are only consonants and writing poetry using only the letters v, o, w, e, and l. The prose has the feel of language poetry anyway and it doesn't surprise me that Bök is a Canadian sound poet.

390. Pure War by Paul Virilio and Sylvere Lotringer
Received: 28 February 2009
Started: 5 March 2009
Finished: 22 March 2009
My second wave of Virilio intake continues with this, probably where I should have started back when I was doing my dissertation (and I did, actually, though the book was recalled to the library right after I started it, and it didn't concern his writings on time, art and the accident as much as other texts). This is where "pure war" was defined — how peace, or rather deterrence, replaced war yet is a war of its own. Technology and speed are the culprits, unsurprisingly, and Virilio discusses the accident here though not as much as in later texts. These books with Lotringer are so amazing because they are so casual and conversational — I need to track down *Crespuscular Dawn*, which is the third. This is the 2007 reprint of *Pure War*, which has two further conversations tacked on. One is from 1997 and discusses the end of the Cold War of course and the first WTC attack; the second is from 2007. Over the whole book, a ton of ideas are thrown out — more than anyone can follow — and due to the conversational nature, the topic switches a fair bit. Lotringer does a good job of organising Virilio's mind and I think I read this thinking about the exhibition I just saw at the Fondation Cartier, about population density and migration. One particular point that stuck out was something about how Einstein knew the atomic bomb was only the first bomb, and that the "information bomb" would follow — PV suggests a "demographic bomb" will be next, as the third bomb, and the exhibition seemed to explore that a bit. I went a bit nuts in Paris and bought a stack of Virilio books but I might take a break before I attempt another.

391. Pilgermann by Russell Hoban
Received: 9 March 2009
Started: 9 March 2009
Finished: 29 March 2009
Pilgermann reminded me a bit of *Xavier: Renegade Angel* (really!) though without the humour or the stupidity of the main character. But Pilgermann is definitely similar in the way he roams the earth exploring questions of theology, the spirit, the body, perspective, war, and other Big Ideas. Hoban is such an insane writer and even though this used normal English prose, it was loaded with references to the Bible and Koran, and was generally very scholarly. I didn't have a lot of fun reading this but there were some interesting questions and occasionally beautiful passages, in the way that a Bosch or Brueghel painting can be beautiful. I can see, from this and *Riddley Walker*, that Hoban is really interested in how knowledge evolves. Despite the crazy medieval bleakness or the narrative, with all of its violence and maggot-infested tax collectors, this is really a classical novel in the way Pilgermann muses on all of the ideas crammed in here. It's too bad I don't know more about history and religion, because a lot of references went over my head and I just skimmed past them in an effort to finish this. For some reason this made me want to re-read *Dictionary of the Khazars*, I guess because it's set in a similar time period and also about the conflicts between Christianity, Islam and judaism.

406 I'm curious to try *Kleinzeit* next, if I can find a copy around here.

392. Speak: A Short History of Languages by Tore Janson
Received: 20 March 2009
Started: 29 March 2009
Finished: 30 March 2009
This pleasant blast of non-fiction is a layman's guide to historical linguistics, focusing on Indo-European languages specifically. Janson writes pretty straight, and is a bit repetitive. He goes out of his way to be politically correct, making no value judgements on any language. But then he makes judgements on the value of great literature, seemingly using it to validate languages somehow. Of course the story of language is the story of civilisation, following human development both economically and intellectually. The nasty aspects of colonialism and exploitation are dealt with, specifically in the chapter looking at the current dominant spread of English. The last chapter attempts to predict the future, with plenty of caveats about how ridiculous it is to try. Overall, it's a good book of "popular linguistics" though I think I would have liked more trivia about interesting/obscure languages.

393. Cold War Hothouses: Inventing Postwar Culture, from Cockpit to Playboy edited by Beatriz Colomina, Annemarie Brennan, and Jeannie Kim
Received: 31 March 2009
Started: 31 March 2009
Finished: 3 April 2009
When I was staying in Paris, my friend had a copy of this that he had borrowed and I flipped through it a bit, thinking it seemed really interesting. Then, my wife brought a copy home form the library (it caught her eye while browsing and she thought it looked interesting) so I figured that was a sign and I had to read it. This collection comes out of Princeton and looks at post-WWII American cultural change, generally reflecting Jameson's ideas of postmodernism, where the emphasis on time and history are replaced by surface and space. The topics varied from intelligence testing to National Park advertising to *Playboy*'s reconceptualization of the male interior. There was an underlying theme in some of these essays about trying to mechanise humanity, and I felt like these topics wouldn't be out of place in an Adam Curtis documentary. The article about Beat space was pretty good too, though focused really just on *On The Road* — as someone who appreciates the Beats but is slightly annoying at their canonisation, it was nice to read something that dealt with Kerouac without elevating him too much. The essay about plastic and Monsanto was pretty funny, as 'The House of the Future' reeks of the paleo-futurism that is rather in vogue right now on the blogs I read. The *Playboy* article is a real tour de force, exposing Hugh Hefner's ideas and lifestyle as the adolescent dreams that they are. None of these essays was particularly specialised, so it was an easy read. I like books that are accessibly academic (if it's a field that I don't have a background in), especially when they're curated well as this one was.

394. The (Diblos) Notebook by James Merrill
Received: 24 May 2003
Started: 3 April 2009
Finished: 4 April 2009
It's great when I buy a book, it sits on my shelf for six years while I cart it from Pittsburgh to Kentucky to Glasgow to Helsinki, and then I finally read it in less than a day. And it was great. It's interesting to me when people who are primarily known for their poetry also write novels; I always look for hints of their poetic style. I'm not familiar with James Merrill's poetry but it seemed like this book was an attempt to really use prose for its distinction in form. The meta-fictional idea — that it is the draft of a novel — is fairly commonplace to me with all of the other stuff I've read, but it was good here, as it made this novel about writing itself, a theme that I am always interested in. However, i think the middle section was the most interesting, when this device was mostly abandoned and a more traditional prose style took over. The character who lived most of his life in Greece, stumbling around a Greek restaurant in New York looking for some authenticity was very familiar and made the novel's shifting geographies resonate.

395. I Am Not Jackson Pollock: Stories by John Haskell
Received: 30 September 2008
Started: 4 April 2009
Finished: 5 April 2009
Haskell's writing falls somewhere between historical fiction and extremely speculative film reviews. He uses sweeping, bold sentences suggesting what a famous artist,

actor or other historical figure was feeling in these miniature dramatizations, often revolving around old films. It's a daring approach that has some great moments, especially the title story, which dissects Pollock's dysfunctions succinctly and non-judgementally. This type of writing can often annoy me, but I guess it's not really any different than Robert Coover writing a novel with Richard Nixon as the narrator. The best story is the composite of several Orson Welles characters, where the various films blend together and the supporting characters are given complex characterisations. It's the Welles characters that remain shadowy and mysterious, and it's an interesting balancing act. I don't know that I'd read anything else by Haskell in this style but presumably he's more versatile.

396. The Burma Chronicles by Guy Delisle

Received: 30 September 2008
Started: 5 April 2009
Finished: 5 April 2009

Delisle's year in Burma is under quite different circumstances than his time in North Korea. Here, he's a housebound husband while his wife works for Doctors without Borders. Subsequently, the book takes on a much more domestic tone, with the little vignettes feeling more like episodes from a life than part of any grand narrative. The observations are much more focused on general daily life than on portraying the situations of dictatorship, though there is a proper amount of information stuck in, generally experiential. *Pyongyang*, because
260 its set in the most absurd and horrifying place on Earth, is perfect for the graphic novel form because cartoons are a natural way to describe absurd situations. This worked too, but with a totally different vibe, more like the autobiographical style of Kochalka or Huizenga. The oppressive-
32 ness of the Myanmar regime is definitely interesting, and the few parts it leaks into Delisle's life are fascinating if not scary. One thing that this book did was make me feel really amazed by the efforts of MSF/Doctors Without Borders (which Delisle describes plainly, without being preachy). I still need to read his book about China which I think I'm going to order from the library.

397. 2666 by Roberto Bolaño

Received: 3 February 2009
Started: 7 April 2009
Finished: 16 April 2009

I have many thoughts about this, both related to the content of the book and the external context of the work. The 3-volume nature of this paperback edition completely affected the way in which I read it. For one thing, it didn't "feel" long at all — really like three, or five, separate works that all arced with a severe velocity. At the end of each volume I was gripping the book excitedly, anxious to read what I could. Bolaño's stylistic experimentation is quite subtle — as a friend pointed out in a comment, the Oscar Fate part is modelled after *Invisible Man*, and I think the last part was definitely influenced by post-war Germanic literature (at least the little bit that I've read). The long digressions and monologues seemed like miniaturised Thomas Bernhard novels, and of course no epic novel is complete without addressing Nazis and the Soviet Union. It is strange how for a novel so open-ended, I found this to be incredibly satisfying. It definitely has a grand scope, which is why it reminded me at times of *Hopeful Monsters*, though it was a very different novel. 60
I do actually think all of the hype — and it seemed immense, given all the lit blogs I was reading in the year leading up to its publication — is quite justified. It's similar to *The Savage Detectives* in that Bolaño's style is familiar (and this is actually the third book 351
of his that I've read) but also quite different in that it took on more universal themes and was a much more 'mature' work. I'm excited now to read the mountains of blogs and online materials that I wanted to avoid until I had finished the book.

398. The Winshaw Legacy: or, What a Carve Up! by Jonathan Coe

Received: 5 March 2004
Started: 21 April 2009
Finished: 22 April 2009

This hardback has been sitting on my shelf for years so I finally decided to read it, just so I can get rid of it. Coe's novel is intricately plotted and rather ambitious in its scope, yet it suffers from too many problems for me to say that I enjoyed it. I think it's supposed to be a satire but the anger was so pointed that it just ends up as a polemic against Thatcherism and the entire British establishment with no shades of subtlety in it. But the biggest problem for me was the style of writing — it was obvious, at times childish, and had that simplistic quality that a lot of mainstream British fiction has (which really irritates me — also like that horrible *Mr. Y* novel I got 353 at the airport, or that bad Russell Hoban 275 novel I read). The insane contrivances of the plot are one thing, but forgivable; it's really when Coe writes dialogue that I wanted to put the book down. In the hands of a creative stylist this novel could be good, or even amazing — it has the scope of something like *Against the Day* or *The* 243, 822 *Recognitions* or *Infinite Jest*. The stabs at 109 humour fall flat too; at least I tore through it quickly, compelled by some strange curiosity as to how the narrative would unfold.

399. The Idea Of Home by Curtis White
Received: 7 August 2005
Started: 23 April 2009
Finished: 27 April 2009

I realised midway through this book that I love Curtis White. I've consistently enjoyed almost everything I've read by him. I looked back over old listings and found that I wrote a lukewarm review of *Requiem*, though 171 over time I've come to significantly upgrade my feelings for it. I enjoyed *Memoirs of My Father Watching TV*, though somehow it must have slipped through the cracks as I read it during dissertation time (when I was trying to unwind) and its not on my original 2006 Excel spreadsheet either. Anyway, in my review of *The Middle Mind* 153 I mentioned his irreverence and stated that 'I didn't think academics were supposed to do things like that'. I thought that a lot during this book too which is somewhere between a collection of short stories and a novel. In some ways this was a very loosely organised mess, with some fantasy, satire, and personal reminiscing all vaguely about the suburban California town where White was raised, or more accurately the aura around the town. There were some sections that I found more compelling than others, and most were very funny. But there's a real literary talent evident in White's writing, one that is definitely descended from American authors who master space and voice. Though there isn't much dialogue, the book is very conversational, even in the extremely pomo-style bits. Though White is very much his own writer, there are some definite influences on display here, most notably Donald Barthelme. I think this has encouraged me to buy some second-hand copies of his other books and maybe re-read *Requiem*.

400. The Areas of My Expertise by John Hodgman
Received: 11 September 2008
Started: 30 April 2009
Finished: 5 May 2009

Funny. This is the type of thing I used to read in high school — from the 'humour' section at Waldenbooks — and this was an excellent entry into that genre. Hodgman has a real gift for the absurd so it would be interested to see him try his hand at something more 'literary' — but then again, it's okay if he doesn't.

401. The Afterlife: A Memoir by Donald Antrim
Received: 30 September 2008
Started: 5 May 2009
Finished: 5 May 2009

Antrim's turn to non-fiction is a bit surprising, as his novels are rich with dark humour and surreal, exaggerated situations. The darkness is certainly here, though there is not a trace of humour — it's like he decided to prove that he was a serious writer, and he succeeds greatly. This chronicling of his mother's dysfunctional life is complex, powerful and severe. The writing is succinct, surprisingly reserved, and highly emotional at the same time. I was reminded a lot of Franzen's autobiography while reading this, although Antrim's was 271 much less self-centred (a difficult thing to achieve when writing about one's life) — at times, Antrim himself seemed to disappear from the narrative, a real accomplishment given the format. I tore through this almost completely in one sitting, and was really impressed with some sections, particularly the way he chronicled his own developing taste for literature with adolescent eroticism. I think this is Antrim's best book, which is surprising, but then not really that surprising once you think about it.

402. Bottomless Belly Button by Dash Shaw
Received: 30 September 2008
Started: 6 May 2009
Finished: 6 May 2009

Despite Mr. Shaw's request (at the front of the book) to take a break between each of the three parts, I tore through this in one sitting, which although it is a graphic novel, was still fairly exhausting. Shaw's narrative is long but it's not a sweeping epic; it's localised in scope, focused on the complex dynamics of one family spending a week together. The comic form is perfect

for this because Shaw likes to draw maps, cutaways, and use textual footnotes over his images. It's a style that may be annoying to some, but it wasn't overwhelming and he often let the art tell the story, especially on the sparser pages. Reading a huge comic — I'm not even sure how many hundreds of pages this was — is an investment so I felt quite sucked into the story. I couldn't help but think about Wes Anderson's work and *The Royal Tennenbaums* in particular,
15, 21, 83, 168 though there's none of the quirky, brainy humour (or really much humour at all). i read this like I would read a film, perhaps because of the visual nature of it or perhaps because it shares the concerns and preoccupations of a lot of filmmakers of this milieu. Not knowing anything about Dash Shaw (I've never seen any of his other work apart from a few pieces in *MOME*) I'm not
377 sure how personal this is, but I'm not sure that matters to me. Because of the size of the work, he was able to really explore the other characters and make this more of an ensemble work. The only part that felt a bit incomplete to me was the narrative of the celebrity romance that was supposed to be some sort of meta-fictional comment on the main storyline (I guess).

403. The Accidental Evolution Of Rock'n'roll: A Misguided Tour Through Popular Music by Chuck Eddy
Received: 28 May 2009
Started: 3 June 2009
Finished: 7 June 2009
I used to have this book, years ago, but I got rid of it because I found it mostly unreadable. Lately I've been on a bit of a Chuck Eddy kick again (I've been paging through the amazing *Stairway to Hell* around the house) so I grabbed this when I saw it. On a re-read, I really enjoyed it, as I've learned to accept his weird tastes and even enjoy his musical obsessions (Kix, Teena Marie, Def Leppard, Silver Convention, etc.). While a lot of these short pieces just connect pop songs that have similar lyrical themes, he really has a way to explode what might seem like a vapid song into a major thought form. There are some very bizarre inclusions (and omissions) here but again, I've come to actually enjoy that about Eddy. At times, the writing actually approaches a Theory of Rock Music much like Joe Carducci's (though not as focused
233, 445 or brilliant). And by the end, Eddy manages to include quite a bit about himself in these pages. Besides the autobiographical information scattered throughout, he also discusses his own social attitudes, giving me an image of a slightly awkward music freak who still hasn't come to terms with his inability to socialise at parties, etc. This was a good find and worth a straight read-through, though it will probably serve as an oddball 'reference' book from here on out.

404. Dune by Frank Herbert
Received: 22 August 2008
Started: 7 June 2009
Finished: 11 June 2009
As sci-fi epics go, *Dune* was cool in some ways but I found parts of it really tedious. Most people seem to think that Philip K Dick's prose is horrible but Herbert is somehow acclaimed as a classic writer — yet I would take PKD's writing any day over this. I'm sure this is a great allegory about race, religion, the environment, and other things — but I didn't really focus on that. Most of the dialogue was actually annoying, pretty much formulaic explanations of Herbert's mythology (which is cool, don't get me wrong) and the overall narrative was pretty much devoid of suspense, as it was just a series of prophecies playing out. There was a lot of "sci-fi bullshit" in here — invented language, ideas and objects that I really enjoyed (as I don't use the term 'sci-fi bullshit' in a negative way' at all) but I don't know that I can bring myself to read the sequels. It will be cool to finally see the David Lynch film though.  784

405. Enjoy Your Symptom!: Jacques Lacan in Hollywood and Out by Slavoj Zizek
Received: 30 May 2009
Started: 12 June 2009
Finished: 9 July 2009
This has probably been the best Zizek work I've read to date. I would probably say this is the definitive Zizek, although it doesn't contain any of his writings on politics. The premise is that he is explaining the ideas of Lacan through Hollywood films, though in his typical fashion he doesn't adhere to his own rules — one chapter is about a Raymond Chandler novel, and some are about non-Hollywood films. I found a few parts of this absolutely fascinating — the extra chapter at the end on 'Why is reality always multiple?' (dealing with *The Matrix*) was probably the part I  148
understood the most, and the sections on phallophant were awesome. In particular I found it refreshing to hear a philosopher take on *The Matrix* by stating that most

philosophers overanalyse the film (no shit!), and the best way to watch it is to just enjoy it, and it actually argues that the Wachowski's vision is incomplete and inverted — a nice rebuttal to all the seers who claim its the first/ultimate 'postmodern' film. The book is a slow read though I stayed with it. Only during chapter 'Why is every act a repetition?' did I get completely lost with the philosophy, because my background isn't strong enough. Still, a lot of the ideas are sinking in and as usual, the writing style is so brash that I was entertained consistently. I had originally planned to watch a lot of the films he discusses here, like Chaplin's *City Lights* and the Rosselini films, but Zizek's explanations are good enough that I don't feel the need to actually watch them to understand his connections. The *Pervert's Guide to Cinema* documentary,
1270, 1336 which I've been watching alongside this,
takes a similar but much more simple approach to dissecting film — however that is more concerned with basic Freudian ideas while *Enjoy Your Symptom* is much more complicated and Lacanian.

406. Kleinzeit by Russell Hoban
Received: 30 May 2009
Started: 9 July 2009
Finished: 10 July 2009
This is Hoban's second novel, and stylistically nothing like the others that I have read, though I am figuring out that versatility is one of his traits. Here, Hoban has written an absurdist novel that conveys Barthelme's approach towards illustrating language's role as a signifying force with playful, detached Beckettian whimsy. The whole novel is very snappy. It moved quickly, with short chapters of just a few pages, giving it an episodic feel even though it's quite a linear narrative. Various conversations with inanimate objects inject a lot of humour, and there's a weird conspiracy/mystery angle that deals with the act of writing itself. I really, really enjoyed *Kleinzeit*, as it's the type of novel I always have fun reading, and I think it is a pretty good example of this type of writing. The heavy topics are present, but instead of being stretched out and combed through like in *Riddley Walker*, they're treated as symptoms of a maniacal world. Though Kleinzeit is not a character that is particularly fleshed out with human traits in a writerly way, he serves well as an absurd, allegorical character.

407. The Rest Is Noise: Listening to the Twentieth Century by Alex Ross
Received: 28 May 2009
Started: 13 July 2009
Finished: 23 July 2009
Alex Ross's book about 20th century classical music seemed to be a general survey of the field, but by the end it emerged as a book about the fate of composition as an art form after 100 turbulent years. I went into this a bit sceptically, cause I've read some of his writing before and seen his blog, and I've not been too impressed. But I was quite taken in by the way Ross writes — he has a magnificent command of narrative non-fiction and had me enthralled by the story of Shostakovich's struggles in a way that Vollmann failed to achieve through *Europe Central*. Ross is really able
to describe music, and he will analyse a 272
piece technically, saying how it moves from A-minor to C-sharp or something, but in a way that actually gave me an idea of what it sounds like without actually hearing it. I figured it would go downhill in the final chapters as he attempted to describe the contemporary composition landscape, but fortunately he keeps it short and takes a pretty progressive view (in my opinion) of the challenges facing the art today. I never thought I would be interested in Strauss, but this book made his story quite compelling. World War II is of course the centrepiece, and the relationship between art and politics is explored quite actively. Whether he intends to or not, Ross paints a convincing argument that totalitarianism, particularly Hitler's involvement with classical music, stained the art form in a way that it never recovered. Though his accounts of post-war composers like Benjamin Britten, the minimalists, and Feldman are very well written overviews, they lack the magnificence of the old masters: Stravinsky, Strauss, Sibelius, Mahler, etc. Of course we've had more time to canonize those composers and the world treated them differently in their time, but I think the war had something to do with it too. Compared to Kyle Gann's book on American 20th century
composers, this is a lot less academic but 52
maybe more driven by Ross's own biases, though he keeps a fairly objective appearance, at least on the surface. And plus, the scope of this is the entire Western classical tradition — parameters that I figured would annoy me, but since that's how it was laid out when I went into it, I accepted this and truly enjoyed it.

408. Life, End Of by Christine Brooke-Rose
Received: 12 May 2009
Started: 23 July 2009
Finished: 25 July 2009
I've been meaning to read something by Christine Brooke-Rose for some time, and I used to have the *Omnibus* with her four best-known novels in them, except it was lost when I moved. I grabbed this super cheap off eBay; it turns out that it's her last novel, or something like a novel. It is a book about death and old age, as the title would imply, but it's positioned somewhere between novel, essay, and autobiography. I found this to be rather hard to put down, despite being plotless and difficult. There's a lot of experimental forebears that I could compare it to, most notably Gaddis' *Agape Agape* but also
47 the writing of David Markson and Joseph McElroy; a lot of the book concerns the act of fiction, and the nature of Character vs. Author. There are many passages about language, comparing words and forms in various European languages, but it isn't too didactic. Despite all of these lofty concerns, in 115 pages *Life, End Of* manages to feel complete and self-contained. Obviously it's full of underdeveloped ideas, but that just serves to make it more interesting. Maybe it's because there was so much "food for thought" that I found this strangely uplifting, or inspiring — instead of bleak, cynical and depressing (which, on the surface, it is). Brooke-Rose's writing definitely inherits a lot from the experimental masters and you can certainly tell she lived her life in France, besides the setting. I'm definitely going to seek out more, perhaps starting by replacing the lost *Omnibus*.

409. Television by Jean-Philippe Toussaint
Received: 30 September 2008
Started: 1 August 2009
Finished: 1 August 2009
My first Toussaint novel was pretty lighthearted and I tore through it in one day. His writing style reminds me of early Nicholson Baker, in the way he celebrates the mundane. He lacks Baker's more whimsical, humorous asides (surprising too, since I thought the French did that well) in favour of a more austere, matter-of-fact style of description. It is definitely comic, particularly in the situations the narrator gets embroiled in, which aren't ha-ha funny but more subdued. The idea of television invades almost every page, though by the end I had forgotten about this supposed obsession because I was drawn into the narrator's academic struggle. This seems like a novel without much purpose, but the beauty is in the details, and the whole theme of television is a bit of a red herring — it's neither a critique nor a polemic, just something to base a novel around.

410. The Occult by Colin Wilson
Received: 30 September 2008
Started: 27 April 2009
Finished: 1 August 2009
My Dad gave me a copy of this years ago and I read some of it but lost it; the $1 copy was too good to pass up, for all I know it may have even been the same copy I lost somewhere in Pittsburgh. Anyway, this was kind of maddening to read. I have a big interest in the history of the occult, and Wilson attempts to approach it fairly intelligently, but he loses the plot quickly. There are so many points in this book where I just wanted to throw it down in disgust at his utter lack of reasoning or logic. There's a fuck of a lot of research that went into this, though I wonder about some of his sources. There's many points where he'll describe some ridiculous magical power that someone was supposed to have any then say "Clearly, the truth of this matter is beyond dispute." It is? Why? I'm perfectly willing to dispute much, if not all of this. But then, I guess if I'm going to be reading the literature of the occult I'm going to have to just accept the pseudoscientific bullshit that soaks this stuff. And while this rendered large sections of this book annoying, the middle section about "adepts and impostors" was great. Reading about Cagliostro and the Comte de Saint-Germain was fascinating and I'd like to read more about these legendary magicians/con-artists. I have *Mysteries*, also by Wilson, on my shelf, and I have a suspicion I might enjoy it a bit more than this, so that's where I go next.

411. The Bushwacked Piano by Thomas Mcguane
Received: 11 September 2008
Started: 9 August 2009
Finished: 9 August 2009
Sunday train reading, read in one sitting. And what a great time it was! This is McGuane in a far more comic mode than *Ninety-two in the Shade* — this was so rich in the way it painted an American land- 306
scape it felt like a cross between Thomas

Pynchon's best descriptions of counter-cultural lowlifes (particularly *Vineland*) and 235 Stanley Elkin's panoramic view of America. The plot was zany, as slapstick as the best of them, but grounded in a fairly realistic scenario — at least, there was something plausible about it all. Actually, Charles Portis might be a better comparison. McGuane chooses his words wisely and manages to pack the novel with a lot of depth, capturing the America I wish still existed, down to the marrow — while keeping the novel overall short and light to read.I'm probably going to end up reading everything by McGuane now because this was so completely awesome that it makes me want to devour more.

412. Stop Me If You've Heard This: A History and Philosophy of Jokes by Jim Holt
Received: 9 August 2009
Started: 9 August 2009
Finished: 9 August 2009
My wife bought this slim volume chronicling jokes from a something historical perspective. It was a quick, fun read — I tore through it in one short session at a train station bar — and it had some great jokes buried throughout it. The stuff about Gershon Legman almost sounded too implausible to be real, though my wife tracked down one of Legman's volumes, so I shouldn't doubt Holt's scholarship. I sort of wish this was longer, but it's not really that type of book.

413. Inherent Vice by Thomas Pynchon
Received: 14 August 2009
Started: 15 August 2009
Finished: 30 August 2009
A new Pynchon book is always a cause for excitement and this was a lot of fun to read. It's definitely "Pynchon lite" but there's nothing wrong with accessibility; it actually shows his versatility as this captures the turning point of the hippie movement in a comic way similar to *Fear and Loathing in Las Vegas* but filtered through a Raymond Chandler novel. I wonder if Pynchon just wrote this for fun; it lacks the density of *Against the Day* and even seems to go 243, 822 out of the way to explain things in a way that none of his other books have, not even *Vineland*. It's sad to think that this 235 may be his 'worst' book but that's in no way an indictment of it; it's great to have a beach book by Thomas Pynchon and this one slowly spirals outward into weirdness (though never committing fully). I wonder how much I'll re-read this — it's fun, and it's nice to revisit fun things, but there's not much to untangle whereas two years after finishing *Against the Day* I remember only glimpses of it, and I've still never finished *Mason and Dixon*. Plus there's a 524 billion other unread works on my bookshelf by writers who are not named Thomas Pynchon.

414. And Your Point Is? by Steve Aylett
Received: 14 August 2009
Started: 31 August 2009
Finished: 6 September 2009
I generally agree with a friend's take on this; it's disappointing, and there's not much joy in parodying academic writing styles. Having been through graduate school in literature I've read many, many essays like these, though none were as entertaining, since they weren't about the fictional works of Jeff Lint. This is a great idea for a sequel to *Lint* since a second biography wouldn't 376 accomplish much, and there were a few completely brilliant passages. But if there was one line that made me laugh out loud, I would have to wait a page till there was another, as opposed to the continual genius and hilarity of the first book. I did like the references to 'New Weird America' musical artists beginning on p.79 and running for a few pages; I guess Aylett's musical taste is pretty clear.

415. Motorman by David Ohle
Received: 14 August 2009
Started: 6 September 2009
Finished: 7 September 2009
I bought this book because Ben Marcus wrote the introduction, and read it quickly, intentionally making it last over two days to savoir its greatness. Before I read *Motorman*, I didn't think there was anyone who wrote like Marcus, but now I can see what a major influence Ohle is. That's not to put down Marcus's writing at all — both are absolutely fantastic writers, and two of the most imaginative I've ever read. Ohle reinvents everyday language in a similar manner, drawing from inevitable associations similar to the Language poets, though with a fairly strict adherence to plot. I would call this novel 'absurd' but that's only because 'absurd' is the best word for describing this type of fiction. Though I laughed a lot, it's not really funny — nor is it really about playing with form of syntax. There's actually no real relationship between *Motorman* and

any other work of literature ever (apart from Marcus and maybe, maybe Brautigan) — it stands as a very singular entity, but remarkable not just for it's singularity. You can read this in a zillion ways — trying to draw some sort of concept or commentary from it — or just pulling images and sensations from the language. I am definitely going to check out Ohle's other work (though this is apparently his best novel).

416. Mischief by Chris Wilson
Received: 20 August 2004
Started: 8 September 2009
Finished: 12 September 2009
Only slightly more than five years on the shelf before I finally started this. I think I picked this up originally because it was recommended highly by the Complete Review website, though it was way out of print and hard to find — and I found it for £1 in Hay-on-Wye, so I figured why not. And during my many moving-related purges of cheap books I never read, this always survived the cut because I knew I'd never find it again so cheap. Anyway, I finally read it and I really did enjoy it, though not the first half. This is a very British type of satire that pulls its punches a bit; instead of painting the portrait of a world gone mad, it indulges in rambling monologues and direct addresses to the reader. I don't know how it pulled a rare A+ rating from the Complete Review because this felt like a superior version of that style of fiction that is popular with the British middle class (Jonathan Coe, Mark Haddon, Zadie Smith); good, but nothing more than that. I did like it, and would recommend it as a quick read, but I don't think it was completely brilliant, though maybe some of its subtleties were lost on me.

417. Watchmen by Alan Moore
Received: 14 September 2009
Started: 14 September 2009
Finished: 14 September 2009
I wanted to re-read this after seeing the movie so I put it on hold at the library, 735 where I was 86th in the queue for an English copy of it. Well, it finally came in and I tore through it in one sitting, remembering it strangely as a mix of the first read (from the summer I lived in Govan) and the film. *Watchmen* is really worth of all of its acclaim and reading it again made me realise how complete of a text it is. Beyond the concept, I realised how fantastic Moore's actual writing is. A lot of the monologues and narration struck me as overly dramatic my first time through, but now I actually see a lot of power to it, and occasional poetry that transcends all of the limitations of the genre. If anything, *Watchmen* is an argument for the comic medium because Dave Gibbons's art is consistently strong in being an essential part of the storytelling. The cold war setting is so central to it that I can only imagine what sort of impact this must have had in the mid 80s. There is an incredible streak of pessimism running through *Watchmen* also, but its the most inspiring pessimism — the blackest darkness of outlook where the most powerful ideas can develop. I almost wonder if a lot of the ideas were lost on me when I read this at 24, just because my own approach to life, politics, ethics and compromise has evolved so much in the past five years.

418. A Supposedly Fun Thing I'll Never Do Again: Essays and Arguments by David Foster Wallace
Received: 17 September 2009
Started: 17 September 2009
Finished: 19 September 2009
DFW hung himself just over a year ago, and I can't believe how much I still miss him. Not that I ever met him, but in recent years my love of his work slowly increased till it reached the point where I considered him to be the foremost literary voice in my world. The thing is, only *Infinite Jest* and *Brief Interviews* do anything for me  109  438 as fiction; it's his nonfiction that really shines and created his reputation, perhaps because it's so much easier to feel like you know him through it. I used to have a copy of this back in the day and I wanted to re-read it, so I ordered it from the library and rather quickly moved through it. I had forgotten how incredible his prose could be, which explodes right off the bat in his essay about being a teenage tennis prodigy. The famous essay on television and fiction is only slightly dated because of cultural changes that followed; I think it's remarkably prescient. And the stuff at the end about how the future of fiction needs to find away around the pervasive irony portrayed by television is really spot-on — it foreshadows the work of Wes Anderson, and of excellence in television like *The Wire* or *Mad Men* — programs which break away from the all-encompassing Image-Fiction he talks about. The essay on Lynch was something I skipped before, because I hadn't seen *Lost Highway* then  — here, I found it to be probably the best 638

analysis of David Lynch I've ever seen, with a really insightful look at his method of filmmaking (and also very entertaining to read). Everything in this collection is great but the crowning jewel is the title piece, the account of a week spent on a Caribbean cruise ship. I had memories of this being completely amazing and it is, though it's sadly too short (though it's not actually short at all). The writing in *Consider the* 343 *Lobster* seems to pick up from this point and I really fucking hope that a third vol- 538 ume comes out one day that collects all of his miscellaneous stuff. (I'm sure it will). Till then, I have these two books to clutch while I mourn his passing.

419. The Jade Cabinet by Rikki Ducornet
Received: 11 September 2008
Started: 20 September 2009
Finished: 1 October 2009
This was the first Rikki Ducornet novel I ever actually finished and I really enjoyed her style, which was part expressionist/ historical and part fantastical like *In Water-* 214 *melon Sugar*. She created a really intense narrative that sort of reminded me of that *Winner of the National Book Award* book 380 because it was about a terrible marriage narrated by the sister of the victim. However, Ducornet structured the entire book around air and wind, being the fourth novel in a series based on the four elements. This doesn't get cheesy at all, instead providing an artistic base for which she can pull out antiquated words and very tactile, yet unreal images.

420. Log of the S.S. the Mrs Unguentine by Stanley Crawford
Received: 14 August 2009
Started: 2 October 2009
Finished: 6 October 2009
My first foray into Stanley Crawford proved to be a pretty rewarding one. *Log of the SS the Mrs. Unguentine* sounds like a completely insane bit of fantastical or absurd fiction from the get-go, being that it's narrated by a woman who lives on a giant floating barge with her husband on which they have turned it into some sort of landmass and built some kind of a biodome. But despite a few very surreal passages (such as the birth of their child), this is really a novel about a failed relationship. Crawford chose to only give Mrs. Unguentine's point of view here but he does a marvellous job of fleshing out her character, even given the short length and absurd setting. He certainly paints Mr. Unguentine to be somewhat monstrous, but the complexity of a marriage (and the true loneliness in solidarity) is fully present. Some of the descriptive passages were uniquely beautiful, even if they were in the middle of a section describing some errant behaviour between the couple. I suspect that reading this again when I'm a lot older will have a pretty powerful impact on me, though even now I felt a real gravity to it. Which was cut with the bizarre scenario to make some weird hybrid fiction really unlike anything I've ever read before.

421. First As Tragedy, Then As Farce by Slavoj Zizek
Received: 28 October 2009
Started: 2 November 2009
Finished: 9 November 2009
I couldn't pass this up because it was about the economic crisis and 9/11, though it wasn't really of course (I should have known better). I mean, it sort of was about that but really this is Zizek's attempt to reconfigure communist thought in reaction to the events of the past 10 years. The timely nature of this is what interested me, plus the usual Zizekian wit and analysis (which was up to his usual standards). There's a certain pragmatism in Zizek's writing here that surprised me — even though he is critical of Obama for just putting a new face on the American empire, he grudgingly admits that it is a better face and seems willing to compromise. The psychological aspects of Communism are investigated in the second part, looking at two different interpretations of Hegel through political thought — the Singaporean/Asian model of authoritarian capitalism and then the Haiti revolution. While overall slim, this was a fun read and one I would probably go back to consult for anecdotes (if not quotes).

422. Born to Run: A Hidden Tribe, Superathletes, and the Greatest Race the World Has Never Seen by Christopher McDougall
Received: 9 November 2009
Started: 11 November 2009
Finished: 12 November 2009
Mixed feelings about this. I found this compelling, and really eye-opening because I never had the slightest interest in distance running before; the downside was that the writing was piss-poor, trying to be edgy and stretching journalism into that category

which is too personal and annoying. The parts I found most interesting were the section about how terrible shoes are for running, and the evolutionary theories that humans evolved the ability to run marathon+ distances so they could hunt prey to death by exhausting them. This makes me want to start running, too, though that's unlikely to happen.

423. People's History of Sports in the United States: 250 Years of Politics, Protest, People, and Play by Dave Zirin
Received: 28 October 2009
Started: 13 November 2009
Finished: 14 November 2009
I have been waiting a long time for a book like this, so I guess it's only reasonable that I'd be disappointed. Actually, this was good, but I wish it were longer and more comprehensive. I always like Zirin's columns (even if his podcast personality is a bit annoying) but in book-length form, his writing style really suffers. The prose is so basic and each section so short, that I really wanted a lot more depth. And he quotes far too much — some quotes go on for a page or even two. He's definitely researched it well — there are portions where he pulls out some really obscure figures that I was fascinated to read about — but there still wasn't enough. This overall felt a bit like a textbook. The longest and most detailed section was on Muhammad Ali, which isn't surprising since Zirin had written a book about him before. I do like the analogy between Ali and Michael Jordan — that Jordan's refusal to use his celebrity for any sort of political purpose is a metaphor for the difference in mentality between the shallow, apathy-driven 90s and Ali's Vietnam-driven era. Zirin really focuses on woman and minorities throughout the book, perhaps ignoring some of the other political factors such as executive decisions and direct government interference (things touched on a few times for sure, but not enough). Maybe someone will pick up this idea and write a longer study of politics and sports; I guess the topic is as underdeveloped in journalism as it is in actuality.

424. Rock/Music Writings by Dan Graham
Received: 28 October 2009
Started: 10 November 2009
Finished: 16 November 2009
It's really great this collection was made available (even if it mostly reprints from a mid-90s collection published by MIT press) because Dan Graham's writings on rock music defy any easy categorisation, yet are thought-provoking and actually fun. The earliest writings in here tend to follow a more free, experimental style (as they often accompanied art catalogues or appeared in unconventional places) and this view of classic rock, while it was happening, by one of the world's leading practitioners of conceptual art, is as jagged and biting as you'd imagine. The two essays about the Kinks in particular are great, because Graham is obviously struggling to justify his own enjoyment of the band through a theoretical framework, but dismantles his own arguments through fragmentation and obtuseness. The writings during the punk era resemble somewhat more traditional essays, though Graham has the freedom to write without any need for intellectual rigor or academic rules. Maybe this is actually a bad thing, but 'the End of Liberalism' and 'Punk as Propaganda' seem to really grasp Britain's changing attitude towards race and it's own crumbled empire in a way that I think few others really got during the time. You can file these in the same category as whatever *Lipstick Traces* goes in, except this is somewhat less pompous — though every bit as freewheeling and anti-academic. Someone who takes this stuff more seriously would probably find a lot of holes to pick apart here, but I view Graham as an artist, not a writer, so perhaps I'm more forgiving. I saw the video of *Rock My Religion* at the CCA a few years ago and I hated it because I thought it was an incoherent mess bogged down by poor-quality technical skills and intentional amateurishness/video artefacts. Reading the text in essay form doesn't make things any clearer, really, but at least there aren't glitchy videos in the way. The last long essay is about Bow Wow Wow and Malcolm McLaren's exploitation of child sexuality, which refers back to the (excellent) earlier essay about feminism and new wave, but through a much more critical lens. I'm not too familiar with the Bow Wow Wow saga but Graham's writing is riveting — confrontational but not too angry, pointed but readable.

425. Salt: A World History by Mark Kurlansky
Received: 22 September 2009
Started: 24 September 2009
Finished: 25 November 2009
Yeah, I just read a 450-page book about salt And it was pretty interestin! Kurlansky really hits it out of the park in terms of scholarly effort. He investigates the role that salt played throughout human history, peppering the book (ha, ha) with recipes from the past. The majority of the food-based uses he described were for meat or fish, which I don't eat, so I'm not likely to try any of the recipes. But the segments on the role the salt embargo played in the American Civil War and French revolutions was fascinating, as well as the more recent history of Tabasco sauce and Chinese cooking. I'm not sure if I will have the energy to tackle Kurlansky's similar book about the history of cod, but this was a really great read (though I drew it out over two months as a part-time read) and I would heartily recommend it to anyone.

426. Blink by Malcolm Gladwell
Received: 23 November 2009
Started: 25 November 2009
Finished: 25 November 2009
I tore through this in one sitting, and enjoyed it, I guess. This is that type of popular nonfiction writing, similar in style and tone to *Freakonomics*. Popular science, yes, or rather popular psychology, but Gladwell's investigation of snap-decisions and quick judgements is occasionally fascinating. A few sections really floored me, like the marriage counsellor who developed a system to analyse normal conversations between couples, and the therapist who measured where an autistic person's eyes looked when watching *Who's Afraid of Virginia Woolf*. 404 I've always enjoyed Gladwell's writing online and in *Times* articles, and I found him equally entertaining in a book-length format. I will probably check out his other books but I think it's time to get back to *Imperial* as my current nonfiction read....

427. Asterios Polyp by David Mazzucchelli
Received: 31 December 2009
Started: 4 January 2010
Finished: 4 January 2010
While visiting New York, I was pretty much couch-ridden at my friend's place due to influenza, so I read this much-anticipated graphic novel that I had seen compared to Pynchon (for some reason). It was a bad comparison, but that's not to say the graphic novel wasn't totally stunning — *Astrios Polyp* is one of the most remarkable achievements of long-form graphic novel I've ever read, surpassing *Bottomless Belly Button*  402  711 (though I still haven't read David B.'s stuff, or *Blankets*, etc.). Anyway, this is the story of an architect, but it's hardly *Atlas Shrugged* — instead it looks at love, loss, and modes of thinking, while structured around a dead twin story in a parallel narrative. Astrerios, as an architect, is obsessed with spatial relationships, and Mazzucchelli uses the comic form to explore visual ideas that language can only hint at. The art is constantly shifting between bubbly, *Archie*-comics like figures to dark, tortured nightmare sequences, yet it jells. This is one that will sink in slowly and I'll surely have to re-read it to dwell on some of the relationships between the characters, which feel fully dimensional yet familiar stereotypes at the same time.

428. Outliers: The Story of Success by Malcolm Gladwell
Received: 18 January 2010
Started: 30 January 2010
Finished: 2 February 2010
I liked Malcolm Gladwell enough after *Blink*  426 to read another one, though these are probably best saved for airplane trips or other 'light' reading situations. This isn't to denigrate Gladwell — he's a perfectly good writer, who is actively trying to explore intriguing ideas. There's just something a slight bit condescending about his style, as if he's writing down to me, repeating things that are obvious and trying to make sure I don't get 'lost'. It makes it run smoothly though, and this definitely falls into the same hybrid type of nonfiction as *Blink* was in — science, psychology, self-help and a bit of history as well. I can't say that I enjoyed this nearly as much, probably because it just wasn't as interesting, but I still tore through it pretty quickly. The section at the end about his grandmother was the most boring part for me, though I could tell he calculated that to have some sort of emotional/personal gravitas which is why he put it at the end.

429. Sex, Drugs, and Cocoa Puffs: A Low Culture Manifesto by Chuck Klosterman
Received: 27 January 2010
Started: 30 January 2010
Finished: 4 February 2010
This is the first time I've ever read anything by Klosterman, whose contributions to the *BS Report* podcasts I really enjoy. His writing is along the same lines — "middlebrow" insights into popular culture and music, with a humorous outsider/everyman style. This type of writing is easy to devour and I admit that I now want to read all of his other books, though I will probably have to buy them as the library system doesn't really have them. While this is like an accessible, watered-down approach to cultural criticism, it's hard to fault Klosterman because he puts on no pretensions and writes with a real honesty. One of the interludes, consisting of 23 questions to ask a potential lover, was totally hilarious; surely the highlight of the book. Essays about *Saved by the Bell* and a Guns n Roses cover band are easy entertainment, but good anyway. Actually, I'd even say they're great. So what next?

430. For Esme – With Love and Squalor. by J. D. Salinger
Received: 9 February 2010
Started: 10 February 2010
Finished: 13 February 2010
I checked out all non-*Catcher* Salinger books from the library after he died. I forgot how great this was, which makes me excited to read *Franny and Zooey* and *Raise High* cause I have never read those before. 432 431 As this goes along it gets a bit more ambitious. 'For Esmé – With Love and Squalor' is strangely autobiographical and sentimental, but still manages to work in the precocious child that every great Salinger story needs. But the last two stories get me the most — 'Dr. Daumier-Smith's Blue Period' because it's such a straight bit of comedy — and 'Teddy', which is just stunning. I really appreciate the details here — just small sentences, inflections, and especially the dialogue. Writing about privileged East Coast people isn't something that I can usually connect with but maybe because of Salinger's influence over so much literature to come, it works for me.

431. Franny and Zooey by J. D. Salinger
Received: 9 February 2010
Started: 14 February 2010
Finished: 15 February 2010
Here I am, again reading a Salinger book that I should have read years ago. This blew me away: completely, and totally. I am kicking myself for waiting so long to check this out. The prose is precisely perfect throughout; the dialogue is spot-on, making him a peer of Gaddis in capturing American speech. The amount of ideas that Salinger is able to pack into such a short book is astounding. Zooey is such a stunning character, through all of his arrogance, though Franny of course dominates both stories, even though she barely speaks compared to her loquacious brother. Zooey's interactions with his family are brutally cruel at times, yet I somehow forgave him. Perhaps because his intelligence and talent shines through and it makes him so likeable; perhaps because Salinger manages to convey the complexity of family life in such a short amount of prose. The spiritual/Eastern aspects of the Jesus Prayer etc. could be read as the overarching theme, and Franny reaching some sort of enlightenment in unknowing, but I actually was most struck by the sorrow underneath everything. Zooey is a success, a talent, a force; yet his indirection and posturing perfectly captures one's early 20s. I'm excited to read *Raise High the Roof Beam* now. 432

432. Raise High the Roof Beam, Carpenters and Seymour: An Introduction by J. D. Salinger
Received: 9 February 2010
Started: 15 February 2010
Finished: 19 February 2010
The final foray into Salinger's oeuvre is pretty intense, and strange when taken as one novel. Though narrated by the very thin stand-in for Salinger himself, *Raise High* is all fun and games (and perhaps the most enjoyable writing of Salinger's published works) while *Seymour* reminds me of *Agape Agape* by Gaddis.  47 It's not quite stream-of-consciousness but it's certainly the most freewheeling and experimental work of Salinger, and it's packed with a lot to untangle. I would say that ultimately *Seymour* manages to be about Salinger himself, though through the guise of his fictional surrogate, though through the guise of that fictional surrogate's brother. If the purpose was to create a more enigmatic view of Seymour Glass than to shed light,

well, it succeeded.

433. Imperial by William T. Vollmann
Received: 14 August 2009
Started: 12 October 2009
Finished: 24 March 2010
It's with great pride that I finally fill in the "finished" column here, because who doesn't want to brag about reading a 1300 page book (even if it took five months of on/off reading to get through it). Actually, I only read 1130 pages of *Imperial* because the last 150 pages were notes and sources, which is to be expected for such an immense piece of scholarship as this. *Imperial* (the book) almost defies description as much as the region called Imperial that Vollmann fanatically spent a decade researching. There are so many things going on with this text that it's impossible to know where to begin. The effort/research involved is staggering, but with Vollmann being Vollmann, it doesn't adhere to academic rules. Though he is a scrupulous historian — getting into microhistories of obscure lettuce farmers from the 1940s (and even hiring private detectives to attempt to help reconstruct these forgotten lives), his instincts as a fiction writer take over. There is most notably the frequent use of poetic repetition throughout the book. WATER IS HERE. THE DESERT DISAPPEARS. I have never been cheated out of a dollar in my life, etc. But beyond that, there are over 200 chapters that vary from tightly reported economic history, to wildly personal anecdotes, to serious investigative journalism, to poetic/romantic reconstructions or even historical fiction at times. The sheer weight of this work is seriously astounding; even as I spent five months going through it (and I'm familiar with Vollmann's intensity), I was continually shocked at how crazy some of this is. It's amazing what he finds in this marginalised corner of California — he is able to construct analogies on so many levels it almost blows open the possibilities that this could be done elsewhere, anywhere. Most obviously, we have an exploration of America as it's defined by the edges — with Mexico's Southside looming just over the border, and the constant negotiations of identity that occur throughout the book. We also have a very strong theme of delineations and demarcations, as the recurring trend in the history of Imperial County (or at least Vollmann's history, which is so wide-angled it's easy to think this is complete) is the way that men have organised and defined space. Vollmann does it himself repeatedly, of course, though the entity he calls "Imperial" is far more than the mere county. The role of water as an economic false Jesus (and a poetic symbol as well) is ever-present, and the (mis-)management of this resource is a narrative that snakes through the whole thing. On top of all of these themes you have some wildly entertaining chapters, particularly when he places himself at the centre of them. Vollmann rafts up the horribly polluted New River taking water samples to have analysed for toxins; Vollmann trying to discover if there really are secret Chinese tunnels under the city of Mexicali (a 100+ page chapter that is in some ways the book's centrepiece); Vollmann outfitting himself with a hidden camera in an attempt to expose the exploitation that may or may not occur at the *maquiladoras*. Of course with any book that is going into this much detail, things are significantly more complicated than they might seem on the surface. I'm really, really glad I've read this. I've never been to Imperial, or even California, and I didn't think that this could possibly be interesting. Now I consider myself to be practically an expert on the topic, in a joking way. I've learned about the profit margins of the lettuce trade, Mexican border-area outlaw ballads, the business dealings that led to the Colorado River Company, and a zillion other bits of arcana that probably no one has ever sought to document before. But beyond the mere history, Vollmann infuses everything with the quality that makes something "literature" and not mere reporting. There are passages of writing that are stunningly beautiful — a few that are shockingly personal, and his gift for empathy and moral clarity shines through everything. In short, there has probably never been a book ever quite like this and reading it was a phenomenal experience.

434. How German Is It = Wie Deutsch Ist Es: A Novel by Walter Abish
Received: 24 August 2003
Started: 23 February 2010
Finished: 18 April 2010
Yeah! Bought this seven years ago, gave it to a friend when I left the US, took it back at New Years, and finally started reading it. And why did I wait so long? *How German Is It* is actually a very difficult novel to assess, because it plays with so many ideas and refuses to assert a viewpoint. It's ambitious, and a bit crazy, for an American

to write a book that attempts to dissect the essence of Germanity — especially when, as I read later, Abish had never been to Germany when he wrote it! But if you put aside all of the factors about his "right" to write such a thing, you do get a novel that confronts the topic of identity head-on. Beyond the explorations of guilt and responsibility, I was really taken with Abish's style. It reminds me a lot of Joseph McElroy — both in the way he structures his sentences/dialogue and the way the novel's voice continually moves. Additionally, it mined similar paranoid/thriller territory as *Lookout Cartridge*, and also about 2/3 86 of the way through the book I stopped really caring about those elements. This was a continually spiralling-out narrative — the long middle-section of the book, set in Brumholdstein, was really weird in the way that it kept expanding it's focus to new characters. I ultimately felt a bit confused about this book, but then the final scene was so striking and on-point, it pulled everything back into focus.

435. Milk It: Collected Musings on the Alternative Music Explosion of the '90s by Jim Derogatis

Received: 6 April 2010
Started: 7 April 2010
Finished: 18 April 2010

I was at the library and browsing the music shelves when I saw this, and on a whim I checked it out thinking "it might be fun to read about Nirvana and Smashing Pumpkins". I guess it was, though it did little to change my opinions about 90s mainstream rock music. I definitely have an opinion about Jim DeRogatis though — that he is an ego-driven fool who occasionally has insights into rock music but spends most of his time trying to stake out his own claim to cultural capital. There are a few great pieces in here — like the argument he has with the singer of Third Eye Blind — but generally the writing is turgid, but trying to be edgy. I hated most of this music when it was happening and reading more 'insider' pieces doesn't lead to any regrets. I enjoyed his takes on R.E.M. — though several pieces which don't talk about the music at all, but instead obsess over how carefully R.E.M. controlled their own image. A lot of these pieces strike me as sour grapes. Little of the music that mattered to me in the 90s was mentioned, apart from one review attacking Guided by Voices for writing too many songs. I still enjoyed this, though, just as I enjoyed the Metallica documentary. 616, 1591 There's no end to the entertainment value of reading quotes by Courtney Love or Billy Corgan. These are extreme, excessive people and credit to DeRogatis for obtaining the access that he did when they were in their prime. It's really funny how he got fired from *Rolling Stone* for writing a bad review of Hootie and the Blowfish, and then includes this review here as if it was some heroic act of defiance — when he just gave it a 2-star review.

436. The Darker Nations: A People's History of the Third World by Vijay Prashad

Received: 25 December 2009
Started: 16 May 2010
Finished: 23 May 2010

I didn't enjoy the first 100 pages of this, because Prashad begins the book by describing the many conferences of Third World nations that met throughout the 20th century. But as I got into the second and third parts of the book, I understood his organisational structure and realised that section 1 was the only truly upbeat material I would find. And even those conferences, while inspiring, are little more than words and plans, all shot down by the cruel realities of history. This is a people's history, which means that it does not resemble a conventional history — this does not actually describe the colonial histories of Third World nations let alone the pre-colonial. But this is successful in the way Prashad sees patterns in Third World history and maps out each chapter illustrating examples of the various pitfalls required for Third World solidarity. He analyses the different types of military coups, contrasting the strong general-based authoritarian military coups (Pakistan, Chile, Indonesia) against the "colonel's coups", a military coup that does not alter the social fabric of the country (Egypt under Nassar, or Hugo Chavez). I also learned that OPEC originally formed as a somewhat radical leftist solidarity movement with deep ecological concerns, though that was quickly corrupted and it just became the economic cartel that it is today. He investigates the problems of an economy based on one product, and gets slightly philosophical when discussing border disputes between fellow Third World nations. Prashad knows he is preaching to the converted so he doesn't spend too much time outlying the atrocities of imperialism, though he certainly doesn't gloss over them. In his conclusions, he looks at the practical reality created by the neoliberal states against the 'darker nations', and clearly believes that we can learn from the mistakes of history. So while I wouldn't call this an uplifting read, there is such empathy for these people that it actually takes on a warmth, despite the fairly academic style.

437. The San Francisco Tape Music Center: 1960s Counterculture and the Avant-Garde by David Bernstein and Johannes Goebel
Received: 28 October 2009
Started: 1 May 2010
Finished: 2 June 2010
I loved this; it's written somewhere between an academic history and a social history, and edits together shorter pieces instead of trying to establish some 'authority', which is the way music/art histories should be. This book almost prioritises the social narrative over the technical achievements, which is exactly what I wanted to read. The interviews which make up the second half of the book are awesome and inspiring; I felt really excited reading them — not necessarily about making sound myself again, but about the general spark of creativity that I long to feel again. I wrote a longer review of this on my own website so I'll keep this one relatively short, but I will definitely be thumbing through these interviews again.

438. Brief Interviews with Hideous Men by David Foster Wallace
Received: 15 June 2010
Started: 16 June 2010
Finished: 4 July 2010
When Wallace died I put this on reserve at the library and it finally came in for me about a year and a half later, by which point I had forgotten that I had reserved it. But good timing, cause this was great to revisit after being transformed into an unabashed DFW fan (along with everyone else) in the intervening years. The centrepiece of the book, the titular stories, are amazing and were particularly good to read after having just seen the film adaptation; the writing is clearly a unique thing, but reading this made me appreciate the film more, which I never thought I'd say. As to the other stories — there are dazzling examples of his style everywhere, and in some places they work better than others. 'The Depressed Person' may be the single greatest thing DFW ever wrote (at least in terms of fiction), and I also love 'Adult World' and the pop quiz 'Octet'. Having read a bit about his artistic struggles, I know that Wallace was really bothered by his own quirky use of language and his stylistic flourishes such as footnotes, technical language, and humorously distancing scientific-speak. He was really struggling to write something "real" and human, which I guess drove him to his end — but for me, I think he was getting there. The pain that rings throughout 'The Depressed Person' isn't dulled by the detachment of the style — if anything, it's emphasised. And while 'Adult World' ends up being a totally deconstructed mess in the second part, the first part is as genuinely moving a study of sexual inadequacy/futility as you'll see anywhere. As always with DFW, humour is the red herring; the last brief interview, about the hippie rape, is provocative, emotionally disturbing, and strange in it's formal construction, and the only traces of humour come from the spoken style of the interviewee, which places the whole piece into an uncomfortable arena that is quite daring. Also — 'Forever Overhead', about the boy on the diving board, is I think one of the most bare, autobiographical bits of Wallace's fiction in his entire oeuvre. I'm still counting the days till *The Pale King;* in the meantime, this was a good holdover, and I just grabbed a new copy of *Infinite Jest* (hey, it was a buy 2 get 3rd free sale and there was nothing else eligible, really!) so maybe a third read through that will fill the time....

879

458

439. The Book of Basketball: The NBA According to The Sports Guy by Bill Simmons
Received: 1 July 2010
Started: 1 July 2010
Finished: 5 July 2010
Reading 700 pages about a league that I don't follow tested my patience, and by the end I was pretty tired of his forced pop culture analogies, sexist frat-boy humour, and obsessive list-making. This is the William Vollmann *Imperial* of books about basketball, and it's an intense feeling to read 450 straight pages of Simmons listing the 96 best basketball players of all time, only to immediately follow it with long chapters ranking the best teams of all time, and then the ultimate dream team. And for a book based around an utterly stupid idea — that there is a 'secret' to winning, which turns out to be 'teamwork' over statistics — Simmons spends most of the book bombarding the reader with stats, which I just started glossing over after the first few pages. But who am I kidding? I really enjoyed this. I read it in four days and I can only dream about if he would write

433

a book about the NFL (or if there was a similar book about hockey or association football by someone with the same level of knowledge and passion as Simmons has for the NBA). I guess that's what comes down to it — Simmons really does love the NBA, probably more than anybody, and it really shows here. And I can now say I know a million times more about the league than I did last week — and I'll be curious to check out ESPN Classic now, especially to read about some of the names that I've now familiarised myself with.

440. Wilson by Daniel Clowes
Received: 21 June 2010
Started: 7 July 2010
Finished: 7 July 2010
The long wait for new Clowes material has come to an end, but sadly, *Wilson* was devoured in one exciting session, and now I guess it will be a few more years till I get something new. This proceeds stylistically from the last few *Eightballs*, though without quite as much of a spider web narrative, instead focusing on one character and storyline. Clowes sticks to a rigid, single page format for each episode, with a punch line in the last panel of every page, a technique that is hilarious and brilliant in its rhythm. Of course, this isn't a pleasant tale, and Wilson is barely evolved from most of Clowes's fucked up, socially repressed characters. His arrogance and negativity shines through everything, even his moments of utter vulnerability, and this is the misanthropic streak that I love about Clowes. The colour palette is beautifully chosen; some episodes are drawn in different styles, much like the *Ice Haven* book, which makes it feel strangely cinematic. I think this has been criticised for being somewhat of an emotional flatliner, but I think that's exactly why I loved it.

441. I'm Not Stiller by Max Frisch
Received: 20 September 2008
Started: 3 June 2010
Finished: 9 July 2010
I wrote a longer review of this and then wiped it; my thoughts are bit disjointed, probably cause I read half of the book, put it down for two weeks while I was away, and then returned to it. But, I loved *I'm Not Stiller*. It continually shifted and confounded my expectations — I went into it thinking it was gonna be like *Camp Concentration* or Kafka's *Trial*, but then it shifted gears a lot. A lot. You can formally assess this as a brilliant study of identity, or a celebration of fiction and storytelling. It was not nearly as dystopian as I expected — in fact, it celebrated the everyday through the long domestic-based passages. This is a work about reinvention and confronting one's past, and the construct of the narrative kept things fresh. The tone shifts completely in the final coda (part two), which is understandable as there is a different narrator. But it's almost shocking in how different it becomes, and I was left slightly stunned and thinking I should read the rest of Frisch's work.

442. The Education Of The Stoic by Fernando Pessoa
Received: 19 July 2010
Started: 21 July 2010
Finished: 21 July 2010
This is a very slim Pessoa piece that works as a natural companion to *The Book of Disquiet*. Although the text itself is really only about 35 pages (filled out with some appendices of all other known writings by Pessoa's Baron of Teive heteronym), it's quite satisfying, because like *Disquiet* you can linger on every little passage. This is again a book about uncertainty, but Teive has resigned himself to suicide and reflects on the dangers of committing to any position. I would say it's the most ambivalent book I've ever read but I'd probably still save that for *Disquiet*; but thinking again about how consciousness and identities are not so much fragmenting but multiplying, Pessoa now seems to me like possibly the most contemporary writer imaginable (and he died in 1935!). Although a good chunk of this was wrapped up in his dissection of three poets and their sexual problems (none of whom I read), this still had some amazing passages. And while seeming on the surface like it would be depressing, it's really not. Pessoa is so amazing because he really wrote fiction from the inside-out (for lack of a better term) — there is no narrative, and nothing happens, but the fiction is in the thoughts and the construction of the author.

443. Voodoo Histories: The Role of the Conspiracy Theory in Shaping Modern History by David Aaronovitch
Received: 25 June 2010
Started: 10 July 2010
Finished: 25 July 2010
Aaronovitch's book looked compelling, but it turned out to be little more than a

standard sceptical rebuttal of the world's most popular conspiracy theories. It certainly began in a promising way, with *Protocols of Zion* and an alleged anti-Stalinist conspiracy, and I thought the book would actually explore what it's subtitle promised. But the rest of the book, dealing with the *DaVinci Code* crap, JFK, 9/11, Whitewater, 135 the Kelly affair and the Birthers, was just a boilerplate (yet intelligent) dismissal of these theories — but not in enough depth to be truly entertaining. At the end of the book, Aaronovitch finally starts to establish a social theory of conspiracy theories — basically, that humans inherently look for narratives and conspiracy theory emerges from those who have suffered political and social defeats and feel like they have no efficacy. Which is all well and good, but maybe the subtitle should have been "How human natures shapes conspiracy theory" instead.

444. Swimming to Cambodia by Spalding Gray
Received: 24 April 2006
Started: 24 August 2010
Finished: 31 August 2010
I grabbed this at a really good, cheap bookstore in Leeds a few years ago but never sat down and read it. I was familiar with a lot of the monologues before, but after the workshop in Mooste with Giles, where

440

we showed the beginning of *Swimming to Cambodia*, I felt like reading this. The written version of it is significantly longer than what's in the film, and that's only about 15% of the book, which is filled out with some other (excellent) monologues. There's something a bit odd about reading monologues that are clearly meant to be performed — Gray as a writer has an obviously conversational style that doesn't always translate perfectly to the page. But his sense rhythm is undeniable, and I can't help but hear the words booming out in his voice. '47 Beds' was maybe my favourite piece here — I'd love to hear/see the performed version of it. 'Terrors of Pleasure' and 'Sex and Death' I had heard before, though reading them took me back to high school when I read a lot of humorous, first-person narratives like this (though I can't really think of any examples right now). I think this is motivation to re-watch all of the films now, though finding the time for that might be difficult.

445. Rock and the Pop Narcotic: Testament for the Electric Church by Joe Carducci
Received: (already owned)
Started: 11 October 2010
Finished: 20 October 2010
I was itching to re-read this after using a short section from Chapter 1 in the seminar I organised in Tampere. It's been a few years but time has been kind to my memory of Carducci's treatise on rock music. But not kind enough — this really blew me away the second time through. I think my first reading was partially about dealing with his politics, and now that I approached it for the ideas I had no problem putting my disagreements aside and just thinking about the points he was making. What's so amazing about this book is that it's a look at the actual musical elements of rock, but also a brilliant insight into the culture surrounding rock. It may feel at times like his 'Narcorockcritocracy' chapter is just petty insider whining, but actually Carducci makes a pretty compelling argument that everyone has basically gotten it wrong. He cares so much about the critics because they have created the structure of the rock world that negatively impacts the music, through the effects of the 'pop narcotic'. Carduci's taste is really distinct but impossible to pin down and really fascinating at the same time. The 'Psychozoic Hymnal' section is pretty astounding, for the sheer number of potential bands to investigate — and his part on the early 90s is probably the most confounding. I was trying to think about how things have changed since this was written (around '94) and I'm not really sure what to think — I'm not sure how accurate my own interpretation of the rock press would be since I haven't read *Rolling Stone* since high school. Anyway, I still say this is the best book about rock music ever written.

446. Darconville's Cat by Alexander Theroux
Received: 20 September 2008
Started: 14 July 2010
Finished: 4 November 2010
It took me forever to read *Darconville's Cat*, which is forgivable because I've had no time for reading and it's 700 pages long. But I also got pretty unmotivated for large parts in the middle of this book. My first tendency is to say it would have been better at half the length, but then the bloat is the whole point. This is as densely erudite as anything I've read by Gaddis or other

masters; it didn't take me long to start letting the references bounce off me because it was too overwhelming. You could spend a lifetime annotating this, or creating a concordance of it. The plot wasn't anything special; this is a book for savouring the actual prose. Theroux is quite funny and the early parts of the book made me think the entire thing was going to be a somewhat juvenile mockery of Southern culture and the types of shitty liberal arts colleges that this was set in. It gets wrapped up in its own melodrama, and then the insane Dr. Crucifer enters and things take on a quite different tack. I wish I didn't find so many of those long chapters tedious but it was hard not to skim — yet they are also the best parts. This is an incredibly dark and misanthropic book that I'm sure pretty much autobiographical — the moral question of a professor boffing one of his students is skirted, no doubt for Theroux to cover his own ass; it then comes down to a thin excuse on which to hang inventive wordplay and ridiculousness. Right near the end there's a chapter that is about twenty pages of ways to inflict harm upon a woman, and it actually outdid Sorrentino at list-making brilliance. By my own self-defined rules of the bookshelf this is gonna travel around with me forever, since it's good enough to warrant a re-read or at least referencing, and it's sadly way out of print.

447. Strange Days Indeed: The Golden Age of Paranoia by Francis Wheen
Received: 25 June 2010
Started: 6 November 2010
Finished: 11 November 2010
Again, Wheen delivers an enjoyable book that managed to be a popular history without being too introductory or repetitive. *Strange Days Indeed* specifically recaps the 1970s and the way paranoia seeped into politics and popular culture. Though written obviously in hindsight, Wheen steers clear of huge sweeping pronouncements apart from his frequent assessments of Richard Nixon's personality. I particularly enjoyed how he balanced Nixon's mental unravelling with Harold Wilson's Britain, and cited a lot of behaviours that were similar without making any grand claims. Most of these chapters left me wanting more, which isn't something I can say often. I liked *How Mumbo-Jumbo...* a lot too, but that got bogged down in its own rants against pseudoscience — freed from that polemic, *Strange Days Indeed* was an overall stronger book, I think.

448. The Fight by Norman Mailer
Received: 24 August 2007
Started: 13 November 2010
Finished: 18 November 2010
Somehow, I have never read a word of Norman Mailer in my life and I have never really been interested in doing so. But this topic was interesting and it was a charity shop find from several years ago that I was tired of having clutter up my shelf. This is a pretty remarkable book, no doubt due to Mailer's style. He's exploring two immeasurable egos in Ali and Foreman, but also while boasting a pretty strong writerly ego himself. He injects himself into the narrative so overtly that I was a bit surprised because it reminded me of the whole 'new journalism' thing that I thought was much more recent, though Hunter Thompson is another precedent (and Thompson appears in the book, with Mailer saying some fairly dismissive things about him). The actual meat and potatoes writing is phenomenal though, particularly when describing the actual bout, which I found insanely compelling. It's time to watch the documentary about this fight now.

449. W, or the Memory of Childhood by Georges Perec
Received: 19 July 2010
Started: 19 November 2010
Finished: 20 November 2010
It will sound pretentious but whenever saying the title of this book I should really pronounce it as "dew-bluh-vay", because that's the French *W*, which is a double *V* after all, not a double *U*. It's important here because this is a book about a double vie, two lives, or rather two memories intertwined chapter by chapter. I was so obsessed with Perec for years, and even was intending to do a PhD at one point about him, yet somehow I never read this, which is probably his greatest book! It's the most straightforward and beautiful of his works, a memory of childhood in wartime, yet with the war distant, even absent. Perec's retelling of his youth is more about memory itself than the experiences of growing up a displaced Jew in wartime Paris. He uses the form of the story to tease out different approaches to recollection, uncertainty, etc., particularly when reprinting a passage he wrote about his parents 15 years previously, with annotations and corrections. The fantasy of W, set in parallel italics, is strangely childlike (with it's bureaucratic sports obsessions) yet dystopian. It falls apart from the initial setup (of the mysterious stranger in the

bar) and just becomes an elaborate fantasy that is all structure, no heart; it's not what I loved about *W*, but yet it's an essential component.

450. At Home: A Short History of Private Life by Bill Bryson
Received: 22 November 2010
Started: 23 November 2010
Finished: 29 November 2010
Bryson nails it again, this time writing a history of the world from the perspective of his house. It's good, not as good as *A Short*
88 *History of Nearly Everything* (or whatever that was called), but done in that great Bryson style — which manages to make anything, absolutely anything, interesting to the point of being fascinating. His usual humour is almost non-existent here but that's OK, because I'm too busy learning about staircase accidents, the life of 19th century London chimney sweeps, and the history of canned goods. I can't help but compare this to James Burke's best television work, though minus the probing, questioning insight about change and fear. But nothing will ever live up to those standards, so it's best to enjoy *At Home* for what it is. The structuring device of his household is a bit misleading, because he really just uses each room as a loose starting point to riff about whatever he is interested in — there's sometimes a direct relationship and other times it feels like a very tenuous connection. But everything in here is researched to death, almost staggeringly so for a work of popular scholarship.

451. Homicide: A Year on the Killing Streets by David Simon
Received: 25 June 2010
Started: 4 December 2010
Finished: 6 December 2010
I knew this would be a fun read but I didn't expect it to be so compelling. But, I don't know why I wouldn't expect that, since I devoured *The Wire* with pretty much the same enthusiasm. It's clear where so much of that show came from — character names galore, specific dialogues, and situations throughout all 600 pages almost felt old hat to a fan like me. Simon's talent as a writer is also impressive; he is far more flamboyant than you might think from his journalist roots. This was a nice paperback edition published by Canongate in the UK, with three afterwords, by Simon and some of the detectives in the book.

452. Neither Here nor There: Travels in Europe by Bill Bryson
Received: 28 July 2010
Started: 7 December 2010
Finished: 10 December 2010
When I said goodbye to someone I met back in July, he gave me this Bryson paperback just because he didn't want to take it with him. I haven't read this since probably high school so it was fun to revisit, especially after living in Europe myself for the past 5 years. Reading this right after serious, mature Bryson made it feel like a real release. His humour so relies on stereotypes that it would be easy to take it as borderline racist, except everything is cast so ridiculously and with a gentle edge. Or maybe I just like him. It's particularly interesting to read about Europe in 1990, with different currencies, Yugoslavia, and the need for visas — all concepts which I have never dealt with much or at all. Bryson is hilarious but not actually a great travel writer — he has some insights, for sure, but also mostly writes about the restaurants he goes to and his annoyances on trains and in hotels. The account of Sofia is fascinating and he's not afraid to say that in some places he just didn't really feel like doing anything (such as Istanbul), which I guess is a more realistic approach to travel writing. I'll read this again in ten or fifteen years probably.

453. Eating the Dinosaur by Chuck Klosterman
Received: 14 December 2010
Started: 14 December 2010
Finished: 14 December 2010
Klosterman is so great. I ripped through this in one sitting and I wish it were ten times longer. The essay about American football is amazing, and one of the most unique looks at the game ever. There's also great writing about ABBA, Weezer, Werner Herzog, Nirvana, Pepsi, and Garth Brooks. This didn't have the extreme hilarity of *Sex, Drugs and Cocoa Puffs* and a few of the  429
pieces felt half-assed, but even a half-assed Klosterman is pretty entertaining.

454. Freedom by Jonathan Franzen
Received: 13 December 2010
Started: 15 December 2010
Finished: 21 December 2010
Sitting down to review *Freedom* feels almost as daunting as it must have been for Jonathan Franzen to write it. I can't even imagine the immense pressure on

him, after the smash success of (and fallout after) *The Corrections*; the heat is on him
54 to be THE great American novelist, this generation's Mailer, etc. What's actually the most interesting aspect of *Freedom* is this pressure — and the inevitable disappointment that must come when it's finally produced nearly a decade after his commercial breakthrough. It's purely external factors, then, that led to any enjoyment I found reading this, which was not much, though there are some bright moments throughout. It starts off with a bang — the book is structured very symmetrically, with opening and closing sections written largely from the POV of minor neighbour characters, and the opening chapter is rather dazzling. It's when Franzen begins to sink into the meat of the story that I started to find fault with *Freedom*. It's clear that Franzen is trying to tackle everything here — the scope is immense, and though the narrative focuses on one family, Franzen tries to paint a definitive portrait of the past decade in American life. His attempts to merge the political machinations of the Bush era with the Midwestern family who are the subject of this novel are clumsy and forced. He simultaneously tries to portray the moral decay of America during the 00s while navigating the complex compromises that are unavoidable as a participant in late Capitalism, and it doesn't come off even half as deft as, say, *Arrested Development*. Actually, *Arrested Development*, though a comedy TV series, is like a far better version of *Freedom* is trying to do. Franzen himself (who I have a lot of sympathies with, as I [and pretty much only I] loved his autobiography) spends far too many inches trying to justify his own displacement from popular culture. Writing a Bright Eyes concert into a novel is a way to comment on his own age, and feeling out of touch; even more glaring are the several times characters comment on the change in communications with texting, mobile phones, Twitter, etc. as compared to older generations. It's almost like he tried to inject his messy diary entries into a grandiose novel, but instead of widening the scope it just comes off as awkward. Which brings up the dialogue — *Franzen* is a well-known critic of William Gaddis, but he could learn a few things about the human voice by reading him. The conversations in *Freedom* are horribly awkward, forced, phony, bland and boring. So while I definitely enjoyed parts of this — some elements of the story had me genuinely engaged — the most interesting aspect to me was how much of Franzen himself was laid bare, though clearly hiding behind things. Here's a writer who is terrified of his responsibility, trying to come to terms with his own aging and his own moral conflicts. *The Corrections* is a great book because it was hilarious and miserable at the same time; this book hits neither of its highs or lows, almost like it's trapped in a self-medicated band of normalcy. But, does the great American novel have to be about the emotional sufferings of affluent white people? I certainly appreciate that in the work of someone like Wes Anderson, and I did love *The Corrections*, but here I found myself unable to be interested in any of the characters, almost like they were portrayed so realistically they became boring. Gross, exaggerated caricatures may be easier but they're also more enjoyable to the reader. It's not Franzen's fault he has been successful, and I think with his last book, it was deserved — but I wonder how much better this had been if he had hid behind a pseudonym.

455. A Smugglers Bible by Joseph McElroy
Received: (already owned)
Started: 2 January 2011
Finished: 23 March 2011

And finally, at 9:46 AM on the 23rd of March 2011, I finish reading a book for the first time in 2011. You who have me (to use a McElroy turn of phrase from *Lookout*
Cartridge) will understand that I used to 86
be quite an active reader, but lately I'm starting to resemble an active collector of books instead. This is not the place to offer excuses about why I don't have the time or inclination to read as voraciously as I used to, but rather the place to enter my comments on *A Smuggler's Bible*, reading #2. The first time I read this was probably about ten years ago, and it's scary to realise it's been so long — when I was buying up recommendations from Internet mailing lists, using half.com to the point of obsession. For the past decade I've considered McElroy one of my favourite writers, but I'm not sure exactly why. I haven't read all of his work, and some of his texts are so incredibly challenging that I'm not sure what I actually get out of them. 2011 seemed like a logical place to re-evaluate, especially as I've trucked my shitload of books to yet another country. I've justified dragging around so many obscurities for just that reason — obscurity — claiming that it's not easy to walk into a library or bookstore and replace, say, *Lookout Cartridge* (especially in Estonia). But if my list of "can't live without" faves is now so vast as to include the complete works of McElroy, Mathews, Perec, and others, I really have

to continually engage with these texts to justify such an un-zen existence. Watching all the Godard films in order gave me a passion for this chronological approach, so why not take McElroy down the same path? This allows me to finally read *Hind's Kidnap*, re-read the others (especially *Plus*), and hopefully finish *Women and Men* this time — and as a treat, I get his new collection of short fiction at the end.

So, *A Smuggler's Bible*. My memory was that this was one of the more 'accessible' of McElroy's texts and I guess this is true, though I don't know how that actually matters. In some ways, the framing of this "story" is merely an excuse for JMcE to dive into various styles and voices and explore semi-autobiographical territory while hanging it around a vaguely ambiguous, mysterious plot. Or is there a plot? Like *Lookout Cartridge*, such elements are distracting and irrelevant, yet provide a compulsion to keep going. There are clues that don't add up, but that's not the point. If there is a point, it's the exploration of consciousness, and the complex depiction of David Brooke through his constructed memories of others in his life — a way of writing around an actual subject. Pure literary impressionism, right? Because McElroy isn't an absurdist and has almost no comic traces, he doesn't seem to fit with the other big names of postmodern American literature (Barth, Pynchon, Coover, etc.); his books are every bit as laced with Gaddis-like erudition, but it's woven so cohesively into the text that it doesn't feel like namedropping or referencing. Though published in '66, this is a novel set in the early 60s, mostly around 1960, so I found myself imagining this juxtaposed in the world of *Mad Men*, which was kinda useless as a mental device since David Brooke's world is about as far away from Don Draper's as possible. The first time I read this I left with the sense that I was missing something, narrative-wise; this time I let the words flow over me, but because I dragged out the reading of this over 2.5 months (mostly in little bursts on the ferry or whatever) I wasn't able to completely immerse myself the way I wanted to. The final section, written as Brooke's father Halsey, was incredible — one of the most unique and beautiful passages that I have ever read. McElroy is such a masterful stylist, though his style isn't flashy — it's a slow burner, that reaches a beautiful climax here. I love writing that can be strange and evocative, which this is, but it does so in such a focused way that it's strangeness doesn't even feel strange. I think I finished *A Smugger's Bible* reading #2 feeling like I can definitely justify carrying this battered paperback around for another ten years at least (this is the same edition I read the first time, and the pages are starting to fall out and the back cover is hanging on by just a few threads).

456. The Anthologist: A Novel by Nicholson Baker
Received: 17 February 2011
Started: 17 February 2011
Finished: 27 March 2011
Good ol' Nicholson Baker. There's something reliable about his books, even though he likes to take chances and write differently. *The Anthologist* falls into the *Mezzanine*/*Box of Matches* style of his books, where the novel exists entirely in  194, 467 87 the narrator's home. And by home, I mean head. *The Anthologist*'s narrator, poet Paul Chowder, is no more or less Bakerian than any of his other narrators. This novel is a book about poetry, in some ways the *Poetry for Dummies* mentioned near the end. Throughout his everyday procrastinations, Chowder explains his passion for four-beat metre, looks at different rhythms in classic poems, and celebrates his favourite writers. Chowder's tastes are different than mine so I found some new names to possibly investigate (though I don't know if I actually will) and I loved every page of this. The 'plot', besides the procrastination, involved Chowder's girlfriend and his longing for them to get back together. This pain was felt throughout the book, but never overly discussed — just mentioned enough to convey a proper lingering emotion. Baker, you've done it again!

457. FreeDarko Presents: The Undisputed Guide to Pro Basketball History by Bethlehem Shoals and Jacob Weinstein
Received: 4 April 2011
Started: 5 April 2011
Finished: 11 April 2011
I loved this; after receiving a big Amazon stash, it was the first thing I went for and I actually wanted to steal myself away from the events I organised in Helsinki last weekend to read more of this. At around 200 pages, this is a much shorter read than the Simmons book, but in many ways it was far   439 better. Certainly, the quality of the writing was better — the FreeDarko collective is a group of truly brilliant basketball fans, and

while Simmons has just as much passion for the history of pro basketball, this book is better because it has multiple perspectives and far more intelligence behind it. The graphics and statistics are brilliantly put together, and quite innovatively designed — they're so snappy that it's easy to ignore the insane level of statistical research that went into this (the graphic showing every fight in an NBA game is particularly mesmerising). I've become way more interested in pro basketball over the past season (since it's been an awesome, fascinating year) so this game at a good time for me — and I'll definitely read it again.

458. The Pale King by David Foster Wallace
Received: 14 April 2011
Started: 15 April 2011
Finished: 4 May 2011
It's been almost three years since Wallace took his own life, and in the intervening time he's grown in stature to my own mind, where I not only consider him to be the most important writer of my time, but *The Pale King* is the most I've ever anticipated any book. With this anticipation comes expectation, which I didn't want to have, so I then tried to overcompensate by lowering my hopes and figuring that in an unfinished state, how good can it be? After now reading it, I understand why it took so long to assemble, and of course I'm left longing for more, which is inevitable (*Infinite Jest* had the same effect on me, and it was twice as long and finished). Of course I loved it, but it is frustrating that it's only 500 pages — so many characters are started, trajectories plotted, and then nothing. I don't want resolutions — I know enough about his style to expect that — just more meat and flavour!

There's an article about DFW that ran in either the New Yorker or New York Times over a year ago which looked at what he was going through in the years leading up to his suicide. I think that's really the key to his whole work; I'm going to re-read it now, but I remember specifically that he struggled with his own writing, which he felt wasn't actually connecting to anyone and conveying anything human. I think that hung over me the whole time I was reading this, because I really perceived this as a much more emotionally connecting work than *IJ*, without compromising DFW's style, love of jargon, bizarre narrative structures, and discordant voices. The long first-person narrative from 'Irrelevant' Chris Fogle , placed (at least by those who posthumously assembled it) as the centrepiece of the book, is substantial enough to be its own novella and in some ways the heart and soul of it all. There are long conversations (particularly the exchange between Meredith Rand and the neutral, emotionless GS-9 at the end of the book) which aren't concerned with literary tricks or humour — and actually try to explore human relationships and a sense of identity. The biggest thing for me is that *The Pale King*, which is about boredom, is not nearly as bleak or pessimistic as *IJ* (though I should say that the first time I read *IJ* I wasn't affected by its pain and desolation, and on a second reading I realised it was the saddest book I ever read — so maybe that will happen here too). But as his notes, appended to the book to hint at where the novel might have one, indicate — DFW wanted to find a bliss that comes through boredom. So I think there's actually something hopeful about it. Of course, one problem is that he can make anything seem interesting, and the nuances of the IRS office structures, tax codes, and other bureaucratic structures are completely wonderful to get lost in. Being set in the 1980s forced him into a more realistic timeframe, though he still manages to work in ghosts and psychics; his own authorial presence has actual value instead of merely being meta-fictional gimmickry, and those chapters are the most entertaining in the classic footnoted style that I've come to love. I've had some bleak times myself lately but I can't even pretend to understand what he was going through, and *Infinite Jest* must have been fairly cathartic, to chronicle such despair and devastation in such a grandiose manner. *The Pale King* is definitely coming from the same place, but also carries the pressure of success in the same way Jonathan Franzen's last book did. While this is a far better (and more interesting) work, I wonder if his own self-imposed and quite stringent writing standards possibly made his situation worse. This is a stupid thing for me to speculate about, but it's impossible to read a book by a recently-suicided writer, especially if he's one of your favourite writers, without wondering about such things. I can't help but be sad and even a little angry at DFW for choosing to do what he did, and not finishing this — were he still with us, we could have at least 30+ more years of his genius. I realise how hideous and selfish this sounds.

459. How I Escaped My Certain Fate by Stewart Lee
Received: 20 May 2011
Started: 20 May 2011
Finished: 29 May 2011
A friend loaned me this given my recent surge of interest in stand-up comedy, and it really hit the spot. I wasn't particularly familiar with Stewart Lee but after reading this I have to call myself a big fan. These are basically the transcripts of three of his sets, with lots of annotations and interstitial chapters explaining his inspirations and experiences in the world of British stand-up comedy. Stand-up doesn't translate well to paper, but Lee realises this and really it's the footnotes that make this, though it make this take far longer to read than it should have. Lee is very pointed about social issues and has figured out a real place for himself in comedy, but he also has amazing taste in experimental music so there's frequent comparisons that are pretty great, such as "the Mighty Boosh are like Sunny Murray's drumming on those early Albert Ayler records", and there's also an appendix about Derek Bailey. I don't know most of the comedians that he's friends with and/or inspired by, but that doesn't matter so much; what was really great was the way he would go into deep analyses about different jokes, and things he would do live to respond to the audience. If I was going to attempt my own stand-up set (which has crossed my mind, in a low-pressure open-mic setting maybe) then this is more or less a manual on how to do it.

460. Chuck Klosterman IV: A Decade of Curious People and Dangerous Ideas by Chuck Klosterman
Received: 5 April 2011
Started: 26 June 2011
Finished: 3 July 2011
Klosterman's *IV* combined mostly essays he wrote for SPIN and other publications with a brief bit of fiction at the end. I enjoyed the fiction far more than I thought I would, but it's just the beginning to a novel he never finished and it just left me wanting more. The essays throughout the book weren't as enjoyable as the ones in *Eating the Dinosaur* or *Sex, Drugs and Cocoa Puffs* due mostly I think to being adapted to fit other publications' formats, length, etc. I did really dig the chapter about the North Dakota indie scene even though it was totally uninteresting to probably most of the readers. The 'hypotheticals' throughout are funny of course.

429

453

461. Blank Spots on the Map: The Dark Geography of the Pentagon's Secret World by Trevor Paglen
Received: 5 April 2011
Started: 20 July 2011
Finished: 22 July 2011
I was looking back over my listings and realised that I never logged this, which I read mostly on the train from NYC to the Adirondacks. Paglen's book was primarily an attack on Pentagon secrecy, with a paperback-edition afterword that blasted the Obama administration for failing to achieve the transparency they campaigned on. This wasn't Area 51 conspiracy stuff but looked specifically at sites that were officially denied for years and the types of military testing that goes on in them. In its most grandiose moments it got into postmodern spatial theory and psychogeography but really only as a dusting.. I liked this but wasn't blown away by it.

462. Born Standing Up: A Comic's Life by Steve Martin
Received: 26 July 2011
Started: 28 July 2011
Finished: 30 July 2011
I found this on a clearance rack for 50 cents and since I am so interested in comedy right now (and always had a ton of respect for Steve Martin), this was a fun read. I was glad to discover a work that was extremely honest, as Martin's stand-up personality wasn't that at all. The origin of his comedy was described quite literally as an epiphany while writing for the Smothers Brothers, and his explanation of the idea of anti-comedy is completely spelled out and articulated. The most fascinating parts of this were the ones about his father, which all resolves at the very end into a classic happy ending. I read this quickly and then discussed it with my mother, who also had read it and loved it.

463. Fargo Rock City: A Heavy Metal Odyssey in Rural North Dakota by Chuck Klosterman
Received: 3 August 2011
Started: 3 August 2011
Finished: 3 August 2011
Autographed copy. Finally I get around to Klosterman's first book, and the one his reputation rests upon. I expected this to be a memoir about growing up in North Dakota, which is very slightly is, but really this is a dissection of 80s pop-metal through that unique Klosterman viewpoint

— ie: writing intelligently about things not typically considered to be intelligent. I read this in pretty much one sitting, at the airport and on my flight, and enjoyed every page. I hadn't thought about *Use Your Illusion* or the Scorpions or a lot of these things in years, so it was a bit nostalgic for me even though I was never really into this stuff.

464. Griftopia: Bubble Machines, Vampire Squids, and the Long Con That Is Breaking America by Matt Taibbi
Received: 6 August 2011
Started: 6 August 2011
Finished: 7 August 2011
Taibbi's latest book is an attack on the contemporary American financial system, but it also finds time to skewer the Tea Party, a group who he (rather correctly, in my opinion) finds most frustrating than infuriating because their anti-elite sentiments are based in reality unlike most other issues on the right. This book definitely gets into the nitty-gritty of credit default swaps, commodities future speculating, and other aspects of financial arcana, but he does so in his usual entertaining way. I can't even guess how many times the word 'asshole' must appear in this book, but there really is no reason to mince words about these fuckers. I was worried this would stir up some rage in me that I have no outlet for, and I was right. These people are true monsters, criminals of the worst kind because instead of cunning, they are incompetent, and receive no punishment but rather benefits. I'm pretty disillusioned with national-level American politics right now and this (plus all the horse-shit going on with the debt ceiling) is leading me to feel like maybe I will never vote again. Incidentally, this was the first book I read in its entirety on an electronic device (the iPad) and I found the experience surprisingly pleasant.

465. The Broom of the System by David Foster Wallace
Received: 20 July 2011
Started: 20 July 2011
Finished: 9 August 2011
I had mixed memories of Wallace's first novel, and when I was looking for something to read on the train to the Adirondacks (cause I actually had nothing with me) this was the most interesting thing in the train station bookstore. And since I've subsequently become a huge fan of DFW I thought this might be fun to revisit. Well, maybe it was fun, but a better term would probably be 'spotty'. This was his PhD work and it's really clear in how up and down it is, as well as some of the preoccupations with sexuality and race (the depiction of the novel's only [minor] black character is pretty much straight-up racist in the use of exaggerated Ebonics). This novel is relatively lightweight and it actually suffers from being too focused — there needs to be more a more expansive world, and more characters — instead, nothing is left to chance and the way all of the characters come together just feels cheap. The surreal aspects, such as the giant desert in the middle of Ohio, are the more enjoyable aspects and I wish he had committed to a fucked-up parallel reality here as much as in *Infinite Jest*. Of course, the main thing missing from this that is present in his later works is the sadness. There are a few brief passages in *Broom of the System* that have some of the magic, but most of the novel is bogged down in bad dialogue. I admit that I didn't even want to finish it, but I kept holding out for some sort of payoff that wasn't there. This is time I could have spent reading *IJ* for the third time.

109

466. The Instructions by Adam Levin
Received: 5 April 2011
Started: 11 August 2011
Finished: 17 August 2011
Wow, *The Instructions* was an intense experience. I got sucked into Levin's narrative and tore through this over a long weekend, anxious to get to the conclusion. This heavy tome at first appeared to be a poor man's *Infinite Jest* or another entry into the child genius category (along with that Mark Haddon book, *Ratner's Star*, *The Last Samurai* and lots of other things). But it didn't take long before I realised that neither of these comparisons were accurate. *The Instructions* is a wonderful, masterful world but (though some parts were definitely funny) hardly the comic masterpiece I would expect from a novel of this size. It was deadly serious, really, and steeped in difficult issues, of which the messianic 10-year-old narrator proved to be a great device for exploring. I'd be really curious how someone actually raised in the Jewish faith would take this, because I'm really not sure what viewpoint Levin is writing from. At it's most genius moments, I realised how Gurion's mother played a major role in his persecution complex, and I read it as a criticism of such a viewpoint. But then again, I am critical of that attitude myself,

109 311
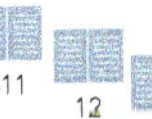
12 97

so I'm not sure if this is my own bias getting in the way. The explosive final 150-200 pages are pretty unbelievable and written in an almost sports-journalism way, making it the most compelling long fiction passages I've read since the murders section of *2666*. This is really something powerful, 397 and I think it's something I'll go back to, at least in passages, though the prose itself only reached magical moments through it's place in the whole work. On a practical note, I'm disappointed in how poorly the hardback survived — the white pleather is filthy after just 5 days of reading, mostly in my house, and the book is practically falling apart already. Or maybe that's just from how tight my fingers were grasping the pages. Now on to read external criticism and reviews!

467. The Mezzanine by Nicholson Baker
Received: 5 April 2011
Started: 19 October 2011
Finished: 25 October 2011
A nice re-read of *The Mezzanine*, purely because I was going to lend this to someone and thought "Wait! I want to re-read it first!". This never fails to please me; I forget how embedded the humour is in this, as Baker clearly knows that the majority of the footnotes are ridiculous in wonderful ways. The last footnote, where the narrator finds the Polish study of shoelace fibre tension, is like a money shot — but also we can't forget the list of things thought about per year and the frequency, with things like "Friends, don't have any" hidden in the list. This is obviously far more autobiographical than one would think, and as dated as some of the passages are (such as the memory of paper straws which is totally non-existent to even my generation), it's still such an utter fucking delight that I can't not rejoice that it exists.

468. Libra by Don DeLillo
Received: 28 September 2011
Started: 2 October 2011
Finished: 25 October 2011
I borrowed this from a friend as for some reason I've never read it, despite sort of being into DeLillo and being a mild JFK assassination buff too. I was really impressed with *Libra*; he took the difficult task of inhabiting such a loaded historical figure and delicately picking aspects of the assassination record to highlight, and he did it deftly. There was a whole lot of moving the plot here — the more 'literary' passages tended to fall to the wayside as it became more about the intricacies of the conspiracy. DeLilllo is masterful though in how he humanises Oswald, but not fully; from everything I had known about the person it seemed perfect, almost without conjecture (despite being entirely conjecture). The final chapter attempts to be this "from a different voice" technique that he did with *The Names* but without as much stylistic experimentation, but it's a great 219, 482 cap to the novel and probably the biggest emotional moment. The typically DeLilloan dialogue was perfect when it's being spoken between Guy Banister and David Ferrie — these shadowy, not-quite-human figures are exactly the type of character that his novels are built around. This definitely comes out of the style that *Players* and *Running Dog* were built from, but more 30 61 successful than I remember either of those being.

469. God Lives in St. Petersburg: and Other Stories by Tom Bissell
Received: 28 September 2011
Started: 22 October 2011
Finished: 31 October 2011
Bissell's been writing video game criticism for *Grantland*, and even though I'm not really interested in video games I've been enjoying his writing more than anyone else on the site apart from maybe Bill Barnwell. My friend knows him and lent me this collection of short stories, which is autographed by Bissell. All of these stories are about Americans in former Soviet Central Asian countries for some reason, and are pretty bleak in their portrayals of both the Americans and the countries. It's written with that same wry expatriate cynicism that my friend himself has and I may be developing, and the criticism of the Americans is so strong that these stories don't feel problematic in dealing with other cultures. Bissell can write, of course! His fiction is just as good as his video game pieces, though of course totally different, yet still drawing me in completely. As dark as most of these stories are, they're still quite hilarious, particularly 'The Ambassador's Son' which has a brash attitude that always conveys a fragility beneath the posturing. Good work for sure, and I'm excited to check out Bissell's other books, particularly his one about video games.

470. Extra Lives: Why Video Games Matter by Tom Bissell
Received: 10 November 2011
Started: 10 November 2011
Finished: 10 November 2011
I realised already that I like Bissell a lot, as evidenced by how I've consumed his video game criticism for *Grantland* despite not being a gamer at all. Bissell has insights into the art of video games that actually make me want to play them a bit. In some ways, I think this is therapy for Bissell to justify how's he's pissed away so much of his time playing games, but he's clearly truly interested in the form and potential, and his criticisms are generally spot-on I think (even though I haven't played them to be sure). He approaches video games as a literary writer would, which is to emphasise their impact on society and culture rather than become fixated on the technical aspects — though he does have an appreciation for great design. I wish I had met him with he was living in Tallinn and hanging out with my friend, though he seemed to be quite busy playing *Grand Theft Auto IV* and doing tons of cocaine. But I hope he comes back to speak at our bookshop, as my friend seems to think he will.

471. American Tabloid: A Novel by James Ellroy
Received: 19 November 2011
Started: 19 November 2011
Finished: 1 December 2011
This is my first experience reading Ellroy, who I always avoided I guess because it seemed like popular crime fiction, which is not a genre that ever interested me. I was wrong — Ellroy is a master stylist, fairly experimental in his minimalism and with some incredible depictions of violence and brutality. He deftly welded fictional characters into historical events, and the conversations with J Edgar Hoover and the Kennedys actually feel natural, and as realistic as can be. The book is massive and the plot is almost overwhelming, but the three lead characters are so compelling in their moral oscillations that I think I'll read the sequel.

472. You Shall Know Our Velocity by Dave Eggers
Received: 3 May 2008
Started: 19 December 2011
Finished: 23 December 2011
I grabbed this for 20p at a library sale 3.5 years ago and it's been sitting on my shelf awaiting a re-read ever since. Having a bookstore is actually motivation to clear these shelves as this book is better off in Slothrop's than Ptarmigan; I can sell this for probably 4.50–5€ and more importantly own one less book myself. I loved this the first time through for how frantic and hilarious it was, but this time I enjoyed it more for the strange juxtapositions of the two storylines. The portrayal of mental illness by the narrator is often haunting, though there's also a liveliness to the proceedings that keeps it palatable. The plot is the anchor that everything is wrapped around, though arguably "nothing happens". Eggers' characters are so caught up in their own fantasies that it's not surprising when their travels don't work out as planned; reading this can be frustrating as it's so cavalier and wasteful of experience, which is precisely the point. Lots of things could be said about the way these characters interact with other cultures, etc but I didn't read this negatively (an ex-girlfriend, who read this years ago, really hated it for how 'white' it was, which is also exactly the point, I think).

473. The Three Christs of Ypsilanti by Milton Rokeach
Received: 27 July 2011
Started: 23 December 2011
Finished: 25 December 2011
The premise of this, a work of psychiatric research/nonfiction that has for some reason been reprinted under the esteemed NYRB Classics line, is that in 1959, three mental patients all believing themselves to be Jesus Christ were in the same mental hospital in Ypsilanti, Michigan. The writer, Dr. Rokeach, conducted various experiments in group therapy over the course of two years, which are detailed in this book. This gets into some pretty dangerous territory, of course — conjuring visions of 1950s state medical facilities a la *Titicut Follies* — but Rokeach is such a good writer that his compelling narrative overrides all. There is a good deal of Rokeach as the "fourth Christ", as he admits in his afterword which curiously expresses guilt and regret at this experiment, which he realises was as much about him as the other three. 300 pages of the ramblings of the mentally insane is, as you can imagine, alternatingly hilarious and upsetting. Overall, there's a horror that can't be denied, as the delusions of these poor souls are so overpowering. Yet, Rokeach has a true compassion that comes through, even when attempting

to be clinical and engaging in unethical, experimental manipulations of the three. The eldest patient is barely a presence, with most of the book being dominated by the batshit-insane Leon Gabor, but the middle-aged Christ is fascinating as well. I don't think the most inventive writer of fiction/fantasy could begin to construct concepts as disillusioned as what comes out of the mouths of these three. And while I was entertained by much of it, ultimately I couldn't enjoy myself too much because of the unending nightmare that these people were clearly trapped inside. *The Three Christs of Ypsilanti* is incredible on many levels, not the least that it produces some minor moral dilemma in the reader.

474. The Moviegoer by Walker Percy
Received: 19 July 2010
Started: 30 December 2011
Finished: 31 December 2011
I loaned this to someone I'm dating and she didn't love it, complaining about the misogynistic attitudes, etc. I'm not bothered by them — I mean, this is possibly my very favourite novel ever, certainly in the top 3 or 4, and thus I re-read this in less than a day after she returned it, mostly on the way down to the MoKS New Years. And I loved every second of it, perhaps more than before. I realised how strangely uneven it is — there are sections full of beautiful, clean writing about New Orleans and the strange air and detachment that infects Binx Bollings; but then, longer parts such as most of the business trip to Chicago that are less engaging and make me want to skip them. But in the end, it's all amazing. The way that Binx explicitly draws attention to his aimlessness is so exaggerated that I feel like it's a ruse; but then, it obviously hints at a truth underneath all of the false confidence. It's also curious how his experience in Korea affected him; it's referenced a bit, most notably when talking to his mother, but he avoids committing to strong feelings even about that. But perhaps this explains his viewpoint, his outlook and avoidance of the 'malaise'? Maybe *The Moviegoer* is the quietest anti-war novel ever written.

475. Nobody's Angel by Thomas Mcguane
Received: 7 December 2011
Started: 9 December 2011
Finished: 31 December 2011
Later McGuane is a lot less comic, but no less majestically constructed. This is a total Western, in the way it's about the American west (in this case, Montana) though set in contemporary times and not about cowboys or Indians. This is a portrait of one character, and not much happens in it besides some marital infidelity and some strange encounters with family, but it's full of such great writing that I enjoyed it. The pace really picked up at the end, and I appreciated how McGuane created such a realistic, rounded character instead of the hilarious caricature that is so easy to do (see: *Ray*, by Barry Hannah). I also like how at the end, he actually ended up fulfilling 476 his dreams but it's not really dramatic or important. I have another McGuane on the shelf from the shop that I will probably read due to the scarcity of such a writer in the Baltic region, though it's from even later and I suspect even more 'serious'.

476. Ray by Barry Hannah
Received: 27 December 2011
Started: 27 December 2011
Finished: 14 January 2012
I took my time with this, a bookstore item that I was curious about as it has somewhat of a reputation as least among people who talk about Barry Hannah. I've never read Hannah before, and was surprised at how edgy his style was. But I didn't really like *Ray*, as its misogyny, however tongue-in-cheek and critical it may be, was ultimately overwhelming and actually a bit dull. It's certainly short enough to get through quickly, and maybe that would have been a better way to parse it. There's not much plot, as this is really a sketch, and while there were some dazzling, strange passages, I wasn't amused by the bawdiness. This is another one of those quiet comments on Vietnam, like the McGuane novel I just finished, as Ray's horrible existence 475 follows his service in a horrible war. But I felt this tried a bit too hard for my liking; still curious about *Geronimo Rex*, though.

477. Estonia: A Ramble Through the Periphery by Alexander Theroux
Received: 2 January 2012
Started: 2 January 2012
Finished: 18 January 2012
How does one even begin to assess *Estonia*, a book that feels like it was written especially for me? At times, it felt like it was even written *by* me. I stopped at points and checked that I wasn't dreaming. But actually, this book is a goddamned mess,

a work of lunatic pseudo-scholarship that I can find little in to recommend to anyone unless they happen to also be American expats with a strong taste in eclectic and difficult postmodern literature and also living in Estonia. The first thing to note is the ludicrous number of factual errors in this book, often to the point where I felt like it was intentional. Though wilful alteration of veracity and sheer "not giving a fuck" are two separate things, and I'm not sure which side this falls on. Now that I think 446 about it, *Darconville's Cat* was also just as mad, and a great deal longer, and not about the country I live in, and I loved that too. Theroux is dazzling; his sheer erudition blasts through everything, even when he's buried in his own cranky curmudgeon zone or ranting nonstop about linguistic oddities. There are long irrelevant passages in this book — rants against Israel for 8 pages, or angry platitudes against the Bush/Cheney nightmare — that give me the impression Theroux felt this would be his last chance to ever publish anything, so he crammed in as much as possible even if it had nothing to do with Estonia. But other parts are beautiful, savage and strange, and at times there are the same exhilarating and bizarre lists that populated the (many) pages of *Darconville*. Thought its shocking — if not irresponsible — that this was published without even a rudimentary pass at fact-checking, the very existence of this book pleases me beyond belief, and reading it even more so. I will be referring to this forever, and maybe my overall enjoyment is the reason I took so long to get through it — to savour its sweet, bitter, and generally flabbergasting words.

478. The Tipping Point: How Little Things Can Make a Big Difference by Malcolm Gladwell
Received: 7 January 2012
Started: 7 January 2012
Finished: 19 January 2012
Gladwell's first and most famous book is of course the one that I read last. So maybe that's why it's impact was blunted a bit; I did like this, but not as much as *Outliers* 428 or especially the one of shorter pieces. The Sesame Street stuff and the suicides in Micronesia were the most interesting sections, but I didn't see this as the revolution in creative nonfiction I thought it would be. Borrowed from a friend, though a copy came into the shop the very next day.

479. The Ecstasy of Influence: Nonfictions, Etc. by Jonathan Lethem
Received: 17 January 2012
Started: 17 January 2012
Finished: 19 January 2012
I loved this so much. This is an eclectic collection of Lethem's miscellaneous writings, not entirely non-fiction, and not unaware of its own place as a compendium of his errant ideas. There were some fantastic pieces here, the most famous probably being his Harper's essay defending plagiarism which is entirely made of plagiarized bits. But also some gems such as his writings on cinema and music, and lots of PK Dick of course. Especially interesting are Lethem's own acknowledgements of his success and expectations. He deals with the topics of the literary life in such an honest and insightful way that it's almost brave; there's no trace of ego inflation, even when he's explaining how he was upset by a bad review he got from James Wood in the Times. I have a tremendous amount in common with Lethem, which is maybe why I have always clicked with his writings. He makes his obsessions clear and doesn't hide from them, and there's some great writing on comics to show for it. I tore through this lengthy work really quickly, only skimming the piece about Thomas Berger (who I have not yet read). His 9/11 piece is here too, which is still probably the best writing on the event that I've ever read. But the absolute best piece in here was a very experimental piece for a Fred Tomaselli exhibition catalogue at the Fruitmarket in Edinburgh in 2004, an exhibition I saw and was pretty blown away by (yet never picked up the catalogue so I had no idea Lethem contributed to it). It's a really amazing interpretation of visual art with almost no literal connection, a beautiful example of trans-disciplinary thinking in action. Plus, he interviews Dylan! Great, great, great.

480. The Visible Man: A Novel by Chuck Klosterman
Received: 19 January 2012
Started: 20 January 2012
Finished: 21 January 2012
Klosterman's bizarre novel is an invisible man story with a bit of a debt to Baker's *The Fermata*, though more adept in its portrayal of middle-American isolation. I laughed a lot at this, as the concept was absolutely fascinating and it was employed with Klosterman's usual insights into life and culture. I don't think the plot-driven

ending worked so well and I would have been happy for hundreds of more pages of the middle section, but that's how it goes, and it was a quick read anyway. I was actually a bit surprised at how much I liked this, even though I like everything I've read by him in any genre. There were some brilliant moments that really transcend the more general parts — it's all amusing, accessible prose, but when he gets into these portraits of people in their homes, it's just insanely compelling in it's mundanity.

481. The Art of Fielding: A Novel by Chad Harbach
Received: 22 January 2012
Started: 23 January 2012
Finished: 26 January 2012
Harbach's acclaimed novel wasn't very well written, yet still managed to keep me reading until the end. I would consider this to be Jonathan Franzen-lite; about on par with *Freedom* (but less ambitious), and nowhere 454 54 close to *The Corrections*, though it was trying to be a very different thing. It was actually somewhat messy in terms of focus, and while it ended up being an ensemble novel masquerading as having a single protagonist (at least in the beginning) this caused whatever connection I might have to any characters to disintegrate. The most interesting aspect of this was actually the sports material; basing a novel around Steve Blass Disease (if it had only stayed true to that!) is a great concept, and Harbach did avoid really cheesy bottom-of-the-9th walkoff grand slam hyperbole (for the most part). The fictional college wasn't even very believable (early on we're told that the president of the college knows the names of all 2000 students, which is preposterous) and the too-perfect campus life just struck me as wishful thinking. I guess I read through this because it was easy and I needed a diversion, but I don't recommend it, even in the slightest.

482. The Names by Don DeLillo
Received: 1 February 2012
Started: 2 February 2012
Finished: 11 February 2012
A friend turned this over to Slothrop's; it's the copy I bought her as a graduation gift (which she read, but no longer wanted). I'm going to keep this for now and re-read it as it's been years and I need to see if this is still among my few very favourite books ... yeah, it still rules. And knowing how I felt the last two times, it's gonna resonate more and more in the next few days as I think about it. There's the added impact now that I am also an expatriate living in Estonia where I have dabbled in a social circle sort of like James Axton's (thinking mostly about the bookstore-centred group of weird expats). The displacement, detachment and selfishness of Axton make a bit more sense to me. His outrageous flirting, which is outright harassment, doesn't warm me up to him, yet I don't think DeLillo is trying to make him a protagonist per se, just an observer. Having also been to Greece and India since my last read helps, though I'm not just a fan of this book because I'm impressed by its accuracy of depiction. Really, the power of this book is in how it explores the act of articulation through all of its linguistic obsessions, the muted speech (and thoughts) of Axton, and the way his son is this moral presence throughout. Not to mention his final chapter, which I think is even more impressive than *Riddley Walker* (though it's quite as deconstructive). Is this actually my favourite book? Certainly top 5. Yet I'm gonna sell this copy in the shop cause it's beat to shit and I can always get a nicer one.

483. I Love Dick by Chris Kraus
Received: 11 February 2012
Started: 13 February 2012
Finished: 15 February 2012
Wow. This was amazing, both as an innovative hybrid of personal writing and fiction, and also as a brilliant statement of artistic identity. This is one friend's favourite book ever and I completely see why; there's a million reasons you can go back to it and as an artistic statement of purpose it's remarkable. Kraus writes so confidently that she essentially defines a new genre of feminism here, one that is flexible and realistic yet bold and boundary-exploring. The honesty in this book transcends any fictionalisation that might have occurred and it somehow manages to be simultaneously emotional and intellectual, which is perhaps what is so remarkable about her viewpoint. I will write about this more later when I am more coherent.

484. Escape the Overcode: Activist Art in the Control Society by Brian Holmes
Received: 23 August 2011
Started: 24 August 2011
Finished: 21 February 2012
I found this in the bathroom at Tiib and

borrowed it from its owner back in August. I kept forgetting to finish it, but today I knocked out the last chapter. Taking three months in between the last time I read it made it a bit inconclusive to me, but overall I was pretty impressed with this work. Holmes (who I met at Pixelache last year, and is absolutely brilliant) attempts to explore the role of activism in contemporary art, using the Deleuze and Guattari concept of 'overcoding'. His writing is so straight-forward and lucid that I was able to understand the vast majority of this, only getting lost around the part about Guattari's *Schizoid Cartographies* project, but I've tried to wrap my head around that (unsuccessfully) multiple times before. This book was actually light reading at times — the majority of it discusses individual projects, most of which I was not familiar with, and some that I will definitely investigate. (I watched *Das Netz* after reading Holmes's
1011 chapter on it; there's also a great dissection of Adam Curtis's work). In some places Holmes casually throws around some great ideas, such as his definition of art as an experimental field for the production of subjectivities. I have been interested a lot in how art can respond to 20th century ideas of cybernetics and information organisation, so this was a great thing to read — I wish I had focused on it more, but it will always be in the toilet if I want to give it another go.

485. The Flame Alphabet by Ben Marcus

Received: 13 February 2012
Started: 17 February 2012
Finished: 27 February 2012

Writing about this is proving to be hard. Ironic, really, since this is a book about language becoming a poison and the impossibility of communication. I just re-read *The Names* and in some ways this
219, 482 is like taking it to another level, inventing a link between language and death, and constructing articulation as impossible.

But *The Flame Alphabet* is Ben Marcus significantly reinventing himself, in a similar to manner to how his past work reinvents the meaning of our words. Here, all of that is gone; the prose is, well, prosaic; though there are stunning passages, particularly when describing food, minerals and other natural elements, this is really an attempt to write something more 'real'. What this resulted in for me, as a reader, was pure pain. I found this so brutal and dark that it was at times unbearable, and my initial excitement at having a new Ben Marcus book quickly turned into something oppressive and actually I dreaded reading. Without the beauty of *Notable American Women*'s magical prose, this 190, 571
became something very realistic, despite the fantastic setting and premise. It's maybe too easy to read into this as being about something you love killing you, but it sure resonated with me. More than just being about fatherhood, *The Flame Alphabet* tries to reconcile a lot of pain but offers no answers. There's no hope here — it just gets bleaker and bleaker as it goes on.

By the end I was trying to cling to the parts of this book that were truly amazing — the Jewish holes, for example — and let the misery wash over me. It's also evident that Marcus is trying to address his own challengers as a writer here through the child character and the language-as-poison device. In some ways I am proud of him for trying to push his craft to a new level, largely abandoning what made his first two books so earth-shattering. But this isn't a stab towards accessibility at all — it's a maelstrom of psychic demons that really got into my head as well, and attained a physicality rarely felt in English literature. I probably sound like I hated this, or I am dismissing it, but far from it — this was unforgettable experience and in some ways reinforces my faith in Marcus, even if I don't actually want to ever read it again.

486. Dry : A Memoir by Augusten Burroughs

Received: 25 February 2012
Started: 27 February 2012
Finished: 28 February 2012

Burroughs is pretty compelling; I really enjoyed *Running with Scissors* since it

combined a really fucked up story with 330
pretty great humorous writing (to the point of extremity) and this was a similarly quick read. The middle third threatened to become a soap opera, and the ending was almost too over-the-top sentimental/emotional, but then it was still undercut with the sharp wit and self-effacing style that makes Burroughs so good. I should organise a course around books about alcoholism — this, *A Fan's Notes*, *Under the Volcano* ... hmm, what else?

103 277

487. Kingdom of Fear: Loathsome Secrets of a Star-Crossed Child in the Final Days of the American Century by Hunter S. Thompson
Received: 2 March 2012
Started: 2 March 2012
Finished: 5 March 2012
A bunch of Hunter S. Thompson books came into the shop and I picked this one up to read over the weekend. I've always felt that the problem with Thompson is that his writing is actually really uneven, particularly towards the end of his life. This is the very end, constructed as an autobiography of sorts, but really a mishmash of odds and ends lying around. The theme is presumably post-9/11 America seen through HST's eyes, but some of the pieces date back to the 80s and 90s. This fragmented nature is actually what I liked most about the book, though there is very little to dazzle. I was struck by how honest Thompson is throughout, even when spinning obvious bullshit (like about how he nearly blew up Jack Nicholson's house and left a bleeding elk heart in the door). The mythology around him was largely the embellishments of others, and he manages to dispel some of it without directly doing so. There's a lot of material about his sexual assault case in 1990 that comes off as sour grapes, but he makes a strong case for his innocence (mostly convincing, at least as much as is possible given that I wasn't there and have only heard his side of the story), and the archival stuff from *High Times* about it is strangely compelling. So overall I'd say I liked *Kingdom of Fear* even though it wasn't particularly *good*; if you go into this expecting something actually cohesive, then you might want to look elsewhere. I suspect the best book about Thompson's life is going to be written by somebody else — maybe some of the other biographies out there will be more illuminating.

488. How to Archer: The Ultimate Guide to Espionage and Style and Women and Also Cocktails Ever Written by "Sterling Archer"
Received: 5 March 2012
Started: 5 March 2012
Finished: 5 March 2012
Downloaded this before bed, and read it before falling asleep. Spin off humour books from TV shows aren't usually something I'd read but this was funny enough for what it was. I would have preferred an audio book so at least I could hear Jon Benjamin's voice, but I heard it in my head anyway while I was reading it. Probably the most embarrassing thing I've read in a decade.

489. Senselessness by Horacio Castellanos Moya
Received: 5 April 2011
Started: 5 March 2012
Finished: 6 March 2012
This was stunning — a lightning strike of a novella that deftly balanced horror, mental dissolution, sexuality and comedy. *Senselessness* is a novel of avoidance, though it doesn't work; it intentionally juxtaposes sleazy male sexuality with genuinely terrible atrocity, in a way that smashed into my brain due to Moya's style. This book was a series of extreme run-on sentences, which flowed quickly and naturally, like a true fountain of consciousness. It felt real, and hilarious, and it hurt at times to laugh. The narrative propels towards a resolution in absentia, and it's a punch in the gut. This really didn't feel like any Latin or Spanish-language writer I had read before, not did it feel like a descendent of the Joyce/Gaddis/Barth rivers. It's a singular masterpiece, readable in about an hour, and riveting on every page.

490. Zombie Spaceship Wasteland by Patton Oswalt
Received: 5 March 2012
Started: 9 March 2012
Finished: 11 March 2012
Patton Oswalt's book is surprisingly great — he clearly has talent as a prose writer, far above average for a non-writer, though I guess comedians are writers who just work in an oral form by default. The book veers between autobiographical sections and goofy, funny stuff like fake wine lists and information about hobos. The funniest of these sections were his script doctor's notes for a fake film called *And Now You May Miss the Bride*, about an amnesia-stricken marriage — but there were other really funny parts throughout. But the personal stuff, though scattered, is really the highlight. The titular essay is a genius theory about teenage misfits, which I heard him lay out in a *BS Report* podcast back when this came out, and I actually wish it was a bit longer and more expanded. The long section about a miserable week spent in a Vancouver suburb is great, though probably a far more universal experience for comedians that we'd hope. My one complaint would be that this felt disjointed and fragmentary — almost as if Oswalt was

not ready to commit fully to autobiography, which I think would have been more enjoyable. In that way, it reminds me of the Hunter Thompson book I just finished, though that randomness suits Thompson far more than Oswalt.

491. Pity the Billionaire: The Hard-Times Swindle and the Unlikely Comeback of the Right by Thomas Frank
Received: 11 March 2012
Started: 11 March 2012
Finished: 12 March 2012
Frank's latest book looks at how contemporary right-wing movements such as the Tea Party have co-opted the rhetoric of the left and the underclasses to define a new narrative of victimisation. This isn't wildly different from what they have done for years with the media, except that here they are mostly abandoning social conservativism and actually misplacing what should be genuine anger at the Wall Street bailouts, TARP, etc. And the lies are even more ridiculous since at least abortion provided a good cover; here, the cries of socialism are just utterly ridiculous and blatantly misleading. There wasn't anything new here for me as I've lived through this and followed it closely, but I wanted to read it anyway because I like Frank's style and have read his other books. This actually gets into some history, going back to the Great Depression, and his lefty roots really show in how he's able to compare reactions of the 1930s to the present. I didn't love this — Frank attacks Glenn Beck often, which already feels somewhat dated, and at one point launches into a takedown of Ayn Rand, which is entertaining but a bit tangential. But overall, I'm glad I read it as it was quick, and Frank managed to get through the book without patronising anybody (which I don't think I could have done). I'm glad that Frank has crossed into the mainstream market successfully, but part of me wishes he was still writing more about culture and its political machinations, which was a really unique and brilliant niche that *The Baffler* carved out. I guess this book *is* about culture and its political machinations, but not in the same way.

492. The Information: A History, a Theory, a Flood by James Gleick
Received: 27 January 2012
Started: 27 January 2012
Finished: 14 March 2012
Subtitled 'How We Got Here', Gleick has created a massive overview of information in the modern era. The book is scholarly, yet populist — the kind of intelligent non-fiction that is probably (sadly) disappearing from bookstores. Because I've always had an interest in the history of computing, I was familiar with the stores of Ada Lovelace, Alan Turing, etc. — but Gleick did not present them as just another history of how computers and the Internet emerged, but rather an overall view of information as a concept. I actually thought this was going to be much longer but the last 40% of the book were all notes (and because I read this as an e-book, a process which is becoming increasingly more common and normal to me) I didn't realise this, so it felt like a sudden ending. The chapter on Wikipedia was particularly great, as it looked at the underlying absurdity that lies beneath such a project, and the frightening ways in which problems self-correct themselves. This is sort of a beach book for nerds, but Gleick avoids making any predictions or other hyperbolic statements, so it ends up being just really, really good.

493. The Raw Shark Texts by Steven Hall
Received: 3 March 2012
Started: 11 March 2012
Finished: 15 March 2012
Ultimately, I'd categorise *The Raw Shark Texts* into the genre of 'Guardian books', which is my derogatory term for these popular British novels that are depressingly middlebrow, but unfortunately what passes for literary culture in the UK today. I include this alongside Zadie Smith and that one terrible Russell Hoban novel I read, and the *Curious Incident of the Dog* and *What a Carve-Up!* and all similar works. And that's not to say that I don't enjoy reading some of these, but that I don't think they are ultimately anything special or memorable on an artistic level. I'm such a snob! Hall's novel starts off very promising — I love amnesia as a theme, and the descriptive prose was quite evocative, particularly when writing about loss and memory. Then things get crazy, in a *Southland Tales* style, but in a way that lacks a pull. I need something to make me want to inhabit these imaginary worlds, at least temporarily, and *Raw Shark* was too focused on defining it's own rules, which it doesn't even do well — it's vague, and continually used the word 'conceptual' as if just saying that word is enough, without actually knowing what that concept is. By the end, it had descended into just

275 311 398

611, 773, 836

a fantasy/adventure story, albeit one with interesting objects around. I enjoyed reading it though, but I wouldn't recommend it or ever want to read it again.

494. I Don't Care About Your Band: What I Learned from Indie Rockers, Trust Funders, Pornographers, Felons, Faux-Sensitive Hipsters, and Other Guys I've Dated by Julie Klausner
Received: 15 March 2012
Started: 15 March 2012
Finished: 18 March 2012
The comedy press was kind to this, and I started it cautiously, knowing a friend didn't like it. I didn't either, maybe even hating it, but hate is a strong word and I managed to finish this, even though I realised about halfway through that there would be no payoff. To some extent, I was engaged by reading a memoir by someone who is exactly my age and from a relatively similar background; her cultural concerns, which to her credit were the backlighting rather than a backdrop, resembled my own in some places. I don't fault Klausner for structuring a novel around her sexual history, though I can see why this is an easy point of criticism, at least from the Bechdel test angle. It's great that Klausner is sex-positive and writes unapologetically about this, and maybe her constant unmet desire to be fulfilled by a male could be viewed as some natural human need for a partnership instead of a culturally-constructed dependency. But ultimately, this wasn't particularly funny. Klausner spends the early chapters creating a persona of herself as a sympathetic teenage misfit, and then later in life, proceeds to berate some of her flings for similar traits that she herself would have been picked on for when younger. Part of my problem is that I recently read *I Love Dick,* 483 which is about as masterful as anything I've ever read in dealing with feminine emotional space and sexuality (though I admit, I've read little, and want to change that). Kraus is no less personal and not much more intellectual, but she describes an emotional life that is tied in with her creativity and sexuality, and the process, articulates an amazing definition of identity. Klausner comes off really just like an R-rated Liz Lemon from *30 Rock*, only more aggressive. It's certainly not my place to proscribe what personality types define womanhood, but I see Liz Lemon as a critique, not a hero. Klausner is someone who spends 210 pages admonishing men for not being able to get over themselves when she can't get over herself either.

495. Killing Yourself to Live: 85% of a True Story by Chuck Klosterman
Received: 5 April 2011
Started: 18 March 2012
Finished: 21 March 2012
I'm working my way through everything Klosterman has published, because it's a bit like candy to me. This was maybe the most enjoyable as it was the most autobiographical, and also came as a nice antidote to Julie Klausner's wretched book. 494 This drive across the country is really an excuse for Klosterman to lay out his weird pop culture and music obsessions and dwell on the women in his life. I hadn't read anything this personal before by him and was glad for it because it was a nice snapshot of a 31 year old with various musical obsessions and differing levels of social detachment. I actually found myself taking this slowly so I could savour it. Totally fun and worthy of a re-read.

496. Downtown Owl: A Novel by Chuck Klosterman
Received: 22 March 2012
Started: 22 March 2012
Finished: 24 March 2012
Klosterman's first work of fiction is like a more superficial, less 'literary' David Foster Wallace, and I'm surprised I never made the connection between the two before. Of course, they write from completely different perspectives, but both have a love of pedantic exposition and an absurd ability to juxtapose sadness with humour. This is Klosterman's North Dakota novel for sure, and wraps up as a marvellously entertaining ball of existentialism, though I felt unsatisfied. I wish he had spent less time trying to emphasise the isolation of these small communities, and also dropped the anachronistic narratorial asides. But the portraits he creates are compelling and I found this as entertaining as everything else he's ever written.

497. House of Holes by Nicholson Baker
Received: 26 March 2012
Started: 26 March 2012
Finished: 27 March 2012
As erotica goes, or maybe straight-up pornography, this is the most absurd, lunatic, ridiculous writing I've ever encountered. Baker tops even the blue movie scene of

240 *Tlooth* here, and I must admit that I greatly enjoyed it. If you want to read about people transported to magical spaces via their own dickholes, women masturbating with screwdrivers, cock transplants, and pinecones that inspire anal sex, this is your work. The language is absurd, and there's a weird undercurrent of commerce behind everything — Baker's sexual fantasies cost the characters money, sometimes more — and because of that there's a creepy dystopian vibe to it all. That, when juxtaposed with language that's often too over-the-top to be arousing, makes this a really weird and uncertain mixture, almost like it's designed to create a guilt or conflict in the brains of those with purely prurient interests. For that reason alone I thought it was amazing, and certainly better than *Vox* or *The Fermata*, though I haven't read either of those since the 90s.

498. Franny and Zooey by J. D. Salinger
Started: 26 March 2012
Finished: 28 March 2012
I felt like reading this again and I downloaded an ebook of it and blasted through it while in Poland, which was a nice juxtaposition against the definitely un-Glasslike surroundings in the villeage of Skoki. There's such a momentum to this story even though nothing actually happens, and I can't quite figure out what the 'Franny' section at the beginning is really for, as Salinger seems to use it only to establish Franny's personality and give us the context of her teenage heartbreak. Burgeoning maturity is so universalised here despite the affluence of the characters, and it's an America that I myself never lived in but sure can imagine. We put a quote from Bessie Glass on our Slothrop's gift vouchers, 'You can't live in this world with such strong likes and dislikes', said of course to Zooey, and I wonder if Salinger actually agrees with her. The flawed hero has never been more perfectly cast than Zooey Glass, and his affectations were so booming that it was like he was in the room with me.

499. Fear and Loathing: On the Campaign Trail '72 by Hunter S. Thompson
Received: 6 March 2012
Started: 28 March 2012
Finished: 1 April 2012
I guess I'm on a bit of a Hunter Thompson kick, and this is the work of his that I've always most wanted to read — I eventually just broke down and bought a copy locally since I couldn't find it online (though every other one of his books seems to be available). In this, I was surprised to discover something far different than I expected. Thompson's coverage of the McGovern campaign is actually extremely journalistic, and not as 'gonzo' as you'd believe. There's definitely a sharp, irreverent edge, but it's mostly inside-baseball talk about Democratic party machinations, which I found to be fascinating (and relevant to today's electoral system). There's a depressing vibe of course, but interestingly, Thompson doesn't talk about Nixon much at all — the October section of the book is essentially excised and the Democratic ticket is the real emphasis. This is actually pretty amazing, and I think McGovern himself called it "the best account of the campaign and also the least accurate". It might be worth reading Crouse's *Boys on the Bus*, which we have in the shop right now, to compare. McGovern's primary was so similar to Obama's 2008 run that it's scary, except Obama knew how to avoid the mistakes McGovern had made, and then ended up destroying his credibility and installing the same ol' shitbags anyway once he won. But it's fascinating anyway, and also surprising how 40 years ago wasn't any less cynical than today; just maybe more neurotic. If you actually need proof that HST is a great writer, this is the place to go; he's brutally honest and doesn't spend much time trying to project a wild man image, instead capturing a pulse that is quite radical for political writing and impressively timeless.

500. Gascoyne by Stanley Crawford
Received: 28 July 2011
Started: 16 March 2012
Finished: 7 April 2012
I really enjoyed *Gascoyne*, and how can you not? It never slows down, attaining a velocity that makes it feel like radical artwork. But it's nothing too innovative — just a genre-bending mashup of crazy sci-fi, proto-cyberpunk 'tude, and a strange take on outlaw/beat narrative. Having read the beautiful, longing *SS Mrs Unguentine*, this  420
is a different beast entirely. I would have read this much more quickly except I didn't take it to Poland and got distracted by other things. I think this was Crawford's first novel and it definitely has a youthful exuberance to it, even if the protagonist is an elderly man. The obsession with speed, cars, and violence recalls the work of the Futurists more than any American hot-rod culture; it's very strange in it's cultural niche and funny at times, in an absurd way.

I didn't LOVE this but I enjoyed it greatly, and it was an easy, fun read even if I didn't care much about the workings of its hard-boiled plot.

501. Where Art Belongs by Chris Kraus
Received: 6 March 2012
Started: 14 April 2012
Finished: 18 April 2012
I was seduced by this, due to it's attractive cover and being by Chris Kraus. It's in Semiotext(e)'s *Interventions* series, though I'm not sure what is interventionist about it. This is a series of short essays about different contemporary art practices, beginning with the Tiny Creatures scene in Los Angeles, and also dealing with the work of the Bernadette Corporation, contemporary attitudes towards video, and a sex workers tour that Kraus herself participated in. It seems fairly disorganised, almost like she collected a few different essays that were loosely related. The subjects of these essays all somewhat integrate art and life in a way that feels natural to me, being of my age and with my own lifestyle, though clearly this is out of step with traditional art practices. There's nothing particularly radical about it, at least for me, but Kraus's journalistic style is as wonderfully open as *I Love Dick* was, so there's a strong integration of her personal warmth with extremely subjective yet insightful analysis. While overall I would call this a bit lightweight, and maybe not remarkable enough to be drawn together into a bound volume, I greatly enjoyed reading it, and maybe it's better that she avoided a strong, unifying conclusion.

502. Chasing the Sea: Lost Among the Ghosts of Empire in Central Asia by Tom Bissell
Received: 18 April 2012
Started: 18 April 2012
Finished: 21 April 2012
Bissell does it again, and I realise that he's done it in multiple genres. This is a book about Uzbekistan, and it's fascinating, top-quality travel writing. Bissell confronts his own demons about his failed Peace Corps run, and his return is laced with outrage and humour. His writing is stunning at times, conveying a distant and disturbing country that's intriguing as well as horrifying. The purpose of his journey is ostensibly to write about the Aral Sea crisis, and it takes him 340 pages to get there, before abruptly ending. In the meantime, he spins his experience into a general travel book, a narrative of Central Asia that makes me want to visit despite the chaos. Bissell's writing about the environmental catastrophe that is the Aral Sea is focused and powerful, and he doesn't hold any punches against either the Soviet regime responsible for the problem or the Karimov regime that's furthered it. I only wish this was longer, and it's made me think how I should read more travel writing.

503. Gulcher: Post-Rock Cultural Pluralism in America (1649-1993) by Richard Meltzer
Received: (already owned)
Started: 21 April 2012
Finished: 23 April 2012
Grabbed this off the shelf for a re-read as some friends online were discussing it; this time through I was completely blown away. I can't remember when I read this before — I'm guessing around my freshman or sophmore year at Pitt? — but now I'm even more into these pranky anti-writing shenanigans. At times I wondered why I was reading it, or why anyone would write some of the pieces. The bottle cap collection is great, the few bits actually about music are stellar, the irrelevant sports rants are hilarious if you can follow them, and the chapter where he calculated the missing numbers in the free throw statistics from a smudged Topps basketball card is the best of all. This is conceptualism, I'd say, though it's too fun and creative to fall into Kenneth Goldsmith's 'uncreative writing' genre. Because it's hilarious! I'm really glad this is back in print — it's a real masterpiece of sorts, and addresses a narrowly disappearing generation.

504. A Year With Swollen Appendices: Brian Eno's Diary by Brian Eno
Received: 17 April 2012
Started: 25 April 2012
Finished: 19 May 2012
I savoured this. Eno's diary, kept in 1995, is simultaneously simple and magical. I've always been a fan of Eno, but this cemented my appreciation of his life and work. For someone occasionally portrayed as overly cerebral and "pretentious" (the takedown of this term he executes in one of the many appendices), this is actually written with great honesty and humility. I loved the insight into his creative life, and I found it inspiring without any particular point sticking out. Some days, the mere

mention of what he made for dinner, or the walk he took with his children was enough to inspire me. The appendices are hit and miss, but a few are brilliant, such as his analyses of defence spending, axis thinking, and celebrity charity. What a brilliant book — this is something I'm going to have to get for myself to read again, for the 'open randomly' value is quite high. Absolutely amazing.

505. Seven Days in the Art World by Sarah Thornton
Received: 9 May 2012
Started: 10 May 2012
Finished: 22 May 2012
A friend (for some reason) loaned me this, which is a look at the art world circa 2004-2006 written from the perspective of a sociologist. This angle proved to be a good one, as there was little ass kissing or attempts to seem knowledgeable. I found this pretty rewarding, especially given my recent work — I usually say that I am not part of the world of contemporary art at all, but I run alongside that word occasionally picking and choosing aspects of it to partake in. With my trip to Documenta in a few weeks it's probably good that I have at least a passing knowledge of this world. I was pretty bored by the chapters on *Artforum* and Art Basel, yet I found the looks at the Christie's auction and the biennale fascinating. Thornton isn't particularly critical of this giant world of shit, though its contradictions are certainly not lost on her. My favourite chapter was the one on Michael Asher's crit at CalArts, for one thing because I have been freelancing for CalArts for over two years but know little about the institution; my 'boss' there (I guess, though I never had contact with him) is discussed in that article as well. The net affect of reading this was to make me more knowledgeable about the art world, though I don't know if that's a good idea — maybe my naiveté keeps me insulated from this stuff. I generally think of 'art' as a much broader concept than the fine art-based practices described here, and likewise I see there being multiple infinite art worlds instead of a singular one, so I would have titled this *Seven Days in An Art World* but that's a minor quibble I guess.

506. On Photography by Susan Sontag
Received: 28 December 2011
Started: 24 January 2012
Finished: 24 May 2012
Started this before the new year when a copy came into the shop, but then someone bought it so I borrowed a friend's in order to finish it, but then shelved it for months before returning to it in a "I better clear off the loan shelf so I can then clear off the stuff I borrowed from Slothrop's so I can then clear off the few hundred books I own and haven't read yet." Anyway. I've only read bits of Sontag before in short essay form, which is what this was too, though all of the essays were about photography. This was good reading, even in this broken-up fashion, as I've been mildly into photographic theory, more so than I'm actually into photography. This wasn't quite as conceptual as Vilém Flusser, though got into similar topics about the camera as 225 an instrument of control, etc. Sontag got much more into the art world agendas of photography, specifically the relationship that photography has to surrealism, etc. She touched on specific work by most of the big-name 20th Century photographers — Cartier-Bresson, Adams, Stieglitz, Arbus — and ended with a chapter of fun, provocative quotations. I don't know if I took anything away from this as a whole — the issues of photography and representation are quite complex and occasionally contradictory — and in some ways I think Godard's *Letter to Jane* might say it better  than anything. 873

507. The Postmortal: A Novel by Drew Magary
Received: 22 May 2012
Started: 22 May 2012
Finished: 24 May 2012
Drew Magary is pretty much the funniest writer on the Internet, but this novel wasn't nearly as enjoyable as any random Deadspin Funbag. I thought this Philip K Dick-style plot would be mixed with his irreverent humour, but instead he tried to play it straight, and created a novel that is easy enough to read but not compelling enough to actually enjoy. There's something a bit lazy about the whole thing, almost hardboiled but without the fun aspects. I don't meant to rag on him too hard because he's clearly trying to be more than a guy who writes about poop online, but there's honestly nobody better out there at that, so I would be happy with a 600 page book of Funbag letters to read while

pooping myself. Better luck next time.

508. Absurdistan: A Novel by Gary Shteyngart
Received: 24 May 2012
Started: 24 May 2012
Finished: 29 May 2012
Absurdistan seemed trapped between being a nothing's-sacred satire of contemporary life in the former Soviet states and a genuine political critique. I wasn't sure how to ultimately assess this book, which was fun and entertaining enough but didn't actually succeed in being as funny as it thought — in other words, it expected to coast on its own humour for large parts when I actually found the characterisations lacking. The non-fiction writing of Tom Bis-502 sell's Uzbekistan probably does a better job at portraying this mentality than Shteyngart, who also put a thinly veiled version of himself in the story. But, entertaining enough for sure.

509. The Psychopath Test: A Journey Through the Madness Industry by Jon Ronson
Received: 9 June 2012
Started: 9 June 2012
Finished: 9 June 2012
Jon Ronson is always nonfiction-candy and *The Psychopath Test* is no different than his other books. As usual he interjected his research with his own not-always-believable comic exchanges, which worked great here because the material was so dark. There's a bit of ramble before it becomes clear what he's getting at, and the test itself is a small part of the book. I read this on the bus from Riga to Tallinn so it went quick but provided the entertainment and diversion I wanted. There are some really genuinely intriguing bits of criminology discussed here, and maybe I should crack open that Colin Wilson book I have to follow this up.

510. Invisible Republic: Bob Dylan's Basement Tapes by Greil Marcus
Received: 30 May 2012
Started: 30 May 2012
Finished: 11 June 2012
The second time through I found *Invisible Republic* much more enjoyable. One reason is that I no longer let Marcus's embellishments bother me, but instead treated them as his writing personality and I really found the writing quite moving at points. The other reason of course is that I've become way, way into the Basement Tapes since the first time I read this, even visiting the (yard of the) house they were recorded in. The historical writing about Dock Boggs, Frank Hutchinson, Clarence Ashley, etc. is actually fantastic — it has the same mix of speculation and accuracy that Tosches's awesome book about Emmett Miller has. The only times I really couldn't 268 take this was when Marcus would write things about how, say, Dylan's version of 'Ballad of a Thin Man' live in Manchester captured the turbulence of America's civil rights struggle in between every piano chord, etc. The overblown desire to inflate great music by nailing it to every historical event that is happening is like an unsubtle episode of *Mad Men*, but when you get past that, there's a pretty great take on the music that shows Marcus can really listen (and not just overthink). This came into the shop and I was going to read it and return it, but I think I will actually keep it, partially because the reference material in the back is so valuable (the breakdown of all *Basement Tapes* songs).

511. Deer Hunting With Jesus by Joe Bageant
Received: 11 June 2012
Started: 11 June 2012
Finished: 16 June 2012
I wasn't wildly impressed with *Deer Hunting for Jesus*, which started out as a folksier, more personal version of *What's the Matter with Kansas* but ended up just being a long 172 rant against American 'heartland' culture. Of course I agree with Bageant, but 250 pages attacking born-again fundamentalists in Winchester, VA gets repetitive. Instead of offering any real suggestions, he just repeats the same rants that I spent the Bush years saying myself. His authority rests on that he is from this town, his brother is a preacher now, etc. but it just makes him come off as a dickhead. I finished this because I hate leaving easy things unfinished but it was a waste of an afternoon for sure.

512. The Sleepwalker by Margarita Karapanou
Received: 13 February 2012
Started: 18 June 2012
Finished: 21 June 2012
Karapanou's novel is unique in it's genre-shifting and accessibility, with some really dark undercurrents and the creepy Greek island vibe of DeLillo's *The*

219, 482 *Names*. But the similarity ends at the murders; where DeLillo's book is about what is not said (despite being about language), Karapanou's is explicit. According to the translator's notes, the original Greek is a hodgepodge of various dialects and voices, so this is an example where the real power of a book is lost in translation. It has an ensemble approach, with only one real protagonist (clearly the stand-in for the writer) and a possibly realistic depiction of expatriates in the Greek islands. The high level of homosexual characters, most of whom are portrayed as fickle and creepy, suggests a judgemental view from Karapanou, though I also suspect these characters are based on people she actually knew (which doesn't excuse anything). The magical realist elements were unevenly spaced, which led this to feel like a genre-shifting experiment. The writing was lucid and direct, and I think she had quite a reputation in Greece before her death; I don't know that I'm super motivated to read anything else by her, however.

513. Love and Hydrogen: New and Selected Stories by Jim Shepard

Received: 26 July 2011
Started: 23 June 2012
Finished: 3 July 2012

Shepard's story collection was dazzling, though as with any short story collection, not every one was totally enjoyable. At times I was amazed that he could 'pull it off' — there's some incredible conceits here, such as writing from the perspective of John Entwhistle or John Ashcroft, both of which are done very well. The tone shifts from light and comic, like in the opening story, to quite emotional and powerful (the story about the volcano researcher and his emotionally disturbed brother attains a genuine sadness and pain that's quite impressive) but nothing is ham-fisted or distraught. This is a long way from John Updike's endless stories about boring couples; Shepard really gets adventurous with his concepts yet it never comes off as *McSweeney's*-style quirk or novelty. The title story, an imagined clandestine gay relationship between two *Hindenburg* technicians, is particularly stunning, and the best thing about all of these stories is that the end before they exhaust their ideas. I should read more short stories in general, and certainly more Shepard. He's no relation to the V-3/Vertical Slit guy, by the way. 1587

514. The Spirit of Disobedience: Resisting the Charms of Fake Politics, Mindless Consumption, and the Culture of Total Work by Curtis White

Received: 5 April 2011
Started: 3 July 2012
Finished: 6 July 2012

I like Curtis White lots, and this started from a great premise — that most attitudes critical to capitalism, ie: the left/liberal tradition, deny their essential spirituality, which is also their downfall. This leads White to a rejection of Reason and Enlightenment thinking as a polar opposite of the religious mania that has taken over America, and he cites Thoreau most notably as being one who realised the soul as essential to dissent. The middle of this book mostly turns into an attack on contemporary America (written in 2006) and the environment-pillaging, me-first anti-Christian ethos pushed by both parties. It's not exactly anything new, and while compared to *Deer Hunting for Jesus* this is practically nuanced, I started to tire of 511 it. The examples drawn from pop culture (*Office Space* and *DaVinci Code*) were fun in a Zizek-like way, though less intense; I 135 wanted a bit more of that, actually. I definitely need to see more Fassbinder, though. The last section of the book consists of three interviews, which were not incredibly enjoyable — James Howard Kunstler being the most interesting. I felt like White really built this up as a major philosophical work and then got too distracted pointing out flaws in American society to really make a grand step forward intellectually, though there's a lot here to work with.

515. The Imperfectionists by Tom Rachman

Received: 26 July 2011
Started: 23 July 2012
Finished: 25 July 2012

I was genuinely impressed with *The Imperfectionists*, which deftly wove together an accessible ensemble narrative that did a lot of subtle and impressive things. Rachman is going to be somebody to follow; while I thought this was going to be fairly lightweight, by the end I was shocked at how much it managed to achieve in a relatively short page count. I liked how it took the obvious route of commenting on the death of traditional media, but by showing how much our own lives are intertwined with it all. The various characters come and go from each others' stories and it's a classic unreliable narrator device, just fragmented into multiple points of view. I now look forward to whatever he produces next.

516. End Zone by Don DeLillo
Received: 6 March 2012
Started: 28 July 2012
Finished: 30 July 2012
This is DeLillo's second novel and even though it was written 40 years ago, it seems like the game of American football hasn't changed that much. I loved this; I was shocked at how compelling the writing was, for DeLillo really knows what he's talking about when it comes to the sport, and the many levels of jargon and slang are perfectly suited to a writer like him. The idea that any college football players would talk like this — like Don DeLillo characters — is ridiculous — but this book seemed to be aiming at a humorous effect, with distinct jokes and situations which were mostly successful. The middle section of the book, describing the game itself, is set apart from the rest of the novel, and contains some of the most perfect sports writing I've ever encountered. The typical concerns of a DeLillo protagonist are evident — fear of death, nuclear obsession, etc. — but what makes this so remarkable is how DeLillo avoids the on-field comparisons to war, instead relegating that topic to a parallel narrative. This was a good read to anticipate the NFL season; it has some passages that are absolutely brilliant, yet tossed-off and lacking the weight of his later writing, which actually was pretty nice for once.

517. A Guide to the New Ruins of Great Britain by Owen Hatherley
Received: 13 February 2012
Started: 4 April 2012
Finished: 4 August 2012
Owen Hatherley writes from that British Marxist viewpoint which *The Guardian* used to represent — I guess he's one of the last dying vestiges of that paper's tradition. *A Guide to the New Ruins of Great Britain* emulates Pevsner's architecture guides but from the post-Blair perspective, mocking the failures of New Labour's aesthetic vision. Each chapter takes a specific city and chronicles some of the most egregious council estates, pedestrianized shopping districts, public buildings, and other such things. This was a long read and I put it down a few times, because while I had visited most cities in the book, I didn't have a deep familiarity with any of them besides Glasgow and Newcastle. The Glasgow chapter was the money shot for me, and it really accurately details the conflicts apparent within Glasgow architecture. Hatherley's tone is sharp, and his politics are unabashedly socialist (he frequently discusses public work commissioned with political intent, and has a clear passion for old-timey socialist workers' art and lore), but he is actually quite fair. There's grudging praise for a few buildings, and he doesn't beat a dead horse. Reading about architecture isn't my favourite way to experience it but his erudition, research, and interesting asides (into Newcastle politics, of the cultural makeup of Sheffield, and others) made this overall worth my time.

518. Portnoy's Complaint by Philip Roth
Received: 21 August 2012
Started: 22 August 2012
Finished: 25 August 2012
A copy of *Portnoy's Complaint* came into the shop, and since a friend and I were just talking about it, I decided to re-read it before putting it out for sale. The second time through I found myself feeling like I was reading it for the first time. I remembered it being hilarious, which it was, but I didn't really see it as such a horror story. This is truly a nightmare of a man trapped inside his own head, and while it's played for classic Jewish, psycho-sexual laughs, the amount of repression and anger is devastating. It's not a tragedy — it's enormously fun to read — but I'm impressed at how much of a double-edged sword it is, at points. Conflating sexual repression with Jewish identity is nothing new, but you gotta love parts where he's jacking in it bed while reading Freud. I should really read something else by Roth, but I'm strangely uninterested in the rest of his work.

519. Norwood by Charles Portis
Received: 18 August 2012
Started: 18 August 2012
Finished: 26 August 2012
This was a fun revisiting of Portis's first book, which I read in e-book form mostly on the plane. Portis really is a master of a comic style — his matter-of-fact depiction is what makes this so great, even more than the amusing characters and scenarios. Also good to read this en route to America cause it's about as American as writing can be

520. And Here's the Kicker: Conversations with 21 Top Humor Writers on their Craft by Mike Sacks
Received: 26 August 2012
Started: 26 August 2012
Finished: 26 August 2012
I'd wanted to read this for awhile and was delighted to find a copy online. This helped pass the 9 hour flight between Helsinki and Chicago. I generally love reading interviews — after all, that's what I'm going to be doing as a big project in March in Helsinki. This worked so well because it balanced contemporary comedy writers like Robert Smigel against people who wrote for Milton Berle. The current of comedy hasn't really changed — what rides through all the interviews is the level of professionalism and commitment to the art. Because this was about writing, rather than performing, it had a focus that made it worthwhile — a bit more honed than, say, an episode of *WTF*. Daniel Clowes was a nice addition too, and makes me realise how important the original run of *Eightball* is to me. I skimmed the tips for writers trying to break into comedy because I'm not particularly interested in that, but the rest of this was brilliant, and I'd happily dig through another volume.

521. Magic Hours: Essays on Creators and Creation by Tom Bissell
Received: 30 August 2012
Started: 30 August 2012
Finished: 1 September 2012
Bissell's latest book is a collection of his various short nonfiction pieces, usually for magazines. It profiles various creative types and is collected under a concept about creation, but this is a bit of a reach as it's fairly hit and miss. For as probing as the essays about Herzog or Jim Harrison may be, there are also long rants against Robert D. Kaplan. I like Bissell's writing so much that I really enjoyed this, and wished it was longer; luckily, I get to meet him in a few weeks and have that experience to look forward to. I was thrilled to discover a long essay about Tommy Wiseau and *The Room*, which was actually the highlight of the book for me — it probably explains the appeal of *The Room* better than anything else I've read, and better than I could realise it myself. I wanted more on David Foster Wallace but it was perfectly succinct and didn't belabour the point. And the essay on the videogame voiceover artist was surprisingly compelling.

740

522. Mainlines, Blood Feasts and Bad Taste: A Lester Bangs Reader by Lester Bangs
Received: 26 August 2012
Started: 26 August 2012
Finished: 18 September 2012
I downloaded the second Lester Bangs collection while hanging out in O'Hare airport, having forgotten pretty much everything inside in the intervening years. The first section of this is filled with some creative writing from Bangs — stream of consciousness stuff, mostly, describing some horrible experiences drunk at biker parties, etc. The music writing takes up most of this book and at the end there are some more essays about larger themes such as politics, society, and the future of art — but it's all pretty ramshackle. I had forgotten how amazing of a writer Bangs was — not just a masterful stylist, but his insight into music is incredible, often cutting to the core of things but managing to balance his opinions with genuine descriptive power. His canonisation in the pantheon of rock criticism is entirely justified, and he's far less 'gonzo' than I actually remembered (though still hilarious and entertaining). A good read throughout — there will be pieces in here I go back to, for sure.

523. Nineteen Seventy-Four: The Red Riding Quartet, Book One by David Peace
Received: 19 September 2012
Started: 19 September 2012
Finished: 21 September 2012
David Peace's Red Riding quartet is a highly-regarded set of grizzled crime fiction in the style of James Ellroy, so when a nice set of all four came into the shop I took a chance on the first one. I was very impressed — this was a compelling, nasty chunk of writing that was more Ellroy-like than I could have imagined. Peace writes in the same short, declarative style, with most paragraphs only one sentence; a minimalism for sure which serves to exacerbate the horror and misery of the tale. The Yorkshire atmosphere adds a level of roughness to everything, and while at times I felt like Peace went out of his way to tell the reader what was on the radio, etc. Whether I will read the others remains to be seen.

524. Mason & Dixon: A Novel by Thomas Pynchon
Received: (already owned)
Started: 6 March 2012
Finished: 2 October 2012
Once again, trying to get through this, the one Pynchon work I've never conquered. • Wow, it's finally over. It took me ages, though I would put it down for months, and I never travelled with it (which are the times I get the most reading done, on transit) because it was just too heavy. I read it mostly with the Pynchon wiki alongside but not entirely following it. Unfortunately, this slow method with so many breaks meant that I didn't really get the most out of this — I enjoyed it, greatly, but had trouble staying engaged after going 2 weeks without reading it and then coming back. I think this is one friend's favourite Pynchon novel and I can see why, but I can't say I'd have much appetite to read it again. There was so much to digest and this is not really the place for a proper analysis. Obviously the surveyors' lines and demarcations are the frame on which Pynchon hangs his wonderful, maddening ideas — thus reflecting man's continual efforts to understand and control the world. This world of Mason and Dixon is so modern, despite being 17th century — while he's not necessarily bothered by anachronisms, the language is really there for him to experiment with, and his erudition is of course unquestioned. But this is really a book about our contemporary life, showing the roots of it all and the lines (yeah?) that travelled into the 20th century. Certainly the aspects of American consumer life are present throughout — food, drink, clothing, and technology (for its time) — suggesting that the root of our modern passions is in the founding of America. And there's a lot about race mixed in as well, not just the ugly history of control (which is the eternal Pynchon theme — the preterite vs. elect, and power) but the benevolent flavours shown throughout by all the British, Indonesian, French, Chinese, Swedish, and American characters that pop up. Among all the adventures — the talking animals, saucy 17th century women, ghosts, etc. — is real warmth, almost as if Pynchon feels more affection for Mason and Dixon than any other characters in his other books. The artifice of this was ultimately so thick that it will scare me away from a re-read (whereas I'm really excited to have another run through the comic book that is *Against the*
243, 822 *Day*) but I'm so, so glad I pushed through. It's also interesting to think about this (and
109 *Infinite Jest*) being published as perhaps the last great pre-Internet encyclopaedic novels. Though 1997 was of course the Internet age, it was released before the Internet had saturated our lives — yet it emerged as this dense web of information, now naturally suited for things like wikis to be annotating it. That *Mason and Dixon* is primarily, to me, about our modern life and technology specifically, feels somewhat relevant, though I know that Pynchon didn't intend this to have anything to do with the Internet (in fact, it's easy to imagine him not even knowing about the Internet). Anyway, that's some food for thought and I hope I can remember to take some things from this. But what next?

525. Men in Space by Tom McCarthy
Received: 10 September 2012
Started: 21 September 2012
Finished: 3 October 2012
Tom McCarthy's second novel feels like it was put together from notes and written mostly before *Remainder*. It's lack of 370
focus is the central theme — disjointed, loose characters who occupy the 'space' that is Prague in the early 90s. Throughout the intrigue generated from various seedy plots intersecting, nothing jells, and no characters even emerge as more than mere sketches. Attempting to centre this around art shows McCarthy's own background, but it fails to reveal anything about the art world or Prague itself. An atmosphere is definitely created by writing around the story, not just writing the story, but by the final pages I was completely disinterested in anything that had gone before. I appreciate the effort — this feels like something I would have tried to write at some point — but it just doesn't work as a novel.

526. Birdseye Bristoe by Dan Zettwoch
Received: 12 September 2012
Started: 5 October 2012
Finished: 5 October 2012
Mixed feelings about *Birdseye Bristoe*. I like Zettwoch's work and this is the first really full long thing he's done, but I'm not sure if it added up to much for me. There's lots of what I like about him — getting lost in the details, the diagrams, the minutiae — and this was blended with a nice teenage, Midwestern sense of imagination, with pages such as the ice cream/soda drink explanation which are fantastic. But then when added together into a longer narrative, it felt a bit incoherent. The story was dull and I guess that wasn't the point, but

then why bother constructing it at all, if not to have something to hang the details on? The book was printed well and I like the ramshackle-yet-obsessive style he draws in, but as I'm starting to think about shelf space issues, I don't know if this one will survive the next purge.

527. Abandoned Cars by Tim Lane
Received: 12 September 2012
Started: 7 October 2012
Finished: 10 October 2012
Tim Lane's style is formally a bit like Dan Clowes, and he inhabits that same lost-noir sensibility that infused Clowes's earlier work, like the Lloyd Llewellyn series. But where early *Eightball* is submerged in biting, ironic humour, Lane's stuff is much more serious. The ugly faces and monotonous urban landscapes in this collection are portrayed with an almost wistful longing rather than a misanthropic rant. I'm reminded a little bit of the comic in the liner notes of Sun City Girls' *Dante's Dis-*
316 *neyland Inferno* — a tough-talking, dark edge of the bar kind of male misery. The little sketches and vignettes of *Abandoned Cars* are interlaced with weird one-page portraits, characters who never seem to go anywhere and who we are supposed to draw our interpretations from out of the barest of visual clues. The recurring autobiographical piece about jumping a train for no apparent reason is the heart of the collection, as Lane finally turns his lens inward and puts forth something young, yearning and honest (though in hindsight). In the end I wasn't disappointed that I read *Abandoned Cars* but I'm not sure I would recommend it, or ever go back to it.

528. Big Questions by Anders Nilsen
Received: 12 September 2012
Started: 28 October 2012
Finished: 30 October 2012
Big Questions is a real masterpiece of the comic form; a true achievement, and a surprise as well. Being familiar with only his *Monologues for the Coming Plague* and a few odds and ends, I thought of his work as more conceptual anti-everything absurdist stuff. But *Big Questions* is a beautiful work of American pastoral comics. The big questions aren't really obvious here — what I thought was going to be 600 pages of birds talking philosophically had so many less words than I expected. Nilsen has no problem ripping off 20 pages of amazing wordless images, and some of the rhythms, particularly the more violent bits, were brilliantly executed. There's a lot of themes at play here, but innocence is an overwhelming one; what is known and not known, by not just the finches of the narrative but by the idiot character, makes a story that is more unsaid than said. Such a simple world is not easy to execute over this duration but Nilsen rises to the challenge — there's a confidence throughout, as well as a mastery of the art form that really surprised me as I thought his style was fairly crude and minimal before. As long-form graphic novels go, this might be one of the best I've ever read — I'm glad I took it as a full-on assault here instead of breaking it up over ten years of individual issues.

529. Fear and Loathing in America : The Brutal Odyssey of an Outlaw Journalist by Hunter S. Thompson
Received: 3 October 2012
Started: 8 October 2012
Finished: 31 October 2012
I may have enjoyed this more than any other Hunter S. Thompson I've ever read. Being his collected letters from some very vital years in his career, there's a lot of action even though he was too busy to write many letters during some of the more active times in the book — the '72 campaign and his own mayoral attempt. The honesty is astounding — and even though half of this book is HST arguing about money, it's pretty amazing to see how he lived and think about the life of a freelance writer. His relationship with Acosta plays out here — it had really deteriorated by the end of Acosta's life, and the last few letters back and forth are quite sad, both of them shouting at each other over potential movie rights to *Fear and Loathing in Las Vegas*. The fan letters are great, as are his friendships with George McGovern, Pat Buchanan and Jimmy Carter. 241, 292, 428, 526 I suspect these are carefully edited because there isn't actually much about his personal life — his wife lost a baby and that's mentioned, but written around, and there's only passing mentions of his son (though a few letters to his mother and brothers, at least early on). The one annoying thing here was how heavily footnoted this was, with 90% of the footnotes being unnecessary because I already know who Tom Wolfe and Henry Kissinger are. But editorial complaints aside, this was awesome and I'm curious now to read all of the pieces he wrote during this time for various magazines, etc.

530. X'ed Out by Charles Burns
Received: 12 September 2012
Started: 3 November 2012
Finished: 3 November 2012
I'm so glad that Burns is back with some new work, except it's going to be a long and excruciating process waiting for this all to happen. *X'ed Out* definitely continues the vibe of *Black Hole* as there is extremely fucked up imagery crossed with a youth-gone-wild aesthetic; this gets into territory of the unreal that *Black Hole* only began to hint at, and I think we're in for a wild ride. When reading this I forgot how gross and uneasy Burns's work makes me feel, but that's one of the main draws. The second volume came out a few days after I got this so at least I can devour that soon.

531. Birchfield Close by Jon McNaught
Received: 12 September 2012
Started: 4 November 2012
Finished: 4 November 2012
Another rave recommendation from a friend, this took only a few minutes to read but lingered with me a long time after. McNaught's pointillist style is restricted to a two-tone colour palette and this works in almost purely abstract narrative, with a rhythm that is utterly captivating. The small repeating boxes feels like an influence from Chris Ware but I think there's something much more European at work here. There's something almost mystical here, and I'm really bummed that this copy got somewhat water damaged during the trip home because the print fetishist in me adores this package. I should stay up on what McNaught does; he's based in Bristol and feels like a singular voice in the comics world.

532. The Man Who Grew His Beard by Olivier Schrauwen
Received: 12 September 2012
Started: 6 November 2012
Finished: 8 November 2012
I really dug Schrauwen's collection because his style is pretty unique and the stories gave just enough to be thought-provoking without being overly obvious. Visually, Schrauwen's work recalls the *Little Nemo* comics from 100 years ago, but also makes me thing of Gauguin. The works deal with imagination and the act of creation itself, and can be as austere or psychedelic as necessary. The final chapter felt like the end of an episode of *Xavier: Renegade Angel*, though there's not much humour or absurdity — instead it's very cerebral, and obtuse while somehow maintaining playfulness.

533. Exotica by David Toop
Received: (already owned)
Started: 5 November 2012
Finished: 15 November 2012
This had been in my parents' basement forever and I brought it back to Estonia figuring I could unload it in the shop. I started reading it and got sucked in by the first few chapters, which are an insanely bizarre blend of fiction and fantasy but in David Toop's style of writing about music — resembling the semi-academic tone of British music writing found in *The Wire*, but with a flair for mysticism. This style disappears as the meat of the book begins — a dissection of the idea of the 'exotic' in music, mostly looking at Les Baxter, Martin Denny, and mid-20th century American pop culture that borrows from Hawaii, Polynesia, etc. The research is good and the tone stays creative throughout, with a constantly shifting focus that is musical itself in feel. But it's only at the end when this more experimental tone returns, and only then for brief passages before being interrupted by appendix-style chapters about American blues and the King of Thailand's clarinet record from the 60s. This is really two different books jammed together, but I wish Toop had been able to follow his more colourful impulses even if it would have been at the expense of coherence. Also, this has a bunch of interviews in the middle with artists as diverse as Nusrat Fateh Ali Khan, Ornette Coleman, Bill Laswell, and the Boo-Ya Tribe, and none of the interviews really do much to support the book and should have been excised. Still, this has vastly increased my appreciation of Toop and I think I should check out his more recent books, particularly the last one which sounds great.

534. The Rings of Saturn by W.G. Sebald
Received: 8 November 2012
Started: 16 November 2012
Finished: 22 November 2012
Somehow, I've gone this long without reading Sebald. There was an essay excerpted in my course at Glasgow that dealt with the German repression of the Second World War, but that's about it. This was marked down super cheap at Apollo and I took a chance on it, as the premise sounded like

my kind of thing despite my general fear of post-war Germanic literature as being "too heavy". Well, this was amazing. This was exactly the kind of book I love — something that is between genres, not really literature at all but a rambling travel essay that delves into obscure bits of history. Some of the digressions are quite arcane — silk farming in France in the 1700s, for example — but others are better known, like the story of young Joseph Conrad. It's really personal, as if he's writing about his experiences through the lens of these historical figures — and I think the blurb on the back put it best when it called the book "long-distance mental travel". As someone who's been missing the UK a lot lately, the East Anglia seaside walks were lovely and I also loved how freely associating it was — the historical narratives were often indistinguishable from Sebald's own voice, an interesting technique that really pulls you into things. I'm probably going to read everything he wrote now.

535. A Naked Singularity: A Novel by Sergio De La Pava
Received: 24 July 2012
Started: 22 November 2012
Finished: 29 November 2012
The much-heralded *A Naked Singularity* was pretty gripping — I tore through the last 300 pages in one night, unable to put it down, not wanting it to end. The acceleration towards a conclusion (even if it's inconclusive) is unsatisfying not in a traditional narrative sense, but because it feels so rushed and I wanted so much more. I'm sure this is getting tons of comparisons to David Foster Wallace, and it's hard to deny the influence. This is most obvious in the long conversations, which veer into irrelevant digressions yet still contain the honesty that Wallace's writing does. But de la Pava is not as careful or calculating as Wallace, often letting bizarre jokes take over (which aren't always successful) and not creating as complete of a portrait of the real/surreal/hyper-real/whatever. I read this being compared to *The Wire* somewhere too, and certainly the machinations of the criminal justice system are complex and the question of morality is every bit at the centre of this book as it is in the TV series. But while *The Wire* attempts to indict the entire American society as culpable in the destruction of itself, *A Naked Singularity* stays with one character. While there are certainly pointed, political moments in this book (the war on drugs is not treated kindly, nor is the death penalty), it's Casi's own compassion here as the heart and soul, and what compelled me to keep reading. I would maybe quibble that Casi's mental dissolution and his complicity in the caper are not really connected to anything concrete — I think de la Pava is vaguely suggesting that a combination of many cultural and financial things are at play, such as workplace pressure, television/popular culture, and/or romantic emotional duress. Regardless, this is a fantastic, stunning debut novel and I anxiously await whatever he produces next.

536. In Search of the Blues by Marybeth Hamilton
Received: 14 September 2012
Started: 30 November 2012
Finished: 2 December 2012
A friend loaned me this book which I thought was going to be about the lives of early/seminal blues musicians. Instead I found a fascinating chronicling of the white scholars, collectors and enthusiasts responsible for popularising blues music in the mid-20th century — so it's a book about the meta-blues. This was actually far more interesting to me, especially as the false quest for 'authenticity' was even more prevalent then. The anthropologists, archivists and collectors described here are all fascinating and Hamilton does a really good amount of research into their lives, and most importantly their attitudes. Many of their approaches were insanely racist or at least problematic, and even in the 40s it's interesting to see how they dealt with these charges. The final chapter, on fanatic blues collector James McKuen, was probably the most interesting to me because it made me think about the subculture my father was part of during his teenage years, though off by a decade or so. Not nearly as much biographical info was available on McKuen as, say, John Lomax, so it's a bit shorter than the other chapters and ends abruptly, but it's great anyway.

537. Wait Until Spring, Bandini by John Fante
Received: 30 November 2012
Started: 3 December 2012
Finished: 9 December 2012
The only Fante I read before was *Ask the Dust*, probably when I was 16 or 17, but I always had a soft spot for him in my mind. Despite the fact he influenced Bukowski so much (which isn't his fault) I loved *Ask the*

Dust and now, 16 years later, was similarly impressed by *Wait Until Spring, Bandini*. As I'm currently applying for Italian citizenship through my ancestry, it was timely and topical to read about Italian-American bricklayers in America in the first half of the century. Fante's style is clean and simple, clearly why he was an influence on the Beats (or maybe the missing link between Hemingway and them), and it made the perspective shifts between different family members feel coherent. The juxtaposition of adult and adolescent drama worked, but it was really the writing — stark, strong, and balanced on an emotional edge — that carried this through. I should check out the rest of the quartet some day.

538. Both Flesh and Not: Essays by David Foster Wallace
Received: 13 December 2012
Started: 14 December 2012
Finished: 14 December 2012
I thought this last collection of DFW non-fiction would be scraping the bottom of the barrel, but it wasn't, and when I saw it in the shop I couldn't resist. Besides, I'm sure they'll find more stuff out there and we'll get the true barrel-scraping in the near future. About 1/3 of this I had read before, such as the great *Terminator 2* essay and the Federer piece, which is considered his non-fiction masterpiece though I'm not sure why (it's excellent, but short, and I think he's written a lot better). One of the longest pieces in here was a detailed analysis of *Wittgenstein's Mistress* which was the high point for me, as I've become (over time) a massive fan of Markson's novel; reading DFW's take was actually thrilling. And it's not often that I would describe reading a book review as a thrilling act. The usual bout of sadness I feel when reading him now wasn't there, not just because these were mostly light pieces, but because I think I'm at the point now where I can enjoy his work without being overcome by that. The section about grammar was actually helpful to me, and the short piece on sexuality in the time of AIDS was possibly the most insightful thing he ever wrote about human relations. The only essay that dragged a bit for me was the look at math-based fiction, but 14 out of 15 is a pretty winning rate.

539. The Sweet Smell of Psychosis by Will Self
Received: 23 December 2012
Started: 26 December 2012
Finished: 26 December 2012
Always been curious to read Will Self, and this was in the shop and stupidly short (I think I read the whole thing in about a half-hour). But not much to say; this fable about decadent London media magazine/cokehead types didn't speak to me in the slightest. The lusty language (which I think Self is known for) wasn't particularly creative and if anything, he writes like a man who hates sex. Nothing ventured though, so nothing lost.

540. As She Climbed Across the Table by Jonathan Lethem
Received: 24 October 2012
Started: 26 December 2012
Finished: 11 January 2013
I was very impressed with this, which I started reading very slowly (sad, but I have given no time for books the past few weeks) and then devoured in sudden rampage. Knowing as much about Lethem as I do, I expected this to be more Philip K Dick style sci-filings, and certainly there was a Dickish (?) core here. But the prose unfolded to be an introspective, yearning book about lost love that was more drenched with the personal than at first glance. Some passages reminded me of DeLillo, but the warm, beautiful DeLillo I rarely can find. The quirkiness that the opening chapters hinted at quickly falls away and this turns into something painful, yet hopeful.

541. Gringos by Charles Portis
Received: 9 December 2012
Started: 9 December 2012
Finished: 19 January 2013
Re-reading *Gringos* was somewhat disappointing, even though I think it's a great book and in some ways, Portis's greatest accomplishment. But it's certainly his least humorous, and I really do value the humour in Portis's writing first and foremost. Some of the descriptive passages were stunning, though, and he managed to create really complex characters with few words, and all filtered through such a distinct first-person narrative. I re-read this because there's a new collection of his miscellaneous writings available but it will be some time before I order a copy (or find it locally); thus, I'm trying to revisit the books I read some years ago. I don't think I was in the right mindset

for this, however — I've been too preoccupied to dive into books lately, which is a shame and something I hope to correct when the clouds clear.

542. Stop-Time: A Memoir by Frank Conroy
Received: 27 July 2011
Started: 24 January 2013
Finished: 26 January 2013
Conroy's memoir is fantastic; he wrote it while fairly young, so it covers life until he began college. As someone who thinks (often) about autobiography being a potential trap, Conroy managed to write something beautiful as well as compelling, despite having nothing particularly eventful in his upbringing. This is no *Heartbreaking Work of Staggering Genius* — though there are some complications, such as his father dying young and disharmony between his stepfather and mother, Conroy was not a particularly troubled child. But he weaves a beautiful portrait from episodes, presented in an irregular sequences, of adventures such as becoming a yo-yo champion to smoking cigarettes in his boarding school. The most compelling passage is in the centre, where he runs away, attempting to hitchhike to Florida, at fifteen; I realised I love stories where people go on the run without understanding why and then return. The appearance of serious mental illness in his sister, coming at the very end of the book, opens up the possibility of some real darkness, but then it ends — leaving a strange, hanging feeling. A hangover of innocent adolescence, perhaps?

543. Insurmountable Simplicities: Thirty-nine Philosophical Conundrums by Roberto Casati & Achille Varzi
Received: 24 July 2012
Started: 4 February 2013
Finished: 5 February 2013
This was a cheap pickup from the discount rack but proved to be rather disappointing because I expected it to be thought-provoking in a completely different manner to the way that it was. These 'philosophical inquiries' were little vignettes about logic, contradictions and paradoxes — mind games, and hypothetical situations, that were sort of fun at first but dragged as it went on. Most of these were so abstract that they resembled a child's riddles, and the interstitial excursions into 'philosophy' were so brief that even though I wanted pop-philosophy, it wasn't enough. This made me want to re-read *Metamagical Themas* instead, which has been sitting on my shelf unopened for the past 15 years or so. So maybe it's time for that; this, however, will be relegated to the sell pile.

544. Exiled from Almost Everywhere by Juan Goytisolo
Received: 28 January 2013
Started: 28 January 2013
Finished: 7 February 2013
A short, intense read, Goytisolo's book is an indictment of the current times, attempting to reconcile radical politics with electronic culture. Goytisolo does this through a series of short, attacking chapters, one or two pages each, outlining a loose narrative about a terrorist consciousness that inhabits various physical and virtual beings. The story isn't important, but the poetic renderings of this zeitgeist are quite remarkable, especially for an older writer. This is more than just a rant at the narcissism of Internet users; it's a genuinely dark look at an inevitable future, using literature as the platform on which it can riff. I liked this a lot, even though it didn't matter when it ended (it could have easily gone on 300 more pages); the short bursts were like gunfire, echoing the violence underneath everything (and also aping short-attention-span formats such as blog posts).

545. Nomad's Hotel: Travels in Time and Space by Cees Nooteboom
Received: 31 December 2009
Started: 7 February 2013
Finished: 9 February 2013
I was very impressed with Nooteboom's approach to travel writing, which comes from a very literary tradition. Nooteboom is much more known as a novelist, but this collection of shorter travel pieces, mostly for magazines, spans over thirty years and covers a variety of topics from the classical history of Venice to a potrait of the Gambia in 1975. One complaint is that I had to flip to the end of each piece to see when it was published, which affected how I read things. The look at Iran just before the revolution was striking and really made me wonder 'what if'; the pieces on Mali and the Gambia were more interesting to me than his writings about Europe. Nooteboom reflects on a lot of heavy topics here — the weight of war, the effects of colonialism, and the isolation of Western Ireland; it was travel writing unlike anyone else I've ever read, determined almost like William

Vollmann but with the same lust for living that's found in Theroux or the other greats.

546. Logicomix: An Epic Search for Truth by Apostolos Doxiadis
Received: 31 December 2009
Started: 10 February 2013
Finished: 10 February 2013
Trying to clear off my shelves particularly of unread (or rarely revisited) graphic novels, I tore through this in a day. This highly acclaimed look at the story of 20th century logical thought is built around a fictitious lecture by Bertrand Russell, who serves autobiographically as the main character in this chronicle. The writers and artists frequently insert themselves into the story, showing how they are arguing about the creation of the story, providing a meta-element that adds nothing to the work except for momentarily transporting us to the present day. Drawing parallels with the *Oresteia* is a nice touch but I found it a bit clumsy, almost like a desperate attempt to incorporate Greek traditions into this. This was well done and a pleasant read, but ultimately nothing special.

547. Paradise by Donald Barthelme
Received: (already owned)
Started: 9 February 2013
Finished: 10 February 2013
This is one of Barthelme's last novels and it seems to be a compendium of various devices that he experimented with throughout his career. The chapters are short and stylistically diverse, feeling at times like you are reading *Forty Stories* but with an overarching plot throughout. This effect is stunning. The story — an architect (no doubt influenced by Barthelme's own father) in his mid-50s invites three sexy women to live with him, where he proceeds to live the typical male fantasy. But there's little prurience here, with Barthelme instead highlighting the interactions between the women, the dreams of all four, and the protagonist's struggles with his ex-wife and 18-year old daughter. This is completely a novel of the 1980s too, filled with references to various cultural and political events at the time. This milieu is essential to *Paradise* for it allows Barthelme to critique American culture, drawing parallels between material desire, career ambitions, and human sexuality. And it's all a bit ho-hum, which is the point. Everything is honest between Simon and the three women, and they are given full personalities throughout the book, and this seeming fantasy proves to be rather dull; when they leave, it's almost a non-event, a return to zero. The most significant plot point in the book, i think, is when Simon gets involved with another woman briefly — a poet, with red hair, who seems to symbolise the 'mature' relationship that is expected of him. But it too fades into nothingness, a landscape of the everyday that is not dark or bleak, but instead just neutral. It seems like Barthelme's argument is that fulfilling desire is ultimately disappointing, but he even does this without bashing one over the head with it. There are verbal tricks galore — conversations taken out of context, Q&A sessions, the usual Don B tricks — and yet it avoids the pure absurdity of his early writing and manages to really probe the middle-aged male mind through it's stylistic excesses — perhaps the truest accomplishment of this wonderful novel.

548. Dead Cities: And Other Tales by Mike Davis
Received: 28 October 2009
Started: 10 February 2013
Finished: 21 February 2013
What I thought was a book-length study of urban decay turned out to be a loose collection of various pieces by Davis, written throughout the 90s and published in 2002 (with a preface written about 9/11). Davis is such a brilliant writer that I stayed engaged through most of these pieces even if they didn't interest me, but the title was misleading — only the middle section of this book really talks about the death of cities — but then, "and other tales" is the subtitle so I should have looked more closely. Some interesting essays for sure, particularly one about the environmental effects of cold war weapons testing in the American west (and a group of activist photographers dedicated to illustrating these atrocities). The look at Compton, CA is disturbing, as one can imagine, yet fascinating to me, especially as I've been away from America for so long and I have forgotten really what inner city drama is like. But I ended up skimming a few of the longer essays, as there is only so much interest I have in the politics of Los Angeles — and the last section of the book is quite technical in the realm of geology, which is theoretically intriguing (I didn't know Davis had that in him) yet not something I was feeling like I could invest my time in.

549. Fear of Music: Why People Get Rothko But Don't Get Stockhausen by David Stubbs
Received: 21 February 2013
Started: 23 February 2013
Finished: 23 February 2013
This book addresses a topic that I talk about constantly with others who straddle both worlds, and I was looking forward to some further insight into the issue. Stubbs is affiliated with *The Wire* and this shows somewhat through his writing, but he's very competent and injects a nice bit of his own personality into this. But the only part of this book actually worth reading was the last 20 pages, the 'Conclusions' section. The first 100 pages are just a recap of the 20th century, attempting to weave the story of music and the story of visual art into a double-helix, but of course in 100 pages he's got to be choosy, which makes the whole thing frustrating. But I don't need a 100-page recap about the history of experimental music and art; I want to explore the reasons why people's willingness to be open and tolerant ends when it comes to sound and music. The conclusions aren't anywhere beyond what I've already discussed with others — the lack of academic criticism, the difficulty in monetising music, and the issue of mass-replication vs. the original. One thing he didn't talk about is the role that music has in shaping youth culture; I think this is key, at least in my own upbringing — musical taste defined our friends, fashion and lifestyle choices (or at least for me). He tries to talk about the difficulty of 'unpleasant' sounds as being unpalatable for many people, and the amount of effort involved in understanding contemporary experimental music, and there's no way around this issue — it's a fact. But the deeper reason for that might be that music is sold to us as a leisure-based commodity, and art is not; no one (except a weirdo like me) is going to put on Stockhausen as background music while cooking. Or in a perfect world everyone would — or in a perfect world, maybe there would be no background music? But I'm digressing; I was really disappointed by this, as I was hoping for case studies, interviews with different viewpoints, models, theories etc. — maybe that's a book that I'm going to have to write myself. The actual printing of this book was a mess too — Zero Books seems like an intriguing imprint but this had the feel of a rush job, with very inconsistent punctuation/formatting and pagination.

550. Isle of the Dead by Gerhard Meier
Received: 12 February 2013
Started: 26 February 2013
Finished: 2 March 2013
This was in the shop and was Dalkey Archive and slim, so I borrowed it. I'm finding myself drawn to Germanic literature now — though this is Swiss, it's Swiss-German and written in the same placid, contemplative style as Sebald's *Rings of Saturn*, though this was clearly intended to be read as fiction. Plot-wise, nothing happens except for two men walking through a town, one talking constantly and the other listening. That's a good enough premise for me; Meier fills these one hundred pages with memories, thoughts about nature and mortality, and the history of art — it's fiction as a frame/excuse to hang ideas on, not unlike David Markson though much, much more traditional in construct. Throughout there is something celebratory, yet melancholic, about the world the two characters live in; some parts are just beautiful and others seem to be meaningless digressions. But perhaps this instability of communication is one of the things Meier was trying to illustrate. I don't know, but I was grateful for the experience. I've been reading in a bit of a blaze lately but this is one that I think I'll hold onto and revisit when I am feeling more attuned to it's genteel pace.

534

551. To Skin a Cat by Thomas McGuane
Received: 12 February 2013
Started: 2 March 2013
Finished: 4 March 2013
There are so many of these 80s McGuane Vintage Contemporary paperbacks kicking about, and they're full of rewards. These short stories were written in the 80s as he was settling into Montana and making the transition away from a comic Americana specialist into the more, I hate to say "mature" but for lack of a better term, yeah, mature writing. There's still a lot of laughs in here, manifested more as a joy de vivre than straight-up guffaws. And there's a lot of serious matter too, dealing with teenage pregnancies, alcoholism, and class issues galore. The ghost of Portis's *Norwood* seems to be living in the pages of 'Dogs', and the final story ('To Skin A Cat') is epic, uproarious in its momentum, and with a real darkness underneath the adventure. I'm on a bit of a short story kick lately so this was perfect medicine.

156, 519

552. The Terrible Threes by Ishmael Reed
Received: 20 September 2008
Started: 3 March 2013
Finished: 5 March 2013
The sequel to *The Terrible Twos*, *Threes* 346 is set in the late 90s (though written in the late 80s) and takes the dystopian American vision of *Twos* a step further. There's a lot of plot here and less exaggerated ranting and nonsense, which made this pass quickly. If you want to imagine an America where Reagan's presidency was viewed retroactively as "left-wing", this is the book for you. Reed's tongue is sharp and his wit is rampant, though given how things actually unfolded, it's an odd parallel reality — Reed vastly underestimates the culture's obsession with celebrity and the media seems to be portrayed in an almost benign manner, but hey, I don't expect him to have predicted the Internet or anything like that. Technology takes a backseat here, making this more like *Infinite Jest* than what actually 109 happened, but he's correct in his vision of "post-race" America. And the point of this was not to predict the future but to create a sharp, edgy fantasy that reflect upon the history of America's political underbelly since the Kennedy assassination. Great stuff; not quite *Mumbo Jumbo* in terms of 114 scope/impact, but what could be?

553. Koula by Menis Koumandareas
Received: 8 June 2010
Started: 5 March 2013
Finished: 6 March 2013
This very short read (it would only about 50 pages if it wasn't double-spaced) follows a short affair between a middle-aged Greek woman and 21 year old sleazy type. It's an emotional window into middle-aged femininity, as written by a middle-aged Greek male, and wasn't the most exciting thing to partake in. What was best about it was the deep sadness of what wasn't written about — the surely horrible monotony of her marriage and family life, and the drudgery of her job, which makes the young man seem like such an escape. I guess this was a pretty good portrait into how we project what we want to project onto people, written with realistic and sensitive language — but this is not my type of book (I only grabbed it in the first place cause it was published by Dalkey Archive).

554. Assisted Living by Nikanor Teratologen
Received: 17 January 2013
Started: 10 February 2013
Finished: 7 March 2013
I have encountered plenty of shocking, transgressive writing — Burroughs, *Fuck* zine by Randall Phillip, Peter Sotos — but Teratologen's book probably takes the prize. I like extreme things, and his use of language is fresh and inventive (at least in the translation of this Northern Swedish dialect, which is apparently the best thing about the original) which kept me from getting bored. After about 250 pages it started to feel like a bit of a chore, because the constant anal rapes and murders of children weren't shocking anymore— but then it finally ended on a great epilogue, so I'm glad I put myself through it. Shock value alone can't carry a text, but there was something mystical about the weird Scandinavian backwoods created here — no doubt meant as some investigation into the idea of evil, done in a far more entertaining manner than, say, *Twin Peaks*. This might also be one of those books that I read just to be proud that I did.

555. The Book of Leviathan by Peter Blegvad
Received: (already owned)
Started: 12 March 2013
Finished: 12 March 2013
I filled a box with my very favourite books to loan to a friend while I will be travelling — "The Fail Selection". This process, of course, made me want to re-read everything, but on the train down to Tartu I only had time to revisit this. It's actually been some years since I read this cover-to-cover, and immersion works well for Blegvad's weird, dreamy world. So many of these strips are just illustrated puns, and I never before realised how much the style of the strip affected its overall impact on me. In the hands of a classic American newspaper cartoonist, a lot of these would be nothing more than a one-off laugh, but with Blegvad's cerebral dressing, it attains some higher plane. Having quotes from classical literature accenting the jokes helps — rather than being showoffy, it forces one to think deeper about language, image, and meaning. I don't think I can sound too overboard with my passion for this collection — I only wish the rest of the Leviathan strips could be made available somehow, because the introduction claims there are much darker ones left out of the book, with

only the intro chapter here representing that, and while there's not as much to laugh at there, the visual style and use of comic form for experimenting in perception and representation is remarkable. I also realise how extremely rooted in the English language this is, and how it might not be very enjoyable for someone who has English as a second language, even if they are a fluent speaker.

556. Artificial Hells: Participatory Art and the Politics of Spectatorship by Claire Bishop
Received: 26 February 2013
Started: 5 March 2013
Finished: 19 March 2013
I dropped way too much money ordering this from Amazon because I felt like it would be a good time to read this, at this relatively 'low' point in my own work (or at least, a time of transition and reflection). This is Bishop's history and critique of social practice, which was odd to read for me since I've been considering myself to work in this field for a few years now, yet I know little (or nothing) of its history/theory. I admit that I went into this defensively, because I knew Bishop was going to come from the art theory angle and probably attack the projects that I found the most inspiring. Actually, there was little in here that I was familiar with, as the meat of the book is a history of participation in art, going back to 1917, with long sections on Argentinian and Czech entries from the 1960s through late 1980s — most of which was fascinating to read. But it's really only the first and last sections of this book that were what I wanted, which were her analysis of contemporary participatory art and also her problems with it. I am constantly saying that I don't care about art and I don't know anything about art, which is only true when compared to the people that I spend most of my time with. My own desire to work as far away from the art world as possible is what I always saw as a strength of our work here — it ideologically allows me to feel like I am actually making connections between people and affecting some sort of small change, however minuscule. 'Preaching to the converted' and all that goes with that phrase, well, it's something that is always on my mind and probably overtly steers my efforts. In Bishops's book, I didn't even reach the end of the first chapter before I had this completely thrown in my face, as she points out that without a strong critical aspect of 'art' in a project, it risks being merely a 'social project'. This would be all well and good with me, except she points out that the Neoliberal governments (particularly under New Labour) are only interested in supporting 'art' that has a measurable social impact, and therefore there is no more room for so-called 'pure' artistic research. I have come to only be interested in art that looks outward, which I realise now means I follow the social critique of capitalism, rather than the artistic one (as defined by Chiapello and Boltanski). But Bishop has made me think that my approach runs the risk of being exploited by the same structures I am hoping to challenge, and at the expense of the innovative art that has given me such a reason to exist. I've been struggling for a long time with how to balance these tendencies — wanting to connect vs. wanting to experiment with boundaries, etc. — so I supposed this conclusion wasn't far off anyway. But yeah, that's Chapter One.

Luckily I didn't have my world rocked too much more after this. As I said, most of the book was a history of art that I wasn't familiar with, some of which I found interesting, but with descriptions of many projects that I did not take an interest in. She spends a whole chapter describing artists such as Santiago Sierra, whom I generally find interesting, but talking about how, to use him as an example, he hires people to be part of his artworks. She considers this to be 'participation' in some way (and I do not), and overall I probably only found about 30% of the projects described here as being relevant to what interests me, what I consider 'social practice'. Additionally, the sphere of live art and performance is only touched upon lightly, yet I think it may be the most relevant area where participation reaches the highest form of the 'participation ladder' (a great anonymous graphic from the 60s in the back of the book, which I have to scan). Only towards the end did she begin to tackle the pedagogical element that has crept into recent art, citing some precedents by Beuys before getting into three contemporary examples, none of which sounded remotely interesting or relevant to what I consider to be participation-based culture. (Though I do think Thomas Hirschorn is mostly fascinating). She also avoids getting into trans-disciplinary work entirely, making this disclaimer at the beginning, which is probably where my interests mostly lie. She also says in the beginning that she's going to ignore relational aesthetics entirely, without really explaining why. So in the end, I'm not really convinced by anything in here enough to re-think my game plan; or maybe I'm discovering that I really am not an artist, but a social programmer (or something like that). This world that I occupy space in (however unknown and irrelevant Ptarmigan may be) is a parallel to Bishop's (possibly more intellectually rigorous) art world, with some overlap which I am mostly grateful for. My world desperately needs a history and critique, but I'm too involved to have the perspective. I'm happy to have read this and will likely cite it repeatedly as I try to figure my shit out over the next few months.

557. How I Became One of the Invisible by David Rattray

Received: 26 February 2013
Started: 19 March 2013
Finished: 25 March 2013

Rattray was a friend and inspiration to Chris Kraus — she mentions him frequently in *I Love Dick*, and I had noted down a quote 483 from him, 'Love can become a holding pattern for tattered ends of memory, thought and experience' which had stayed with me for some time. I ordered this from Amazon, and it's pretty much out of print and I had to wait almost a month to get it; when it arrived, I found it was curiously laid out in a fairly hard-to-read typeface in what seemed like unusually cheap printing for Semiotext(e). Anyway. This started off in a fury, being a memoir of his early drug-fuelled days with Alden Van Buskirk and other marginal beat figures and lowlifes. As an alternate history of American bohemia, I've never read anything like it; these first two chapters were incredibly immersive. This era of the American avant-garde — in-between the beats and the hippies — is of great interest to me, and reminded me in parts of Brautigan's *A Confederate* 256, 558 *General from Big Sur*. But after this, the book changed into a rather varied collection of essays, largely about poetry, which made the overall book a bit discordant. Most of these pieces were great — plenty on Artaud and translation, with rich and esoteric references throughout. Rattray's insight into poetry is unique, and I really had my interest piqued in Émile Nelligan and Rene Crevel (who I have a book of 628 sitting unread here for a decade), staying engaged with essays on them (and their curious lives) despite not having actually read their work. By the end of the book, it swings back towards the mystical-outsider perspective for the eponymous piece, and when taken as a whole, I'd say this book often left me breathless, despite it's uneven nature. Why this isn't more well known or in print is beyond me — well, I suppose the content is of marginal interest to most people. I'm now in the mood to read more memoirs from these times; perhaps *Ringolevio* is next. 559

558. A Confederate General from Big Sur, Dreaming of Babylon, and the Hawkline Monster by Richard Brautigan

Received: 4 September 2012
Started: 28 March 2013
Finished: 29 March 2013

Really just bought this to re-read *Confederate General* though maybe I should try these other two, which I read in high school and don't remember fondly. • *Confederate General* was delightful a second time, as it's really a wistful buddy story/memoir that takes great pains to showcase its alternative way of life. The attitudes towards women aren't particularly progressive, but I tend to forgive things from this time period, especially as it really helps to construct the character of the narrator and the friend. Brautigan has a way of writing through things; of casting an absolutely absurd image that is provocative and hilarious, but not without something sublime. I see a lot in common with David Berman's best Silver Jews lyrics; it's strange I never made this connection before. For a book where nothing really happens much, there's a lot going on here. The final chapters portray a magic lackadaisical lifestyle and the absurd multiple endings are a precursor to *Trout Fishing*. 213 Glad to have been to this literary Big Sur again, especially during this long, long winter.

559. Ringolevio: A Life Played for Keeps by Emmett Grogan

Received: 27 March 2013
Started: 27 March 2013
Finished: 2 April 2013

Emmett Grogan's "autobiography" was probably more than 50% outright lies but contained one obvious truth — that Grogan was a totally fucked up and complicated human being whose own account of his life doesn't even attempt to resolve the contradictions. This was written in a gonzo, almost primitive style that starts in the early 1950s and doesn't touch down until the late 60s, throughout which young Emmett steals, murders, fucks and extorts his way around the world, before spending the second half of the book dealing with the Haight-Ashbury scene and all its fallout. He somehow manages to boost and take down the 60s at the same time, and his quest for anonymity and against publicity is clearly just a complicated ego manifestation. It's good to see that someone was being critical of the youth movements at that time, even while operating from inside them, but unfortunately this critique doesn't get too deep. I'm curious to really understand what his beef with Abbie Hoffman was, but I guess we'll never know since Grogan OD'd in the late 70s. I enjoyed every page of this.

560. Everything and More: A Compact History of Infinity by David Foster Wallace
Received: 3 August 2011
Started: 2 April 2013
Finished: 4 April 2013
This, the final book-length work of DFW's that I hadn't read, was a joy to experience, like all of his non-fiction. I was scared off for years because, let's face it, this is barely for non-maths geeks, but maybe because I'm such a fan, I found it mostly accessible. The man obviously had a gift for making anything seem interesting, but I actually completely handled all of the maths in here at least until the last 30 pages or so. It was only when finally getting to Cantor's set theory that I began to feel lost, but perhaps this is due to fatigue more than anything. I haven't thought about these concepts since high school, mostly, though I do occasionally pull Hofstadter's *Metamagical Themas* off the shelf, just to dabble around in it; these more metaphysical aspects of theoretical mathematics are of great interest to me, and can be genuinely awe-inspiring. DFW clearly shared that view and his writing is infused with a true enthusiasm which at times goes far beyond what a so-called 'popular science' book should be — his frequent personal footnotes about his own high school maths teacher being a good example. Vollmann wrote something for this series too which I am curious about now, though I imagine it's a far different beast.

561. Americana by Don DeLillo
Received: 9 April 2013
Started: 9 April 2013
Finished: 13 April 2013
Americana is stunning, and I find it hard to believe it's a first novel. Of course, there's rough edges, but this is an epic book, one of the best DeLillo works for sure, and it seemed much larger than its 283 pages (or virtual pages, since I read an .epub format). The first third, which is all *Mad Men* and detached cunning, flails about somewhat, trying to set up what I expected to be some sort of road/travelogue. But the curveball comes with the middle section of the book, a hallucinatory mishmash of family history and other memories, trapped in-between plot points to echo the narrator's in-between existence. The power struggles, clever conversations and moments of sexual intrigue come and go, and what's left is a classic postmodern narrative structure: that of disintegration and dissipation. The ending scenes are almost shocking, but are more of a conclusion than the sudden about-face I thought at first. *Americana* might be one of the first true post-1960s novels I've read. Vietnam hangs over it, both unspoken and explicitly referenced throughout, yet the absurd idealism of 60s icons such as Richard Brautigan are in the rear-view mirror. The encounter with the dropouts on the Indian reservation, at the end of the book, is an obvious example — it's not a showcase for these alternative lifestyles, nor a judgement — if its a critique, it goes both ways. But the road movie section of *Americana* is distant and ungraspable, caught up in recollections, tangents, and disengagement. The main character here is ensnared in the pressures of a competitive work environment, and in media as well, which is perfectly in-tune with the decline of all other American industries and the rise of a media-based economy that was just happening at the time of writing. Stylistically, this felt extremely akin to Joseph McElroy, particularly *Lookout Cartridge*,  86 but with DeLillo's pacing and strange dialogue instead of McElroy's linguistic consciousness. There are many attempts at humour, some successful and some not, just like with *End* Zone; this early in his career,  516 DeLillo's signature apocalyptic themes are only a nascent suggestion (which in many ways made them more effective). This felt extremely complete yet extremely fragmentary at the same time; whether this was an intentional accomplishment or not, I'm not sure, but it succeeds entirely.

562. Apathy for the Devil: A Seventies Memoir by Nick Kent
Received: 14 April 2013
Started: 14 April 2013
Finished: 17 April 2013
This ranged from bad to excruciating, but

it was a fast read and contained enough entertaining stories about legendary 70s rockers that I didn't abandon it. I actually finished this two days ago and was thinking about all sort of excoriating daggers I could write here, but what's the point? Kent is a bad writer and a petty parasite of the music business who wrote this book to try to convince everyone that he was well liked by Led Zeppelin and the Stones. Even though he takes great pains to point out his youthful follies, it's clear that he has barely matured and his self-serving junkie habits have persisted into middle age. I was expecting this to be a somewhat more bittersweet memoir of British life in the decade, but that was only really the first chapter, because then it's just partying with Iggy Pop and the Sex Pistols. On top of everything, Kent's taste in music is so predictable (he refers to prog rock as the "opiate of the masses", as he clearly lived in some alternate world where Red Noise were selling out stadiums and his poor Rolling Stones languished in commercial obscurity) and his treatment of women is just as barbaric as the supposed traditionalism he thought he was fighting against. He did mention a weird party in California where Neil Young was challenging other musicians to come up and shred on guitars with him, and he outlasted Jimmy Page and some other titans — if that even actually happened, but since Kent, by his own admission, spent most of the decade strung out on smack, it's hard to say what was reliably reported here.

563. Austerlitz by W.G. Sebald
Received: 22 April 2013
Started: 22 April 2013
Finished: 26 April 2013
This was a lot like *Rings of Saturn* and also a lot different, in that it was more explicitly a work of 'fiction', in that it embraced a fictional character and most of the book was a long autobiography told in monologue. Structurally this was like that one Thomas Bernhard book I read once, but Sebald packed the same observations on architecture, place, and history into Austerlitz's story that he did in his own *Rings of Saturn* expedition. The frequent use of photos throughout is an interesting device, because they didn't really seem necessary; but for a book that is about searching for history, they served as some desperate attempt of documentation, frequently out of weight with their significance in the "plot". This is a German writer tackling the Holocaust, but he writes entirely around the event, yet not out of fear. And for what was in some ways the most rambling book I've ever read, it was far from sloppy, attaining some precision through it's run-on sentences and unformatted pages. It became difficult at times to keep track of what was Austerlitz's story and what was the narrator's own words, since this eschews quotation marks, but I think that was intentional — another comment on history and provenance. I might be forced to order copies of his other work unless I can find a good source online, but I think I'll do that post-haste.

564. Mrs. Ted Bliss by Stanley Elkin
Received: 26 April 2013
Started: 26 April 2013
Finished: 10 May 2013
It's been a long time since I read some Elkin; this is his last novel, and deals with old age in a typically Elkin manner — it's funny, wordy, and sympathetic, though slightly cartoonish. Mrs. Ted Bliss is a unique protagonist for contemporary fiction, being an 80-year-old retired Jewish woman living in a Florida condo. Elkin's knack for descriptive prose is at a peak here, as is his ability to create bizarre, unrealistic dialogue and plot structures that seem fantastic. Here, I didn't really let myself get wrapped up in the vague intrigue he continually hints at, probably because I've read enough of his work to know it won't amass to anything. This is drawn-out and episodic, and the ongoing interactions with various men hint at some sort of longing for companionship that he is probably trying to put forth, despite Mrs. Bliss's seeming independence. There's a lot of kvetching throughout, as to be expected (as well as a lot of Yiddish language I had to look up) but I'm a fan of his writing, so I committed to it and found it enjoyable, if a bit odd to read in this setting.

565. Three Novels: Molloy, Malone Dies, The Unnamable by Samuel Beckett
Received: 5 April 2011
Started: 12 April 2013
Finished: 15 May 2013
Replaced copy lost in the move from Glasgow. I never made it all the way through this before, so the first 2/3 was essentially a re-read, though I read it as new. *The Unnameable* was such a chore to get through, as I found it's discordant rhythms the problem (not the language or

style), that I still kinda feel like I only read the first two even after spending all this time with this. I took this slow, reading a few pages a day on the beach, making this possibly the first book that I read outside for 100% of it. Amongst all the bleak earthy squalor, I found a lot to love here, even in *The Unnameable*, which seemed to be about the loss of meaning as much as *Molloy* was about the loss of communication and *Malone Dies* was about the loss of identity. That is, if these books are 'about' anything, which is probably a flaw on my part, trying to graft traditional interpretive/associative strategies onto Beckett. But what else can I do? I only learned how to read one way; we all did — and that makes it more incredible that Beckett actually impacted so many readers. It felt the most like Beckett's own voice in the last book, writing somewhat personally, with the spirit of decay throughout, or maybe that's just an easy guess since it's so much about the act of fiction and the references to *Murphy*, *Watt*, etc. I'm
195 struggling here. • It's hard to really say much about the trilogy, being such a massive literary event and also one so resistant to being unlocked. For large passages I just gave up and went along with the flow, sometimes letting the words wash over me like a bath. The individual moments I liked the most were often wrapped up in the more regulated, process-based passages, like when Molloy goes on for two pages about moving stones around in his pockets. These elements of delight were nice reprieves from the otherwise unrelenting despair that pervades this. *Malone Dies*, the centrepiece, is the most curious book perhaps, being structured around three recollections or maybe one delusion, and with a structure that disintegrates more notably than the others. In many ways, as a student of the absurd, this trilogy is essentially Genesis — and trying to 'read' it, meaning to understand and process it, can be the most absurd act of all. Yet there's a reason that this not only remains in print, but it is considered the cornerstone of prose for a writer who won the Nobel Prize for literature. I can't decide if I'm glad I read this, at least in this context — that I went to paradise as an artist in residency and spent all my sacred outdoor time buried in this. I don't feel it made any creative impact on me; in fact, the most valuable purpose to reading this was so I could be happy that I have finally read it. But will it affect my life, work, or philosophy? Probably not, unfortunately.

566. The Lime Works by Thomas Bernhard
Received: 2 March 2003
Started: 28 April 2013
Finished: 23 May 2013
The Lime Works probably repeats it's title hundreds of times as the lime works of the main character, Konrad, are central to his mental unravelling. But Bernhard chooses to tell this story sideways, as a novel constructed of hearsay, built primarily through an unnamed, mysterious narrator (who nonetheless refers to himself or herself in the first person a few times) recalling Konrad's story via an interlocutor, Fro. This device allows the novel to become many things — a portrait of small-town communication, for one. But this is also about the act of creation, as Konrad is driven mad (we presume) by his quest to write an impossible scholarly work about hearing, and his wife becomes the unfortunate victim of his madness. But though we are told of the murder in the opening paragraph, and the novel purports to be a hearsay-based explanation of the deed, we don't get any more indication as to the motive. Instead, this becomes a study of procrastination, intimacy, power/control and language. I think I really liked this, and it was a relatively fast read when I bothered to spend time with it. But I should have just torn through it in one sitting, instead of breaking it up over weeks, as Bernhard seems to get momentum going and build to a peak.

567. A Field Guide to Getting Lost by Rebecca Solnit
Received: 16 May 2013
Started: 16 May 2013
Finished: 24 May 2013
It's been years since I read *Wanderlust*, but I remember it fondly. I saw this on display in a selection of books recommended for the critical tourism symposium here at Nida, but since I couldn't take them out of the mediateque I downloaded a copy instead. This is ostensibly a series of essays riffing on the topic of being lost, both in terms of orientation and in terms of purpose, but really is just a catch-all term to collect some loose writings of Solnit. But that's okay, because she's such an interesting writer that I'll accept any pretence to read this material. There are pieces here about art and film (Yves Klein and *Vertigo*, though the

latter is more about Hitchcock's depiction of 468
San Francisco) and quite a lot of personal writing. A long elegy for a deceased punk rock friend is rather touching, as are her

writings about family and her own love affairs, though she maintains a respectable authorial distance, even when addressing such personal material. This is a warm, imaginative and creative book that somehow straddles travel writing, creative non-fiction and essay forms into something that probably through its diversity isn't for everyone. But I'm going to keep an eye out for more of her work, certainly.

568. The Mooring Of Starting Out by John Ashbery
Received: 22 December 2009
Started: 15 April 2013
Finished: 25 May 2013
I don't usually list poetry as having a start and finish date, as I never read from cover to cover. But in this case, I did, and somehow *The Mooring of Starting Out* was perfectly timed to match the dates of my residency at Nida Art Colony, as I finished it on the last day I was here. This is a collection of Ashbery's first five books of poetry, which is a monumental accomplishment in American poetry, so much that trying to write about it here seems silly. The earliest poems in *Some Trees*, from the get-go, showcase his incredibly stylistic voice, though many here are more accessible than his writing is usually perceived as. He displays a fondness for sestinas and other traditional forms, even while dismantling them, and there's a real kinship to Wallace Stevens. By *The Tennis-Court Oath*, the Ashbery legend is on full display. This is a book that explodes with confidence, with adventurous experiments such as 'America' and 'Europe' (the former of which reminds me of Butor's *Mobile*) 762 while there's a bit of humour and parody at play in other works. *Rivers and Mountains* begins to take on an awareness of its times, with military imagery and concerns less cerebral, more grounded in the world. I read a bit of this every day on the roof terrace while drinking my coffee, and sometimes I had to just let poems wash over me; others, such as 'Civilization and its Discontents', were practically crippling in how much they affected me. *Rivers and Mountains* ends with 'The Skaters', an absolutely hurricane of a poem, and the first part of which is as pure of a statement of purpose as you'll ever find in postmodern writing. I've read this before, of course, yet this time I was struck by how elusive it was, despite seeming to confront its own artifice head-on; the narrator (or whatever you would call it) is shifting and ungraspable. *The Double Dream of Spring* begins to introduce his prose poems, which make up the entirety of *Three Poems*; oddly, despite being much more a prose-orientated reader, I found these often too difficult to get through. *Three Poems*, particularly 'The System', seems almost resolute in being straight and non-poetic, and I found this the most rewarding of the later works; it demanded a concentration that we often take for granted, and is probably one of the more remarkable works of introspective writing there is.

569. The Way the World Works: Essays by Nicholson Baker
Received: 26 May 2013
Started: 26 May 2013
Finished: 6 June 2013
Joy of joys, a new collection of Nicholson Baker essays! I had read some of these before, but was delighted to read them again, especially the dissections of Wikipedia and the Amazon Kindle. The long piece about his pacifist view of World War II is obvious if you've read *Human Smoke*, 326 though he states that he didn't write that book intending to put forth this argument, but that he came to it later. Either way, it's explicit and convincing, and it's pretty powerful stuff coming from a man who writes books about escalators, dildos, and fireplaces. His look at video games is like a bizarro version of Tom Bissell and I kept laughing while imaging the 50-year-old Baker mashing Xbox buttons. I actually thought he was a bit older that he actually is, so that's good news — I hope to have at least two more decades of his writing to enjoy in the future.

570. Cooked: A Natural History of Transformation by Michael Pollan
Received: 11 June 2013
Started: 12 June 2013
Finished: 17 June 2013
There's a lot to like in Pollan's latest book, though at times his writing feels like a place I've been to before. Like his most successful books, *The Botany of Desire*  309 and *The Omnivore's Dilemma*,  364 *Cooked* is organised around four chapters, representing the roles of fire, water, air and earth in cooking. Though the 'earth' chapter is a bit of a stretch, it's about fermentation and talks with Sandor Katz as well as this intense nun who makes cheese. I loved reading this and it made me feel a renewed commitment to sourdough bread and fermenting things; even the barbeque chapter had me

engrossed, though I'm not planning to start eating pork. Pollan brought a bit more of his personal life into this book than usual, talking about shared cooking experiences with his wife and son, but kept it from being about him. His arguments are essentially the same as always — that industrial food is killing us, and that the spiritual benefits of cooking and eating real food are immeasurable beneficial — but he wasn't beating me over the head with them, and I agree anyway.

571. Notable American Women by Ben Marcus
Received: (already owned)
Started: 31 May 2013
Finished: 18 June 2013
A re-read that I took slowly, picking this up when in the kitchen or sitting on the balcony. Having read *The Flame Alphabet*
485 more recently (and having felt that it paled in comparison to this), I noticed a lot of similarities between the two. Actually, I'd say that *Notable American Women* is the halfway point between *The Age of Wire*
123, 286 *and String* and *The Flame Alphabet*. Much of this book is preoccupied with *Wire and String*'s lists, glossaries and redefinitions, while the first and last chapters, dealing with the "Ben Marcus" figure from a parental viewpoint, gets into the dark, ugly territory of his newest book. This was also far more unpleasant than I remembered, though enjoyable of course because of the overall brilliance of the writing style. I was just re-watching some old Tim and Eric episodes and I started to wonder why I find invented nonsense terms like "Taargus" and "Corwin's Crouch" hilarious in Tim and Eric, but I see it as serious, high art in this book. And actually, I started to re-interpret *Notable American Women* from a more humour-based viewpoint, which honestly made it even better. This approach to artifice is complex enough to serve in multiple forms; these systems and devices are made even more ridiculous because they are so formally presented. This is still, I think, my favourite American novel since *Infinite Jest* but I'd have to really dig through these archives to say that confidently.

572. The Last Novel by David Markson
Received: 26 April 2013
Started: 26 April 2013
Finished: 19 June 2013
Markson's *Last Novel* is actually Markson's last novel, but not one of this best. Given that all of this post-*Wittgenstein's*
Mistress books have followed essentially 63
the same format (a loose series of notes about past writers and artists), this sounds like a thin criticism, as how can one be better than another? But this didn't engage me nearly as much as *This Is Not a Novel* 17
or the others. If any theme emerges, it's the judgements of one artist or writer of another's work; this is full of dismissals, insults or otherwise mistaken judgements. Perhaps Markson is lashing out against his own career being overlooked, as he never found anything approaching mainstream/commercial success, though to be honest, given how uncompromising and experimental his writing is, he should have been happy to achieve what he did. Or maybe I'm completely wrong to read any sort of bitterness in this. Though it's short, it took me awhile because I didn't really feel engaged, and I eventually remembered I hadn't finished it and went back and read the second half in about an hour. I never read his early, more conventional novels and maybe I should check them out, but really I want to re-read *Wittgenstein*.

573. American Hardcore: A Tribal History by Steven Blush
Received: 19 June 2013
Started: 19 June 2013
Finished: 24 June 2013
Oral histories are pretty easy to read and this was no exception; the different voices by so many of the major players of the day assembled to give a pretty convincing portrayal, despite the best efforts of "author" Steven Blush to destroy this book with his own terrible writing. His interstitial segments were painful, but not enough to diminish the value of this book, which really chronicles an incredible segment of American music that has never been well documented or canonised. My own interest in hardcore was deeper than I realised, as long sections describing obscure bands that I never heard (or only heard once) reminded me of all those years sitting around with friends back in Pittsburgh and hearing them swap stories about the hardcore legends who inspired them. Blush's decision to cut things off at 1986 is a valid one, I think, as there are lots of great second-wave bands but too many terrible ones, and boundaries have to be drawn. That book will someday be written, I'm sure, and then we can learn about Moss
Icon, Current, Cap'n Jazz, Bastro, and all 1703
the other nooks and crannies of the punk/

HC world. I do thank Blush for being reasonably open-minded here, not dismissing any band from his book because their music wasn't "hardcore" enough — he certainly seemed to recognise the dead-end of a limited sonic scope and seemed to respect Black Flag, Bad Brains, and others who tried to do something more interesting. Of course, his connection was through No Trend so that might explain lots. By organising the chapters into locations, he actually portrays 'scenes' quite well, and I hope accurately; we see each major dot on the hardcore map as being motivated by a distinct reason (LA: music, SF: politics, DC: social values, Boston: beating the shit out of people) and his diversions into smaller regional scenes is fascinating (I never knew Charleston, WV had a good record store or that Indianapolis ever had any bands at all).

574. Getting Even by Woody Allen
Received: 30 June 2013
Started: 1 July 2013
Finished: 5 July 2013
Textbook comedy, though actually it's not a textbook at all. These early examples of Allen's comedic writing shine with a clever wit that somehow feels contemporary while also being very much of its time. Allen's knack for old-timey, almost vaudeville slapstick mixed with existential despair is evident throughout, whether it's a detective hired to find God, or the memoirs of Hitler's barber. Most of these were published in *The New Yorker* and are all short, making this fun to dip into for quick laughs. I'll have to check out his other prose soon, which I imagine can only get better, though his 'problematic' nature also makes it somewhat difficult to really enjoy this fully.

575. Night Soul and Other Stories by Joseph McElroy
Received: 5 April 2011
Started: 12 June 2013
Finished: 6 July 2013
I haven't spent much time with McElroy in short form, apart from his short novel, *The Letter Left To Me*. This collection doesn't cite when the stories were written, but they feel recent, though McElroy's early novels were so mature that it's hard to really pinpoint things. This collects some real doozies. 'Character' and 'Canoe Repair' are adjacent and feel almost like different versions of the same idea, where memory takes on a textural form in prose that is absolutely dazzling. The opening cut, 'No Man's Land', places us squarely in an urban environment that deals eloquently with trust and expectations, and like many stories in this book, deals with a child and an adult's interactions. This is most notable in the title piece, which closes the book as a beautiful, stunning depiction of a man being affected by his infant son. It's simultaneously moving and tense, and it's almost a shame to have to wait till the end for it as many readers may not make it through the preceding stories. There's a bit of sci-fi in 'The Last Disarmament' and 'Annals of Plagiary' is immediately relatable. I haven't read everything he's published yet, but almost everything (*Women and Men* and *Hind's Kidnap* continue to elude me, though I've read over half of both) and this might actually be the best book of Joseph McElroy there is. I admit that I've been reading a lot more short fiction lately than I usually do, but there's something about *Night Soul* that really showcases everything that makes him such a great writer, and while requiring less of a commitment than his full novels. I'm embarrassed that this sat on my shelf for two years before I opened it because he's supposed to be one of my favourite writers. Reading this reminded me that, yes, he certainly is.

576. The Atomic Bazaar: Dispatches from the Underground World of Nuclear Trafficking by William Langewiesche
Received: 4 July 2013
Started: 5 July 2013
Finished: 7 July 2013
I totally ripped through this account of illegal nuclear weapons trafficking. Langewiesche, who writes often for *The Atlantic*, takes an edgy tone that is pessimistic and dark, but given the subject matter, I actually finished this feeling much better about my own security. Pakistan is really portrayed as the key danger in this world, as their shady government continually tries to play both sides of the game, and one famous nuclear scientist pissed off the wrong people and had to be made an example of. There's no real political point of view here — Langewiesche is hardly pro-American empire; yet I admit that I actually, for one of the few times in my life, felt happy for the United States and their efforts to police the world on nuclear terms. As futile as their efforts are ("throw money at the problem" being the main course of action), there's still some reassurance that at least the US's might acts as some sort of deterrent.

577. The Collected Stories of Lydia Davis by Lydia Davis
Received: 13 April 2012
Started: 14 February 2013
Finished: 11 July 2013
It feels epic to work through this, which compiles everything Davis wrote at the time of publication (2009), which is probably over 200 stories, though I didn't count. A lot of these are one page toss-offs, some even one sentence, which are often funny and usually brilliant and sometimes quite forgettable. I liked most of the longer stories in here, especially the historical 'Lord Royston's Tour' and 'Helen and Vi: A Study in Health and Vitality', or maybe I just remember them more. Davis is formally extremely experimental and this benefits many of the stories (though occasionally detracts). My tendency was to linger on the pieces that have more emotional cores, such as 'The House Plans' or 'What You Learn from the Baby'; she seems to have a deep understanding of human interaction, and even when describing something in a detached manner, she taps into something universal (similar to how Wallace's artifice amplified the real). I've always liked Davis's work but never really immersed myself in it before, and even though it took a long time to work through this, it was always delightful, for her frivolity and accessibility carried me through even some of the less engaging sections. There's really something remarkable and singular about the way she writes, and I'm actually curious to dive into her novel next even though I've just read 731 pages of her.

578. I Wear the Black Hat: Grappling with Villains (Real and Imagined) by Chuck Klosterman
Received: 11 July 2013
Started: 11 July 2013
Finished: 12 July 2013
I ripped through Klosterman's newest quickly, but loved every page. This is supposed to be an investigation into the idea of the villain — a cultural evil rather than a pure evil — but is really just an excuse for Klosterman to riff on things he spends his time thinking about. In this case, that would be the Oakland Raiders, Perez Hilton, Hitler, performance-enhancing drugs in sports, bands he hated as a child, Bill Clinton's legacy, and Bernhard Goetz. It's hilarious, of course, and thought-provoking in that charming and superficial way that Klosterman is the master of. I wished this was longer because it felt like an extended version of one of his *Grantland* pieces, which themselves are never long enough, but maybe I just have a bottomless appetite for Klosterman.

579. The Power of Flies by Lydie Salvayre
Received: 4 July 2013
Started: 16 July 2013
Finished: 20 July 2013
I don't know anything about Salvayre but since it's on Dalkey Archive I picked it up and tore through it. This is a murder mystery written from the inside out, as a series of monologues of the deranged killer held under custody. His sociopathy unfolds quickly, and we visit numerous obsessions, most notably the philosophy of Blaise Pascal but also personal habits, cleanliness, sexuality, etc. The character is intriguing at first, but I found myself bored as I don't find mental illness particularly interesting these days, and the murder aspect, while unarticulated, isn't that compelling either. Salvayre has a nice style that veers between rant and very clean, calculated prose without warning; this formal diversity gives the novel a nice momentum that, coupled with its short length, concluded exactly when I felt that it should have. I'm not motivated to explore more of her work, but I did find this to be a good example of unusual fiction, and though I'm left wanting a bit more I don't regret reading it.

580. Those Guys Have All the Fun: Inside the World of ESPN by James Andrew Miller
Received: 20 July 2013
Started: 20 July 2013
Finished: 24 July 2013
This type of oral history is a fun, easy, engrossing read. I don't know why I decided to read this — I don't even watch much ESPN, but it was interesting and put together well, without pulling any punches or protecting anybody. The interstitial writing was pretty high quality and while it's written clearly in admiration of ESPN, it doesn't shy away from the controversies/ problems. The egos of the on-air talent shine through, though the manoeuvrings of the executives kept my interest more than I would have guessed. Once they reached the more modern sports era which I was familiar with, I was less intrigued — I preferred the early 80s stories of producing highlights shows by the seats of their pants. I love that Berman had to address

the 'You're with me, leather' story and Kornheiser comes off as far more of an intellectual than I ever took him to be. The sexual harassment and other shenanigans were of course the juicy bits, and, well, there could have been more of that.

581. Chronic City by Jonathan Lethem
Received: 13 April 2012
Started: 26 July 2013
Finished: 30 July 2013
Compared to the novel that preceded this, this is a real about-face — Lethem finding his footing again, though I don't think I really loved this until the very end. I've never read Bret Easton Ellis and probably never will, but I felt that the first half of this novel conformed to my preconceived notion of what Ellis's writing is like (perhaps motivated by knowing that he and Lethem were friends). This starts as a novel immersed in the cultural connections of New York City, where the references to obscure art and pop culture are so thick that it becomes impossible to separate the real references from the fictional ones; Lethem does a great job of creating a half-real cultural world that feels believable and true. It wasn't clear to me at first that this is entirely a sci-fi novel, in a parallel universe, as I assumed the use of Gnuppets instead of Muppets, for example, was a copyright issue; but then, about 500 pages in, there's a reference to the World Trade Centre still standing, slipped in surreptitiously, and I realised finally what Lethem was really up to. A passing reference to Vonnegut's *Sirens of Titan* should have been a clue. The last two or three chapters of this are a near-total shift, recasting everything in a 'holy shit' feeling that is gradual, not sudden. Everything I thought about *Chronic City* turned out to be wrong; the child actor stumbling through a meaningless life narrator seemed like an easy character, a product of the mind of a young 'now' writer like Lethem — but then, all of my reservations about that fell away. The Perkus character I assumed was modelled after Richard Meltzer and also makes a shift into the source of pity, though I'm not sure how it all adds up. You have the same themes that are in most of his novels — fractured romantic relationships, amnesia, etc. — but with Manhattan as a central character. Like his biggest influence,

9, 210 *Dhalgren*, this is a pure city-book, though the Manhattan is elusive and fictionalised — even given the small amounts of time I've spent in the city, I can tell it's not the real one. This isn't perfect — some parts are extremely overwritten (but then other passages are just so spot-on perfect that they're almost breathtaking) and it's definitely a bit long. I'm not sure what it all adds up to — just an entertainment? But I'm compelled enough to keep reading everything Lethem publishes (and looking at his work, I realise that I've read all of his books except *Girl in Landscape*) for now, and given how terrible *You Don't Love Me Yet* was, this is a real return-to-form.

632 291

582. Monsoon: The Indian Ocean and the Future of American Power by Robert D. Kaplan
Received: 4 July 2013
Started: 17 July 2013
Finished: 30 July 2013
I am very interested in this part of the world and know what I'm getting with Kaplan, though after reading Bissell's takedown of him, it's hard not to be annoyed at some of his writing style. This was constructed around an exploration of how the Indian ocean region will affect America, which I didn't really care about; when I filtered out that pro-American bias, I was left with a work that was half travelogue, half history, with a few fascinating parts (Oman, seriously, what an interesting place!) and a lot of filler about Chinese development politics. It made me miss India, of course, but also I realised how much has changed in the nine years since I was there. He doesn't claim to give more than a surface look at the very complicated social dynamics of Indonesia, and the breakdown of Sri Lanka's political struggles was appreciated. Ending with a chapter on Zanzibar was a nice move as Kaplan suggests it's the truest melting pot of the Indian Ocean region.

583. Farther Away by Jonathan Franzen
Received: 3 August 2013
Started: 3 August 2013
Finished: 6 August 2013
A hit-and-miss collection, for sure. Franzen seems much more natural with non-fiction and after the disaster that was *Freedom*, 454 this is a real pick-me-up. The title piece is probably the winner, being some hybrid travelogue, personal essay, and eulogy for David Foster Wallace. Wallace is a ghost throughout this book; plus, there's a longer piece that is literally a eulogy for him, delivered by Franzen at his funeral, which is remarkably honest and occasionally difficult to stomach. But Franzen himself is less interesting; in his early 50s, he seems

to have settled into his role as a birdwatching literary figure, occasionally obsessed with his own place among a community of writers that is likely more in his imagination than anything else. There's some book reviews here that are often entertaining, such as his passionate rave about Alice Munro and his insight into *The Laughing*
430 *Policeman*; and a few failed attempts at creative nonfiction, namely the interview with New York State which I skimmed through. This was far less thrilling than his first two books, and could have used some editing, but had some moments for sure and as always, when he's not striking a pose, he actually has some great things to say, especially about the art of writing.

584. Autumn Rhythm: Musings On Time, Tide, Aging, Dying, And Such Biz by Richard Meltzer

Received: 6 August 2013
Started: 6 August 2013
Finished: 9 August 2013

There isn't much Meltzer on the free download sites, but this relatively recent book was there for the taking, and thus I took. Supposedly a meditation on aging, *Autumn Rhythm* is actually a rambling, unedited mess with occasional moments of brilliance and a lot of filler. Meltzer's musings on his parents are the darkest and most powerful parts of the book, but in the meantime you have to get through a lot of stream-of-consciousness poetry and pedestrian observations about being 'old' (though much is written in his late 50s which is hardly ancient). The more lucid, nostalgic passages are the best — one highlight is a recollection of hearing the white album for the first time, on the radio, listening with other members of Soft White Underbelly, where his genuine excitement from that time carries through 40 years later into the writing, without any posturing. And some of the shorter bursts attain the brilliance of *Gulcher*'s madcap screeds, but only some
503 — and the tone isn't sustained consistently. But whatever — it's a short read, it's still Meltzer, and it's probably inspired me to return to *The Night Alone*.

585. Lipstick Traces: A Secret History of the Twentieth Century by Greil Marcus

Received: 26 October 2002
Started: 10 August 2013
Finished: 14 August 2013

I've been going through and tossing out books, trying to get rid of things I've already read, or will never read, or never re-read. I thought about tossing this, but it's been so long since I read it (since at least before 2002) that I decided to dive into again and see if a decade+ of my own involvement with art/culture would give me a better reading on this. *Lipstick Traces* is a really ridiculous book, and that's entirely due to Marcus's style of writing. He tried to write something well researched and informed, but impressionistic, rather than academic; there's no real 'argument' here except for his view that the Sex Pistols, the Lettrists, and the Dadaists were all channelling the same current. This is just his reading, and it's not one that can be proven or disproven, so it leaves *Lipstick Traces* feeling, in the end, like one man's messy PhD notes — enjoyable riffs, certainly, particularly if you are interested in the material, but ultimately too academic to be a fun read, and too poetic to be taken seriously as an academic work. It's not even a popular history of Dada through the Situationists (though it might be the closest we have) because of his non-linear style. Marcus's 'secret history' concept is one of those terms like 'pataphysics' that just becomes a thin framework on which you can hang essentially anything you'd like. ('Psychogeography' is another.) This isn't inherently problematic, but Marcus's 'secret history of the 20th century' is just a way to connect a bunch of his interests, culminating in Johnny Rotten's existence, which he spends the first half of the book raving over almost reverentially. The final result is a great, great book that's only real value is it's well-researched anecdotes about Isidore Isou, Michel Mourre, Debord and other agents of his 'secret history'. The biggest problem I really have is that Marcus belongs to that class of people who just takes pop music way too seriously. Maybe at the time 'Holidays in the Sun' really did feel like a culture-shattering event, but it's still just a pop song, created for the purpose of selling records. I grew up on this stuff, but now in hindsight realise how silly it all seems — to read a revolutionary statement into a pop single.

586. The Sporting Club by Thomas McGuane

Received: 4 September 2012
Started: 10 August 2013
Finished: 21 August 2013

I've been meaning to read McGuane's first novel for ages, and I found it less overtly slapstick than I expected, yet still infused with a wild, comic sensibility. The two characters drive a plot forward and he portrays them with a wry sophistication that is perfectly placed, at times amazing for a first novel. The Upper Peninsula of Michigan comes across like an insane, wild frontier which I guess in some ways it is; this is a pretty sideways depiction of masculinity, with Quinn as the central omniscient character somewhat reserved and detached from his feelings, even when his thoughts are narrated.

587. The Way of the World by Nicolas Bouvier
Received: 15 June 2012
Started: 18 August 2013
Finished: 5 September 2013
My father raised me on a steady diet of travel writing, yet that's based really on recent stuff: the late 80s to the present, or maybe not even the present since I don't actively read much in the genre anymore. Thus, I was surprised that *The Way of the World* was not just an incredibly compelling read from the 1950s, but one of the best travel books I've ever read. It helps that this is much more of a ramshackle adventure than the studious, learned travel writing of Paul Theroux or his ilk. Bouvier and Thierry's adventure was much closer to *On the Road*, only non-fictional and minus the beat affect, which is a good thing in my opinion. The writing in here is incredibly vivid, as Bouvier has a minimalist style with occasional flourishes of colour and an uncanny ability to capture emotion. His story is more like that of someone caught in a whirlwind, leaving a small footprint on his travels and focusing on the experiential instead of trying to assert their own identity. Maybe this is just a curious Swiss-French jouissance; I don't think an Anglophone would write this way at all, and that's clear even in translation. I read this very slowly because I've been too busy with paid work to be able to dedicate much time to books (plus the eye strain problems I've been having), so it was possibly to savour this just as Bouvier savoured the Persian sunset or the sweet Turkish figs.

588. Secret Rendezvous by Kobo Abe
Received: 30 September 2008
Started: 6 September 2013
Finished: 9 September 2013
I don't even know where to begin in unravelling this extremely dark sexual nightmare. It begins from the same premise as many Murakami tales — with a woman disappearing, in this case taken from the narrator in a Kafkaesque state-sponsored removal. He's drawn to a hospital to find her, where he becomes a pawn (or unwilling instigator) of a variety of extreme sex-based experiments, involving masturbating doctors, nurses with rape delusions, and a man who has half the body of a horse (and two penises). The often grotesque elements present in contemporary Japanese sexuality (at least from what I can pick up on through manga and horror films) is in full force, but I'm not sure what Abe is trying to do here. There's nothing titillating here, nor do I think that was his intent. This is a bit of a piss-take on bureaucracy, with the hospital surely functioning as a stand-in for society in general with rules, roles, and codes; the medical setting also jars nicely against any sort of eroticism that would otherwise be present. This is a dark side of surrealism for sure, similar in tone to his *Kangaroo Notebook* (which I always thought was his most insane, gonzo work, though this is equally fucked) yet it's never not fun. This recurring theme of lost love in so many Murakami books and also here makes me wonder about the Japanese family structure and their commitment to romantic, monogamous love — the loss of the wife seems to be the true horror (and her fate in the epilogue, possibly, is quite gruesome), more so than having your penile impulses transmitted to a horse-man.

589. Inherent Vice by Thomas Pynchon
Received: (already owned)
Started: 6 September 2013
Finished: 21 September 2013
I read this voraciously when it came out and actually couldn't remember much about it, so while waiting for *Bleeding Edge* to hit stores in Finland, I thought I'd dip into this again. *Inherent Vice* is such a romp that it doesn't resemble a Pynchon novel except in little glimpses; it's a comedy-detective-noir throughout and the ending gets so caught up in the action that it leaves style behind and just gets to the nuts and bolts. In retrospect this is a really, really minor work for Pynchon, even more than I thought from the get-go. The central joke, "Doc is stoned", is beaten into the ground and while the plot is beautifully constructed, the light nature even downplays the usual themes that Pynchon infuses into his writing. If I sound like I'm complaining, I don't mean that

591

— this is fun, absolutely engrossing and under any other writer's name this would be more celebrated. I think it outpaced similar deconstructed detective stories such written by Stanley Crawford or Jonathan 500 Lethem, though really, Pynchon isn't even really deconstructing anything. He has no real reason to mock the genre, and without having to prove that, he's able to just write. This is so dialogue heavy that Pynchon has less room to write those brilliant, strange passages which established his style in his early books; when they come, they hit hard, and this early-70s California is really something he knows. The ending is quite beautiful, as in all of his books, and this is probably the most autobiographical of anything he wrote, at least I think so. The violence in the book is written in a way that really puts a cap on the 60s, so this also recalls *Gimme Shelter* and any of the other 28 dark works of the time (Hunter Thompson?) but somehow, despite the obvious requiem for these times, this book feels celebratory.

590. 39 Microlectures: In Proximity of Performance by Matthew Goulish
Received: 23 October 2013
Started: 23 October 2013
Finished: 23 October 2013
Re-read this on the bus trip to Pori. I forgot how enjoyable this is; Goulish's vagueness doesn't bother me nearly as much as it did the first time through, probably because I still had the cloud of my academic life around me then. I particularly liked the bit about criticism, where he states that the critic cannot change anything about the work, but rather that the critic is likely trying to change their own self. The guy seems to have a really good outlook on gender, and I think I feel much closer to Goat Island's approach at this point in my own life and practice. I forgot how the endnotes are almost half the length and they're just as enjoyable as the main text, in a way.

591. Bleeding Edge by Thomas Pynchon
Received: 8 October 2013
Started: 8 October 2013
Finished: 29 October 2013
Bleeding Edge reads, at points, like an extended experiment in what he began with *Inherent Vice* — what I suppose

413, 589 should be called "late Pynchon" stylistically, marked by a very straight-forward single character-driven narrative, an almost classical mystery/detective plot, and the weirdness and popular culture infused throughout in a manner that makes it extremely accessible. And extremely fun. This is the first Pynchon novel set in a time that I can distinctly say I lived through, and his capturing of the 2001 pop culture zeitgeist is stunning, exactly because it's not something we would expect Pynchon to be aware of. This is his *Microserfs*, in a way, depicting digital capitalist culture in an earlier stage that already feels incredibly distance, only 12 years later. That the lead figure is such a complete, fleshed-out female character makes it easy to overlook many of the cartoons that otherwise populate this (the Russian spies, the sleazy men, the leftie conspiracy theorists...) and there's a sense of feminine solidarity, particularly in the closing pages that's unlike anything seen in his previous work. I read a zillion reviews of this before I was able to get my hands on a copy, so I had some preconceived framework before I went into it, but I don't think anything influenced my enjoyment (at least, not too much). What's really strange is how this deals with 9/11 in such a sideways manner. It's clearly the central event of the book (as the mysterious intrigue reveals itself to be nothing conclusive) yet he doesn't go all-out describing it, nor does he avoid it. There's elements of American life at that time I completely forgot about (such as the constant wondering if things would be 'normal' that year, Halloween and Thanksgiving for example) and the truther/conspiracy element is probably the most pronounced, but even that is weird. Contemporary conspiracy theory is arguable influenced *by* Pynchon; for him to come out now, writing about 9/11 conspiracies, feels strange, like an artist doing a cover version of someone doing a cover version of their self. This might be the first Pynchon novel where even I, an unabashed fan, wondered a bit "What was the point?" when it was all over. Still, the ride was pretty satisfying.

592. Marvel Comics: The Untold Story by Sean Howe
Received: 11 November 2013
Started: 11 November 2013
Finished: 15 November 2013
I started reading this on the ferry for something fun and light and found myself getting way into it, as it stirred up so many memories of Marvel comics read around age 11-12. I kept flipping over to Google and Wikipedia to look up details about characters and storylines that I barely

remembered, so it was a good trip down nostalgia lane, and I think it's time I watch the last few X-Men films that I didn't see. Howe's book doesn't pull any punches, though at first I thought it was, as it seemed to be portraying the Stan Lee of the 1950s and 1960s very sympathetically, and seemed to gloss over Steve Ditko's role in the creation of Spider-Man. But as the story developed, and the issue of creator rights and royalties comes to the forefront, Howe is (I think) fair and accurate in his reporting of the controversies. The classic 60s Marvel creation myths have been told so many times, but the 1970s era is what I found most fascinating, partially because I was only vaguely familiar with it. My own Marvel knowledge is the mid-80s until where things totally went off the rails and they launched new *X-Men* comics with 700 different collectible covers, so it was great to read about what I had missed and also how drugged-out and psychedelic that earlier era was. I became really nostalgic for the classic Chris Claremont-penned X-Men titles, which I was around for the tail end of (I remember deciding at age 12 that when Claremont left X-Men it wasn't going to be as interesting, and apparently I was right); I had no idea about his creative love-hate relationship with John Byrne, or how absent Stan Lee was from the day-to-day operations of Marvel since the mid-70s. The emergence of Jim Lee, Todd McFarlane and the supremely awful Rob Liefield is portrayed as the true end of Marvel's ability to hold their own universe together; the 90s-era unravelling sounds so horrendous that it doesn't make me wish I had kept reading any of them. McFarlane sounds like a dumb jock, and I was hoping for more of an attack on Liefield's steroid-fuelled style, as well as his inability to draw legs/feet in correct perspective and his obsession with putting pockets and pouches all over the characters. It's ultimately a very sad story and Howe doesn't get too caught up in Marvel's own bullshit about superheroes as contemporary American myth; he focuses on the corporate and creative battles and leaves the rest to the imagination. Jim Shooter is portrayed as probably the most divisive figure in the history of the company, but it does seem to me like he was at least dedicated and probably just lacked people skills. I'm going to seek out what anthologies and omnibus formats I can find for some of the 70s X-Men titles specifically, though I have zero interest in anything that came after my own departure from comics collecting. I have five or six different copies of *X-Men* #1, and several with the stupid fold-out cover, somewhere in my parents' basement, along with a million other people who bought into the hype. I didn't realise it at the time, but I was drawn to Claremont's soap-opera emotion-based X-Men, and not at all interested in Scott Lobdell (or whomever) creating characters like Cable and Bishop, who are just ultra-violent guys with big guns; additionally, I think the fatigue of the limited-edition silver-ink covers and rising costs affected me, even as a pre-teen, which apparently was a sentiment shared by many other people. What's most shocking about Marvel Comics is that they still don't sell that many comic books — only a dedicated cadre of a few hundred thousand buy the most popular titles, and the real money is in the films and merchandising, which thankfully Howe doesn't spend too much time delving into ("Oh yeah, Spider-Man with Tobey McGuire came out and it was a big hit" is essentially all he says about it).

593. A Carrot is as Close as a Rabbit Gets to a Diamond: Captain Beefheart Interviews and Texts, 1966 — 2001 by Captain Beefheart

Received: 12 September 2012
Started: 30 November 2013
Finished: 24 December 2013

This is a collection of interviews with and articles about Beefheart, collected by some rabid fans. I love this type of semi-official rock scholarship, which in some cases (*The Acid Archives*) dwarf most academic attempts. As one can imagine, Van Vliet is a continually entertaining interview subject, and this book delivers endless quotable lines and fascinating viewpoints. There's some pieces by well-known writers like Lester Bangs, Byron Coley and Kurt Loder; there's a recurring encounter by Dave DiMartino that is pretty insightful; and some TV interview transcripts with Letterman which made me dial up the clips on YouTube. The one thing that became repetitive is that most of these articles began with a very similar recap of Beefheart's career, so I got very tired of reading the same information over and over in different forms. The post-music interviews are some of the best, and Coley's 1999 Spin article is one final career re-cap that really focuses on *Trout Mask* and in some ways revises the standard history as Beefheart set it down, as it came out around the time of the Revenant box during which John French's side of the story was becoming prominent. (DiMartino's last interview is overly concerned with Henry Kaiser's allegations that Beefheart did not deserve sole musical composer credit, and is probably the only time that Van Vliet directly addresses them, though nothing is really direct with Van Vliet). For such a complex figure, somehow a really full portrait emerges over the years, and I'd say I have a better understanding of the guy. It's easy to read through his showmanship and myth-making, and the bits where real insecurity comes through are powerful, because while I don't personally want to inflate the myth any more than necessary, Van Vliet is still one of the most singular figures in the history of American art. The final interview is a conversation with Bono via telephone, recorded by Anton Corbijn, and I don't really understand the context of it, but it's bizarre and rambling and left me somehow wanting more, and sad that he is no longer with us.

594. Terrestrials by Paul West
Received: 28 January 2002
Started: 2 September 2012
Finished: 26 December 2013
Bought in 2002. Started ten and a half years later, and then finished over a year after that. You'd think this was some massive, unapproachable epic from the amount of time it took me to get through its 388 pages, but not really. Sure, West's prose is dense and difficult, among the more challenging stylists of late 20th century literature I've ever read. But it's always lucid, and the conceit of this book is laid out in its prologue (that the book is narrated by an extra-terrestrial from Alpha Centauri) though it's not necessary to realise this to enjoy it. The journey of Booth and Clegg shifts locations and viewpoints multiple times, sometimes coming off as a harrowing adventure story and sometimes like a slapstick road movie. There's no particular logic to these shifts but the story is compelling and both characters quite fully fleshed out, though because its the view of an extra-terrestrial it raises all sorts of issues about fictional characters in general. I just liked West's prose; sometimes I struggled to stay engaged but once they returned to America, I found the last half of this really easy-going. I'm not sure why I put this down for a year because it's best as an immersive experience, which the two halves combined to form. For a fairly short novel, there's quite a lot addressed here, most interesting for me the threat of power structures to one's sense of masculinity. The final passages descended into sexual fantasy, which felt like a relief after such an austere first 350 pages, but also seemed to logically support the narrative at that point, if there is actually logic. West has written a bunch of novels, all of which seem to be ultra-obscure as he has disappeared from history, though this really could stand up against the more well renowned accomplishments of American postmodern literature.

595. The Unwinding: An Inner History of the New America by George Packer
Received: 26 December 2013
Started: 27 December 2013
Finished: 9 January 2014
I appreciate what Packer tried to do in *The Unwinding*, which is to deliberately ape the style of Dos Passos' *USA* trilogy to create a nonfiction work that attempts to describe what's been going wrong with America in my lifetime. It's an impressive bit of nonfiction, and I like the way he laid it out — the "newsreel"-style interludes, while lacking the experimentalism of Dos Passos, server as nice interstitial breaks, and the weaving stories are constructed with expert timing. But where Dos Passos's newsreels were a striking evaluation of the emerging American media, Packer's feel a bit desperate — his attempts to include Twitter tweets and rap music lyrics are clumsy, and he fails to convey the fragmented nature of today's popular culture. The other big problem I had with the book was the quality of the writing. I think he's trying to take a very omniscient, very simplistic narrator position when describing the changing beliefs of these people, but it feels condescending at times, or even just bad — like a high school book report. But then other passages are expertly composed. His proximity to the subjects seems to dictate it; weirdly, I found his slightly sarcastic biographies of Oprah Winfrey, Jay-Z, and Newt Gingrich to be more successful than his intimate portraits of Tammy Thomas, Jeff Connaughton or Dean Price. This is non-fiction, after all, and when borrowing structure and tone from fiction it becomes a dangerous game. Packer's own ideology is clear but when he tries to empathise with right-wing or Bible-thumping people, it feels demeaning, as if he cannot hide his contempt. I think this is a good book and worth a read, still. It doesn't claim to be the absolute, all-encompassing portrait of American decay, and it often writes "around" major events without tackling them directly. It's not a history book, but an emotional narrative,

and by the end it does feel very successful, somehow complex and satisfying despite being so fragmented. But it's not as good as, say, watching all five seasons of *The Wire*, which by focusing on one city (and by being fictional) achieves many of the same goals in a far more compelling and intimate way.

596. The Dick Gibson Show by Stanley Elkin

Received: (already owned)
Started: 9 January 2014
Finished: 13 January 2014

A re-read that was a pleasure, even as this battered copy bought a decade ago in Cincinnati fell apart in my hands. I should give it some appropriate send-off — a burial, or a burning with ashes to be scattered over the radiowaves/cosmos of Southern Finland. In my memory, which is a constant battle for superiority over all the other books I've read, this was my favourite work of Elkin's and the re-read confirms that sentiment. It's a bit messy and lacks the complete grandeur of *George Mills* or the 83, 709 sweeping Americana of *The Franchiser*, 62, 341 but there are bits of both, as well as some hilarious verbal play. I think this book is best read as being about distance, and the way media can become an emotional wall, to be designed to isolate even while seemingly bringing us together. As true as it rings today with our online exhibitionism, this novel is set largely in the 1950s and confined exclusively to radio technology, yet I still took a lot from it. As much as Gibson tries to exist beyond a self, through his constant traveling and identity changes, he's haunted by the few recurring characters — his lost love from New Jersey, or the paranoid fears of the psychotic psychologist that follow him around unresolved for a decade. This is a much more sophisticated book that it may seem on the surface. It's funny, yeah, often incredibly so, but the pieces add up to create some fantastic negative space. I'm such a sucker for the now-vanished America chronicled in this book (and *The Franchiser*) that I might be inflating its value somewhat through the household, everyday existence that Elkin infuses into Gibson's callers. The long story of the dodo hunt on Mauritania might seem unrelated, or a too-obvious metaphor, but it's hilarious and weird and shows how much scope one writer can pack into any work of imagination if s/he tries hard enough.

597. The Archaic Revival by Terrence McKenna

Received: 12 February 2005
Started: 9 January 2014
Finished: 26 January 2014

This collection of interviews with and essays by Terrence McKenna was published in the early 90s and mostly contains material from the late 1980s. The topics are varied, but not that varied — psychedelic plants and shamanic techniques are at the root of almost every piece in here. McKenna was a brilliant guy and he's able to talk about pretty far-out topics in a way that isn't alienating, even when literally talking about aliens. His approach to psychedelics is probably the most reasoned and sophisticated one I have come across; he warns against any non-plant-based substances, and even thinks that psychedelics should be restricted to those who are able to actually learn and benefit from them, rather than a way for 18-year-olds to get zonked. When he gets into some of his more far-out theories, like "the end of history" (different to McKenna than when Fukuyama was saying it around the same time) or his Timewave Zero nonsense, I get lost — but not so much because he's a raving lunatic, but because his fuzziness gets the best of him, though he thankfully owns up to it and never claims anything to be true. So really, for a guy writing about flying saucers, this is exactly the way I want it to be. It's not Von Daniken pseudoscience, but certainly a speculative approach to cosmology, but I tolerate it because he's not dogmatic and like Robert Anton Wilson, there's some great ideas in here. It's been a decade since I took psilocybin and I have been thinking about it again, which is why I picked this up. McKenna's account of traveling to the Amazon to find ayahuasca in the late 60s reads like a great travel piece, with reasoned results that were somewhat surprising and certainly not sexy. The essay on the Voynich manuscript is totally great, though its only relation to the rest of the book is that I guess it's about esoteric knowledge that may possibly be extra-terrestrial in origin (though that's a stretch). Even still, I somehow never knew about the Voynich manuscript before, and it makes the *Codex Seraphinianus* just seem derivative by comparison. The chapter near the end about the emergence of virtual reality technologies is laughable now, as it was written in 1990, but I can forgive McKenna for his enthusiasm and he's probably lucky to have died before seeing Second Life. It's frustrating that people who are willing to actually explore important topics such as psychedelic consciousness so easily get drawn into theories like Timewave Zero; McKenna was about as empirical and scientific as they come, at least when he started out, so it's a shame that he ended up being marginalised by many as only a druggie nutcase. Of course, psychedelics are about having your ontological identity ripped out from under you, so I guess if you hold back on your post-psychedelic thoughts then you're really wasting the potential of communicating to the masses.

598. Flight to Canada by Ishmael Reed
Received: 7 April 2011
Started: 17 January 2014
Finished: 29 January 2014
I didn't love *Flight to Canada*. It picked up from *Mumbo Jumbo*'s radical reimagining
361 of American history, criss-crossing timelines and logic, and directly addressed the idea of the Underground Railroad and slave liberation movement. I can't really pinpoint what I didn't enjoy this time around — I've read enough of Reed by this point to be used to his crazy dialogue, bizarre character constructions and ironic takedowns of media and celebrity. This just wasn't that funny, and the plot didn't move me — it felt more like he was going through the motions, though there were a few good moments.

599. You Are Not a Gadget: A Manifesto by Jaron Lanier
Received: 6 February 2014
Started: 6 February 2014
Finished: 7 February 2014
A friend lent me this and I read most of it in the car on the way back to Helsinki. Lanier is a computer scientist from the early days of the Internet who was actively involved in VR research in the late 80s. Now he's taking a philosophical tone, and has written this book to stake out his views, which are mostly against "open culture" and cloud computing. This is written like a computer guy would write — it's organised very tightly into sections, with descriptive headings and summaries before (which would allow you to skip certain chapters if you want to). There's some very strong material in the beginning — part 1 is entitled 'What is a person?' and is fiercely critical of social networking because of how it changes us — a theme we discuss frequently at Pixelache and will likely organise some activities around. I loved the parts of this book that tapped into my own recent thoughts, such as said section, and his overall disappointment at the open-source movement's conservative nature. Lanier seems to be as disappointed in technology as I am, and puts forth a beautifully written argument that what Alan Turing really gave us with his test is a merging of the spiritual and the humanist realms to stand against the computationalism of today (whereas before the spiritual and humanist views were at war). I think he's absolutely correct in his analysis of the insidious advertising and marketing techniques of Internet-based content aggregators, and how techno-elites are separating themselves from the masses, and how our own complicity in this is deeply disturbing. But about half of this book consisted of arguments about intellectual property, in particular music, which were dull and un-engaging. Not that Lanier is necessarily wrong, but his relatively mundane statements about content creation and digital replication are nothing I need to hear anymore (though I admit my own background, coming from the super-uncommercial 'underground' (or whatever) of music and art, changes my priorities entirely). I was most annoyed by his need to reassure Silicon Valley libertarians that he's not advocating socialism, and while I recognise his own viewpoint is more sophisticated, I wish he had taken on more of the political ideals that shape Google, Wikipedia, etc. He makes the superficial mistake of conflating Marxism with Stalinism and almost completely dismisses it, which is a shame, as a Marxist approach might offer one direction to combat the problems he highlights. Back in high school I read Clifford Stoll's *Silicon Snake Oil*, and this is a far better book than that, though dealing with similar ideas (though a lot has changed since then); I would genuinely recommend this to people who maybe aren't realising the depth of their own web 2.0 "expressions". But it still felt a bit like philosophy-light; I would have been more curious to see an analytical look at cultural shifts on a deeper scale, encompassing political and economic shifts and incorporating the developing world into his purview.

600. The Journals of Spalding Gray by Spalding Gray
Received: 18 January 2014
Started: 18 January 2014
Finished: 9 February 2014
Getting through *The Journals of Spalding*

Gray was as tough as watching the last Soderbergh documentary on him, for even though he was a narcissistic, self-absorbed alpha male, his work made me feel a closeness to him, like someone I knew. (Which makes it funnier that I really didn't get into his work until years after his passing). These journals emphasised this false closeness even more so, and it's an indispensable piece of the Gray canon, even though the editors really had their work cut out for them. Gray journaled sporadically throughout his life, and the more active and turbulent times had few entries, so the editors had to fill this in with long biographical passages. As a result, this is halfway between biography and autobiography, though I guess everything the man did was an autobiography anyway. And everything the man did was for an audience, including journaling, which he cops to at a few points. This makes it very readable, though you have to wonder what they left out. Though I knew a lot about him, this clearly fills in missing pieces — the details of his relationships with Elizabeth LeComte, Renée Shafransky and Kathie Russo in particular. The mess in the early 90s after he married Shafransky but had fathered a child with Russo is probably the most intense part of it all, giving more insight than *It's a Slippery Slope* on its own provides. The transition from 1970s young, sexually adventurous Spalding Gray into late 90s family man, a man so enamoured by the existence of his own son that it turns almost creepy, is a wonder to read. And the final section, detailing his repeated suicide attempts, while mostly written by the editors, has a few excerpts that are just brutal to endure. I didn't realise the ugliness of the very end of Spalding Gray — the Soderbergh film
1015 is more abstract on this topic (in a tasteful way), but the last year sounded so insane and horrible for his family that I felt absolutely devastated just reading it. I really wish there were some videos out of there of his last monologues, or everything he did from *Morning, Noon and Night* on — maybe I will order the books so I can at least read them.

601. Escape Velocity: A Charles Portis Miscellany by Charles Portis
Received: 18 February 2014
Started: 18 February 2014
Finished: 1 March 2014
I only read about half of *Delray's New Moon*, the play that takes up a chunk of this, because I found myself having trouble focusing on the script — I guess reading drama is a skill I let atrophy. The rest of this was great, though. I've been wanting to get my hands on this since it came out last year but I wisely waited until I could get it from the library (as my reducing-possessions goal is making me really cautious, keeping which books I will actually purchase to a minimum). Jay Jennings carefully compiled just about everything he could find by Portis, which includes a few hilarious short stories; an austere, beautiful memoir of his childhood; and some miscellaneous journalism. The journalism ranges from local Little Rock stories to his front-line reporting on the civil rights struggles in the 60s, which is surprisingly gripping yet still written with that Portis cadence. A long piece on the country music scene in Nashville, circa 1965, was oddly compelling, and since there's nothing else by him left to read, this is really a great service that Jennings did. The end reprints some essays about Portis by others, including the *Believer* article that launched my interest in him back in 2003, and the only known interview with him, which is primarily about his work for the *Little Rock Gazette*. I will definitely revisit *The Dog of the South* soon. 93

602. Berg by Ann Quin
Received: 26 February 2014
Started: 28 February 2014
Finished: 14 March 2014
I've always been curious about Quin, and a recent re-evaluation on some blog made me finally order this. Some consider *Berg* to be a classic of experimental British literature, and while I didn't find it particularly experimental, it was extremely British. Quin's writing was very Joycean, lifting its style from certain chapters of *Ulysses* but transforming the Dublin setting to Brighton. As a portrait of Brighton it's incredible; though there are only scarce descriptions of the town or landscape, I felt like I was back there, though not possessing any murderous desires. Maybe I'm reading into the Britishness of this too much, but I felt a strong undertone of class here; the depiction of Judith and Nathy's lifestyle felt sharply rendered, and Berg himself, while the centre of everything, is barely present. His existence is rendered only by his quest and the scattered memories of his mother, and the effect is brutal; this is a very dark, very unpleasant book. I found a more direct line between *Berg* and the social realist films of the 60s coming out of Britain, than to any sort of experimental

tradition beyond Joyce. There's not a trace of absurdity, though the severe vibe of Genet was likely an influence. This was a short book but I took it slowly; it was worth savouring, and there's something intangible about the whole experience that has really resonated with me.

603. Glyph: A Novel by Percival Everett
Received: 11 March 2014
Started: 14 March 2014
Finished: 16 March 2014
Why is the 'precocious child' such an oft-used device in the literature of my generation? Everett's novel takes it even further, as his hero comes out of the womb with a full adult intelligence, genius-like even, with a mastery of philosophical though — yet is voluntarily mute. The first half of this book unfolds at a breakneck pace, with Everett's scattered form mostly supporting the narrative. He attacks Roland Barthes beyond mere critique, using *Glyph* as an all-out assault, and fills the remaining spaces with strange poems and thought experiments that I couldn't quite determine the seriousness of. I was reminded of *I Heart*
372, 454 *Huckabees* — a fun pseudo-intellectual romp that used larger thoughts to enhance a rather traditional structure — though I think Everett was reaching for something loftier. I really enjoyed reading this, tearing through the whole thing mostly during one trans-Atlantic flight, and it's made me curious about Everett's other work — though I'm not sure if this was actually good. It felt a little bit like intellectual fast food, as it really seems to evade any reading beyond a reinforcement of biology and family patterns despite the supposed genius of its narrator. Everett has a talent, for sure; I'm not sure if this is a minor work of his quite prolific output but I will try to find others, for sure.

604. SPECTRE by Laurence A. Rickels
Received: 10 March 2014
Started: 16 March 2014
Finished: 17 March 2014
Rickels's curious little book attracted my attention when I read a review of it in the *Los Angeles Review of Books*, so I ordered a secondhand copy. This was a silly thing for me to have read, though, as it's based almost entirely on the Ian Fleming Bond novels and very little on the films; I've never read a Bond novel (though I've seen probably all the films) so this fascinating psychoanalytic literary analysis went right over my head. Furthermore, Rickels is very rooted in the writings of Klein, so pretty much every other chapter was about Klein and thus I ended up reading 100 pages about things I only had a vague knowledge of. Still, Rickels is a great writer, and I'd call him 'clever' but that sounds condescending. He uses sharp puns and an edgy style — the kind that wins awards in British literary criticism, though my sense of Rickels is that he's a real outsider, writing about German culture, psychoanalysis and other such matters. I have only a light interest in psychoanalysis and certainly not to the level that Rickels applies it, but I'm still glad I read this, if only to introduce me to the concept of *acedia*. I should have ordered his book on Philip K. Dick instead, given that I've read most of the Dick novels, but instead I got his book about California, a place I have never been to. Maybe this approach warrants an analysis of its own.

605. Last Evenings on Earth by Roberto Bolano
Received: 25 June 2010
Started: 19 March 2014
Finished: 22 March 2014
I just watched Leos Carax's *Boy Meets* 1339
Girl, and though I didn't intend for this to relate, reading this book of Bolaño stories really fit the mood I was in after that. Pretty much everything in here was striking, if not completely dazzling, set in Bolaño's world where literature rules over everything but with a driving momentum that was serviced by the shorter form. Some, like 'Vagabond in France and Belgium', recall the device of the mysterious obscure author used so well in *2666*. Others are written with what looks like, on the surface, to be a Robbe-Grilletesque *nouveau roman* form — of detachment and characters named A and B — but are actually much richer, laden with the weight of poetry, heat, and violence always lurking just underneath. This is what he does well and he's at his best here; this ranks up there with *The Savage Detectives* as some of his best work (and features the narrator Arturo Belano in several stories). A few seem to be just chronicles of a life, or experience — 'Anne Moore's Life' is long and seeming without purpose, yet probably the most affecting story in the book; 'A Literary Adventure', 'Last Evenings on Earth' and 'Phone Calls' are all completely astounding in different ways. I should probably just read the last few translated titles and then revisit *Savage Detectives*, which 351
I barely remember at this point.

606. A Visit from the Goon Squad by Jennifer Egan
Started: 17 February 2014
Finished: 2 April 2014
I started this on my way to America and forgot about it; appropriately, I finished it at a different airport. This was good and also nothing to get too excited about. Egan seemed to be writing a bunch of short stories that she tried to loosely link together, but sorry, that doesn't make it a proper novel. This had the curious effect of being too short and also too long; some chapters went on forever, with no resolution or real value, while others I could have stayed inside forever. She has an innate ability to capture modern life, which is a valuable asset for a contemporary novelist. However, she also tries to project into the future and write about technology in a way that feels too speculative, and her chronicle of labels and bands feels desperate, trying to be too hip. I did enjoy this, but it was definitely an airport book — yet I'm convinced Egan can write something wonderful next.

607. The Culture of the Copy: Striking Likenesses, Unreasonable Facsimiles by Hillel Schwartz
Received: 28 July 2007
Started: 21 March 2014
Finished: 20 April 2014
This was something I picked up randomly during a period where I was buying books obsessively, and fairly haphazardly — when it wasn't safe to let me near the gift shop of a contemporary art gallery. I had this on the shelf for years, and finally got around to starting it recently, as part of my doomed quest to read everything unread and sell most of my books off before the end of the summer. Wow — I won't be selling this one. I love books like this: essays that are somewhat historical, somewhat theoretical, and highly stylistic. It all ends up being extremely entertaining, and I took this slowly in order to savour it. The book looks at the idea of 'copy' throughout various themes, from twins to doppelgangers to portraiture and ultimately to genetic cloning, stopping for all manner of digressions along the way. There isn't a central argument here, as much as a personally curated tour through history's ephemera, and in doing so it gradually attains a strong voice. I read that Schwartz just completed a massive 900 page study about the history of noise (meaning unwanted sound, rather than the genre of music) which I immediately ordered.

608. Heartsnatcher by Boris Vian
Received: 11 March 2014
Started: 2 April 2014
Finished: 22 April 2014
Heartsnatcher is a textbook example of French absurdist literature, reminiscent of Samuel Beckett's trilogy, the works of Alfred Jarry (unsurprisingly, as Vian belonged to the College of Pataphysics) and of course Lautremont. I ate this stuff for breakfast when I was younger and I always enjoy something constructed like this, where there's a pastoral scenario undermined with violence, darkness and disturbing sexuality. It's hard to know what this adds up to, besides a perverted mockery of psychoanalytic techniques and a cynical view of the family. But I don't pressure myself to find too much in works like this, which are at their best when they create an imaginative scenario that is simultaneously horrifying and inviting. Vian's best known work is *L'écume des jours*, which 
maybe would have been a better starting 1382
point, as this was his last book and it feels somewhat unfinished, but I can always read that next. While I'll always love extremely absurd work (especially books like this, which are less reliant on humour and genuinely try to create new emotions through the descriptive language and plot), I think I was craving something more grounded while reading this and thus I took it slowly and didn't rush through it, though it was an easy read. But you can't read *The Movie-* 
goer every day; and I much prefer fucked 155,
up anti-establishment literature of the past 287, 474
to easy contemporary fiction that attempts to document this particular milieu.

609. On Us by Douglas Woolf
Received: 11 October 2013
Started: 22 April 2014
Finished: 24 April 2014
Douglas Woolf, where have you been my whole life? This small self-published novel starts off with such a strange and unsettling tone that I had to brace myself for what I expected to be a challenging slab of experimental fiction. But after a few pages I started to guess at Woolf's intent, which was (I think) to construct an omniscient portrayal of someone who has slipped through the cracks of American life — not a Bohemian per se, but a writer; no one radical or even that fascinating, but yet-undescribed. As this short tale expands from a sweet romance to a bizarre road trip and ultimately to something very strange and almost sci-fi, there's never any conflict

or drama. It's a sketch, where the pleasure lies in the details and the work stands out as something incredibly singular, yet very much in the league of certain other lesser-appreciated American writers from the 70s, specifically Stanley Elkin. I wanted more from this. I will seek out and consume the rest of Woolf's bibliography now.

610. Homo Faber by Max Frisch
Received: 28 August 2008
Started: 25 April 2014
Finished: 27 April 2014
Frisch continues to amaze me; this was maybe the best of his three novels that I've read (though *Man in Holocene* is really
266 something spectacular too) and quite reminiscent of Walker Percy's *The Moviegoer.*
155, 287, 474 It's not as light, and the protagonist is somewhat more sympathetically portrayed, but it has this same sense of detachment and wandering though on a more fantastic, global scale. I loved how Frisch would spoil the plot intentionally and undercut and sort of mystery/buildup, leaving just the strange narration of Herr Farber to carry things along. When it takes a highly emotional turn in the second part it fits and rounds out the midlife crisis portrayed here. This is about as 'modern' and 20th century as a novel can get, set in 1957 and filled with air travel, post-national identity and unconventional family relationships, with the spectre of World War II hanging heavy over everything. But it's fun — I blew through the first 100 pages in a flash, and only made myself slow down when I realised I was approaching the end. In all of the tales of alienation I've read, there was something really powerful here, maybe in the way it crescendos into something very real and sad, and this is due to Frisch's careful construction and language.

611. Torpor by Chris Kraus
Received: 11 October 2013
Started: 28 April 2014
Finished: 5 May 2014
How odd to find a Chris Kraus book at a charity shop in Stockholm — but I'm glad I did, because I've wanted to try Kraus's "fiction". After a few pages I remembered that *I Love Dick* was technically "fiction"
483 too and thus *Torpor* was about the same level of fictional, though far less mind-blowing. In this story, Kraus actually bothered to change the names of her and her husband, but there's no mistaking that this is a thinly disguised bit of biography. This is primarily concerned with the onset of middle age and the desire for motherhood that comes biologically, while built around a time-broken narrative of Kraus and Lotringer — excuse me, Sylvie and Jerome — going to Romania in the early 90s hoping to illegally adopt a refugee. The travelogue takes over at times, and the utter misery of Kraus's marriage is pushed just under the surface, which is an effective technique as it bubbles throughout and sets a general sense of sadness and, well, torpor. It's remarkable that she would write a book so honest and raw about her marriage to Lotringer, and then publish it under him on Semiotext(e). I think this would be enjoyable even without that layer of external information, but I couldn't really separate the 'real' people from the fiction here. The depiction of 90s Eastern Europe and all of it's attendant politics and controversy is pretty solid, and the way she contrasts it with the banalities of contemporary art/philosophy society (she doesn't write about the various gallerists, curators, or artists in this book with any sort of reverence, let alone Felix Guattari) is carefully done. I'm glad to have read this as I really do think Kraus is an exceptional talent, existing beyond any sort of genre barriers; though this isn't *I Love Dick* (what could be?) it was still worthwhile and I think
I'll seek out *Aliens and Anorexia* next. 787

612. Beautiful Losers by Leonard Cohen
Received: 6 March 2014
Started: 6 March 2014
Finished: 15 May 2014
I finally finished this, which I've gone to several times over the years, but I'm not sure what to think. I love Leonard Cohen's writing and this sets him free, fully unrestrained, roaming through language and tearing up conventions, transgressive in its sexual content (for the time) and occasionally breathtaking. I didn't find a lot to click with here, though I enjoy the mythology of early Canadian history (as Vollmann deals with lots in his *Seven Dreams*) and 
the stream-of-consciousness moments 116
afforded Cohen a freedom not found in the relatively boundary-driven structures of his poetry and songs. This would probably surprise a lot of people who only know his hit songs, but the darkness and desperation oozes out of his best albums (which is why I love *Death of a Ladies' Man* so much) 
so I found this strangely familiar territory 1788
(though I've also started this several times over the years).

613. The Jokers by Albert Cossery
Received: 5 April 2011
Started: 14 May 2014
Finished: 22 May 2014

I didn't love Cossery's writing, but I didn't hate it either. It just simply was. There are some interesting ideas here about dissent and violence, and it's all done in a nice ensemble-style narrative that portrays the diversity of life in Alexandria (where this was set, though I only know that from the preface) in a surprising way. Egypt in the mid-60s was apparently a lot more liberal than I realised, and the various 'jokers' whom this chronicles are portrayed if not heroically, then sympathetically. But it's too light to add up to anything substantial, and Cossery's prose is occasionally a bit too rigid to reflect that chaos and dynamism of Middle Eastern urbanity. I felt like this was meant to be satirical and dark, but it pulled its punches and ended up being nothing remarkable.

614. Leaving the Sea: Stories by Ben Marcus
Received: 26 February 2014
Started: 23 May 2014
Finished: 12 June 2014

It's probably a testament to how dark and gruelling I found *The Flame Alphabet* (as
485 well as how preoccupied I am with everyday life stress right now) that I waited a few months to start this, a new collection of short stories by someone who is probably my favourite active writer. *Leaving the Sea* contained a little bit of everything that Marcus does, including some things I didn't know that he did. The book is divided into sections by theme, starting with a few relatively conventional stories that explore family, professional and sexual insecurity in a manner that is no less brutal than *Flame Alphabet*, if less fantastical in setting. The familiar Marcus style of *Notable American*
190, *Women* appears later in the volume, and
571 it culminates in a long story called 'The Moors' which seems to summarise a lot of themes into one place. I really loved 'The Father Costume', previously available only in an expensive art edition, which may be the perfect amount of the *Wire and String*
123, style that he seems to have mostly moved
286 past. 'Leaving the Sea' the story is a Molly Bloom-esque spiel that is maybe the bleakest point of the book, yet invigorating in its difficulty and uncompromising nature. There's not much sunshine here, but I'd still call myself a rabid fan.

615. Night Film by Marisha Pessl
Received: 11 June 2014
Started: 11 June 2014
Finished: 25 June 2014

I started reading this after it came up as a suggestion from Amazon, showing how gullible I am when it comes to auto-generated taste algorithms. If I had noticed the comparison to Stephen King from the get-go I wouldn't have bothered; of course, I ended up sucked in, the classic 'guilty pleasure' if I believe in such things, but I don't (I'm not ashamed of any of my pleasures, but there was no pleasure here). *Night Film* is a poorly written book that takes an intriguing premise (experimental horror film director is reclusive and possibly murderous) and then unfolds the plot in a formulaic and badly-written procedural which, by the end, left me just glad to get it over with. So why did I keep reading? I guess I wanted something entertaining, and I read most of this while travelling so I can use the holiday/beach book excuse. I don't feel the need to justify my media consumption habits anymore (I'm only mildly ashamed of all the cruddy comedy films I watch) but I don't want to admit that I actually enjoyed any of this, but again, I read it through to the end. Maybe I sound here a bit like when Radiohead's *Kid A* came out and *The Wire* reviewed it in this very roundabout way, basically trying not to admit that they enjoyed it. I guess I felt a comfort in easy prose and the new Hillel Schwartz book was far too heavy to drag all the way to Bulgaria....

616. Making Noise: From Babel to the Big Bang and Beyond by Hillel Schwartz
Received: 28 May 2014
Started: 27 June 2014
Finished: 4 August 2014

I can't believe I finished it. I've read a lot of lengthy tomes, but somehow *Making Noise* felt special. It might be due to my own inability to concentrate lately, though I've had more or less ideal conditions for reading it; I can't even count how many hours I whiled away in the windowsill of the Ptarmigan office with this cradled against my lap. At 852 pages, Schwartz's work is an epic study of noise (in the sense of 'unwanted sound') in a cultural history format, and the style was similar to *The Culture of the* 
Copy. Ultimately, I think his prior work was 607
probably the stronger book, but maybe that's just because I didn't have the stamina to consistently stay focused on Schwartz for a longer period. This is an amazing work

of scholarship and yet it's so digressive and idiosyncratic that I can't imagine what value it would have for anyone beyond entertainment or being a starting point for further research. One review on Amazon suggested that almost every sentence here could be a PhD topic in itself, but actually it's the paragraphs that are thematic — the notes, kept online to avoid ballooning this to 1500 pages, are for each paragraph and I'm sure you could spend a year each investigating any of these sources. Throughout this journey I've learned about 17th century London prostitutes, New York City's history of anti-noise activists, theatre designers in the 1800s, and a zillion other things that don't always seem completely relevant to 'noise' but are certainly fascinating. I think Vollmann's *Imperial* might be the only other 433 book I've read that is anything like this in terms of how vast and encompassing it is, with regards to an authorial vision or perhaps mania. I took this to the beach a few times, spilled water on it, and generally treated it badly so even though I only spent a month with it, it looks like the book itself survived some sort of war — which is how I feel somewhat, as a reader.

617. Debt: The First 5,000 Years by David Graeber
Received: 6 August 2014
Started: 6 August 2014
Finished: 8 September 2014
I took this much more slowly than I thought, as I tore through the first 120 pages at MoKS and then switched to a digital version and found myself slowing down. Graeber has interested me ever since I read his essay on 'bullshit jobs' and the subsequent interview in Salon. His anthropological approach to studying economics means he is far less bound by ideology and orthodoxy, and thus can put forth a theory like this, which is quietly radical. Graeber rejects the conventional history that a barter system led to the establishment of paper money, and then to credit/debt relations, showing with a great deal of supporting evidence that the truth is very much the opposite order. He cites Western examples such as the Irish slave trade as well as present-day tribal/indigenous situations, and the subtext is that the very foundation of economies is built on human suffering and exploitation. Being written just after the "crisis" helps to sell his points, about how ridiculous the profit/wage imbalance has become and how the true moral route would be to NOT repay debt. The final chapter, covering 1971 to the present, could stand alone as a brilliant summary of our situation since the US dropped the gold standard, at least until the final pages which take on a polemic, anti-globalisation stance which actually distracts a bit from the vision he's presented. This isn't overly academic at all — it's a layman's guide to a topic that few of us have ever thought about distinctly, but probably should. His writing style is extremely accessible, almost like "popular anthropology" if there is such a thing.

618. Taipei by Tao Lin
Received: 25 June 2014
Started: 25 June 2014
Finished: 9 September 2014
Great writing reflects experience, and I can't deny that Tao Lin is chronicling some shared existence that's probably relatable to many people. This book is just begging for me to judge Paul's behaviour — to cast my own personal ethics against his endless cycle of drug binges and Internet commenting. I'm trying to withhold this impulse, and when I do that, I must admit that I'm impressed. I mean, there's something here — a type of writing that is pretty much without precedent, in that it bears no discernible influence of literary traditions past (or concern for how it will be regarded). Is this actually a great book, hiding in the Xanax'ed trench of dulled senses? This doesn't give a shit about stirring passages of prose or romantic, starry-eyed wonder; it's probably the best summary of this type of lifestyle I've seen (with the only thing close being maybe some of those mumblecore films I love so much) and it's not nihilistic, either. The absolute lack of attitude is probably what I found so confounding, and hard for me to wrap my head around. I feel old, reading this, which I probably say about a lot of things, but in this case I'm actually sort of in awe of it.

619. The Notebooks of Malte Laurids Brigge by Rainer Maria Rilke
Received: 11 March 2014
Started: 4 September 2014
Finished: 17 September 2014
Rilke's words never fail to stir me, though I lost interest in the second half of this. The first half was more or less a continental version of *A Portrait of the Artist as a Young Man* with some spooky tendencies and less guilt. There were some great, contemplative passages in this section,

particularly about death, written with the winking naiveté of a fictional youthful voice; other sections, like anything having to do with the actual plot of this (if there is one) were hard to engage with. I'll take Rilke's poetry over his prose, though maybe it's just that I wasn't in the right frame of mind to take this on.

620. Asterios Polyp by David Mazzucchelli
Received: (already owned)
Started: 20 September 2014
Finished: 20 September 2014
Re-read in one sitting as part of my quest to pare down how many books I have, particularly comics and graphic novels which I tend to get rid of reluctantly. I always look at them and ask myself the question "will I ever read this again?" Well, I did and enjoyed it again but will be glad to let it go. I think the parts that annoyed me the first time around — specifically the more abstract parts — were my favourite moments here. The decision to have every character in a different drawing style and font (as well as the meticulous colour schemes) tried to add a rational, structural feel that the narrative was critiquing. I like what was left out of the story — though the tension of his marriage is felt, the very end is occluded. Conceptually, this is phenomenal, even down to the design of the book itself; the allegories aren't cryptic (with Orpheus being directly in the plot, plus the Greek nature of Polyp) but it's not simplistic. The thing that felt a bit underdeveloped is after we learn that Polyp has recorded his own life with cameras — we see the tapes burn up in the opening pages — and I guess that sense of letting go is what leads to his decision to disappear, but it doesn't feel congruent or fleshed out enough.

621. Microscripts by Robert Walser
Received: 5 March 2014
Started: 10 August 2014
Finished: 21 September 2014
As I gradually begin to read more literature originally in the German language, I wonder why I keep migrating towards Swiss or Austrian writers over ones actually from Germany. Walser's *Microscripts* are fascinating conceptually, in a manner akin to outsider art or an obscure underground musician who left a largely indecipherable body of work. But Walser is considered to be one of the major writers of the 20th century, even if his work has gone in and out of fashion. Thus, I'm not sure if this was the best starting point for him — if these little ventures are indicative of his style, or an oddity. Maybe I should have started with *The Assistant* or *Berlin Stories* first. But I really enjoyed this, loving some of them, and they were short enough that I could quickly pass over the ones that I didn't care for. I was surprised by how playful and affect-driven these were. They reminded me of Lydia Davis, not just because of the brevity (an obvious comparison), but in the way that they could build themselves around a concept or thought and sustain it for the perfect duration. Having just read Rilke's *Malte Laurids Brigge*, also German language modernist writing from around the same period, I felt both to carry a contemplative nature about the field of literature and writing throughout — this is work that is totally dependent on the history of literature rather than some free-standing construction. But where Rilke's novel is wrapped up in youthful passions, Walser is writing from an older, more stoic perspective, and still managed to employ a variety of voices throughout. This is a book I'm going to hold on to (as I'm getting rid of much of my library now) and flip open to when I'm looking for subtle pleasures; I think it can fit nicely next to Pessoa or *Mr. Palomar* as a book that may keep providing dividends the longer I stay connected with it.

577

619

622. Dockwood by Jon McNaught
Received: 11 March 2014
Started: 21 September 2014
Finished: 21 September 2014
This is McNaught's best work yet, I think — it's somehow more connected to the 'real' world, yet without sacrificing any of it's contemplation. It's concerned with work, chronicling a kitchen worker and a paper-boy's daily routines, but also has moments of sky-gazing wonder, without ever leaving the confines of the mundane. Visually, it's a treat — the larger format book allows him to pack more of his small panels on each page, and the colour palette is the same as in his other works and also printed with great quality. This work really identifies itself as being part of Britain, with the presence of Topshop and Tesco advertising in the background and the speech patterns of the few bits of dialogue present. The real star is the background — the landscape, trees, skies and power lines of the fictitious Dockwood. Absolutely stunning.

623. The Snow Leopard by Peter Matthiessen
Received: 10 September 2014
Started: 10 September 2014
Finished: 29 September 2014
What a beautiful, beautiful book. Matthiessen writes about the natural surroundings of Nepal in 1973 with a calm yet lush flavour, celebrating the colours and movement as he sees it. As a travelogue, it's a first-rate documentation of an experience that few readers could ever hope to undergo. But the journalistic edge blends into an introspective, Buddhist-influenced sense of presence, making this somewhere between philosophy and a personal mourning over the death of his wife. Her presence haunts the book without weighing it down, and Matthiessen is incredibly human, whining about petty annoyances caused by his travelling partner while simultaneously reflecting on the absurdity and beauty of existence. The snow leopard itself serves as the quest at the heart of this, though in true Zen fashion, it's really not important if he actually sees it or not (spoiler alert: he doesn't). This is one of the best works of nonfiction I've ever read.

624. Music: What Happened? by Scott Miller
Received: 25 September 2014
Started: 25 September 2014
Finished: 1 October 2014
The great Scott Miller of Game Theory/ Loud Family (R.I.P.) compiled CDs representing the best of popular music for every year from 1957 to 2009. The book is simply his notes on each selection and why he chose what he did, which eventually starts to build a narrative of one man's engagement with music throughout his life. His writings on the 60s and 70s are fantastic; the 80s start to parallel his own career in the industry and his tastes become more idiosyncratic, but it's all great. I actually skimmed the last few years as I knew nothing about any of the music from 2005-2009 and his choices seemed (knowingly) removed from the paradigm of popular culture by then. His choices are great, when I knew them — who else besides me would choose two Flop songs? I already loved Miller but this boosted him in my view, and now I'm even sadder about his passing.

625. Cosmos and Pornografia: Two Novels by Witold Gombrowicz
Received: 4 September 2012
Started: 2 February 2013
Finished: 6 October 2014
I never read Gombrowicz before and knew he was a Polish absurdist, but I didn't expect this to be so dream-like and engrossing. *Cosmos* sucked me in by constructing a first-person narration built around mundane, mysterious things. His style is elliptical, yet realistic — there's a lot of long list-like runs of nouns (a common trait I find among writers I like) and I'm wondering if he was a bit of an influence on Nicholson Baker's fiction. As the novel progresses, it gets darker and darker, culminating in something confusingly deranged that I didn't expect in the slightest — yet still, sort of it's about 'nothing'. There's a lot of mystery in here, none of which adds up to anything, which is precisely why it's so great. This translation was re-translated by combining the French and German translations, and while it sufficed, I'm curious about the newer, direct-from-Polish translation, which is what I'll find if I ever re-read this. There's lots of potential for use in action-based performance or non-performance collaborations, as this whole 'search for meaning' thing is wonderfully deconstructed. [4 February 2013] • And *Pornografia*, wow — another stunner. This was DARK and twisted and somehow agile in it's perversions. Gombrowicz was wise to title this *Pornografia* because it's certainly about the deep, forbidden impulses that separate pornography from normal sexuality. This isn't about sex at all, or at least not on the surface, but about power, violence and manipulation, mining the essence of pure prurience. I like that Gombrowicz uses his own name for the narrator, but doesn't shy away from implicating himself in these activities. I'm not really sure what the point was to set this during the war, but maybe there's some deeper Polish context here that I didn't pick up on. I also loved the tone here — this was written in a matter-of-fact way, rather without embellishments or overly emotional asides, despite directly addressing a perverse longing; it's a balancing act, for sure, though this wasn't the supposedly better translation that is now available. I need to read more of his work — a friend says that the diaries are really his masterpiece, so I should see if they're available in English. [6 October 2014]

626. In the Fascist Bathroom: Punk in Pop Music, 1977-1992 by Greil Marcus
Received: (already owned)
Started: 4 October 2014
Finished: 8 October 2014
I think I read this (or most of it) a long time ago when it was called *Ranters and Crowd Pleasers;* approaching it now, from an older perspective (and having formulated a lot of my own thoughts about class, politics, and music's relationship to them) I got a surprising amount out of this. This is a collection of various pieces Marcus wrote throughout the 80s, theoretically addressing the spirit of punk in popular culture but getting pretty tangential (at least, I failed to grasp what was punk about Cyndi Lauper). Marcus is a genius in many ways, and his obsession with Leeds-based British post-punk bands hardly wavers throughout the years. There's a whole lot more about Elvis Costello than I particularly cared for, but the rest of this was pretty enjoyable. A few pieces on the 486 Mekons and Lilliput started to feel almost repetitive, but some were written in a satirical manner that made this almost like Bangs or Meltzer — a tendency I didn't know Marcus had in him. Other artists were surprising to appear here — the Iron City Houserockers were mentioned quite a few times, though not enough to make me curious enough to investigate. Marcus, of course, thinks way too hard about pop music and overblows the significance of many of these things, but if you aren't prepared for that you shouldn't read him. The pontificating 585 here isn't as loose as in *Lipstick Traces*, and thankfully the fall of the Soviet Union (and grunge) passes with hardly a mention. I wouldn't mind a whole book of his 'Real Life Rock Top Ten' lists that were frequently excerpted here; there's some musical curiosities buried within, plus it's intriguing to see how he felt about, say, a late-80s Wire record when it was initially issued.

627. M: Writings '67-'72 by John Cage
Received: 22 September 2014
Started: 22 September 2014
Finished: 22 October 2014
This collection of miscellaneous Cage writings (the first of three) is largely mesostic-based, interspersed with the brilliant and sporadic 'Diary: How To Improve the World (You Will Only Make Matters Worse)'. This is uneven, but with a few wonderful moments; the mushroom diaries are fantastic and just abstract enough; the lengthy 'Mureau' (a cut up piece combining the I Ching and Henry David Thoreau's writing, which ends up being a somniferous and highly experimental celebration of natural sounds through language) is fucking amazing and the real centrepiece. There are more mesostics throughout the book that were in a crazy art deco typeface and I actually found them hard to read so I started skipping them. The most surprising thing, content-wise, was how much this book attempted to address the political and social concerns of the time; 1967-72 was a hell of a time to be a gay artist in America, and what really shocked me was how much Cage flirted with Maoism here. In the introduction he writes quite openly about the attraction of the cultural revolution, and the earlier sections of 'Diary' have some moments that make me feel like I don't "know" Cage — not that I expected a nuanced viewpoint on totalitarian repression, but that he might reject the Communist orthodoxy as much as he rejected that of the Academy. He doesn't out-and-out endorse Mao here, but he certainly seems to be blinded a bit by the potential and the rhetoric, and I guess this is also what happened to Cardew. On to *Empty Words* next.

628. Putting My Foot in It by Rene Crevel
Received: 13 April 2003
Started: 9 October 2014
Finished: 1 November 2014
Crevel is a tough read. His prose is nuts, and I'm sure not easy to translate. This, published in 1939, forcefully integrates surrealist creative approaches with politics and sprinkles it with tons of cultural references, a filthy sense of humour, and some wordplay. I found myself drifting off and not really paying attention, but that's fine, cause there isn't much plot here. It started to feel like a chore by the end, but I think I'm looking for something a little more focused lately. Which isn't to say that this is a sloppy mess — Crevel's iconoclasm is remarkably scrupulous, and his attacks on Church, sexuality, and politics are still inspiring so many years later. The penultimate chapter seems more like a diatribe, and of course if I were more familiar with European aristocracy of the early 20th century, there'd surely be even more to appreciate. Of the surrealist writers I've read, Crevel might be the most accomplished in terms of prose; this is a far cry from automatic writing, and the absurdity comes with a potency that transcends mere randomness. Still, I don't think I'd ever read it again, but I could see

myself thinking a few years later that this was really remarkable and I didn't appreciate it enough.

629. On the Natural History of Destruction by W.G. Sebald
Received: 27 October 2014
Started: 27 October 2014
Finished: 2 November 2014
The main essay in this is Sebald's famous Zurich lecture, on the repression of World War II in Germany (and a lot more), which I had read 9 years ago in my postgraduate course. The book filled this out with some after-thoughts, mostly regarding the response he received to it, and then three short pieces dissecting German writers who attempted to deal with the legacy of the Third Reich. I didn't get a lot out of these pieces, not being familiar with the writers, beyond the general attack-dog mode Sebald was in. But re-reading the Zurich lecture was a pleasure, though maybe pleasure is the wrong word because it certainly isn't a fun topic. Even in this mode, Sebald is primarily writing as a literary critic and thus his scope is limited — I'm sure there is a wealth of literature that could be cited were this a more academic context. Still, even in the most direct, discursive mode, Sebald writes with a quiet rage, an intense probing that never breaks its veneer of wisdom. I know that the leftist activities of 1970s Germany was very much in reaction to the revelation of the legacy of the Third Reich and the repression in popular culture, but Sebald doesn't even mention Baader-Meinhof or anything like it. I've always perceived this writing as the most 'important' of Sebald's work, even if it's so different from his other books, though maybe I'm wrong here, as compared to my enjoyment of the others this felt slight.

630. Dissident Gardens by Jonathan Lethem
Received: 3 November 2014
Started: 3 November 2014
Finished: 10 November 2014
Maybe I was just starting to get into this when I reached the end. Or perhaps this just wasn't very good. I'm not sure; it could be that, like many other books, *Dissident Gardens* grows in my esteem over time. I think it's certainly Lethem's most ambitious novel, though I should really read *Girl in Landscape* just to have read them
632 all and therefore be able to make such judgements. But what was he really trying to accomplish? The political basis of this wasn't real politics, but rather how ideology can affect family life. It aspired to be an epic portrayal of an unconventional family, with the double-whammy of Judaism and Communism mixed in, but it came up short of being engrossing. This was somewhat due to the fragmentary, non-linear nature of the book's flow, which didn't serve any real purpose except being unconventional (and not even so much, by 2014 terms). It just felt like things were missing, and it was hard to really care about any of the characters in this ensemble. I really do think Lethem is best when he incorporates sci-fi elements into his work. His writing suffers when attempting to chronicle today's youth movements, just as *You Don't Love Me Yet* 291
was actually pitiful to read; the depictions here of the Occupy characters felt clichéd, like a man in his 50th year is trying to seem relevant but unable to actually connect to anything. This is what I imagine later Philip Roth books are like, though I might just be basing that on the title *I Married a Communist*. Lethem's Philip K Dick fascination is nowhere to be found here (unless I missed some veiled reference) and I wish he had brought back some reality-bending elements. I wonder if he feels pressured to write more 'serious' novels? *The Fortress of Solitude* was fun first and foremost, and this was just a drag to get through. I'm hoping he can bounce back again (as much as I hated *You Don't Love Me Yet*, *Chronic City*
was sort of great and keeps going up in 581
my estimation after more time has passed).

631. Revenge of the Lawn: Stories 1962-1970 by Richard Brautigan
Received: 3 November 2014
Started: 8 November 2014
Finished: 12 November 2014
It's been years since I read this — possibly since high school. It stands up for sure among Brautigan's best, at least of his most absurdist-leaning stuff. (I should really check out late Brautigan, especially his last book). These stories of course recall other short-form experimentalists, particularly Barthelme and Lydia Davis, though there's the whimsicality throughout that Barthelme lacks, and not a trace of darkness. As fun as these are, quite a lot of them (there are about sixty in all) deal with Brautigan's childhood in Tacoma, Washington and are laced with an ironic nostalgia. There are missing chapters from *Trout Fishing in*
America, followed by "Well, there you have 213
it, the missing chapters from *Trout Fishing*

in America" and that conversational, almost idiot-savant tone (which is so iconic in his writing) saturates this entire short book. The introduction is well-written, apart from the assertion that *In Watermelon Sugar* is his
214 worst book (it's his best!), and also argues that 'The Scarlatti Tilt' is the greatest short story ever written. Well, it's pretty good. I hit up Brautigan just about once a year now and he's like a drug that I need.

632. Girl in Landscape: A Novel by Jonathan Lethem
Received: 10 November 2014
Started: 10 November 2014
Finished: 17 November 2014
The last Lethem novel that I hadn't previously read, this was very much in his PK Dick-influenced sci-fi mode, and read immediately after the overreaching *Dissident Gardens*, this was something I
630 appreciated. Here, he constructs a future-planet scenario that is used as a backdrop to explore racism and construct a thriller based on community conflict, with a few layers of sci-fi overtop. The titular character is presented with strong neutrality for a 13 year old girl — she isn't particularly innocent nor are we meant to pity her. The deep sleeps she succumbs to because of the alien atmosphere are written in a lucid, beautiful way that makes then rather inviting; her unsure relationships with the other adults, upon waking, are caked in confusion and unknowing. In a way this is "straight" sci-fi, but I prefer the smaller Lethem.

633. The Culture of Lies by Dubravka Ugrešić
Received: 20 August 2004
Started: 21 November 2014
Finished: 8 December 2014
This was sitting on my shelf for years and I never quite took enough of an interest to flip through it until now. I was delighted; Ugrešić's collection of essays, written during 1991-1994, lay out her views on identity, nationalism and culture. Though this deals with a Southern European situation twenty years ago, she might as well be talking about contemporary Estonia; small-mindedness and stupidity are everywhere and the parallels (particularly in regards to the manufactured "traditions", here being Croatian folk dancing but again it could be the Estonian singing festivals) were stunning. This is powerful feminist writing as well, though only a few essays directly addressed gender; the way in which she can balance a scrupulous, pinpoint argument with a strong emotional reaction is not only skilled but it made these pieces feel unlike anything I had ever read before. This English-language edition included two appendices written in 1998, including a glossary where she explicitly lays out her views on nationalism, Yugoslav identity, and related topics to make sure the reader is 100% clear about how she feels. She never wavers from her stance as a "writer"; these essays sometimes deal with culture and the arts directly, and sometimes don't, but always take a literary viewpoint. This position doesn't compromise her arguments but if anything strengthens them, as the larger perspective that she implies is undoubtedly evident. Of course, I agree with her, but even if I didn't I think I'd be impressed by the depth and breadth of her erudition. The numerous references to other Yugoslavian writers were intriguing though I don't know if I am motivated to try anyone in particular.

634. Have a Nice Day: From the Balkan War to the American Dream by Dubravka Ugrešić
Received: 24 August 2007
Started: 9 December 2014
Finished: 17 December 2014
The other Ugrešić book on my shelf is also non-fiction, compiling a series of newspaper columns she wrote while living in America during the early 90s. This has that fun "stranger in a strange land" feel, even though she was dealing with the war in Croatia and Serbia during this time. Her a-national stance never wavers and though she addresses the conflict, it's primarily in exposing how Americans reacted in ignorance or false sympathy. This made the whole book feel someone light, though also angry; it's a weird combination that was almost whimsical at times. Ugrešić again includes an appendix that lays out a more vehement stance on the Balkan conflict, this time in the form of a letter to someone. I'm still impressed by her sophistication and moral compass, though this was a significantly lighter work than *The Culture of Lies* 633
and I'm curious to read her fiction next.

635. Wolf in White Van: A Novel by John Darnielle
Received: 16 December 2014
Started: 17 December 2014
Finished: 19 December 2014
I love the first decade of this man's music so

much, and while I haven't been as close to him in recent years, I was curious about this. I have no doubt of John's writing talents (I'm going with a rare first-name use here, since I spent some time talking with him in 1997, corresponded for a few years after, and last saw him in 2004), either in song form, or in his *Last Plane to Jakarta* zine, or various online writings. *Wolf in White Van* far, far exceeded my expectations, and I wonder if that's due somewhat to how familiar I am with his use of language. This isn't what I would have expected though, at least not ten years ago, if I heard that he was writing a book — I would have presumed he was going to tackle some sort of failing-romance social realism plot about a doomed couple (like most of those first-decade songs). Instead, it's a book about adolescent isolation, propelled into adulthood but stunted at the same time, which I guess has popped up in his recent songwriting somewhat. This was structurally extremely innovative — a winding, propulsive text (despite nothing really happening), that moves both forward and backwards at the same time. In this age of the nerd, where the outcasts of my adolescent time are now celebrated in popular culture, *Wolf of White Van* presents an alternate escape without any of the fawning or careful documentation of the subculture. The structure, as well, is integrated into the book in a flowing way so it's not some sort of gimmick or overshadowing device. The Mountain Goats song that was lodged in my head while I was reading this, on a loop I couldn't break away from to fully concentrate, was oddly enough the cover of 'Hellhound on My Trail' from *Nothing for Juice*. Maybe that sense of paranoia was somewhere in the novel's game, Trace Italian — 'gotta keep moving' — as opposed to the in-this-world storyline, where narrator Sean was about as stationary in his life as one could imagine since his accident. Or maybe it meant nothing. Anyway, this is a fucking great book, probably the best novel I read from this year (though I don't think I read many 2014 books). John Darnielle's prose has these moments of lucid precision that capture the same dramatic slice of experience from so many great Mountain Goats songs, even if they only appear in the margins — descriptions of the light, or some stray weeds growing near the side of the road. Though this plot is something new for his writing, this overall American experience is something that he has managed to craft over all the years, through all of the songs, and the expanded form of the novel really allows for a complete viewpoint to be fleshed out and a certain dignity honours the character. And it's a dark trip indeed, though in a surreptitious way, not looking for some teenage misery or drama to bathe in. Most tellingly, it's his refusal to explain 'why' what happened happened, which makes this so refreshing. I think he's run the risk in the past of proclaiming a false grandeur onto the characters in his songs, a distinct form of irony that can work for something like 'The Best Ever Death Metal Band from Denton' but would cheapen a long-form prose. He doesn't even come close to that here, as the focus seems to be on the human experience as shaped by culture, rather than the cultural presence of human archetype. After I finished this I was reading some reviews, curious how it was received (quite well, it seems), and I found one that embedded a YouTube video of a younger Darnielle performing 'Going to Georgia' in front of a rapturous audience who screamed along with every word (including the spoken bits). It's been awhile since I've sunk into those early Mountain Goats songs but I cried a little bit watching this, mostly due to my own nostalgia and artistic self-identity, which this man really affected. Like Sean in *Wolf of White Van* and his Conan books, I had those early Mountain Goats albums, 7"s and tapes; *The Hound Chronicles* is my Cimmeria, and the tiny community of nerds collecting Shrimper tapes in the late 90s were a community united by something so impossibly tiny and obscure that it made us strong (even if we didn't even really know each other or communicate). Reading this, I guess, was like feeling that whole relationship to be inverted somewhat, but without dwelling too much on it and getting in the way of the artistic expression that drew me in to Darnielle's web to start with.

636. The Engineer of Human Souls by Josef Skvorecky
Received: 26 May 2009
Started: 22 December 2014
Finished: 7 January 2015
It was good to finally tackle it after having it collect dust on my shelf for so long. I'm woefully uneducated in Czech literature apart from the Milan Kundera novels I read in high school, so I approached this with pretty much a blank slate, knowing only that it was quite well regarded and somewhat long. There were a ton of characters here, all emanating from the memories and letters of its narrator, a clearly

thinly-fictionalised version of Skvorecky himself. But since there was really no plot, or at least not anything linear, I didn't worry so much about keeping these all straight, instead just enjoying the ride. *The Engineer of Human Souls* is set, I guess, in late 70s Canada where the narrator, a famous yet exiled Czech novelist, teaches English literature to some undergraduates. The framing device of the novel is a five-chapter structure modelled after a writer being taught in the class — Conrad, Hawthorne, etc. — but really the story lurches between the narrator's present day and his memories of being a factory worker in Nazi-occupied Kostelec, as well as some later memories of the Communist occupation. While this deals with heavy subject matter, concerning itself primarily with ideology and being an unflinching attack on all forms of it, the tone is relatively light. There's a lot of humour, some bits more successful than others, and a raunchy, Bohemian turn. Though the narrator is too proud to acknowledge it, a real loneliness seeps through, emphasised by the bittersweet nostalgia for his first love and the numerous letters of people we are never really introduced to and don't really understand. The various run-ins with secret police and North American-based Czech spies are mostly comic; if there's a viewpoint here, it's that the instruments of totalitarianism (left or right doesn't matter, as Skvorecky seems equally contemptuous of both) are idiotic and buffoonish in their day-to-day operations. Because I love sprawling, messy, twentieth century novels, I dug this; I could see where it might be frustrating if one required a bit more narrative thrust, but I'm used to it. It felt not unlike Gaddis or Sorrentino in that sense, though the style is not as formally experimental. The WWII-based sections are undoubtedly the most compelling, in particular the interactions with Nadia and the American Nazi supervisor who catches and strangely supports their subterfuge. It's almost like Skvorecky believes in a human goodness throughout all of the systems and structures created to control us; I'd argue that he's an optimist, though maybe he would have been in denial himself.

637. Nothing but Blue Skies by Thomas McGuane

Received: 25 January 2013
Started: 7 January 2015
Finished: 20 January 2015

In charting the fall and fall of Frank Copenhaver, McGuane achieves something very difficult to write about — a treatment of male middle age crisis time that is compassionate and honest while still being edgy and (very, very) funny. I think this is my favourite of all the McGuane novels I've read, set in Montana like most of his later books and written with a wisdom that comes through patience. Though the chapters are very short, and the actions are often energetic and irrational, there's some sort of calm oration at work here. Set around 1990, this doesn't shy away from the cultural reference points of the time, and though Copenhaver is an ex-hippie who sold out and became a businessman, there's not a whole lot of hand-wringing over lost ideal and changing attitudes. The internal conflict generated by society's expectations is certainly the engine that drives his actions, but this is really about a man falling apart when his wife leaves him. That he falls apart in such a pleasant and hilarious manner is to the reader's benefit; but the levity doesn't take away from the tragedy, even though a super fun time is to be had (as a reader) throughout. As always, McGuane is able to toss out a stunning depiction of some natural feature in the Montana landscape, then immediately cut to some mundane small-town personal interaction, and end it with a wry joke. But rather than create a discord, it all comes together into a style that is so carefully crafted it's hard to even notice what went into it.

638. Impossible Vacation by Spalding Gray

Received: 3 February 2015
Started: 3 February 2015
Finished: 8 February 2015

I first read this ages ago, maybe before I had ever seen any of Gray's monologues (I have a very vague memory of seeing him interviewed on some talk show, maybe Letterman, around the time this came out, and I was interested in him from that). Now, having immersed myself in the rest of his output, this feels much less like the novel I remembered and just like an extended autobiographical monologue. It's silly that this is considered fiction merely because he changed his name in it, but I'm sure some other details were embellished or altered as well. But the result isn't that different from any of his other work really — it's a tapestry of his mind, as he careens from one life experience to another, all haunted by the suicide of his mother. Despite all of the typical Spalding Gray neurotic energy, there's a strange lack of affect here. His descriptions of wandering India while completely sex-crazed are all fit into a frame of recollection, making these experiences seem almost quotidian by the end. There aren't any tremendous highs or lows here, but maybe due to its length this is his definitive written work.

639. Leaving the Atocha Station by Ben Lerner

Received: 8 February 2015
Started: 8 February 2015
Finished: 9 February 2015

I remember reading a review of this a few years ago when it came out. Someone who used to come into the bookstore to talk to me a lot said that he thought it sounded like a perfect depiction of my generation, or something like that. Usually that would turn me off but I remembered the title and started reading it on a whim. What I discovered was something viciously funny and strangely sympathetic, despite essentially being a first person narrative of a sociopath. A friend was saying something, I think in a performance he did, about how it doesn't really matter to him anymore whether art is 'good' or 'bad'. I've been having similar sentiments lately; maybe it's a by-product of my descent into popular culture, or maybe it's some advanced stage of burnout. The narrator's admissions of how he feels unmoved by art and his lack of conviction for his own work was great music to my ears; it was funny, but also so real, and definitely mirroring something I've been feeling, at least somewhat. Maybe this is because it felt so natural, and so ingrained into him, but it wasn't a spectacle or any attention-seeking gesture. The myriad lies of his narrative are all so tiny that even when they build up to be bigger they still aren't really a big deal, or at least not what this book is about. Nor is this really about the identity of an American performing a different self abroad, though that's certainly part of it. I guess there isn't any one central topic of meaning behind Lerner's brilliant book, which is maybe one of the reasons it's brilliant. Ultimately, it's an artistic coming of age story, which I believe there is a German word for that I can't remember. Or maybe this really is about a sociopath, though there's enough self-awareness and concern for how he appears to others that he can't be so easily pigeonholed. The obvious 618 comparison to this would be Tao Lin's *Taipei*, except this found a middle ground between totally detached self-annihilation and a conventional narrative. I realise now that I'm personally from a different era than these protagonists, and I'm trying to react to that without overreacting, and to take these works on their own merits, not mine. In Lin's case I was really sceptical but with this I loved every minute.

640. The Stain by Rikki Ducornet

Received: 27 February 2009
Started: 26 January 2015
Finished: 17 February 2015

Clearing out my backlog of unread books may be a quixotic task but I guess I have to keep at it. I didn't find this too enjoyable; Ducornet's first novel is a dark mockery of horror-Gothic literature, attacking superstition, religion and small-town life from within. I was into the first half of this, but at some point I lost interest in the quality of the prose (which is the best thing going for it) and found it just a chore to finish. This occupies the same demented French village setting as Beckett's trilogy or Boris 565 Vian's *Heartsnatcher*, yet without as much 608 humour as those. I've now read three different writers doing postmodern deconstructions of the 1800s French village, without ever having read a "normal" example.

641. The Black Dahlia by James Ellroy

Received: 18 February 2015
Started: 18 February 2015
Finished: 21 February 2015

This was a world away from *American Tabloid* 471 though only about a decade separates them. This is much closer to what I imagined Ellroy would be like, which is still marvellously entertaining and a nice respite from trying to bash my way through *The Making of Americans*. The gore was still pretty nasty but the prose much more fleshed out; this is practically overflowing with language compared to his later style, though to be honest, I got a bit bored with the writing. The plot was beautifully constructed and I can understand why this is such a classic of the genre, but it definitely was of a genre, which is not necessarily a bad thing but not a unique, depraved and inspiring worldview like *American Tabloid*. I will probably read the rest of the quartet eventually too but I think I'm more interested in going back (forward?) to *The Cold Six Thousand* and *Blood's a Rover* next. Maybe I can read all five of these before I finish Gertrude Stein. But first I think I'll watch DePalma's much-derided 1433 film adaptation.

642. The Flight of Icarus by Raymond Queneau
Received: 24 May 2003
Started: 22 February 2015
Finished: 28 February 2015
Lightweight-as-usual Queneau, this time being a tad like *Exercises in Style* because it's a bunch of short chapters, though all are in the format of a play. This is another entry in the legacy of *At Swim-Two-Birds*, *Mulligan Stew*, etc. where the characters 33 rebel against the author. Here, the title is a clever joke because Icarus's flight is not in the sky (well, at least not until the last page) but from the text itself. We get the writer hiring a detective, a lot of intrigue between Icarus and some other characters, and the whole setup imploding on itself in a way that doesn't really matter. As always it's playful and fun, not so much linguistically as structurally, which is Queneau's modus operandi. Nothing really blew my mind here, but I was much more inspired by these things a decade ago and thus felt my same nostalgia for the days when meta-fiction and deconstruction rang my bell.

643. Point Omega: A Novel by Don DeLillo
Received: 18 February 2015
Started: 4 March 2015
Finished: 9 March 2015
I haven't made too many forays into post-*Underworld* DeLillo (nor, come to 720 think of it, did I ever finish reading that one) but maybe I should. This novella — barely over 100 pages and with well-spaced large print at that — somehow managed to capture a lot of his ideas in an almost perfect distillation of his style, while staying fairly structurally innovative and having hardly anything actually happen in the story. The narrator is as detached and distant as many of his best voices from past novels, despite having very human forays into fantasy and sexual abandon; the subject of his book, Elster, is a hybrid of the shadowy figures that occupy *The Names*, *Players* and *Mao II* 209, 730 30 219, 482 (all three of which *Point Omega* reminded me of). But while you could argue this is incredibly underwritten, essentially being a short story bookended by a piece of art criticism, it's the restraint and lack of engagement that seems to perfectly capture the culmination of forces so explored in past books (isolation, war, power, family breakdown) without actually discussing any of it. In short, I thought this was amazing because I took it in the continuum of DeLillo's career, not because I saw it as a standalone book. It left me wanting more, but I don't know what else would have been necessary.

644. American Purgatorio: A Novel by John Haskell
Received: 8 March 2015
Started: 10 March 2015
Finished: 14 March 2015
I read Haskell's short story collection (*I Am Not Jackson Pollock*) years ago and liked 395 it, but I sort of forgot about him until I saw this mentioned in a review of the new Ben Lerner book. Though I haven't read the 645 Lerner yet I took a detour into this, which was similar in spirit to *Atocha Station* but maybe a little bit more complete, and 639 strangely beautiful in its prose. I'd like to see a course offered on 'the detached male', because this defining characteristic of today's literature started a long time ago, and includes some really powerful works, such as *The Moviegoer*, which this is absolutely a descendant of. I expected 155, 287, 474 something predictable and was surprised; some of these themes, such as the missing woman and the unreliable narrator, have been beaten to death, but Haskell played with these expectations and did so in a way that didn't rely on irony or trickery. Everything here was straight and honest, written in the easy first-person cadence that Darnielle's *Wolf in White Van* had, and therefore I devoured this quickly. Books that 635 start with 'American' seem to have higher stakes, like they must be iconic and full of grand sweeping proclamations. *American Purgatorio* is worthy of this, being a compendium of the downtrodden, the outsiders, and the otherwise marginal forms of existence (not unlike a Kelly Reichardt film). There's an accurate yet personal portrait of contemporary American consumer culture in there too, and not without criticism, though it's hidden between the lines. Shades of *Spoorloos* too, but again, just on the surface. Wonderful.  265

645. 10:04: A Novel by Ben Lerner
Received: 18 February 2015
Started: 18 March 2015
Finished: 25 March 2015
After finishing *10:04* I'm not sure whether to proclaim Ben Lerner my favourite American writer since Wallace, or to revel in the sadness and emptiness of this time. Certainly, as a 34-year old white male coming from a liberal middle class American background with a strong interest in literature, there's a

lot for me to relate to here. As stunning as *Atocha* was for taking cynicism and detach-
639 ment and trying to render some truth in it, this went further while struggling openly with the question of meaning and purpose. There's no trickery here, just Lerner writing about himself "skirting between fiction and fact" (to paraphrase) and capturing a distinct period in his life, coming off a successful first novel and trying to write a second. It's an inherently unrelatable experience for me to relate to, and it works because he writes in a way that is so beautiful, strange and familiar. I compare him to Wallace because both writers strike me with some shocking force of experience, this capturing of what it means to be alive in a particular moment. Lerner's depiction of his writing residency in Texas feels so sincere and unabashedly selfish at times that I realised, at that point in the novel, how complicated the question of 'sincerity' actually is and whether it even mattered. *Atocha* made me think of Tao Lin's *Taipei*
618 644 when I read it, and Haskell's *American Purgatorio,* which I just finished as well, but are any of these books expressing anything than emptiness and drift? Maybe that's an accurate portrayal of the post-postmodern age but I'm not sure that it's enough. Lerner puts this question front and foremost in both books, presumably by dealing with the issue of fraud and authenticity, but that's actually a red herring. *10:04* is really a book of identity construction, with so many negotiations regarding fear, performance, and ego that it's best to just ride along with it. I haven't felt this much joy while reading a book since, well, *Atocha*; before that, I don't even know how long. I may suspend any criticism for another time and right now just be happy that someone is writing something that feels so perfectly attuned to my sensibility.

646. Eminent Hipsters by Donald Fagen
Received: 16 September 2014
Started: 14 April 2015
Finished: 23 April 2015
I wish Donald Fagen would write more! *Eminent Hipsters* collects some short pieces, of which some felt very familiar (I swear I read the piece about Jean Shepard before, somewhere online probably) and others, which were a pleasant surprise. The meat of this is a tour diary from 2012, which is funny and acerbic, but brutally honest about touring in a rock band at age 64. I actually expected this to be a bit nastier, given what I heard about it when it came out; somehow I didn't find it quite so extreme, despite the fact he seems to hate everyone in the world who was born after 1960. The first few pieces in the book, about the Boswell sisters and growing up listening to jazz as a child in New Jersey, are wonderfully written. There's tons of curmudgeonly 'old man yells at cloud' content here, but he owns it, and I went into this not only expecting such a tone but actively desiring it — and I was not disappointed. His insight into music and culture isn't really surprising if you're familiar with Steely Dan lyrics, but it's still almost thrilling that he can stretch out into such a contemplative, bittersweet and yet acrobatic style of long-form prose. I've read so many accounts of growing up in the 60s and coming to terms with one's identity through music and culture, yet Fagen seems to stand alone, an experience that was far different from hippies and punks and everyone else I've read. The boy and teenage Fagen is appropriately cast in hindsight as a confused, half-formed identity and the Fagen of today is so clearly self-assured that I really wonder about everything in between. Now I'll dream that he'll product another book of memoirs during the heyday of Steely Dan (and I'm not even really a big fan of them).

647. Open City by Teju Cole
Received: 27 March 2015
Started: 27 March 2015
Finished: 24 April 2015
It's not often that I read a recent novel and think of it as an 'instant masterpiece', but this is definitely that. As excited as I have been by Ben Lerner's two novels, *Open* 639,
City is on another level entirely. At first this 645,
seems to be connected to Lerner's work, being the internal narration of a lonely male wandering a city. But this establishes itself as Sebaldian rather than jaded or narcissistic; Julius (the narrator) navigates his life in a contemplative form that takes time to reflect on Yoruba traditions, Mahler's symphonies, and current European racial issues among many other things. There's no trace of bitterness or irony, and it's a more direct descendent of *The Moviegoer*, Pessoa,
and the adrift flaneur. But Cole seems to 155, 287, 474
be rejecting any sort of navel-gazing assertions about modern life, thus making *Open City* feel like a work of high modernism rather than post-post-whatever. There's a shocking twist near the end that is delivered in the same calm style, so it softens or rather sidesteps the drama, which maybe

amplifies its power in a Gestalt way; yet even without this turn I would still feel this to be a marvellous work of literature, even if nothing 'happens'. As the main character is a middle-class Nigerian immigrant living in New York, it feels like this should be more focused on racial issues, but it's not 'about' that (though it doesn't shy away from the displaced, complicated ethnic identity of the narrator). Amazing.

648. Ice by Anna Kavan
Received: 1 March 2015
Started: 14 March 2015
Finished: 26 April 2015
Kavan's most celebrated novel is an odd beast; the forward places it in the genre of 'slipstream', which was apparently invented well after Kavan's death to define a certain type of science-fiction that was more speculative and surreal and less focused on space opera. I never heard this term before and think it's a silly one, but there's no real comparison for the dark, dream-like horror of *Ice*, a mix of dystopian fantasy and quest novel. The creeping ice age of the book sets a cold tone, of course, but the style of the prose does as well — this is matter-of-fact depiction of environmental horror, totalitarian rule and civil unrest, related by the narrator as a backdrop to his confusing pursuit of a woman, the reason for which we are never completely clear about. Throughout there are various interactions with power structures, including possibly the woman's husband and/or captor — killings, subterfuge, battles, and escapes become commonplace in the short 140 pages of the novel. There's barely any dialogue and what's there is told through the narrator, so it becomes clear that we are dealing with someone potentially insane and certainly single-minded, though the motives for his actions aren't really clear. I can't say this was fun, or inviting, but it's certainly a remarkable book especially given Kavan's own troubles — most of her late fiction apparently consists of writing about her tormented mental state, and this is a cry for help that can't even grasp its own anger.

649. Before the Storm: Barry Goldwater and the Unmaking of the American Consensus by Rick Perlstein
Received: 26 April 2015
Started: 26 April 2015
Finished: 1 May 2015
A pretty great time overall, though it suffers from what affects all works of popular history — generalisations must be made, and a strong narrative requires some ironing out of the nuance that is undeniable in the rolling ball of chaos that is our world. With this caveat, I found *Before the Storm* incredibly gripping, not just in the masterful way Perlstein painted the birth of the modern conservative movement, but in how it captures the now almost completely disappeared mid-century America. It was arguable at its peak in the late 50s and early 60s, before corporations homogenised not only our aesthetics but our culture as a whole. Goldwater comes off as a more complex figure than I ever imagined — reluctant to enter the presidential race, and while conservative to his core he also feared the even more whackjob extremists like the Birchers, while simultaneously requiring their enthusiasm. That he was a personal friend of JFK is surprising, and he seemed to genuinely believe in states rights without being a straight-up segregationist or racist. Although maybe he was just savvy enough to know he needed to come down on the correct side of history. The cast of side characters here is wonderfully rendered as well, though Perlstein's near reverence for LBJ is a bit over the top. Nelson Rockefeller truly comes across as a genuinely passionate figure, if out of touch, and I never realised how the Republican party before Goldwater was really just a pro-business party, mostly liberal socially, and more or less like today's Democratic party (except more effective and without being as morally compromised). The post-nomination Goldwater campaign is actually kind of hilarious to read about, it's so inept — the sheer number of gaffes would have killed any of today's politicians in a heartbeat, though you can also point out how much different the media handled things then. Actually, this is visibly the point where the right turned against the media, for their accusations of liberal bias rang true, or at least true enough for the media reported on Goldwater's insane statements objectively, which seemed certainly to them as biased. Nixon is a fascinating shadow throughout this — I look forward to reading *Nixonland* next — and 656 Reagan emerged in the 11th hour as the future star of the movement. Although Perlstein's bias shines through and this is clearly meant to chronicle a point where American electoral politics changed forever (and it did for sure), this also serves as a solemn requiem for the once great political party of Lincoln, hijacked by its worst impulses

and today genuinely hammering bigger nails into the coffin of the American empire. This also gets me simultaneously excited and depressed about next year's election, though I've already decided I won't vote for a Democrat unless Scott Walker is the GOP candidate and he actually might win.

650. The Emigrants by W.G. Sebald
Received: 26 April 2015
Started: 26 April 2015
Finished: 6 May 2015
Here's Sebald reminding me a bit of Thomas Bernhard, for his portraits of these emigrants are constructed largely from memory but with some parts taken over by the voice of the subject, suddenly shifting to the role of the narrator. The repression of WWII's atrocity is again the subtext of this book, but uses very personal stories (of which I'm not sure how fictional they actually are) and some great photographs (all presented in that ghostly reconstructed way) to bring them together into something really beautiful and complete (yet small) by the end. If I were to put *The Rings of Saturn* at one end of the 534 Sebald spectrum, this might be the other, more explicitly fictional, though still blurry (and *Austerlitz* in-between).  563 Somehow, he managed to put himself front and centre (writing directly about his own biographical experiences in meeting these emigrants) but also as a ghost who haunts the memories of these other people. I can't say I connected with any of these characters as an emigrant myself, though I'm not Jewish and this isn't World War II, so clearly there's no common ground. But the question of identity and statehood is deconstructed through the shifting roles these people played over their lives, and Sebald's own bittersweet recollections. I maybe wasn't in the greatest state of mind for this right now, because I found myself aware that I was reading some amazing, breath-taking passages, but it felt like something I should go back to in the future when I'm more prepared to interact with the text.

651. My Life and My Life in the Nineties by Lyn Hejinian
Received: 2 May 2015
Started: 2 May 2015
Finished: 7 May 2015
My Life is Hejinian's masterpiece and one of the major poems of the Language movement; this is packaged together with *My Life in the Nineties*, which uses the same concept but stands alone. The format of these prose poems is structurally significant — each year of her life is represented with one chapter, each containing the number of sentences of the total years of her life. I don't think these were in chronological order, though it's hard to tell, because the writing is so cryptic and memories and associations flow and intersect with their adjacent sentences; it often seems like a very primal, early image is suggesting an early childhood year, but then there's often a very 'adult' sentiment immediately following. The tone shifts throughout, feeling at times like the Benji chapter of *The Sound and the Fury* and a flowing, immersive tone. *Nineties* is a bit of a different feel and has some insights and thought-experiments sprinkled throughout, and I'm glad these were kept separate — *My Life* is long enough, and just when it feels it's about to collapse under its own weight, it ends. I think *My Life* deserves its reputation; I'm interested in reading some of her essays and nonfiction now.

652. Nomad Codes: Adventures in Modern Esoterica by Erik Davis
Received: 4 May 2015
Started: 4 May 2015
Finished: 18 May 2015

653. Ubik by Philip K. Dick
Received: (already owned)
Started: 18 May 2015
Finished: 18 May 2015
I read through *Ubik* in one sitting. This wasn't the first Philip K Dick book that I ever read, but one of the first, and thus my memory was dusty. I was pretty into this, as I had forgotten enough to still be dazzled by the twists, and the way it starts to melt upon itself as soon as maybe 25% through makes it pretty nonstop in terms of pace. This feels like a novel saturated in capitalism significantly more than his other works, with the Ubik adverts throughout and the protagonist's completely skint existence (where his lack of poscreds makes him a second-class citizen, even compared to the machines that rule the techno-society). I found myself imagining this as a film, though it would be in some ways unfilmable. I think I enjoyed the 1939 stuff much more than *The Man in the High Castle*'s World War II revisionism, though the latter isn't actually set back then. This helped immensely pass the 8.5 hour flight from Manchester to Chicago.

654. Lucky Alan: And Other Stories by Jonathan Lethem
Received: 18 May 2015
Started: 18 May 2015
Finished: 23 May 2015
There's some uproarious moments in *Lucky Alan*, especially when compared to the joylessness of *Dissident Gardens*. 'The King
630 of Sentences' is Lethem at his best, playful and absurd, and the experimental edge of 'Their Back Pages' is even exhilarating. There are stories that are less pleasurable — the titular one tries too hard to capture some serious NYC literary vibe, and I skimmed through the one about the guy in the hole, even though I liked the idea of it. 'The Porn Critic' maybe finds the perfect balance, and 'Pending Vegan' is a near masterpiece. It's a short collection and the highs are so high that it carried me through, though the lows were hard to endure. I love that Lethem has never completely abandoned his more fantastical edge, even as he's become increasingly acclaimed; I think he's at his best when it's just slightly uncanny, such as in *Chronic City*. These sto-
581 ries don't last long enough to develop this creeping, unsettling surrealism but serve more like explosive blasts of it.

655. American Innovations: Stories by Rivka Galchen
Received: 18 May 2015
Started: 18 May 2015
Finished: 29 May 2015
Tackling so many short stories at once is unusual for me; I just read the Lethem in parallel and will probably start the new Donald Antrim, which I should have already started so I could be massively confused by them all. This collection really impressed me. I was already on board with Galchen after *Atmospheric Disturbances* but this
630 shows she's more than a one-trick pony, though that same nearly extreme level unreliability persisted in almost every story. All of the stories in here (I think) were written from a female point of view, which isn't remarkable since Galchen herself is female, but after *Atmospheric*'s very male narration, it's curious to see a writer shift through gender consciousness so directly. This happens immediately via the first story, and the emotional avoidance reoccurs in a later story about a husband leaving the narrator, who seems more concerned with replacing the Parmesan grater. Nothing here is normal, but nothing is too edgy either — the prose is straightforward yet sprinkled with a few dazzling images, though it's more between the visual elements (if that makes any sense). Not everything is great, but that's true for pretty much all collections; the average is quite high throughout, and I may even prefer her writing in the short form.

656. Nixonland: The Rise of a President and the Fracturing of America by Rick Perlstein
Received: 23 May 2015
Started: 23 May 2015
Finished: 18 June 2015
Perlstein's second book picks up right where the first left off and makes it clear that this is about NixonLAND rather than 630
Nixon himself, which is fine because there's already a million books about Nixon the person. Of course, Nixon is still the central character, and the book makes a lengthy argument for his divide and conquer politics as being the predominant agent for social change in late 20th century America. The epilogue has a somewhat heavy-handed bit about Nixon's "Silent Majority" and how that created a cultural divide in America that persists today. It's changing somewhat, now that the Vietnam generation is no longer front-and-centre, but I think it's a fairly correct way of looking at things. But the reason for this is not because of a fundamental essence of the American people, but because the culture was shaped by this view — so by simply saying it repeatedly (by both the politicians and the media), it became true. This is a long book and it goes into huge lengthy passages chronicling the violence and unrest that took place during these years, so it functions as a fairly solid historical overview of the era. So much of the art and culture that I grew up inspired by was fomented by this turbulence but it's hard to imagine what it was like to live in it; I'm not sure if this helped create that sense in me — that American life was ripping apart at the seams — or the non-stop grouping of these situations overemphasised it. There's a lot to juggle in writing this and he mostly succeeds, though the scope is so much wider than the Goldwater book that it's by definition a bit less coherent. We get a lot of inside looks at Nixon's mind set, and his utter paranoia which is probably underemphasised (if anything), in a way that almost explains Watergate (though only the tip of that iceberg is chronicled here). As we read about the Vietnam atrocities and both the outrage and support of it, it's all well and good, but Perlstein fails to get at the

real reasons for Vietnam's escalation and downfall — the defence contractors and elites who were profiting so much from it and their subsequent disillusion. As much as we're told that Nixon himself knew the war was hopeless, and how saving face was so important to his administration, we don't hear a word about those who actually created it. But I still enjoyed this — it wasn't the gripping page-turner that *Before the Storm* was, but kept me going and I'll definitely take on the Reagan book next. This
693 probably makes a good companion piece to *Fear and Loathing: On the Campaign*
499 *Trail '72*, which is still the best book about American politics I've ever read.

657. Wilson by Daniel Clowes
Received: (already owned)
Started: 26 June 2015
Finished: 26 June 2015
Been re-reading some random "recent" Clowes (and I think this is his most recent work, being 5 years old). Was talking about this with a friend back in Pittsburgh who said that it was being made into a film; I remembered it being more slight than it actually is. The formality of it is rigid and adapts the method of varying the style of the art from chapter to chapter that the last two issues of *Eightball* did. As a narrative, I appreciated how complete it was in its brevity, having major plot devices occur off-page, and really committing to the six panel format (with the gag in the last one). The gags too are rarely actual jokes, but just extremely bitter, assholish contrarianism, but it quickly, after the first few pages really, builds up this most Clowesean of characters. I can't see how this will work as a film without just becoming formulaic or overly sad, but *Ghost World* worked well as cinema, which I didn't expect either. I wish he'd do *Eightball* again, as I think that's my all-time favourite comic series, but supposedly he's at work on a large graphic novel and I have faith he'll come through.

658. The Emerald Light in the Air: Stories by Donald Antrim
Received: 19 June 2015
Started: 19 June 2015
Finished: 29 June 2015

659. Fade Out by Douglas Woolf
Received: 5 June 2015
Started: 27 June 2015
Finished: 5 July 2015
I've been hungry for more Douglas Woolf since reading (and loving) *On Us*, so I
ordered a bunch cheap from half.com 609
when in the states. This is his first novel and allegedly his most popular, as it seems to have been kept in print by Black Sparrow for all these years. It's a wry, darkly comic adventure about an elderly man with creepy tendencies, going on a road trip with an ex-boxer friend, clearly out of his mind but portrayed sympathetically and in a way that makes it slightly enticing. It wasn't ha-ha funny, nor did it possess the strange stylistic rhythms that made me enjoy *On Us* so much, but there was something remarkably readable about it, and Woolf's ability to convey meaning through what he omits is ever so strong here. This was written in the late 50s and thus I imagined that same slightly unreal pallor over everything described that I find some dominant in portrayals of the 50s, which is probably just the residue of too many viewings of *Back to the Future* when young. But this is remarkably sympathetic to the elderly, and given that Woolf was a young man when he wrote this it's an odd choice and probably explains why he never found an audience among the avant-garde or youth movements of the time. I'm a sucker for mid-century Americana and you get this, particularly during the hitchhiking passages which remind me greatly of Elkin's great novels such as *The Franchiser* and *The Dick Gibson Show.* 62, 341 71, 596

660. Slow Fade by Rudolph Wurlitzer
Received: 30 June 2015
Started: 30 June 2015
Finished: 5 July 2015
I thought this was going to be a counterculture classic, but it was much more subdued than I expected, reminding me slightly of Barry Hannah or McGuane, though not quite as poetic. There was such a sadness and longing here, despite the cool, hip nature of the writing and the fairly flowing storyline. It was odd how Wurlitzer didn't commit to a single main character, instead splitting it over three, though the filmmaker father was clearly the most troubled and most central as well. Was he supposed to be based on Coppola, or Otto Preminger, or no one in particular? I felt like this was a good read after just watching *Serial*, since
this also seemed saturated in post-hippie 1466

lifestyle choices, though with a far less reactionary viewpoint. After finishing this I saw that it was published in 1984 which is way later than it felt. This seemed like a mid-70s viewpoint, and only the mention of the

Clash made it clear that this had to occur later. Indeed, this felt so insulated from Reaganism and even the popular trends of the cinema and music in those years that I wonder if this was written much earlier than when it was actually published. This made me want to read Wurlitzer's other books, especially *Nog* which Pynchon was a big fan of, and his non-fiction/travel book — and I should see the films he wrote the screenplays for.

661. Speedboat by Renata Adler
Received: 2 June 2015
Started: 9 July 2015
Finished: 14 July 2015
Though *Speedboat* is a short novel (173 pages), it took me a relatively long time to get through it. That's because the prose is so extremely (as my friend put it, when convincing me to read it) "punchy". Adler constructs her novel out of little short bursts of anecdote, plotlessly revolving around a journalist 'character' who is navigating her life and professional relationships in the mid 1970s. I guess you can call this an experimental novel as it reminds me of Joseph McElroy conceptually, but stylistically all I could think about was DeLillo, DeLillo, DeLillo — I wonder if she was an influence on him (or vice-versa). I don't make that comparison primarily because of the sense of detachment present here (though the narrator only lets her emotions slip through in bits and pieces) but the way these moments assemble into some grand patchwork quilt of what it was like to be alive at a moment in time. I think this documentary aspect of literature is one that I'm extremely attracted to, and thus I'd actually rank this among the best books I've ever read, no exaggeration. Unlike DeLillo's works, which always resonate with me after I finish reading them, I felt a continual thrill to dive into *Speedboat*'s universe, even though the characters are irrelevant (and blur together) and again, nothing happens; even the chapter divisions feel arbitrary. It was a thrill I had to mediate, with short bursts of reading. I had incredible difficulty concentrating on this, and I've read plenty of other plotless books and it's not like the prose was actually difficult itself; I think I was maybe not in the right frame of mind for this right now at the laziest point of the summer. This only leads me to speculate what a re-read, when I may have a better mental environment, might be like.

662. The Third Reich: A Novel by Roberto Bolaño
Received: 1 February 2015
Started: 15 July 2015
Finished: 30 July 2015
Even minor Bolaño is compelling to read. This is a fairly conventional novel, narrated by a detached asshole who is no less navel-gazing than his usual narrators, but this time immersed in war-themed board games rather than Spanish-language poetry. I read this a lot on the beach, which is why it took so long — and also that the ending chapters dragged on forever, beating the story to death and continuing with exposition after there was nothing really left to gain from it. But it was a good setting for me to read this, since it takes place in a Spanish beach resort, and this rhythm of holiday life is something he nailed really well. The mystery wasn't really much of one, yet this still somehow felt like a thriller, ironically commented on throughout by the presence of a bad detective novel the narrator's girlfriend is reading. Once the war game takes over I lost interest, and I couldn't really understand what he was trying to do there. But this was primarily enjoyable, in a laid-back way that I kind of needed, and it's motivated me to dig through the rest of his published English translations, though since they are releasing pretty much every scrap of paper he ever scribbled on, maybe I should be careful.

663. Nazi Literature in the Americas by Roberto Bolaño
Received: 3 August 2015
Started: 3 August 2015
Finished: 5 August 2015
I'm pushing myself to read the rest of the Bolaño catalogue and this one was brilliant and inspiring in a different way than his others. Actually, it's Greenaway's *The Falls* that I would compare this to more than anything, as it's written as a reference guide, comprised entirely of biographies of fictional writers which of course intertwine and create a whole surreal parallel universe. There's no sci-fi concept here, but simply political ideology, which is what unites all of these writers (as the title indicates), though Bolaño doesn't fuck around with this too much. These characters are all grotesque in their own ways, and some of the works they supposedly created sound fantastically fascinating, in the way that fake books often can. I think back to the idea I had to write a novel in the format of a *Trouser Press*-style record guide, constructing a totally

227

88

fictional music world where narratives are
told through releases and reviews; this is
a bit like that, though with some weirdly
resonating moments beyond being just an
intellectual game. The last chapter is the
longest and is a draft version of *Distant*
313 *Star*; the index and bibliography are even
more entertaining than the main text. I
don't know if I can genuinely say this is a
greater work of literature than *The Savage*
397 351 *Detectives* or *2666* but for me, it occupies
the same hallowed ground.

664. Tripticks by Ann Quin
Received: 4 June 2015
Started: 8 August 2015
Finished: 9 August 2015
Ex-library copy. Looking to read something amazing? *Tripticks* blew my mind.
I totally dug *Berg*, but this, written at the
664 other end of her unfortunately too-short
career, was another beast entirely. This is an insane experimental novel loaded with cunning and momentum; transgressive without being "look at me" transgresssive; so ahead of it's time that I don't know even what to compare it to. It's not really science fiction, but it exists in a fantastic reality that is built entirely from the monotony of consumer capitalism. Quin writes brilliantly, unrecognisable stylistically from *Berg* except for the strong emphasis on parent-child relationships (and not in a pleasant way at all). For a British woman to create such a strong American male voice is impressive, even if the narrator is far from a protagonist. There's not really a plot and the disjointed timeline makes it hard to tell what is actually happening, if anything, but this was such a beauty to read I would have accepted any structure. Maybe this would be like if J.G. Ballard was a better prose writer; the back cover calls this 'pre-punk' and compares it to Kathy Acker; I can see the reasons why, but it feels even too singular for that. Wow.

665. The Return by Roberto Bolaño
Received: 3 August 2015
Started: 11 August 2015
Finished: 15 August 2015
I know that *The Return* was all of the stories from Bolaño's first two Spanish-edition
short story collections that didn't make it
605 into *Last Evenings on Earth*, so therefore I
knew I was reading lesser material, at least in the eyes of his American editors. I think that did make this less enjoyable, and I wonder if I would have felt the same way if I hadn't known that. *The Return* has a few very good stories — I think my favourite ones were the porn star reminiscing about her relationship with John Holmes, and the football player narrating about the African player — and a few forgettable ones too. His alter ego Arturo Belano appears a few times, in 'Detectives' (which tries to build a narrative using only Tarentino-style snappy dialog) and 'Photos' (which I found somewhat incomprehensible) and Bolaño writes as himself in the final story, about Enrique Lihn. The goofiest is probably the dead body telling about how a famous French designer fucked his corpse, and it's nice to see the lighter side of Bolaño (though it still attains a solemn, wise manner). I'd definitely flip through this again but it doesn't feel like something that had to be devoured from cover to cover.

666. The House of Ulysses by Julián Ríos
Received: 5 April 2011
Started: 2 May 2015
Finished: 16 August 2015
I took my time reading this, which claims on the back cover to be 'a comic extravaganza' but was really nothing more than a series of notes on Joyce's *Ulysses*, technically the musings of a classroom of graduate students studying the text. This blended actual Joyce scholarship with *Room 237*-style ridiculous leaps of faith and interpretation, though since I haven't read the source text for many years, I had trouble distinguishing the two. Not that it really matters — *Ulysses* is the birthplace of all modernist over-interpretation and that's not shocking assertion, and if Ríos's goal was to mock this I don't think it was successful
because, really, does it matter? Or maybe,
again like *Room 237*, this is supposed to be
celebrating the pleasure of literature and 1084, 1157
the supposed ridiculousness doesn't really
matter. I'm not sure, but I guess I enjoyed this, though I mostly read it when in the laundry room downstairs. This contains a chapter-by-chapter summary of *Ulysses* so it satiated my desire to re-read the original for some time, I think, not to say that this was in any way the same experience, but it at least refreshed my memory. And in a way, I think it instilled another appreciation of Joyce's genius, though maybe it's just more a reminder of this. Ríos is apparently one of Spain's foremost postmodern writers and I sort of wish I had chosen a different novel of his — one where his own talents might have been more obvious.

667. Ice Trilogy by Vladimir Sorokin
Received: 27 July 2011
Started: 22 May 2013
Finished: 23 August 2015

The dates here will indicate that it somehow took me 2.5 years to read this, though that's not true at all; I read most of *Bro*, the first novel on this trilogy, while at Nida in 2013 and then never was engaged enough to finish it. I picked this up again as part of my quest to rid my shelves of books I don't want to keep, and tore through the rest of it in about a week. I'm not sure what to think about this; I found long parts tedious and repetitive, and the whole overall concept to be a bunch of irritating new age faux spiritualist bullshit. But now that it's finished, I'm not really sure how to take the "plot" behind it all, and maybe I missed the whole notion of satire until the very end. This is a real mishmash of styles and voices, very intentionally done so to reflect the fragmentation of the 20th century and the moral corruption of Russia; the metaphor of ice cracking is probably in play here, too. And some of Sorokin's prose (at least as passed through this particular translator) is invigorating and entertaining, pulpy in an enlightened way (no pun intended) and kept me turning pages quickly, caught up in the momentum of the dialogue even though I wasn't the slightest bit invested in the story. This book doesn't really have any people in it; I mean, there are tons of characters but not even the slightest attempt to flesh them out, apart from maybe the first 1/3 of *Bro*. I love the idea of parallel histories, and the 20th century in particular, though I'm more accustomed to Pynchon's cracked handling of history's secret speculations (and his use of the Tunguska event in *Against the Day*, which I couldn't
243, 822 help but think about throughout this, is seeped in mystery and ambiguity which is more my style). At times I was infuriated by this seemingly pro-Eugenics, almost fascist devotion to the Brotherhood that the prose seemed to endorse; I also don't like sci-fi where a bunch of prophecies are foretold and then things come true for no

404 apparent reason (such as *Dune*). Yet now that I've finished it, I keep thinking about it, and I wonder if maybe this was pretty great, especially as I am interpreting the climax in a way that suits my own personal outlook. I think I definitely want to read more of Sorokin, though who knows if I ever will.

668. Ya! and John-Juan: Two Novels by Douglas Woolf
Received: 9 June 2015
Started: 25 July 2015
Finished: 28 August 2015

These two short novels — novellas, really — are collected together in one volume, and I took some time between them. *Ya!* was a great time, similar to *On Us* in terms of it's narrator being a thinly-autobiographical 609
stand-in for Woolf, existing on the margins of the American economy. There was a lot of creepy family stuff here, so whenever it would be sort of funny there would be a strange, dark undercurrent to cut against the laughs. The final chapter was surprisingly absurd and nonsensical, and felt alive. *John-Juan* was a funny title for me since my flatmate is named Juan; this was even looser of a narrative, practically hallucinatory at times. There's a good ear for dialogue here and the depiction of a man out of place was welcome, but it just wasn't quite enough for me to really love it.

669. Book of Numbers: A Novel by Joshua Cohen
Received: 23 August 2015
Started: 23 August 2015
Finished: 31 August 2015

This has gotten a lot of press lately and is being hailed as the latest great American novel of our time, being praised especially for its handling of the digital age. I can't say that I agree, though I didn't hate this; I found it occasionally compelling and certainly ambitious, but falling a bit short in key ways. The reality of *Book of Numbers* is pretty much like ours and there's only a mild amusement derived from reading fictional version of Julian Assange and Google. Almost half of the book is taken over by the Principal character's dictation, and I suppose there's a literary version of

Persona going on in places when it's not particularly clear who the first person sig- 1131
nifies, but that's about it. I don't require dazzling experimentalism, or exceptional emotional depth, but a little from either column seems important to me if you're going to be the great American novel of our time. This was lacking in both; the closest bit of honesty I felt was the narrator's porn addiction and misery with his ex-wife, but even this was beaten to death with her blog entries, which were I think supposed to be like Molly Bloom's soliloquy in the Internet age. Honestly, I thought *Taipei* by Tao Lin did a far better job of capturing the way we 618
use GChat and Skype as part of our daily

life. When *Book of Numbers* tried to weave a shadowy, mysterious thriller plot it was at its worst; when it dealt with the narrator's fear of insignificance, I really enjoyed it. There is probably a genuine critique of techno-capitalist exploitation in here, but it was so obfuscated by the text's various layers that I couldn't really follow it; what it mostly felt like was a company history of a bizarro Google, which made the resulting novel feel like a less funny, less focused season of *Silicon Valley*.

670. Purity: A Novel by Jonathan Franzen
Received: 5 September 2015
Started: 5 September 2015
Finished: 13 September 2015
This was actually okay, or at least a bit better than his last book. But like *Freedom*,
454 *Purity* opens with a great rush of beautiful language before proceeding into more quotidian territory. The first chapter had some phrases that made me posit that perhaps Franzen is a great writer, but a bad novelist; this didn't turn out to be the case, as the book-like conventions here (plot, characters, shifting viewpoints) ended up being the strongest aspects. This is the second book in a row that I've read which uses WikiLeaks as a major inspiration, though the political intrigue is really minor here. Instead, it's a book about personal relationships kept hidden, and mostly about terrible parenting. All of the mothers in this book are awful, extreme monsters, to the point where I started to question if the novel was a bit misogynistic. There's a genuinely good air of paranoia at play here, though it's a distinct form of it, not like from a 70s film nor really reflecting today's entrenched Deep State; the paranoia here emanates from personal mistrust and fear, and Franzen did an excellent job trying to capture that. There's a lot more kindness here than in *Freedom*, as well — the titular hero is truly a sympathetic character, and I didn't feel that Franzen was trying to grind an axe about today's kids, nor express some great outrage at the morals of America. It's actually a much smaller book, in that sense, though structurally it's huge, proceeding through several locations and time periods. I still think he gets caught up too much in explication, and wish there was a bit more style here. Maybe I just haven't forgiven him for dissing Gaddis, but there are long sections of this where the prose is so plain I was questioning why this is considered great 'literature'. One very obvious reference to himself was the worst meta-fictional intrusion, but it was easily ignored.

671. Visit Sunny Chernobyl: And Other Adventures in the World's Most Polluted Places by Andrew Blackwell
Received: 28 August 2015
Started: 28 August 2015
Finished: 2 October 2015
I found this while killing time in Kallio library and read it casually, taking a long time to finish it because the festival got in the way. This ended up being an enjoyable read, not straight travel essays but infused with the writer's personal story and neuroses, but not too much that it became annoying. The sites he chose to visit are all fascinating in their own way, so it wasn't difficult to stay engrossed. The oil sands in Canada were perhaps the most interesting part to me, as I didn't know anything about this issue before, and the great Pacific garbage reef is terrifying to learn about, though I suppose that chapter is the most unsatisfying. It seems that writing this book ended Blackwell's long-term relationship, or at least he casts it that way, which gave the later chapters a slightly manic, desperate edge that's not usually found in these types of books.

672. Satin Island by Tom McCarthy
Received: 3 October 2015
Started: 3 October 2015
Finished: 4 October 2015
Wow, holy shit, what a book. I liked *Remainder* a lot but wasn't prepared for this, which 370
seemed to grab the idea of the novel by the throat and squeeze until there is no possibility left unexplored. And it's so taut, so perfectly assembled, that though it's only 150 pages it felt as complete as any of the great, thick postmodern American classics of the 20th century — more complete, even. There's a lot to unpack here and in so many ways there is nothing actually happening here. I suspect McCarthy has packed a lifetime of secrets and layers into this, as he mentions in the afterword that there are many references and things ripped off throughout. But this doesn't feel like mere game playing — this instead feels like a deft encapsulation of many ideas and theories, written in a novelistic way without much actual plot, and as saturated with our contemporary concerns as anything else I've read. I was thinking about halfway through the long, strange story of the woman being unconventionally interrogated at a protest about how different of

an approach to identity and self McCarthy takes compared to, say, Ben Lerner. While I loved *10:04* and *Leaving the Atocha Sta-*
639 645 *tion*, they are prime examples (perhaps the best examples, actually) of a writer who inflicts his own personality into the novel to the point of blurring lines. This is a pretty common device in today's fiction and no doubt a symptom of my generation's obsessive narcissism. So for McCarthy to write from a first-person perspective without the slightest trace of autobiography, but to still maintain something warm and human, is all the more remarkable. And this is why I think I was so blown away by this — it has the structure and tone of a DeLillo novel (shadowy corporations; the narrator doing some obsessive, bizarre, probing under the guise of research; detached sexual affairs) but felt at times almost like Pessoa in it's diligence to the mysteries of existence. The closing description of the Staten Island Ferry is transcendental, magical prose that somehow is synchronised with the edgy, Ballardian observations that appear earlier. I think I'm going to buy a paper copy of this because it's something I'm going to want to go back to again and again.

673. To Our Friends by The Invisible Committee
Received: 27 August 2015
Started: 27 August 2015
Finished: 10 October 2015
This is the second book by the Invisible Committee and I guess their first one, *The Coming Insurrection*, was kind of a big deal so I should have read it first. This makes a case for the nature of revolutionary leftist action in today's climate, by trying to argue that the moral question of radicalism replaced the strategic question of how to achieve it, and thus the left is always undone by its claim to legitimacy. It's a pretty interesting starting point and throughout they make some good case studies, using a lot of what's happened recently in Greece (though not that recently — this predates the crazy events of this spring and summer) and Italy. Probably the idea I enjoyed the most, which wasn't even a major point, was that government itself was not longer the source of power, but the infrastructure that we exist on. I guess that's a bit like deep state theory, though a bit less malevolent, and I liked the example of Euro notes having abstract drawings of bridges and aqueducts on them instead of people as a proof of this.

674. The Brightest Thing in the World: 3 Lectures from the Institute of Failure by Matthew Goulish
Received: 4 November 2015
Started: 5 November 2015
Finished: 5 November 2015

675. The Illogic of Kassel by Enrique Vila-Matas
Received: 7 November 2015
Started: 7 November 2015
Finished: 21 November 2015
I've never read Vila-Matas before, but I really should have sooner, as he seems like the type of literary trickster I enjoy. This is a slightly fictional work about his participation in 2012's Documenta, and ends up being a dissection of an elderly avant-garde writer's understanding of contemporary art, as well as a snapshot of a distinct experience. It's hard to say which parts are fictionalised and which aren't, but that doesn't really matter. It starts full of subterfuge and mystery and ends up being a completely straightforward personal essay about his experiences in Kassel. I can't imagine that I would enjoy this if I hadn't also been to Documenta and seen many of the works written about, but I also think what I liked was how Vila-Matas approaches things from his literary perspective and is completely unconcerned with all of the empty bullshit that surrounds art. It's really personal and yet really quite elusive at the same time, as I found myself wondering why anyone would construct these thoughts in the form of a 'novel', which this arguably isn't. This is packed with references to art, cinema, and literature throughout, and I think it's maybe one of the closest in terms of format to the work of Sebald (and Sebald is himself discussed here). Vila-Matas's erudition is never under question, but the way he's able to process his lifetime of culture in the realm of the unfamiliar (contemporary art's context in 2012) is impressive, particularly in the way he writes an openness that could almost be naiveté if it didn't demand a respect. This is surely a minor work of Vila-Matas but I tackled it because of its length and my own connection to the content.

676. Quicksand by Steve Toltz
Received: 21 November 2015
Started: 21 November 2015
Finished: 30 November 2015
Toltz's second novel was a whirlwind of energy, and I felt myself carried through it like as if I was riding a wind. This is a very funny, very assured work that despite

its energy never feels like an assault. We switch between two characters, mostly focused on one, but chronicled by the other, in a very black comedy of contemporary life, set in Australia (though it never feels particularly Australian to me). There are quite a few topics that I would have preferred to see more fleshed out, such as the police force and the art teacher, but we keep returning to Aldo and his tragic self-destruction. It's impossible not to enjoy this, and the momentum probably covers up some of the weaker bits of the writing. Toltz's prose is so current, yet distant from the navelgazing self-absorption that covers so much Ameican writing now. This made me think of D. Keith Mano's *Take Five* as 121 another novel about an alpha-male unravelling, though not quite as mean-spirited. Even when this descends into poetry and the weird testimony at the end, it never feels any less like one clear authorial voice. This didn't get reviewed as positively as his first book so I might check that out soon as I could easily enjoy a few hundred more pages of his writing.

677. Pages from a Cold Island by Frederick Exley

Received: 15 September 2015
Started: 1 December 2015
Finished: 4 December 2015

I was really surprised by Exley's second book, because maybe I don't remember  *A Fan's Notes* as well as I thought I did 103 — was it this raunchy, bawdy and over-top-top with its male chauvinist viewpoint? My guilty admittance here is how much I enjoyed this. It's structurally pretty much  the same as Lerner's *10:04*, but written in 645 1972 and thus caught up in the dramas of the time (Women's Lib, McGovern, and Norman Mailer reigning over all as the king of literature). I never have read anything by Edmund Wilson except a few parts of *To the Finland Station*, but this book, essentially a fawning bit of hero-worship, motivates me to do so. Despite my ignorance of Wilson's life, I enjoyed every page of this and I'll likely seek out his third book. The depiction of Wilson, as told via his daughter and assistant (via Exley), really build up the "great writer as difficult man" image, which reading in my current state of mind seems to stem from the relative isolation of the literary profession. Do these personal habits emerge from solitude? Exley, despite frequently banging students (or at least claiming to), probably headed this way himself, but without the level of success or acclaim of Wilson. Parts of this were so cringe-worthy by today's political correctness — the out-and-out misogyny of his obsession with taking down Gloria Steinem would have him rightfully ostracised today, except there was a strong sense of self-doubt throughout it, as if he knew he was a bag of posturing hot air while he was embarking on this interview. I would have liked to hear more about his time at the Iowa writer's workshop, which only ends up getting the last short chapter and being primarily about him screwing a student, but maybe that's in the third book.

678. Information Doesn't Want to Be Free: Laws for the Internet Age by Cory Doctorow

Received: 6 December 2015
Started: 6 December 2015
Finished: 9 December 2015

I wanted more from this. Doctorow has positioned himself as a prominent voice advocating for Internet freedom and I don't mean to diminish his efforts, but this didn't offer anything new to the discussion. I was hoping for a few philosophical stirrings like in that Jaron Lanier book I enjoyed so much, but it was more like the boring parts of that book which discussed intellectual property. I agree with him on everything he wrote here, of course, but this felt almost remedial. I should have used the time spent reading this focusing on the Clarice Lispector stories, or something more fulfilling.

679. Pitch Dark by Renata Adler

Received: 12 December 2015
Started: 12 December 2015
Finished: 14 December 2015

Did I love *Pitch Dark* as much as *Speedboat*?  661 Yes, I think so. This is a somewhat more straightforward work, though that's not to say it's a conventional novel in any way whatsoever. But, stuff actually happens here, and while the fragmented, peristaltic lurching of her first novel was wonderful, the Molly Bloom like slip-and-slide that she reaches during a few of the extended passages here is undoubtedly exhilarating. You know, I'm actually a pretty terrible reader — until I read Muriel Spark's afterword, I didn't even realise that this was a book about a relationship. That's cause Adler writes all around the relationship, mentioning it for sure, but not discussing any of the details whatsoever. The middle passage, describing a strange rental car experience in Ireland, is the most weirdly compelling yet mundane thriller I've ever read; the final section reminisces on friendships and passing professional acquaintances in a way that seems so detached, yet invested. There is much more of a straightforward and emotional core to this, perhaps a result of the inevitable 'maturing' over a few years or maybe because Adler didn't want to repeat herself. I'm actually sad that she never wrote any more fiction, though she's still alive, so she still might, I suppose. I have been thinking recently about Sebald and how his unique style has likely influenced today's hot English-language novelists such as Lerner and Teiju Cole. But Adler's two novels aren't a million miles away from his style, at least on a structural level. I suppose the blurring of fiction and non-fiction essay was inevitable, and Sebald is of course a completely different beast, but both of these writers attempt to capture subjective experience on their own terms, and it's a beautiful thing to behold.

680. The Dewey Decimal System by Nathan Larson
Received: 14 December 2015
Started: 14 December 2015
Finished: 16 December 2015
Fun and pulpy, but not bad at all — this is a romp through a semi-dystopian New York City, narrated by a hardboiled black hero whose memory is fragmented but his skills are highly specialised and heroic. Would maybe make a good film, as it's written in short paragraphs of often only a single sentence, reminding me of Ellroy's late style (though a lot more fantastical in content). The plot concerns hiding war criminals, femme fatales, and assassinations attempts so it's fairly standard stuff. I read a good review of the latest in this trilogy and thought this would be something fun to read when I want a break from Gaddis, and it served the role admirably. The world here was nicely underwritten, and the tone reminded me a little bit of Steve Aylett though nowhere near as whacked-out linguistically.

681. Goodbye, Columbus : And Five Short Stories by Philip Roth
Received: 12 January 2015
Started: 8 December 2015
Finished: 17 December 2015
This was the first book Philip Roth published and about half consists of the titular novella, and then five short stories making up the rest. I can understand why Roth's reputation was built upon *Goodbye, Columbus*, which encapsulates every stereotype and preconceived notion I have of the man. Of course I've only ever read *Portnoy's Complaint* (twice) and have had no real interest in reading the rest of his work, apart from being able to tick a box of being 'well-read'. I enjoyed *Columbus* and the first two short stories but found my patience wearing thin as we went on. I liked how attuned Roth was to class issues in *Columbus*, and these chronicles of reformed Judaism in mid-century America have a sharp attention paid to minute details, even if they feel a bit obvious at points. Yeah, the guy can write — but the neuroses are buried mostly compared to *Portnoy*, and perhaps I like things to be more explicit. Being a goy myself probably means I have somewhat less of an appreciation of these stories, but I think I've absorbed enough Judaica in my life through popular culture, living in Pittsburgh, friends, etc. to understand the issues of family, mothering and sexual guilt on display here (which is not altogether alien to the Catholic upbringing I had myself). Overall, not a bad find for 1€.

192, 518

682. Woodcutters by Thomas Bernhard
Received: 14 December 2015
Started: 16 December 2015
Finished: 19 December 2015
Wow, was this brutal. I knew what to expect in terms of form, having read some Bernhard before (in my mind his books are all one long, unbroken chapter without paragraph breaks) but I didn't expect this sort of bitterness. I often get frustrated with the vapidity and arrogance of the artistic world, but never to the extent of this, which was a book-length rant against theatre people. It was very much rooted in early 80s Vienna and particularly the theatre world, which I know nothing (and care nothing) about, but I found plenty to relate to. The bile on display here was made even more potent by Bernhard's choice italicisations, for example *intellectual conversation*, where the mocking tone just drips off the page (or the iPad screen, in my case). As the entirety of this novel is set at one *artistic party*, although filled with flashbacks and digressions, it reminded me of those party scenes in *The Recognitions* expanded to book-length, though I haven't reached them yet in the re-reading of Gaddis I'm doing in parallel to this, so maybe I am remembering them wrong. I think *Woodcutters* triumphs not just because it's so cutting, but because it relentlessly interrogates

the relationship between the self and art, seeking the genuine, so it really is a lot like Gaddis in that sense. Bernhard's writing is as lucid as the earlier books, though there is far less description of the natural world or even physical details — it inhabits the attitudes, beliefs and social behaviour of its characters, all filtered through this narrator's extreme misanthropy. Assuming this narrator is a thinly disguised Bernhard, I felt somehow that the experience of age of the narrator almost justified these attitudes, though maybe I'm just an equally miserable bastard.

683. Everything You Always Wanted to Know About Curating* But Were Afraid to Ask by Hans Ulrich Obrist
Received: 17 December 2015
Started: 17 December 2015
Finished: 19 December 2015
This is a messy collection of interviews with Obrist, turning his interview project around on himself. It doesn't actually really tell you anything about curating as an art form (which is fine) but a bit about the man, or at least whatever image of himself he puts forth to the art world. The guy is surely brilliant and fascinating, but he's so rooted in the format of the art exhibition that it's hard for me to take much inspiration from this. I love how involved he is with architecture and other fields as half of the endless torrent of names dropped here are not fine art practitioners at all. But at the same time, Obrist's best quality — that he is so supposedly ground-breaking and brilliant within the confines of the art world — is also what turns me off, because I just really am not that interested in the celebrity culture of these big name artists, however much I might enjoy and appreciate their work. So I found myself anxious to get through this, hoping for some inspirational idea to emerge. The editors tried to be aware of his repetitiveness (which is not a criticism, as this is comprised of so many different interviews that it's inevitable that there will be repetition) by underlining passages that recur, suggesting that these repetitions are in fact 'outward spirals'. But I found them to be merely repetitious. If I had ever gotten my 120-hour nonstop talk show to happen (a failed project of mine from back in 2012), it probably would have just been considered a rip-off of Obrist's 24 hour interview marathons. I wish this guy would release podcasts or something because it would more enjoyable to listen to him talk to people than to read this.

684. Black Mountain: An Exploration in Community by Martin Duberman
Received: 17 December 2015
Started: 17 December 2015
Finished: 21 December 2015
A surprisingly enjoyable read, this history of Black Mountain College was written in 1971 and thus had the benefit of using primary sources for most of it. However, the author doesn't dig as deeply because of this, so for example, when the second rector resigned in disgrace after getting arrested for a homosexual cruising incident (in the early 40s), he disappeared completely and broke off all contact with Black Mountain alumni, though he was surely still alive in '71 and thus could have been found with more effort. A minor quibble; this is an otherwise excellent work that really illuminated the legend of Black Mountain, de-mythologizing it while also providing a clear description of its activities and organising principles. It's fascinating how conventional and even conservative this was in the 30s when it started. Though today it's remembered as a haven for experimental practitioners like Cage, Cunningham, de Koonig and Buckminster Fuller, these people were relatively minor figures who were only there for some of the summer sessions in the late 40s. Charles Olson really took over operations by the end, but by this point it wasn't a college anymore, but more like the open-form artist residency centres of today. Most of the book chronicles the fights and schisms between the different factions, as well as the institution's financial struggles. It's somehow both comforting and sad that Black Mountain College wasn't necessarily that different from the art and culture organisations I've been involved with myself. I read this hoping for some tips and/or inspiration as I look forward to planning (with my colleague) our next venture, but really there wasn't a tremendous amount of ground-breaking thoughts in here. Still, it was worthwhile to read and I feel richer knowing more about this, historically.

685. To Hellholes and Back: Bribes, Lies, and the Art of Extreme Tourism by Chuck Thompson
Received: 23 December 2015
Started: 23 December 2015
Finished: 24 December 2015
Not a good book, but a quick easy read of something that was for some reason in the Nida library's fiction section, though this is travel writing, technically. But it's travel

writing with an ATTITUDE, as Thompson is a loud, abrasive American who has taken the 'hellhole' angle to frame a humorous travelogue of journeys to the Congo, India, Mexico City and Disneyworld. I read this because I was curious about his take on India, which was the most moderate part of this, I suppose, but still pretty much without any merit. The all-out attempts to be funny, almost like a Dave Barry book or something, annoyed me because it's trying to be so edgy and failing completely. Thompson's 'edge' just comes off as whiny, self-centred American chauvinism, though he occasionally turned an entertaining phrase (such as when he described the Jaisalmer heat as 'ball-wilting' and then in a footnote, described his testicles as a resembling a wet bunch of romaine lettuce). The chapter on Mexico City is the only one that brims with any joy or life, and is probably the least racist of them all. Yes, the non-stop touts in India are extremely irritating, but instead of complaining about them for five chapters, maybe Thompson could have written something indicating a unique perspective or insight into the country. I guess when you start off with the term 'hellhole' you're already showing your cards. The final section, on Disneyworld, was an attempt to critique American culture (maybe as a balance to all of the borderline racism in the other chapters), but it ends with him admitting that he loved the experience. Fuck this guy. But, it was a quick and easy read and I wanted a break from 'smart' stuff.

686. Wall to Wall by Douglas Woolf
Received: 5 June 2015
Started: 25 December 2015
Finished: 26 December 2015

609 *Wall to Wall* strongly resembled *On Us*, perhaps even being a rewrite, but this was OK by me; the two books taken together (or apart) are exemplary works of what I love about Woolf. The protagonist of *Wall to Wall* was slightly younger than his others but no less drifting. Published, I think, in the early 80s, this had the stigma of Vietnam all over it without being overtly about veterans. The America depicted here (largely highways and Arizona) feels sleepy and stuck, just like the character of Vivien, who longs to escape. When I think

374 about works like *Revolutionary Road*, which deconstructs the Salinger trip of American affluence, they seem to define a world of literary insularity that Woolf, I assume, stood opposed to. The people here are certainly not New England WASP types, but neither are they degenerates or junkies as Bukowski or Burroughs would chronicle. Instead, they're stuck somewhere in the cracks between, when there existed an American society that was still possible to disappear into entirely. Claude's roaming adventure is completely without purpose or map, yet it's worthy of being written about, whether it's the stunning descriptions of these sleepy Arizona towns at night or his interactions with other travellers, old friends, and family. There's no violence or nastiness here — Claude comes across as a pretty OK guy, if a bit aimless, and maybe this is a celebration of that freedom — a freedom which comes from youth, though perhaps at the end we feel the tentacles of family pulling him back in.

687. Poking a Dead Frog: Conversations with Today's Top Comedy Writers by Mike Sacks
Received: 21 December 2015
Started: 21 December 2015
Finished: 26 December 2015

It felt like I had read this before — the Daniel Clowes interview felt so familiar that I had to check *And Here's the Kicker* to make 520 sure it didn't already appear there. This deviates slightly from the earlier volume by being more explicitly geared towards aspiring humour writers than I remember *Kicker* being. The interviews are the best part, and in-between are short blasts of prose from numerous comedians and writers offering their advice. I skimmed these, as I am not looking to break into the humour-writing business, but enjoyed the interviews throughout. Bob Elliott, Tom Scharpling, and Roz Chast in particular had good insight, and there was enough about the secret past comedy world that this should hold me over until I can get my hands on a copy of the Kliph Nesteroff book that just came out.

688. The Nightmare of Participation by Markus Miessen
Received: 25 December 2015
Started: 25 December 2015
Finished: 27 December 2015

This was an excellent book, though frustrating by nature, as Miessen's hypothesis rejects any logical answers or a conclusion. Miessen is a young architect, seemingly from the crazy interzone between contemporary art practice and theoretical architecture, and thus his starting position is one that I can easily relate to — that the idea of consensus decision-making as currently practiced in most cultural and political forms prevents anything meaningful from being achieved. This book is a search for a more conflict-based form of participation, one that Chantal Mouffe called 'agonism' as opposed to 'antagonism'. The centrepiece of the book, and the best part, is a lengthy interview with Mouffe, whose post-Marxist approach to collaborative political practice is brilliantly innovative. There's also a brief look at a German politician who Miessen feels is a practitioner of post-consensus Leftist politics, and a good essay exploring the failure of the academy in today's context. There's an interview with Obrist at the end that felt almost obligatory and is just about how great they think Cedric Price is, so I'm not sure of the relevance, and then finally Carson Chan dissects the whole book in an afterword that is extremely critical of the book as a whole. This was much more about political engagement than any specific discipline such as architecture or art, which I guess is a more high-level way of thinking about participatory knowledge production. It was written without any academic pretence as well, which I think helped significantly in making this readable and fairly light. I don't know if I have gathered any conclusions myself beyond what I already thought about and feared, but the ideas here were clearly articulated throughout.

689. Game Urbanism: Manual for Cultural Spatial Planning by Hans Venhuizen
Received: 27 December 2015
Started: 27 December 2015
Finished: 28 December 2015
I picked this up while flipping through the Nida library's small section on architecture and got sucked in. This is a catalogue of projects by Hans Venhuizen, a well-known Dutch architect and urbanist. His definition of 'cultural planning' is not traditional planning, but an organic approach that tries to make space for already existing cultural trends rather than being proscriptive. But it's still spatial planning, and thus the projects he demonstrates are still realised in some form in the public sphere. The 'handbook' section of this was the most interesting, as it contained some lightly theoretical models, some practical descriptions of scenarios, and then some great marginalia detailing many of his projects that addressed the relevant topics. A lot of these were ironic and playful (such as a society to preserve McDonald's signpoles) but never cynical. The examples in the second half are expanded descriptions of a few of these projects, with lots of photos. I liked his term 'concept manager' for a person trying to create agile urban plans without being either top-down or bottom-up in nature. This was designed as a cool 'art' book with large photographs and disruptive typefaces, and while it wasn't as bad as a lot of things going on now with a hip design aesthetic, I found myself wishing it was presented more straightforwardly. But I'm a curmudgeon. In a way this was a nice, semi-relevant counterpoint to the Miessen book.

690. Map Addict: A Tale of Obsession, Fudge & the Ordnance Survey by Mike Parker
Received: 27 December 2015
Started: 27 December 2015
Finished: 29 December 2015
I picked this up thinking it would be a "Guardian book" (non-fiction category) which, I guess it was — very broad non-fiction about something middlebrow and smart, in this case, cartography. But I loved reading this and was so thoroughly entertained by it that I'm sad its finished and I actually called up my Dad to recommend it to him. Though it's probably too British for him — Parker is totally obsessed with obscure British locations, and I am too, so I was thrilled by his obsessive notes on the changes in Ordnance Survey maps of obscure Lincolnshire waterways and other such minutiae. It's a really personal book describing one man's obsession, which he seems to have parlayed into a career as a Radio 4 personality, but it doesn't come off as contrived in the slightest. Parker's enthusiasm is infectious and while there is no real purpose or argument to this book, it's well-organised into chapters about topics such as the history of OS maps, erotic and pornographic place names (I particularly like that many medieval towns had a street where prostitutes worked called 'Gropecunt Lane' or some variety), and a screed against satnav systems. I became incredibly homesick reading this, which causes me to reflect why I still think of the UK as 'home' when I only lived in Scotland for 3 years of my nearly 36 on this earth. Oh, also he confirms that the BBC used the shape of the Kintyre peninsula as to what is the acceptable level of tumescence that can be shown in a penis on TV — which I always thought was just an urban legend.

691. The Road to Little Dribbling: More Notes From a Small Island by Bill Bryson
Received: 9 January 2016
Started: 9 January 2016
Finished: 16 January 2016
I've grown up with Bill Bryson, so I was thrilled when my Dad told me he had a new book, and one that returns to his travel-writing roots as he journeys around the UK again. It's officially billed as a sequel to *Notes from a Small Island*, two decades later, and comes at a time when I've been missing the UK more than usual. Bryson's sense of humour feels as familiar as that of a family member or close friend, and now that he's in his sixties it's amazing how little it has changed. I'm referring only to his style of humour — exaggerations and fantasies and obviously ridiculous interactions that are fictionalised — as opposed to his general outlook, which has definitely aged. The curmudgeonly aspect is definitely something central here, even mentioned in the press blurb, but it felt more extreme than ever from Bryson. I know that even in *The Lost Continent* the far younger Bryson still kvetched and whined about things — but in this one, it's just non-stop complaints about the UK's celebrity culture, the behaviour of fellow tourists, the Internet, and every other imaginable aspect of daily life. In fact, I'd say that this was less a travel book and more the demented ranting of an angry, yet hilarious old man — there are page-long passages that have no connection to whatever picturesque hamlet he is walking through, about such topics as booking hotels online or people littering. When Bryson calms down and focuses on what he does best, it's sublime. He travels an idiosyncratic zigzag through England and Wales, only venturing into Scotland at the very end, and visits really small towns and less well-known tourist destinations. He often talks about an attraction and then fails to actually find it, because he gets tired or something else comes up, which is amazing that he left those sections in the book — his lack of adventure is endearing and even slightly aggressive against the traditions of travel writing. Throughout the book there's an assortment of facts about history, archaeology, and British cultural life that Bryson writes about in his inimitable way, with his true talent showing: his ability to infuse obscure facts with warmth and passion, in a cheerful, accessible way. This is even, at times, a bit like Sebald's *The Rings of Saturn* done in a very accessible (and far less deep) way. Contemporary Britain is such a beautiful and complex mess, falling apart under the ravages of a horrible government yet still so stuffed with wondrous arcana that it remains fascinating, and somehow he manages to capture it, benevolently (despite the complaining) and accurately. And its sad, slow decline is explicitly discussed; given that Bryson will probably never write another book about the UK like this, *Dribbling* feels a bit like a eulogy. But a mostly funny one; even if this is maybe his 'worst' travel book, it was still a pleasure all the way through.

692. The Book of Ash by James Flint
Received: 12 November 2015
Started: 1 January 2016
Finished: 17 January 2016
I forget where I came across Flint's name, but he was surely being compared to some of the heavyweights of contemporary literature, and I think I saw him referred to as an unrecognised genius of contemporary British literature. I ordered this for £0.01 + postage, but I should have gone for the more adventurous *Habitus* (or just not bothered at all). *The Book of Ash* is compared to DeLillo on the cover, and I can see DeLillo writing a book with a similar theme (radiation and nuclear waste) as this. But that's about where the possibility ends, because DeLillo would never suffer from the overly telegraphed and unimaginative prose. The key word here would be 'obvious' — Flint's narrator is so straightforward and his exposition so clunky that I spent the first half wondering if this was some intentional device. But it didn't go anywhere, just unfolding a sprawling quest narrative built upon some (admittedly interesting) themes, using completely bland dialogue and exposition. This felt like it was tailored to get a film option (and I think it would be an excellent film, actually) but was such a chore to get through that I wish I hadn't bothered. Still, I might try *Habitus* as a friend coincidentally bought a copy recently and that looks to be a bit more adventurous.

693. The Invisible Bridge: The Fall of Nixon and the Rise of Reagan by Rick Perlstein
Received: 28 December 2015
Started: 28 December 2015
Finished: 31 January 2016
Perlstein's books keep getting longer while the time period they cover shrinks; this was 1200 pages, and only covering about

649 three years. While I still think *Before the Storm* is his best book, I absolutely loved this and tried to find time (as the last few weeks have become more busy than I have been for awhile) to sneak to a quiet corner and lose myself in this. The formula is the same — a deft, colloquial chronicling of America's recent past, built around the rise of the modern right-wing, mixing in popular culture and other touchstones of the times. Perlstein's own bias has been clear since the first book, but even among the figures of the left he is often excoriating; the only two figures across all three books that seem to be portrayed completely positively are Lyndon Johnson and Barbara Jordan, and I may be forgetting complaints he made about Johnson. Carter is shown to be a completely fraudulent opportunist, a huckster just looking to straddle whatever it took to achieve power, and it makes me re-evaluate my feeling that his administration is the only one of my lifetime (albeit only briefly, during my first nine months) that could ever be defended. Reagan is nothing but a self-aggrandising hack from the very beginning, and just as in *Nixon-* 656 *land*, there's exactly the right amount of biographical information about him here. If the ultimate destination of these books is where we are today, then *The Invisible Bridge* shows the roots of so much that came later: Clintonism/triangulation, the direct-mail movement written about by Tom Frank in *The Wrecking Crew*, and ultimately 368 I guess the blowback of what's happening now with Trump. I can't wait to read his next book, which will likely be 3000 pages and only about the second half of 1976.

694. A Whore Just Like The Rest: The Music Writings Of Richard Meltzer by Richard Meltzer
Received: (already owned)
Started: 1 February 2016
Finished: 19 February 2016
I'm really trying to convince myself that I'm going to toss 60-70% of my books this summer, donating them to Nida, so I started filling boxes hoping to make some shelf space in the meantime. This has been collecting dust for years, since I first got it sometime after it came out, and as it's been awhile since I dabbled in some Meltzer I decided to re-read it before getting rid of it. Except now I'm not so sure I want to get rid of it. Sure, it's in print, and I can definitely order another copy if I really get desperate, but there are some short pieces in here that are such absolute genius that I could see myself wanting to refer to them and quote them in my own future work. This is presented pretty much chronologically, yet divided into thematic sections anyway, with each introduced by Meltzer in the present-day (or the date when it was published). Though this is supposed to be entirely music writings, he slips in some other work, most notably a long, angry rant about white supremacy written in the aftermath of the LA riots (which was powerful and still Meltzerian to the core). There's some record reviews from the mid 70s that are so wildly anti-everything they really belong in *Gulcher*; there's also quite a lot of sexist and misogynistic shit, though 503 he admits these attitudes required refining once punk came around, and he somehow comes across as still having pretty strong ethics, even if he's complicated. Meltzer is probably closer to Carducci than any of the other rock writers in the pantheon, not at all politically, but in his ability to see through bullshit and really assess things on his own terms. He displays a great understanding of music as art, if not as actual music, when he actually bothers to write about sound. I actually would have liked more about jazz and avant-garde classical, if that's where his interests went in the 70s, but what we get is good. The penultimate chapter is the masterpiece, a long essay called 'Vinyl Reckoning' which uses random bits of his record collection to review his life through nostalgia and memory, with some wistful and angry bits about past relationships and a whole lot of ranting about Christgau and Greil Marcus. It reminded me a bit of the PME-Art 'The DJ Who Gave Too Much Information' performance, both in structure and in how I wished it would have gone on forever. This isn't quite as delicate but Meltzer is an extremely different personality to the PME-Art people, and anyway I'm just a sucker for people who write about musical memories. This is the piece I could see myself going back and reading often, so that's probably why this will escape the great book purge.

695. Supergods: What Masked Vigilantes, Miraculous Mutants, and a Sun God from Smallville Can Teach Us About Being Human by Grant Morrison
Received: 29 February 2016
Started: 29 February 2016
Finished: 6 March 2016
Morrison's masterwork on superheroes was hard to put down, though about halfway through it shifted from being a thoughtful

extended essay about the deeper mythological themes of superhero comics into a personal autobiography of his own career. But Morrison's life is so deeply integrated with the comics industry, and his impact on it has been enormous, so I didn't mind this — and the lines between the industry and Morrison's personal story became very blurry as it went on. Surely, a heavy-handed editor could have reined him in, but would Morrison have ever gotten anywhere if he listened to editors? Given his reputation as an acid-head mystic, *Supergods* is surprisingly lucid, grounded in an astute analysis of cultural trends that is really well-integrated with his own anecdotes, beginning with his dreamy-eyed upbringing in Glasgow's Govan district and through his slow progression into the writing world. The book is divided into ages — the Golden, Silver, Dark, and Renaissance — and he manages to weave together a history of the industry which, while I already was well-versed in it, managed to be engaging anyway because of his fresh take on some of the familiar stories. He is diplomatic, even when criticising the direction of some of his colleagues and former collaborators, and maybe spends a little too much time explaining the motivations behind some of his own decisions but that's a minor quibble. I actually would have liked more of his analysis of some of the more obscure characters and offshoots from the Marvel/DC universes, and maybe a little more inside baseball about what it was like to work for the different companies (though he is pretty up-front about his struggles at Marvel, and seems to take Image for what it was, admitting he wrote a few issues of *Spawn* just for the cash). Of course, this made me want to dig into more comics, especially Morrison's own and some of the Warren Ellis stuff I haven't yet read.

696. The Utopia of Rules: On Technology, Stupidity and the Secret Joys of Bureaucracy by David Graeber
Received: 7 March 2016
Started: 7 March 2016
Finished: 13 March 2016
As much as I loved *Debt*, *The Utopia Of*
617 *Rules* goes even further and actually had
a pretty big impact on my thinking about the new cultural initiative I am working on. Graeber does what he does best, which is to open up a topic that I never really thought about deeply and approach it from a radical, leftist anthropological perspective. Like *Debt* unmasked the threat of violence that enforced debt repayment, here he illustrates how the same threat works to reinforce bureaucracy. What I liked most was the personal anecdotes sprinkled throughout, such as his work with an anarchist collective in New York City. There
was an appendix that was about *The Dark* 
Knight Rises which didn't so much serve a 1061
purpose other than to rant about the film; I got the feeling that Graeber just really liked writing it and wanted to include it, although it only tangentially deals with bureaucracy. This was absolutely great from start to finish.

697. Splendide-Hôtel by Gilbert Sorrentino
Received: 2 March 2003
Started: 1 March 2016
Finished: 16 March 2016
It's misleading that this shows it took me fifteen days to read it — really, I read it in two sittings as this is extremely short, not even novella-length. And also I'm ashamed it sat on my shelves for THIRTEEN YEARS almost to the day before I finally gave it a shot — because it's an amazing text, one of the best experimental novels I've ever read. Sorrentino structured twenty-six chapters around the letters of the alphabet, inspired by Rimbaud but only really theoretically because without having read Rimbaud since high school I was still able to enjoy this immensely. There is definitely an experimental structure though the writing, that while stylistically bold, isn't a stream-of-consciousness mess (at least not consistently so). Actually, this felt not unlike a blog, though of course decades before such things existed. There were moments of beauty, occasional social commentary, and some hilarious lists as only Sorrentino could do; some fake songs and texts were described, the titles of course hilarious but suggesting a world I wish existed. I read this so I could get rid of it, but it's so short and enjoyable and barely takes up any space that I think it'll be a keeper.

698. Cosmic Trigger I: Final Secret of the Illuminati by Robert Anton Wilson
Received: (already owned)
Started: 10 March 2016
Finished: 19 March 2016
I loaned this to a friend awhile back and then took it back, thinking that it was time. This is definitely a good thing to re-visit every few years, and actually I think a lot of what I thought was in here was actually in

the second or third volume. So much of this is actually about RAW's relationship with Timothy Leary and while there is a lot that is problematic about it, if you actually take the true lesson from this (which is not to believe in anything) then it's easy to avoid Chapel Perilous. I actually really appreciated now the autobiographical components — RAW talking about trying to raise his family in Ohio and the change in his own thought process that he underwent through drugs and other experiments. It's hard to know if all the stuff about Sirius and alien visitors is meant to trick gullible readers, or if RAW genuinely thinks these coincidences are significant. It serves to diminish the book's capabilities as a fundamental philosophical text, but maybe that's just another game he is employing. Actually, this is a lot more grounded than I remembered it being, and it didn't make me feel like I had to stretch my own view of reality too far in order to comprehend Wilson's world. Maybe this is because *Cosmic Trigger* (and *Illumina-*
232 *tus!* even more so) had such an impact on my way of thinking that re-reading it produces a numbed "So what?" effect, since I'm essentially already seeing things this way. Still, it's like re-reading the Bible or some other fundamental text.

699. Vertigo by W. G. Sebald
Received: 20 March 2016
Started: 20 March 2016
Finished: 22 March 2016

700. Panama by Thomas McGuane
Received: 4 September 2012
Started: 18 March 2016
Finished: 25 March 2016
This is McGuane's outlier, a sarcastic, bitter book which amplifies the extreme self-indulgence of his other protagonists and is vaguely about McGuane himself, though he was never a celebrity on the level of the narrator of this novel. *Panama* dispensed with sentimentality entirely, and the fallible and endearing foibles of the characters

411 637 in *Nothing But Blue Skies* and *The Bushwhacked Piano* are absent, replaced with pure bravado. Except I still think there was a lot of weakness in Chet, and he's certainly not a hero. The frank and callous depiction of his actions had the same recklessness as *Blue Skies*'s most exhilarating parts, and I think there's a certain type of male momentum that McGuane chronicles better than anybody. I'm a bit sick of white male viewpoints at the moment, and while McGuane's novels are extremely white and extremely male, there's the same kind of self-deprecation found in a lot of today's well-written television comedy (*Girls* and *Broad City* leap to my mind). This made me think I should read *Great Jones Street* as it's the only early DeLillo I haven't read, 704
and it's also about a celebrity coming to terms with things.

701. City on Fire by Garth Risk Hallberg
Received: 20 March 2016
Started: 20 March 2016
Finished: 30 March 2016
I fell for the hype — when a writer gets paid two million dollars for his first novel, you have to think something must be redeemable about it. Now, a few hours after finishing all 968 pages of it, I'm asking myself not only if it was worth the time (I'm pretty sure it wasn't) but if maybe I just don't like the majority of today's popular American fiction. This was way, way, way too long — it could have been cut in half — and rather lazily written. The plot was so based on connections and coincidences between the characters that it was preposterous, and the overstuffed cast all spoke with the same voice. But I kept reading, because some parts of this were extremely compelling and I wanted to see what it would all amount to. I feel like Hallberg calculated exactly what to do in order to write a critically acclaimed book; he put in just enough gripping plot twists to make it easily optionable for a film, and situated everything in 1977 New York, so it could be about PUNK, because that's trendy, right? Well, among the kinds of people who buy books today, I guess, though I'd imagine that most people in their early 20s could care less about Hallberg's less-than-faithful recreation of the Bowery or CBGB's during the era of Patti Smith, Television, and the Voidoids. I know that he's my age, so he's writing about an era that took place before he was born, but plenty of writers have been able to achieve that — it's called historical fiction. Hallberg was just flat-out lazy with it, only sprinkling in references to popular culture or political events of 1976-77 when he seemed to remember to, making it feel like a cooked meal with spices haphazardly thrown on at the end, rather than during the actual cooking time. The book is entirely about white people apart from the gay black character, probably the book's protagonist if there is one, but one whose own backstory feels also tacked on with an unnecessary trip to Georgia in the middle, written as if to insulate oneself

from the criticism of under-developing said character (and in the process, emphasising the underdevelopment via the tone-deaf prose style and utter inability to imagine life for Southern blacks in the 70s). This book felt completely tailored to tick the boxes of the youthful obsessions of people my age: zine culture, gritty 70s NYC life, and anarchist communes. But I've moved on from being excited by an otherwise rote mystery story just because it namedrops Richard Hell. Ironically, Hallberg is at his best when writing about the wealthy WASP family at the centre of the narrative; depictions of their 1960s youth come across not unlike depictions of Salinger's Glass family, suggesting that Hallberg should stick to what he knows. The Long Island working-class families and the gutter punks seem one-dimensional by comparison, though they get plenty of prose inches to have all of their parental issues dug through. I probably sound overwhelmingly negative when I actually tore through this rather quickly and did enjoy parts of it, but the resulting disappointment was massive and the more I think about this, the more I'm convinced Hallberg is a genius only for writing the type of easily digestible, button-pushing, easy narrative that gets inevitable referred to as 'ambitious' just because it's long and has a complex plot, and then getting two million dollars for it. His prose style reminded me of Jonathans Lethem and Franzen, the former maybe because of the New York/music setting and the latter because the novel is ultimately so fucking bad, like *Freedom* (but will be similarly showered with press, attention, and the inevitable proclamation of being an important new literary voice). This is so incredibly middlebrow and I really wanted more, stylistically mainly, though Hallberg has the ability to write well — he just doesn't consistently do so. When he gets away from pure exposition and canned dialogue, and actually lets a bit of poetry into his sentences, the effect is chilling — he describes the feeling of urban space so well that it's haunting and grounding at the same time. And the aforementioned Hamilton-Sweeney flashbacks, while they don't feel even remotely like an original contribution to literature, at least wear their influence well. The last 150 pages is the 'thriller' section, where the inertia of Hallberg's careful chronology and non-linear reveals for the previous 800 pages finally spirals out of control and contributes to a real sense of madness, which echoes the NYC blackout he is chronicling. However, by this point, I just found it all irritating, and I wanted it to end — the big payoff never comes, there are no more surprises that matter, and I really found myself wondering what this book ultimately had to say about New York, art, music, life, our time now, that time then, or the act of storytelling itself.

702. Psychedelia and Other Colours by Rob Chapman
Received: 31 March 2016
Started: 31 March 2016
Finished: 26 April 2016
I had high expectations for this lengthy study on LSD's effect on culture (or at least that's how it was presented). What I got was yet another book about the same old 60s bands you've read about a million times, as Chapman's emphasis on culture was about 90% rock-music based. Thus, the first chapters were the most interesting, discussing some antecedents to rock, such as the San Francisco avant-garde; then, the British side (which Chapman was much more deeply immersed in) had some intriguing observations about music hall culture's descent into the psychedelic era. Most of the middle sections of the book were just more takes on the Beatles, Hendrix, Jefferson Airplane, the Grateful Dead, and the usual suspects. Chapman does have a good insight into music and had some unconventional opinions, and his knowledge was deep enough that he highlighted some less frequently celebrated bands, so I can thank him for turning me on to Blossom Toes. The Beatles are his favourite, by far, and while he probably writes some unorthodox things about them, I'm personally completely sick of reading, hearing, or even thinking about them. I'm probably being too hard on this — it was an easy read, though I took my time with it, and I wish he had done a wider study on psychedelia outside of the Anglo-American world. It's also dubious what Chapman considers to be 'psychedelic' — he is occasionally somewhat presumptive about certain artists using or not using drugs, and I guess it's a wider concept than the drug itself, but he spends the early chapters focusing specifically on how LSD spread to cultural communities.

703. The Irresponsible Magician: Essays and Fictions by Rebekah Rutkoff
Received: 26 April 2016
Started: 6 May 2016
Finished: 11 May 2016
The Irresponsible Magician is slim and didn't take very long to read, but it left me

feeling slightly insane and unsure of what I
experienced. I'm often tempted to conflate
this type of structural confusion with genius,
and proclaim this to be amazing and masterful, but it might just be cryptic enough
(and generally widening the boundaries
between genres) that I would be rushing to
praise because of my own insecurity about
comprehension. Which is not to say this
is experimental stream-of-consciousness
nonsense or impenetrable prose; quite
the opposite, as Rutkoff's few pages are
extremely carefully chosen, word for word,
with a pinpoint accuracy. I ordered this
after reading a review on the *LA Review
of Books* that described this as a work
somewhere between fiction and criticism,
without bothering to distinguish which bits
are which. And it's clear after reading it that
this is a type of hybrid writing that feels
totally alien to anything in the literature
field, though not so strange in the art world;
even Sebald's cloaking of his essays under
a fictive umbrella retains a stoic presence
that Rutkoff utterly dismisses. That review
compared this to Kraus's *I Love Dick* as well
483 as a handful of other 'hybrid' works that I
will check out as well; I can see the similarity
in styles as well as in the viewpoint of a
female American artist using prose as an
extension (or substitute) of (for) her visual
art practice. Rutkoff employs many celebrities from popular and fine art culture almost
as characters; the strange interviews with
herself are almost comic in the way they
draw in real-life figures, a manner which
some could call irresponsible (hence the
title?) yet here, they become larger than
life and illustrate a worldview that manages
to touch on personal and family influences
as well as being a reflection on her place
in the art world. The longest piece in the
book, and by far the most straightforward,
is a triplicate essay exploring the experimental cinema of Gregory Markopoulos,
the poetry of H.D. and Rutkoff's own travels
in Corfu. It's a beautiful, sinewy essay that
winds up feeling focused though it doesn't
have to; maybe this is just in comparison to
the rest of the book. Throughout everything
are a series of photographs, reproduced in
this Semiotext(e) edition in bolder-than-real
colours, making me feel like I'm holding an
inkjet-printed Asian restaurant menu. It's
not always clear what these photographs
and artefacts have to do with the writing
— in fact, it's almost never clear — and
that's probably why I don't feel 100%
comfortable assessing *The Irresponsible
Magician* as a whole. I'm glad I bought
this because I think it's something that will
warrant a re-read; it feels like it might be
as much of a treasure map as something
like, say, *Kew. Rhone*, and also continually
provokes new avenues and openings. No
matter what the final assessment may be,
this is a damned impressive work that feels
really unlike anything else I've read to date.

704. Great Jones Street by Don DeLillo
Received: (already owned)
Started: 8 May 2016
Finished: 13 May 2016
The last of the pre-*Underworld* DeLillo
books I haven't read, *Great Jones Street* 720
was clearly a transitional work between the
comic contemplations of *End Zone* and the
greatness that was about to come. Though 516
to be honest, having read all of these books
over a period of 18 years or so, I don't
really remember them all so well — my
recollection of *Ratner's Star* is spotty at 12
best and I remember *Players* being amaz- 30
ing and *Running Dog* being a throwaway 61
— or was it the other way around? After
finishing McGuane's *Panama*, I thought to 700
read this as it's also about a rock star, but it
couldn't be more different; instead of being
an inward-focused seriocomic portrait, this
was a device on which DeLillo could attach
his various preoccupations, and had little to
do with the idea of celebrity or music. There
were some funny bits — the song lyrics felt
a bit like a man releasing his energy — and
the whole intrigue-laden plot with the drug
took over the end of the book, though it
didn't really interest me. But mostly this had
strange characters speaking in the way that
DeLillo characters speak, dissecting their
strange place of existence in mid-1970s
America, and with some brilliant, beautiful
and spooky passages.

705. The Hour of the Star by Clarice Lispector
Received: 14 May 2016
Started: 14 May 2016
Finished: 18 May 2016
Lispector's last novel is very short and very focused, being the chronicle of a lost soul, written from the perspective of an unclear and very unreliable narrator. But this is far from a typical modernist 'unreliable narrator' novel, as it feels more like a work of philosophy, beautiful in its mundane depictions of Brasilian working class life and probing a healthy spirituality in the uncertainty of its assertions. *The Hour of the Star* feels so elusive, as if the entire text is under a shroud of darkness, though maybe

that's just the influence of the title on the novel itself. I've been working through her collected stories off and on for some months, though I don't think I'll ever finish reading them all because Lispector's prose seems to defy linear reading, at least in that collection — it's better to dip in and out, more like a work of poetry. While this was a more concentrated burst, it still felt blurry, without edges to grasp onto. Perhaps that's because the narrative itself is a bit of a red herring — I'm not clear how much of the Macabéa character is connected to Lispector herself, or the narrator Rodrigo, or if all of this is about fantastical identity and fiction itself. Either way, it was an incredible experience and one that felt like a light respite from an otherwise hectic month.

706. Omega Minor by Paul Verhaeghen
Received: (already owned)
Started: 22 October 2015
Finished: 7 June 2016
Finally! *Omega Minor* is a weighty tome, but at 691 pages it shouldn't have felt as long as it did — I've read far longer books in much quicker time periods. Of course I put this down for long periods at a time, eventually returning for one concentrated burst during which I knocked out the last 150 pages in a day. This Belgian novel follows in the tradition of sweeping historical epics centred around World War II, though it's more rambunctious and loose than anything else I could compare it to.
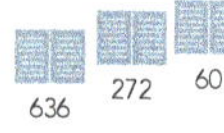
636 272 60 Like *The Discovery of Heaven*, *Hopeful Monsters*, *Europe Central* and *The Engineer of Human Souls*, the devastation of the war and the holocaust hangs over the following centuries. But where those books work with matters theological, romantic, or political, *Omega Minor* seems more interested in interrogating the idea of fiction itself, shifting its voices from character to character until they blend together in a confusing morass. I ultimately would say I really liked this; Verhaeghen's style was powerful, yet familiar; after reading stuff like *City on Fire* recently, it was nice to feel
701 the weighted restraint of a European style, although restrained this was not. There's tons of bawdy sex, poetic outbursts and even some thriller elements, and that it all comes together plot-wise into a big finale is nice (though not necessary). This is obscure and will probably remain so despite Dalkey's translation; it's too dense for anyone except those committed to contemporary world literature, and exists only in that market of books which cannot get noticed by the masses no matter how brilliant they might be. Which is a shame, because *Omega Minor* is a far more masterful work than many other more popular/acclaimed titles; it emerges from the now-traditions of postmodern literature while having a scope worthy of its heft.

707. But What If We're Wrong?: Thinking About the Present As If It Were the Past by Chuck Klosterman
Received: 13 June 2016
Started: 13 June 2016
Finished: 15 June 2016
Another incredibly pleasurable Klosterman book, this one examining the possibility that fundamentals about how we perceive art, science, and politics might be wrong. It's a great premise for a philosopher, perhaps, but with Klosterman's unique set of interests, he's mostly concerned with how the present might be perceived in the far future, and the most memorable sections are the ones about literature, rock music, and television. On science he's a bit shakier, though he interviewed plenty of public pop-intellectuals (such as Neil DeGrasse Tyson) and the resulting book is probably the most thought-out and 'mature' of his work. I think I enjoyed it the most of anything I've read recently from him; one chapter in particular deals with the Phantom Time conspiracy, which I love and he has ruminated on it precisely the same way that I have — and it's always nice to read things you agree with, but written in a way you wouldn't say yourself. The footnotes are often hilarious, but actually he peppers jokes throughout the main text as well, which would disqualify this from being taken seriously, but does Klosterman ever seem concerned with that?

708. Patience by Daniel Clowes
Received: 16 June 2016
Started: 20 June 2016
Finished: 20 June 2016
New Clowes work is always a cause for celebration and this one actually snuck up on me as I haven't been paying attention to the comics world lately. *Patience* is the longest single work he's done, I think, and at first seems like an abrupt departure, being a sci-fi/time-travel story with psychedelic visuals and a fatalistic romantic focus. But really, these are territories mined before — the death ray issue of *Eightball* and *Like a Velvet Glove* certainly had sci-fi elements, and there's always been

a bittersweet truth behind even the most angry-seeming panels. Still, the ironic detachment of the younger Clowes is subdued. Yet the inherent sadness of the white working class life is in full-force; the scenes of *Patience* set in 2006 are every bit as social realist as anything he's ever done, and having a time travel narrative overtop doesn't affect the misery, played now more for sympathy than to show contempt. I hesitate to say that Clowes has become warm and intimate, as we are still kept at arm's length, but it's a definite step away from the bitterness that saturated all those great issues of *Eightball*. Time travel is always fun and this focuses entirely on the interlocking plot instead of the confusing mechanics of it, all while narrated by his hard-boiled protagonist. I found myself deeply drawn into the story, which explodes off the pages with a brighter colour palette than he usually uses and some fun sci-fi futuristic elements (but not too many as to be distracting or gimmicky). The freaky, outsider weirdos that populated all of his previous work are certainly present, as is that damaged masculinity he's been portraying ever since Lloyd Llewellyn. And the melting body/psychedelic panels were a real new direction for Clowes, at times resembling old *Doctor Strange* comics — not an influence I ever thought I'd see in his work! I guess my one complaint would be that this isn't very funny — it's certainly not without humour, but the machinations of the complicated plot (which, I must say, is masterful, with not a meaningless detail in the whole book) pushed that aside. With Clowes, the humour is usually more in the outlook that ha-ha gags (*Wilson* excepted) 440, 657 and this is all about the story (story being something that, to be honest, *David Boring* could have used more of).

709. George Mills by Stanley Elkin
Received: (already owned)
Started: 21 June 2016
Finished: 6 July 2016

I decided to revisit this, as I like to spend some time with Stanley Elkin once every couple of years or so, and I've kept this on my shelf for the last thirteen years anticipating the inevitable re-read. I didn't completely 'get' this the first time through, but I knew one friend loved it and many people consider it to be Elkin's magnum opus. This isn't as immediately gratifying as *Dick* 62, 341 71, 596 *Gibson* or *The Franchiser*, but plays by its own rules about what a novel should be, and I think I would now agree that this is Elkin's masterpiece. But that's a weird word to use to describe a work from someone who so aggressively defies the conventions of what a novel should be, while still adhering to its surface-level form. *George Mills* is stridently sloppy, and intentionally digressive, to the point where its excess is what must be celebrated. The scope is also huge — spanning 1,000 years — starting right away with the opening section, a definite departure from Elkin's comfort zone (mid-century American culture, usually Midwestern) which he somehow pulls off. The deliberate anachronisms, crass dialogue and whimsical plotting made it so I forgot at times that I was reading a 'period piece' set in a salt mine in Poland in the year 980. And the majority of the novel, set mostly in modern-day (or at least early 1980s) America and Mexico, are more familiar territory for Elkin, though his comic nature is somewhat mellower here, if not outright subdued, than in his other works. The long digressions into side characters are for flavour rather than to service a punch line, and the nature of his prose is so rich, cutting at times against the low-culture speech he so faithfully renders, that it was occasionally off-putting. This is a very sideways meditation upon predestination, inheriting Pynchon's absurd theme of the preterite vs. the elect, but infused with a very American blue-collar mentality. Labour, class and ultimately belief are the real subjects of *George Mills*, though in the end Mills (and Elkin himself, I think) refuse to commit to a coherent viewpoint. This uncertainty is reached in the most scrupulous manner possible, however, and long passages of this are such a pleasure to read that they could work as miniatures (and I wonder if maybe they began as short stories). In a more conventional plot structure, a book like this might collapse under the weight of these ambitions, but because *George Mills* rejects conventional plotting and structure, it actually works well. Ideas leak out of the edges of every chapter, and the reader is the only one who is going to scoop everything up. This could be taken as a criticism, and indeed my own enjoyment of Elkin as a writer is probably the reason I'm giving him a green light on this, but it also resembles the open-ended forms of so many great postmodern novels. I'd say Elkin is somewhat of a bridge between modernism and post-modernism, and that's the most evident here out of everything I've read by him (which would be a few of his novels twice, and a few others not at all, so I should dig out the rest).

710. Odd Number by Gilbert Sorrentino
Received: 13 April 2003
Started: 2 July 2016
Finished: 7 July 2016
This is the first book in the *Pack of Lies* trilogy, and now I'm curious to read the others, if I can find them. According to the flap, this is modelled after a Greek chorus, though I would have never picked up on that myself; it's in three sections, collecting information about a large group of shady people, centred on the cultural world, pornography, and a possible murder. The first section is the most fragmentary, made up of incomplete sentences, though actually it resembles actually human speech, as if we are getting only one side of the conversation. The remaining two chapters follow a more standard interrogative form, a bit like the 'Ithaca' chapter of *Ulysses*. There's a ludicrous amount of characters, and they're thrown at the reader without any actual characterisation, so it starts to pile up and becomes quickly impossible to keep it all straight. I'm not sure if that's what Sorrentino intended — if I had taken notes and kept all the possible connections straight, maybe it would have been more rewarding — but I've read enough Sorrentino to know that he's not interested in such conventional narrative attributes. This is all about sex and specifically the commodification of it, though it's not really erotic in its own right, with all these sexual connections referred to rather than described (although he seems to have a real fetish for feminine attire). There are only a few list-like sections, which is something I remember absolutely loving about 33 *Mulligan Stew*. *Odd Number* is similar to that book in that it's main theme is the questioning of fiction itself, which is probably Sorrentino's major motif (based on what I've read by him); it also satirises the lives of Bohemians and cultural types (writers, artists, actors) just like *Imaginative Qualities of Actual Things* did, or Bernhard's 682 *Woodcutters*. Though everyone in this book sounds pretty sketchy, it doesn't feel as much like an attack on these types, but rather a giant web of mystery that is intentionally empty, with the main apex of those mysteries possibly being false. The last chapter feels like it's throwing in even more characters that weren't previously mentioned, or maybe they were and I wasn't paying enough attention — but I could see Sorrentino just adding more names for the fuck of it. I enjoyed this, though it's anti-structure somewhat rejects the compelling read vibe; I wonder if the next two books build on these characters more, or just on the concept.

711. Epileptic by David B.
Received: 21 June 2007
Started: 7 July 2016
Finished: 10 July 2016
There's a reason why this is so celebrated — it's an extremely intimate memoir, pulsing with sadness to the point where it becomes energetic. Beauchard merges his brother's tragic epileptic life with his own development as a creative, and their two inseparable paths are chronicled without any need for flashy plot twists or too-precious analogies. His style is very dark — meaning, lots of ink, where the characters exist primarily in negative space — and this emerges as a distinct visual language which draws from his childhood obsessions with violence yet recasts into a fantastic sphere for the many dream sequences. I have no excuse for waiting so long to read this, especially as I dragged it from country to country with each move, and it didn't take that long once I finally started. Though it's a meaty, hefty experience, as dense as *Bottomless Belly Button* or *Big Questions* even with a smaller page count. 402 528, 856 French cartoonists have such a nice style of autobiography, or at least Guy Delisle is not so different in how he puts his fears forward, yet still manages to be standing to the side of the main 'action'. *Epileptic* is generally regarded as one of the greatest graphic novels of its time and I would say it's pretty worthy of the praise; I should check out *Babel* next, though to be honest his inky style is something I should have taken more slowly because it's not so easy to read fast.

712. The Nick Tosches Reader by Nick Tosches
Received: (already owned)
Started: 7 July 2016
Finished: 10 July 2016
I've had this for years, always filed next to the very similarly-structured Meltzer collection which has recently been read cover-to-cover and tossed on the pile of future Nida library donations, so I figured why not extend the same courtesy to Tosches? As with *A Whore Like All The Rest*, I've 516 dabbled in this over the years but never gone straight through. And I still haven't, really, because I found myself skimming some of the bits near the end (the ridiculous play, the Sonny Liston stuff). Tosches really started out mining the same vein of

absurdity that Meltzer did, but then got pretensions of being a 'serious' writer; Meltzer *is* a serious writer, yet he doesn't give a shit about the literary canon, and there's the difference. That's not to say that there aren't amazingly enjoyable parts in here; the early reviews and pure fabrications have a certain touch of madness to them. His pig-headed misogyny is more full-on than I realise; Tosches is unapologetic about including some sex-crazed ravings which should embarrass a mortal man. The collaboration with Meltzer, *Frankie*, is the highpoint of these — where the purpose is not to titillate but to celebrate obscenity, which it does with great aplomb. I am actually a bit curious now to read his book about Sindona, and maybe even the Dean Martin book; I'll pass on his fiction, thank you, and it was nice to re-read a page from *Where Dead Voices Gather*, which I remember extremely fondly. This doesn't really work so well cover-to-cover, as it loses its energy, but it doesn't justify sitting on my shelf for the rest of eternity, so to Lithuania you go!

713. The Wrong Place by Brecht Evens
Received: 12 September 2012
Started: 12 July 2016
Finished: 12 July 2016
Clearing out my graphic novels for future Nida donations, I actually sat down and read this, which I bought because I was so into the use of watercolours, previously only flipping through it. I do really love the art, but the story feels a little lackluster, concerning a group of young people gravitating around a disco-based social scene. It's chock full of silly behaviour, without much to really say about the nature of these interactions. For such a beautiful, fluid visual style I was hoping for something a little dreamier, in terms of content, and not just people going to parties and nightclubs. The sex scene in the middle though, oh my god; it's brilliantly rendered, using the just-out-of-focus nature of watercolours to create an overlaid, multidimensional depiction. I think it's these pages that convinced me to buy this, and if I ever re-visit it, that's what I'll go to, not for any prurient interest but just for how spectacularly the act of coitus is rendered. But the narrative meanders around its central character, presenting him first as a mysterious cipher and then finally introducing him and deflating any such intrigue; from this point on I just tried to immerse myself in the scenery, which is beautiful when spare, and even more beautiful in the chaotic crowd scenes. It's a bit surprising to me that this is a Flemish artist because the names and scenarios feel extremely American, but then again, the world is global.

714. The Best American Comics 2006 edited by Anne Elizabeth Moore and Harvey Pekar
Received: 30 September 2008
Started: 12 July 2016
Finished: 13 July 2016
Another anthology that's been taking up shelf space for years, and really, there's nothing that remarkable in here that makes me feel I need to keep it. The 'Best American' series is a hit with my father, who has years of the Essays, Travel Writing and Short Stories in his library, but I don't think he's likely to take to comics. This is co-curated by Harvey Pekar and thus skews a bit towards the typical male alternative comics artist — R. Crumb is here, probably out of obligation, and other big such as Chris Ware, Ben Katchor, Jaime Hernandez and Joe Sacco. It's not all men, though — Lynda Barry has a nice piece about the nature of creating (which is where she started to head around this time) and Alison Bechdel is present, which also feels a bit obligatory. The difficulty in reformatting all of these stories into the shape of the collection shows in a few places — the wonderfully surreal 'Rabbithead' by Rebecca Dart is out of place with so much white space around it, and the works of Chris Ware and David Heatley are so tiny that I can barely read all of the text. Heatley's work, a recollection of short vignettes about his father, is probably my favourite piece in the whole book, though you could argue it's really derivative of Ware (especially when placed alongside the Ware selection in this volume). There's absolutely nothing from the commercial superhero comics genre (though a few deconstructions of them, by Joel Priddy and Gilbert Shelton), which actually feels kinda fucked up — maybe they would have had difficulty getting printing rights from Marvel or DC, but if you're not including them in something called the 'Best American Comics' (and you aren't throwing the word 'alternative' in your title), you're not being that comprehensive.

715. Collected Fiction by Louis Zukofsky
Received: 1 May 2003
Started: 10 July 2016
Finished: 13 July 2016
It's hard for me to get past the typeface that Dalkey Archive chose to use for half of this book — a barely-complete, nearly unreadable font that resembles the old MacOS system menus, only desiccated. But I nonetheless slogged through it, figuring that any book I've kept around for thirteen years unread, even unopened, deserves some of my attention. The first half of this is *Little*, Zukofsky's only novel, published in 1970 and about a child violin prodigy, not even loosely based on his son Paul (who wrote a hilarious afterword, threatening legal action and including annotations to the novel that indicate the real-life incidents or characters the text was based on). This is a fabulously inventive bit of writing, descended from Firbank's playfulness but with a lot of insane proper names and onomatopoeic conjunctions. The story isn't super exciting to me, but that Zukofsky kept my interest is commendable, and this was offset from the far superior-looking type in the original novel. The other half of the book is a reprint of *It Was*, a collection of 4 pieces written between 1932 and 1961, and they are wildly erratic. The titular story is rather beautiful, almost pastoral; the second piece is a farce about cocaine addicts, which sticks out like a sore thumb against the rest of the book (but is strangely enjoyable). 'Ferdinand' is the longest piece, which is a fairly fluid tale of emotional development mixed in with slightly confusing world politics; I didn't stay interested the whole time but there were some majestic passages, and I didn't mind taking it in a fragmentary form. The final piece is the most experimental of the whole book, built around the dictionary but even less sensible than *Alphabetical Africa*. Even though this was the type of writing I was looking for, and expected the whole book to be, I must admit it tested my patience and I found myself rushing through it all just to get it over with.

716. $20,000 by Bill Drummond
Received: 24 June 2010
Started: 16 July 2016
Finished: 18 July 2016
$20,000 comes between Drummond's famous post-KLF work (burning £1mil, etc.) and his less-heralded Fluxus-style compositions as The 17. Its preoccupations fit right into this timeline, dealing with his emerging interest in choral music, sense of geography, and an honest dissection of creativity. And while it's ostensibly the document of another one of his provocations (where he decided he no longer wanted to own a Richard Long print, so was trying to sell it for $20,000 at which point he promised to bury the money at the place where the photograph was taken), it really is mostly a wonderful, idiosyncratic travelogue of the UK around ten years ago, a time where I was getting to know the country myself. Having recently seen *Imagine Waking Up Tomorrow and All Music has Disappeared*,  1550 I feel a little more on the wavelength of Drummond as a person than I ever did before (still never having met him) and thus I felt the true beauty in his approach to life, seeping through these pages. This actually functioned as a much better 'trip up Britain' chronicle than Bryson's recent *The Road To Little Dribbling*,  691 and with that country currently closer to complete social and political collapse than ever before, it made me really sad in places. Drummond's musings on the art world are also great to read, and surprisingly nuanced; of course, no one can really back up the talk like he does, but he still maintains an enthusiasm for pure creativity despite all he has experienced. He particularly harps on the way that London dominates the British art game and he expressed great interest in those who choose to stay in smaller cities. There's a big rant at the end about the idea of Britain and how he feels it's obsolete, and that he considers himself a "UK'n", which he distinguished completely from the classic idea of Great Britain; again, in the wake of Brexit this all feels really different (or maybe right in line with what he is saying). It's funny, too, without being as over-the-top nutso as *Bad Wisdom*,  167 and maintains a proper Discordian spirit throughout while also being really honest, which is something hard to achieve. I need to track down the sequel to *Bad Wisdom* but it's rather pricey and the whole idea here is to get rid of books. This is one I'll probably be keeping.

717. Inverting the Pyramid: The History of Football Tactics by Jonathan Wilson
Received: 25 June 2010
Started: 11 August 2016
Finished: 21 August 2016
Clearing off the shelves again, this was one I didn't take to Nida since they weren't likely to have or want a 'sport' section in their art

library. So I finally ploughed through it, also to get excited about the new Premier League campaign which just began, and because I've meant to read this for, well, six years. My old flatmate recommended it the last time I was in Glasgow and I bought a copy on his recommendation, and yeah, he's right — this is great. Wilson uses the formation as the basis for explaining how the game evolves, but this is far more than just a bit of intricacy about 4-5-1 vs 4-3-3 etc.; it's really about the social development of the game, snapshotted through some famous historic matches. He moves chronologically and geographically, highlighting the eras when one country's approach dominated the game (the Austrian era, the Hungarian era, the Italians in the 60s, Dutch "total football") and brings things up to modern times, more or less. There's also a great deal of background information about the key figures, mostly coaches, but Wilson isn't one to insist that a good system can trump brilliant players. Actually, that conflict is essentially what he presents as the struggle at the soul of the game, and while I can tell he leans towards believing in tactics over talent (as evidenced by the attention given to Valeriy Lobanovskyi's Dynamo Kyiv/USSR sides, and the somewhat condescending coverage of the Brasil 1970 side) it's mostly presented fairly. This made me curious to read a deeper history of football, one that might be more complete beyond just tactics, as there was only minimal mention of the Shankly/Paisley Liverpool years (of great interest to me), and neither Sir Alex Ferguson nor Arsène Wenger are mentioned at all, which seems a bit shocking.

718. The Game of Our Lives: The English Premier League and the Making of Modern Britain by David Goldblatt
Received: 23 August 2016
Started: 23 August 2016
Finished: 7 September 2016

717 After reading *Inverting the Pyramid* I wanted to read another book about football. I knew Goldblatt's history of world football was really well regarded, so I went into this expecting it to be a bit more popular-focused than critical. I was pleasantly surprised by his approach to chronicling the current state of football culture in the UK, using the Premier League as the central character but also looking quite in-depth at lower league football, and the Scottish & Welsh games. There's a lot here if you're a nerd for English football history, though it's really focused on the last twenty years and only dips into folklore when necessary. Goldblatt takes a very critical approach to the commercial impact of the game, and his politics aren't hard to determine; large sections of the book are spent chronicling the financial impropriety of smaller-division clubs, and an entire chapter is dedicated to the FA itself and the failed attempts to reform it. His view of the national team is fair, which is to say negative, and he highlights the media's role in creating-ruining the Premier League without overemphasising it. This will have the net effect of making me read his history book, which will make three football books in a row, unless I take a break first.

719. Zero K by Don DeLillo
Received: 6 September 2016
Started: 6 September 2016
Finished: 11 September 2016

I was really impressed with *Point Omega* 643 and the first half of *Zero K* is similar. Two men – one fascinating, rich and powerful, and the other our narrator — are in some very isolated setting exploring a concept that is quintessentially DeLillo. In this case we have a father/son relationship, and the topic is death, but rather than *White Noise*-style 220 existential dread, we're talking about cryogenic preservation and the post-humanity movement. This is a perfect topic for DeLillo and he tackles it in his unique way, which is to directly confront while seemingly not writing about it at all — that fierce style which is ponderous, yet light. It's like if he wrote the screenplay to *Ex Machina*,  1517 which would have been an improvement, for sure. But there's a bit more meat on the spine here, as we then follow our narrator back to New York for a period of drifting through his life, hovering around his short-term relationship and her son, who is a standard DeLilllo precocious child-figure. At first this felt tacked-on, like some residue from one of his other books, or a device he turns to in order to fill space, but ultimately there was a really beautiful convergence, which took place at the site in the first part (which is actually called The Convergence). What's new here is that I felt a lot more warmth than usual — the narrator's feelings about his father's treatment of his mother are brought out explicitly, and the sense of 'detachment' that always affixes itself to DeLillo narrators is subdued. The man is 79 now but he's still got it; this stands against any of his best works and feels incredibly relevant for this moment in history, as the shadows of Peter Thiel and his gang of creeps loom behind our capitalist death trip. There's a definitive choice made here, a viewpoint not avoided and no cop-outs at play, but the man knows what he's doing and it's a joy to read him.

720. Underworld by Don DeLillo
Received: 11 September 2016
Started: 11 September 2016
Finished: 9 October 2016
Wow, I didn't even realise until now that I started reading this on September 11th! Finally, I can cross *Underworld* off the list of weighty, unread tomes — my recent rekindling of DeLillo-love made it hard to keep avoiding this, though I wish I wasn't so focused on 'getting through it'. For all the acclaim this has received, I never quite understood exactly what this book was about — reviews and blurbs never talked about an actual plot — and now that I've finished it, I can see why. There's not really a plot at all, except for the loose, non-linear story of the baseball's travels through the late half of the 20th century. In my freshman or sophomore year at Pitt, I got about 250 pages through this before abandoning it; now, all month I was joking that I had been literally reading this 'since the 90s'. My recollection from then was that the opening 60 pages, later re-published as *Pafko at the Wall*, was undeniably the greatest passage of writing DeLillo ever achieved and the rest of the book was a mess. Now I can't say I feel so strongly about *Pafko*, but I'd upgrade the rest of the book to at least a "brilliant mess", or maybe a "brilliant masterpiece that I never want to read again". I think this is the most free and experimental book that DeLillo has written (though I still have two more novels to go before I can say for sure), but he's unable to completely abandon structure, and I suspect this came together from two or three unfinished novels jammed together. I wish he would have just let himself go completely and written something more like Michel Butor's *Mobile* — a literary land-
762 scape of America, though with DeLillo's preoccupations, would be a dream book for me. Instead, there's a sorta-main character (Nick Shay) who is sorta like all the other detached white male protagonists of

219, 482 220 561 643 209, 730 719 his books (*Americana*, *White Noise*, *The Names*, *Mao II*, *Point Omega* and *Zero K* for sure could in many ways be about the same person), and there's a sorta-climax in the book's last 150 pages (before the epilogue) which chronicle's Shay's early years in the Bronx in 1952, building up to a weird accidental crime that is supposed to be some dramatic moment but instead feels like an unnecessary, conventional plot element. That's a novel in itself, and then all of the intersections with secondary characters, such as the tragic spectre Esmeralda (who I suspect will re-appear in the short story collection I'm about to start) or the historical figures pad out the rest. As it was published, this gets written about as a chronicle of the culture of Cold War America and that's a beautiful thing — and really, the Cold War itself is nothing more than a shadow until the book's epilogue so it's absence (in being referred to directly) that makes it even more effective — but I wish this didn't feel like such a chore to get through. It may just be that DeLillo isn't a writer who benefits from length; I found *Point Omega* and *Players* to be some of

his strongest work, and they are very short 30
books, and his pensive probing of technology and speed doesn't require Pynchon-esque encyclopaediaphilia. But like many of his books, especially my all-time book-BFF *The Names*, *Underworld* has a slow burn. A day after finishing it, I'm feeling haunted by it, and thinking that there is some pretty incredible stuff inside that maybe I could have let sink in more if a) I wasn't so focused on getting through this and b) I hadn't read it during such a busy time in my own life. It would be too easy to say that DeLillo uses the 1951 baseball as a symbol of America's unravelling, but the central conceit of the book is not far from that reductive summary, and I'm really torn as to whether this would have been better without any centre at all. I love how he can probe subcultures (even imagined ones) that feel so extreme and removed from the lives we lead, yet strangely believable as some symptom of whatever times he's writing about. The dalliances with real-life culture here (*Cock-

sucker Blues*, or the depictions of Lenny 343
Bruce & J. Edgar Hoover) are really strong; like *Libra*, I think DeLillo is unusually apt

at writing about historical figures. I found 468
myself recalling Douglas Woolf's strongest work (such as *On Us* or *Ya!*), though with

very different aims. I don't think I ever made 609 668
the connection before but I would actually compare DeLillo to Paul Virilio somewhat — both are seers of speed and simulacra, and probably both influenced in the same way by their Catholic upbringing (I am assuming that DeLillo as an Italian-American grew up Catholic, though again I'm thinking about how little I know about the man himself). There's so much more that went through

my mind in some places that I should really start keeping notes again when reading (like in Evernote or something) because it feels like I'm doing a disservice to myself and anyone else who might be reading this when I let things escape. I'm diving right into the short story collection next, and then *Comopolis* and *The Body Artist,* 723 725 because at this moment I can't get enough of the man (I'm gonna re-read *Mao II* and *Players* after that!).

721. The Angel Esmeralda: Nine Stories by Don DeLillo
Received: 11 September 2016
Started: 10 October 2016
Finished: 16 October 2016
DeLillo's recent novels (at least until *Zero* 719 *K*) have been quite short, and the short story form generally serves him well. This proceeds chronologically, containing nothing earlier than 1977 (which is a shame — I wonder if he didn't feel that his early short stories were as strong — or maybe there just weren't any?!) and a heavy emphasis on the post-*Underworld* era. The early stuff was unsurprisingly great, including one set in a space station. The titular story is another view of incidents from *Underworld*, a bit like the *Alexandria Quartet* approach 375 to plural retelling, and it's packed with emotion yet avoids heavy-handedness. It's justifiably the centrepiece here. I found it hard to concentrate on the long story about the students stalking their teacher's family, and a couple reminded me of Updike, or at least my idea of Updike, which is "somewhat dull stories about middle-class white people". But I'm not complaining — DeLillo writes beautifully in all of these, and even when they failed to grab me in terms of narrative or larger concerns, they were brief enough. 'Hammers and Sickles' was one of the funnier ones, dealing with the recent economic crisis yet having that edge, suggesting a global covert conspiracy (or just two rogue agents). There's a real creepy undercurrent throughout, as unsettling as his best work and to be honest, it being something I have missed from his more recent fiction.

722. The Circle by Dave Eggers
Received: 24 August 2016
Started: 18 October 2016
Finished: 21 October 2016
When my father told me that he read this I was shocked — he never reads fiction, but he said he enjoyed it. I guess I enjoyed it somewhat, or at least I consumed it quickly, but I don't think this was remarkable. It's a fairly obvious bit of moralistic sci-fi, kinda like a Vonnegut story ('Harrison Bergeron') or really obvious cautionary tale. I'm already predisposed to be critical of social media and how it affects human behaviour, but this doesn't really offer any insights — it just plays out like you would expect it to. I expected much more from Eggers, because *Heartbreaking Work* I remember as being moving and *You Shall Know Our Velocity* was so fun I read it twice; for a guy who 113, 472 has built himself into a modern-day literary scene titan, his style is really bland. I love when direct, obvious writing can be powerful (see: Hemingway, or James Ellroy), but this was just rudimentary — like something written at a sixth grade level. If his goal for dumbing it down was to reach a mass audience to spread his message ("social networking is bad!") then he probably shouldn't have chosen a novel, because what novels reach mass audiences besides *50 Shades of Grey* or *Harry Potter*? The characterisations are so thin that it's hard 21-24, 89, 193, 259 to excuse; if Eggers is trying to get into the mind of a modern-day American woman then I feel sorry for those in his life. His protagonist is so devoid of personality that the half-hearted attempts to complexify her are just cheap, easy outs (father has MS, likes to go kayaking alone, etc.). Having her fuck the mysterious figure at the heart of the novel, if anything, is kind of misogynistic, like this is the only way she can connect with someone, and she is ultimately just another objectified and controlled victim of power. Even if that's the point, it's clumsily executed. This really didn't need to be 491 pages, but thankfully it went quick. This might be a fun film, and maybe Eggers wrote this intending to get it optioned, but that's about the best I can say here.

723. The Body Artist by Don DeLillo
Received: 24 August 2016
Started: 22 October 2016
Finished: 23 October 2016
Here's DeLillo writing what seems like a huge departure from his usual topics — taking the perspective of a woman, and directly addressing loss and grief. I don't know anything about the man personally or if he had a close death around the time this was written; it could also be that as the follow-up to *Underworld* he wanted to try something radically different. It's a 720 novella, really, and despite it's brevity it packs a punch. The entire novel is set in the domestic space of a woman who is 36

years old, and who passes time watching a webcam of a highway in Kotka, Finland (!). This behaviour is the only thing that feels typically DeLilloan here, except for the protagonist's career as a performance artist (described by a journalistic excerpt, and recalling the section of *Point Omega*
643 that describes the video installation) and the general difficulty of the book. If this is the beginning of 'late DeLillo' it's clear that he is turning away from writing about cults, terrorism, media, and the weight of history and towards the internal, human side of consciousness, using technology to amplify the disconnect (or detachment) that is the trademark of all of his characters. Some may find this a slight entry in his bibliography, no doubt due to the length and the lack of big, easy plot points, but I thought this was haunting to read, moving at points, and creepy (with the disabled visitor aspect) in a way that makes it about serious mental instability, yet calm to read. There's forces at play here between the tranquil, almost methodical description of Hartke's quotidian daytime behaviour (and her body-based exercises) and the extreme strangeness of the man-boy in her mental space. I may not have appreciated this if I had read it back when it came out, but now I found lots to savour; once again, I'm somewhat shaky after finishing it, letting it's power slowly reverberate over my own body.

724. Cannonball by Joseph McElroy
Received: 2 January 2016
Started: 5 June 2016
Finished: 24 October 2016

I didn't give this book the justice it deserves with my reading habits; I voraciously devoured the first 1/3 of it, then put it aside as other things came along, mostly a summer spent coding, plus all the DeLillo. So returning to it was distant, uneven, and with pieces missing, which pretty much mirrors the plot. The first few chapters of this are breath-taking, and then it fragments more and more. Or was it me? I confess I had to read the Wikipedia entry afterwards to really understand what all had happened, which is due not so much to my gap in time, but to the difficulty of McElroy's style. For a man in his early 80s, he's incredibly in touch with the voices of younger Americans (or at least my perception of them, since I am pretty distant from that world too); this,

86 like *Lookout Cartridge*, has elements of suspense and intrigue but sidesteps anything typical in favour of a dense web of memories and associations, put together by the narrator as he recalls his friendship with Umo and his experiences with his own family growing up in California. That this is staged in the Iraq War should probably be read as a meaningful act of protest, though what judgements he's making about it, I can't say. I actually feel so wrapped up in confusion about this novel, while simultaneously feeling like it was something remarkable that I would recommend, even if its a half-hearted recommendation since I didn't really read this the right way. The lost Dead Sea Scroll at the centre of the book's non-mystery might be read as some sort of comment on American values or a wry wink at the pseudo-intellectualisation of history by popular culture, or maybe not. I'm actually ashamed at how much I still struggle with McElroy — I've read almost all of his books, and started the two I haven't finished, so why am I still struggling to form a coherent understanding of writing? I guess it's because he gives just enough to get started — because these novels are truly set in the synapses between brainwaves, it means that they resemble human elements enough that resisting the urge to make sense, to complete the map, is a real challenge. At times, as I confess I've done with many of his other books, I simply throw up my hands and go along for the ride, letting the words wash over me like a waterfall. There are some stunning pages here, somewhat 'stream of consciousness' but mimicking the rhythms of the human voice, media tones, and other eavesdropped sonorities. Or maybe I'm overthinking this and I should just take it for what it is, a somewhat intellectual, experimental, novel version of the film

Three Kings. 394

725. Cosmopolis by Don DeLillo
Received: 23 October 2016
Started: 23 October 2016
Finished: 26 October 2016

Cronenberg's film really weighed over me as I read this, though I didn't imagine Rob- 1516
ert Pattinson in my head, since I forget what he looks like already (bland, attractive?) — but Paul Giamatti as Benno Levin is unforgettable. Maybe I should read all literature while imagining Paul Giamatti as the characters. It would certainly work for some writers (Beckett, Joyce) and be pretty interesting for others (Shakespeare, Faulkner, Austen). The film really was almost a direct translation to the screen, as except for the surreal movie-extra scene before

the end, this is (as I remember) more or less the screenplay already, except with DeLillo's sardonic observations between the dialogue, many of which Cronenberg translated as well into visuals. For a slight book (131 pages), this was pretty dense, and definitely retained much more of the classic 723 DeLillo feeling than *The Body Artist* did. This electronic edition had a few reviews prepended, which were all negative, one of them calling this 'a step backwards'. In comparison to *The Body Artist*, it certainly seems like a retreat, back to the affectless world of powerful people and personal conspiracies. But I didn't find that to be problematic; this was a really spot-on take on late capitalism, issued without the usual moral judgements (though I believe that DeLillo is quite clear about his feelings about working people and the victims of globalisation, just doesn't express it through obvious left-wing terminology). This was written after 9/11 but set a year before it, and somehow New York manages to be both the central star of the book but also fairly anonymous (apart from some roads and other landmarks, all of Packer's pit stops are anonymous, fictionalised places), as if any other mega-city could stand in its place; this is the usual DeLillo male protagonist, this time in city form. Packer is of course the centrepiece, but is paralleled by the dark undercurrent of Benno Levin throughout, with the 'confessions' interleaved in the cross-town limo journey. Levin really completes Packer, but not in a standard have/have-not way. Maybe the bad reviews are because the protagonist is so difficult to empathise with, impossible actually, and critics are always so fixated on likeability and other such niceties. And they're fools, because *Cosmopolis* is great; if it would have come earlier in his career, say before *Underworld*, then it would be universally hailed as a masterpiece. There was an essay I started reading about Edward Said's notion of 'late style' and how writers such as DeLillo, Pynchon, and Roth changed their approaches as they got closer to death, which reflects fears of their own mortality, etc. I don't really buy it here — this prose is as lucid and haunting as anything he would have written twenty years previously, and fucking hilarious as well. I've now read all sixteen of DeLillo's novels, but I'm feeling more in awe of him than ever before, so I'm actually going to keep going and re-read some of the older 30 209, 730 ones like *Players* and *Mao II*.

726. One Summer: America 1927 by Bill Bryson
Received: 24 August 2016
Started: 27 October 2016
Finished: 5 November 2016
As a Bill Bryson fan since age 12 I usually read all of his books out of obligation, but when this one came out I either missed it or just forgot about it. I had no doubts it would be a compelling, page-turning bit of non-fiction and it delivered completely. I always love the bits in his travel books where he goes on weird digressions telling about some historic thing, always relating it to the social context of the day, and then gently pointing out how amazing it can be in a modern context; this was basically 500 pages of that, and a general overview of 1920s American culture at the same time. I didn't learn about anything I didn't already know about (Lindbergh's flight, the Sacco and Vanzetti trial, the 1927 Yankees, etc.) but certainly discovered all of these things to a much greater depth than I could have ever imagined. I was looking for a popular history, not an academic one, so I have no quibbles about whatever simplifications or generalisations that Bryson made here. But then, I guess he always gets a free pass from me.

727. The Partly Cloudy Patriot by Sarah Vowell
Received: 24 August 2016
Started: 5 November 2016
Finished: 7 November 2016
I never read Vowell before — well, no more than a few pages — and just know her as an annoying voice from middlebrow NPR America. Yet somehow I thought this might be worth reading, especially as preparation for the Democracy event at Temporary. But, yuck, what a waste of time. The only thing really interesting about this book is that it was mostly written after Bush was elected but before 9/11, so during that brief window when the left was angry but still felt like we had some possibility of stopping it all. There was one chapter obviously shoved in after 9/11 happened but it's somewhat incongruous with the rest of the book, which talks about inane shit like her crushes on Clinton and Gore and generally was the type of writing to make me feel the red states are justified in their resentment of coastal liberals such as Vowell. This type of personal essay feels to have largely receded, or at least migrated mostly to digital space, where they are at least killing less trees. I think I hate Sarah

Vowell as a writer. That's how bad this was. And yet I still finished it, out of some delusional quest to close out as many entries as I open here.

728. The Flamethrowers by Rachel Kushner
Received: 10 October 2016
Started: 10 October 2016
Finished: 27 November 2016
Wow, I'm impressed — enthralled, really, by what a driven, focused and ultimately pretty thrilling novel this was. With this, Kushner rockets to the top of my list of young (meaning, under 50) American writers to be 701 excited about. Compared to *City on Fire* (which I would only do because it's set in the same time and place), this is clearly a great literary statement as opposed to an ambitious work of easy fiction; yet despite the acclaim for *The Flamethrowers*, it's Hallberg who got a million dollar advance. Well, maybe she's selling shit tons of copies of this too, I don't know. She should — it is rightfully a work of great passion and vision, capturing contemporary American culture's trajectory by situation itself 30 years in the past. Maybe the ramblings about motorcycles, 60s radicals, and Italy seem quirky, but I think this was expertly pulled together into a narrative that has a stunning momentum, yet finds time to explore murky areas of feminism, political ideology, and economics/class. There's a very wide geographic scope here, as if the settings of Bonneville Salt Flats, NYC, and Milan keep trying to pull the book in different directions. For some reason I felt the vibe of early Richard Brautigan in the opening passages, maybe because they were set in the Western US, though far from his absurd tone. The novel manages to weave an interesting plot that doesn't require suspense or mysteries to be solved, instead inhabiting the mysterious emotional sphere of the narrator, who holds nothing back from us yet remains elusive. I love these types of sinewy protagonists, and while this could possibly be criticised for being a bit too loose or digressive, I actually was happy to drown in its ambience throughout. I will check out her first novel next and hope she can follow this up soon, and that the success/pressure doesn't collapse upon her like so many other successful literary stars.

729. The Daily Show (The Book): An Oral History as Told by Jon Stewart, the Correspondents, Staff and Guests by Chris Smith, etc.
Received: 28 November 2016
Started: 28 November 2016
Finished: 30 November 2016
Reading this was like smoking crack, I guess, though I've never smoked crack — I mean it was incredibly gratifying and I just wanted more. I've seen every episode of *The Daily Show* since sometime during 2004 when I started to connect with it, and during my first years out of the US it became a vital lifeline to connect to my home culture. Stewart's been celebrated by everyone almost ad nauseum, but rightfully so — in the final pages here, someone claims that he has forever altered the cultural and political life in America, and that's a pretty bold claim but hopefully true. Oral histories like this are remarkably easy to read and this one was a lot more compelling than the ESPN one, since I felt really connected to the material. Re-living so many of the episodes and segments that I had loved was great, but also revisiting the ugly, awful political decade that just passed was intense, in the way that I felt a sense of outrage again. The interviews here are really candid, and the book's constant admiration for Stewart is actually strengthened by the moments where people honestly talked about his darker sides. I got sad again that he isn't on the air anymore, but also really happy that he stepped out when the time was right, because he never let the show get stale or weak. I think I felt already very clear about what Stewart was trying to do, though reading it articulated explicitly by him (and other crew members) made me really appreciative for his sensibility and how much it probably has led to an awakening among many people. It was frustrating reading how often he was accused of cynicism when he was actually trying to do the exact opposite, and near the end when Dan Bakkedahl claimed that Bernie Sanders probably owes a lot of his success to Stewart, I sort of understand what he was getting at (even if that's a bit hyperbolic). I don't think this recent election has necessarily changed anything either. I've been watching Trevor Noah since he started until the past few weeks, and while it's certainly lacked the vitality (and anarchy), it's trying to be a different show, and I'm going to get back into the habit of it, because that's what it is — a habit, at this point. Anyway; this was great.

730. Mao II by Don Delillo
Received: 28 November 2016
Started: 28 November 2016
Finished: 7 December 2016

Mao II is a tricky one. I looked back at when I first read it, assigned by David Pascoe for the 'Writing the Disaster' seminar at Glasgow Uni, and I didn't have much to say — though I was much more sceptical of DeLillo then. Here, coming back to it after going through a semi-binge of the man's work, it feels powerful and prescient, which is how time eventually marinated my initial memory. There is no other writer whose work resonates so much after I have finished reading it. I'm certainly not a beginner any-more with him, having read all of his novels, but even now I found myself struggling to stay engaged with the plot, and occasion-ally questioning why I regarded this one so highly — but then, just a few hours after fin-ishing it, I'm having the 'Holy shit!' mental stimulation that his work always provides. I was a bit surprised to realise this was pub-lished in 1991 as I thought it to be a book from 1989 or so, which is probably when a lot of it was written, but that's because it's so much a product of the 1980s. Considering this as such, then DeLillo's 80s books are an infallible quartet that must rank among the most accomplished successive novels that anyone has ever written (*The Names*, *White*
468 220 219, 482 *Noise*, *Libra* and this) and this decade is bookended by books that are concerned largely with terrorism and violence. But while *The Names* deals with secret, ritual-istic violence on the personal level, *Mao II* is about mass-market terrorism, specifically of this Islamic flavour, and about crowds. That this was written before 9/11 and the Internet is crucial, and it makes the book feel like a transmission from another time, yet no less rewarding than something tackling the contemporary era. The major contrast he explores is between art and politics, by setting a Salinger-esque reclu-sive novelist as the primary character (which also suggests that *Mao II* is among the most personal works of DeLillo, as much as he's capable of writing about himself).

The aforementioned 'plot' — the mach-inations of writer Bill Gray, his assistant Scott, Scott's lover (and ex-Mooney) Karen, and the photographer Brita — is not super compelling. Something that I've come to admire about DeLillo is the way he will lay out all of the ingredients but refuse to do the cooking himself. A more obvious nov-elist would try to explicitly spell out what he wants to do here, but without being lazy, DeLillo is content to sketch out a scenario and trust the reader to draw the rest. It's admirable and not just any writer could pull it off. His language is calm and deter-mined, and that coldness which he's often accused of is honestly a virtue in a situation like this. It's not so interesting to me what these people are doing, but it provides a framework to explore the value of art in the age of mass media and spectacle.

Like *Underworld* (which opens with a spell-binding re-telling of a historical event, 720 merely a prologue unconnected to the "real" story, also set in a baseball stadium), *Mao II* starts with a passage describing Rev. Moon's mass-marriage in Yankee Stadium. It's a dazzling passage, and makes me wish the man had published more journalism. The end of the cold war and Fukuyama's 'end of history' bullshit was all happening around the time this was written, and while these events aren't explicitly dealt with in the text (since the Lebanese terrorism angle grounds this deep into the Reagan years), it's something I felt, particularly with what's happening in the world right now. The interest in crowds permeates this book, yet there's no attempt to really get into them. Though we see them on TV, hear about them — even the Hillsborough disaster is mentioned — it's all through the viewpoint of the very isolated individ-uals in the novel. While I think an earlier version of myself would criticise DeLillo for trying to write around his topic and using standard novelistic fodder (writing about other writers, etc.), now I see this as a brilliant mirror. Gray's final appearance is laid against the leader of the terrorists in Beirut, whose child soldiers wear masks with his own face on it. This interest in the cult of personality (the book is called *Mao II*, after all) persists throughout much of DeLillo's work, and maybe the world step-ping into a more decentralised form of ideological poison in recent years is another reason this feels like it's from a different era.

Yet all great classics of literature reflect upon today, and this is as amazing as some-thing written by Shakespeare or Joseph Conrad. I think this is my favourite or sec-ond-favourite of his books, overall, and I'll try to go back to it for inspiration in the future. It's not as quotable as some of his other works, but this may also perhaps be a strength — there are less profound pronouncements, and a concentration of ideas that isn't overreaching.

731. What Color Is the Sacred? by Michael Taussig
Received: 28 November 2016
Started: 28 November 2016
Finished: 10 December 2016
A friend recommended Taussig and he was right, how great! I'm going to have to read more by him. Taussig is an Australian anthropologist, but much of his writing defies conventional categories, and *What Color Is the Sacred?* is clearly one of those. The first 1/3 of this was mesmerising, the type of free-flowing, erudite soliloquising that I love and can't find enough of. I would probably compare Taussig most to someone like Hillel Schwartz, and that's not a bad thing at all. This meditation on colour starts with Goethe and runs through Burroughs, Walter Benjamin, Virginia Woolf, IG Farben and various anthropological touchstones. The middle section is the longest, going through the work of Bronisław Malinowski (who I was not familiar with), in particular deconstructing some photographs from Malinowski's anthropological work in Melanesia. I know this is like Anthropology 101 but as I wasn't familiar, I struggled somewhat — I still haven't read *Tristes Tropiques* yet, so I have lots to learn on the topic. The third section tackles Proust, a major hole in my modernist background, but I've read a lot about Proust before and found some ideas here exciting even without having read him — in particular, the relationship between memory and colour, which Taussig manages to connect to class. It wraps up nicely by getting into Nazis and gas chambers, and Taussig views the emergence of chemical colour/dye synthesis (particularly through colours like Prussian blue and indigo) as a major step in modernity's mastery of the intangible world. I'm simplifying a good bit but that's because the argument isn't really the point here — there's just a lot of associations and fun packed into this, much like *The Culture of the Copy* (though not quite as dazzling) and makes me definitely curious to read either his book on mimesis or the one about cocaine next.

732. Indecision by Benjamin Kunkel
Received: 24 August 2016
Started: 12 December 2016
Finished: 13 December 2016
I remember this being talked about some years back as a popular novel and for 50 cents it was worth the gamble. Kunkel's only fiction (as far as I can tell) is a hilarious romp about a narcissistic white male slacker set in 2002, travelling from New York City to Quito, Ecuador. It's anchored by this character's archetype, one that has saturated fictional creations by white men of the past two decades. I laughed a lot, though it felt easy and familiar. The best parts were the dark, Oedipal stuff with his sister, and some of the clever turns of phrase, though I kept feeling like I was reading a relic, even though this is only a decade old. This is definitely a post-9/11 novel in a way, and I recalled an essay I recently read proclaiming the era between 9/11 and 2010 (roughly) to be the era of 'random', where popular culture struggled to find a sensibility that encompassed the state of confusion and (to coin a phrase) hopeless affluence that permeated America. This maybe fits into that, but then the story changes in the end towards something so strange and almost polemical that I thought it was a joke. A quick look at Kunkel's other books on Amazon indicates that it was not, and maybe this novel is really about Kunkel's own coming-of-age. But, wow, fuck, has the political landscape changed in the last few years — the democratic socialism espoused by the book's narrator at the end already seemed rooted in pre-9/11, Seattle WTC, Indymedia-type activism which didn't quite fit with the War on Terror setting of the novel. Read now, in the closing weeks of 2016, it feels woefully inadequate to address the issues of today, and I'm not even getting into this whole 'post-truth' shit. But ultimately, this was fun.

733. The Stack: On Software and Sovereignty by Benjamin H. Bratton
Received: 20 December 2016
Started: 20 December 2016
Finished: 24 December 2016
This is an immense work of scholarship, a theoretical masterpiece that will actually change the way I see the world, which is praise not given lightly. Without risking hyperbole I wonder if this could even be an epoch-defining theory, so that we may divide intellectual thought into pre- and post- Bratton. OK, maybe that's getting ahead of things, but *The Stack* was absolutely mind-blowing in the way it tied together so many trans-disciplinary threads into a cohesive 'Theory of Everything', without feeling like it was stretching for credibility. This was so beautifully written, yet so extremely dense, that I felt trapped by it, and the four days it took to read went by slowly even though it was really only 365 pages. But then there's the notes, which I read concurrently, using the two-bookmarks

system I've used before while reading *Infinite Jest*. Bratton's model of the Stack 109 is a cross-section of the world we already live in, an 'accidental megastructure' of planetary computing that takes some of the ideas I've dabbled with reading before (futurism, political analysis, the Anthropocene of course, and even some of what Jaron Lanier was talking about in *You Are* 599 *Not A Gadget*) and ties it all together in an incredibly complete way. I was able to stay with everything, though I had to learn about stigmergy and synthetic catallaxy along the way. The subtitle of this book is 'on software and sovereignty' and the latter term is really the key to understanding Bratton's whole vision — at least the parts of the book that are questioning and forward-thinking. The middle section of the book is taken up by the slow process working through the Stack itself and the structure of the book, though it works from the bottom-up, is interwoven throughout all of the other parts like the theory suggests. It was stunning how many sources, anecdotes and viewpoints he presented here and it feel almost like nothing slipped through his fingers. The 'interface' layer of the stack I found the most difficult to follow, as Bratton talked primarily about GUI and Augmented Reality, and by the time I got to the 'user' layer I was become worn down. Yet I was still thrilled, and impressed as much by his scholarship and wit (some of the notes were downright hilarious) as by his sense of optimism. Bratton is careful to avoid kneejerk reactions and is critical of the left's tendency towards Ludditism or flight as a strategy; also, the amount of speculation in this text is just the right amount, not too wild while consistently opening doors. Wow — fucking amazing, and maybe this will be the experience I take the most from this time in Nida.

734. Biografi: An Albanian Quest by Lloyd Jones
Received: 24 December 2016
Started: 24 December 2016
Finished: 25 December 2016
A fascinating find in Nida library's 'Land/Place/Site/Tourism' section, this is a travel book written by a Kiwi writer in 1993 about post-Communist Albania, specifically structured around his search for Petar Shapello, a village dentist who, due to his uncanny physical resemblance, functioned as Enver Hoxha's stand-in throughout most of the dictator's life. This is merely a structuring device for Jones's travels around Albania, though he does find Shapello and even Nexhmije Hoxha. As a writer, Jones has little interest in swelling passages of descriptive beauty, nor the generalisations about the people that characterise so much travel writing, particularly when dealing with developing areas. This is a refreshing style that feels like slightly askew journalism, and made for a fun, quick read. Without dwelling on anything too much, Jones highlights how absurd conditions were in early 90s Albania, but not in a way that's mocking or condescending — the chaos bubbles up through the short chapters and the story told is really about Jones and his (often mundane) travels from village to village. If you're seeking a deeper, anthropological study of the Albanian people you should look elsewhere, but it also doesn't come off as smarmy or self-centred like so much edgy travel writing tries to be. I've always been mildly interested in Albania and this made me even more curious; I'd like now to read an account of the last 25 years, to see how this country has changes since the uncertain post-Hoxha years — or maybe I should just go visit.

735. A History of the Baltic States by Andres Kasekamp
Received: 25 December 2016
Started: 25 December 2016
Finished: 27 December 2016
Given that I've lived in this region for eight years, I really should have read this sooner. Kasekamp's work is a basic English-language overview of the three Baltic States beginning from the medieval times and working up to 2010, when this was published. I learned a ton, though the names and dates started to come so quickly that I still couldn't tell you, for example, exactly why the Lithuanians invaded Saaremaa in 1270 or exactly when Samogitia merged with Livonia. But it was good enough, and since it was heavily weighted towards the 20th century, this also provided a nice refresher course on what I knew from visiting the Occupation museum and general cultural intake from living in Estonia. I would have liked some more descriptions about what people's lives were actually like in the earlier times, as the first few chapters are basically fact dumps and only starting in the 19th century does he say anything about cultural life, but I don't know how rich the sources are. And, I'm looking at 1000 years of history in 180 pages, so that's probably not possibly anyway. The chronicles of the first republics are fascinating — I never

realised that they became authoritarian police states after just a few years — and he manages to convey a sense of horror about the brutal Soviet occupation without being heavy-handed (and he also is not a Nazi apologist like so many other Baltic people I've met). I never realised that Tallinn was still called Reval even into the early 20th century, or that the *Kalevipoeg* was essentially invented in the 19th century just to create a shared cultural document. A lot of this stuff (the ancient battles between the Poles and Lithuanians and the other factions) really just goes to illustrate how artificial all identity is, which I tend to forget at times. That simultaneously made me feel proud of the Baltic States for achieving independence against all odds (and the stories of the late 80s efforts are inspiring and beautiful) while also really disappointed at how nationalistic these independent nations have been, and how poor their choices have been in terms of economic policy (especially in Estonia which took the harshest 'scorched earth' approach to privatisation possible, and suffers now from it despite everyone's fantasy that a barely taxed tech industry is capable of building a society).

736. The Easy Chain by Evan Dara
Received: 4 April 2011
Started: 17 July 2016
Finished: 28 December 2016
I started this earlier in the summer and for some reason forgot about it, so I brought it along to Nida (for the second time in a year — I think I brought this to finish reading during the short visit in July, and failed to read a page since) and donated it to their library, deciding to finally finish it for completion's sake. Which isn't to imply that it wasn't enjoyable or good — it just slipped through the cracks of my attention span during personally busy times in the last half-year. I remember this pseudonymous
44 writer's first book, *The Lost Scrapbook*, very fondly, though it was ages ago when I read it; this follow-up is similarly great, with the same Gaddis-like mastery of dialogue and modernist narrative structure as the first one. There's a plot here which follows a mysterious figure who comes to Chicago and then leaves, and the book is essentially about the cloud of chaos and confusion he caused, formed from a variety of disparate voices and fictional sources whose provenance isn't always clear. Actually, *The Lost Scrapbook* may be a better title for this tome, due to it's collage-like nature, which at times descends into wildly experimental prose (there's about 40 pages of repetitive poem-lines, like punk lyrics, near the end, as well as a Molly Bloom-like stream-of-consciousness final chapter). Dara, whomever he is (some online sleuths think he's Richard Powers, but I'm not sure, and why does it even matter since novelists have so little impact on popular culture anyway? [unless he's secretly Kanye West or something]), has written a deceptive novel which seems to be milder in scope than it actually is — we get a deep critique of identity, politics and the environment, and family issues here, all woven into a relentlessly uncompromising patchwork of references and allusions. I didn't quite unravel the mystery, if there is one to really unravel, which I attribute to my six months in between pages 350 and 351 here; I should have done better justice to this, which is something I find myself repeating quite often about literature lately.

737. The Interventionists: Users' Manual for the Creative Disruption of Everyday Life edited by Nato Thompson and Gregory Sholette
Received: 28 December 2016
Started: 28 December 2016
Finished: 29 December 2016
A title like this really speaks to me, but it was a case of false advertising. This is the catalogue from an exhibition at Mass MoCA in 2004 featuring a who's-who of political 'interventionist' artists from the time, mostly focused around North America but with a few Europeans (and no one from outside of the Western world). Apart from an essay or two, this was primarily photography of the works and interviews with about 2/3 of the artists in the show. There was very little of value here — the interviewees were all asked identical questions, which meant that even the more thoughtful answers were somewhat lost in the repetition of it all. Like Bishop's *Artificial Hells*, I was troubled by how much everything in here still func- 556
tioned as artwork in galleries, even when trying to be street-based, nomadic, or the 'experimental university' section. That's not to say that the work presented was bad — some of it seemed quite great — though it also felt rather subsumed by the politics of the late 90s and early 00s, which has so recently felt extremely distant to me, maybe due to the tumultuous events of 2016. The worst thing about this, though, was the graphic design, which was like a Play-doh version of Chris Ware; it was just

appalling and cast the entire book in a childlike, amateurish light. I was hoping to at least pull a few ideas from here, or to get back into thinking about my own projects (which, while at Nida, have receded into the distant corners of my consciousness) but apart from a quote by the Critical Art Ensemble about how it's impossible to have spontaneous experiences inside of cultural institutions, I found myself unable to relate to anything in here whatsoever. Which might mean it's time to find a new line of work. (Oh, I've known this for some time anyway).

738. The Anthrobscene by Jussi Parikka
Received: 29 December 2016
Started: 29 December 2016
Finished: 29 December 2016
This is really a bound pamphlet, not a book, and its 60 pages are packed with a lots of ideas about the materiality of digital media and the environmental effects as such. Plus, a middle section attempting to redefine the concept of 'deep time', which I was unable to follow. Parikka's talk at the HYBRID MATTERs symposium last month was simultaneously great and pointless, so I was a bit curious to read him, and this bite-sized chunk was much more palatable than *A Geology of Media*, which this is essentially an introduction to. Maybe I'm
733 a bit spoiled after *The Stack* but I really wanted some deeper ideas to be explored here — what it ended up being was just reiterating the damage and destruction our digital lifestyles cause w/r/t rare-earth mining, environmental disasters, etc. — that's the obscene Anthropocene of the title, but that's also not really a big idea since the whole concept of the Anthropocene (which, let's face it, is one of the most overused terms in contemporary thought) already implies that. I was hoping that 'Anthrobscene' could be used for something more fun, and possibly naughty. I don't think I'll venture to his other work anytime soon but maybe this was meant to be 'light'.

739. The Wretched of the Screen by Hito Steyerl
Received: 31 December 2016
Started: 31 December 2016
Finished: 1 January 2017
Steyerl's collection of essays didn't impress me as much as I had been led to believe, though it had some salient insights. It started strong, talking about the loss of linear perspective as the bird's eye-view becomes more commonplace in the age of Google Maps and video games. She seems to write best about media, being a theorist descended from Villem Flusser and McLuhan's lineage, and these sections were the book's strongest. The manifesto on the 'poor' image was also fantastic, yet too short; whenever she started to really get going, the essays would end and I'd be faced with a bunch of interesting endnotes and wanting more 'meat', particularly in the 'Spam of the Earth' essay. Some broader topics, like the politicisation of art, felt more like starting points and huge topics that could be books of their own. But she's definitely brilliant and these are written more in a creative essay way than as a work of theory; perhaps after the dry density of *The Stack* I wasn't prepared for 733
the more free-flowing associations and references. This isn't to say she's a wild stylist, but would probably be on the midpoint between Bratton and Rebekah Rutkoff. I 703
anxiously await more from Steyerl, hopefully a full-length book!

740. A People's History of Modern Europe by William A. Pelz
Received: 1 January 2017
Started: 1 January 2017
Finished: 11 January 2017
I was craving some more history after the Baltic book and this seemed like fun, being modeled (like so many others) after the Howard Zinn classic. Pelz manages to pull off a competent surface-level history in 200 pages, starting in the medieval times and heavily weighted towards the 20th century. But there's no way this can really succeed as anything more than a simplistic overview with links to further reading. I felt like I was reading a high school history textbook throughout, albeit one with a heavy leftist angle, and the book focuses primarily on France, German, England and Russia. I don't think the Baltic states are mentioned once and Scandinavia gets only passing mentions, but I don't know what I would do if I had to condense this much into such a short book. There are parts which feel like digressions — the role of women feels like it's shoehorned into the different chapters, and there are surreal diversions that go on for several paragraphs about trivial matters (such as an anecdote about the sexism encountered in the 1960s by a British academic) which, while generally interesting and illustrative, seem a bit odd when entire countries are left out. I suspect this 'people's history' label gets thrown

around and lots of them are written — I also downloaded a people's history of the American empire — but I probably could have taken a deeper dive on a more niche topic instead of browsing through this for the past week.

741. A Gambler's Anatomy by Jonathan Lethem
Received: 11 January 2017
Started: 11 January 2017
Finished: 13 January 2017
As I started this, I looked at that page in the front listing all of the other works by the author and realised that Lethem hasn't 125 written a great novel since 2003's *The Fortress of Solitude*. 581 *Chronic City* was pretty good, and this was pretty similar in the way that it employed a realistic viewpoint for 90% of the text, and then threw some supernatural/sci-fi elements into the dark corners. In the case of *A Gambler's Anatomy*, those would be the main character's possible psychic abilities, though maybe this was just a fantasy (though it would make some of his omniscience hard to explain). But these powers aren't particularly useful, as the gambler in question is shuffled through all manners of indignities — financial, sexual and physical — before ending up more or less right back where he started. Is this a dark, cynical take on reinvention, ultimately putting its faith behind predestination? Or maybe Lethem is just going through a mid-life crisis of his own. A one-sentence description of this story would sound insanely bizarre (or Charlie Kaufmann-esque): 'A slightly psychic professional backgammon gambler develops a rare brain tumour' — and I'm not sure if it's to Lethem's credit or detriment that he's made this story less quirky and exciting that that would suggest. His depiction of student culture in Berkeley feels really rudimentary — but I've never been there so what do I know? — and his femme fatales are written a bit like nerdy male fantasies trying hard to not be so obviously nerdy male fantasies. In the end I'm not sure what it all added up to, but I enjoyed it, probably a lot more than any of his novels in the past 13 years. In many ways I feel like Lethem and Franzen have just become the new macho class of white male writers, even if they're incredibly self-aware about their privilege and their literary preoccupations. As a white male myself who has read most of their books, I still give the upper hand to Lethem by a comfortable margin, but I wonder if he's spinning his wheels a bit now. All of his early books, even if they were so heavily indebted to Dick and Delaney, are still pretty amazing (at least in my memory) but now that he's a big-deal writer I feel like he keeps writing books because he has to, and maybe has amalgamated his influences too much. Still: pretty good work this time!

742. Extrastatecraft: The Power of Infrastructure Space by Keller Easterling
Received: 13 January 2017
Started: 13 January 2017
Finished: 14 January 2017
After *The Stack*, I was hungry for more 733 of something similar and Easterling is quoted multiple times by Bratton in that, so I hoped this would be in the same vein. And I guess it is, though it was far less overwhelming and not as strong of a 'statement' as I wanted. Not everything can be that epic, and I don't mean to diminish *Extrastatecraft*, a creatively presented theory of 'infrastructure space' with a decidedly leftist angle. Easterling writes somewhat more conversationally than Bratton, though the subject matter means a lot of jargon is unavoidable. She establishes her model throughout six chapters, but I was expecting something that fit together like a puzzle (again, like *The Stack*) so it was a bit of an adjustment from my preconception. The 'zones' being things, and here the acronyms almost become overwhelming, but there's a lot about sovereignty at play and it really opened my eyes to how insane 'free trade' actually is. The chapter on 'disposition' is probably the most original element of Easterling's theory, and this echoes throughout the rest of the book. The broadband chapter is almost entirely about Kenya, which is a curious choice and feels more like a case study than a cornerstone of the work, but actually compelling if you are interested in such matters. The 'quality' chapter is where things started to feel like a salvo from *The Baffler*, with ISO and their standards emerging as a real villain, and the absolutely insane ISO9000 being dealt with especially (I had no idea!). What really pulled this all together for me is the way she finished the book with a look at dissent and how the left can attempt to disrupt extrastatecraft, which was treated as a series of theoretical assertions and models, and therefore actually felt like a blueprint rather than wishful thinking.

743. Zama by Antonio Di Benedetto
Received: 14 January 2017
Started: 14 January 2017
Finished: 18 January 2017
Zama was pretty good but I didn't start to really enjoy it until the weird, ragged final section. This was written in the 1950s but is set in Paraguay in the 1790s, and is written from the first-person view of its eponymous character, a complicated figure which is sort of a hero and sort of just in-between. This is a book very much about the brutal ways in which men treat women, though it didn't feel like it was expressing a particularly feminist nor enlightened viewpoint. At the same time, it didn't feel to be endorsing or embellishing Zama's misogyny, and maybe I'll attribute my uncertainty at the cultural differences and change of affect that happens via translation. The three sections are set in 1790, 1795 and 1799 and find Zama in three very different situations. It chronicles his misadventures while commenting on not just gender and sexuality but on politics, race, and class, and while he's no warrior of the working people he also feels like an odd fit for the colonial times, being too Paraguayan to be Spanish but yet not noble enough to take on leadership roles. Di Benedetto was a fairly obscure Argentinian writer and this was peppered with that placid, genteel description of nature that I for some reason associate with South American writers. Bolaño was apparently enamoured of di Benedetto, though Borges and Casares tower so heavily over that country's literature that he remained relatively unknown outside of his own country, which this NYRB Classics edition tries to address.

744. The Nix by Nathan Hill
Received: 17 January 2017
Started: 18 January 2017
Finished: 18 January 2017
Hill's novel is a pretty impressive debut, though long and uneven. One thing I wouldn't call it is overambitious, though at the beginning I though it was going to be a wild, sprawling mess; it actually pulls itself together relatively well and the diversions into side characters are nice bits of comic relief. I enjoyed elements of this, though one thing about reading a 664-page novel in one sitting (while on a long flight, but still) is that you can really commit to the worldview. And that's maybe the reason I would be the most critical of *The Nix* — that world is limited, and I tend to like things that imply future possibilities and paths yet untraveled. This is essentially just a story about fate and circumstance, wrapped up with some of-the-moment concerns (politics in the modern era as reflected back on Chicago '68, sexual abuse and childhood trauma, the state of literature and entertainment, and how technology mediates our communication/expression) and told in a straightforward style that characterises so much popular American fiction today. It's so easy to see the influence of the big names of white male America literature from the last two decades or so; Franzen is probably the most obvious, as this felt really simliar to *Purity* in the way the plot was constructed, but there's also the usual DFW marks (the 670 long unbroken paragraphs of the Pwnage and Laura chapters would have made this a poor man's *Infinite Jest* if the main story hadn't been so quotidian). 109  One theme I felt was trying to emerge was a general frustration with consumer capitalism in the way it presents the illusion of choice without real alternatives (such as the comment that all NES games were just 'move to the right' and the aggravation of the mother when trying to shop); this was nicely done, and made up for the clunky bits, such as the (to be honest, awful) ending and the ridiculous suggestion that a high school prom DJ in 1968 would have played the VU's 'Venus In Furs'). 587 The first 1988 chapter, describing the boy's friendship and interactions at school, was beautiful and hit exactly onto real-life experiences I've had, which made me want more. The modern day sections were injected with humour and satirical elements; it's really the 1968 sections that felt the weakest, in terms of prose. Still, I liked reading this and couldn't have picked a better large novel to tackle on a flight.

745. The Corn Wolf by Michael Taussig
Received: 28 November 2016
Started: 18 January 2017
Finished: 22 January 2017
This collection of Taussig essays was probably even more delightful than *What Color Is the Sacred?*, although the first half was a bit 731  tricky to concentrate on. The leadoff essay is about the Corn Wolf from *The Golden Bough* (which I've only read excerpts from), as discussed by Wittgenstein as a theory of language, now modified by Taussig to look at different ways about writing; this double-analysis was pretty alien to me, not being familiar with the original material, so I definitely had a struggle a bit with it. His method of 'nervous system' writing vs. 'agribusiness' was (I suppose)

demonstrated in practise by this book itself, and the standout would be the essay on humming, which was dazzling and idiosyncratic and Taussig at his best. In the second half of the book, things become a little more lucid, with the 'Alphabet of Iconoclasm' being my favourite thing in here by far, and then a great essay on obscenity and finally a recollection of his time in Columbia in the early 70s, a mix of personal memoir, anthropology, and political intrigue. I still wish I knew a bit more about fieldwork and 20th century anthropology (much of this book draws heavily from writings of people like Malinowski, who was also a central figure in *What Colour Is the Sacred?*), but Taussig is the kind of writer who creates openings and new avenues to explore.

746. Something to Be Desired by Thomas McGuane
Received: 19 January 2017
Started: 22 January 2017
Finished: 23 January 2017
More McGuane, who feels like an occasional yet constant presence in my life. This is another entry into his saga of Deadrock, Montana, his own Yoknapatawpha Country, and again follows a complicated and irascible white male. Lucien, the focus of *Something to Be Desired*, isn't a million miles away from Frank Copenhaver of *Nothing*
637 *But Blue Skies*, which is the novel that followed this. Here we find a rags-to-riches story, where our hero vacillates between two different women, one a definitive *femme fatale* (in that she keeps murdering people), and the other being a typically McGuanian woman who struggles with Lucien's weaknesses but also doesn't give up too much of herself. There's a strong emphasis throughout on outdoorsy activities, beginning with young Lucien in the late 50s as his own fucked-up father abandons him and returns. This behaviour is carried forward and that's the cynical core to this novel, that the traumas of our childhood are replicated to the future generations, but there's such hilarity throughout that this misery goes down smoothly. I think this and *Blue Skies* together are my favourites of his work (though I haven't read his most recent few) and this mid-80s period is where he really shines. I wonder if you could argue that McGuane is a feminism-friendly author, not that he really understands women or tries to write about them, but because he is so sympathetic to their situations and chronicles such institutionalised sexism/abuse. Or maybe that's just me trying to impose my own biases onto this reading. The dialogue, when it's present, is hilarious, and the story shifts quickly throughout time, which really emphasises its anarchy. God, I fucking love Thomas McGuane.

747. More Curious by Sean Wilsey
Received: 22 January 2017
Started: 24 January 2017
Finished: 29 January 2017
This is a nice collection of non-fiction that proceeds with a punchy style through a variety of topics, some more interesting than others. It's bookended by pieces about Marfa, Texas, a fascinating place for sure, but Wilsey doesn't make me any more interested in it than I already was, especially as the first one is really just a chronicle of a Chianti Foundation summit of architects that just sounds surreal and strange. There's a fantastic essay about skateboarding and growing up with *Thrasher* magazine, and a long travelogue about a road trip that's probably the high point. Other topics include NASA, John Updike, and football (the essay about watching the 1970 World Cup on VHS was somewhere else before, probably in the *Thinking Fan's Guide to the World Cup* that Wilsey edited, though I was 229
happy to read it again. This could maybe have benefited from some tighter editing, but it worked well overall mostly because his style was fresh (without becoming tiresome) and he kept a sense of humour throughout all of his topics, without succumbing to the usual McSweeney's snark.

748. You Don't Know Me but You Don't Like Me: Phish, Insane Clown Posse, and My Misadventures with Two of Music's Most Maligned Tribes by Nathan Rabin
Received: 26 January 2017
Started: 29 January 2017
Finished: 30 January 2017
A fluff read but that's all I was looking for, *You Don't Know blah blah blah* was an interesting premise and I figured Nathan Rabin would be decent enough to sustain it — I enjoyed his 'My Year of Flops' series, and figured he has a somewhat insightful look into the larger issues of pop culture. Unfortunately, this is a total mess, and what starts off with a lot of potential eventually succumbs to the whole personal journalism scourge that my generation is generally cursed with, and is just a bunch of self-indulgent crap about his drug use and love life. The Insane Clown Posse parts are

far better than the Phish parts, and while the class distinctions between the two fan bases could be a good building block for understanding today's music subcultures, he fails to go anywhere beyond a superficial reading. Both of these bands peaked, both commercially and artistically, a long time before he started to follow them, and his 'Stockholm Syndrome' appreciation of their music is constantly undercut by his need to seem knowing and hip. The result is a book that manages to be condescending to its subject and its readers at the same time. The Juggalos are fascinating, no doubt, but not really any different than, say, the kids in *The Decline of Western Civilization* 30 years
1473 earlier, just with worse music (which is also a subjective opinion). The sense of community and brotherhood that these kids have built for themselves is genuinely admirable, and they are endemic of what's happened to America socially under neoliberalism, though Rabin never gives any more than an armchair pundit's commentary on this. The long chapters about traveling around and seeing Phish are really boring, as the druggie culture and the music are given equal weight and neither is particularly interesting to me.

749. Normal: by Warren Ellis
Received: 30 January 2017
Started: 30 January 2017
Finished: 2 February 2017
When at Copacetic last week I was talking a bit with Bill about how I find many of the big-name comics writers to be overrated. I like Grant Morrison and wouldn't deny Alan Moore's talent, but even the best of Morrison's work (*The Filth* or *The Invisibles*) is just "pretty good" to "slightly great", to me. Ellis is someone I've come to because of his email newsletter, which I read every week even though I'm not that into his writing (having read the first 10 issues of *Transmetropolitan* and also *Crechy*). So I feel an interest in him personally, and especially the company he keeps, if not his actual work. Trying to rectify that, I figured this 80-page novella would be a nice quick read, which it was, and it was enjoyable too. Yet I don't think it was a masterful work of fiction or anything close — just a nice diversion with a few good dystopian/sci-fi questions, but nothing mind-blowing. I loved the idea of a retreat centre for burned out futurists, and the types of characters in this book reminded me of some of the more interesting people I've met over the years on the fringes of arts culture. The protagonist is from a more sinister place but in such a short novel Ellis never really got me particularly interested in his backstory or motivations. The best parts here were the conversations of the patients at Normal Head, and the surveillance drone plot was fairly standard and not anything that expanded my thinking — which should be goal #1 from good comics/sci-fi. In a way I feel like the main experiment here was to write a serialised novella, and it's certainly not a bad effort by any means. Yet I just hunger for something a bit more.

750. Megg & Mogg In Amsterdam (And Other Stories) by Simon Hanselmann
Received: 27 January 2017
Started: 8 February 2017
Finished: 9 February 2017
I don't think Hanselmann's work is life-changing, but it's totally funny, and the last Megg & Mogg book I got is apparently worth 150€ now, so I'm probably going to sell it after re-reading it. This is a larger collection in hardback, and it's mostly more of the same — endless stories of these fucked up characters taking drugs and abusing each other. At some point there starts to be some actual gravitas to Megg's sadness and the impossibility of their relationship, but whenever that happens, Werewolf Jones usually shows up and wrecks some havoc. In a way this is like an advanced iteration of the *Krazy Kat* formula, but with the concerns of today's youth (chemicals both external and brain-based, the futility of motivation in late capitalism, etc.). A couple of these short one- or two-pagers are absolutely fucking hilarious, such as Werewolf Jones' adventures in airport security. The closest Hanselmann gets to true greatness is when the humour and sadness slam into each other like fists, which does happen, but he seems too intent on subverting any actual growrth. The longer 'Amsterdam' story is OK, feeling like a turning point in the overall narrative, but the whole opus is ultimately pretty disposable. I'd probably hold onto this one if I ever wanted a re-read just because it's long and thick and contains a lot of different material.

751. The Lucifer Principle: A Scientific Expedition into the Forces of History by Howard K. Bloom
Received: 22 January 2017
Started: 31 January 2017
Finished: 10 February 2017
Ugh. This was on my list for *years* — I'm not sure where I first heard about it, though I remember a housemate was really into it, so maybe he owned a copy when I lived in Lexington. Big theory-of-everything books appeal to me, especially when written by academic outsiders, which Bloom definitely is; that the Atlantic Monthly press published this is a near miracle, given how shaky it is as a work of scholarship. So, yeah, I would say that I was extremely disappointed by *The Lucifer Principle*, though I forced myself through the last 100 pages just to conclusively dismiss it. I can see where Bloom's lack of academic principles (or at least peer review) hurt him; if this was some really weird reality-bending theory a la Robert Anton Wilson, he could get away with it, but what this ends up being is a work of amateur anthropology/sociology that shows its time period more flagrantly than I would like. I expect a certain amount of obsolescence from any book with a scope this big (politics, behaviour psychology, economics, military history, and religion all play big parts here) that was written before the Internet, 9/11, and whatever the fuck we're going through now. But what dated this aren't the assumptions about human progress (for who could fault Bloom for not being able to predict all that stuff?) but rather the generalisations about race and gender. To call this Islamophobic would be mild, but rather than admit his prejudices, he cloaks his screeds in a bunch of assumptions that border on pseudoscientific, such as stating that Islam is inherently a violent belief system. There's also a section where he cites the non-acceptance of homeopathy as an example of the orthodoxy of Western scientific beliefs, without bothering to cite any of the studies that (even in the early 90s) failed to show a shred of evidence for homeopathy's effectiveness. What's good here is the simplified accounts of history, particularly non-Western accounts of strife in medieval China, early 20th century South America, etc — which genuinely educated me somewhat, as my knowledge of non-Western history is spotty to nonexistent. The book has a remarkably neoliberal outlook for something that purports to be an anti-establishment viewpoint; Marx's writings are repeatedly disparaged in a way that emphasises the less relevant idealism of Marx over the many things that he got right. And the overall argument here, the so-called Lucifer Principle, is nothing more than an extended riff on the same 'human nature' bullshit that people always cite to justify their worst impulses. This would maybe be a good thing to read if I was still a teenager, as the short, punchy chapters have a certain appeal, though the overall text is a bit to dry to be engaging even as entertainment.

752. How Soccer Explains the World: An Unlikely Theory of Globalization by Franklin Foer
Received: 22 January 2017
Started: 11 February 2017
Finished: 15 February 2017
At 75 cents it was worth a gamble though I meant to blast through this in America and not waste precious suitcase weight on it. But I didn't get around to it and decided to bring it anyway because I do enjoy books about football and this purported to be a 'theory' about matters economic, social and cultural (beyond the game itself). The subtitle was a bit of an overstatement, as what this really is, is a book of essays about various topics around the game from a liberal American perspective. Foer is smart and knows his stuff when it comes to the game, and while it's still written for an American audience who probably knows very little about the game, these occasionally over-explanations didn't hinder my enjoyment of this. About half of this was great — mostly the parts where Foer integrated himself with some truly nasty people, such as Old Firm fanatics in Glasgow, or Red Star Belgrade's super violent hooligan squad (with their connections to proper Serbian war criminals), or the Jewish Chelsea supporter. The chapter about the old Austrian Jewish team was interesting though only a starting point for a more general discussion of Judaism in sport; the chapters on Barcelona and Iran were less worthwhile, and the final chapter about the American 'culture wars' already felt incredibly dated. This came out about a decade ago and that chapter was already rendered obsolete by the surge of interest in the Premier League, Champions League and the World Cup all across America (not to say the large TV rights contracts taken by NBC, Fox, etc which is the real sign of success or failure for sport). So while I learned very little about football, this was a decent-enough stab at pop-sociology,

though I would have preferred a crazy mad-scientist-like 'theory' as I was led to believe by the subtitle.

753. Europeana: A Brief History of the Twentieth Century by Patrik Ouredník
Received: 9 February 2017
Started: 9 February 2017
Finished: 17 February 2017
A short, sort of fun novel, that really isn't much in the way of fiction, Ourednik's 120 page text re-tells the events of the 20th century in a non-linear, storybook way, and somehow stirred a sense of awe in me even though it was clear what he was trying to do and it could easily have come across as snarky or twee. The writing style reminded me of fun French literature like Perec or Queneau, yet the subject matter was pretty dark and the creative element came from how he danced around topics and focused on what he chose to focus on. Ourednik was Czech so there's that feeling of Eastern European absurdity here, particularly when recounting the horrors of war and juxtaposing them against capitalist consumer behaviours and how the changing attitudes believed in different ideals throughout the century. The last few pages take a swipe at Fukuyama because why not — and it's almost like the novel knows that it will be read in the future and will let our own experiences be its proof. This was something I meant to read a long time ago and I thought it would be longer, like some dense epic, though of course history is epic enough already. In a weird way I would see this as a novel even though it's more like a personal vision of history; it's certainly very writerly and stylised, and it would never be actually useful as a reference text.

754. Otaku: Japan's Database Animals by Hiroki Azuma
Received: 27 January 2017
Started: 19 February 2017
Finished: 23 February 2017
This was an odd choice — Bill brought it up when I was telling him about *The Stack*, and while it's definitely a work of theory, its scope is significantly more limited — but then again, all scopes are going to be limited when compared to Bratton. This is a work of cultural theory about the subculture in Japan known as 'otaku' — essentially, the pop-culture obsessed, predominantly male youth who revolve around the axis of anime/sci-fi/manga/video games. Azuma has two main arguments here, and they are discussed repeatedly while informing about some of the aspects of otaku culture, such as moe-elements in characters. His first argument is where the term 'animals' comes from in the title, as he followed Kojeve's reading of Hegel that ascribed animalistic tendencies to American culture and snobbish ones to the Japanese — the otaku, we are to believe, are rejecting the snobbery and tradition (of which seppaku was a classic example) in favour of a more hedonistic embrace of fiction. The second argument is that of the 'database narrative', which is a rejection of the grand narrative (in the Lyotard sense), which is pretty obvious. There's some good bits about simulacra here, especially in terms of characters and fantasy elements where the world and character are in some ways more important than the actual narrative or meaning; this is echoed of course in American comic-con geek culture too, and I wonder what influenced what. So this was pretty standard postmodernism 101, and it was fine and had some insights for sure, and had copious notes that made this a two-bookmark read (which is possibly the only real thing it had in common with *The Stack*). This ended with a chapter about HTML and the web, which talked a lot about the semantical nature of HTML versus the presentation layer of CSS and how this was generally misused; I didn't really get the point or relevance though. Overall: OK, and the one amazing thing is that this was a bestseller in Japan about 15 years ago, which is amazing for what is technically a work of theory, even if it's one about pop culture.

755. Sky in Stereo by Sacha Mardou
Received: 27 January 2017
Started: 19 February 2017
Finished: 25 February 2017
There's not much new material here in *Sky in Stereo*, as the entirety of the 2 individual issues are here with some prequel material and maybe a slight-reordering. I'm not going to drag them out and compare because this isn't the Rosetta Stone, but rather a pleasantly intimate coming of age story set in mid-90s Manchester, from a female perspective. Mardou's art is soft and accessible and her ear for dialogue really conveys life in the UK as I imagine it, and draws many societal archetypes from my own experience in the UK a decade later. It's so easy to default to self-indulgent outsider sadness in the non-superhero comics genre, and Mardou is definitely coming

from that side, but there's a wisdom of hindsight here, even though she clearly keeps the narrative rooted in the emotions and worldview of its setting. The new material talks about an upbringing by a mother who converts to being a Jehovah's Witness and the suggestion for part two is that Iris will be in a mental institution, so I'm curious to see when volume #2 comes out, though I think it will be a long, long wait. I really do like her work but owning both individual issues and this graphic novel feels superfluous, so if anyone wants them, let me know.

756. Vanishing Voices: The Extinction of the World's Languages by Daniel Nettle

Received: 17 February 2017
Started: 17 February 2017
Finished: 26 February 2017

For some reason, I put tENTATIVELY, a cONVENIENCE's Goodreads profile into my RSS reader, so I sometimes browse through the endless list of sci-fi novels he reviews. He covered this work of popular anthropology a few weeks ago, calling it one of the ten most important books of his life, and then listing the others, two of which were books he wrote himself. Anyway, I was curious and a work about endangered languages sounded like my cup of tea so I hunted it down online and gave it a go; it's a nice counterpoint to
745 731 the Michael Taussig books I recently read, which makes me think that I'm going to be reading more and more anthropology in the near future. *Vanishing Voices* was actually pretty straightforward and had little inside to blow my mind or even surprise me. The book started out by explaining just how serious the problem of language loss is, and then explaining how important different languages are to the character of the people that speak them. The concept of 'killer languages' was introduced and English is of course the biggest killer; this led to some interesting anthropological data about different places in the world, with the Celtic languages being nothing new and the part about Papua New Guinea extremely interesting. The last section gets into a theory about how 'think local, act global' needs to be the way to preserve languages, which was more or less a standard re-tread of globalisation's many sins, while somehow arguing that people could pursue increased developmental opportunities and still preserving their own languages (though this was not really that clear of convincing). Not bad, overall, but I felt it was a bit repetitive and I was hoping for more details about historical language extinction; I definitely don't see why tENTATIVELY, a CONVENIENCE was so blown away by this, but then again, I don't know the guy.

757. The Argonauts by Maggie Nelson

Received: 25 February 2017
Started: 25 February 2017
Finished: 1 March 2017

Thanks to a friend for reminding me to check this out — I suspect he's turned to it in those final moments before becoming a father, as pregnancy and birth is a major theme here. Without having that in my life I still found this to be stunning, remarkable, and groundbreaking (three words I use all the time, but applicable here) while being approachably conversational in tone at the same time. It's an incredible achievement, but one that feels light, like a diary or monologue revealed to a larger audience. I wonder if 2017 is going to be the year that feminist theory goes mainstream, because this has gotten a lot of attention, and they're making a fucking TV series based on *I Love Dick* (a work with which this shares much territory 483
— an attempt to find a distinctly feminine form of writing that does not shy away from emotional response yet is rigorous, learned, and boundary-pushing at the same time). *The Argonauts* tears down every assumption one might make about Nelson, an accomplished poet with deep roots in academic gender studies, who is in a relationship with a transgender artist that makes up the primary framework of this book. Over this frame we explore issues of parenting and responsibility, health and body, the shifting political landscapes, and a relentless interrogation of sexuality that directly confronts the public narratives which have become so familiar w/r/t concepts such as 'queer', 'gender', 'kink', etc. It's hard not to be awed by the amount of intimacy on display here, which isn't much to do with Nelson and Dodge's relationship (though there are no pseudonyms and the issue of privacy seems irrelevant) but rather the direct application of fear to the text. Which isn't to imply that this is a cowardly book, or one written in retreat, but one that unabashedly lays out the tremendous fear involved with child-rearing, commitment, and the general situation of being female under a patriarchy. (And a passage about a stalker, as well.) This e-book wasn't able to format the quotes as the print edition did, so they were all replicated and attributed as

an appendix, which maybe detracted from the book somewhat, or maybe it didn't — there were long italicised passages which felt like poetic intrusions but were later shown to be, say, from her partner's diary entry or much more esoteric sources. There is no way you could accuse this book of lacking a scholarly glow, as Nelson is an impressive polymath and cites numerous major thinkers, sometimes in anecdotes about encountering those thinkers directly. This is beautiful and I'm really happy to have spent a few days with it just now; it's so rare that the personal experience can be made so compelling without feeling self-indulgent or insular, especially in our age of extreme narcissism.

758. Anathem by Neal Stephenson
Received: 24 February 2017
Started: 24 February 2017
Finished: 6 March 2017
Two different people raved about this novel in the past six months and I've been trying to enjoy Stephenson again ever since I read *Cryptonomicon* whenever that was, probably close to 15 years ago. That was a nerd masterpiece, a book I had trouble putting down, but subsequent attempts to read his historical fiction ended in frustration, as he tends to write long-winded explanations of historical philosophical thought without much concern for it being an actual story. *Anathem* still had plenty of those digressions — many of the conversations in the book went on for 20 pages and were built around Plato's cave argument, though transposed to his invented world. But this overall was a pretty masterful work of world building, a story as epic as *Lord*
53 *of the Rings* and with almost as much of a mythology created around it. For the first 50 pages I was getting frustrated by what I often call 'sci-fi bullshit', although I usually mean that term in a positive way. It reminded me of that one *Rick and Morty* TV bit where they show you how to make a 'plumbus', as I was dragged through a ridiculous amount of invented jargon and nonsense, and it wasn't until 100 pages in or so that I realised there was a glossary in the back, which helped. At some point I grasped most of the world Stephenson created and just went along for the ride, and a ridiculously baroque ride it was. This hero's journey traversed time and space and had moments of political intrigue, arctic adventure, and theoretical mindfuckery; it was really masterfully plotted and came together in a satisfying way. Stephenson is a bit of a nutcase and his writing captures some of the worst personality traits of some IT people I've known, taken to extremes — though I also mean that in a good way. He writes well enough to move a story along, if not in a particularly literary manner, and I felt the same rushes of energy I had while going through my Philip K Dick phase — where I would be happy to steal away any bit of time from my 'real' life in order to plop on the sofa and get back to the book. I've been warned by another friend that *Seveneaves* is terrible, there's no way in hell I'm going to attempt the Baroque Cycle again, and *Reamde* looks 
kinda mundane; there's always the much 760
beloved *Snow Crash*, or maybe I can just 
wait another decade before reading my 793
next Stephenson work. This really was great, though, and a great example of what sci-fi — excuse me, *speculative fiction* — could and should be.

759. Hello America by J. G. Ballard
Received: 24 February 2017
Started: 8 March 2017
Finished: 13 March 2017
In between the time I finished reading this and the time it took me to write these comments, I had a conversation about Ballard with a friend at Noku Club in Tallinn. He agreed with me that Ballard is amazing and yet not enjoyable to read; he copped to reading Wikipedia summaries of most of his books, which he found to be sufficient as compared to actually reading them. I wish that I could say I feel otherwise, with the same passion that inspires me to frequently defend Philip K Dick's much-maligned writing style, but I can't really bring myself to do that with Ballard. I still think I want to read more of his work, because while his prose is not inviting in the slightest way, there'a so much that is notable about his ideas and I do think in this case a Wiki summary wouldn't suffice. How great is this concept? It's the late 21st century, about 100 years after America had to be abandoned due to an energy crisis and climate effects which took place after the Bering Strait was dammed. All Americans migrated to Europe, and the former US is a vast, unoccupied desert. This novel follows a small exploratory expedition, which slowly moves West, discovering all sorts of craziness (audio-animatronic Presidents, a gang of Indians with names like Heinz and Pepsodent, and ultimately the current acting president of the US, Charles Manson). The style of the book mirrors an

old adventure novel for children, as the protagonist is a wide-eyed Americanist stowaway from Ireland and throughout the novel he's treated like a child, with all characters speaking to him in broad, patronising tones, without Ballard ever dropping this facade. And that's a stylistic choice I applaud, even though I still struggled to find the actual chapter-by-chapter reading of this to be engaging. I much preferred the harsh, affectless brutality of *Crash* (which 211 also takes a lot more chances with regards to then-living historical figures such as Elizabeth Taylor, and the then-daring use of a narrator named James Ballard) but still had to stop and admire how fucking mental and fun this was. There's plenty of ways to see this as clairvoyant, not just presaging the celebrity nature of our politics but climate change and bioterrorism as well; the next president of the US in this book's universe would have been the 45th, bringing things up to right about now in terms of timeline. So despite the fact I was not even remotely in love with the prose, I think this has motivated me to read some more Ballard, at least some of his major works like *Atrocity* 764 *Exhibition* or *Concrete Island*. I wonder if all of his novels entropically decay into chaos and violence; I sort of hope so.

760. Reamde by Neal Stephenson
Received: 7 March 2017
Started: 8 March 2017
Finished: 16 March 2017

I've read about 1900 pages of Neal Stephenson in the past few weeks, which is about half of the length of *Rising Up and Rising Down* by Vollmann; should that be next? It would be good to clear it off the mental-shelf before starting *Bottom's Dream*. Anyway. *REAMDE* is fiercely situated in the 'techno-thriller' genre, a category I would stay away from entirely if I didn't remember the similarly-classified *Cryptonomicon* being so fucking compelling sixteen or seventeen years ago when I read it. This was actually far less geeky than that, and far less intense in terms of mythology than *Anathem*, using the device 758 of the MMORPG as his place to pack all that crap. And actually, he does this in a fun and light way, as the D&D-style fantasy elements referred to in the game are mentioned mostly for humorous value, I think. But this was a far more intense book than either other Stephenson tome, or anything else I've ever read by anyone, really; at least, if 'intense' is defined as cinema-influenced action. This took awhile to get going and it seemed pretty formulaic at first — former hippie turned Silicon Valley billionaire, token black/female protagonist (whose motivations were occasionally explained with lazy writing like 'Because she spent time in a refugee camp as a child, she had trouble trusting people' [paraphrase]), Russian mobsters, and technically-accurate mentions of Linux, etc. Then everything takes off, and for a few hundred pages I was pulled into an unbelievably gripping story with incredibly high stakes, fantastically suspenseful writing, and characters who begin to develop more and more with each page. I found myself several nights in a row staying up until I just couldn't keep my eyes open, til 2:30 or 3 AM, just tearing through the pages anxious to find out what would happen next. This wasn't the best book I've ever read, but I think it was the most exciting, and it helps that Stephenson is too intelligent to resort to easy, common-denominator literary techniques or simple explanations. What annoyed me (and this is a minor quibble) was the way that characters would debrief each other throughout the book on the situation as it unfolded, which was done I think to make sure that there was no ambiguity whatsoever about what was happening and keeping the reader close to things — but it always felt repetitive because he had just chronicled the events being described, and this book was over 1000 pages. In the story no character was as omniscient as the reader so there were elements to their recaps that were wrong/missing, and those holes were generally responsible for their subsequent actions. The tremendous violence in this book was never soft, cartoonish, or gory; it felt powerful and necessary, and also served to constantly ratchet up the pulse. There were a lot of ideas that could have easily gotten lost under all the action; the identities of race, nationality, and borders are very prevalent and yet Stephenson doesn't moralise or simplify things, but the fictional T'Rain world that most characters escape to provides a fun metaphor for the Other, and also adds fascinating wrinkles into the plot. My biggest complaint would be how quickly it all ends — I mean, it's 1054 pages and the final shootout-hunt goes on for at least 100 — but after it does, things are just over and wrapped up with a tiny epilogue. No 'good' characters die here, apart from some really minor ones who are introduced late and without giving us any chance to build a relationship with them, and the final wrap-up is so tidy it's actually unrealistic. But what I really don't get is why we spent hundreds of pages learning about the T'Rain world's war between those who put earthtones on their avatars and those who use bright colours, and the tension between the two fantasy writers who built up this mythology. Of course it's an obvious metaphor for the good vs. evil battle at the centre of *REAMDE* — and while such distinctions are explicitly proclaimed (in the game-world) to be arbitrary and insufficient, the al-Queda/ISIS terrorists here in the real world are less ambiguous. This whole construct feels a bit underdeveloped, or maybe I'm just missing something — I don't think Stephenson is criticising MMORPG culture as he rather adeptly embraces its patterns of behaviour — but clearly he's fascinated by the ideas of fiction and role-play, and its ties to commercial action (the sums of real money passing through the game were staggering). There's also a nice irony in setting the final shoot-out around the house of a total survivalist gun-nut in Idaho; in *REAMDE*, their insane paranoia about al-Queda invading their farm actually takes place, though I hope this isn't mean to be an endorsement of said lifestyle.

761. Lincoln in the Bardo by George Saunders
Received: 1 March 2017
Started: 1 March 2017
Finished: 22 March 2017
I always thought of Saunders as an 'NPR' kind of writer, which is my own snobby bias coming into play, just because he seemed to be celebrated by the same people who get excited over Sarah Vowell books. I couldn't have been more wrong, as *Lincoln* was more insane and awesome than most recent American fiction I've read, and I was super into this. I understand that his short stories are not quite this fucked up, and I'm sure they couldn't be similar since this required the long form structure in order to function. The plot is bonkers enough on paper but the way he implemented it as a bogus oral history (though mixed in with a few genuine historical sources, I think) was a stroke of genius and beyond just the pleasure of concept and artifice, there was a great deal of humanity in here. I love when someone can evoke something relatable from the most out-there of concepts, and this also avoided being hagiographical at all, towards Lincoln or anyone else. Worthy of the hype, glad this got as much attention as it did, no doubt due to Saunders' existing fame, but it's still amazing that a mass audience read something this experimental.

762. Mobile by Michel Butor
Received: 11 March 2014
Started: 16 March 2017
Finished: 3 April 2017
The first time I read *Mobile* was during that year I lived in Kentucky, yet I somehow forgot to list it here, though I remember somehow checking it out from the UK library (I think non-students could obtain borrowing privileges). Coming back to it many years later, it's not quite as experimental as I remembered, though that's not to say that it isn't extremely fragmentary and suggestive. It moves by its own logic, driven by maps and written as if by the ultimate armchair traveler experimentalist, but it's very much the work of a foreigner at play in a strange land. There's an almost forced modernity at play, in the way that the endless repetition of radio noises and small-town advertisements and commerce are as much a part of the steady rhythm here as the pastoral descriptions. I think I felt a significantly darker pulse now, or at least compared to my memory of it; sadly I didn't jot down my thoughts then since I didn't list it here, and now I'm writing this a year and a half after the re-read since I'm filling in some missing comments. So once again *Mobile* has to stay just out of my immediate grasp, a masterpiece of experimental fiction that recedes into background noise by design, and will forever resist my attempts to summarise it. As I've been away from America myself for a long time, there should have been a distance to relate to via Butor's own very French viewpoint, but the passage of time since this was written overrode this. Today this would be an endless stream of Applebees, Sav-a-lots and Taco Bells, for that's the real small town America, the one that irritating coastal media people write about in such a condescending way that it's no surprise Trump got fucking elected. Maybe, in the style of de Toqueville and Baudrillard, there should perodically be a French viewpoint published regarding whatever cultural and economic zeitgeist is going on.

763. Universal Harvester by John Darnielle
Received: 25 March 2017
Started: 25 March 2017
Finished: 8 April 2017
Universal Harvester was a lot less familiar of an experience than I expected. I devoured

635 *Wolf in White Van* since after decades of knowing Darnielle through his songwriting and other nonfiction/Internet screeds (and in person a few times), I felt a familiarity with his voice and his preoccupations. This, despite being his 'Iowa novel', is so drenched in ambiguity that I never felt myself wanting to stay involved. The four-part structure is a bit messy too; it's the relatively focused and small second part that has the most momentum, but whenever it moved back to the videos plotline, I lost the thread. It may be somewhat due to my own disjointed nature while reading it (it was started while in Stockholm and paused for almost two weeks while I recovered from an eye injury), but I didn't love this; I wonder if there is something far more sophisticated a play here which I didn't pick up on, because I'm so fragmented myself right now. I liked the 90s setting and the focus on the technological apparatus of this so distant time (such as Gateway 2000 computers and Tripod.com websites); the fast-forward to the present-tense didn't serve to do much except tie together the already wispy plotlines into something even less satisfying than I expected. If there is a novel here about belief and loss in the Midwest, I would like to read it again; I wonder 744 if the parts of Hill's *The Nix* maybe did this more successfully. What also got me is that the whole mysterious videotape footage plot is something that I would have gone crazy about years ago; I was even trying to write really similar narratives myself back when I lived in Pittsburgh. So maybe I have changed, or maybe I wanted it to develop the fantastic elements a bit futher.

764. The Atrocity Exhibition by J. G. Ballard
Received: 19 March 2017
Started: 31 March 2017
Finished: 9 April 2017
Here we go — finally, I find the Ballard book I should have discovered a long time ago. *Atrocity Exhibition* was stark, brutal, and unrelenting, but it was the audacity of its form that most impressed me. This reprint edition was annotated by Ballard himself after each chapter, and these annotations were in many ways the best part, full tangential ideas and a remarkable distance from his own creation. A lot of this was 211 reworked as *Crash*, and some of the concepts here (such as 'The death of affect') took me back to my seminars at Glasgow Uni; I wish this had been assigned instead of *Crash*, or that I would have read this earlier, because I likely would have become obsessed with Ballard while younger. This is really a collection of experimental story-forms with some recurring characters and a terrifying internal geography/logic, tackling the accelerated culture of the late 1960s in a way that doesn't even really seem 'dated' as much as like a window into a parallel world we could have lived. So much is predicted here in terms of celebrity culture, technophilia and violence, but Ballard's style is so bold that it feels more like fragmented documents of some alien transmission rather than a cautionary tale. Astounding.

765. Tree of Smoke by Denis Johnson
Received: 19 March 2017
Started: 19 March 2017
Finished: 12 April 2017
We had a thick hardback copy of this sitting around in Slothrop's forever and I was always curious. Johnson has an almost cult-like reputation and apart from reading half of *Fiskadoro* years ago, I haven't been familiar with his work. What always scared me away was the size of this, and the topic (Vietnam), but in paperback it seemed a lot less intimidating. Getting into this took some time, perhaps because I wasn't used to Johnson's writing style, which I would describe as stark and harrowing, yet economical in terms of word choice. Not exactly minimal, but rather the opposite — incredibly lush, descriptive, and with some strange images that left me feeling spooked — but without an excessive word count. Maybe this is why the book feels so dense, because it's still 600 pages and a lot happens, and to employ a cliché, every word counts. After reading a few lengthy and celebrated (but clearly over-hyped) novels such as *The Nix* and *City on Fire*, it was really satisfying to 744 701 read a thick American work that was packed with masterful writing, and not obvious, kiddie prose. This is a book that doesn't fuck around, despite its winding focus and sometimes uneven dips into the lives of side characters. Johnson is unflinching in describing the brutality that men can do, but this didn't feel like a typical war story, and there's very little actual combat in it. It uses military intelligence officers rather than combat soldiers for its main track, and this allows a more complete and perhaps much more damning portrait of the US's involvement in Southeast Asia than another blood and guts war tale. This was written during the Iraq war and he doesn't try to hide

the parallels, but doesn't beat the reader over the head with them; pointing out the evils of American imperialism has been done many times, and I felt like Johnson was seeking some sort of deeper, almost religious significance here. By the end, I was hooked, and I loved how little Johnson needed to rely on traditional dramatic tropes. His style really carried this, I'd say — it's not particularly 'difficult' or obtuse or even overtly unusual, and the distinctions of his approach didn't really make themselves clear to me until it was over. Yet somehow, despite being grounded in 'reality', it felt extremely psychedelic; I felt the sweat, the heat, and the bugs even though there weren't a lot of page inches given over to describing them. For as much as the Vietnam War has been the major defining schism in the American culture of my lifetime (probably only just beginning to fade from consciousness now as the Boomers are starting to wane in power), this feels like a different take on it, unconcerned with making grander cultural points. Maybe this is another reason I found this so masterful — it felt like a genuinely fresh perspective (Johnson is my father's age which means he was of the age to go to Vietnam, though I don't know if he actually did).

766. Whiskey Tango Foxtrot by David Shafer
Received: 19 March 2017
Started: 16 April 2017
Finished: 22 April 2017
An easy airport book which maybe I should have saved for a flight, but I avoid air travel these days. This thriller was compared to Neal Stephenson but it's nowhere near that level of technological sophistication, historical erudition or writing ability. I found
722 it far closer to Dave Eggers' *The Circle* both in theme and mediocrity, and the schizo blogger, sexy non-white female lead and narcissistic celebrity archetypes are always fun if not particularly original. I love 70s pop culture that was influenced by Watergate and distrust in the government so I might as well dabble in what's made today — this is clearly part of a wave of work inspired by Snowden's revelations and the general
733 sense of Bratton's Stack concept, at least as far as it trickles down into everyday parlance. The one sci-fi stretch here — the 'eye test' — is actually a cool concept, and when the novel starts to really get crazy in the 'gang is getting together' way, it had some promise for being fun. But then it just ends, which makes me realise there's a longer game here, a whole series of books, and maybe I should just wait for the film but I could see myself reading the inevitable sequel just for the hell of it.

767. A User's Guide to the Millennium: Essays and Reviews by J. G. Ballard
Received: 19 April 2017
Started: 22 April 2017
Finished: 23 April 2017
This is a collection of essays and reviews by Ballard, mostly culled from *The Guardian* or other UK newspapers, and spanning from the early to mid 90s, though a few pieces from the late 60s are included. I was hoping for something a little bit more powerful here, but there's probably a reason this collection is rarely talked about, and that's because the writings are generally about small topics, though it's still thoroughly enjoyable. For as much as he's considered to be a pulp or sci-fi writer, his erudition is vast and it shows here; he's capable of reviewing scientific literature, poetry, or cinema with equal capabilities. A few book reviews were fascinating and his musings on science fiction show how seriously he took his role in that genre, and how he genuinely sought to push his work towards new areas of thought. There's also some autobiographical work, mostly reminiscing about his youth in Shanghai, which makes a nice companion essay to *Empire of the Sun*. What I really felt hanging over this book was the non-presence of the Internet; this was published when the nascent web had yet to reach elder statesmen such as Ballard, and I couldn't help but feel its absence — not in a negative way, not at all, but in how much it has influenced journalism and nonfiction writing since these pieces were written. Even within some of the book reviews, Ballard drops some radical ideas, almost as asides (such as wishing that there was more sex and violence on TV, as he sees pornography as freedom) and it's great to think about these viewpoints being smuggled into the newsstands of John Majors's Britain.

768. The Secret History by Donna Tartt
Received: 19 April 2017
Started: 24 April 2017
Finished: 29 April 2017
So this is what Donna Tartt is like; I always figured she would be someone I could read via airport bookstore or secondhand sale, and the years have ticked by without that happening, though the (semi-)recent buzz

873 about *The Goldfinch* reminded me to get around to reading her finally. I've still never read Bret Easton Ellis or most of the other hyped authors of that era, though I guess Jonathan Lethem was part of this gang, in a way. *The Secret History* was a long and densely plotted 'campus' novel that was much more exposition-based than I could have ever imagined. Lately I've been really focused on style, and I've indulged in a lot of popular, acclaimed 'mainstream' fiction and found most of it fairly bland in that category; Tartt is no exception, though as this was published in 1992 I guess it's more of an influence on contemporary American writers than an example of them. I'm not saying Tartt is a bad writer — quite the opposite, as she displays a wealth of talent in terms of description and mood. But she overtells the story, with zero ambiguity, and leaves nothing to the imagination. It's almost a bit like reading Dickens or some other pre-modern storyteller, which sits maybe with the classics theme of the novel, but probably padded what should have been a 400-page novel to 600 pages. I almost gave up after the first 100 pages, which chronicled a narrator's excursion into a posh Vermont liberal arts college and was soaked in the environment of the delusional white academic. I'm really not in the mood to read more books about the fantasy of a life in literature and letters, even if these kids are deliberately portrayed as naive and a bit dangerous to themselves. I know there was far less of a focus on diversity in 1992 but race isn't really the issue — it's more this prep-school atmosphere, a written version of the Whit Stillman/*Metropolitan*
1311 scene, which descends from Salinger and that whole lineage, and you would think is in some way actually representative of the American experience for more than a tiny handful of well-off people. But once I started to get into the story, and realised Tartt was trying to write about class directly but through immersion, I realised she was doing it pretty effectively. This is an inside-out murder mystery, and she handles the 'thriller' components of the story deftly without there really being much suspense or action. It's enough to drive forward a story over which she fleshes out a number of characters that are fairly damaged in different ways, and the small-town setting only serves to emphasise the twisted version of reality they live in. A contemporary reading of this could show how this is entirely a book about privilege, what white people can get away with, etc — the posh version of *The Night Of* or something akin to it. But I don't think Tartt was aiming for any activist statements, just trying to explore the psychological effects of crime (not unlike Dostoyevsky) with a non-ironic embrace of melodrama and some teen angst thrown in as well. It's a pleasurable balancing act and a page-turner too — as the group starts to unravel I found myself rather perversely enjoying their misery, since there were few if any people to feel sympathetic about.

769. Into the Maelstrom: Music, Improvisation and the Dream of Freedom: Before 1970 by David Toop
Received: 23 January 2017
Started: 5 May 2017
Finished: 7 May 2017

Here's a joke review in one line: shoulda been called *Into the Malestrom*, ha ha ha! There's no denying the world of free improvisation is extremely male-dominated, and as this focused on pre-1970 free improvisation it was even more so, but at least Toop was aware of this and made more than a few references to the situation. I generally loved this, and for the same reasons that I originally didn't like *Ocean of Sound* back when I read it in the late 90s or whenever it was. Then, I wanted a linear history of ambience and drone in music, but what I got instead was a loose history punctuated with creative nonfiction and Toop's own subjective associations. Nowadays, I realise the futility of trying to impose a chronology on creative thought, which is not only futile, but somewhat immoral, I'd say. Toop's writing captivated me here; there's still a semi-structure and I learned a ton of information here, but I also felt like I was really reading David Toop's thoughts, which were informed, provocative, and passionate. Additionally, his first-hand experiences described herein, mostly drawn from his own career as an improvising musician, served to relate the historical context to the now and also introduce some much needed diversity. The other big complaint I have would have been remedied if he had included the true geographic scope of the book in the title, which is England. There are plenty of passages about American jazz musicians, such as Ayler, the New York Art Quartet, Lennie Tristano, Coleman, etc — but they pale in comparison to the metres of print given over to what was brewing in England in the late 60s, specifically London (though the Sheffield-born Derek Bailey gets plenty of attention). This is fine — its an incredible lineage of music and it's great to read about, say, young AMM romping through the halls of the RCA — but maybe specifying that would have been a bit more fair to the reader. Toop promises in the next volume to cover continental European improvisation, Japanese musicians, and a lot more, so perhaps this will be balanced out when it's viewed as a complete work. But, yeah, *Into the Maelstrom* was a great read and inspiring as well — I've gone back to listen to *Karyobin*, *Withdrawal*, and other works by Spontaenous Music Ensemble because the book makes an argument that John Stevens developed one of the most truly original and democratic methods of group playing not just of its time, but ever — and listening to these again, I can really hear them in a different way. And that's really the greatest accomplishment that one could have when writing about music, I suppose — to provide a new way to hear. There's little tidbits about the larger contexts of literature, avant-garde art in America, Japan and the UK throughout these times, and of course the relationship between jazz and 'non-idiomatic' improvisation, however fraught with tension it might be. There's also a lot of content about musicians who I was previously only barely familiar with, or not at all — Joe Harriott, Alan Davie — and some new ways of writing about existing music that I know well. When he actually describes the music, it's fantastic, and I wish there was more of that. Toop seems to agree with many hardline improvisers that recordings are not super important and just documents of the ephemeral moment, which is the core of free playing, and when he mentions records at all they aren't particularly central (and the discography given in the back is wonderfully idiosyncratic). The many conflict-driven debates about the nature of improvisation, which seemed to me at times to dominate discussion of the UK 'old guard' (who are of course the new kids in the timeline of this book) are written without malice; though it's discussed how Cage and Stockhausen disliked improvisation, these divisions don't feel as intense as they often did when discussion them myself with other musicians who I have crossed paths with, and that's also great — it's refreshing that Toop can find a tolerance for different viewpoints within his enthusiasm. Ultimately, *Into the Maelstrom* served to re-excite me about playing with others, listening, and believing in music, which is an impressive feat in these times. That it was written in such a masterful manner makes me want to go back to this as a work of reference, however idiosyncratic it might be.

770. The Sellout by Paul Beatty
Received: 29 April 2017
Started: 29 April 2017
Finished: 10 May 2017

Kudos, Mr Beatty — you've managed to drive a giant bulldozer right through racial sensitivity at a time when America's tensions are reaching a boiling point. *The Sellout* is the opposite of subtlety, a satire so obnoxious that it felt at times like a violent assault on my own sense of decency, and I'm someone who is pretty indecent to begin with (I never feel 'offended' by anything). It's a *Putney Swope* for our time, I guess, with the same 'fuck it' sense of absurdity and jokes coming so fast that it actually took me awhile to get through  this. And the jokes are mostly great — not 48, everything hits, but the overall impact is as 458, 602 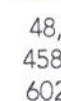 full-on as *Assisted Living* and the sting is felt. When I wasn't laughing I was enjoying the narrative, which is shocking if you want to be shocked and genuinely provocative  if you're not. 554 I found the love interest to be the weak link, but that's judging it by a conventional grading system which is somewhat irrelevant here. While the idea of re-segregating a city might seem like mere shock value, there's enough psychology at play here with the narrator's father to suggest deeper motives; I think it would be too easy to just say this is about 'race' when it's about so much more, such as belonging, community, power, and even the media. I'm more likely to re-read this than other books because of the yuks, but I might check out *Slumberland* next because Beatty writes in a way that makes want to know more about him and I suspect he hid behind the narrator here, and that one might be a bit more autobiographical.

771. Hav by Jan Morris
Received: 28 April 2017
Started: 28 April 2017
Finished: 16 May 2017

How absolutely wonderful it was to read *Hav*! I actually am not familiar with Morris's travel writing directly, but her influence is incalculable and she has clearly influenced probably ever travel writer which I have ever read, so her style felt immediately familiar, even authoritative. Of course, this is a novel, but one written in her own style, chronicling two journeys to the fictional city-state of Hav, the first (and main book) published in 1985 and then a novella-length sequel from 20 years later. This might seem like much ado about nothing since there is nothing particularly fantastical here, nor

does she show her hand too obviously, so it's really like reading a book-length travelogue from a place that could be real, but isn't. But everything lies beneath the surface in this book, much like in Hav itself. This is a fascinating document of a world on the brink of globalisation, where east meets west in a territory of dubious ethnic origin and frequent occupations. The Hav of 1985 is a remnant of a previous century, where citizens of former empires can live out their days under the fantasy that the world is not quickly changing. The fictional characters, traditions, and scenery are a pastiche of Morris's travels and there is a deeply heartfelt yearning for these wonderful and chaotic contradictions, written with the knowledge that such places will soon be transformed into a soulless global infostream. I could even detect possibly a subtext about occupation and identity, knowing that Morris is Welsh; the differing classes of the Havians in some ways resemble a more eccentric version of the British Isles. I was also reminded a lot of Wes Anderson's *The Grand Budapest Hotel*, though I have never read Stefan Zweig whose novels inspired that film; still, the pan-European culture mash and the
1341, 1342 sense of a place existing out of time, absurd and ridiculous as it struggles to keep up a appearances, was similar enough. *Hav of the Myrmidons* updates Hav's story to 2005 and it's here that Morris starts to let her sharp edges show a bit more obviously. By this point, Hav has been taken over as a Singapore-like police state, with an enforced fake ethnic identity, farcical state censorship and secret police, and a whitewashing of actually existing class structures. Complete with shithead English tourists at the hotel breakfast! Morris really shows her understanding of the modern world and it's political/economic machinations (not that anyone would have doubted her) and I liked how there was even a special economic zone in Hav 2.0, a weird shipping port that was in search of traffic. Shades of *Extrastatecraft*!

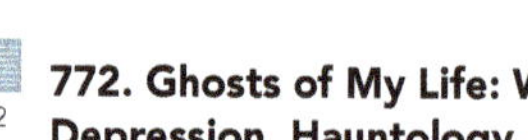

742 **772. Ghosts of My Life: Writings on Depression, Hauntology and Lost Futures** by Mark Fisher
Received: 10 May 2017
Started: 10 May 2017
Finished: 16 May 2017
This is a collection of writings by the guy who ran the k-punk blog (now deceased) around the topic of 'hauntology', a term originally used by Derrida but co-opted here to refer to a feeling of nostalgia for obsolete technology and a longing for lost futures. The opening essay was so amazing that I braced myself for what I thought might be a awe-inspiring book, but as he got into it, it was really just a collection of essays about music and some other cultural items, many taken from his blog. And while they were mostly pretty good reads, and occasionally brilliant, the book suffered from the same problem that affects Greil Marcus and a lot of other writers — basically, they take pop music way, way, way too seriously. With that aside, I loved a few of the pieces, though I found a few others overblown. I could have left the Joy Division one behind, but the titular essay (about Goldie and David Sylvian's Japan) was written with such a personal passion that it really worked (even though I have little interest in either artist). I found the writings on film generally thought provoking, though oddly more so from the essays on films I didn't like (*Inception*) or haven't seen (*Patience (After Sebald)*) than when reading about films I liked (*Content*) or loved (Patrick Keiller's *Robinson* trilogy). I let my own  music biases dominate my reading, so I 919  admittedly was pretty bored reading about Burial, but significantly more interested in 892 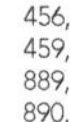 Black to Comm and the Ghost Box label. 456, 459, 889, 890, 965 It was nice, I guess, to read an interview with old acquaintance James Kirby (the Caretaker) and I wish I was still in touch with him. 'Depression' is one of the subtitles here, and in the first essay Fisher mentions how the hauntology concept is related to depression, which he suffered from, and he contrasts melancholy with melancholia though I already forget the difference. He committed suicide in January of this year and I knew this before I started the book, so I was expecting to feel a real current of hopelessness throughout (like I get when I read Wallace now) but actually, I found mostly enthusiasm for his subjects. I know I should have read *Capitalist Realism* first since that's the book Fisher's reputation is based on, so I guess that can come next.

778

773. Chuck Klosterman X: A Highly Specific, Defiantly Incomplete History of the Early 21st Century by Chuck Klosterman
Received: 18 May 2017
Started: 18 May 2017
Finished: 20 May 2017
A new Klosterman collection is a cause for celebration, and this (as the title indicates) is most like *IV* in terms of how it's

put together — selections of his various nonfiction writing from magazines and Internet sites, with some new introduc-
460 tions and reflections on them. I read most of these already in *Grantland* but I didn't mind reading them again, particularly some of the more insane essays (the examination of every KISS album; questioning whether Popovich's decision to sit Duncan, Parker, and Ginobli during one regular season game is a key to understanding one's views on the universe). There's nothing totally mindblowing to say here — some pieces I enjoyed more, some were less memorable, and ultimately I devoured this quickly and with great relish. I do miss *Grantland*, though.

774. The Towers of Trebizond by Rose Macaulay

Received: 22 January 2017
Started: 13 April 2017
Finished: 24 May 2017

Macaulay's novel is an eccentric tale of a woman's journey to Asia Minor in the late 1950s and it falls somewhere between being a proto-feminist novel, a goofy comic take on class and religion, and an actual travelogue. It worked well being read in parallel with *Hav* and I only noticed after finishing it that Jan Morris wrote the forward to this edition. Macaulay's sense of humour was great, and truly out of step with the
771 more cynical bite found in much of today's literature; she's never cruel or mocking, but aware of a general ridiculousness in many personalities. I'm sure this could be torn apart for its attitudes about race and the Other from a 2017 perspective, but for it's time it's actually quite progressive, and the Aunt and the Reverend make a great (and misguided) pair of Anglican-feminist warriors. There's a real sadness at the core of *The Towers of Trebizond* in the way the narrator's love interest is dealt with, almost entirely as memories and longing, and then with a brutal ending that comes just after some silliness about trying to teach an ape how to drive. I think Macaulay was really aware of the problems of the British Empire and its legacy of entitlement, or maybe I'm trying to read a favourable interpretation here, but it's definitely a solid example of British humour at its best.

775. Post-Punk Then and Now edited by Kodwo Eshun, Gavin Butt, and Mark Fisher

Received: 20 May 2017
Started: 20 May 2017
Finished: 30 May 2017

More Mark Fisher (again, I'm skirting around *Capitalist Realism* which is supposed to 
be amazing), 778 here as editor/organiser of a conference about post-punk in London, 2014. The book is essentially the transcript of the conference, a series of interviews and lectures with audience questions, and thus it has a cohesive voice that would probably more fragmented if it was a collection of essays written in other places. I never could have dreamed when I was younger that this period of music would be studied so deeply and become so institutionalised — I remember as a kid being excited to find any music books in the library that even mentioned the Pop Group or **Mission of** 
Burma 117 in passing; here I'm finding the topic done almost to death, presented with an academic focus that can really suck the life out of this. But I enjoyed reading parts of this; the interview with the Brasilian post-punk artists was good, as was the Polish one, since I knew relatively little of that scene. Lydia Lunch's performance/Q&A is sort of hilarious and sort of sad; she's so far into her character even in 2014 that it's remarkable, though not something I would aspire to be. Still, she has managed to carve out a career doing what she wants completely on her own terms, which is admirable. Other highlights: the long interview 
with Gee Vaucher about Crass's artwork; 695
Green Gartside's analysis of Scritti Politti's legacy; 1317 Sue Clayton talking about *The Song of the Shirt* (which I really must see), 35 years later. Less exciting: Fisher talking about the Jam to the point of obsession (does it really matter now who Paul Weller voted for in the early 80s?); the in-depth description of every issue of *Vague* fanzine, from the West Country. Reading this simultaneously made me feel inspired again my the music of this time, while also making me glad I escaped the British academic life myself. Such a contradiction, come to think of it, is pretty much 'post-punk' in a nutshell. I suppose in 30 years there will be conferences on Witchhouse or the Insane Clown Posse, and hey, why not? You gotta study the past to get a grip on the present.

776. After the Tall Timber: Collected Nonfiction by Renata Adler
Received: 16 May 2017
Started: 16 May 2017
Finished: 5 June 2017

Another collection that I somehow didn't write about at the time; today is the day of closing out empty book comments. Adler has become one of my favourite writers, as her only two novels immediately rocketed into my pantheon and the friend who recommended her in the first place said that her nonfiction was even better. This certainly wasn't as challenging as *Speedboat*, 661 but it resonated with a powerful moral clarity that was refreshing to read and felt like something missing from today's journalism. This is spread throughout her entire career and it contains some really historically fascinating content, such as a dispatch from a Southern civil rights march and a piece about the atrocities in Biafra. There's some sniping about the *New York Times* which in the hands of a lesser writer would be too 'Inside Baseball' to enjoy, but here served as a crucial signpost illustrating that paper's fall from greatness into the hideous embarrassment that it is today. Most memorable to me (a year after reading it) was the content about the Clinton impeachment, and Adler shows how insanely fucked up that impeachment was in terms of being a logical legal argument, even though I despise Clinton. 'Formidable' would be the best word to describe her writing — she's hard as nails, and I would be absolutely terrified to be on the other end of her. I don't think I can even compare her to many other journalists in terms of ferocity, tone and precision. Fucking great.

777. This is Memorial Device: An Hallucinated Oral History of the Post-Punk Music Scene in Airdrie, Coatbridge and Environs 1978-1986 by David Keenan
Received: 22 May 2017
Started: 5 June 2017
Finished: 9 June 2017

Goddamit, David's book is fucking amazing. I assume that it will get read by a decent audience, since it's published by Faber & Faber, and I hope that its topic isn't too esoteric — because I would bet this has a good chance of winning the Man Booker or some of those big deal literary prizes, especially given the frequency that post-punk has been a motif/theme of recent contemporary fiction. And this novel approaches Pynchon or Gaddis in terms of how dense it is with references, David being David and all, with obscure free jazz and Japanese psych names scattered throughout this supposed account of Airdrie's early 80s post-punk scene. But this goes well beyond superficial namedrops, managing to be a portrait of a fictional music scene that contained patterns so real to me that I easily forgot it was fiction, and got completely drawn into the world. I've never doubted David's talent as a writer, even if his music reviews sometimes tend towards hyperbole (pot, meet kettle) and his interest in beat writers is felt maybe a bit too strongly, but I was really blown away here. By having each chapter written by a different character, he set himself up to fail at accurately conveying 30 different voices, yet he somehow pulled it off, and with just enough magic and mystery throughout. There's an occult underbelly here, but also the day-to-day reality of West Scottish working life, and the balance is perfect. The fiction he created is magnificent, all anecdotes and experiences without a central narrative, and it really is remarkable in how it portrays an individual's relationship to their experiences and how we convey these things, I've never actually been to Airdrie but I've been to enough other similar towns to really be hit by this, though of course I never lived in them; still, even looking at the neighbourhoods in Pittsburgh that I lived in, I am struck by something familiar. The local environments all have their heroes and villains and these paths are universal in a way. Knowing David and his forceful opinions, I'm pleased that he holds back from portraying these local obscurities on a value system, and that they are allowed to celebrate their local stardom through is words. Really, really fucking great.

778. Capitalist Realism: Is There No Alternative? by Mark Fisher
Received: 10 June 2017
Started: 10 June 2017
Finished: 10 June 2017

I finally read this, and, wow, it was as great as everyone says. I didn't realise how short it was — 81 pages — but it's completely satisfying and covers and amazing amount of territory. In many ways, Fisher just amalgamated a lot of things that were already in the air, but with his unique obsessions of culture and memory. But it's not overbearing — there are only a few brief diversions into Kurt Cobain and contemporary television's trafficking in emotion, for the subject of today's capitalism stays central. This takes Jameson's ideas and goes a good bit further, updating for the technologically affected environment of today but also genuinely seeking solutions. The chapter about his experiences teaching teenagers in Britain was so spot-on to the problems of youth culture there that I was actually moved by it, and the final chapter's suggestions for ways out of our predicament are genuinely some of the most optimistic writing I've read from the left, and after the election the other day and everything else going on in the world, don't seem so far-fetched. It's tragic that Fisher didn't leave behind more writings, though I suppose the K-punk archives are rich for mining and we'll likely see a few more books come out before it's all said and done. I think this really would be a great book for anyone to read, especially people who fear theory or political writing, since it's accessible and stimulating; I would recommend this in a heartbeat, or even insist on it.

779. Dispute Plan to Prevent Future Luxury Constitution by Benjamin H. Bratton

Received: 10 June 2017
Started: 10 June 2017
Finished: 18 June 2017

More Bratton! But this is far from the theoretical mindfuck of *The Stack*, more like an 733 *Incesticide* of the man's thoughts and writings, assembled by e-Flux into a collection that (like the Hitero Steryl one) is spotty by 739 definition, though still very worth reading. I think because Bratton's more theory-heavy writing is so dense and unrelenting, I need to really immerse myself. At Nida, I had to really give myself to *The Stack*, in a way that I'm not even sure I could have managed if I tried to read it while at a normal time/place in my life. Similar, the longer and most impressive essays in *Dispute Plan* were lost on me. The central piece of this book was a long exploration of violence and architecture, but still scattered with references to all manners of cultural and political phenomena, and I really couldn't stay with it. The more sketch-based pieces were the most enjoyable, such as the travelogues on Indonesia and Kazan, as they also seemed to have the most personal flavour and were not trying to hammer in some sort of grand observation. Parts of this even felt like experimental fiction, which I guess was the intention, though it didn't assemble into a meaningful whole. The piece about chromopolitics started the most promising though I can't even remember where that one ended up; this is kinda what happens here, as this short collection has so many possible directions to travel that it didn't erally work for me as casual reading. Nonetheless it was a deeper glimpse into the guy's mind, and certainly more connected to his work in speculative design; I'm now way more curious about John Frum, Xefirotarch, and surgical automation, even if the writings on these topics here presupposed a good deal more knowledge on them then I already had.

780. Between Dog and Wolf by Sasha Sokolov

Received: 24 January 2017
Started: 15 May 2017
Finished: 20 June 2017

This was amazing, but not easy. Sokolov's novel was long considered untranslatable, and of course I'll never have any idea how accurate this was, but the results are still astounding. It's a highly experimental novel not so much in form (it follows a pattern of interleaving narrators with some intentionally bad poetry occasionally stuck in) but in style, as one narrator writes in a pidgin dialect with malapropisms, portmanteaus and other such devices throughout. This narrator has a hell of a voice, which distinguishes him from other such characters in the history of avant-garde literature; it's enhanced greatly by the setting, the forgotten life of the Soviet Union. I took this slowly, but despite my own patience I struggled to grab onto the narrative that was promised to be there, instead bathing in the language and artifice. The poetry was actually pretty good fun — more enjoyable to read than the stuff in *Pale Fire*, and just the right amount of it. Sokolov left quite a legacy between this and his more celebrated (but more traditional) first novel, and it's great that this exists in English. Mostly I feel the need to push myself back towards reading experimental literature, a process which fell away quite a bit over the past few years and thus was difficult for me.

781. Jane: A Murder by Maggie Nelson

Received: 22 June 2017
Started: 22 June 2017
Finished: 23 June 2017

Nelson's brief experiment examines the murder of her aunt by a probable serial killer in 1969, a few years before she was born, and is a mixture of poetry, prose, and excerpts from her aunt's diary. This could have gone in any wild direction — maudlin, speculative, emotionally distraught — but it doesn't, staying focused without being rigid or bound to a strictly journalistic form. Nor does this veer into the genres of true crime, memoir, or mystery, even though it has traces of all of these. I have a lot of time 757 for Nelson after reading *The Argonauts* and 782 will surely move on to *The Red Parts* next, the semi-sequel to this. This had the feel of a fantastic artistic research project, one formatted into a fluid codex instead of a messy exhibition, and it could really be an example to those working in similar personal forms. The personal connection is obviously why this was written, but it doesn't overwhelm or become too navel-gazing. And it's short, but long enough, revealing the incident's influence over Nelson's own upbringing through evocations rather than many direct explications.

782. The Red Parts: Autobiography of a Trial by Maggie Nelson
Received: 23 June 2017
Started: 23 June 2017
Finished: 24 June 2017
It's the companion to *Jane*, sure, and since I'm always more comfortable reading prose than poetry I'd have to admit I found this more rewarding. Taken with all the true crime dramas coming to Netflix, *The Red Parts* is a nice antidote, being so obviously personal and written by someone who is as brilliant as Nelson. The overall accessibility of this makes it something that could be recommended to a larger audience, but it was still infused with enough digressions to be more like a personal essay than a true crime book. Her connection to the murder as well as the existence of *Jane* sidesteps 781 any of the moral quandaries usually raised by such matters, and she seems to have treated her family's feelings respectfully; of course, her own emotions are wildly present and not exactly irrational. The mystery underlying this is interesting, but what Nelson does delicately is question the overall presence of sexual violence, without this turning into a polemic. I can't deny that there's anger here, but it was an anger that wasn't visible unless observed from an angle.

783. More Alive and Less Lonely: On Books and Writers by Jonathan Lethem
Received: 3 July 2017
Started: 3 July 2017
Finished: 3 July 2017
It's nice to have another collection of Lethem's nonfiction, and this one specifically collected bits written about other writers and literature (with a tiny bit of bleed into the film arena). It's edited by a third party, and divided into different sections based on theme. I always like Lethem's passion, enough that it can carry some of his lesser fiction, and this showed a much more broad range of influence than he's written about previously (though Philip K Dick is very present here, of course). Maybe it's because I read this on planes and in airports but I was really open to reading about more obscure writers that I hadn't previously been familiar with, such as Thomas Berger, who he writes about his personal relationship with in a way that's a big braggy but also trying to be humble. Throughout a lot of these pieces I felt Lethem struggling to deal with his own relevance and place in the literary canon as his career was developing, yet it wasn't as irritating when I read that from other 'young' writers. Some of the reviews have little to do with the book under review as they have to do with Lethem himself, such as the Chester Brown review which is just full of Lethem raving about how Brown is the greatest artist ever, but that's the nature of journalism of his time, and everything in here was short enough.

784. Clans of the Alphane Moon by Philip K. Dick
Received: 12 July 2017
Started: 18 July 2017
Finished: 20 July 2017
While visiting Glasgow, an old friend had a box of books that he was trying to get rid of and I took a few, mostly ones that I had already owned and given to him when I left. So the circle of book-life continues except I just re-read *Clans of the Alphane Moon* while at Allenheads and now I'll leave it there for someone else. This is an odd Dick novel to re-read, not because it wasn't great, but just because it's rarely cited. I remember that this was a book dealing with mental illness, which it does very obviously, as the Alphane moon is divided into a ghetto/caste system built around paranoia, mania, depression and other ailments. But reading it now in the wake of Brexit (which a year after the vote is pretty much all people are talking about here), it works well as a crude sci-fi allegory about race and division, and not one that is without hope. The protagonist at the centre is a Dickian damaged male, taking illegal drugs to work two jobs at once, and with his id raging out

of control and sexual urges dealt with quite explicitly (though he is not involved in the book's strange, brutal rape scene which I totally forgot about and which is written in an almost devilish way). No one would ever accuse Dick of being progressive in terms of sexuality or women's issues, but this book, with it's fixation on breasts and nipples and weird jokes hidden beneath the dialogue, seems especially demented. The telepathic slime mold from Ganymede is the emotional centre of the book (weirdly) and reminds me of Glimmung from *Galactic*
319 *Pot Healer*. I loved reading this again and I hope I don't slip into another Dick hole (ha ha); as much as I'd love to re-read them all, there's so many other books I could be reading instead.

785. Haunted Weather: Music, Silence and Memory by David Toop

Received: 23 January 2017
Started: 22 June 2017
Finished: 25 July 2017

This is an awesome book about experimental music and as it was published in 2004, it feels like a perfect summation of the 'first' phase of my own musical life, or at least the years where I was actively investigating experimental music of the past and then-present. It's hard to pin down exactly what the topic of this book is besides surveying the field of experimental music at the date of publication; it feels like a primer of what *The Wire* was covering around this time, as well as incorporating some of the historical precursors, even getting into free jazz and improvisation a bit. The ending chapters have a bit of overlap with *Into*
769 *the Maelstrom*, at least the segments on

199 Derek Bailey and John Stevens, but again, Toop's writing is so great that I'm happy to revisit (or pre-visit, since this came out over a decade before) these topics from another angle. There's the same sort of free-flowing movement from topic to topic, making it a bit hard to grasp how this book is organised, but there's no reason to stop and wonder about that anyway because the prose is so generous and enjoyable. I wish a larger publishing house had printed this, as the typeface was very difficult to look at for an extended period of time, and the paper quality was poor, making this feel like an early print-on-demand book. But I think this may actually be my favourite of the four David Toop books I've read so far, maybe because it feels the most open and fascinated with music and sound and all of its potential. Toop writes in here about a lot of sound artists and musicians, as well as some poets and visual artists, and there is a focus more on recordings here than the book on improvisation had, as that largely eschewed recorded music to be consistent with the philosophy under review. And as this came out in 2004 there's a lot of stuff here that feels a bit dated already, such as the writing about digital music and technological debates of the time (are laptops performative, what is digital silence, etc.) though he's never polemical and seems to (if anything) enjoy all possibilities. I would actually say this works as a nice sequel, or updating, of Michael Nyman's great *Experimental Music: Cage and Beyond*, though to be honest, I read that as a freshman in college which means it's been 20 years now, so maybe I should go back to it myself and see if it holds up. One friend said that Nyman book changed his life and it was pretty influential on me too; if paired with *Haunted Weather* then a novice could be brought right up to the early 00s — and now we just need a good overview of the noise/CDr underground I was sucked into, and all of the other stuff that happened since. I used to be absolutely fascinated with all forms of sound and music, right up until I left the US, at which point I started to jell into a proper scene of my own, by which I mean a scene that was larger than just myself and my few close friends. But paradoxically, being introduced to more interested people and musicians (while also starting my own small career in music) actually narrowed my interests. Maybe that was a process of refining things in order to focus, which was probably necessary at that point in my life, but reading this book made me nostalgic for those years in Pittsburgh, going out to Manny's shows and being excited equally by Jim O'Ro-  1728, 1823
urke, Oval, and Arab on Radar. These days  1803
I'm feeling wide-eyed again — like I don't have anything to prove anymore, and I just want to be inspired and delighted as before. And actually, it's been happening, so maybe *Haunted Weather* also worked so well because it was clicking in rhythm with the mental state I'm in with regards to sound and music. I guess it's on to *Sinister Resonance* next!

786. The Angry Island: Hunting the English by A.A. Gill

Received: 22 January 2017
Started: 25 July 2017
Finished: 27 July 2017

This was a nice, fun read after returning

from three weeks in the UK, mostly spent in England. The cover blurb promised this to be a sassy, vicious attack on English culture, but it was actually much more nuanced and intelligent, being essentially a collection of essays on different topics. Gill, the writer, was technically born in Edinburgh and thus has never identified himself as English, a get-out-of-jail-free card he employs throughout, even though he confesses to having the R.P. (Received Pronounciation, aka BBC English) accent and identifies as a Londoner for all intents and purposes. These identity politics aren't so interesting to me but they aren't dwelled upon. Still, the chapter on accents is pretty great, as is the section on Letchworth Garden City and the bit about sport. When he does sharpen the knives a bit, such as the chapters on humour or the Cotswolds, it's entertaining, but as he says himself in the humour chapter, he's a funny writer who doesn't write actual jokes. There aren't punchlines here, nor any particularly brilliant insights — this comes off, in the end, like having a long conversation in a pub with someone who is reasonably intelligent. I didn't finish it having learned about anything besides maybe the origin of Letchworth and Gill himself, but that doesn't mean it was a bad way to pass the time, and as a 'beach book' (since that's where I read most of it) it was a pleasant and mildly entertaining cap on my time in England. Gill passed away last December, which I didn't know until after finishing it, not that it makes a huge difference on how I received it. In some ways he felt like a significantly milder, more accessible Jonathan Meades, which means I should probably move on to the two Meades books I bought while in England.

787. Aliens & Anorexia by Chris Kraus
Received: 22 July 2017
Started: 27 July 2017
Finished: 28 July 2017
This perfect little masterpiece is again presented as a novel, but is even less fiction-rooted than *I Love Dick*, to which this makes a nice companion piece. Kraus's writing again moves through layers of autobiography and references to art and philosophy; here, Simone Weil is the primary concern and as I'm not really familiar with her I learned a great deal, especially as Kraus focuses more on Weil's biography than her philosophical writings. So much of this book is about Kraus's struggle to make a film that no one was interested in anyway. This frustration with being a mediocre artist carries through in the S&M phone conversation plotline, a nice example of how this text twists and turns in on itself. By now I'm used to Kraus's voice, so I'm not longer confused by the apparent lack of plot, drama, or resolution. This is fiction that is about the act of creativity itself, while simultaneously interrogating the superficiality of the commercial art world and the monstrous men (Aliens) who populate it. And then anorexia is presented as a different sort of disorder than how it's usually thought of — as a radical reclaiming of the body. I wasn't convinced by this and I'm not sure that Kraus is either, but it was a beautifully rendered argument and the titular topics served as a cohesive double-helix to structure the book around (while also mirroring her themes, gravity & grace). The closing film treatment is really different than what I imagined her film was about while reading it; it serves as a sort of Dear John letter to her artistic ambitions, and feels distant from all of the self-reflection (which I wouldn't call narcissism) and sexual indulgences that populate the book. What I'm most struck by is how resolved Kraus is with her fears + desires — there's no posturing here, no sense to define oneself as a steely visionary. She clearly just longs for connections and intimacy with others, and is remarkably honest about these desires. At the period where this book takes place her marriage has just turned into some sort of formal relationship (and I remain fascinated by the fact that Lotringer publishes these books of hers that feature him, not rendered positively) and this isn't even commented on much; it is what it is. It's absent of drama, absent of plot, and absent of easy reference points, yet *Aliens & Anorexia* is something special that I suspect will gain in my estimation as time passes.

788. Tomorrow and Tomorrow by Tom Sweterlitsch
Received: 27 January 2017
Started: 28 July 2017
Finished: 30 July 2017
Pittsburgh porn! Recommended by a friend, of course, or why else would I know about this? Sweterlitsch worked for the Carnegie Library for the Blind for years though I don't remember him from my days in the library system; this novel claims on the cover to be like a mashup of Chandler and Dick, but it's not really close to either. The premise is that Pittsburgh was destroyed by a nuclear bomb and now has

been reconstructed in virtual reality as a museum/monument, and the protagonist is an insurance investigator who lost his wife and would seek out past insurance claims from the VR-Pittsburgh. This wasn't bad, though I can't imagine it being appealing to anyone who isn't from Pittsburgh. It reeked of the annoying localism that drove me crazy about Pittsburgh — the way we would champion mediocre local bands and never dream of anything higher — and this is saturated in references both geographical (a key location is 3138 Dobson St third floor AKA Copacetic Comics) and cultural (namedropping of bands like Centipede Eest and Shade (!) is pretty amusing, as well as numerous real-life things such as Copacetic and the *New Yinzer*). As someone who also left Pittsburgh about as long ago as the book's apocalyptic event was set, it mirrored something in me as I remembered a life I don't really think about much anymore except for my annual(ish) visits. But otherwise it was a fairly ho-hum thriller plot, which tried to deal with loss and letting go in its most effective sections. Sweterlitsch is actually a pretty talented writer and I appreciated the way this future world was built on today's technology with very few leaps requiring suspension of belief. Sexual exploitation and violence has become so commonplace in his future America, with the president a porn star and every waking minute an assault of sex-based advertising, that the protagonist's chastity comes across as a strong moral quality, even though it's never explicitly dwelt upon. Pornography so prevalent that it becomes mundane is one of the best things about this future world (maybe we are already there?), and it emphasises the goodness and empathy of the hero, especially as he mourns his dead wife and tries to help the Albion character. There's some less successful clichés here — the evil Republican donor, crazy psychiatrists, and secret sex-abuse rings controlled by the powerful — but it made for a convincing page-turner with a compassionate centre.

789. The Administration of Fear by Paul Virilio
Received: 22 July 2017
Started: 22 July 2017
Finished: 3 August 2017
I used to be much more immersed in Virilio's ideas but now it's been some years since I read him. I was in the mood and this is one that is written in the style of an interview, so it's quick and sort of fun. I read this in one sitting while on a plane, and unfortunately I can't remember any specifics about it now, which probably illustrates that I read too much too quickly and it's all ultimately a waste of time. Hmmm.

790. Museum Without Walls by Jonathan Meades
Received: 22 July 2017
Started: 30 July 2017
Finished: 7 August 2017
Meades in prose is a wonderful thing, every bit as erudite and sharp as his television programmes. This is a collection of essays largely about architecture and the built environment, and it rambles through a variety of topics organised into sections. His use of language is grandiose and occasionally it becomes a bit of word salad, or maybe 'culture salad' is a better term since I'm not always able to grasp the deep references to UK cultural life, especially those from previous decades. He's somehow fiercely educated about these topics without being a proper academic, and he's able to maintain an irreverence that isn't necessarily comic but sharp and coy. Compared to the biographical material in *Encyclopaedia of Myself*, I think I slightly preferred this, as it feels like the definitive collection of Meades' worldview. It's remarkably thick too, and an odd choice for the beach, where I perused most of this.

836

791. The Record Store of the Mind by Josh Rosenthal
Received: 19 January 2017
Started: 11 August 2017
Finished: 18 August 2017
Rosenthal runs the Tompkins Square label and self-published this book which is somewhat of an autobiography through music, though erratically organised and bound only by his eager, guileless enthusiasm for obscure Americana. He's not a great writer — this has the style of YouTube comments, or blog posts – but that's somewhat forgivable because this is delivered so honesty, like the polar opposite of the John Olson book I shelved it next to. Rosenthal chronicles a bunch of country/folk/jazz musicians who he is passionate about and had various levels of interactions with, such as Tia Blake, Robert Lester Folsom, Ron Davies, Charlie Louvin, and Bill Wilson. Most chapters contain extremely enthusiastic writing about these artists and their work, which often sounds generic or at least product of their time, but he always finds something

to celebrate. And then the chapter usually ends with some story about how he met the artist, and then they died. It gets repetitive, but then there are a few chapters about his own life that are the most enjoyable, though his limitations as a writer are most obvious here. His childhood in Syosset, NY and high school friendship with Judd Apatow is an interesting chapter; his work for Columbia records in the early 90s is another though it reads as a bunch of namedropping; the chapter entitled 'Gigs' which ends with five pages listing every concert he went to, less interesting for sure. (I realise my hyprocrisy here).The title and intro promised this to be about record stores but stores aren't mentioned so much throughout, though recorded music is the major theme and I'm glad at how much this turned me on to some new (to me) music. My favourite chapter was the one about Raccoon Records, a short-lived subsidiary of a major that the Youngbloods ran for a few years which released some inexplicably weird and great stuff — I've already listened to Jeffrey Cain's *For You* online and I totally love it. Near the end he provides a list of his favourite records, which is mostly obscure 70s folk-country but also has some random things in it (David Sylvian's *Secrets of the Beehive* feels like an odd fit), and I'm looking forward to pillaging the Internet to hear many of these, too.

792. Mathematics: (A novel) by Jacques Roubaud
Received: 27 January 2017
Started: 4 August 2017
Finished: 19 August 2017
Mathematics is the third branch of Roubaud's *"the Great Fire of London"* project, which includes the novel *The Great Fire of London* that I never finished reading, as I found it slow and depressing. This seems like a different beast, being (on the surface) about the pursuit of mathematics but like the other book I half-read, really being a playful investigation of personal memory. I wonder if this book is structured to mimic the study of mathematics itself, because it's heavily convoluted, with footnotes/ 109 endnotes that make *Infinite Jest* seem simple. I had to read this with three bookmarks at times, and the narrative of the first two-third concerned his 1950s pursuit of university-level mathematics studies at the time of the Bourbaki movement. Roubaud's struggle with the Bourbakis is the main subject of the book's prose, but I think that's misleading, because this is a book that writes around the self. The endnotes feel drawn out and repetitive and I started to get really frustrated reading this, especially as I chose it to take to the beach for several days, and because (like *The Great Fire of London*) I didn't have the patience to put up with Roubaud's digressions. But finally, the last chapter drops the constant references and chronicles a memory from Roubaud's military service, and at this point (and only then) does *Mathematics* start to truly lift from its moorings and become something. And I wonder if this was intentional, to echo the way math itself can be when learning it, where only after years of hard work can one break through to the sublime. The death of his wife isn't explicitly mentioned at all here (at least I can't remember it) but because I'm familiar with his other work, I felt it hanging over the text, especially as Roubaud tried to dance around his emotional responses to the events of his youth as he chronicles them. I found the most enjoyable parts when he dropped the supposed narrative and just had fun, like the long silly play between the Tortoise and the Hare in the endnotes, which intentionally mashes up and obfuscated Xeno's paradox with other philosophical arguments. I haven't changed my feelings about Roubaud, that he is ultimately a frustrating writer, but this difficulty is something he clearly embraces and does so without stylistic, prose-level difficulty, which is quite welcome.

793. Snow Crash by Neal Stephenson
Received: 24 June 2017
Started: 19 August 2017
Finished: 21 August 2017
I've read a lot of Neal Stephenson this year, and now finally this, and I understand why it's considered a classic. This is the most fun and spazzy Stephenson novel I've read and it's descended from the Gibson 'cyberpunk' thing for sure, but it has a lot of other ideas that take it towards different directions, none of which it fully commits to. There's some typically pedantic Stephenson exposition, like everything about the Sumerian language metavirus plot concept, which is detailed by having the hero talk to a Librarian AI, which was clumsy and boring. I loved the bleak anarcho-capitalist world portrayed here, which presages Bratton's theories of future sovereignty by a few decades, and is pretty spot-on 733 at capturing where we are headed. And this was funny — with lots of zany ideas tossed out and discarded, reminding me

a bit of Pynchon's most hyperactive style. The action sequences were good but something he would far improve on by the time he got to *Reamde*; here, there's
760 a lot of adolescent boy fetish stuff, like swordfighting and super machine guns, but that's a motif of the genre, I guess. I found the first half of the book a bit more enjoyable, as the pleasure for me was in teasing out this future world and figuring out how it functioned; when it turned into thriller mode it was still good, but I found the whole metavirus thing kinda stupid, a grandiose overreach to infuse some intellectual content into a narrative which honestly didn't need it. I tried to read Gibson a few times but always found him tough going — slow, and hard to engage with. There was a bit of 'fuck it' absurdity here, not exactly a mockery of the cyberpunk ethos but also the sense that it didn't have to be taken too seriously, which truly liberated the book from its influences. One of the fun things about reading a book that was published 25 years ago is seeing what aspects of future tech Stephenson got right. The Metaverse is just a photorealistic Second Life, and Google glass exists here; I suspect history will prove him right in terms of corporate sovereignty, and Trump is doing his damnedest to make sure the US government goes this way. But then Stephenson totally failed to anticipate wi-fi or mobile devices, which makes this idea of people lugging around computers and 'jacking in' to wired ports in order to communicate on the Metaverse really silly and actually kinda nice, something weirdly anachronistic about a novel that takes place in the future.

794. Nature Stories by Jules Renard
Received: 27 January 2017
Started: 14 August 2017
Finished: 29 August 2017
It's hard not to be charmed by this little quirky book, a collection of short reflections on the French countryside published orig-

inally in 1896. Renard is like a proto-Lydia
577 Davis, not just because of these stories' brevity, but in the way that they jump between styles. It's almost like he took each animal depicted here as a challenge, and it comes off as so extremely French, much like the way Queneau darts between form in *Exercices de style* or like a whimsical Michel Gondry script. I particularly enjoyed the cluster of birds at the end, and while Renard enjoyed personifying the animals, it never devolved into spiritualism or anything close. The illustrations by Pierre Bonnard are as much a part of this book as the writing, and together it makes a beautiful, slim package that I took my time reading, savoring each story as I watched the summer begin to end.

795. Essays by Wallace Shawn
Received: 27 August 2017
Started: 27 August 2017
Finished: 29 August 2017
Wallace Shawn's writing is perhaps exactly what I imagined it being. I haven't seen *My Dinner with Andre* for a long time but
I remember Shawn espousing a thoughtful 485
rationalism that sometimes jarred against Gregory's more emotional flights of fancy. This collection of essays hews to that style, being a tight 111 pages that are almost evenly split between writings on politics/morality and writings on art and theatre. The first half is the political half and almost everything comes from the Bush years, railing against the Iraq War and Cheney and Rumsfeld and all of those nasty motherfuckers. It's crazy how far away that all seems now, though I still stand by my belief that that administration was far worse and more criminal than the shitheads in there now, who are just incompetent grifters. Anyway, Shawn tops it off with a decent interview with Chomsky that actually is a nice transition into the writings on drama and poetry. Nothing here is too academic or didactic; there's an almost amateurish feel to things, which makes for a nice and easy read, though maybe a tiny bit middlebrow. A good interview with Mark Strand appears in the second half which talks about the different voices of poetry and why we read it; that was probably the high point and what I'll remember from this, if anything.

796. Kill All Normies: Online Culture Wars From 4Chan And Tumblr To Trump And The Alt-Right by Angela Nagle
Received: 4 September 2017
Started: 4 September 2017
Finished: 5 September 2017
After hearing Nagle interviewed somewhere and reading a few reviews, I didn't expect much from this, as I thought the main gist of what she was writing about probably came across in those excerpts. But actually, *Kill All Normies* had a lot of meat to it, especially for such a short book. Nagle really dove into the toxic world of

online alt-light/alt-right shenanigans and not only dissected the turn towards right-wing transgression on a macro-scale, but placed it all into a context of cultural and political theory. Since tons of popular and established journalism outlets have been covering the 'alt-right' since the election (everywhere from *Slate* to Samantha Bee to the *New York Times Review of Books*), I was pleased that Nagle actually applied an academic understanding to these trends, situating 4chan and the incel movement as a belated reaction to second wave feminism, and with a nice dose of Gramsci in there too. Her chronicling of online misogyny was unpleasant to read but probably even more unpleasant for her to explore — while I was aware of this shit, I never forced myself to read so many detailed accounts of rape/death threats and harassment at once, and it took its toll on me. Nagle is extremely critical of what she calls the 'Tumblr left', the masses of overly-sensitive identity warriors who she blames for enabling the cultural backlash against this type of inclusion. She manages to do this from within a left-wing angle, siding overtly with Mark Fisher's 'Exiting the Vampire Castle' polemic and arguing, quite sincerely and convincingly to me, that the left needs to find a way out of identity politics if it is to ever move forward again. I could see some people taking issue with this critique but it was preaching to the converted for me; what's impressive is how she threads the needle of criticising left-wing behaviour without invalidating their beliefs or intentions, and without overshadowing the right who are the true subject of the book. This is timely, too — Yiannopolis is a key figure but this was published after his downfall, and the second chapter on the nature of transgression is probably the book's strongest. The ending section on the 'manosphere', the Proud Boys/Gavin McInnes bullshit and MGTOWs and all those creeps, was the most disgusting to me (even more than the racial/nationalist stuff, which I think is just employed as shock value for a considerable number of the people), but Nagle really strongly suggests that all of these people would go away if they were actually able to have relationships with women, which I'm sure is somewhat (but not completely) true. I have been interested in trying to understand the new right since the election, and this helped contextualise the new culture wars significantly more than any of the online journalism (of which the Triple Canopy piece on Anonymous some years back is still one of the best). Did this book make me feel any better? Absolutely not, and I'm convinced the left (at least in America) will never be able to get on top of the culture wars, unless sheer demographics win out in a generation or so, if we last that long. The near-victory of Corbyn is clearly the blueprint for how the American left needs to progress, but the Democratic party is standing in the way of that, and I'm sure they will never win another major election unless they embrace actual left-wing values. There's nothing in *Kill All Normies* about these topics at all, but I finished this thinking even more about how disgusted I am with the Democrats because they let all of these morons swing an election.

797. HHhH: A Novel by Laurent Binet
Received: 2 January 2017
Started: 23 August 2017
Finished: 9 September 2017

Binet really pulled off something magnificent with *HHhH* — a work of history masquerading as a novel, which directly addresses the reservations about fictionalising such things, yet doesn't let these reservations sideline the narrative. And it's hella compelling too; the last few bits of action were genuinely a thrill to read, and where I realised how Binet managed to benefit from all of the tricks of a novelist (emotional connections with characters, slow buildups, etc.) without actually really writing anything fictional at all. I was reminded a lot of the prose of William T. Vollmann – not so much *Europe Central*, which is cited here, but more his intense approach to nonfiction and journalism, like some of the parts of *Imperial*. It's history without really giving a fuck what the rules of history are, though Binet is scrupulous to the core and takes no liberties without outlining exactly what those liberties are. He even manages to bring his own personal connection to Prague, the woman he was living with while writing this, and the subject matter itself to the text, but again, it's a nice layer of dressing. We live in an era where metafiction elements and postmodernism are so infused into our lives that we take them for granted, but in *HHhH* I really felt like this everyday approach to textual experimentation was beneficial. When I finished this I felt triumphant, and I wanted to go out and kill some Nazis. And anything that makes someone feel like killing Nazis is undoubtedly a Good Thing.

272

433

798. My Cat Yugoslavia by Pajtim Statovci
Received: 2 September 2017
Started: 2 September 2017
Finished: 10 September 2017
It's rare for a Finnish novel to get such international acclaim but even more rare that said novel was written by an Albanian immigrant to Suomi. *My Cat Yugoslavia* had some very impressive moments, and was at its best when capturing the story of the mother's arranged marriage in Kosovo and her subsequent struggle adapting to life in 1990s Finland – this is the story we need here, and it's rendered beautifully, with some very dark passages. The intertwining story in this helix is the one more obviously autobiographical for Statovci and this had all of the fun postmodern tropes like the titular talking cat. I actually found this a bit less compelling, especially the cat part, which only occupies a small part of the narrative and is just a reminder of what abusive relationships can be like. The attempt to bring both narratives together regarding the father's death and the visit to Kosovo felt a bit clumsy, and not even really necessary — the novel was already accomplished and moving, and therefore just felt like a deux ex machina that is underwritten and left me feeling a bit distant. There couldn't be a more succinct novel in existence to symbolise Finland's progressive/left/multicultural atmosphere right now and as a member of that culture I wish I had felt a bit closer to *My Cat Yugoslavia*. Instead, I found myself wishing that it was less overtly fictional, which is not something that I often feel with literature.

799. Conditions On The Ground by Kevin Hooyman
Received: 27 January 2017
Started: 10 September 2017
Finished: 13 September 2017
Great, great stuff — *Conditions on the Ground* was a small self-published comic/zine that is collected here in its entirety in a beautiful hardback book with a nice colour cover and inner leaves. Hooyman approaches comics like the greatest of the contemplative stoner class; Anders
528, 856 Nilsen comes to mind for sure, but there
are many others. The many stories in here are sometimes very short, just a one page gag, but rarely ha-ha funny; often they are rambling meditations on consciousness that probably don't hold up to a sharp philosophical scalpel but are fun and refreshing to read. Longer stories don't necessarily have any more dramatic impact but I love this — these 'small' stories, and the world he creates. His moustachioed stand-in is a warm blanket on which he can wrap all sorts of insights; sometimes the supporting characters are so absurd that their ruminations take on a hilarious glow, such as a Swamp Thing, or cheerleaders. Visually, Hooyman is the master of the line — his long, sinewy strokes make incredible scenery, and it feels clean, while active, and nothing like the sloppy/messy trend in comics that I usually find annoying.

800. The Rise and Fall of D.O.D.O. by Neal Stephenson and Nicole Galland
Received: 10 September 2017
Started: 11 September 2017
Finished: 14 September 2017
I couldn't resist more Stephenson, and this was a time-travel story so I figured I would like it. Actually, it's pretty terrible — the premise of 'magic is real' is so infantile that it wasn't even fun as a speculative fiction, and the characters were thinly sketched out, yet masqueraded as possessing a complex vibe that fell apart under further examination – a weakness that most of Stephenson's books suffer from. I guess the co-author primarily writes historical fiction, and this was about half that, so I'm not sure who is more to blame for the book's deficiencies. It's certainly a lighter book than anything else I've read by him, and there were so many similar patterns from his other works. The climactic action sequence was like the best parts of *Cryptonomicon*
or *Reamde* (and certainly the best part of 760
the book); the characters even felt familiar, like the overeducated beautiful heroine and the trench coat sysadmin geeky white male. Stephenson really loves inventing complicated acronyms and jargon (*Anathem*!)
and this book allowed him to do plenty, 758
under the guise of US military codewords; the middle 1/3 of this book is primarily built around that stuff, through memos and other supposed documents, though it also manages to play games with government bureaucracy and this is actually a pretty fun part to read, I must admit. The jokes are usually too obvious and drawn out too long, but it was amusing and compelling enough to get through, and I kinda wish they could have made a time travel book that didn't need to tie it to a half-assed take on occultism. I guess this is just an airport book and it's OK to write something a bit more silly, but even if magic was real and time travel was possible, still none of this

makes any fucking sense and the suspension of disbelief required to understand why the characters were doing what they were doing, even by the novel's own crooked logic, was enormous. I'm really tempted by *Seveneaves* but my friend insists it's a fucking awful book and I probably should cool it on Stephenson for awile, after this. This was a nice counterbalance to all the WM Spackman I'm reading in parallel.

801. Typewriters, Bombs, Jellyfish: Essays by Tom McCarthy
Received: 25 September 2017
Started: 25 September 2017
Finished: 1 October 2017
McCarthy as a nonfiction writer is an intriguing concept and I went into this expecting probing, quasi-technofuturist essays about speed and time. What I got instead was a collection of rather hardcore literary essays, any of which could function as a successful academic paper in the style familiar to me at Glasgow Uni over a decade ago. This collection goes through a variety of topics (Kafka, DeLillo, *Ulysses*, Gerhardt Richter, *Tristram Shandy*, Zinedine Zidane) with a few recurring targets. Mallarmé seems to be quite an obsession, and as I'm not familiar with him, I felt a big hole in my own understanding while reading. McCarthy has a keen symbiosis with French literature of the wondrous, ponderous kind which makes
370 sense, because of *Remainder*; chapters on Toussaint and Robbe-Grillet were a joy to read, even without knowing most of the texts under discussion, because of his enthusiasm and ability to draw connections within the authors' work, across different disciplines, and into the contemporary era. There is still a strong sense of extra-textual influence, relating to the changing world we are in, which is when I remembered that this is the same writer who banged out something as brilliant as *Satin Island* in a way that felt effortless to me, at least as a reader. He has a keen understanding of space, from a theoretical perspective as well as a stylistic one, and especially the more experimental, roving essays ('Kool Thing, or Why I Want to Fuck Patty Hearst') feel aware of their construction as an *objet d'art*. An Ed Ruscha image adorns the cover and Ruscha's act of throwing the typewriter from the car inaugurates what is probably the best essay, or at least the one that feels the most insane in terms of all of the stuff he pulls together. A closing chapter on Kathy Acker is also timely given the sudden resurgence of interest in her work (I can't believe how hyped Chris Kraus's new biography is, but I'm happy for that) and ties her directly to Kristeva and other theorists, but perhaps most significantly points out how Acker began publishing pretty much as the whole thing we now call 'theory' was just coming to dominate literature and academia. This was occasionally a challenge to stay focused on, especially when writing about texts that I was unfamiliar with, but that's one of the things that makes McCarthy such a genius — his ability to melt difficult concepts into something palatable, all served up in a way that provokes wonder and inspires curiosity.

802. The Weird and the Eerie by Mark Fisher
Received: 1 October 2017
Started: 1 October 2017
Finished: 4 October 2017
I think I've run out of Mark Fisher books now; this was a bit like the Tom McCarthy book I just read in that it's really a collection of literary criticism, though in Fisher's case it also covers cinema and television, and everything is tied into the bipartite topic of the title. Rather than being a collection of previously existing work, everything seems to be written specifically for the purpose of this short volume, as the essays refer to each other throughout. Topics include Lovecraft, David Lynch, Philip K Dick, Nigel Kneale, and Daphne Du Maurier; the film criticism has much more positive views of *Interstellar* and *Under the Skin* than I felt

when watching them myself, though not enough to encourage me to revisit them. 1402 1447
This lacked Fisher's sharp political viewpoint, and because of that I enjoyed this far less than any of his other writing, as it felt sort of lightweight and a bit obvious — I don't think I left *The Weird and the Eerie* with any more insights into either the weird or the eerie.

803. Psychedelia: An Ancient Culture, A Modern Way Of Life by Patrick Lundborg
Received: 22 May 2017
Started: 1 October 2017
Finished: 12 October 2017
This is about as epic as a work of nonfiction can get, and it was hard to put down. I thought Lundborg's study on psychedelia would be better than the other one I

read that was mostly just about well-known 702
psychedelic music, and it surely was, but it was so much more than I imagined. This is

a complete survey of the entire concept of psychedelia, merging anthropological content with cultural history, with a grounded questioning of the nature of not just the psychedelic experience, but also the entire lifestyle. I feared this would be like a lot of drug-related literature and that it would make wild speculations, but this was pretty much up to an academic standard. Lundborg's writing is fantastic (and it's referenced throughout with enough fascinating content in the endnotes that I did the ol' double-bookmark trick here) and almost on the level of Hillel Schwartz's books in
607, 616 terms of non-institutional research quality. This guy's understanding of psychedelic music went far beyond the layman's (after all, he compiled *The Acid Archives*) but he doesn't overstate the obscure psych records of the 1970s, instead declaring this the period where psychedelics went 'underground' and people started to really devote themselves to the lifestyle, producing fertile yet overlooked results. The history of Owsley and his street acid, or the scientific questions about ayahuasca's psychoactive properties, or the use of the trip as a form of therapy — these are certainly stories that have been written before, but they are synthesised so well here into a work that offers a full understanding of the nature of these experiences without being prescriptive or pseudoscientific. Even the last three chapters, which attempt to forge a theory and model for the experience, are careful not to make proclamations about spirits or anything non-empirical, but just focusing on the shared elements of subjective moments. This book was just over 500 pages, but they are large pages with very small type, making this more like an 800-page book if printed normally. I'm planning another psilocybin experience myself in the near future so I wanted to read this first to have some new context, and now I'm not only ready but actually pretty excited for it. I was struck by how literally every single name mentioned in this book, and it's hundreds of them, is a male one (apart from two female partners of researcher couples — Masters & Houston, and I forget the other). Maybe I'm extra sensitive to patriarchal environments but I wonder if the history of psychedelia really is entirely male dominated, or if men are just the strong personalities who made their mark in the public eye (Timothy Leary, Terence McKenna, etc.). I now see the entire nexus of psychedelia as one created and shaped by men, and I wonder if there is someone working on a feminist reading of the movement that can define a female trip experience (such as, for example, the way that Laura Mulvey defined a new feminist theory of cinema).

804. Summer of Hate by Chris Kraus
Received: 22 July 2017
Started: 13 October 2017
Finished: 15 October 2017
The last (so far) of her four novels, *Summer of Hate* is the most directly novelistic, in that it actually can pass as fiction and not as thinly disguised autobiography mixed with theoretical digressions. Of course, the lead character is still a stand-in for Kraus, working in the art world but having carved out a modest academic career and with a French theorist husband whom she is in an open marriage with. The other lead character is a male black-Hispanic ex-addict who struggles to stay clean and sober, not so much in the realm of substance use but in terms of the watchful eyes of the law. Set between 2004 and 2006, this book is ultimately a compassionate, left-wing critique of the justice system in America, using an underwritten yet strangely believable relationship as the core and contrasting this with the moral decay of Bush's America (which feels already like so long ago now), and also featuring the corrupt and crypto-fascist Maricopa Country sheriff's department under Joe Arpaio, truly one of the worst living Americans. Written primarily from Catt's point of view, the story investigates relationship dependencies, primarily from a financial angle, and creates an almost dystopian portrayal of life under parole, as a person of colour with little access to privilege might experience it. Kraus does an effective job of contrasting his lifestyle with the world of Catt's, which is of course my world and the world that most of the readers will come from; however, it doesn't oversaturate this contrast, allowing itself to fall into beautifully descriptive rhythms, distinctly emanating from Kraus's familiar
voice as I experienced in both *Torpor* and  611  787
Aliens & Anorexia before this. Paul's character felt a bit plastic to me at times, so focused on the straight and narrow, yet I found the details of Albuquerque real estate management weirdly compelling. This scales back the authorial diversions into her own insecurities, which I supposed is a good thing — Catt/Kraus by this point has her shit together, apart from the dangerous interaction with an S&M partner which starts the book. I suppose, given how things end, there's a dark message

of inescapable control that men have over women, which is really the only way to link together Catt's frightening interaction with 'her killer' and the slow draining nature of intimacy with Paul. It's explicitly stated, which maybe isn't necessary, but Kraus isn't always the most delicate of novelists. This feels far more conventional than her other work, though I enjoyed it immensely; I want more of the hybrid form of writing that made her famous, but I don't fault her for doing what she wants to do. If I had the time to re-read Gaddis's *A Frolic of His Own* it would be an interesting comparison to this, at least in terms of being about justice and privilege, though I think honestly at this point in my life Kraus's book resonates deeper with me, even if it's not going to be celebrated as much by the English departments of the world.

805. 2023: A Trilogy by The Justified Ancients of Mu Mu
Received: 17 October 2017
Started: 17 October 2017
Finished: 22 October 2017
The Discordian event of the year! Or was
232 it? *Illuminatus!* is maybe my all-time favourite book or at least the one that had the biggest influence on me; it's even more obviously an influence on Cauty and Drummond, as it's been all over their output, and let's face it, they've accomplished a lot more than I have. So after 23 years of inactivity the JAMs return with a novel, one that is so influenced by Shea & Wilson's classic that it's practically a cover version. I can't imagine many people deriving any pleasure from this book unless you are also deeply interested in Discordian thought, obsessed with *Illuminatus!*, and take British pop music a bit too seriously. I'm ultimately not sure if this was good, tremendously pointless, or both. I had fun reading it, but again, I fit the microdemographic for this. It's not even really worth unravelling the meta- layers, as this was written supposedly by a 'Roberta Antonia Wilson' and essentially combines a cyberpunk/dystopian novel with absurdist nonsense (like an electro band made up of fish) and then inverts everyone's genders and makes it a utopian novel instead. That dys/utopian twist might be the most interesting thing about it all, but it's mostly just fun to spot all of the references. The documentary on Drummond shows his work in The 17 and it's clear that he's been heavily influenced by Fluxus approaches lately; what I loved was how hopeful, strange, and beautiful a lot of those compositions were. I was hoping for something similarly sublime to have crept into *2023* but it's ultimately too deconstructed and meta-fictional to really attain any emotional resonance.

806. Nobody Move by Denis Johnson
Received: 9 October 2017
Started: 18 October 2017
Finished: 23 October 2017
After *Tree of Smoke* this was a weird
diversion, not just for me as a reader but 765
for Johnson as a writer since this was the follow-up to that massive statement. Originally serialised in *Playboy*, *Nobody Move* is a straight crime/noir novel, built almost entirely out of dialogue and with the usual thug baddies, regular Joe hero, and femme fatale. There's very little descriptive writing here, a shame after *Smoke*'s ability to really transport me to a foreign land; it's almost like Johnson just wanted to blow off some steam and write a genre work. I've never read Elmore Leonard yet still have a feeling that Leonard's take on pulp is far more rewarding than this, which was just, well,
fine. I need to read *Jesus' Son* and some 
of his earlier works; this was ultimately just 821
something to pass the time and contained nothing even remotely memorable.

807. The History of Luminous Motion by Scott Bradfield
Received: 5 June 2017
Started: 23 October 2017
Finished: 25 October 2017
I read this in the late 90s, when I was an undergrad, on the enthusiastic recommendation of a WPTS DJ who seemed to recommend a lot of things to me during our brief friendship. I remember loving it, and then forgetting all about it, and I never checked out any of Bradfield's later works even though I saw *What's Wrong With America* at every secondhand bookshop I visited, for years — it was the R.E.M. *Monster* of books. This seems to be highly regarded in almost a cult way as I see its name pop up occasionally and recently discovered that there's even a forgotten film adaptation from the 90s. On a re-read, I understand the appeal, and the dark humour of the style struck me now, but I don't know if it clicked with me so much when I was in college. The novel is narrated by Phillip, a sociopathic 8-year-old boy who dabbles in drink, drugs, the occult, and violence while maintaining a fervent devotion to his addict/trainwreck of

a mother. This does the whole impossibly precocious child thing that has become a fairly standard device among contemporary writers, though this came out in '89 97 so it predates *The Last Samurai*, though 12 it reminds me more of *Ratner's Star*, but that's probably cause this is also a Vintage Contemporaries edition. Bradfield's writing is slightly gonzo while also drenched in poetic rhythms, bubbling with a feminine consciousness that tonally juxtaposes its content with its delivery in a manner that might not appeal to everyone. While it's funny to read a 12-year-old girl lecture the narrator about Marxism and the patriarchy, they comes mixed with soliloquies about light, and nightmarishly psychedelic dream sequences, all brimming with the untold potential of childhood. This is a brilliant novel, worthy of its cult following, as it brought me back to feelings and sensations of my own youth, even though Phillip has little resemblance to an actual child let alone me, and the 80s broken home California setting couldn't feel further from my own experience. There's such a velocity to this narrative, even though it ultimately resolves in a sort of conventional way, but along the way there's comedy, tragedy, horror, and prose which is just beautiful and flowing. It might feel a bit empty – Phillip's search for 'luminous motion' might just be a great phrase the author stumbled upon and employed to give this novel the appearance of more depth – or maybe it's a masterful depiction of familial trauma. It was a joy to revisit and I feel a bit like I belong to a secret club, for fans of this book. Why Bradfield's career sputtered into obscurity after this is a mystery, one that probably won't be resolved until I read something else of his, which won't happen anytime soon since I'll never find any of those here. (Amazingly, *Luminous Motion* was translated into Finnish — the library has a copy where it's called *Matka valon virrassa*).

808. Making of Modern Britain by Andrew Marr
Received: 27 October 2017
Started: 27 October 2017
Finished: 5 November 2017
I'm not usually in the habit of reading books by BBC presenters (well, James Burke and Jonathan Meades would be obvious exceptions) but I was in the mood for a popular history of 20th century Britain and these two books proved to be exactly what I was seeking. I read this one first because it takes place chronologically first (covering the death of Queen Victoria to the end of World War II), even though it was published second of the two, and I think it's the superior work. I'm less connected to the time period, of course, but found the machinations of British politics in the 1910s-1930s fascinating, and I think that the deeper roots of modern Britain are more interesting since they're less obviously visible today. Both books cling closely to politics but this one took lots of time to have sidebars on aspects of popular culture, lifestyles, and other factors about British life, not just the political class. Marr is an excellent writer who can manage to make the most mundane aspects of Parliamentary procedure gripping, even when they happened 100 years ago. Both World Wars end up in here and the first one is a bit more harrowing to read about, as first of all the death toll was much higher, and the war was just so brutal its hard to fathom (plus, as is widely understood now, insanely pointless). There are a lot of fascinating political figures — David Lloyd George, Churchill, Asquith, Joe Chamberlain, Ramsey MacDonald — and some others who were not in office, such as Oswald Mosley, the Mitford sisters (wow!) and the woman who ran all the music hall clubs in the Edwardian era whose name I've already forgotten. There were also some interesting social movements that I had no idea existed, some of which seem quite strange today — the Kibbo Kift and the Greenshirts, for example. I know this wouldn't be taken seriously be pro history buffs but I really enjoyed it, and spent long hours poring through it.

809. We the Animals by Justin Torres
Received: 27 October 2017
Started: 6 November 2017
Finished: 10 November 2017
Torres's short novel is really fucking dark, but it's almost a bait and switch. The first two-thirds are really a beautiful memoir of growing up in a mixed race family, written from the perspective of a 7 year old but without even a trace of the precocious genius trick that *The History of Luminous Motion* employed. 807 This was pure innocence, caught up in magic and memory and with really strong prose that conveyed the universe of the 7 year old and all of its ensuing demons, possibilities and rule-structures. And then, when it turns, that impact is rendered all the more powerful; I wouldn't say it cheapens the book in any way, and in fact is probably a much

more personal and cathartic avenue for the author to have taken, but I personally wanted to stay in the backseat with the brothers and see the world slowly make sense. This is a gutpunch for sure, and an impressive work (his debut, I think). Torres came from the Iowa Writers Workshop and this fulfils every stereotype I have of that scene and it's vision of what literature is, though I don't mean that in the slightest bit to be pejorative.

810. A History of Modern Britain by Andrew Andrew Marr
Received: 10 November 2017
Started: 10 November 2017
Finished: 19 November 2017
Marr's first work of British history was still gripping and fun to read but not quite as good as the followup, as it essentially just talks about politics the whole time. While attempting to seem judicious in his opinions, I would bet he is a classic Labour supporter, just from the way he writes about the more modern figures. And while I knew this period more through culture because of its closer proximity to the present, really getting into the details of these politicians and their lives was still illuminating, and I probably now will inherit Marr's depictions of these administrations as the way I think of them. Of course I already considered Thatcher to be the devil incarnate, having lived in Glasgow and directly observing the effects of her class war, but Marr goes into some of her most arrogant behaviours and also attributes her to being extremely lucky in circumstance. He's possibly even more savage towards Blair, and rightly so — even wondering outright why Blair chose to be a Labour politician at all since he was so disinterested in traditional Labour policies. This was published just before Gordon Brown took over so the Iraq War was still a hot topic and the rage is felt here, though he's fair enough to credit him for the Good Friday Agreement and a few other accomplishments. Culture is only touched upon briefly — a little bit about British humour when writing about the 50s, a bit about punk in the 70s, but that's about it — I found it odd that football is hardly mentioned at all, especially the meteoric rise of the Premier League in the 90s or the great run of Liverpool, Aberdeen, and Everton in Europe in the 80s. Marr makes a case that the Atlee government and Thatcher's first two terms are really the only two governments in modern British history that genuinely transformed the lives of the citizens, of course in very different ways. I suppose great history writing should illustrate the future through the past, and this was written far before Brexit, UKIP, or even the recent Tory governments yet contained similar patterns of conflicted consensus. Reading about how Britain entered Europe in the first place, and how contentious that was, everything now seems to make sense.

811. Love, Sex, Fear, Death: The Inside Story of The Process Church of the Final Judgment by Timothy Wyllie, edited by Adam Parfrey
Received: 9 November 2017
Started: 9 November 2017
Finished: 23 November 2017
The Process Church is pretty fucking interesting; who doesn't enjoy an apocalyptic cult with worldwide reach that peaked during the late 60s/early 70s and had major countercultural crossover? This is written as a supposedly objective tell-all, mostly the narrative of Timothy Wyllie, who was a fairly high-up initiate in the Church with some additional testimonies by minor acolytes. Wyllie's narrative reads like a straightforward act of dictation and is almost surprisingly artless given the heavy imagery and provocative graphic design that these guys used in their newsletters. He details his involvement with the Church founders and the main claim throughout this book is that the true cult leader was a woman from Glasgow, Mary Ann MacLean, who did a good job of insulating herself from the public eye to the point where her husband was seen as the true leader. Whether or not this is true, I don't know; Wyllie clearly has a bone to pick with MacLean and she was long dead when this was published, but the testimonies of the others seem to back this up, and the early days are actually quite fascinating to read about. The Process actually grew out of Scientology but then split quite early on, and it shifted into a catch-all spiritualist cult with heavy Malthusian leanings and a wildly inconsistent worldview. As a study in power, it was far more fascinating than being a book about belief; MacLean had the Process pursuing celebrities and much of Wyllie's account is caught up in namedropping of really random figures (MI6 agents, rock musicians, Rashaan Roland Kirk, etc.) to the point of becoming a distraction. Even within his own account, Wyllie is incapable of conveying if he actually believed any of the shit he was shovelling; the overwhelming sense I get is that misfits glommed

onto the movement because it offered a sense of belonging masquerading as self-improvement. Which is essentially all movements, from art-based ones to the alt-right to every other cult, so there was nothing really too shocking here. The most amusing fact is how they eventually just turned into a Utah-based animal care charity, and I wonder how many once radical movements end up becoming quite tame eventually. The other accounts are really piecemeal and became repetitive, and the chapter by Genesis P-Orridge about how the Process influenced thee Temple ov Psychick Youth is the most obtrusive, as he seems to really value elements of their ravings. What I found most amusing was how obviously the Church leaders would retcon whatever they needed to fit their goals of power and security; this seems to be an established behaviour of cult leaders and when it's laid bare it can be quite amusing. I still would love to read a good, objective biography of Hubbard because he seems like the ultimate grifter, apart from the cabal currently in the White House.

812. Your Band Sucks: What I Saw at Indie Rock's Failed Revolution (But Can No Longer Hear) by Jon Fine
Received: 30 November 2017
Started: 30 November 2017
Finished: 1 December 2017
Mixed feelings about this one. It was super enjoyable to tear through this, as this is the closest thing I've ever read to chronicling my own life experience. Which isn't to say that it was much like my life — Fine is 12 years older than me and his indie rock adventures came as part of the generation that influenced mine. But the insecurities he lays bare in this, by far the most commendable aspect of the book, were spot-on parallels to the same emotional growing pains I went through, as well as the strange ego trappings that came with it. Of course, the overwhelming boy's club nature of this world is difficult to enjoy now, but the post-adolescent era he writes about, about going to Oberlin and forming Bitch Magnet, is the strongest section narratively because that's likely the mentality that indie rock culture was forever stuck in. Again, Fine really comes clean about the foibles of youth but without completely renouncing his behaviour, giving this a propelling, slightly nasty edge that might even make it appeal to someone who didn't care so much about the bands. It's especially amazing that he put in his attitudes towards women, which aren't as coarse as, say, the old Big Black tour diary from *Forced Exposure*, but still way out of step with 2015's approach to sensitivity. Most of the book is spent on Bitch Magnet; Vineland hardly gets discussed musically, only mentioned as an example of total failure, and I guess they truly were a failure in that sense since they never even got an LP out. (Which I can relate to.) Coming to terms with one's lack of commercial success can actually be compelling, but Fine never makes it clear what exactly he was after. Money? Fans? Fame? It seems like he spent the intro and first chapters talking about how special and unique the insular, tiny world of indie rock was, then the middle of the book whining about how no one cared, and then the end accepting it. Which is a complete narrative arc, I suppose. Way too many pages are spent chronicling the Bitch Magnet reunion, but of course it was fresher history, and is also an OK travelogue, especially when describing the Asian shows. The chapters in New York where he gave in to dance music and drugs are the least compelling, but I also don't find much of that era of music interesting. Fine still feels really strong about his musical opinions, way, way, way more than I care about mine now (and again, I'm 12 years younger than him); it's almost like admitting that he places way too much emphasis on the purity of rock riffs (or whatever bullshit he goes on about) would fail to justify the dickish ways he treated people in the past (and that's even acknowledging what he owned up to already and apologises for). I guess maybe my own tastes are somewhat counter to his; he reminds me of all those annoying old Pittsburgh guys who are totally stuck in the era that Bitch Magnet came from, getting way too concerned with, for example, what kind of guitar amp someone used and who can play in 11/7 time and being dismissive of warmer, more humanistic music. Maybe it's also that I never really got Bitch Magnet. As a teenager, everyone used to tell me that if I liked Rodan, I should listen to Slint, who Rodan ripped off; and then if I liked Slint, I should listen to Bastro and Bitch Magnet, who Slint allegedly ripped off. That's not the case at all; Fine makes it clear that Bitch Magnet and Slint were peers, but maybe, just maybe, I should revisit *Star Booty* now and check out *Ben Hur,* which I've never heard. After all, I consider Seam's *The Problem With Me* to be one of the genre's high water marks and still listen to it regularly, and I've been rocking Slint's *Tweez* a ton lately, ever since

watching that documentary. But Fine still 1678 finds it necessary to shit on Small Factory in a book published twenty years after Small Factory broke up because he found their live show annoying and indie-pop 'weak'. Taste is subjective, but Small Factory were incredible and a band I'll still be listening to deep into my old age instead of Bitch Magnet. It's all just macho posturing, sure, and I understand because I came from it too – it took me years to escape the Isle of Strong Opinions and it didn't help that I was often surrounded by people who traded in them. Everyone has to work out their masculinity and personal politics, but like stand-up comedy, being obscure and close-knit tends to foster reactionary viewpoints and protectionism. This is really why this book hit home — as much as Fine clearly laid out the motivations of the male indie kid ego, the true story was between the lines. It would be curious to write my own version of this, and I'm sure one of my peers will; anyway, my own maximum involvement with being part of anything wasn't indie rock, but the mid-00s experimental/'noise' world, of which I was really peripheral anyway, though I'm sure it will be written by someone eventually and I may even make an appearance.

813. Strange Rebels: 1979 and the Birth of the 21st Century by Christian Caryl
Received: 3 December 2017
Started: 3 December 2017
Finished: 9 December 2017

I'm in a mood for popular histories after the Andrew Marr, and this was a good followup, 808, 810 being a chronicle of 1979, presenting it as a year that disproportionately affected the future of the world. Caryl's book follows several parallel storylines: Thatcher, the Iranian revolution, the Afghani revolution, the ascension of Pope John Paul II, and Deng Xiaoping's economic reforms in Communist China. Except for the Afghanistan storyline, these all feature unique individuals who led their own forms of revolutions, none of which resembled traditional ones in that they tended to reinforce either free market or theocratic ideas. It's a good premise for structuring a history around and it resonates quite well with today's new right-wing movements, who fancy themselves as anti-establishment rebels even though their goals ultimately just reinforce traditional forms of power. There's none of that here, as Caryl sticks to 1979 (with its effects on the subsequent years addressed in the final chapters) and elegantly weaves together the narratives. His writing is mostly unbiased, as I genuinely couldn't tell his political leanings from most of the book, and only at the end when describing the effects of Thatcher's revolution did I sense a pro-Tory slant (when it's mentioned that the amount of Britons living in poverty rose from 5 million to 14 million during her reign, but that's just presented as an almost dismissed 'oh, by the way' aside, then it's pretty clear that he's drank the Kool-Aid). Caryl shows his mettle in writing about the intellectual underpinnings of the Iranian revolution and the theory of the Islamic State, and despite the temptation to write about the exacerbation of the Islamic fundamentalist movement in subsequent years, he mostly stays focused on the time period in question. Most interestingly is that out of the figures central to the book, the Pope almost seems the most radical, and his anti-Communist political manoeuvring is presented as justification for his era of extreme social conservatism and support for various human rights abuses, with again the only criticism coming as a mention of the child abuse scandals that plagued the end of his reign. Given how depressing all of these 'revolutions' turned out, I found this really pleasurable to read, especially as the United States played almost no role in this story so it was nice to read something not so American-centric for once.

814. Perfidia by James Ellroy
Received: 31 October 2017
Started: 21 November 2017
Finished: 16 December 2017

Okay, I mean, 800 pages is pretty long for any book but I'm not usually fazed by length. But 800 pages of Ellroy seemed especially daunting, not because I thought it would be too experimental or difficult to comprehend, but because I figured the depravity would be overwhelming by the end. But actually, *Perfidia* was way less grisly than the other Ellroy I've read; the wall-to-wall racial slurs were the most difficult aspect of it and they weren't even that bad, just an accurate reflection of the 1940s era. And stylistically, this felt a little bit more 'full' than *American Tabloid*. It's still made 471 up of very short sentences, but they aren't quite as minimal and there's a lot more traditional narrative exposition here. While I find his minimalist style fascinating, I'm not sure if I could have endured 800 pages of it. I find it amazingly ambitious that he's writing a *second* LA Quartet, a massive

prequel, and that the characters in it will appear throughout not just the original Quartet but also through the Underworld USA trilogy; the resulting 11 books, when he finishes them, will be a mammoth literary world and a fascinating fictional appraisal of the hidden mid-20th century American history. I remembered plenty of characters from *The Black Dahlia* and also even a few
641 from *American Tabloid*, but it was a lot, and I found myself wishing I had something like a baseball card for each of them to keep track. *Perfidia* was a pretty good read, which I expected, and addressing Japanese internment is a timely concept now in these racially charged times, though I don't know if that was intended. What it does explore is extreme ideologies, not mere racism; everyone in the book tends towards fascism or communism and the 1941 setting is really sort of exciting, as it's long before neoliberalism began and such ideologies faded out of the realm of possibility. The plot was super complicated, but explained throughout (by what felt like every character, to every other character, constantly), so it wasn't really a mystery nor was it particularly suspenseful. That's a bold move for a 'crime fiction' author, as he instead chose to flesh out the character studies to an insane degree, or at least the four main ones. This might be where the novel fails; all four voices essentially feel like the same narrator, and the omniscience is a bit confusing (Kay Lake's 'diary' explicitly renders all of this stuff in first-person but the others are written third person, and it's not always clear who the narrative is privileging at certain moments). Some of the dialogue is hard to take, either needlessly expositional or sounding weirdly legal. There's ludicrous amounts of intrigue and double-crossing and vigilante justice and coverups and everything else one might expect; by the end every character has been revealed to be totally disgusting and amoral, and the two most sympathetic characters mostly just seem so because one is female and one is Japanese-American. The Kay Lake character does feel like the fantasy of a man who is obsessed with genre fiction but doesn't really know real-life women; she is a sexual libertine in 1941 and portrayed as passionate and emotional, which feels a bit too easy of a 'female' type. The length of this is a bit absurd too — the last 100 pages were superfluous and I would have been happier if this had come in around 600, but it was never hard to get through or anything. I guess there's certain ethics about using real-life figures so much — the novel is about a 50/50 mixture (which the dramatis personae in the back helps keep straight) and considering that Ellroy attributes murders and other crimes to some of them, I really wonder if he based some of this on research or if it's irresponsible conjecture.

815. JPod by Douglas Coupland
Received: 18 December 2017
Started: 19 December 2017
Finished: 20 December 2017
I didn't think this was very good, but it was entertaining and fun to read I guess. I'm not a big Coupland fan beyond *Microserfs*, to which this was so similar it was almost a cover version. I suppose this is more than just a retread, as it updates the techie lifestyle to the mid-00s instead of the 90s, and with the appropriate cultural shifts. But, man, do the 00s seem super weird already, in retrospect. This was written in 2006-2007, so smart phones aren't yet a thing but vacuous pop culture Internet nonsense saturates this book, and instead of a fairly compelling portrait of different, changing people at a curious moment in time (like *Microserfs* was), we just get a bunch of goofball comedy antics. The characters are really one-dimensional and the crazy parents provide the most interesting content, though the characterisations are so boilerplate that it lost any possibility of being compelling. The cut and paste filler around the chapters also failed to contribute anything to the narrative or to even be funny — it's just random nonsense that is vaguely about computers, and it came off as lazy. Worst of all was Coupland's insertion of himself into the novel, albeit as a malignant force, and it's neither metafictionally impressive nor funny — just, again, lazy. It all builds up to him revealing some sort of digital imaging product, which is kinda weird, because it doesn't serve any purpose in the narrative. I can try to find some actual literary value here — the detachment and superficiality of the characters is haunting and prescient; the ridiculous business decisions of the video game company could be taken as satire. But otherwise it's just kinda blah. Apparently this was made into a TV show in Canada but I'll give that a miss for sure.

816. Fantasyland: How America Went Haywire: A 500-Year History by Kurt Andersen
Received: 20 December 2017
Started: 20 December 2017
Finished: 28 December 2017
If this had been what it promised, I would have been delighted – a cultural history of delusion in America, written by *Spy* magazine's Kurt Andersen. But *Fantasyland* fails to get to any real insights on my native people, mostly being a rant against pseudoscience, spirituality, and fantasy. I agree with Andersen for the most part, but his approach actually isn't curmudgeonly *enough*, for example in the manner that someone like Paul Fussel might have written this. I found myself imagining the voice of Bill Maher in my head as I read this, and that's never a good thing (though Maher himself also comes under fire for endorsing medical quackery here). The chapters on the first 200 years of America are the most interesting, as they contained the least redundancy with information I was already aware of, but Andersen just picks and chooses his narrative and it feels lazy and rushed, despite being over 500 pages in total. The book is mostly unsourced, except in the last 20% when he starts to really dig in against fundamentalist Christianity, as he cites numerous opinion polls about contemporary America's beliefs in all sorts of nonsense. This is a case of preaching to the converted, I suppose — I'm extremely critical of alternative medicine and my politics are far to the left of Andersen's, so I found myself rushing through this bored, going "uh-huh, uh-huh" and waiting for something either interesting or hilarious to be revealed. If anything, I found Andersen's arguments a bit too much, but not because they are extreme, just because they are boring. He rants about the turn towards fantasy in popular culture, and makes some good points, but is unwilling to afford anyone the joy of imagination. Strange and magickal thinking is a goal for my life, and when you have someone attacking people who dye their hair for being escapists, it starts to feel stifling. The last 20% I pretty much skimmed, as this covered the recent years and I didn't need to read another analysis of the Internet, Fake News, Trump, the alt-right, etc. I read this quickly but still didn't see any significant insights; indeed, the early parts were the best, and also the funniest, such as when he described Mormonism as 'fan fiction' about Christianity and the writing about 1800s alternative medicine. Having never considered these ideas in the form of a continuum, I did find it interesting that these periods seem to come and go in waves. This may be just how Andersen chose to frame his material, as I never thought of 1900-1960 as a particularly rational "Age of Reason"; his omissions may be the most interesting thing about this. Still, I guess this could be a good gateway drug for the mind of a youngster, to turn them towards skepticism. For me, though, it was just remedial-level reading, which was maybe the right choice given my vision was blurry (in my left eye) while reading most of this.

817. Nocilla Dream by Agustin Fernandez Mallo
Received: 10 December 2017
Started: 10 December 2017
Finished: 30 December 2017
Maybe the best work of fiction I read this year? It's a short read, but I savoured it. *Nocilla Dream* is a really curious and experimental collection of short vignettes, sort of connected, sort of not, but mysterious in the way they are thematically linked. Other short chapters, maybe 1/3 of the entire book, are quotations about technology, science, or other technical matters, presented in a way that they start to feel like part of the 'plot'. There's not enough time to get used to any of the characters, but the scenarios are fascinating in that I don't feel like these themes have been portrayed much elsewhere or at least not so brilliantly, despite being insanely indicative of contemporary existence. It's easy to digest yet sublime in its execution, defining a new way for fiction to emerge from the media stream that is evocative and powerful. It's all extremely fragmentary, but it adds up. I found myself awestruck not by any particular passage but by the way it all added into some sort of snapshot, focused around certainly places around a Nevada highway but also taking us to Singaport airport and numerous other outliers. Writing some sort of comment here is challenging because this is all about the need to summarise and organise, but unlike the fiction of, say, Thomas Pynchon, which would mock such attempts, it's nonjudgmental, unconcerned with completeness or accuracy. Fuck. I'll be thinking about this for ages; next, on to the sequel.

818. Fire and Fury: Inside the Trump White House by Michael Wolff
Received: 6 January 2018
Started: 6 January 2018
Finished: 7 January 2018
I have a master's degree in English Literature. I'm not the most well-read person, but I'm familiar with a lot of the Greek classics, as well as the major works of Shakespeare; I've read *Moby Dick* and Hawthorne and some Henry James and most of James Joyce and Faulkner's Big Four, and Virginia Woolf (and Douglas Woolf too, for that matter) and of course many/most of the grand postmodernists (Gaddis, Pynchon, DeLillo, etc.). I would hesitate to call myself an expert on literature, but I think over the years I have refined my tastes and can evaluate literature critically, with a good understanding of its history and context. With all of that said, I think that *Fire and Fury: Inside the Trump White House* is probably the greatest work of literature that has ever existed. Great literature explores the human condition, and this book has that in spades. As a study in power, narcissism and delusion it's unparalleled, and as an investigation of what Arendt famously dubbed 'the banality of evil', or in this case perhaps 'the Bannonality of evil' it goes much further than I imagined. Seriously, though, this isn't so much a book about Trump but about the power struggle between 'Jarvanka' and Bannon, with Reince Preibus the third party, occasionally switching sides; Trump himself functions more like a natural disaster than an actual character, and is the catalyst for the narrative. I had hesitations about wanting to relive the nightmare that was the past year, but this was so fucking hilarious, absolutely sidesplitting in places, that I'm totally satisfied, even though I never read books by political hack journalists. I can't fault Wolff as a writer — his vocabulary is impressive and this doesn't try to simplify anything; it's a nice device to describe incredibly dumb people using sophisticated language, or at least on a reading level higher than anyone in the Trump family could manage. Perhaps the most flabbergasting thing about the adventures chronicled here is the sheer amount of boneheaded stupidity in that family. Kushner and Ivanka, who have been portrayed by the sympathetic/sycophantic media (desperate to have anyone to pin their centrist-liberal hopes on) as the most intelligent people in the administration, are revealed by Wolff to be perhaps the least intelligent of all, unless you count Don Jr and the other son. This is really a book about Bannon — not Bannonism or whatever his nationalist deconstruction of administration and policy will be called — but Bannon the person, careening through the most tumultuous six months in American political history with a velocity that is almost admirable. I don't want to say he's likeable or the hero here, but he's certainly the centre of the narrative and by far the most interesting person possibly to ever work in such a high position. On the *Deadspin* podcast recently the hosts tried to recall all of the fucked up shit that Trump did in 2017 and they couldn't remember back more than a few weeks, the list was so long. Still, I found myself marvelling that certain elements were not mentioned here, even small details such as how the letter firing Comey claimed that Comey explicitly pointed out three times that Trump was not under investigation. But there was enough hilarious material here for sure, some of which I forgot about — a lot was information I was already familiar with, through the rumours that had leaked in various stories as the year went on, but provided here in the context of who was actually doing the leaking (amazingly, Trump himself is the source of most of the leaks inadvertently because he was too stupid when gabbing to his billionaire friends to request their confidence) they attained a majestic, almost transcendent level of storytelling power. And, again, there are so many amazing moments in this book that you could almost blink and miss Wolff's snide putdowns, such as referring to Kellyanne Conway's 'antifeminist feminism' or the many descriptions of Bannon's disheveled appearance. And, my god, the entire Scaramucci episode! By the end, when Bannon is tossed out and Kelly comes to establish order, I had tears in my eyes — sadness that this administration didn't get to crash and burn a little further, and tears of laughter after reading Bannon's directly quoted rant that went on for several pages. It's also sad that there isn't more Gorka in this book, as he only gets a mention. It's been said a million times that you couldn't make this stuff up, that truth is stranger than fiction and all those other clichés; what's most remarkable here is that this is being allowed to go on. The real damning is not towards Trump (who, let's face it, is just a senile old fraud) but towards those who enable him and continue to support him. The ultimately cowardice and reprehensibility of the Republican Party is not found in Trump himself (the man is not a Republican or anything at all — he is utterly without ideology) but in how no

one is trying to stop him. I know that's not an original observation, but Wolff's book makes this most evident, even though Paul Ryan only barely appears. The other major missing character would be the American people themselves, rarely even referred to; I don't know if this was an intentional stylistic device by Wolff but it worked amazingly well to make this seem like some terrible fantasy or satire, which of course we all know it isn't; it's a terrifying and awesome truth. Some would say that to trivialise such a malevolent and destructive demagogue as mere comedy is irresponsible of me, but this book actually did a lot to reassure me that things are going to probably be OK. I'll still maintain that the Bush administration was 1000x worse than these what these fuckheads are doing now, for the main reason that they were ideologically evil *and* competent (and there's a million dead people in the Middle East to show for it). Trump's cabal are genuinely morons, the ones laughed out of the Establishment, who have even fewer ideas than the GOP leadership (another delightful thing are the multiple times that Trump tries to get Guiliani or Chris Christie roles in his administration, or on the Supreme Court, not understanding how toxic and unqualified they are and that Senate confirmation would never happen). I know the idiot might start a nuclear war via Twitter and the GOP tax bill that just passed is the most egregiously horrendous act of public policy of my lifetime, but that would have happened much more quickly had any other Republican been in the White House. I really feel that we are better off with Trump in the White House being ineffective and destructive to not only the Republican party but to the entire ideology of right-wing populism than if we had a toothless centrist like Hillary Clinton as president, which would stoke the fires of the right even further while continuing the same ruinous, neoliberal policies that got us into this mess.

819. Franny and Zooey by J. D. Salinger
Received: 18 December 2017
Started: 2 January 2018
Finished: 16 January 2018
This may become a standard thing I go through every few years; in this case I was just killing time in the library and saw it on the shelf and felt like re-reading it. Though I

again think it might be time to re-read *Raise*
432 *High* as it's always nice to assign works to life moments and the idea of *Catcher in the Rye* being the perfect teenage book, *F&Z* the perfect 20s book, and *RHtFBC/S,al* the perfect 30s book is just too neat and pat of a classification to pass up – so I better make sure it applies. I had forgotten just how savage and irascible Zooey is, particularly with his mother; somehow the depictions of the New York cultural class in Salinger's books doesn't irritate me as much as in, say, the latest Noah Baumbach film; it's my own bias 
I guess, a big pass I give to him. The very 1463
American approach to spirituality is what really defines this book, and this lunch-buffet style of it that Franny seems to pick from. The weights of the Glass family tragedies are also really saturated throughout, so much that the more crass Zooey lines are undercut with a nasty aftertaste, loaded in repression and pain. The 'Franny' section as well is just teetering on the edge of post-adolescent breakdown, and thinking about it in line of today's information age or whatever, it feels remarkable prescient, as if Salinger in the 1950s was looking ahead to the future psychoses being unlocked by emergent modernism. A bit like *Homo*
Faber, or maybe not at all like it. Despite 610
being rooted in anxiety + cruelty, I really find *Franny and Zooey* fun, which maybe says more about me than I'd like it to. Not sure if this is still in my all-time pantheon, but I'm not sure it ever was or why I still default to such rankings and classifications.

820. Forbidden Line by Paul Stanbridge
Received: 22 July 2017
Started: 25 October 2017
Finished: 5 February 2018
This took awhile to get through, though for being part of the 'difficult fiction' genre, it wasn't actually all that difficult. But it's a real gem, a book I would have never discovered in a million years if it hadn't been enthusiastically recommended to me by a friend, who himself is an old friend of the author, and seconded by my friend's wife. *Forbidden Line* is a contemporary deconstruction of *Don Quixote*, but I didn't mind that so much, for although I never finished *Quixote*, it's influence and cultural impact is something that I'm well familiar with. The two protagonists of *Line* travel from Essex into London on an aimless, modern day quest that probably parallels *Quixote* directly but is really a map of insane linguistic devices, faux scientific theories, and hilarious textual games. This is comic experimental fiction of the highest order, the kind of treasure that Dalkey Archive

usually rescues from obscurity and delivers to slightly larger audiences — I won't be surprised if they reprint this in a decade or two, if print still exists then. There were aspects of this that were sidesplitting and other parts I found difficult to force my way through. Stanbridge is a hell of a stylist, and he captures the pastoral rancour of the Southern people and the fecund squalor of the commonfolk; it reminded me of Beckett as his most shit and shovel, or like being trapped inside a folk tune gone bad. In a way this makes a perfect setting for a post-Brexit novel, and there's a feeling of reverse anachronism here, as we follow Don and Is through contemporary times which slowly start to disintegrate. By the end, all logical constructs have fallen in on themselves, and while it's turn towards metafiction was never exactly a surprise, it was almost a little too obvious. Doesn't matter; there's too much that is rewarding about *Forbidden Line*, though it's obtuse delivery and general sense of being out-of-step with the times will probably limit its audience, which is sad. I couldn't think of anything further away from the '*Guardian* book' classification that I derisively assign to contemporary British fiction that is too easy and crowd-pleasing. Please find this, world.

821. Jesus' Son by Denis Johnson
Received: 19 February 2018
Started: 19 February 2018
Finished: 20 February 2018
My only complaint about *Jesus' Son* is the punctuation in the title, which while technically a correct option, is not as preferable as *Jesus's Son* would have been to these eyes. This book is a cult classic, but that suggests it only appeals to people for whom literature is a cultural affectation, which diminishes Johnson's talent. Which is not to say that I respect any sort of critical canon over the tastes of the so-called cult, but anyway, Johnson eventually came around to be critically adored by the end of his career, as the press around *Tree of*
765 *Smoke* more or less set it up to be a triumph before anyone had actually read it. I thought *Tree of Smoke* was masterful while elliptical, so reading his most-beloved book finally, over two decades after I first meant to, was somewhat of a surprise. There's a velocity to these stories that comes from a completely different place than *Smoke*, and the term 'hallucinatory' is quite applicable here, even if the prose is less psychedelic than other writers. It's hallucinatory in the way short explosions of imagery come like rushes, simulating an actual chemical experience without going overboard in its metaphors. The first-person narrator of each story situates it in a very intimate emotional space, even as they hurtle through rash decisions, irresponsible behaviours, and precarious scenarios. To point out how non-judgemental the authorial voice here seems unnecessary given the long tradition of literature of the underclass (a tradition *Jesus' Son* definitely adheres to, making it equally at home with the Beats, or Lifter Puller lyrics), but I suppose emerging at the end of the 1980s, this actually was quietly radical. Not just to humanise these drifters and addicts, but also to build fiction from their experiences in which their world becomes commonplace rather than a cautionary tale. The story about the baby rabbits dying in the truck was the most memorable, at least until the voyeuristic final story, but all are still resonating with me (though it's such a short collection that they are are still fresh in my mind).

822. Against the Day by Thomas Pynchon
Received: (already owned)
Started: 27 December 2017
Finished: 3 March 2018
Now that I've re-read this and can put it into the context of his two subsequent novels, I see a real trajectory towards lucidity starting here. *Against the Day* is long — really, really long (I would even argue that it's a little bit too long) — but otherwise it's Pynchon writing without gloves on, making no bones about his worldview. Going all the way back to *V* (a novel which is more and more stunning the more I think about it), Pynchon has always been deeply committed to us-vs-them themes, the preterite vs the elect, the oppressed vs the oppressors, etc.; this is the major axis upon which he built *AtD* as well. But this duality isn't just a simple political theme but rather a starting point, which starts to twist into a helix until it becomes the structural motif of the entire book, which eventually implicates time and history itself. That's not to say that this novel isn't deeply saturated in ambiguity, but even this is done in service to the aims of the book rather than being merely stylistically obtuse (not to say his earlier work is obtuse for no reason, but here he achieved a total thematic integration of style and structure). After reading *Gravity's Rainbow* and *Mason*
& Dixon with annotations, I was stunned 336 524

at the historical precision of his novels; *AtD* is no less researched, but deliberately makes the timeline inexact, occasionally anachronistic and contradictory, all to further the blur. Because the blurriness is again a theme, the Iceland Spar mineral is perhaps a stand-in for the mediating power of literature and art itself? There's so much to unpack here, and so many questions. Yet I still feel that this is a book of almost fierce clarity, defining a world that is not quite ours but perhaps impossibly one with it too (the Counter-Earth, of course).

I assume this was begun in the 90s; that he started writing it after *M&D* was published, as the turmoil of this time shows. It was released in 2006, at the height of the Bush-Cheney criminal empire, and Pynchon's own words in his press release made a smirking claim that no similarity between the book and current events was to be intended or inferred. So of course it fucking was, and this is as left wing as an 1100 page postmodern epic can be, at least for one set a century ago. The anarchists and bombers of this book are almost consistently, unapologetically the good guys, and if there are any moral qualms about their violence it's best left for another writer to tackle. Pynchon has other concerns, and they are insane and erudite at the same time. For being one of America's most celebrated and esteemed novelists, he certainly tends towards the cartoonish, and *AtD* has that in spades, most explicitly through the Chums of Chance characters but elsewhere throughout the text.

But this book is shockingly relevant now, a decade after it was published, as the Second Gilded Age is upon is, and the liberal world order that was being constructed during *AtD*'s time is now collapsing under its own excesses (while scapegoating immigration through racial tension). All of that is here; the book is populated by colonial residue, Balkan anarchists, and others who were displaced by Scarsdale Vibe and his cabal (who use technology to further solidify their power — the predecessors of today's tech giants and industrial titans). It's a rather grandiose and fantastic vision that on the surface might seem too absurd to be meaningful, but therein lies the impact of great fiction again — it resonates, and meditates upon our reality. This may be the ultimate novel of late capitalism, perhaps because it's set in middle capitalism, posit then as an era of early unraveling.

For something so sprawling, I keep feeling a pull back towards the Colorado setting, which is really the heart and soul of the book. This is a true Western, and that it succeeds in the adventure angle while also managing the have whole Traverse family dynamic as a compelling plot point is another aspect that makes this a remarkable accomplishment. It's this material that I remembered the most from my first reading, while the latter half of the novel's geographical dispersion I had completely forgotten. Which is a bit of a shame; I read this along with the pynchonwiki.com annotations again, which have only grown in their depth over the last decade, and by page 800 fatigue was starting to set in, so I didn't learn as much about Macedonian geography, Turkish fin-de-siècle politics, or German mathematicians as I should have. It's always there to go back to, of course, but this was a truly exhausting book. At times reading it felt like the single most enjoyable experience I could imagine, and at others it felt absolutely punishing.

And this takes me back to Pynchon's 'late style' of his most recent two books. I remembered this as his difficult, overstuffed magnum opus, which made the shift towards colloquial genre in *Inherent Vice* surprising when it came out. 413, 589 After revisiting it, I'd say *AtD* certainly is stuffed, and one of his three magnum opuses, but it's not really difficult — it has something to say, and it says it, and as someone who has accepted the lack of closure and resolution in postmodern fiction for over 20 years now, I think it's even pretty clear what it says. This book is called *Against the Day* and there's no subtlety to how often it invokes variations of its title, either embedded in deeply beautiful and lyrical prose passages or in the plot points itself, which deal with vector mathematics, invisible cities, bilocation and doppelgangers, air, light, ether, capitalism's disruption of the aforementioned through its arrhythmic pulse of electricity and industrialism, etc. It's a shame that I started to wear down so much towards the end, because the final chapters contain some of the most conclusive statements of purpose, and it concludes with a rather melancholy wrap-up chapter that resists too many happy endings but rather realistically portrays the dynamics of human interaction.

I actually want to read more Pynchon now, which is another dangerous aspect of re-reading him. He's addictive. I want to go back and read *V* again, and also *Bleeding*

Edge. These endpoints of his oeuvre are thick with reflections and refractions of ideas here, from technology and control to the way ethnic groups are portrayed (genuinely with admiration and compassion). But I'm going to resist at least for the time being and get back to all of the other books I have currently unfinished.

823. Air Guitar: Essays on Art & Democracy by Dave Hickey
Received: 9 February 2018
Started: 23 February 2018
Finished: 6 March 2018
My partner randomly grabbed this from her Academy library, thinking that I might like it, and she was right! Hickey is a curator and critic who has been around the art world for a long time, but this doesn't deal with art so directly, or at least not so much with contemporary art. The subtitle 'essays on art and democracy' is a bit misleading, unless you take them all to be about the general state of culture in liberal late capitalism. Hickey is a great writer, opinionated and talented with language but without letting his style overwhelm his content. His more personal recollections about growing up as the children of jazz musicians in the 1950s are the most enjoyable, as well as the two essays where he writes in the voice of others — one as Hank Williams's ghost, and one as the wrestler Godiva from G.L.O.W. These experiments would fail under a less talented writer but Hickey infuses both with a well-paced empathy, which makes them into a weird type of biographical fiction, or fiction-leaning non-fiction, if that makes any sense. Other topics include Liberace and the city of Las Vegas (where Hickey lived at the time of this writing). This was written 20 years ago so I expected it to be more or less obsolete in terms of how the culture world functions, but it held up pretty well, especially some of the more wizened observations about youth movements. I see he just published a second collection, which I'd really like to read.

824. It Still Moves by Amanda Petrusich
Received: 3 March 2018
Started: 3 March 2018
Finished: 9 March 2018
Here's a pleasant enough book by a Brooklyn-based writer who has that youthful bloggy perspective, which makes the writing style feel familiar, as it could be someone who writes for Gawker or Vox or one of the other Internet media companies. I grabbed this off the shelf while I was killing some time in the library, and it was a nice read, if a bit inconsistent. The first half is much more of a travel book than a book about music, and while the stories of Sun Records, Elvis, Robert Johnson etc. have been told before, it's somewhat interesting to read about the tourism industry that's emerged around it all now. Petrusich's theme is 'Americana' but she thankfully takes a sceptical approach to the term, looking at how manufactured and meaningless it ultimately is. Her enthusiasm for the music carries through, as the last few chapters have little to do with travelling and just chronicle the stories of Woody Guthrie and the then-contemporary freak folk movement centred on Brattleboro and Western Mass. That last chapter made this feel like a relic from my own life, as it writes about a lot of people I know and a scene that I used to be tangentially part of — David's 'New Weird America' article is quoted at length, and a lot is written about Matt Valentine and the Brattleboro Free Folk Festival, as if that was some sort of Newport of the era. I guess it was at the time, or at least seemed like some great watershed moment, but a decade later all of that stuff is pretty much forgotten and Petrusich barely describes the music, so someone unfamiliar with it might mistakenly think that MV & EE were actually worthwhile music. I guess I got a little bit nostalgic even though I didn't learn anything; one musician, I think the Fruit Bats guy, says how the public tastes tend to cycle through a desire for acoustic instruments and a desire for more electronic ones. It's an oversimplification but it certainly describes what happened to that scene since this was written, though the effects of the Internet (already mentioned here as breaking down geography-based scenes) are also a factor. Anyway back to the book — fluff reading, ultimately, but the best chapter is the one having nothing directly to do with music at all, instead looking at Cracker Barrel restaurants and the image that they sell.

825. The Murmuring of the Artistic Multitude: Global Art, Politics and Post-Fordism by Pascal Gielen
Received: 9 February 2018
Started: 9 February 2018
Finished: 21 March 2018
A local art professor suggested that I possibly study with Gielen as a PhD in Belgium, so I looked into his work. This was the third edition of this book, which was

more of a collection of essays than a linear theme, though of course everything was connected. I'm not sure that anything here was groundbreaking for me, as I'm already well aware of how neoliberalism leads to the exploitation of artists. Still, there were some great passages here, and his tendency to propose models was sort of fun, particularly the 2-axis mapping of community art between auto- and allo-relational and digestive/subversive. A lot of the more art world stuff was unsurprisingly uninteresting to me, especially the politics of Belgian curators, but despite the art world being the subject of this book, there were still a lot of good ideas present. In the more theoretical sections he attempts to move beyond Bordieu and bring in Virno's ideas of biopolitics, which is something I wish was explored further, as it's interesting to me but I'm not that familiar with it. Gielen's term 'repressive liberalism' ties in nicely with David Graber's book *The Utopia*
696 *of Rules*, and the discussion of ethics at the end of the book, while not necessarily belonging with the overall argument, was really clearly articulated. As Gielen didn't reply to my email, I guess I won't be studying with him any time soon, but it was good to take this in and again it's encouraging me to finish *Empire* (if only so I can move on to *Multitude*).

826. Gnomon by Nick Harkaway
Received: 3 March 2018
Started: 3 March 2018
Finished: 21 March 2018
I've read a lot of long books and I just finished *Against the Day* before this; I
243, 822 tend to like big, sprawling worlds that one can get lost in, where the ideas can barely be contained and the book feels more like a set of unexplored potentials than a taut tale. Unfortunately, *Gnomon*, despite being mostly fun and enjoyable throughout, wasn't this; it was long merely because it was poorly edited, and by the end I just wanted it to be over. Harkaway's vocabulary is vast, but this alone doesn't make for good writing. His tendency to over-explain the plot through redundant infodumps reminded me of Neal Stephenson, except somehow I still couldn't manage to follow what was going on, which is maybe due to my own lack of concentration or possibly a deficiency of the writer; I'll go with the latter hypothesis. Actually, this reminded me of Stephenson in multiple ways, being a technology-based sci-fi thriller with lots of historical fascination, though this was far less fixated on 'hard' tech veracity than something like *Cryptonomicon* was. At about halfway through the book I was actually thinking of it as if it were a hybrid of Stephenson's more ambitious novels and *A Smuggler's Bible* by Joseph McElroy, which is an astounding combi- 11, 455
nation of influences. But as it progressed, the different voices began to repeat and this became much more caught up in it's indictment of a potential future surveillance state (one that does not seem so far away, especially being set in London where CCTV has been ubiquitous for some time) and let its more stylistic pleasures sink to the bottom. I feel like I'm being harsh because there was a lot I liked about *Gnomon* — the ambition is nothing to fault it for, and some of the more ambiguous mysteries held my interest at first. He used mostly female characters here, but his interface to feminine emotion and sexuality felt clumsy (at best) and occasionally it became hard to separate the narrators, though I guess that was the 'point'. His afterward bragged that there were puzzles and layers hidden throughout, yet I didn't feel drawn to unravel any of them. The shark motif was bizarre and surely rooted in some allusions to past works, mythological and/or pop culture-based, but I kept thinking about the first *Dirk Gently* TV season and *The Raw Shark Texts*. Despite these gripes, I'm 493
curious enough that I will probably read Harkaway's earlier works, which are shorter.

827. Essayism by Brian Dillon
Received: 15 March 2018
Started: 22 March 2018
Finished: 25 March 2018
What a wonderful little volume of personal-infused literary criticism! Dillon's analysis of the essay isn't concerned with a precise definition, but with the very essay-like fluidity that wanders, breathes and inhabits possibilities. It's a spot-on example of the essay itself, and rather than get bogged down with its own meta-level intensity, Dillon brings his own experiences into play, as any good essayist should, but taking things a bit further than I expected, especially when discussing his battle with depression. It doesn't get sad-sacky or emotional, but just provides a backdrop to explain, for example, why he was interested in Barthes, or Robert Burton, or any of the other names referenced in this. He stays mostly in the mid-20th century, and deals with William H. Gass, Virginia Woolf, Joan
Didion, and Elizabeth Hardwick as well as 56

862

Sebald, Wallace, and others, but this isn't really straight literary criticism at all. Flowing and precise at the same time, *Essayism* triumphed when it was doing the least, allowing each short chapter to resonate into the space of the next one. Dillon, I think, comes from an art background, but this is very much rooted in the literary traditions and he is well-read without being annoying about it. Again, Fitzcarraldo Editions has struck gold; maybe it's time to read everything they publish?

828. Art Sex Music by Cosey Fanni Tutti
Received: 17 March 2018
Started: 22 March 2018
Finished: 26 March 2018
Ms. Tutti's autobiography/memoir (what is the difference, really?) delivers on the three topics promised by its title, though that title suggests that her personal life is secondary to her work, which it's not. The friend I borrowed this from was correct in her assessment that Tutti is 'not a writer', as the prose ranges from bland to awful. But when describing the most fascinating times of her life — the beginning of COUM Transmissions in Hull through the end of TG in London — it doesn't matter, because her anecdotes are great and the life she led was amazing and admirable. It's only during the inevitable slide into stability and middle age where things drag, which is not her fault — that's life. And a life it was; it's actually incredible how singular and visionary she was, and this book is honest without any braggadocio. The principle villain is Genesis P-Orridge, revealed here to be much more a monster than I ever thought. Of course this is only her side of the story, but she's laid down so many indictments of his controlling megalomania, bordering on violent and criminal behaviour, that it makes the publication of this book all the more important because she needs to set down her story to counter P-Orridge, who is also keen to write a historical record. One would say that he almost dominates this book, which is a sad state of affairs — that the life story of such a groundbreaking female artist cannot be told without revolving around a monstrous (then-) man. Her love affair with Chris Carter, however, almost balances this out, and Carter himself is a bit of a mystery — he has been a part of her life longer than I've been alive and they seem to have a wonderful and beautiful relationship, but his own personality is rarely mentioned, at least compared to Sleazy Christopherson, P-Orridge and so many others who feature in this. It hit me that during the long section at the end about the TG reunion, I was as bored as I am whenever the band reunites in a music documentary; it's actually the chronicles of P-Orridge's horrid behaviour that kept my interest, and I felt somewhat ashamed of that. Tutti's estrangement from her parents is a genuine source of pain that will be forever unresolved, and that actually was a bummer to read about. Her adventures in the art world are also somewhat refreshing; it's great that she is getting the recognition she deserves, and her own methodology, described here as a lack of methodology, is refreshing and unassuming, the kind of approach that is really inspiring. I actually feel envy towards young misfits who might get to experience similar creative blossomings as Tutti did. My own coming-of-age is long past and it took a vastly different route, but if I had her as a role model I would have become a different person indeed. I hope the young'uns can discover her and be influenced in some way.

829. The Bend of the World by Jacob Bacharach
Received: 27 March 2018
Started: 27 March 2018
Finished: 29 March 2018
The first of Bacharach's two Pittsburgh-set novels (I'm sure I'll read the other one) cracked like a whip, bursting with irony, detachment, and a very male energy. It flaunted its political incorrectness and smart-arsed humour, but this was only surface tension that was broken by the aimless sadness hidden inside. The freak/paranormal/conspiracy content was played totally for laughs and the best friend character who espoused these beliefs was never allowed to grow into anything more than a caricature, albeit a massively entertaining one. So when the book essentially concludes at a funeral, there's a surprising impact even though the character who died was not one that ultimately meant much even to the book's own narrative-world. Given that I heard of Bacharach from his very articulate participation on a political podcast, I was surprised how apolitical this book was, though there was an unexplored sub-sub-subplot about Democratic party machine shenanigans at the mayor's office, which I would have enjoyed more of, but am now glad for what it was. I did find this funny, but more familiar; could someone who doesn't know Pittsburgh possibly enjoy this book, where its many references to

places and the culture are unannotated? Because I spent a few years floating around Pittsburgh, employed, aimless and mildly hedonistic, I had a lot in common with the first-person narrator of *The Bend of the World*. I miss those days (though don't wish to repeat them) and a decade after they took place, Bacharach writes essentially the same experience, though mine was boozier and less druggy, and my job was in the public sector, and I had musical and artistic aspirations. This fits right in alongside the other indulgent slacker writer men of today — the Tao Lins and the Ben Lerners — though this had a different flavour, maybe because it was so focused on the comic and didn't feel the need to paint some zeitgeist portrait. I don't really miss Pittsburgh much and this book didn't make me miss it; if anything, it reminded me of the city's insularity and how ultimately grateful I am to have escaped.

830. The Solitary Twin by Harry Mathews
Received: 28 March 2018
Started: 28 March 2018
Finished: 31 March 2018
I wanted to read Harry's last book properly — slowly, savouring it, and on paper — but I downloaded an .epub for now and couldn't stretch its 94 digital pages to last any longer than it did. This is somehow completely a Harry Mathews work, instantly recognisable for its curious choices of words, seeming non-sequiturs, and suspiciously playful construction. But what makes it most Mathews-like is the way it's somehow unlike any of his other books, being hard to compare to any of his prior novels yet unmistakably his. There's an actual plot this time, though the whole book is essentially laid out in dialogue between a few characters set in a seaside fishing village somewhere in New England. It feels a bit like an episode of *Murder, She Wrote* and that's probably intentional. His erudition and whimsy is as flagrant here as in any of his other books, and apart from a few references to modern technology, this could have been one of his earliest works. It's hilarious in places, without jokes, studiously committed to language and style, and also pretty fun. I got sad reading it, for while we only spent 2 days together, he and his work have been very dear to me throughout my entire adult life. I will get a print edition of this the next time I buy books, because it belongs next to every other one of his books on my shelf; then I can dip back in for a second go.

831. The Big Short: Inside the Doomsday Machine by Michael Lewis
Received: 18 March 2018
Started: 30 March 2018
Finished: 3 April 2018
Forgot to chronicle this when I read it; dates are an estimate based on my entry for the 
film re-watch. Enjoyable, sure, as I knew it 1545,
would be. Good popular nonfiction writing 1716
like this is no easy task and I understand why he's such a best-seller. I am unlikely to read *Moneyball* though.

832. Flights by Olga Tokarczuk
Received: 31 March 2018
Started: 31 March 2018
Finished: 16 April 2018
Tokarczuk is quite well-known in Poland but until recently has not been translated; I think this is only her second book to appear in English. *Flights* is called a word meaning 'wanderers' in its native language and that might have been a better title, though apparently it's not exact either, and one review of this stated that the translator's choice of *Flights* was understandable. A good portion of this does deal with travel, air travel in particular, and it captures that sense of transient non-space well. But this is also a book about loss and environment, and after finishing it and having a few days of distance, I really feel its weight. But it's not actually heavy to read — it's light and airy, as the prose darts though a tremendous number of fragmentary chapters. Some are wistful observations from (presumably) Tokarczuk's own voice, which reminds me both in style and content
of Rebecca Solnit's essays in *Wanderlust*. 
But this is definitely a work of fiction, as 119
a few stories are teased out and skipped through across the whole length of the book. There's a great deal of historical fiction or at least fictive embellishments on biographies of Europeans from the past few hundred years. And there's also some untouchable, practically ghost-like protagonists, whose stories are explored at a languid pace and rarely resolved: the man who loses his wife and kids for a few days while on holiday in Croatia; the doctor who has a strange encounter with a widow, etc. Tokarczuk's prose, at least as conveyed through this translator, is wonderfully experimental without being obtuse or stylistically extravagant. The amount of space in this novel gives it buoyancy, which is beautiful

to behold, and occasional philosophically profound statements are tossed off as casually as the more mundane observations that surround them. While I was reading this I felt a bit bored after the first three hundred pages, as the lack of cohesion was losing my interest and I was craving something a bit more direct, or at least 100 pages shorter. But I'm glad I stuck with it, because like the first time I read many DeLillo novels (a writer with whom Tokarczuk shares many similarities), it started to resonate with me much more after I finished it.

833. Insane Clown President: Dispatches from the 2016 Circus by Matt Taibbi
Received: 24 April 2018
Started: 24 April 2018
Finished: 26 April 2018
I can ask myself why I wanted to read this; certainly I'm not interest in re-litigating the 2016 election from any angle, since it already feels almost as culturally monumental as the Vietnam war. But I usually enjoy Taibbi, and in this collection of his *Rolling Stone* pieces during the election, he is able to acknowledge that he has become part of the political class he once criticised, and maintains a healthily, sceptical view towards all of the politicians under study here. The writing is mostly hilarious, but better when instead of tossing witty barbs at easy targets, he merely recites back some abnormal behaviour or moment from the campaign — it's almost as if the less Taibbi adds his own commentary, the more damning it is. He correctly chastises the Democrats for their hubris and arrogance, and in hindsight there's nothing really to add except revisiting the ups and downs of the whole process. Comparing this to the Michael Wolff book, I think that (818) work succeeds slightly more at what this is trying to do, though the lens is wider here and the angles somewhat different. I should check out *I Can't Breathe,* which is apparently brilliantly written and not so much a cash-in/throwaway book as this was.

834. Storm Static Sleep: A Pathway Through Post-Rock by Jack Chuter
Received: 3 March 2018
Started: 23 March 2018
Finished: 10 May 2018
There was no reason to read this except I was killing time in Itis library and it caught my eye and I wanted to read the chapter about Labradford and **Stars of the Lid**. This sat next to my bed forever, and I even had to renew it, so today I just decided to finish it. It's sort of weird someone would write a book about post-rock in 2015, but at least he tried to bring it up to date with later chapters on bands like Tides of Nebula, chapters that I skimmed or even skipped. Chuter's narrative is basic — begin with Slint and Talk Talk, and work chronologically (1933), all while reflecting on Simon Reynolds' coining of the term 'post-rock' and what that might actually mean. The writing was basic, though he actually displayed an aptitude for describing sound that I could have done with more of. There were some bits of trivia about these bands and I would have been super excited about this circa 2000, as music like this this was really the main focus of my life during my first two undergraduate years. I have been going through a mild resurgence of interest in some of this music lately, and have been discovering some bands which I dismissed or didn't hear during their original run, so it was great to read about Pram and Disco (2116) Inferno now. Even though these records are over 20 years old, they feel 'current' to me. A lot of the bands that didn't interest me then (Mogwai, the For Carnation, Trans Am) still are not interesting to me, but I read about them anyway.

835. The Idea of North by Peter Davidson
Received: 15 March 2018
Started: 16 April 2018
Finished: 14 May 2018
Another great find via my partner's school library! This takes it name from the Glenn Gould radio play and the book really dives into its title, and produces a flowing, beautiful exploration of exactly what that idea might be. The north in question is a Western one for sure, and Davidson's 'Topographies' section at the end explores quite directly the norths of Scandinavia, Canada and the UK. Davidson draws from the cultural world almost exclusively, and he seems to be invested most deeply in poetry, citing all sorts of poets from the last few centuries as well as referencing films, visual art, and literature. I think that I've elevated Hillel Schwartz's two books to be the gold standard for this type of (607, 616) cultural history, but Davidson is much more restrained and grounded in his process than Schwartz. After 250 pages, Davidson truly elaborates a clear distinction between the actual north and the idea of north, so this line of thought emerges as an attempt to document subjective experience across

time and place. It's by nature impossible to chronicle 'north' as a reference work, so rather than try to be authoritative, he just goes with his impulses. There were passages that held my interest and others that didn't, and as someone immersed in a 'north' place for essentially my entire life and certainly my entire time living in Europe, it still felt like some conceptual territory was just out of reach. I'm going to check out Gould's piece now (and all of his other radio plays, which somehow escaped my attention until now) and maybe see what else this Reaktion *Topographies* has published (besides my former professor's book).

836. An Encyclopaedia of Myself by Jonathan Meades
Received: 22 July 2017
Started: 2 February 2018
Finished: 15 May 2018
It took me ages to get through this, in part because I kept it in my backpack as my 'on the go' read, and I rarely took time to read while not at home in the past few months. But also, Meades' prose is as baroque as his television scripts, and this memoir of life in 1950s Salisbury is best taken in slow, piecemeal chunks. This aggressively rejects any typical memoir characteristics such as sentimentality or nostalgia, and it also refuses to assess the different standard of life 60 years ago, leaving a chronicle that could almost function as a reference work, despite the strong voice it comes from. The encyclopaedia conceit doesn't really work though, as the alphabetical chapter headings disguise a more traditionally chronological narrative and most are just tangential chapter openings if not outright red herrings. The large number of Majors encountered does make for some comic relief, and despite this being an autobiography, long passages start to feel like one of Meades' documentary works, like when he goes on about the Frenchness of the Mistral typeface for awhile. Even these digressions are afforded an appropriate amount of space in this tightly crafted yet flowing work. His sharp critical approaches to culture, architecture, and food are evident even in this nascent form, and while there's no doubt a lot of that can be chalked up to hindsight, it's still impressive to read about young Meades and his run-ins with neighbours, schoolteachers, relatives, and other random people. While my own childhood couldn't be further from his in actuality, there were similarities in the way that I remember things — those strange fleeting glimpses that stay with you so long and the odd privilege that certain objects and moments receive from the still-forming brain. The prose, while about the most English thing ever (at least half of the references went over my head and the mobile nature of my reading habits here usually prevented me from looking anything up), is exciting. His language is bold and provocative, never lugubrious, and always pointed without bellicosity, a fine needle to thread from such a strong personality. The photographs scattered throughout were just enough to give context and atmosphere without it turning into a full-on scrapbook. Wonderful.

837. Men and Apparitions by Lynne Tillman
Received: 10 April 2018
Started: 10 April 2018
Finished: 18 May 2018
I think I've read Tillman before, but maybe it was nonfiction or something about art — I didn't know she was a novelist too, and this is a rather remarkable exploration of image and gender, but wrapped up in the form of one of those novels where nothing really happens except that we are inside the thoughts of a protagonist. It feels like the format of so much of what I read now, which is a style that has always interested me (see: McElroy, Joseph) and I guess are ultimately the contemporary carriers of Proust's torch, except, well, I've never read Proust. An anthropologist who is exactly my age narrates *Men and Apparitions* and he studies personal, family photos (usually found) and relates them to his own complicated family background and upbringing. Again, nothing 'happens' except for some memories recast by narrator Zeke, including a painful long-term relationship breakup and its aftermath, and it culminates in an excerpt from Zeke's manuscript, a massive anthropological study about men and masculinity. In this case, the explicit gender politics of *Men and Apparitions* aren't revealed until the end, and even still, they're presented in a form of interview subjects, making it like a reboot of *Brief Interviews with Hideous Men*. Zeke, like me, grew up being aware of social politics, gender issues, and feminism, and struggles to define his own place as do many of the interview subjects. I admit this turn comes almost as a surprise, until I stopped to think about it; before that I was caught up in the Flusser-esque deconstructions of

image and performance, as well as Zeke's own issues with his mother, aunt, and mute sister. Tillmann's character is so infinitely relatable to me that I'm impressed she was able to get into the male mind, especially of a character a generation younger than her, and to convey this outlook so honestly and realistically. There's a lot to unpack here, which is why I took this rather slow, but it's neither a ponderous philosophical novel nor a vivacious romp. It's really a beast of its own, and a work that I hope finds an audience outside of art critics and gender studies students. Certainly it feels like it comes at the right time in culture, though I don't think literature like this really has much popular appeal in any era.

838. Lost at Sea: The Jon Ronson Mysteries by Jon Ronson
Received: 18 March 2018
Started: 17 May 2018
Finished: 20 May 2018
Easy, fun beach reading. I've read enough of Ronson that by now I don't mind his smart-alecky faux-naive personal approach to journalism. He even mentions in a later piece that he is often compared to Louis Theroux in the 'humorous journalism' field, and this book, a collection of pieces originally published in *The Guardian* and elsewhere, doesn't veer into any new territory. What this does contain are some fascinating pieces about human delusion, from the Indigo Children movement to Robbie Williams' fascination with the paranormal to a cruise run by a clearly fraudulent TV psychic. As in *Them*, Ronson has a way of gaining the confidence of his subjects only to quietly mock them with his scepticism, a scepticism which almost hides in plain sight but which is the sole redeeming value of his writing. I don't really think of this as serious work even though he addresses some serious topics, and for as constructed as his own persona is in the writing of these pieces, he definitely lets his own morality shine through rather than try to further exploit these people any further than he already is. The guys who cheated on *Who Wants to Be a Millionaire?* are fascinating, as is the disturbing chapter about Jonathan King. So I guess that I've put aside the things that bothered me about his writing now and I can just enjoy this and say that I do really like Ronson overall. Plus, that podcast he did about porn was phenomenal.

839. Men in Blazers Present Encyclopedia Blazertannica: A Suboptimal Guide to Soccer, America's Sport of the Future Since 1972 by Roger Bennett and Michael Davies
Received: 24 May 2018
Started: 24 May 2018
Finished: 26 May 2018
This should have just been a funny sport-related humour book, a spinoff from a podcast that I really like, but it somehow was so much more, and I absolutely loved it. Written in the style of an alphabetic encyclopaedia (making this the second such-styled book by eccentric Englishmen I finished this month), this works as an annotated guide to not just the podcast but to the personas of the hosts. And despite claiming that 'Rog' and 'Davo' are just that — personas they've adapted for *Men in Blazers* — by the end of the book I'm pretty sure that these guys are pretty much who they pretend to be. This oozes with honesty, enthusiasm, and passion, laced with their trademark winking self-deprecation and genuine joy for the material. Certainly I found it hilarious, a book about football crammed with deeply obscure cultural and intellectual references, but not in an annoying Dennis Miller style. But even more so, it was strangely moving, and it served as intertwined, alphabetically organised autobiographies of the two, built around their dual lifelong love affairs with American culture and with the game of football. As an American who went the other direction, I feel somewhat equivalent to their dual cultural backgrounds (although I only lived in the UK for 3.5 years, it still feels like 10 times that to me). The football stuff was deep, though not overly technical, and consistently hilarious. What really crept out slowly was the emotional resonance of these life experiences, whether talking about family, or their relationships with each other. All the fun things you'd expect in a book like this are present — their all-bald, all-ginger, and all-Jewish starting XIs, their list of the greatest World Cup kits of all times, and their individual lists of the greatest overall footballers of all time (which includes, of course, Leighton Baines). They're both consistently hard on Wayne Rooney, which is lovely. These guys successfully bridge the gap between the technical and vernacular approaches to football, mixing in enough cultural traditions and myths to drive the book forward but without falling into cliché or easy assumptions. These guys are a treasure and I wish football-watching friends in the UK knew about them. Davo's attempts to

justify being a Chelsea fan are less than convincing, though.

840. Neoreaction a Basilisk: Essays on and Around the Alt-Right by Elizabeth Sandifer
Received: 25 May 2018
Started: 26 May 2018
Finished: 29 May 2018
The edition I downloaded was published as Philip Sandifer, though it's been republishde under her correct name and pronoun now. This dissection of the alt-right explicitly positions itself against Nagle's *Kill All* 778 *Normies*, which is attacked for rejecting identity politics and semi-blaming them for the rise of the alt-right. More distinctly, Sandifer gets into the so-called 'intellectual' side of the movement, looking at some of the theorists who are maybe not so well known to those just following the sagas of Milo Yiannopolis and Richard Spencer in the mainstream media. The title essay makes up the main half of the book, which works through the theories of Yudkowsky, Mencius Moldbug/Curtis Yarvin, and Nick Land. I was only familiar with Land and hardly at that, except to know that he is batshit insane and somewhat fascinating; I did not know that he took a hard turn to become a neoreactionary, though Sandifer posits that this may be a massive Andy Kaufmann-esque performance prank. Anyway, this essay is fucking awesome even though I was reading criticism of writers whose work I was not familiar with at all. This is a testament to Sandifer's writing style, which is funny, sharp and logical while employing enough crowd-pleasing vernacular to keep me entertained. Her approach is based more on logic than a deep understanding of philosophy, which may be another thing that made it possible for me to hold on. The subsequent essays get into Gamergate, Trump, TERFs, and David Icke, and rather than just attacking them for the easy targets they are, she actually points out their inherent self-contradictions and utter pointlessness. It's funny without being sidesplitting, and thus holds up as a fairly coherent work of criticism. It reminded me a little bit of Matt Taibbi, stylistically, in the way that he doesn't hold back from calling an asshole an asshole, but has more to say than just fanning internet flame wars. The final chapter, on Peter Thiel, was really great because I never realised how empty Thiel's supposed accomplishments are. Sandifer doesn't offer a way out — the first sentence is the book is something about how we must assume that we are fucked, and while she quickly makes it clear that putting some billionaire heads on spikes is really the only course of action she can see, the book is otherwise free of class warfare or slogans. It's a work from the left that really resonates via common sense and decency, and the final conclusion may seem childish — that the entire movement and all of its so-called thinkers are ultimately just incredibly stupid, and that's what is the bleakest fact of all — and we are now forced to fight and refute such stupidity, when they have literally nothing to contribute, on top of all the other shit we have to deal with. The chapter 'Theses on a President' stands out too as maybe the single finest bit of writing I've yet read about Trump. It never once uses his name but works as a biography, anti-hagiography, and indictment of narcissism — and it's funny, too.

841. Sundog by Jim Harrison
Received: 18 March 2018
Started: 23 May 2018
Finished: 3 June 2018
2018: I finally read a Jim Harrison novel. *Sundog* read quickly but its power crept on up me, only really hitting once I was basking in its afterglow. I was always hesitant to dive into his work because I saw him as a purveyor of the classic idea of the great white male novelist, a neo-Hemingway, and that was not an incorrect assumption. But Hemingway was a great writer and Harrison is worthy of carrying that banner, for sure; it's certainly no reason to avoid his writing, providing I balance him out with some different types of writers, which I think I have been doing. This is set in the U.P. of Michigan (like most of his books, I think) and chronicles the life of a character who is basically the 'I was a dambuilder...' verse of 'The Highwayman'. The narrator, probably a thinly disguised Harrison himself, is a familiar type of drifting male id, fucking everything he can, drinking and eating with great gusto, and generally taking himself too seriously. The interesting stylistic choice is how the narratives are fragmented into different voices — the narrator, the interviews with Strang, and the typed-up notes which for some reason were presented in a different typeface. When writing about the natural world, Harrison is unparalleled. The depictions of rivers, creeks, and other water imagery saturate this like that one Ray Bradbury story about the rain, and the narrator's lusty lechery fits in here, feeling as natural as the sunrise by the end of the

book. Of course, this is about manly men whose lives are primarily defined by their relationships with women, and they aren't exactly role models. Once I got past the general sense of ickiness and just gave into the aesthetic, I found myself pretty satisfied by this. McGuane, who was Harrison's friend and contemporary, takes a much more comic and emasculating approach to his protagonists which maybe makes them hold up better in today's climate (one which maybe isn't actually any more 'enlightened' but at least a lot of people are trying). I'm probably more forgiving than most, but I don't think that *Sundog* should be invalidated because of its failure to conform to today's identity politics; actually, there's a lot to take from this and as a portrait of the late 20th century American midwest, it's magnificent. The plot didn't even need to have as much happening as it did; what I took from this was the mood: humid, languid, and inviting.

842. The Mars Room by Rachel Kushner
Received: 18 May 2018
Started: 19 May 2018
Finished: 3 June 2018
This is a hotly awaited followup, as *The*
728 *Flamethrowers* is definitely one of the standouts works of American fiction that I've read in the last few years, and Rachel seems like a far better Kushner to support than Jared. But while *Flamethrowers* was a novel of wild, unbridled freedom, this is a book of confinement and captivity — a prison drama! Like *Orange is the New Black* (a series I've never seen), this takes place primarily inside a women's prison, though with a few diversions into a men's prison and the outside world. Kushner's protagonist strains against the seedy underworld she's stuck in, with an intelligence and taste for literature that seems to be exactly the kind of character created for literary purposes, but it didn't strain believability too much as there's a hell of a lot of street-level grit all over this. I was surprised by how much I immersed myself in this world, even though I found it mostly unpleasant to read, and despite not having much sympathy for anyone depicted. Kushner, I think, aimed for the opposite — an empathetic work that portrays different viewpoints and indicts systems of power, whether legal, penal, or gender-based. The decision to split the narration across several voices is a curious one, as they aren't consistently balanced so the novel is still largely from one viewpoint, and the others I guess try to flesh things out in a classic *Rashomon* kind of way (to refer to another work that I've never seen) but the interconnectedness doesn't serve a larger purpose. Still, she's at the top of her game here, and the novel explores ideas of isolation (either voluntary or involuntary), while questioning all relationships from familial ones (mother-child in particular) to those of cold drug/sex work transactions. Bringing in the Unabomber and Thoreau was done in a subtle manner, which made the compelling, thriller-like conclusion thematically apt. I actually wanted something even more aggressively feminist than this, which is saying something since every male character is tragically flawed if not an outright monster, but there's more to feminism than that, and there may be aspects of female friendship presented between Romy and Sammy that would make more sense to me were I female myself. This also is so contextually American that it felt stifling, at least in comparison to *Flamethrowers*, which felt like a European novel, or at least a novel for Americans in Europe. And her first novel, which I haven't read yet, is set in Cuba, so this portrayal of the non-glamorous side of San Francisco (and a period piece, set in the early 2000s which didn't quite come together for me besides a few references to the Iraq war) is a shift for sure. She's just such a great writer, one who is capable of sharpening a voice to capture today's cultural currents and stylistically bold without being flashy or caught up in artifice, and she's young so hopefully there's a long future ahead of reading her.

843. Bullshit Jobs: A Theory by David Graeber
Received: 4 June 2018
Started: 4 June 2018
Finished: 7 June 2018
If I'm going to try to be objective here (and this is not really the place for that), I would say that *Bullshit Jobs* is the weakest of Graeber's three books that I've read. But in truth, I think I enjoyed reading it more than anything else by him, or by anyone else I've read recently. It certainly wasn't the totally brilliant illumination of *Debt*, but the core
essay from 2013 (of which this book was a 617
significant expansion) was equally illuminating, which is funny because Graeber admits here that it was an essentially tossed-off think piece, just a rant that he didn't expect to blow up. But blow up it did, and this book was the inevitable cash-in, but he thankfully expanded on things enough to justify this venture. The first 2/3 is filled with

many descriptions of bullshit jobs sent in by people who responded to his original essay, and these are incredible to read. I particularly love the absurdity of the workplace, and this is like a real-life anthropological analysis in the same vein as films like *The* 818 1163 *Boss of it All*, *Visioneers*, dystopian novels about bureaucracy, and even the song 'Take Stuff from Work' by King Missile. Graeber tries to set out a clear definition of what a bullshit job is, taking care to separate them from shit jobs and finding key distinctions about the farce, such as that one must pretend the work is meaningful. The stories are hilarious, occasionally incredible, and probably I'll go back and cite this section repeatedly in the future. The last 1/3 tries to place things into a larger frame, and this is probably the more important part of the work, yet somehow where things start to slip. Graeber dissects the labour theory of value as well as the evolution of the quasi-religious belief that work is good for you and should be central to one's life. His view is primarily Marxist, though he's happy to deviate when necessary, and the book ends with a convincing, heartfelt argument for Universal Basic Income. It's not something that I needed to be convinced of, yet it was nice to read this section because it's always nice to read things you agree with. So what's best about *Bullshit Jobs* is how funny it is — the stories are hilarious, but Graeber himself populates the work with one-liners and footnotes which are hilarious in places, without taking over the text and making it feel like Dave Barry or something. There's a sense of joy here, like he really just loved writing this, and is pleased to share it with the readers; the joy of the creator is a nice thing to feel from a work, and it's all the more impressive given that this book is talking about a serious situation with potential consequences. I would even make the case that this might capture the futility of existence in late capitalism as well as anything I've ever read, even if the 'problem' of bullshit jobs is primarily one of the privileged middle class. But the book has some glaring weaknesses that I had trouble ignoring, even through all my laughter. There's a part where he gets into the current culture war, reductively pointing out the resentment of the white working class of coastal elites, Hollywood, etc, and he has little to add to the discourse that I haven't already read in the approximately 37 think pieces per day that float past me already, online. And the generalisations he makes in this book are enormous; the entire book is essentially a big supposition without any actual evidence to back things up beyond the anonymised anecdotes sent in by people in response to the original essay. If you take that for what it is, then *Bullshit Jobs* can be cast as a philosophical work that shines light on an undiscussed aspect of society, and a masterpiece at that; it hopefully will be instrumental in getting enough discussion going to ultimately change the situation (but given that the only solution is a fundamental restructuring of society, I'm not going to hold my breath). As an academic anthropologist, though, he really could do better; *Debt* and *The Utopia of Rules* both contained hard-hitting analy- 696 ses of our lives that drew from much more proper research, and they were stronger for it. Still, this might be the book I'll now tell everyone they should read, because its truth is deep and soul-affecting, and it's accessible as well.

844. Don Quixote by Kathy Acker
Received: 18 October 2017
Started: 24 May 2018
Finished: 12 June 2018

This is the first Kathy Acker novel that managed to finish, and while this wasn't something I traditionally 'loved' I now found myself really curious to read everything else she ever wrote. *Don Quixote* is now the second book I've read recently that's a take-off on Cervantes (along with Stanbridge's *Forbidden Line*), though I also never fin- 820 ished reading the real *Don Quixote* the two times I tried. Acker's version went by a lot faster, though I don't think there is much to do with Quixote here, as was confirmed by an interview I found online where she admits it was essentially random plagiarism without much meaning behind it. Her Quixote doesn't follow much of a narrative but rather an internal quest, ostensibly seeking the meaning of 'love' but using that as a pretense to explore power, the body, sex, loyalty and cultural trends of the 1980s. The book is split between Quixote and St. Simeon, who is I guess the Sancho Panza figure, a character which narrates more than half of the book and changes genders and species a few times, possibly even merging with Quixote herself. Maybe this is one of the points — to probe the boundaries of love as possession, where it also might border on violence or abuse. While a work of 'punk' fiction (according to the blurb on the back), this writing tackles a lot of theory that was emerging in the 1980s, such as Elaine Scarry's work (*The Body in Pain*) and intersectionality as we discuss so often today. Her style is fragmented in a way that places it far closer to today's mediascape than she would have probably considered herself, and its absurd, take-no-prisoners imagery reminds me a little bit of Ishmael Reed's voice. The section near the end where the lines kept repeating three or four times was particularly insane, making me at first think it was a printing error, which captured something akin to psychosis, I guess. In general it was aggressive, textbook postmodern experimental fiction that would hate to be classified as such, and relied on emotional and physical tension throughout to reject any sort of intellectual marginalisation, which leaves it feeling like true literature of exception.

845. Platform Capitalism by Nick Srnicek
Received: 10 June 2018
Started: 11 June 2018
Finished: 12 June 2018

Not what I expected, but good. But I should have expected this, because the title says what it is — a look at the role that the platform occupies in contemporary capitalism. I am seeking to expand my understanding of exactly what a platform is, somewhat putting the cart before the horse as I usually do, as I'm trying to fit my work of the last 5-8 years into a theoretical framework. Meaning, I know what I've done, but I can articulate it better, and it's clear that I have been trying to build platforms for culture that defy the logic and exploitation of capitalism, either as parallel structures with regards to social relations, or as an explicitly oppositional ones. Of course, we failed; reading this, which goes through some of the larger tech platforms and how they work in a wider macroeconomic scope, still provided some illumination. It's a short book, really a long paper, and well-cited with references to business analysis, economic theory and tech news. Srnicek positions the rise of platforms such as Facebook, Amazon and Uber as the natural result of the post-1970 decline in real economy, and while that seems obvious he gives some more insight as to how the low interest rates since the crash have forced investors to seek a higher return on investment, thus leading to greater investment in VC and tech start-ups. The natural depression of wages is the perfect feast for these platforms, of which data are their main component, and the traditional product is often given away for free (Google, Facebook) to yield data, or a low-margin service such as Uber develops to own nothing, outsource everything, and keep pushing down wages and benefits to seek maximum growth. This, like the Graeber book I just read (*Bullshit Jobs*), 
was illustrating things I've been thinking 843
about more clearly, and while written in 2016 this remains quite current. Still, I was looking for a more theoretical definition of the platform, specifically as to how one might subvert or misuse such things, so I should probably go back and re-read chapter 9 of *The Stack* (which is cited here 
with instructions to more or less just do 733
that if the reader wants more thoughts on platforms as a concept). The third part of this gets into how these platforms interact with each other and what the future of competition is, since one aspect of the platform that's key is how they must gravitate towards monopolies to be successful. The future opportunity for 'siloing' their services into contained, unblockable closed universes which keep people locked into their products is already well underway and perhaps the most disturbing trend to me, as someone who has always valued diversity and choice in information services. Srnicek is clearly no fan of the subjects of his book but puts his faith into government, feeling that regulation and the state's ability in terms of monetarism, plus their potential to, for example, create truly non-profit platforms for the people – are maybe the only answer. There's also the potential that the whole system just eats itself, which is much more likely, and already starting to happen, as the precariousness and depression in the wages of the vast majority of people are leaving these massive platforms with fewer potential customers so that the digital divide will grow, becoming basically luxury items for the super rich which feed off of the data generated by the personal habits of us, aka the underclass. Something else that hit me, maybe exactly what I was looking for, was an almost tossed-off paragraph near the end of the book which talks about the problem with building (non-state) cooperative platforms. Srnicek refers to 'the traditional problems of coops' but doesn't explain — I can imagine, though it's something I would like to read more clearly about — only parenthetically stating 'the necessity of self-exploitation under capitalist social relations'. And that hit me like a bomb, again, like someone showing you the obvious; capitalist social relations, of course, this is why Biathlon/Kuusi Palaa failed. We tried to graft a new model for social and cultural production onto existing

capitalist social relations, and thus it was doomed to fail. He goes on to suggest that even if Facebook made their entire platform open-source, 'the weight of its existing data, network effects, and financial resources' would 'fight off any coop rival'. Which, of course it has done before (Ello, anyone?) and even explains 1% of what killed Kuusi Palaa — not that Facebook knew or cared about Kuusi Palaa as a rival, but Kuusi Palaa was a rival for the attention of even its own cooperative members let alone the larger potential cultural community it may have served. Anyway, that's me obsessing over one paragraph which is not even really what the book was about, but this book (which was depressing as fuck but good and worth the quick read it takes) shows me how much more I need to think and write about what happened to us, and hopefully I can not just learn something from it, but perhaps I can actually find a way forward that doesn't just leave me submitting to consumerism, big data, and the allure of middle-class comfort.

846. Die, My Love by Ariana Harwicz
Received: 3 June 2018
Started: 3 June 2018
Finished: 13 June 2018
This great, sharp, and short novel descends from the literature of mental illness and domestic horror — a bit of Heller's *Something Happened*  416 138, 855 crossed with *A Woman Under the Influence*, to make my typical hybrid comparison, except it's a lot darker than either of those, if one can believe it. Harwicz upends the idea of the pastoral setting as idyllic, and writes with such a forked tongue that it attains (at least through the translation from the Spanish) a poetic violence. The short chapters are presented as long, unbroken paragraphs, all internal monologues, and occasionally shifting to another perspective to further disorientate. There's a marriage falling apart, dark sexual subterfuge, and the trappings of motherhood, but the narrator is so unhinged that this goes far beyond any traditional explorations of those themes, towards total psychosis. The unreliability is paramount here, and even when her descriptions of what's happening start to involve the outside world being aware of her behaviour, it still feels like it could all be some twisted fantasy. But I wouldn't classify this as genre horror or another tale of domestic violence — it's much more explosive than that, being an attack on all that is supposedly good and wholesome about our lives. Absolutely amazing, and I'm glad to have a new international author to look forward to future writing by

847. Falling Man by Don DeLillo
Received: 3 May 2018
Started: 14 June 2018
Finished: 17 June 2018
I used to consider this to be the 'worst' DeLillo. Do I still think that? I'd need to  61 re-read *Running Dog* and a few others, and it doesn't really matter anyway, because this is still DeLillo and there's plenty of value here. I was certainly hard on this 11 years ago because I felt like DeLillo was trying to "cash in" on 9/11 as an opportunity, since terrorism is such a major theme of his. But why did I see this as a cheap ploy? Perhaps I conflated it somewhat with the Jonathan Safran Foer 9/11 novel,  188 which I liked at the time but in hindsight was terrible and emotionally manipulative. *Falling Man* is built around a recently separated couple who reunites after one of them survives 9/11, and it's caught up in family-relationship drama with the viewpoint through a typically detached and mysterious male protagonist, as found in most of his books. I don't think this was terrible, but it definitely isn't one of his strongest works. I found myself really bored by the marriage interplay, though their interactions with the wife's mother were probably the most interesting. The presence of a child seems to be something that occurs frequently in post-*Underworld*  720 work and maybe this would have been worth exploring more, though in *Zero K*  719 it feels like we get a better version of this idea. The weakest sections for sure are the historical fiction segments inside the minds of the 9/11 attackers training for their mission; I didn't really feel much to connect it besides 9/11 itself and in a longer book-length study of a historical figure, such as *Libra*,  468 maybe I would have found more to appreciate. The depictions of technology and city life all seem like they were done better before in his earlier books, but no, this isn't terrible; it's certainly a book that's concerned with the intersection of cold political trauma and so-called everyday life, and I can't blame the guy for wanting to write around a topic this big especially, as his past work is a like CV showing his qualifications for tackling it. The Falling Man character himself is a performance artist and he haunts the book like an enigma, getting a bio at the end but in a section that felt superfluous except to illustrate some connection between art,

commerce/fame and politics? Coming just after the acerbic and inspired *Cosmopolis*, 725 it's hard not to see this as DeLillo spinning his wheels a little bit, but that still means he's head and shoulders above just about every other novelist on earth. I read this over two days while lying on the beach at Marjaniemi.

848. Organization after Social Media
by Geert Lovink and Ned Rossiter
Received: 23 June 2018
Started: 23 June 2018
Finished: 26 June 2018
Totally fucking incredible. But maybe not for everyone; this book felt like it was written specifically for me. You see, when I'm not spending my time thinking about football or food, I'm obsessing over the topics in this book. Which is no doubt due to what I've chosen as a career and specifically the way I've spent the last few years. Lovink and Rossiter's book comes out of the Netherlands-based Institute of Networked Cultures which do fascinating projects, and whom should I probably get in contact with. This is somewhere between a work of theory and a manifesto, though it doesn't prescribe a solution. They push the idea of the 'organised network' as the answer to social media and spend much of the book defining what such networks are like, without every really spelling it out. It's only at the very end when they talked about the early industrial music scene in the 80s and how it was connected to mail art and a lot of similar 'underground' movements that I started to really understand. The emphasis here is on building infrastructure, not just events. Lovink was one of the big tactical media people and talks about the successes and failures of that movement, and there's also a plea for a more evolved form of media studies as well as the problems with directly politicising organised networks through political parties. Their outlook is as positive as possible given the state of the world now, but it's not the kind of book you finish inspired and rush out the door ready to start something. The chapter on financing networks, for example, is frustratingly incomplete, and this stuff isn't supposed to be easy. Of course our work with Biathlon was all I could think about while reading this, which is why I'm imploring my colleague to take a crack at this, and while there's nothing in here that I disagree with, I wonder how our situation in Finland might be a little bit more extreme, as the trust factor (officially ranked last week in some study as the most trusting country in the world) is a real motherfucker when it comes to the dominance of social media in the lives of people here. I think our work tried to bridge the event with infrastructure to varying degrees of success, and maybe the attempt to be a platform was our undoing, beyond the fact that we didn't build our network naturally, but in the way that all competetors to platform monopolies try things (and also fail). Obviously I have a lot more to think about regarding this and I'll be writing about this more properly somewhere, but as far as the act of reading this, I can't say I enjoyed a work of theory like this since *The Stack* (to which this makes  a nice companion). 733

849. Social Media Abyss: Critical Internet Cultures and the Force of Negation by Geert Lovink
Received: 26 June 2018
Started: 26 June 2018
Finished: 4 July 2018
Working backwards to Lovink's previous book, this premise seemed great at the beginning but soon devolved into a more loosely themed set of essays of Internet criticism. Still great though; the last essay was essentially an early version of the *Organisation*  book and being two years old now, it 848 already feels slightly dated. It seems hard to read a book that deals with the intersection of politics and Internet culture without talking about Brexit, Trump, fake news, etc. The chapter on Bitcoin was a pretty good analysis and was appropriately critical without even getting into the morally repugnant aspects of cryptocurrency. Lovink's writing has a great balance of provocative and solidly-researched argument, and most chapters started with this same mishmash of quotes and slogans as the other book had, which are just nice accents. I've been quite stricken with a nostalgia lately for the way the Internet used to be, or maybe for the impossible dream of what it could have been (like most nostalgia, it's a semi-manufactured fantasy), and this opened me up to the possibilities that things could be re-engineered away from monopoly platforms and towards something more commons-based and beneficial. However, unlike the more technical youbroketheinternet.org, this works from a theoretical angle that takes into consideration human and organisational behaivour, political movements, economics and psychology. Again, there are no easy answers, but lots of pillars around which thoughts can be organised,

including numerous sources that are all avenues for further investigation. There's a little biography mixed in too, as Lovink talks about his own upbringing as a media artist and the career path he chose during the 90s, which emphasises his call for a strong media analysis of the current digital environment, something that in his view must be included in any sort of building efforts. There's also a great chapter on Jonathan Franzen, which seemed weird at first but is really looking at Franzen's own net critiques, apparently buried in the footnotes of his book of Karl Kraus translations. There's still so much to take in here and place against my own thoughts and energies, and I definitely have a different viewpoint since reading both of these books, probably having to do somewhat with the ideas of agency and choice in why people choose to 'use' any tools.

850. The Reactionary Mind: Conservatism from Edmund Burke to Donald Trump by Corey Robin
Received: 24 June 2018
Started: 29 June 2018
Finished: 8 July 2018
This was only a few years old but Robin put out a second edition to include the 2016 election and changed the end of the title to replace Sarah Palin with Trump. According to the introduction he changed a few more things, and tried to express more of a narrative. I never read the first edition, but this was pretty great — a thorough, scrupulous dissection of conservative thought, written from a clearly left-wing perspective but rarely mocking or taking cheap shots. It's closer to an academic or theoretical work than a typical non-fiction bestseller would be (not that this necessarily sold that well) and is really readable, and not too long. The revanchism under study here ultimately becomes a study of American conservatism, and why not, since that's one thing Americans do undeniably well, though I would like more of a look at modern conservative thought in other cultures. Robin doesn't pull punches though, and is somewhat more deferential to OG conservatives like Edmund Burke than to more recent ones, as they probably at least deserve a little respect for their ideas. By the time we get up to the 20th century and Friedrich Hayek he's a lot more cutting, and fair enough — Hayek's philosophy is significantly more reprehensible than I ever realised, and Robin shows how it descended from Nietzsche and a misreading of Adam Smith. The chapter on Ayn Rand is actually funny, and the rise of the modern movement from Goldwater on is breezed over, which is fine cause I already read three Rick Perlstein  books about it. 649, 656, 693 The last chapter is added to cover Trump and while I'm a bit sick of reading Trump takes, this one actually uses *The Art of the Deal* to determine a cultural analysis of contemporary populism, and to show how inevitable its fall is. So it's a hopeful ending, but we could use more than words right now.

851. City of Quartz: Excavating the Future in Los Angeles by Mike Davis
Received: 18 March 2018
Started: 17 June 2018
Finished: 13 July 2018
An urbanist classic that I've always wanted to read, this made a somewhat odd beach book but for 50 cents, not a bad charity shop find. This was written in 1990 so the biggest thing hanging over it was the generation of shit that's happened since. I've never been to Los Angeles but it occupies a prime position in my mind, and my increasing fascination with it made this a perfect mix with all of the recent television set there, Vollmann's *Imperial*, the  Ellroy novels I've read, etc. 433 Davis works through the history of the city in a non-linear fashion, in a series of chapters that look at power and mythmaking, the two undeniable currents of Los Angeles. The first chapter, which looks at LA noir works and the way it's represented in fiction and cinema, of course recalled Anderson's *Los*  *Angeles Plays Itself*, 1265 another key work in making me so fascinated by the place. Later chapters look at the growth of the Catholic church and what social engineering they've done through manipulating their Latinx followers; the pro- and anti-growth movements of suburbanite homeowners, and finally the rise and fall of the Kaiser steel plant in Fortuna, CA. Davis writes from a fiercely left-wing position, even somewhat radical, and his roving eye never loses sight of the underclasses who provide the bulk of the population in Los Angeles and the surrounding area. If his reputation is mostly based on this work, it's certainly deserved, and I wonder if he's working on a new edition or sequel to cover the last three decades.

852. Pond by Claire-Louise Bennett
Received: 8 July 2018
Started: 9 July 2018
Finished: 13 July 2018
Here's a beautiful, short book that's another entry in the genre of 'plot = person just thinks about stuff', which is the style of so much new fiction that I am reading lately. Bennett's narrator is living alone in a rural place in Ireland, suffering from depression but writing about her experiences in a methodical, straightforward manner that wobbles in places but primarily conveys a sense of trying. It doesn't dwell on any of the topics that it could be about — loneliness, loss, the pastoral — but comes across as a convincing work of internal character construction. There are references in a few places that the narrator is reading a book which I'm fairly certain is Markson's *Wittgenstein's Mistress*, 778 so there's an explicit reference to an obvious influence. But this is not horrific or dystopian in the slightest — reading this so soon after *Die, My Love* is 846 weird because there are a lot of similarities to that too. *Pond* is a remarkable example of fiction at its best, interrogating the now, and positing scenarios for a life that can be fulfilling and independent without too much compromise. It's not escapism — Bennett's narrator doesn't escape from anything, and this feels almost resolutely opposed to easy solutions. On top of everything she's created a fascinating character, whose vocabulary leans towards cold, clinical terminology with an attempted rationality that is ultimately futile, yet non-judgemental, and whose depictions of mundanity are like a less humorous version of *The Mezzanine*. 194, 467 Some might find this claustrophobic or depressing, but I found it a celebration of difficult, eccentric people, the kind who have enriched my life even when they are obviously struggling with their own demons.

853. Hell Bent for Leather: Confessions of a Heavy Metal Addict by Seb Hunter
Received: 8 June 2018
Started: 13 July 2018
Finished: 14 July 2018
This is a bit like the Winchester/UK version of *Fargo Rock City*, 463 except for two differences. The first is that Hunter is actually writing about his experience trying to make it in a glam metal band as opposed to just being a fan or observer. The second is that he is nowhere near the creative thinker that Klostermann is, so this falls flat in more than a few places. The most obvious deficiency is that while Hunter is able to gently mock his adolescent metal years and surrounding culture from the hindsight of evolved aesthetic taste, he does not fully renounce the misogyny and homophobia that was so saturated in this lifestyle. Nor does he deny it — the way he treats women here is abysmal, and there doesn't seem to be any remorse. Otherwise, this is a book with no real purpose — his insight isn't anything special, so it ends up being an autobiography of no one important or memorable. I enjoyed it enough for a beach book that I paid 1€ for at my local shitty itsepalvelu kirppis, but wanted a little more. His attempt to bring his troubled relationship with his father into this was less than convincing; maybe he's just being too English and trying to write around the pain, but it didn't seem so terrible to me and it sounds like he had a decent enough middle-class upbringing (enough to afford to buy shitty guitars often). I enjoyed the earliest chapters, where Hunter describes his early adolescent obsession with heavy metal and trying to be in bands with anyone else he could find out there who was even remotely interested — I certainly could relate to that myself, despite growing up a decade later and on the other side of the ocean. There was certain majesty to being obsessed with music when 13 years old, when the idea of a band and what that band meant was larger than anything else in the universe. It's a way of thinking that kids now will never fully understand, as there's no longer any need to hunt and gather our own cultural touchstones. I also liked his overviews of certain bands and/or scenes, even though the humour was a bit too easy. But yeah, nothing great here; I think I saw this mentioned favourably somewhere, maybe in *The Quietus*, so I'm glad I got a chance to read it but would not recommend this in the slightest. I may start re-reading *Fargo* though.

854. Eileen by Ottessa Moshfegh
Received: 13 July 2018
Started: 13 July 2018
Finished: 19 July 2018
I expected this to be a comic novel, as that's how it was described wherever I read about it, but it was something much different. A slow, drawn-out portrayal of the last week of a woman's life before she runs away, set in 1964, this grew on me until it finally exploded in a surprising climax that was still natural within the world Moshfegh created.

The titular Eileen narrates from the present day, looking back at her anonymous life of repression and misery in the 60s, and I couldn't help but feel a great deal of empathy for her, as she captured the misery of work and family in America in a way that I imagine is still true today for so many. The feeling of repression really consumes this, making it almost claustrophobic, and while some of the drama could be felt almost like an exaggeration from a modern feminist viewpoint, it was well-written without being stylised. Funny, no; nor was it groundbreaking, experimental, or even that awe-inducing of a plot, but there was something compelling that kept me keep hanging on. I'm not sure how this compares to her short stories or her new novel, which sounds great.

855. Something Happened by Joseph Heller
Received: 14 January 2017
Started: 15 July 2018
Finished: 24 July 2018
I've only read this and *Catch-22* by Heller, but I consider this to be a masterpiece, though I guess they both are. A re-read over a decade later shows this to hold up, though I realise what a completely different beast this is. *Something Happened* is so dark as to be almost unbearable in places, and while I found myself laughing frequently, it's only because I have a totally vicious sense of humour and Heller's narrator would shift between cocksuredness and fear so quickly that it actually formed jokes. The narrator is a true monster, and while I certainly didn't read this in 2004 thinking he was a hero, the last 14 years of social progress have sharpened some of the misogynist and racist edges, to the point where this is so caustic it hurt to read. The mentally retarded child is so repressed here, except when Slocum directly discusses his attempts to repress it; I noticed how the chapter ostensibly about him quickly abandons the plot and goes back into a long and lurid dissection of his dalliances with prostitutes and the various ways he mistreats women. Throughout everything there is an almost wistful longing for the woman he worked with when younger, a character that committed suicide; she returns in his adult thoughts to the point of obsession, and I almost mistook it for a genuine emotional connection until I realised that she was simply the only woman he didn't get to possess. The upper middle class office/suburb dichotomy here recalls the earlier seasons of *Mad Men*, and not just because of the workplace sexism and philandering. I wonder if this was an influence on Matthew Weiner, because it indicts the white American dream for its inherent corruption and exploitation as fully as the TV series does. And this was written literally at the peak of capitalism; from this point on, things just have gotten worse in the march to this new Gilded Age we are living in now. I'm not grafting a Marxist perspective onto *Something Happened* — I think Heller's vitriol addresses deeper matters than politics and economics. And it's hard to even tell if this is a moralistic work. It's certainly as outrageous in terms of sex and language as *Portnoy's Complaint*, but like all great modernist novels, it places 192, 518 quite a lot on the reader. As a novel, this is way too long and messy, but I overlook that because it's still such a powerful work — the rare book that is shocking, horrific, and twisted, merely through unmasking the fears that lie behind affluence.

856. Big Questions by Anders Nilsen
Received: (already owned)
Started: 4 June 2018
Finished: 25 July 2018
I picked this up off the shelf before a bird started building a nest on our balcony, but it was such a perfect comment on the situation we're going through that I wonder if I might be slightly clairvoyant. A blackbird has now laid four eggs in the nest and sits on them most of the time, right on the other side of our bedroom window. If we go onto the balcony it usually flies away, though I did manage to spend about ten minutes out there yesterday before she freaked out. When she flies away, she retreats to the tree in the yard and starts swooping back and forth between the tree and the balcony railing while squawking, until I eventually concede the balcony to her. We've left some nuts out for her, which she ate, though the whole situation makes me nervous and I think it's going to end badly. This is a nice backdrop to revisit *Big Questions*, an exemplary graphic novel that also serves as a throughline for over 15 years of Nilsen's style. The early pages are crude, built around absurd jokes, and suggest that the reader will be in for 600 pages of one-liners and wry observations. But the world soon expands, while somehow staying quite small (it never leaves an unnamed, barren landscape containing some only trees, a river, and a house). There is a plot that unfolds quite momentously

though it is ultimately a simple story, but cast in the context of a flock of birds, it's becomes the biggest thing imaginable. The title is rather misleading too, as once the story gets underway, we don't find so many explicitly articulated questions, instead being drawn into a beautiful, pastoral, and dark universe. Reading this again, I can't help but think of *Isle of Dogs* since there's a similar story (downed pliot + talking animals) and the overall emphasis on perspectives is similar (to a staggering degree, here). *Big Questions*, perhaps because of the title or knowing Nilsen's other more ponderous work, suggests it's going to be immensely ambitious in terms of philosophy, but it's really not. The sheer weight of this is deceptive, because it's actually sort of light, despite being full of life and death battles. There's juxtaposition of empathy with the cold reality of the natural world that can be somewhat off-putting, especially as the scenarios suggest escapism, or a detached and fantastic sense of wonder. Nilsen's great achievement here is that he manages to pull so many feelings into one work, and that the centre holds throughout. There's a really honest and straightforward afterword in which he describes not just the evolution of this book but of himself as an artist and adult, and it emphasises how much of a complete work this is. I haven't actually seen any of his recent output since this was published, though.

857. The Communist Horizon by Jodi Dean
Received: 19 July 2018
Started: 19 July 2018
Finished: 26 July 2018
Jodi Dean's work is about reformulating and modernising the conception of communism/Marxism, and this work sets forth a concise definition of what she calls the 'horizon' of communism. This was brief enough that I found it fascinating reading as it drew from social and cultural conceptions as well as more heavy psychoanalytic theory. I'm most interested in these ideas put into actual boots-on-the-ground practice, but she seems to have a good understanding of the popular conceptions of communism and insight into how this might change. She's correct in expressing how American culture equates communism specifically with the Soviet Union, and she brings in her theory of communicative capitalism, which seems to build on Hardt and Negri's ideas with a bit of media theory as well. It's a perfectly valid outlook and one that I essentially agreed with, especially after just reading those
Geert Lovink books and so often thinking 848, 849
about what it is that I think about. Probably the best chapter is where she explored the idea of collective desire and how the left is constantly haunted by its own sense of loss. I often check out when Lacan and his ilk are brought in, but this was definitely getting at something — something about the pull of nostalgia and the difference between depression and melancholy, which actually I think works when talking about political struggles. The weakest section was possibly the last chapter, attempting to address the role of the party but was really just about the Occupy movement. There was certainly a lot to celebrate there, but being that this was published before the 2016 election, it already felt dated or even irrelevant, though certainly the idea of Occupy as a platform-like 'eventual site' can have some legs in the future. If I dive into any more of her work it would definitely be the communicative capitalism theory, which feels adjacent to Bratton and maybe even some accelerationists, though I need to read more about accelerationism.

858. I Am the Brother of XX by Fleur Jaeggy
Received: 26 July 2018
Started: 26 July 2018
Finished: 3 August 2018
The tone is set here in the first story, the eponymous one. This is prose that is cold, blunt and precise, in a style that is nearly violent, and unflinching. That's more adjectives in one sentence than you're likely to find at any point in *I Am the Brother of XX*, a short story collection by an obscure Italian-language Swiss writer which I discovered when randomly reading a review of it somewhere. There are about 15 stories here, none more than 3 or 4 pages in length, and with an economy and experimentalism of language that immediately
made me think of Lydia Davis. But Davis is 577
a much more varied stylist and often writes with a whimsicality that is utterly missing here. This is austere and oblique writing, extremely post-war central European, or at least conforming to my conception of that aesthetic tendency. Jaeggy was supposedly a friend of Thomas Bernhard and I can see a similarity here. She was also a friend of Ingeborg Bachmann, the Austrian poet who is the focal point of the final story here, though I didn't know who she was until I looked her up. There are many historical

figures here, or quasi-historical figures, for it spans time and space and yet somehow all feels united. There's no sympathy present, as it's an utterly cold collection, yet I somehow found a lot of joy in it. We get a chronicle of a cat, and some tourists going to concentration camps, and of course the deranged sibling relationships of the first story; it all adds up to something mesmerising. This was only 93 pages long, but every story, made up of crowded paragraphs packed with short sentences, could have been a lifetime.

859. Stayin' Alive: The 1970s and the Last Days of the Working Class by Jefferson Cowie

Received: 1 August 2018
Started: 3 August 2018
Finished: 10 August 2018

I loved this! Cowie's look at my favourite decade that I never lived in starts off by working through a description of some of the notable moments of labour action across America. I thought it would be a pretty straightforward labour history study, but starting with chapter two it starts to expand its scope and become a lot more interesting. This reminded me of Perlstein's

693 656

Nixonland and *The Invisible Bridge*, as it covers some of the same material such as the doomed McGovern campaign, the Yablonski murders, etc. — but was significantly more fun to read. It's also pretty even-handed in its assessments — while clearly it's a book written from the left, for the left, it doesn't pull its punches in pointing out the absolute shameful ways in which union management and in-fighting committed to the quick collapse of trade union power. George Meany emerges as one of the great villains of the decade, and Jimmy Carter doesn't come off as so likeable either. Ultimately, this is a book about the social changes that white working class people went through, and it's really similar to what we experienced in 2016, only it happened already in 1972 and 1976 and especially 1980. Nothing is new; Trump is just more vulgar than George Wallace was, but perceptions of condescending coastal elites were already in full swing then. I guess all backlashes are pretty much the same, but I still loved reading this. Cowie weaves in some nice bits of cultural history as well, discussing Merle Haggard, *Dog*

1892 489

Day Afternoon and even Devo. I wish the title specified that this was strictly going to cover the American white working class, though I would have read it anyway. I learned a ton here — I had no idea (or had forgotten from the Perlstein books) that from 1976 through 78 there was a major attempt to pass a full employment bill, and the neutered joke of a bill that eventually passed is one of the true tragedies of the time, an utter failure to capitalise on the mandate the Democrats had after Watergate. The utter corruption of the Democratic Party was already in full swing here, and in many ways the Republicans were the more ethical party apart from Nixon (who actually ran a more liberal administration than Clinton did). I'm oversimplifying — there are huge differences now, primarily that globalisation and financialisation run the world — but the political patterns are remarkably similar. The last chapter sums up 'where we are now' (this was published in 2012) and it's pretty bleak, though Cowie certianly doesn't pine for the days when the AFL-CIO pulled all of the strings. This isn't a radical work of history but a really concise chronicling of the time just before I was born, which I only absorbed secondhand through cultural osmosis, so I'm fascinated by it. There's not too much theory here, but he's not afraid to connect things and his eye for cultural moments (such as the manufacture of nostalgia as a reaction to the economic doom) is sharp. The union leaders' behaviour in here actually made me sick — their undermining of McGovern is one of the great unmentioned crimes of the time. Actually, Bobby Kennedy never wanted to run for president and wanted McGovern to in '68 — had he done so and won, maybe we'd be living in a far different world today.

860. The Chapo Guide to Revolution by Chapo Trap House

Received: 21 August 2018
Started: 21 August 2018
Finished: 26 August 2018

Comedy podcasts have held a pretty strong role in my life, but I guess everyone of my demographic is into them at this moment in time. Marc Maron's *WTF* made me feel way better when my marriage was collapsing, though I haven't listened to an episode for years. *Harmontown* occupied the pole position for the last few years, though I also haven't listened to an episode this year, even though it inspired my own talk show and at one point felt really groundbreaking and amazing in terms of emotional rawness mixed with pop culture accessibility. But it's been undoubtedly *Chapo Trap House* for the past year, a podcast that is so much more than just a podcast, understandably the most successful Patreon ever and something tipped (by the media they are so completely against) as being a 'movement'. All I can say is that I had a really shitty first half to 2018, at times feeling lower than I have felt since my marriage broke up, and once again, a podcast provided therapy and a feeling that I am not alone. In this case, it was like discovering that there are actually people who see the world as I do, and they are also a bit younger than me and a zillion times more articulate and brilliant when it comes to conveying their worldview. It's inspiring, not because there's any real hope for this world, but that at least we'll go down in flames laughing together. Actually, there's a lot more hope in *Chapo* than most people realise — they are not cynical, and have a genuinely moral and impassioned way of challenging political thought in American culture. This book was their cash-in, and was given this unfortunate title against their will by the publisher, but there was no way I wasnt going to read it. I did steal a copy for now, as I'll likely buy it later when I have money and/or am In America; they get my money every month already (I'm a Grey Wolf) and they're doing just fine. Anyway. It's crazy that this is the second book I've  read this summer that is a spinoff of a pod- 839 cast and that both transcended the form. I expected this to be something like the *Daily Show*/Colbert books, a goofy mashup of jokes to be filed in the 'humour' section of B. Dalton Booksellers (if such a place still existed), the section that I browsed all the time when I was 10. I guess technically this might be that, except it's way, way funnier than I imaged and again it articulates an impressively in-depth worldview. Almost every sentence was brilliantly funny, and despite Amber Frost's non-participation, it felt like the Chapo gang I know and love. The takedowns of Libs and Conservatives are accurate, true, and lance the corrupted American culture with an ethical tip that is impressive when balanced against the aggressive disrespect they evince towards these figures. We get some dives into history and culture that again are actually pretty good overviews of American malevolence, while still being funny as hell. I laughed out loud so much reading this that I think I was keeping my partner awake. I intentionally slowed down my reading speed in order to savour parts of this. They are preaching to the converted in my case, but if this has even a microscopic effect in bringing a hard Marxist/left viewpoint to a larger audience, then they should get the Nobel fucking prize for it.

861. Novel Explosives by Jim Gauer
Received: 14 June 2018
Started: 14 June 2018
Finished: 2 September 2018
This may be the next great big postmodern American novel, as it's (along with *A Naked Singularity*) probably the most  535 accomplished one I've read in the years since *Infinite Jest* was published.  109 Yet while the writing here was dizzying, dazzling, and encyclopaedic like so many of Gauer's antecedents, I can't say that I found it as engrossing as I thought it would be after the first 100 pages or so. Partially this is because the text became so dense that its 700 pages felt more like 1500, and the long passages describing weaponry and other technical apparatus, while impressive on a conceptual level, were a chore to read and failed to hold my interest. The intertwining narratives here also worked in reverse on me, as the clichéd amnesiac in Mexico plotline interested me much more than the drug runners/action line. In the end that whole saga reminded me of a textual version of *True Detective* (or at least the shootout scenes in each season), though 'literary', whatever that might mean. While I'm criticising it to death here, I do so mostly to justify my own slow progress through this, because I have a feeling I will cite this frequently in the future and recommend it. It's certainly an all-encompassing summation of Where We Are Now, which is what big, sweeping novels are supposed to be. In this case, it connects investment capital to violence and the military/weaponry field, and addresses the role of technology and all of its contradictions in modern life, particularly with regard to loss of identity and self. I should probably write more about what is such a mammoth work, but maybe the problem is that while I recognise and appreciate Gauer's mastery of Where We Are Now, I personally am so disgusted by the state of the world that even a brilliant, hyper-literary rendition of said world fails to move me towards the sublime. Whereas the generation(s) preceding me, the generations that produced DeLillo and Pynchon and Gaddis and even Wallace, are ones that I still wanted to live in, or at least ones that offered me the true potential of imagination while I was in my own formative years. Whatever; this was amazing.

862. Sleepless Nights by Elizabeth Hardwick
Received: 2 September 2018
Started: 2 September 2018
Finished: 8 September 2018
Sleepless Nights is a remarkably bold, brilliant novel that feels a bit like a precursor to a lot of contemporary fiction. The blend of memoir and fiction isn't so interesting to me today during an era where those boundaries are stretched so often I stopped caring about such delineations, but Hardwick's use of language would be stunning in any time. This is a short novel that feels strange in how it moves through a life and memory, with concerns that rotate around identity (as a female on the left) and a distant, non-judgemental style of chronicling ones history. It felt immensely relatable to me, even though I've had very different experiences in my life, perhaps because her memories aren't so journalistic; they are more like invitations, or at least feel like she wants to share her melancholy. It's overall a rather sombre experience, and the title reflects the mood of the piece. I could have probably devoured this in one sitting but I took it slow, stretching its ten parts over a week, trying to savour the language and let it sink into me. Despite this slow approach, it already feels like a ghost that passed through me, leaving me little to hold on to.

863. Bad Blood by John Carreyrou
Received: 11 September 2018
Started: 11 September 2018
Finished: 14 September 2018
This was the fun read I expected it to be, and a good portrayal of the grifter personality that seems to lie at the heart of American history/culture. Carreyrou is a pretty terrible writer, or at least doesn't manage to flesh out his journalistic exposé into very interesting book-length prose. It's good enough to read, though, and becomes a real page-turner. The first 2/3rds are just a matter-of-fact telling about Theranos's founding and shenanigans, compiled through the sources he was able to get on the record. Once Carreyrou personally enters the story it becomes a bit repetitive, as we are introduced to some characters again, as if we had forgotten them the first time through – but once Theranos starts amping up the legal attacks on him and the sources, it becomes a fun *All the President's Men* type of adventure story. The *Wall Street Journal* is not a newspaper that I have any respect for, but it's admirable that Rupert Murdoch allowed Carreyrou's stories to run despite his own conflict of interest. (Maybe he's just in the tertiary stage of syphilis at this point, or maybe he was trying to lose a shit ton of money for tax write-off purposes, as he ended up doing). Carreyrou doesn't try to make big sweeping statements about the grift until the epilogue, but the actions described are enough to show what happens when extreme ambition and narcissism are combined with shitloads of VC money. There's also an inherent criticism of Silicon Valley in general here, as well as the connections fo power and violence throughout (George Schultz is one of the major characters here and is shown to be an absolute moron; Henry Kissinger was also involved). This is a damning indictment of the disgustingly corrupt new Gilded Age we are living through, and despite this book's success, I don't think any of its warnings will be heeded. The trajectory of corruption in America is now at an astounding level, and no one can do anything about it, or at least doesn't want to, with the federal government being the most shining example of grifters imaginable. Elizabeth Holmes should probably get a job in the Trump administration, though actually she was buddy-budy with Obama and Hillary Clinton, because of course she was, because the Democratic leadership will do anything to help jack off tech-sector celebrities instead of caring about actual people.

864. Personae by Sergio De La Pava
Received: 8 November 2017
Started: 9 November 2017
Finished: 18 September 2018
These dates suggest that it took me over ten months to read a 150 page novel. I guess it did, technically, though I stopped halfway through the seemingly interminable play in the middle of this and only picked it back up now, feeling I should finish it before starting his new one. As a followup to a hit debut, *Personae* is a totally different creature, though still engaged with the world of police and crime. This feels so intentionally 'experimental' in nature that I can't say I enjoyed reading it, even though I'm generally up for stylistic adventure. This novel took the form of the 'manuscripts found by a person', which made it a bit like *A Smuggler's Bible* or even that *Gnomon* novel I read earlier this year. In the right hands, such as McElroy's, that can be an illuminating technique. By a weaker writer, it can feel like an excuse to cobble together

11, 455 826

several unrelated, unfinished pieces and pass it off as a novel. De la Pava is a fantastic writer and that shows through in most of this, yet I still found it hard to engage with. The play at the centre of it all was nonsensical but not even fun to read; I guess it could be compared to Beckett, but it seemed to just go forever until I found myself just skimming things. Going back to it months later, I found myself interested again, but not interested enough since it was so long since I had started it. Overall I would have probably been better off just skipping this, for its pleasures didn't outweigh the pain in the effort involved.

865. Mirror, Shoulder, Signal by Dorthe Nors
Received: 8 September 2018
Started: 8 September 2018
Finished: 18 September 2018
This was mild reading, a low-key portrait of a single, somewhat lonely woman living in Copenhagen and trying to learn how to drive. I don't have any idea what Nors's prose reads like in the original Danish, but the translation here is so casual (with phrases like "give props to") that it felt a bit dumbed-down. It was only in the last few chapters that I started to appreciate what Nors was doing here, which was showing a marginalised part of society (though one that rarely engenders any sympathy) and commenting on issues of class (though in the Nordic social democracy sense, so that class is determined much more by culture, education, and family background than by income level), gender, and health. The protagonist translates a Swedish crime writer into Danish (a fictional one, but based clearly on Stieg Larsson), and his spectre dominates the novel, with passing mentions of his grisly violent prose becoming a stand-in abusive relationship even if it's technically just a professional one. The signs of Sonya's unraveling only really start to become present towards the end, as she's otherwise following a standard script for living and feeling anxious all the time, which manifests as the vertigo she experiences. Nors sets this up for a violent car crash that never comes, subtly stirring a sense of anxiety in the reader as well, or at least in me. I wonder if this had been translated more gracefully, if some form of style could have been visible in the prose — then I may have really loved this.

866. The Third Hotel by Laura van den Berg
Received: 23 September 2018
Started: 23 September 2018
Finished: 13 October 2018
I suspect *The Third Hotel* will make many year-end lists and probably top a lot of them. It's probably going to top mine, though I've only read a handful of books that came out this year. Though who, besides professional lit critics, read more than a few new releases per year? Anyway, this was amazing; maybe my favourite American novel since *The Flamethrowers*, 728
and it burns in a very different way than that does. I don't know if over time my enjoyment of van den Bergs's book will diminish in my mind, or if I will feel compelled to celebrate it even further; it certainly is one that sinks in and affects slowly, but I'm just not sure which way it will go. This novel is so spooky in the way it unfolds that it feels totally singular, even though the basic plotline is sort of like an inverted version of any Murakami novel, and the integration of film theory into the narrative also feels like something I've read before, maybe from Chris Kraus or Lynne Tillman. But it's not precisely like anything else, just on these surface levels, and it's like a multi-faceted cube containing many sides through which to examine this text: a travelogue of Cuba, the aforementioned film theory, a general feminist mentality that I probably superficially perceive in all novels written by women, an examination of middle class American domesticity, an exploration of relationships through privacy and secrets. I also feel a bit like years of reading works that eschew clear resolution have paid off, and this is more than just another one, but somehow a step forward in the murky unreliable ambiguity genre. I don't know. I saw this blurbed as a 'future cult classic' and I wonder why anyone would decide it's 'cult', as opposed to just a stunning fucking novel, which is what it is. This also feels insanely 'now' due to the way cinema has saturated our approach to narrative and text, though this writes directly about that, rather than trying to ape cinema's structure or language. In some ways, *The Third Hotel* is a throwback because it doesn't feel so focused on digital communication, and yet by being set in the developing capitalist Cuba it still manages to cast a net around issues of economics and class, without being a distraction to the very emotional mysteries woven throughout the novel. So, so great — I really loved this and it just got more gripping as it went along, even

though there became less to grip on to.

867. No Future For You edited by John Summers, Chris Lehmann, and Thomas Frank

Received: 13 October 2018
Started: 13 October 2018
Finished: 16 October 2018

I thought that *The Baffler* had changed a lot over the years, as the blog I read daily seems to be much more focused on inequality and class issues than the classic Thomas Frank Chicago years. Yet this collection of essays, drawn from the transitional period of *The Baffler* that brought it to today's status as a nonprofit organisation that publishes rather than an indie journal, reveals the continuum of thought. It's really the world that has changed, and this collection, published in 2014, feels almost like essential reading to understand today's cultural and political climate. The old *Baffler* railed against market democracy and the co-opting of culture by the forces of insidious profit, and that's merely reached another stage by this point. There are some heavy hitters here — Frank appears twice, to attack the idea of the city as 'vibrant' in a memorable essay that could come from the 90s critical beat; David Graeber writes a version of an essay about the failure of the future and the utter mediocrity of today's tech; Chris Lehmann and Evgeny Moroznov have some beautiful takedowns as well. Susan Faludi's attack on Sheryl Sandberg and the superficial 'Lean In' movement is hilarious and sharp; the takedown of Vice Media is brilliantly titled 'The Vertically-Integrated Rape Joke' and lays out the sins of Vice long before McInnes and the Proud Boys even came into being. There's a slight risk that these essays might seem a tiny bit dated already, all being published long before the 2016 election, but I found this incredibly enjoyable from start to finish and it serves as a fine document of how we got to where we are. Apart from the Chapo book, to which this makes a some-
860 what more researched companion but no less an ideological peer, I don't see a lot of cultural criticism that combines a hard left viewpoint with such entertaining style. Some of the attacks here feel a bit strange for a publication as esteemed as *The Baffler* to focus on — the *50 Shades* book series, for example — but there's always a powerful underlying point that opens up a wider lens onto popular items and reveals just how sick and rotten American culture is. There's a takedown of Thomas Kinkade which at first seems just like a needless revelation of how awful and kitschy his work is, but as it goes along, it builds a convincing portrait that he was just another grifter, perfectly in line with a culture that produces grifters better than anything else (and now even blatantly filling our government with them). There are some media hit pieces in the back which feel a little too insider to fully enjoy — the attack on *The Atlantic* is the one thing I just skimmed here, not that it was necessarily bad but the only thing needed to destroy that magazine's credibility is being reminded of the fact that they employ Conor Friedersdorf. The final essay examines the legacy of Barack Obama, albeit written only halfway through his tenure, through the viewpoint of the numerous hackjob biographies published about him by that point. This felt at first like the weakest piece but ultimately was the most damning, revealing the Obama presidency for the mediocrity that it was, which at the time this was published, probably felt like a daring move for a writer on the left. I should seek out the second collection of *Baffler* essays and even revisit *Commodify Your Dissent*, which is really a classic.

868. Records Ruin The Landscape: John Cage The Sixties And Sound Recording by David Grubbs

Received: 21 October 2018
Started: 21 October 2018
Finished: 21 October 2018

Read this on the plane. Not bad — David Grubbs writes about avant-garde music and particularly on changing ideas regarding sound recording. His main point is to illustrate how much we are now influenced by recorded music, and that this is a relatively recent phenomenon that goes fairly against what Cage stood for. The extent of this way of thinking really hit me; I personally subscribe to a recording-based understanding of music more than almost anyone I know, and it's hard for me to wrap my head around how 'wrong' this actually is, at least in the views of many composers. Grubbs writes in an accessible way and his references are fairly understandable to me. He is particularly focused on Henry 
Flynt, who is a great example of some- 24, 164
one who was 'discovered' and is primarily known through archival recordings, though that's really an inaccurate representation of his work. A lengthy interview between Flynt and Kenneth Goldsmith is frequently referred to (which I should really listen to), and at the end of the book he dissects

UbuWeb and some of the other archives available online. Grubbs is enthusiastic about this material being made available and doesn't get into the issues of digital sound reproductions or rights, at least not too much. Considering the author's sense of poetics (which I do love, in a certain way) I guess I was a little bit surprised by how grounded this was; while it's not quite an academic-level text, it's certainly for such a niche audience that he probably felt free to write this in whichever way he wanted. This book very much takes on Cage as a central concern — after all his name is in the title — yet it's not overly reverent towards him. But it is written in a way that makes one appreciate other aspects of Cage's writing
627 and thought, and forced me to think about Cage as a musician more than I usually do.

I could at any time while reading this call up any song he mentioned, which I did a little bit; I think it would be amazing to go back through and investigate some of the many early 1960s singles he mentions — enough that I wouldn't mind grabbing a paperback copy of this to use for 'reference'. The other idea that came to mind while reading this is how incredible it would be to write a similar history of UNpopular music, though it's even more daunting since if you measure unpopular music as all music not in this book, it's a nearly infinite strain. Still, something like a music version of Steven Moore's alternative history of the novel (which is two volumes in and still only up to the year 1800) would be incredible, especially if written with the passion and craft that Stanley brought to this.

869. Yeah! Yeah! Yeah! by Bob Stanley
Received: 4 November 2018
Started: 4 November 2018
Finished: 16 November 2018
Stanley's history of pop music (as it existed in the US and UK, at least) is stunning, and I tore through all 963 pages of this and was left wanting more. He set pretty reasonable boundaries: time-wise, it spans the start of the charts in 1952 through Napster, and he considers 'popular' to mean commercial success, so the charts function as a beacon throughout. Even though he wrote about plenty of music I already knew loads about, he wove a narrative thread through each small chapter that ultimately rendered this history as one man's personal vision, albeit a seemingly complete one. His enthusiasm for music is endless and his tastes are far from the standard rock narrative (as you would guess from listening to a Saint Etienne record). Yet he doesn't shy away from criticism; his appraisals of some of music's biggest stars are generous but others are dismissed, though not in a typically dickish, arrogant music snob manner. Chapters on the Bee Gees and the Monkees were among the strongest, plus sections on oddities such as Lou Christie and Rod Stewart left me curious to hear more of their work. By the time the narrative reaches the 90s, he somehow found a way to illustrate a common thread through the electronic and dance styles that started to take over the UK. There's little about the late 90s alternative rock boom, and no rap metal at all, but I suppose he was worn out by the end — I thought there'd be another 100 pages of prose but it was a lengthy index and bibliography. Thanks to YouTube

870. Nocilla Experience by Agustín Fernández Mallo
Received: 15 August 2018
Started: 17 November 2018
Finished: 6 December 2018
As mind-blowing as *Nocilla Dream*, *Expe-
rience* felt a little more coherent but 817
followed essentially the same structure. Narrative threads come and ago, dealing with relationships and art, and there's a lot of sampled material from interviews, films, and media sources. Writing about the experience of reading this is difficult for me. In the afterword, Mallo says that he was trying to translate his 'post-poetry' project into fiction. There's plenty of bits of wonder here — giant anthills, mathematicians living on rooftops, complex conceptual art interventions, a man running from Florida to Alaska — and it also references real-world examples, such as Henry Darger and the Bélmez Faces. It holds together around a slowly expanding quotation from *Apocalypse Now*. So strange, so strange, and yet reading this gave me a feeling of exhilaration, an inspiration I rarely experience from literature lately. This inspiration was not to write fiction at all, but to walk through this world breathing in deeply, exhaling profoundly, and cherishing our personal relationships. While seemingly scientific in affect (though less so than the first book), this work radiates love. I feel after two books like I have a clear sense of who Mallo is. The third book comes out soon, with the whole trilogy in a box set republished by someone larger, and I'm fucking stoked for it.

871. K-punk: The Collected and Unpublished Writings of Mark Fisher by Mark Fisher
Received: 17 November 2018
Started: 17 November 2018
Finished: 9 December 2018

If the cult of Mark Fisher isn't huge yet, it will be after this, the long-awaited posthumous collection. What separates this from most posthumous collections is that the vast majority of content here came from his k-punk blog, which I used to occasionally read. I've now read almost all of his book-published work and I completely understand why he's amassing a following — Fisher is exactly what the left needs right now, which is a clear and articulate voice who is equally rooted in cultural, philosophical, and political matters, and is able to approach almost any subject with a warmth and passion. So this was great, though I'm wondering if I read a 'long' version- it's a PDF I pulled online, which clocked in at 1187 PDF pages. Amazon claims this to be 500 pages and a review I read today on an art blog said it was 800. Perhaps it was something to do with PDF pagination, or maybe this was a pre-release version before it was edited down. I actually think this could have lost a few pieces and been stronger, as it became repetitive. The political section in particular had a few pieces that felt dated, usually in response to specific news items that I was struggling to recall just a few years after they happened. He introduced about 15 essays in a row by explaining his 'capitalist realism' definition (which isn't even his term, originally) and then expounded on it more and more in the interviews section. Of course, these were mostly blog posts, and that's what sort of makes this great. Stripped of the ability to have hyperlinks (though necessary things are footnoted, which I didn't use much since the PDF reader isn't as easy to flip between endnnotes and back as the EPub software), the posts feel strange and it drew attention to just how specific the format dictates the content. It also brings up my own frustrations with the Internet as stoked by the recent reading I did of Geert
848, Lovink's works; the blog culture of 2004–
849 2010 was actually a really supportive and thought-provoking community and I didn't realise how good it was then as the social media monopoly platforms have managed to destroy them as well. Fisher doesn't comment much on this, but this 'lost time' is felt for sure throughout. So, the pieces of *K-punk* are divided into several sections. Writings on books start off and there's a lot of talk about Ballard, which makes sense, as well as Margaret Atwood (who I've never read). The writings on film and television were really surprising, and it's made me take note of a few things to check out. By the time the writings on music come around I've already been well inside the head of Fisher for a few hundred pages, and the stuff that overlapped with *The Weird and the Eerie* (such as the long piece about The 802
Fall) or *Ghosts of my Life* were a welcome 772
refresher course. Fisher was definitely of that mold like Greil Marcus, people who are brilliant and make incredible cultural analyses, but definitely take pop music way too seriously. I started to feel the repetition here, not from the earlier texts as much as within this, but I guess you could make a case for each piece's inclusion. I think this might cover capitalist realism better than the *Capitalist Realism* book
itself, a book that is no doubt brilliant but 778
almost shockingly influential for how brief it is and how much of it specifically talks about British youth and the depression epidemic. I hung around and got through the rest of this, sort of loving it but wanting it to be over, and I'm glad I didn't buy it in the end, even though it may end up on my shelf one day anyhow. There's a section of more emotional rants after the interviews, which includes the famous 'Exiting the Vampires' Castle' and some angrier and kinda funny rants as well. Re-reading 'Castle', I was somewhat struck by how oppositional Fisher is here and in many ways destructive to the cause. The left currently does feel torn between the so-called 'identity politics' which are negatively cast as the tools of 'SJWs' and online call-out culture; and those who believe the project needs to be more class-oriented, to challenge wider structures. Fisher comes out emphatically as on the latter team and I used to be as well, though reading this 'seminal' essay again (it feels quite funny to call a blog post seminal) I feel maybe that both sides need to reconcile, and to do so quickly. Call this an awareness of my own white male privilege, or just realising Fisher's, but my feelings that collective class should trump individual identity issues is certainly easy for me to assert as a white male. Any actual progress in this hellworld is going to need both areas to be worked on, so while I don't repudiate Fisher, I sort of feel like he (and Angela Nagle) needlessly cause conflict by trying to paint Twitter SJWs as tools of the liberal order. We're all in this together and we're all learning. Which brings me to the final section, the introduction to his

unfinished work *Acid Communism*, which was going to be a historical study of the early 70s and how different the sought-after utopia was from how it's been portrayed. I'm not sure that it would have been a great book, as it would be really leaning heavily on the cultural angles that he was so fascinated by, but I guess we'll never know. The introduction ias a great way to end this collection, as he pointed out on I think the last page how our current material conditions of precarity under late capitalism are even more ripe for it to collapse than in the 1970s, but that we no longer have the emotional or existential willpower for that change, so beaten down are we from decades of successful neoliberal implementation. This is certainly true, and something I have thought about at length without actually realising it so explicitly as Fisher articulated it; this might be a major motivation to take from this book as I go forward, trying to find my own path. Anyway; I'm sure everyone is going to be reading this and I'm glad for that, and hope that the million topics I didn't mention in this comment will be discussed at length in the future media outlets of today's online world.

872. Saint Cole by Noah Van Sciver
Received: 7 November 2018
Started: 15 December 2018
Finished: 15 December 2018
Van Sciver's novel is a bleak portrait of a white working class fuckup, struggling with alcoholism and libido issues while trying to make ends meet. It's a story you've heard before, Bukowski 101, and were it not for Van Sciver's artistry it would be unremarkable. But cast in graphic form, it's a totally different beast. *Saint Cole* is predictable and a bit over-the-top in how the protagonist's life goes from bad to nightmare in the course of one day. The dense frames are packed with dark, short strokes and it overwhelmingly conveys a sense of structural claustrophobia. There's no sympathy to be had for the character, and I'm curious how Van Sciver might take on more fantastic, imaginative subject matter instead of these navel-gazing, dark, and extremely male storylines. I also picked up a little one-off diary he put out chronicling a year in the life of the real Noah Van Sciver, and while the dead-end job and general workaholic lifestyle was similar, he managed to downplay any substance abuse issues or rampant misogyny (as you would, if you were publishing your diary). It could be that Van Sciver is actually as dark and fucked up as his fictional creations, but I don't think so — he just sees this as a fascinating subject, whereas I came off from it just feeling bad, even despite the ending. Still — good work here, and I'm curious if he would be good at a really extravagant long-form work.

873. The Goldfinch by Donna Tartt
Received: 3 May 2018
Started: 22 December 2018
Finished: 26 December 2018
Yeah, this was a real page-turner. Having now read 2/3 of Tartt's oeuvre, I can't say I think much of her as a great literary figure, but she sure can craft a yarn, and for holiday reading I was happy to sink into the narrative and let it take me away. But stylistically? Ugh. I hate to pile on to the snobby lit crit assholes who trashed this for being like an inflated children's book with highbrow art details shoehorned in, but I think I felt that way too. Which is fine — I always call these types of books 'Guardian books', which is super fucking snobby of me and something I should stop (hey, I read *The Guardian* too), but that's really where I'd classify this. Having just finished it, I'm thinking that the more interesting aspects of *The Goldfinch* are subtle, such as the way she embraces Russian literature and culture through both the Boris character and the crime/thriller elements near the end. That character also seems like a cliché right out of an edgy action-comedy film, something Shane Black would have penned, which maybe undercuts any depth to this subtlety. One has to admire on some level a best-selling, prize-winning novel that digs so deeply into the art of furniture restoration, and I would be lying if I didn't say I enjoyed reading this. But it's just embellished genre fiction for me, and I guess I'm ultimately more interested in literary style than plot. I hate feeling this way and I hate being so snobby, but this is along the lines of a Jonathan Franzen novel or *City on Fire*, and I guess I find it 
unjust how financially successful these nov- 701
els are while so many literary geniuses toil in obscurity. Tartt's first novel (*The Secret*  
History) was no better, worse actually, and 768
even more saturated in posh New England white person literary fantasy. At least this one references popular culture as much as the Greek classics, and the wild n' decadent Las Vegas chapter finally breaks away from this post-Salinger cultured NYC elitist vibe, which is certainly where Tartt hails from (or aspired towards, I don't know anything about her personally) but just annoying to

read about for me, at this stage. Just make this into a film, please, as that seems to be what it was written for. It could have been way shorter, too.

874. Notes from the Fog by Ben Marcus

Received: 15 December 2018
Started: 15 December 2018
Finished: 30 December 2018

I now think of Marcus as a 'former experimental writer' but that's not really fair. Certainly by now he's made the full transition from the earlier avant-grade tactics of *Wire*

123, 286 *and String* to work that is more concerned with probing emotions and relationships through artifice, rather than being stuck at the layer of language itself. A few pieces in the latter half actually felt closer to his early work in terms of tone, and I found those the hardest to get through, which makes it evident that I've probably grown with him. Or maybe it has to do with the mentality I put myself in after the first few story, which was coldly realistic and brutal in a way I couldn't imagine. The darkness in his work continues but maybe he steps on

485 the brakes a little bit from *Flame Alphabet*, as this is a collection that is rather occupied with the relationship between children and adults, and while there are some total gut-punches (like the eponymous story which closes the book), misery isn't the point. Communication is, which has always been at the root of Marcus's prose; stripped of the objects that previously decorated his writing, only people remain now and the writing takes on a clarity that no longer demands to interrogate meaning, definition, and association. The story about the architects proposing a monument for a terrorist/nuclear disaster was amazing, addressing the art of public emotional manipulation and throwing in some sci-fi/speculative aspects as well, such as the idea to spray a mild drug to alter mental states. That felt like just the beginning of something, yet complete as well, a short story that left me tingling and thinking. But yeah, other parts of this did feel tedious though I was so happy to have some new writing by him that I still devoured it like I was starving for his prose. I'd love a new longer-form work, but novels are starting to seem like the exception rather than the rule for Marcus, which is strange cause I still think of him as a novelist, albeit a very experimental one.

875. Beautiful Country Burn Again by Ben Fountain

Received: 30 December 2018
Started: 31 December 2018
Finished: 5 January 2019

I didn't think I could deal with another take on the 2016 election and Trump, but I'm glad I tried this, because it was stunning. The sheer talent of Fountain as a writer is maybe what separated it from the 7 million other essays I've read online and elsewhere about the current state of America. He's a literary wordsmith of the highest caliber, which is immediately evident in the first chapter's descriptions of Iowa scenery during the campaigning. But the language isn't the only reason this is so incredible — it's the whole package, the way he is able to temper his reporting with emotional distance, strong moral arguments, and an accessible gentility, but also with sharp and occasionally outrageous moments. The structure of this is built around a series of expanded essays originally written for *The Guardian*, interleaved with journals from each month of 2016, titled 'Book(s) of Days'. These are undated, yet chronological reports from the newspapers, done in a matter-of-fact style, sort of; the result is an often-hilarious portrayal of a very weird, absurd time that accelerates towards the Trump victory. Fountain's politics are good, even great. He excoriates the Democratic Party and the Clintons in particular for doing this to the world, and never takes out any of his frustration on Trump's actual voters, which makes his view much closer to mine than, say, my mother's. There's an unwritten sympathy for the downtrodden here, and Fountain repeatedly refers to the country's "largest political party", nonvoters, whom he (quite correctly) does not blame for their apathy. Historical context is everywhere — sections on Ambrose Bierce, James Baldwin, pre-electrification rural Texas, and the slave trade are riveting. There's some hilarious moments, but it never descends into dirtbag left name-calling like Matt Taibbi would do, which shows a restraint far greater than I could ever have myself.

Appendices

Appendix A: Books read in 2001

For some reason (what is the reason for any of this, really?), I kept a list of all of the books I read in 2001, the year before this project began.

I did not record dates or comments, so this can only be presented as an appendix, a 'prequel' of sorts. It nonetheless informs about my literary mind during the earliest years as chronicled in this volume.

Donald Antrim:
Elect Mr. Robinson for a Better World
The Hundred Brothers
The Verificationist

Nicholson Baker — U and I

David Byrne — The New Sins

Don DeLillo — The Names

Dave Eggers — A Heartbreaking Work of Staggering Genius

Amy Fusselman — Pharmacist's Mate

William Gaddis:
A Frolic of His Own
JR
The Recognitions.

James Joyce — Ulysses

Lawrence Krauser — Lemon

Jonathan Lethem:
Motherless Brooklyn
This Shape We're In

Harry Mathews — Tlooth

Harry Mulisch — The Discovery of Heaven

Vladimir Nabokov — Pale Fire

Flann O'Brien:
The Third Policeman
At Swim-2-Birds
The Dalkey Archive.

Georges Perec — Life: A User's Manual.

Arturo Perez-Reverte — The Club Dumas

Neal Pollack — The Neal Pollack Anthology of American Literature

Thomas Pynchon — The Crying of Lot 49

Raymond Queneau — Exercises in Style

John Sayles — Sayles on Sayles

William T. Vollmann:
Butterfly Stories
The Rifles

Appendix B: Books started, but not finished

Of course I don't finish every book that I start. Here are the ones that I didn't get through; some of these I swear that I finished, while others I only went a few pages in.

2002

Aberration of Starlight by Gilbert Sorrentino
New York Is Now!: The New Wave of Free Jazz by Phil Freeman
Jazz: The 1980's Resurgence by Stuart Nicholson
Ambient Century by Mark Prendergast
Future Jazz by Howard Mandel
File Under Popular: Theoretical and Critical Writings on Music by Chris Cutler
1984: Selected Letters by Samuel Delany
In *Recognition of William Gaddis* by John Richard Kuehl and Steven Moore
Flock of Dreamers: An Anthology of Dream Inspired Comics
Phosphor in Dreamland by Rikki Ducornet
Superbad by Ben Greenman
The Futurist Cookbook by F. T. Marinetti
Giles Goat Boy by John Barth
Stupid White Men by Michael Moore
Harry Mathews by Warren Leamon
An Unspeakable Betrayal by Luis Buñuel
A History of Experimental Film and Video by A.L. Rees
The Outsider by Colin Wilson
Ten Tales Tall and True by Alasdair Gray
Hopscotch by Julio Cortazar
The Feverhead by Wolfgang Bauer
A Pattern Language: Towns, Buildings, Construction by Christopher Alexander
Fireproof Women by Ricky Jay
Peter Greenaway's Postmodern/Poststructuralist Cinema by Mary Alemany-Galway
Peter Greenaway: Architecture and Allegory by Bridget Elliot, Anthony Purdy
The Films of Peter Greenaway by Amy Lawrence
La Vie Mode D'Emploi (French Edition) by George Perec
The Great Fire of London by Jacques Roubaud
Things: A Story of the Sixties; A Man Asleep by Georges Perec
Conjunctions: 37, Twentieth Anniversary Issue edited by Bradford Morrow
Film As A Subversive Art by Amos Vogel

2003

Our Band Could Be Your Life by Michael Azerrad
The Ancient Mysteries: A Sourcebook edited by Marvin W. Meyer
An Instance of the Fingerpost: A Novel by Iain Pears
Palinuro of Mexico by Fernando Del Paso
The Duplications by Kenneth Koch
Ulysses by James Joyce
Monstrous Possibility: An Invitation to Literary Politics by Curtis White
Dark Star Safari by Paul Theroux
One-Way by Didier van Cauwelaert
Rising Up and Rising Down by William T. Vollmann

2004

The Ruined Map by Kobo Abe
Almanac of the Dead by Leslie Marmon Silko
Terra Nostra by Carlos Fuentes
India: A History by John Keay
Midnight's Children by Salman Rushdie
Don Quixote by Miguel De Cervantes
The Grand Trunk Road: From the front seat by Brian Paul Bach
The Constants of Nature: From Alpha to Omega--the Numbers That Encode the Deepest Secrets of the Universe by John D. Barrow
Q by Luther Blissett
Book of Lies: The Disinformation Guide to Magick and the Occult edited by Richard Metzger
Alembic by Timothy D'Arch Smith

2005

A Criminal History of Mankind by Colin Wilson
A Bad Man by Stanley Elkin
Quicksilver (The Baroque Cycle, Vol. 1) by Neal Stephenson
Small Things Considered: Why There Is No Perfect Design by Henry Petroski
Nostromo: A Tale of the Seaboard by Joseph Conrad
Conversations Before the End of Time by Suzi Gablik
The Heat of the Day by Elizabeth Bowen
Empire of the Sun by J. G. Ballard
Orlando by Virginia Woolf

Appendix B: The abandoned

2006
Going Sane by Adam Phillips
A Grain of Wheat by Ngugi wa Thiong'o
Titus Groan by Mervyn Peake
True Tales of American Life edited by Paul Auster
The Memoirs of a Survivor by Doris Lessing
*The Writing of the Disaste*r by Maurice Blanchot
The Parallax View by Slavoj Zizek
Bridge of San Luis Rey by Thornton Wilder
Open Sky by Paul Virilio
Circles of Confusion by Hollis Frampton
Something New Under the Sun: An Environmental History of the Twentieth-Century World by John Robert McNeill
W Ou Le Souvenir D'enfance (French Edition) by Georges Perec

2007
The Archaeology of Knowledge by Michel Foucault
A Landscape of Events by Paul Virilio
Filthy English by Jonathan Meades

2008
The Language of Inquiry by Lyn Hejinian
Smells Like Dead Elephants: Dispatches from a Rotting Empire by Matt Taibbi
Explainers: The Complete Village Voice Strips (1956-1966) by Jules Feiffer
The Komplete Kolor Krazy Kat (Volume 1: 1935-1936) by George Herriman
Women and Men by Joseph McElroy

2009
The New Spirit of Capitalism by Luc Boltanski and Eve Chiapello
Ulysses by James Joyce
Cantatrix Sopranica L.: Scientific Papers by Georges Perec
Le Petit Prince (French Language Edition) by Antoine de Saint-Exupery
Dark Paradise by Rosa Liksom
The Practice of Everyday Life by Michel de Certeau
Everything Is Cinema: The Working Life of Jean-Luc Godard by Richard Brody
The Street of Crocodiles and Other Stories by Bruno Schulz

2010
Sewer, Gas and Electric: The Public Works Trilogy by Matt Ruff
What the Dog Saw: And Other Adventures by Malcolm Gladwell
TRIPLICITY - Echo Round His Bone; The Genocides; The Puppies of Terra by Thomas M. Disch
Death 24x a Second: Stillness and the Moving Image by Laura Mulvey

2011
Hind's Kidnap : A Pastoral on Familiar Airs by Joseph McElroy
India: A Million Mutinies Now by V.S. Naipaul

2012
Silence: Lectures and Writings by John Cage
Friction by Eloy Urroz
The Vintage Mencken edited by Alistair Cooke
The School for Atheists: A Comedy in 6 Acts by Arno Schmidt
The Invention of Morel by Adolfo Bioy Casares
Inverted World by Christopher Priest
JR by William Gaddis
The Life and Adventures of Trobadora Beatrice as Chronicled by Her Minstrel Laura: A Novel in Thirteen Books and Seven Intermezzos by Irmtraud Morgner

2013
America's Magic Mountain by Curtis White
On Balance by Adam Phillips
A Drifting Life by Yoshihiro Tatsumi
Selected Poems by James Schuyler
Call It Sleep by Henry Roth

2014
This Is Not a Program by Tiqqun
The Counterfeiters: An Historical Comedy by Hugh Kenner
Vanished Kingdoms: The Rise and Fall of States and Nations by Norman Davies
The Planetarium by Nathalie Sarraute
The Corner: A Year in the Life of an Inner-City Neighborhood by David Simon and Ed Burns
The Hidden Order of Art: A Study in the

Psychology of Artistic Imagination by Anton Ehrenzweig
Capital in the Twenty-First Century by Thomas Piketty
Reading in the Brain: The New Science of How We Read by Stanislas Dehaene
*A Moment in the Su*n by John Sayles
There Is No Year: A Novel by Blake Butler
Deep Time of the Media: Toward an Archaeology of Hearing and Seeing by Technical Means by Siegfried Zielinski

2015
The Making of Americans: Being a History of a Family's Progress by Gertrude Stein
The Collected Poems by Frank O'Hara
Cyclonopedia: Complicity with Anonymous Materials by Reza Negarestani
There by Lance Olsen
The Sheep Look Up by John Brunner
The Complete Stories by Clarice Lispector
Cities and Cultures by Malcolm Miles
The Recognitions by William Gaddis
The Book Of Disquiet by Fernando Pessoa

2016
Madness and Modernism: Insanity in the Light of Modern Art, Literature, and Thought by Louis A. Sass
Nine Lives: In Search of the Sacred in Modern India by William Dalrymple
Jerusalem by Alan Moore
Planetary Modernisms: Provocations on Modernity Across Time by Susan Stanford Friedman

2017
Dark Territory: The Secret History of Cyber War by Fred Kaplan
The Doomed City by Arkady & Boris Strugatsky
Life is a Rip Off by John Olson
Complete Fiction of W.M. Spackman
Unruly Places: Lost Spaces, Secret Cities, and Other Inscrutable Geographies by Alastair Bonnett
Strange Tools: Art and Human Nature by Alva Noë
Birdbrain by Johanna Sinisalo
Empire by Michael Hardt & Antonio Negri

2018
Recitation by Suah Bae
The Invented Part by Rodrigo Fresán
Lovecraft Country by Matt Ruff
The Golden Age by Michal Ajvaz
Midnight's Children by Salman Rushdie
Don't Network. The Avant Garde after Networks by Marc James Léger
A Brief History of Seven Killings by Marlon James

Indices

Index by title *$ – Be*

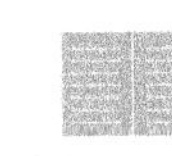

Index by title *Ex — Gu*

Index by title *H – In*

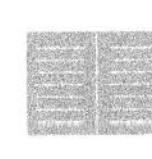

Index by title *Wo – Zo*

Index by author *Aa – Br*

Index by author

Index by author

Index by author Mc – Po

Index by author

Index by author *Vo – Zu*

About the author

John W. Fail is a Helsinki-based artist who works primarily with open-form collaboration. He was co-instigator of Biathlon, a toolkit for experimental and participatory culture production, which was operated at two Helsinki-based platforms. Previously, he was co-director of the 2015 Pixelache Festival. He has had a hand in numerous projects in the Baltic/Nordic region, usually working in the liminal space between roles of artist, curator, and producer. He operated the Ptarmigan project space in both Helsinki and Tallinn from 2009-2014, and has also recorded and performed in various experimental and improvised musical projects since the early 2000s. His work often takes the form of open, trans-disciplinary events, bringing together people of diverse backgrounds to experiment with collaborative creative techniques that focus on discordant and even irrelevant pleasures, without regard for measurable outcomes.

www.ingramcontent.com/pod-product-compliance
Ingram Content Group UK Ltd.
Pitfield, Milton Keynes, MK11 3LW, UK
UKHW050146280726
14058UKWH00007B/857